The Encyclopedia of Origami and Papercraft Techniques

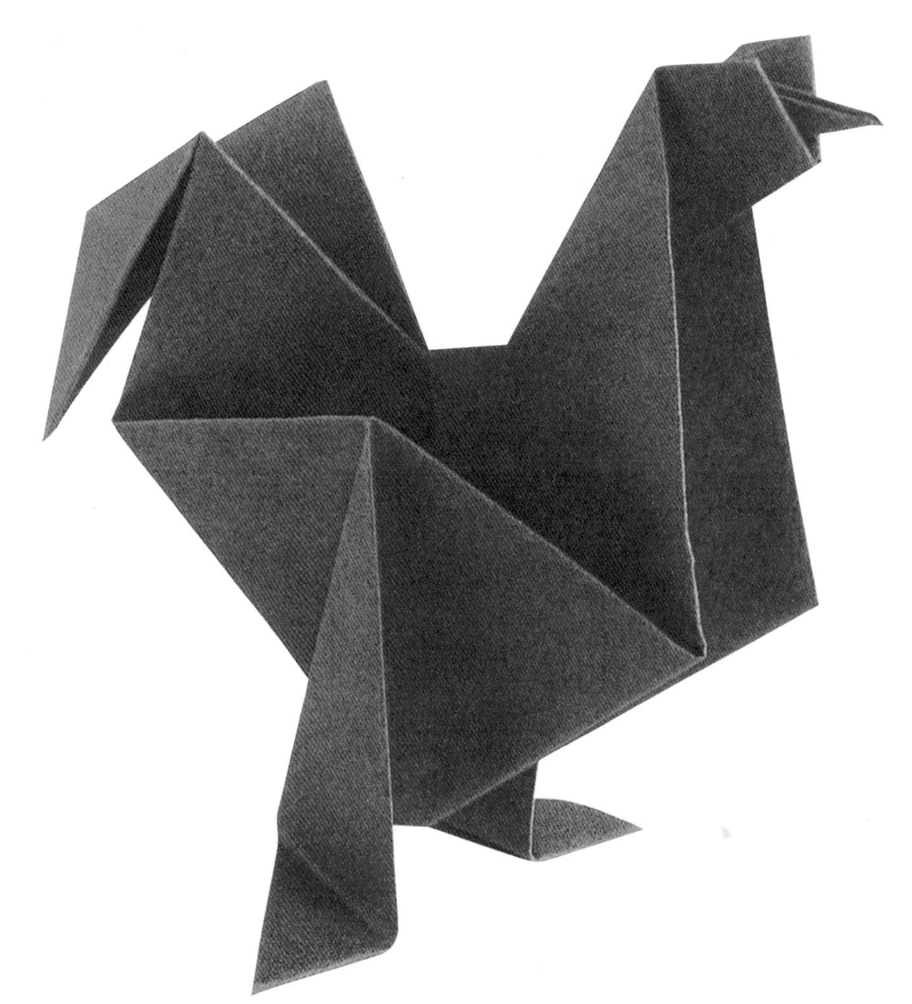

The Encyclopedia of Origami and Papercraft Techniques

Edited by Emma Callery

CHARTWELL BOOKS, INC.

A QUINTET BOOK

Published by Chartwell Books
A Division of Book Sales, Inc.
PO Box 7100
Edison, New Jersey 08818-7100

This edition produced for sale in the U.S.A., its territories and dependencies only.

ISBN 0-7858-0441-2

This book was designed and produced by
Quintet Publishing Limited
6 Blundell Street
London N7 9BH

The material in this book previously appeared in *An Introduction to Puppets and Puppet-making* by David Currell, *The Encyclopedia of Origami and Papercraft Techniques* by Paul Jackson, *Magnificent Mobiles* by Melanie Williams, *Making Masks* by Vivien Frank and Deborah Jaffe, *Paper Airplanes* by Nick Robinson, *Paper Animals* by Robert J. Lang and *Pop-up Greetings Cards* by Mike Palmer.

Creative Director: Richard Dewing
Designer: Peter Laws
Editor: Emma Callery

Typeset in Great Britain by
Central Southern Typesetters, Eastbourne
Manufactured by Eray Scan Pte Ltd, Singapore
Printed by Star Standard Industries (Pte) Ltd, Singapore

CONTENTS

INTRODUCTION

Paper is a common material – we are surrounded by it in our daily lives, and most of us discard hundreds of pounds of it every year. It is prosaic and mundane. Yet, hidden within even the most humble scrap of newsprint lie animals, birds, and flowers galore, all waiting for an appearance via just a few simple manipulations. The techniques by which paper may be transformed into marvelous creatures form the art of origami – just the first section in this wonderful collection of papercraft projects.

There are more than sixty projects in all in this book, and following on from the origami chapter, there are pop-up greeting cards for all sorts of occasions; papier-mâché masks and mobiles; papermaking and decorating ideas ranging from weaving and collage through to stenciling and marbling; and finally ways to cut, fold, and glue paper to make such things as boxes, bags, and puppets.

So, if you want to make an Eskimo paddling in his kayak, a pop-up card to celebrate a twenty-first birthday, an astronaut mask, some specially marbled paper, or a Noah's Ark mobile, look no further. Each chapter starts with a detailed basics section, explaining carefully each technique required for that particular craft, and then there are numerous projects to choose from in order to practice and develop the techniques. Each project is divided into step-by-step text, and there are numerous photographs and illustrations to clarify things still further.

The Star Rating System

To help you choose which projects you would like to work on, each one has been allocated a star rating ranging from the most straightforward to the most difficult.

★ elementary
★★ simple
★★★ average
★★★★ difficult
★★★★★ advanced

ALL ABOUT PAPER

Although it is a common material, sources for the supply of paper may not be immediately apparent. However, with only a little research, a pleasing variety of papers and cards can be found, some of which may inspire paperworks that would not otherwise have been made. The three sources suggested here should all be useful.

ART AND CRAFT STORES

All cities – and towns of any size – have these stores, most of which stock a reasonably good selection of papers.

LOCAL PRINTERS

All printers keep stocks of papers and cards brought in for specific printing jobs, and because they buy in bulk, some sheets invariably remain unused. Prices per sheet will be considerably lower than a store's prices, but you will probably have to buy a minimum quantity.

PAPER WHOLESALERS

Paper wholesalers buy paper direct from manufacturers to sell to users. Many will supply swatches free of charge. If you are able to give a company address for delivery, you may be able to order a large number of sample sheets without charge.

TYPES OF PAPER

Papers and cards are usually developed and manufactured to be used by the packaging industry and commercial or fine art printers. Consequently, a bewildering number of papers are available for particular uses. The complex technical specifications need not necessarily concern the paper artist, to whom the look and feel of a paper is more important, but a few basic paper types and terms may prove useful.

Acid-free paper Paper from which all acids have been removed during manufacturing to improve its strength and color. It should have a pH number of 7.07 or higher and should not turn yellow or become brittle quickly. Wood pulp – the basic component of most paper – is naturally acidic, which is why low-quality, chemically untreated newsprint, used for newspapers and some paperback books, deteriorates rapidly.

Bond paper Paper which has been "sized" (sealed with a glue mixture) to prevent penetration by writing or drawing inks, such as stationery papers. Printing papers are lightly sized and are not usually called bond.

Coated paper Papers coated with an additional surface to give a smoother finish and therefore greatly improve printing quality. A coating of a different color may crack when creased, so color-coated papers should not be scored.

Laid paper Paper with a pattern of fine parallel lines, appearing either as ridges and furrows or as opaque and translucent bands.

Rag paper Paper containing a high percentage of fiber from cotton or linen fabrics, including recycled clothing. A rag paper is usually of very high quality and will fade or turn yellow only with great age. Rag papers are commonly used by artists for watercolors and etchings.

Wove paper Paper with a very faint mesh pattern.

PAPER WEIGHTS

Weight is a guide to a paper's other properties and to its price. In most countries, except the United States, weight is expressed in terms of the weight in grams of a sheet of paper one meter square. Thus, photocopy paper is said to be 80gsm (or 80gsm^2), because a sheet 1m x 1m weighs 80 grams. Thinner paper, such as airmail paper, is approximately 45gsm, and thicker paper, such as drawing paper, is about 150gsm.

Above 250gsm, paper is officially card. Above 500gsm, cards are identified by thickness, measured in microns.

Some papers and cards are unusually compacted or aerated. They appear to have a high or low grammage compared to thickness, which is not necessarily a reliable indicator of weight.

In the United States, paper weight is measured in pounds per ream (500 sheets), known as basis weight, or more often in pounds per M sheets (1,000 sheets). The size of the sheets weighed can vary considerably from one type of paper to another, so there is no consistent relationship between the actual weight of a sheet and its official poundage. However, the most common size for measuring poundage is 25 x 38in. At this size, photocopy paper of 80gsm is 118lb, drawing paper of 150gsm is 222lb, 220gsm paper is 330lb, and so on. Tables are available to make the necessary calculation for other sizes.

The poundage system survives outside the US when referring to traditional high-rag papers, such as watercolor and etching papers, but for all practical purposes, conversion tables are needed whenever US poundage and paper sizes need to be converted.

KEY TO PAPERS

1 paper wholesaler colored paper
2 paper wholesaler added fiber effect
3 paper wholesaler marbled effect
4 paper wholesaler different "colored" parchment effect
5 acid-free
6 bonded
7 coated
8 laid
9 rag
10 wove
11 colored one side
12 colored both sides
13 decorative origami paper

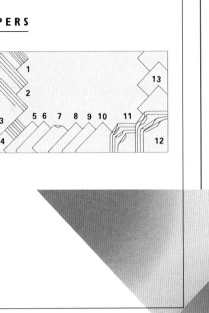

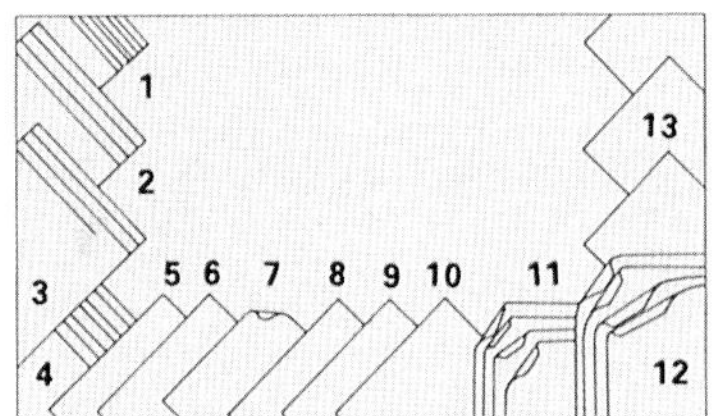

PART I

ORIGAMI

BASICS

Almost all construction work with paper and cardboard must take account of the grain in the sheet. For ease of reference, therefore, and because this matter is so central to all papercrafts (with the possible exceptions of papier-mâché and pulping and papermaking), the use of grain is discussed here instead of being repeated within individual sections. Much of the remainder of the book assumes some knowledge of these matters, so if they are unfamiliar to you, please spend a little time on this section.

All machine-made papers and cards have a grain, formed as the glutinous hair-like fibers that stick together to form the sheet are vibrated to lie in line with the direction of travel of the moving belt that pulls the pulp from the "wet" end of manufacture to the "dry," gradually creating the paper. Handmade papers do not have a grain, as the fibers lie randomly around the sheet.

When drawing or painting on paper, the grain is of little relevance. However, when paper is folded, rolled, torn, or cut, the influence of the fibers lying in parallel can be critical.

TESTING FOR THE GRAIN

1 To find the direction of the grain, bend a sheet in half several times (do not crease it) to gauge the spring.

2 Then, turn the sheet 90°, and bring the other two edges together. A difference in tensions will be apparent. The sheet will bend more easily along the line of the fibers, or "with the grain." It will not be as flexible when bent across the line of the fibers, or "against the grain." If you have never noticed this before, this is a very surprising phenomenon!

CREASING WITH THE GRAIN

The tendency of a sheet to fold more easily when creased with the grain becomes ever more apparent if you use heavier and thicker paper. A crease made against the grain on a sheet of heavy paper will often produce a rough, broken edge at the fold.

So, whenever possible, crease heavier sheets with the grain, not against it. This would apply, for example, to the construction of incised pop-ups, where all the creases are parallel.

A crease at an angle to the grain – particularly if it is one of only a few creases on the sheet – will produce unequal tensions to both sides and distort the surface of the sheet. Therefore, a shape cut out from a larger sheet may have to be orientated so that any creases on the cutout lie parallel to the grain, not at an angle to it.

ABOVE *Here, the top sheet has been creased against the grain to create a rough edge, whereas the bottom sheet has been creased with the grain, to create a smoother edge.*

TEARING

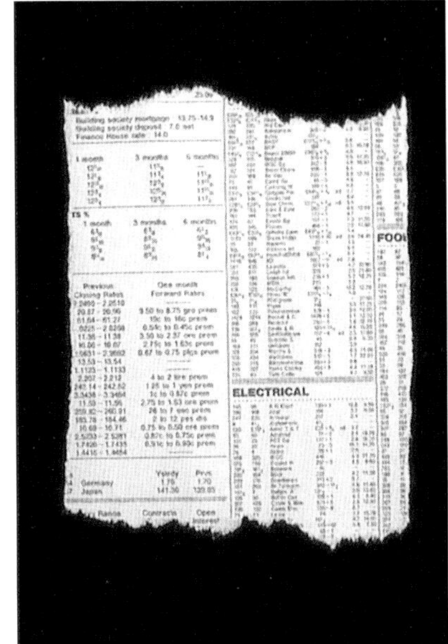
ELECTRICAL

FOOI

As could be predicted, a sheet will tear more cleanly with the grain than against it.

To test this, tear a sheet of newspaper first downward, then across. The difference in the tear is very pronounced.

ROLLING ▲

When rolling cylinders, the paper will roll more readily with the grain, so that tighter cylinders can be formed.

Always carry large sheets of paper or cardboard rolled into a loose tube along the line of the grain. This may sometimes mean rolling one long edge to the opposite one to create a longer tube than may seem necessary, but the paper will be less stressed. Rolling against the grain can leave disfiguring buckle marks on the sheet. When you buy paper, always insist that heavier weights are rolled the correct way, with the grain.

PLEATED FORM ▼

The sheet below has been precreased and collapsed without cuts to create a very flexible form with a remarkable load-bearing capability. It is hand-creased from lightweight paper. The crease pattern is so complex that the direction of the grain has no influence on its construction.

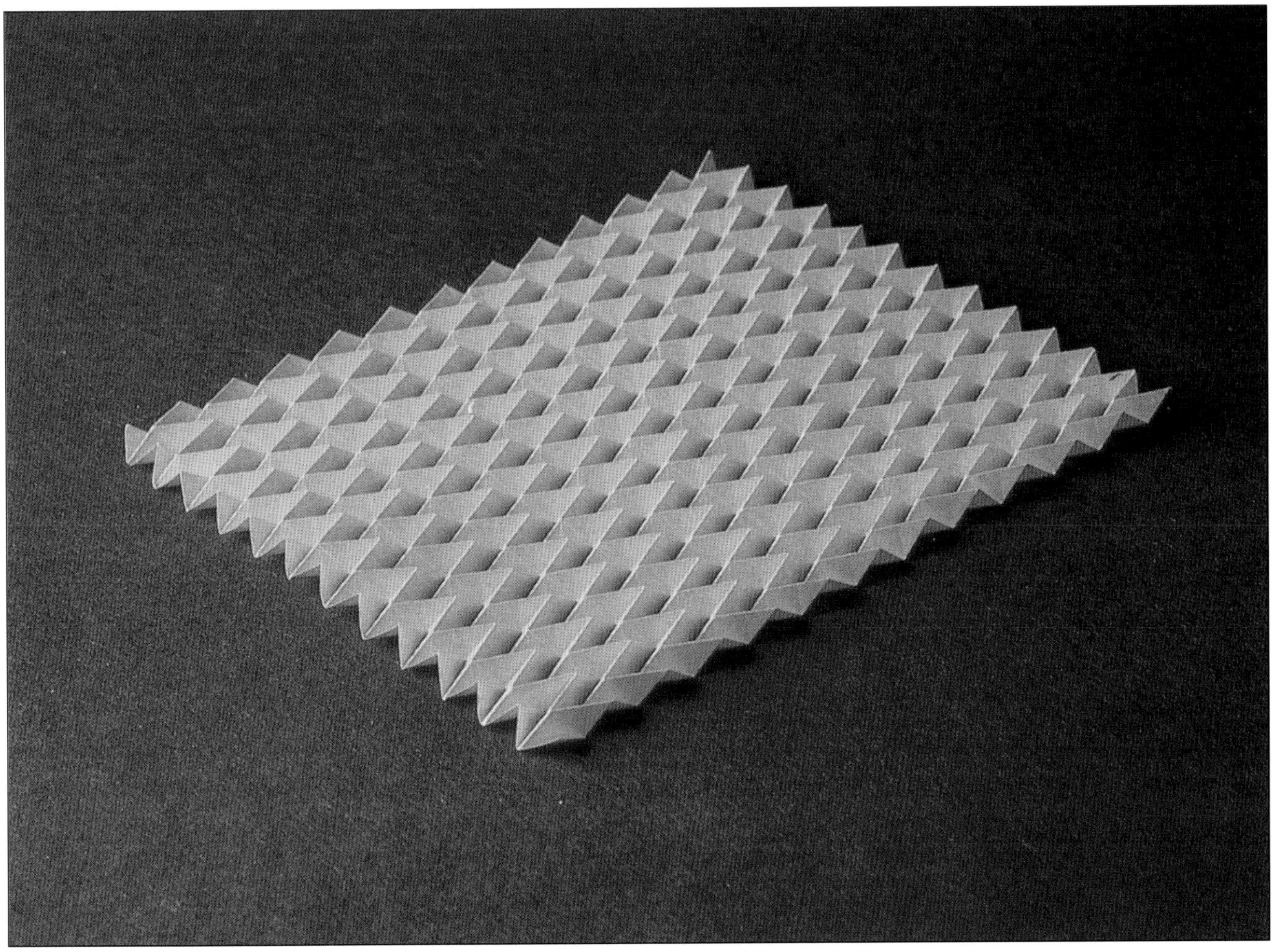

CREASING PAPER

The majority of papermaking techniques involves making creases. As with grain (see previous two pages), the basics of creasing are discussed here, rather than being repeated within individual sections.

Creasing is so elementary that it is frequently done without regard for the best method. One of the following four methods will be ideal for any crease on any sheet. Choice depends on the weight of the sheet and the use to which the crease is being put.

CREASING BY HAND

Before deciding to crease by hand, crease a small piece of the sheet both with and against the grain. If the folded edges are clean and unbroken, the sheet can be creased by hand. If the folded edges are broken, the paper is too heavy to crease by hand and should be scored, cut-scored, or indented (see following instructions).

1 Rest the paper on a smooth, hard, level surface. Orientate the paper so that the line of the crease about to be made runs horizontally from left to right across your body. Pick up the edge or corner nearest to you.

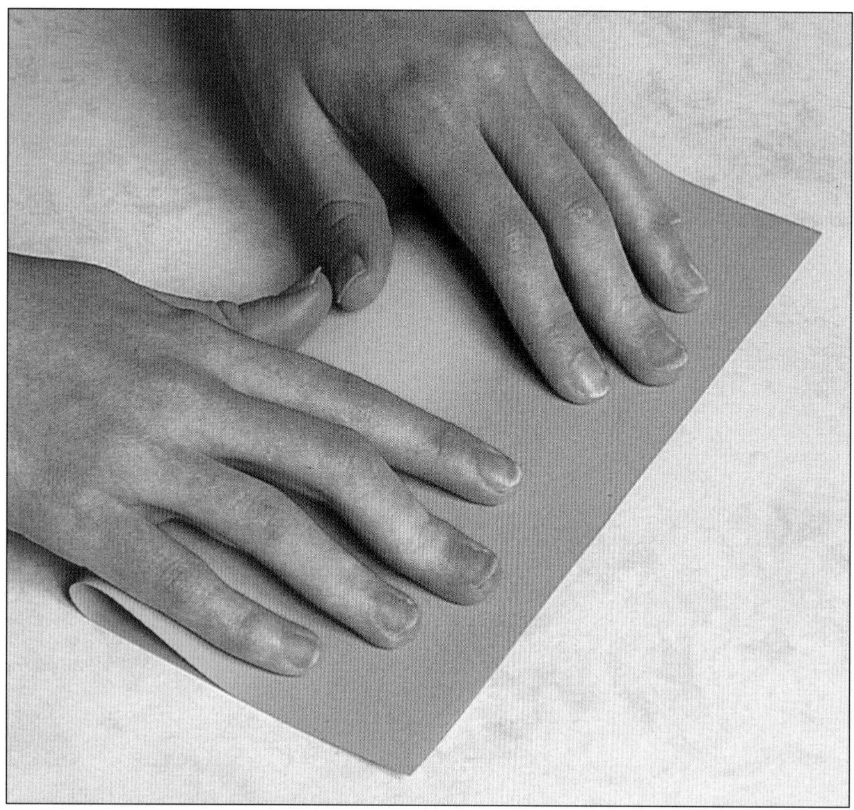

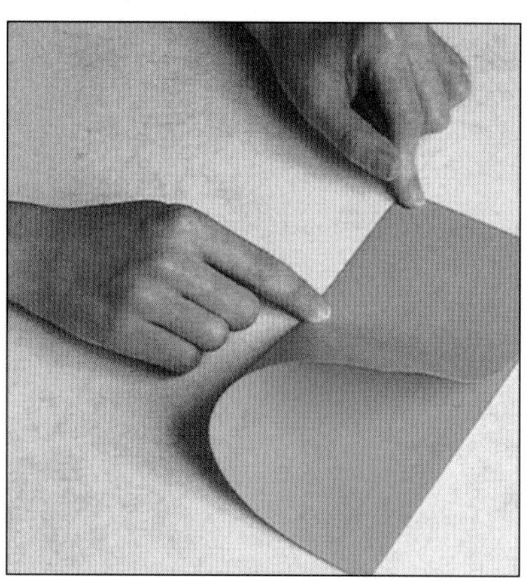

2 Take the edge or corner to whatever position is necessary to locate the line of the crease, then make the crease. Always make sure that the crease is made at the bottom of the sheet, never down the side or across the top.

Not all creases should be made against a surface. Smaller creases, particularly in origami, are best made with the paper in the air.

SCORING

This is an easy way to crease heavy paper and thin cardboard, but has the disadvantage of weakening the sheet at the folded edge, because the surface of the sheet has been cut.

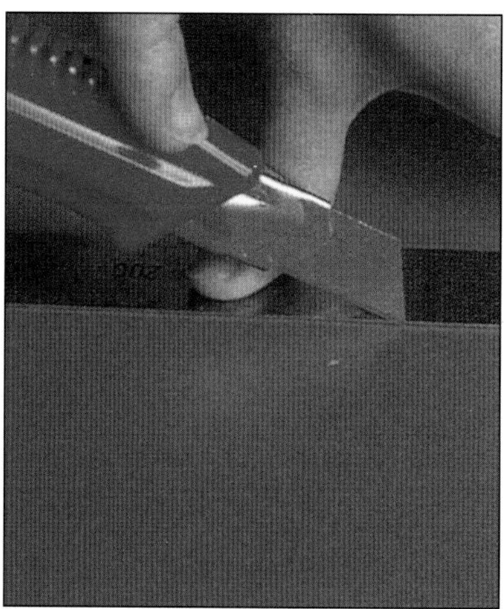

1 Place a metal ruler along the line of the crease and score with a sharp scalpel, cutting two-thirds of the way through the card. Always score on the outer, or mountain, side of a crease.

2 Scoring is ideal for constructing curved creases, which can be made freehand.

CUT-SCORE

A technique halfway between scoring and indenting, cut-scoring should be used either for creasing very thick cardboard or for giving thinner cardboard a particularly flexible crease, such as might be needed on a box lid.

INDENTING

This is the technique used to crease commercially manufactured cartons and boxes. The cardboard is not weakened by scoring, but is indented under pressure along the line of the crease. This is achieved by stamping the cardboard with a metal edge similar to the edge of a metal ruler. The same result can be achieved by hand.

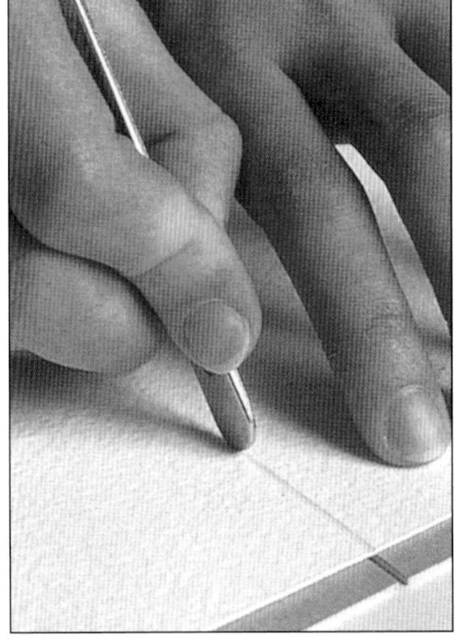

ABOVE *Use thick, strong cardboard. Cut it into two parts, each with at least one perfectly straight edge. Tape each part to a flat backing surface, so that the straight edges are 1/10 inch apart. Lay the cardboard to be creased over the gully between the two parts, so that the line of the crease will exactly follow the line of the gully. Push the cardboard into the gully with a blunt scissor point to form the crease.*

ABOVE *The cardboard is cut all the way through in a series of dashes formed by a knife held against a ruler. The length of the cuts and the distance between them depends on the thickness of the card and the degree of flexibility required, though clearly the longer the cuts, the weaker the card will be. Indent the crease for added flexibility (see above).*

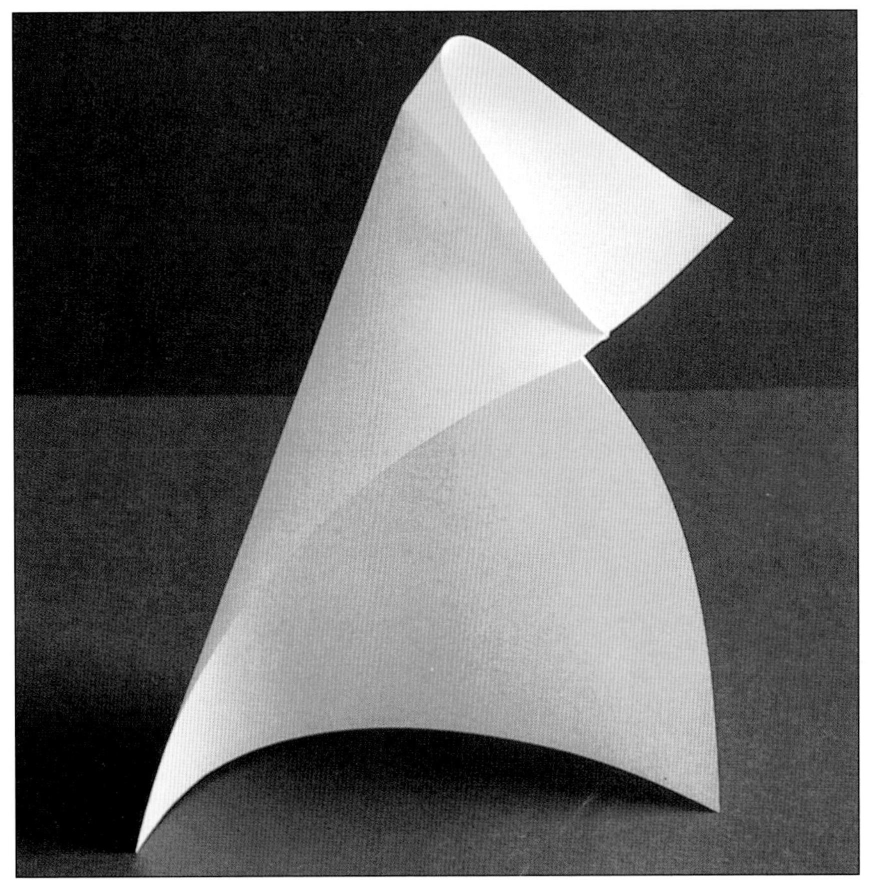

RIGHT Folded Form *(PAUL JACKSON) This simple but surprisingly stable form is one of a long series of "one crease" studies which explored the possibilities of single creases put into a square sheet of paper. The crease here is made by hand on lightweight paper. Its finished height is 6 inches.*

SYMBOLS AND TERMS

Before folding the models in this section, first study the explanation of the symbols and procedures in these pages. Refer back to this section whenever necessary.

Origami folds are communicated through drawings showing the progression of the fold as well as verbal instructions. Each drawing shows two things: the result of the previous step, and what action is taken next. Before performing the operation immediately shown, look ahead to the next step, or next several steps, to see what the result will be.

Verbal instructions are provided for each step and should be used with the drawings. The terms "upper," "lower," "top," "bottom," "left," "right," "horizontal," and "vertical" refer to the dimensions of the page itself: thus "toward the top" means "toward the top of the page." The terms "front" and "near" refer to location or motion perpendicular to the page, that is, toward the folder; the terms "far," "behind," and "back" refer to location or motion away from the folder. The terms "in" and "inward" mean toward the middle of the model; the terms "out" and "outward" mean away from the middle. An edge can be a folded edge or a raw edge, which is part of the original edge of the square. These terms are illustrated (right).

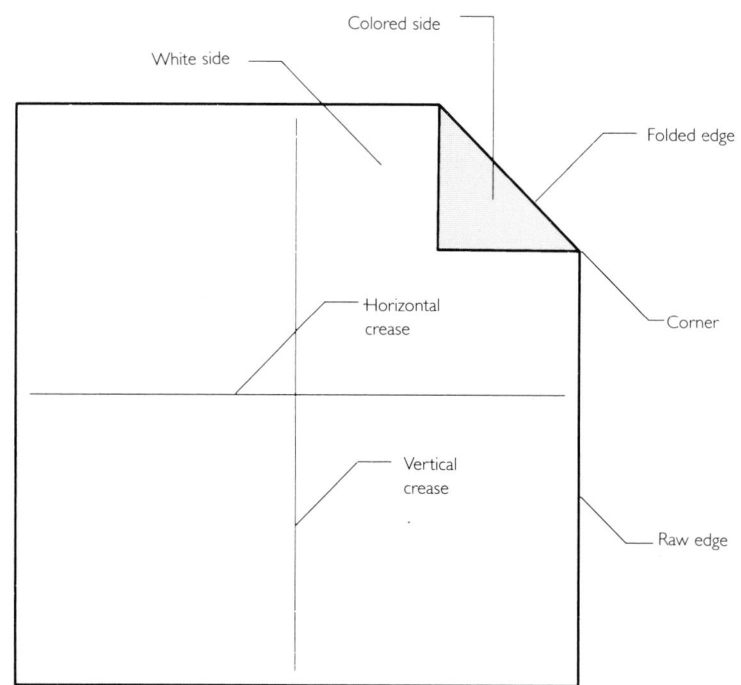

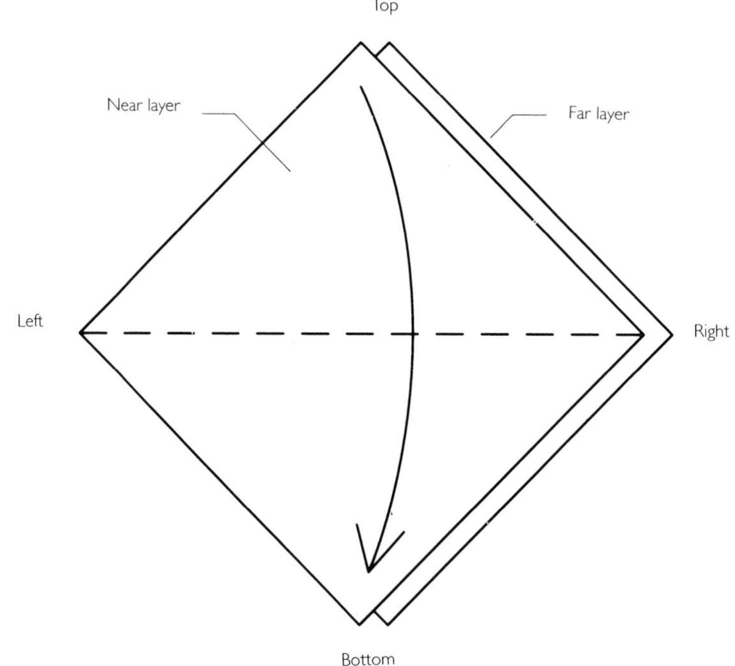

Most of the legs, wings, and other appendages of origami animals are made from flaps of paper. A simple flap has two sides: the spine, which is closed, and the open side, which consists of one or more edges. Some flaps have several layers on the open side; more complicated flaps can have several layers on each side.

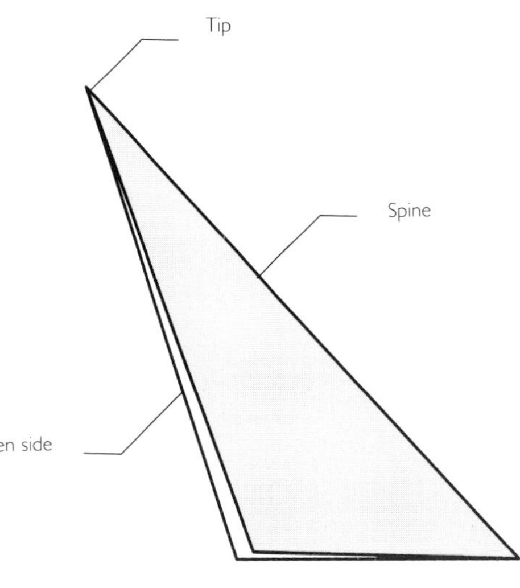

Origami diagrams are drawn as if the paper were opened slightly to display the ordering of multiple layers within the model. However, you should always fold the model so that all edges are made to line up as neatly as possible (unless otherwise instructed).

Fold accurately, making sharp creases. Origami is a geometrical art, and for this reason there is little tolerance for error in the folding process. Small inaccuracies at the beginning turn into large ones as the sequence progresses. The appeal of many models, however, can be enhanced by subtle shaping, rounding, and adjustment of the finished form.

Traditional origami paper is colored on one side and white on the other. All of the instructions in this book are drawn as if there were a colored side and a white side of the paper. Of course, you may fold the models from paper that is the same color on both sides, as are many of the models in the photographs.

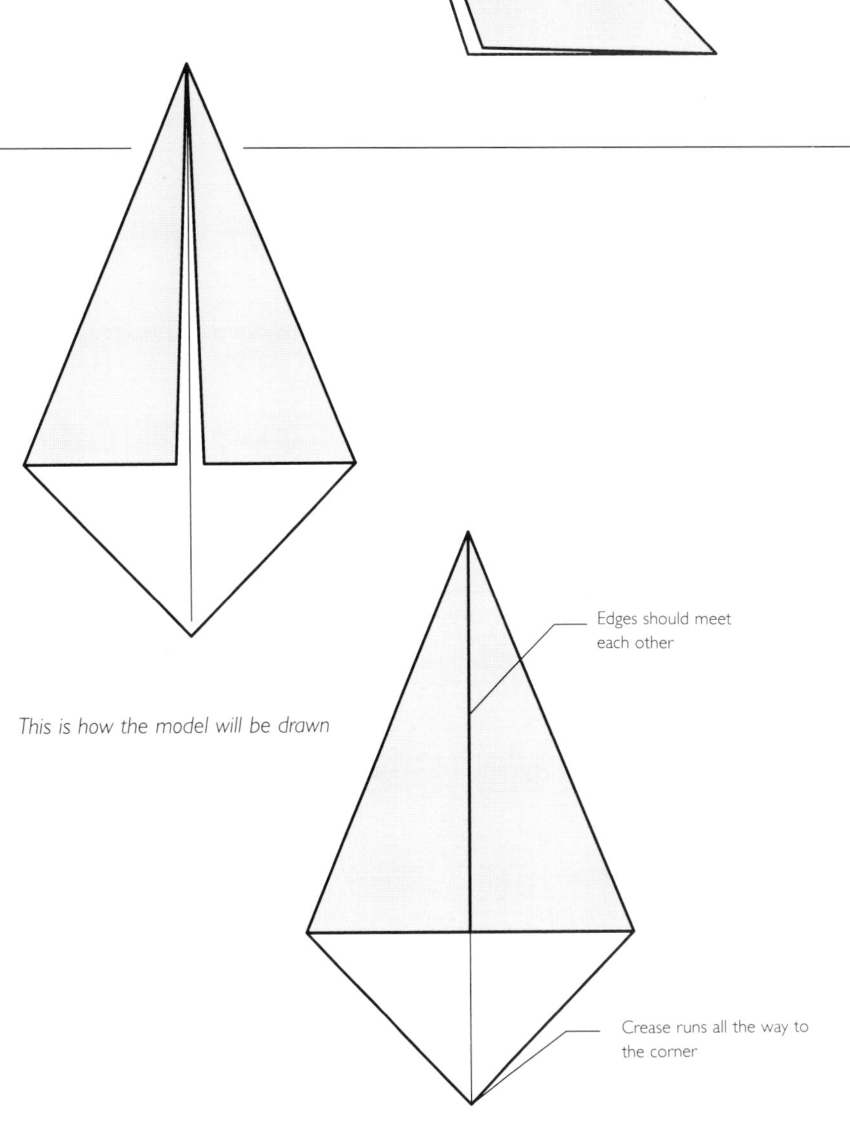

This is how the model will be drawn

This is how your paper should actually look

Several basic procedures are common to most origami designs. These procedures, and the symbols used to indicate them, are illustrated in the following pages.

VALLEY FOLD

When a flap or layer of paper is folded so that the crease forms a trough, that is called a valley fold. Valley folds are the most common types of fold, and in this section, wherever the word "fold" is used by itself to describe an action, it means "valley-fold." A valley fold is indicated by a dashed line, and an arrow with a symmetrical split head shows the motion of the paper. In this example, the top of the paper is folded down to meet the bottom, making a valley fold.

Most of the time, a valley fold forms automatically when you bring one point or edge to another and flatten the paper. In the example opposite, you bring edge AB up to edge CD and when you flatten the paper, the crease automatically forms in the right place.

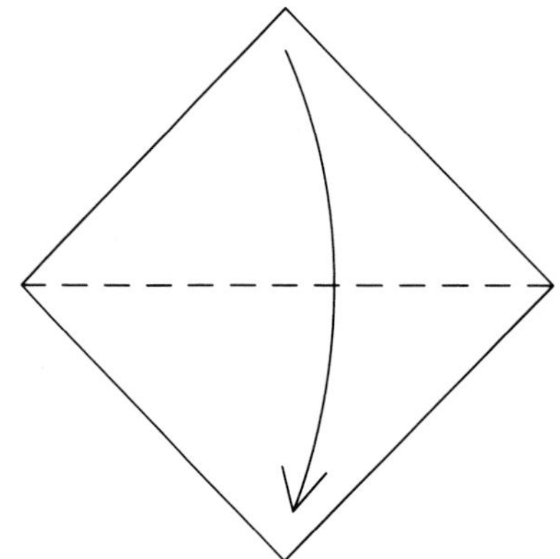

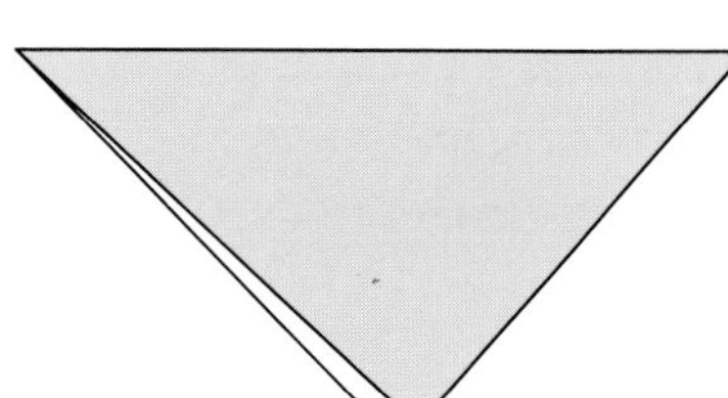

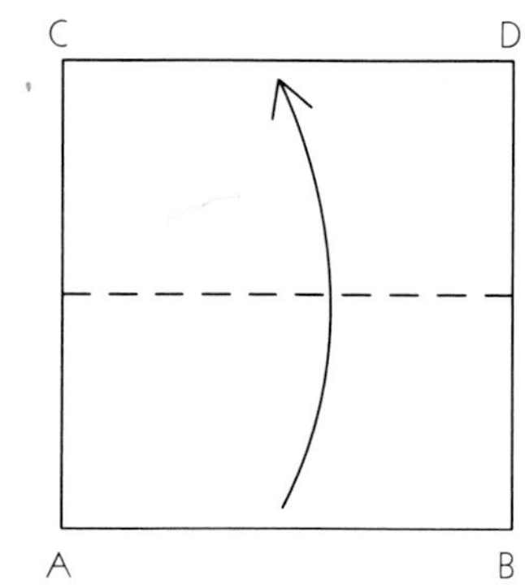

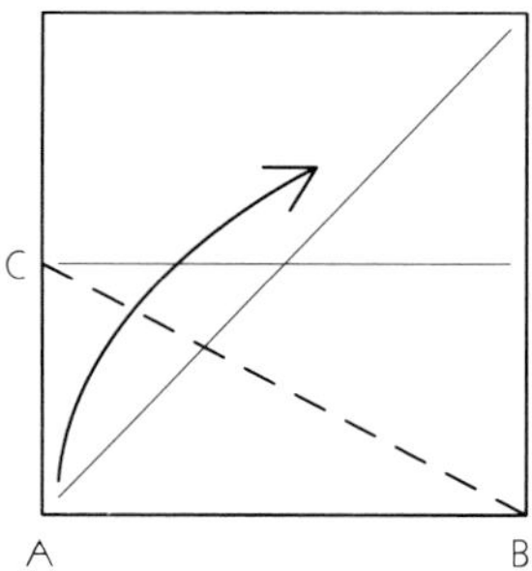

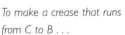

To make a crease that runs from C to B . . .

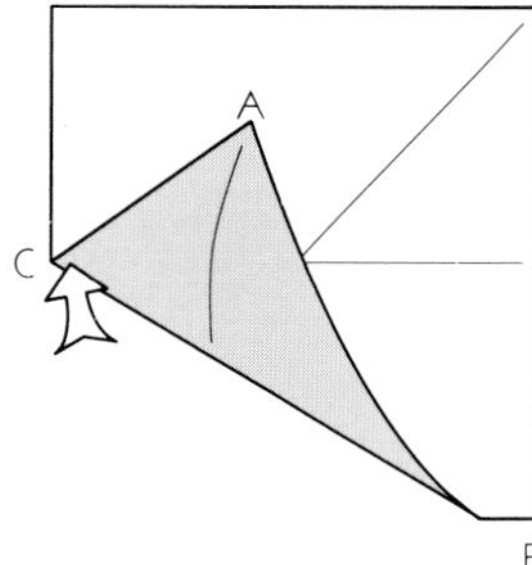

. . . first, make a small pinch at point C . . .

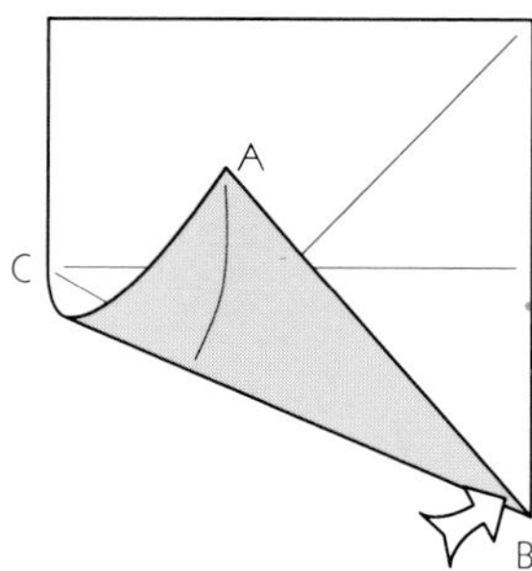

. . . then make a small pinch at point B . . .

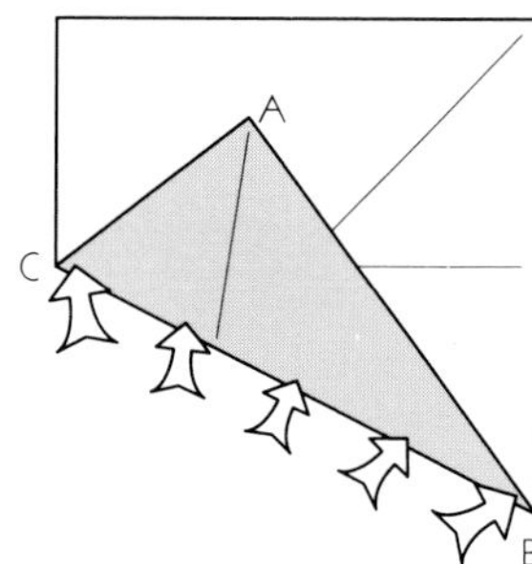

. . . finally, flatten the crease between points B and C, a little at a time, until it is sharp.

It is usually easier to fold a point or edge from the bottom up, as shown above. This gives you a good view of the crease as it is being formed so that you can make sure that it forms in the right place. If the drawing shows a point being folded down, you can rotate the paper so that the direction of the fold is upward. Be sure you return the paper to its original orientation, however.

An exception to this rule arises when you are folding so that the crease goes through a particular point. In this case, you might find it easier to make the crease go through the reference points by folding the paper toward you so that you can see the reference creases.

To make a crease that accurately connects two points, make a small pinch mark at each of the two points, then gradually flatten the paper between them, making the crease sharp a little at a time, until the paper is completely flat.

MOUNTAIN FOLD

When a flap or layer of paper is folded away from you so that the crease forms a peak, that is called a mountain fold. A mountain fold is indicated by a dot-dot-dash line and an arrow with a one-sided hollow head showing the motion of the paper. In general, if the arrow has a split head, the paper starts out moving toward you; if the head is hollow, the paper moves away from you.

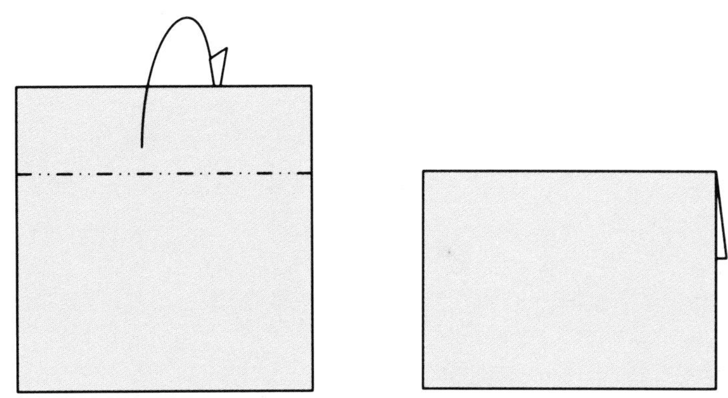

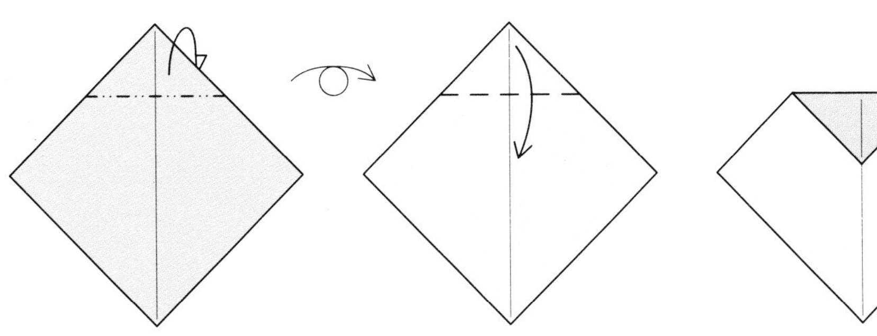

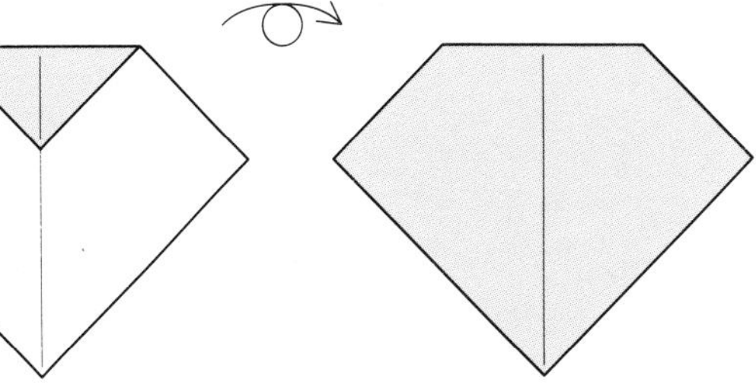

To make a mountain fold . . .

. . . you can turn the paper over . . .

. . . make a valley fold . . .

. . . and turn the paper back over again.

Sometimes a mountain fold is more easily accomplished by turning the paper over to perform it. For example, you can sometimes do a mountain fold by turning the paper over, doing a valley fold, and then returning it to its original position. You should always be sure that you return the paper to the orientation shown in the next drawing before proceeding.

However, a mountain fold is also often used to tuck a flap inside a pocket, in which case turning the paper over is not necessarily useful.

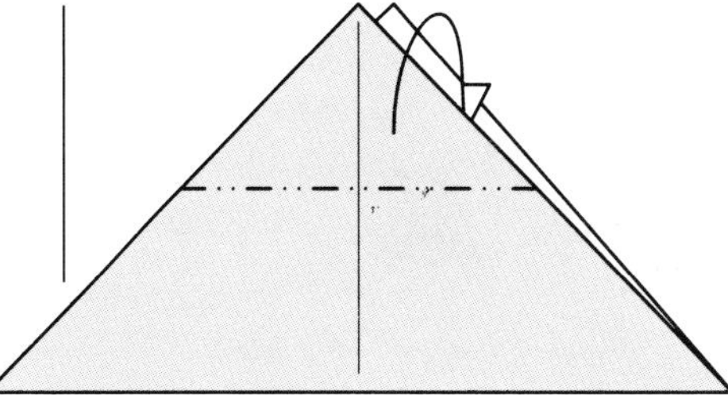

This method won't work if you are tucking the flap in front of another.

X-RAY LINE

A dotted line is used to indicate a fold or an edge that is hidden, and in this respect is similar to the cutaway view. Typically, an x-ray line will be used to indicate the continuation of a fold behind a flap, while the cutaway view is used to show more complicated structures. This example also shows that the mountain fold line may be extended past the edge of the paper if not enough of it is showing otherwise.

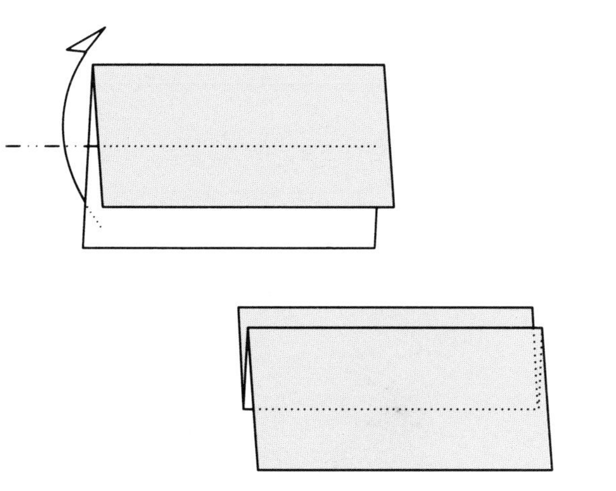

UNFOLD

Sometimes you will need to undo a fold you have made previously. This procedure is indicated by a hollow open arrowhead. You will often do this in the beginning steps of a model, when you are establishing some guide creases for reference.

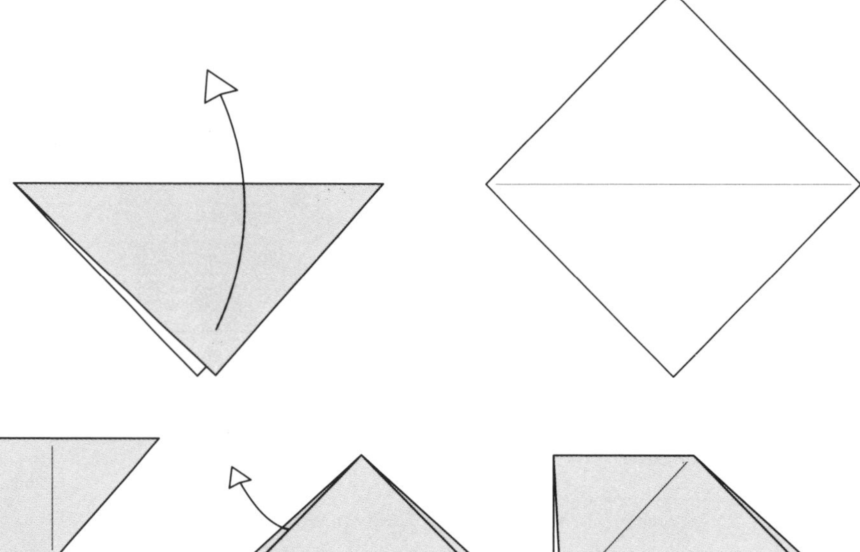

The same symbol is used to indicate that you should pull some paper out of a pocket or unwrap a layer of paper, as in the examples shown here.

FOLD AND UNFOLD

When you are making guide creases, you fold the paper in a particular way and then unfold it, which is normally drawn in two separate steps (one to fold the paper, one to unfold it). Here, the two steps are often combined into one, by using an arrow with a valley fold arrowhead on one end and an unfold arrowhead on the other. This arrow means to fold and unfold. After you have unfolded a step, the creases that remain are indicated by thinner lines. Where a crease meets an edge, there will be a small gap, to emphasize its presence and further differentiate it from an edge. Creases are sometimes used as references, and sometimes used to establish the

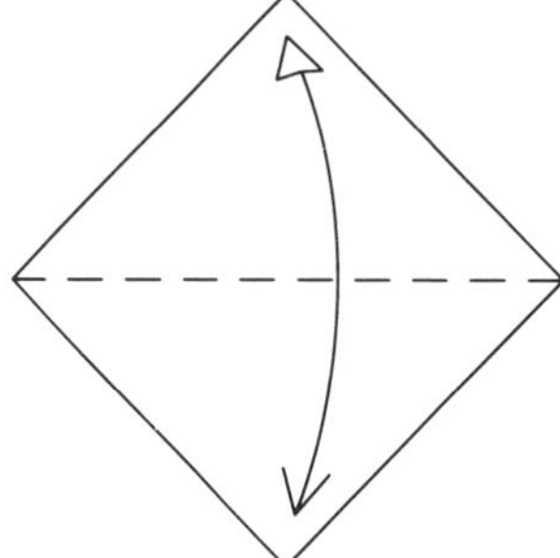

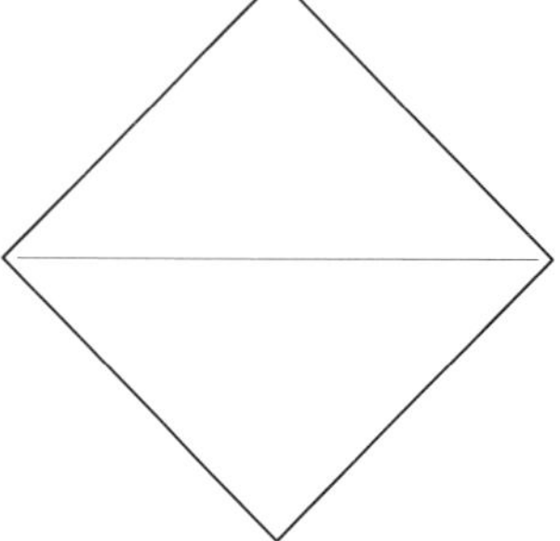

location of more difficult folds such as reverse folds and petal folds.

When you fold and unfold it will often be to make a reference mark. Your final model will look better if the pinch marks are small and unobtrusive. (It will also be easier to follow the diagrams if your paper isn't covered by extraneous creases.) If you need only the point where one crease crosses another (or hits an edge) for reference, then in the diagrams, the crease will be shown as a dotted line along its length and as a valley fold only where you need to make it sharp. The example shown below is a standard technique for dividing a square into thirds; the point where the crease crosses the diagonal divides the paper into thirds.

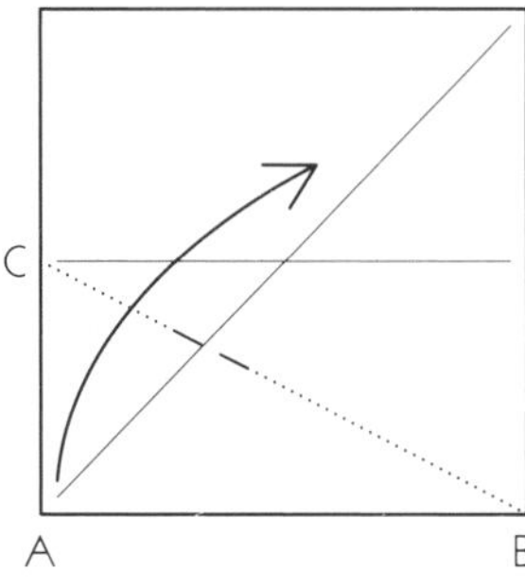

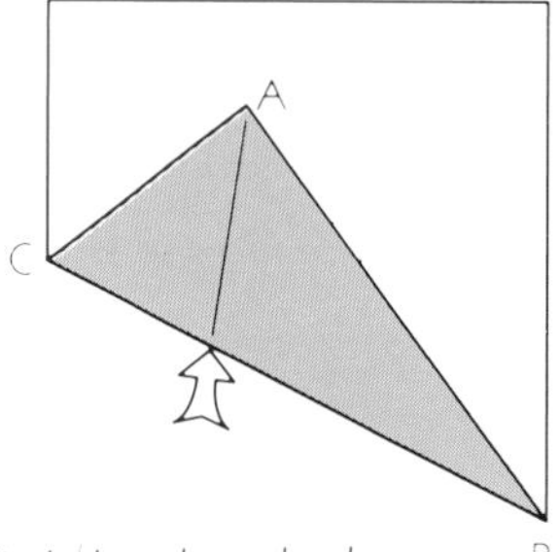

Pinch the edge only where the crease hits it.

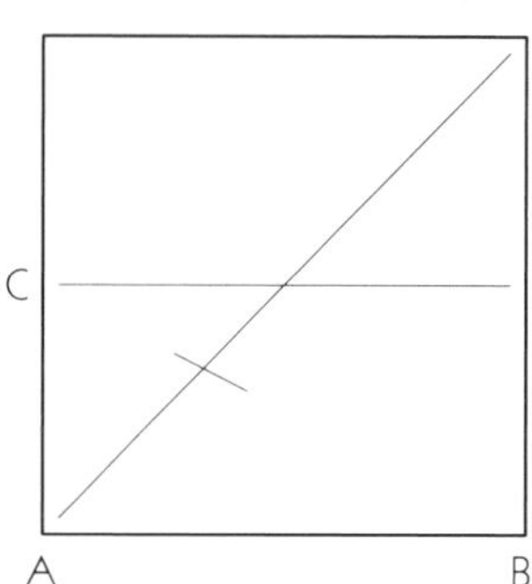

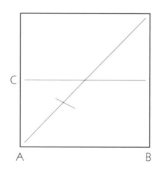

WATCH THIS SPOT

In this section, important reference points are marked with letters, which have a reference in the verbal instructions. Often, the position of a lettered flap in one step can clarify any ambiguity in the previous step.

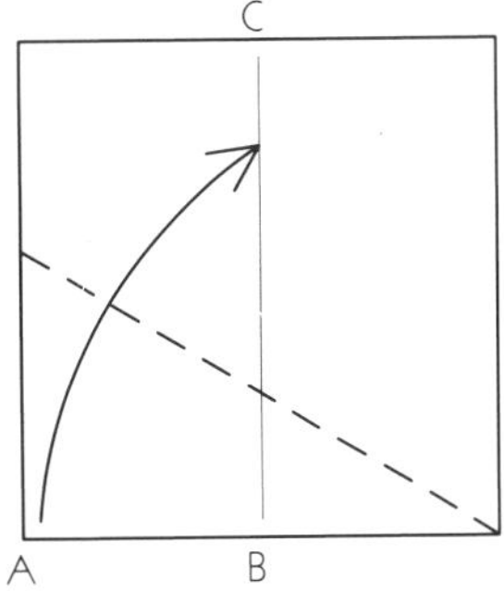

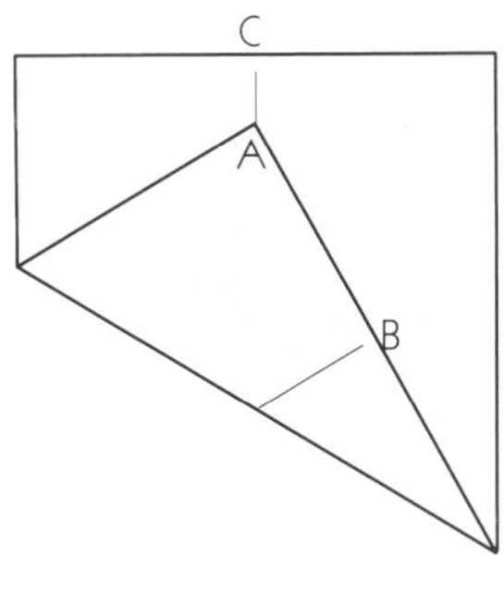

ROTATE THE PAPER

A circle with two arrows indicates to rotate the model in the plane of the page. The direction of rotation is indicated by the direction of the arrows; the amount of rotation is given by the fraction in the centre of the circle as a fraction of a complete revolution. For example, in the first figure above, you should rotate the model one-quarter turn clockwise.

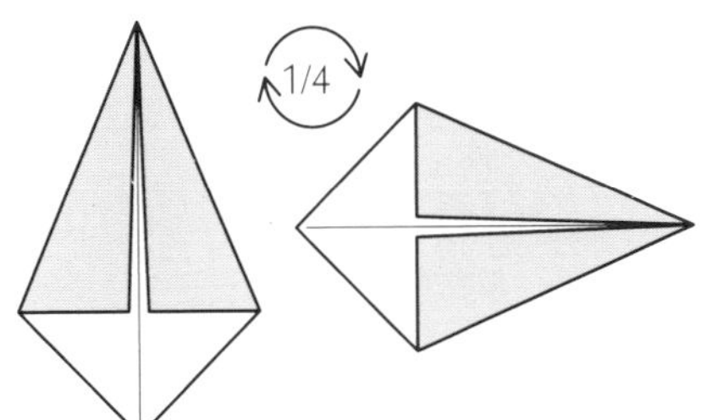

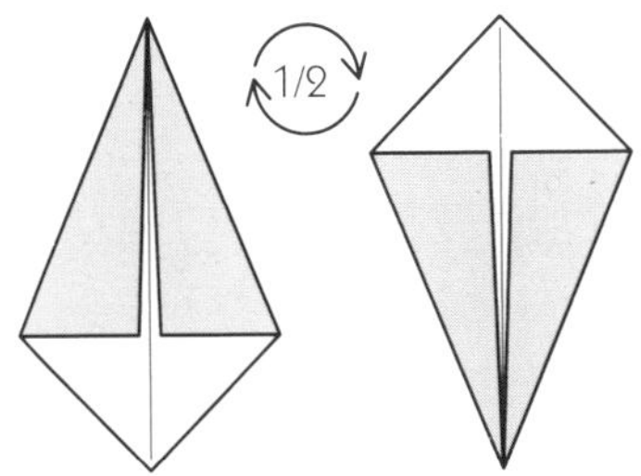

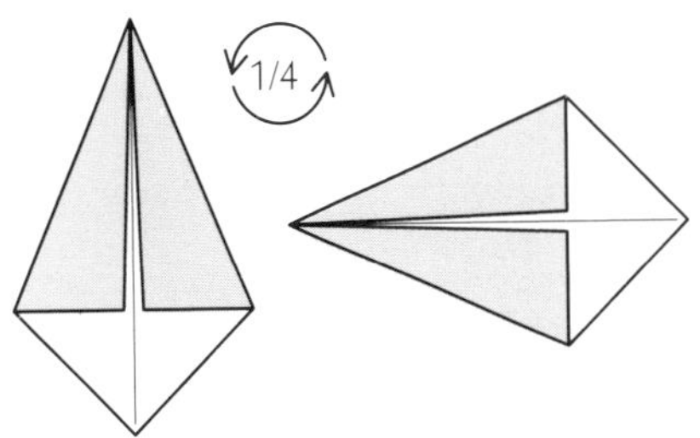

FOLD OVER AND OVER

An arrow that touches down more than once indicates to valley-fold once, and then valley-fold again (and again, if necessary, for as many times as the arrow touches down).

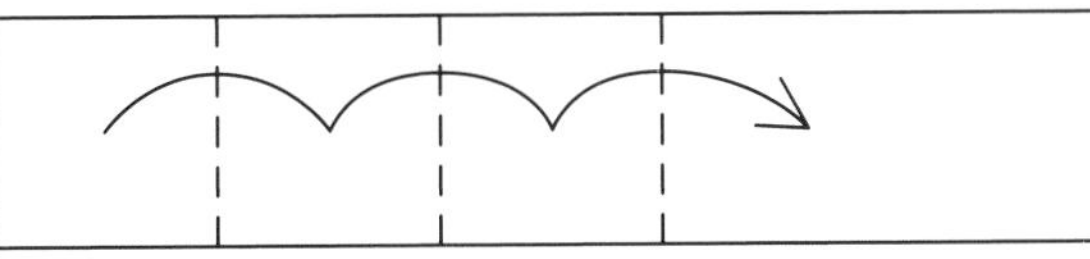

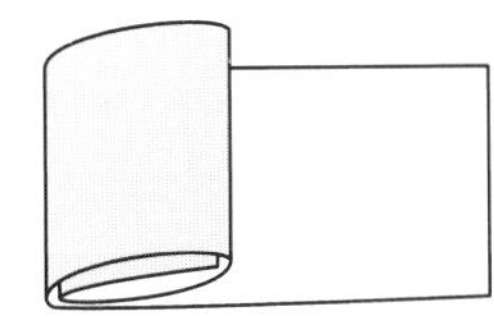

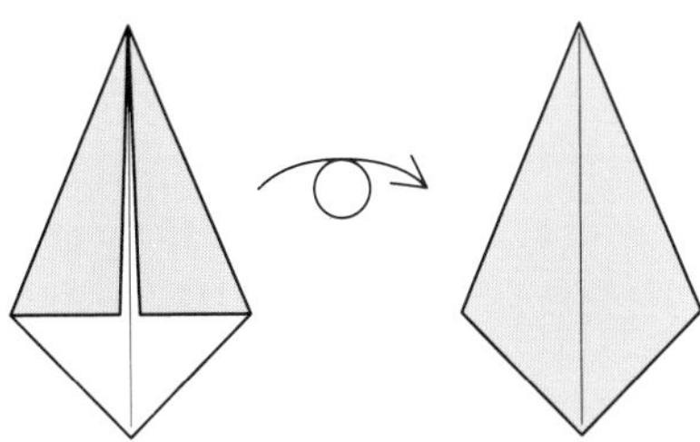

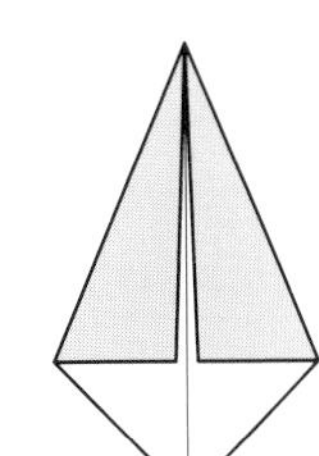

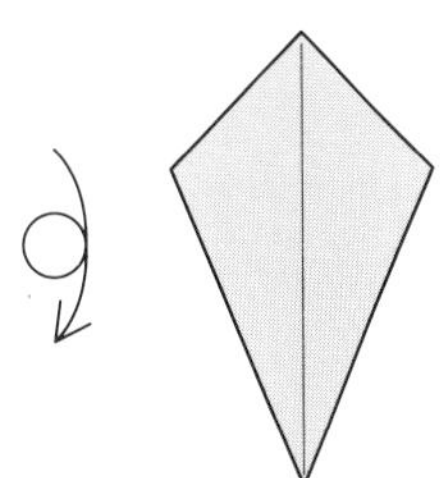

TURN THE PAPER OVER

An arrow that makes a loop means you should turn the entire model over. If the arrow runs horizontally, the paper should be turned over from side to side. If it runs vertically, the paper should be turned over from top to bottom.

CUT-AWAY AND PARTIAL VIEWS

A solid circle is used to give a view of hidden layers of paper, drawn as if the near layers of paper were cut away to expose the inner layers. Similarly, sometimes only a portion of the model will be shown in a close-up view, in which case no edge will be drawn where the rest of the model should be.

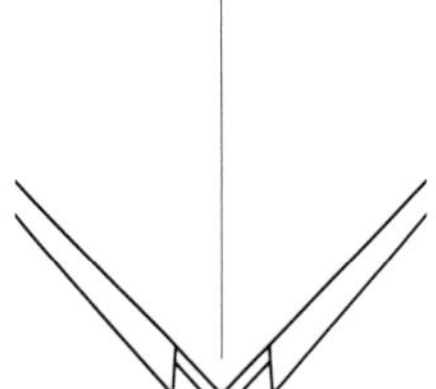

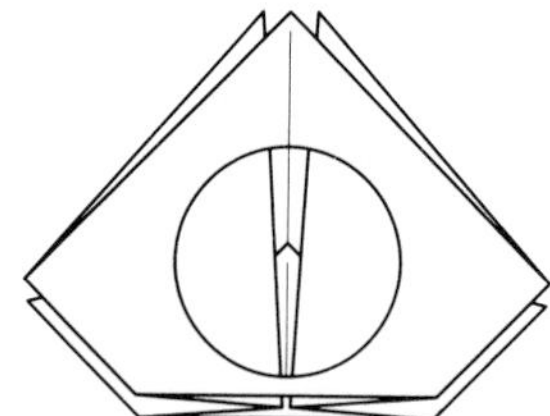

REPEAT STEPS

In many folds, an entire sequence of folds will be repeated on a different part of the model – the most common occurrence is when you do the same thing on both sides of the paper (folding the left and right side of an animal, for example). When this is to be done, the range of steps will be called out in the verbal directions. In addition, a boxed list of the steps to be repeated will appear with a line pointing to the flap or flaps affected. An example is shown below.

When the instructions say, for example, "Repeat steps 1–3 behind," you should turn the paper over and perform steps 1–3 on what is now the mirror image of the drawings. When you have finished, you may or may not be told to turn the paper back to its original orientation. You should always be sure that the paper is in the proper orientation before beginning the next step.

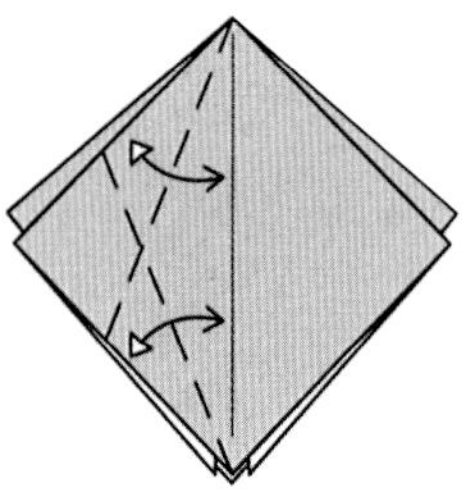

1 Fold and unfold.

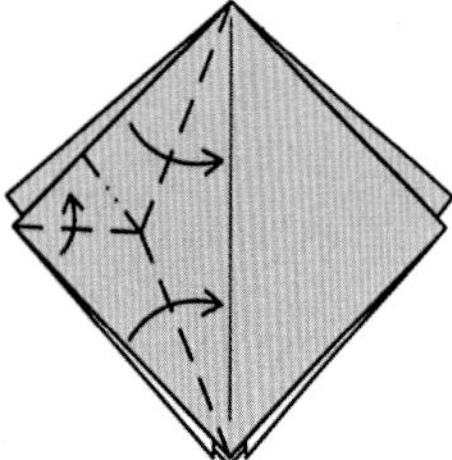

2 Fold a rabbit ear (see page 25) from the flap.

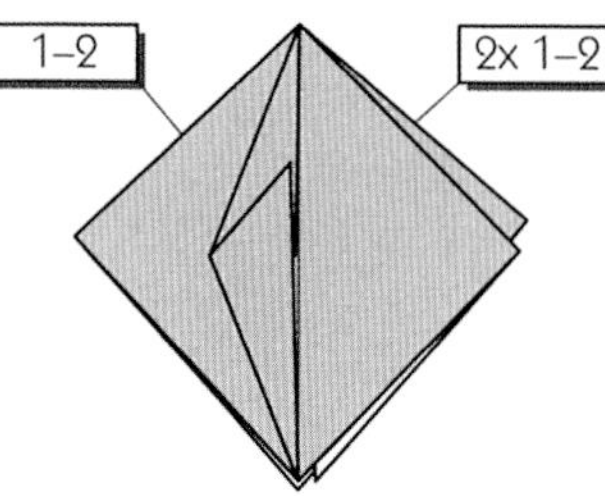

3 Repeat steps 1–2 on the left side and on both flaps on the right. (You should turn the model over to do the two rear flaps.)

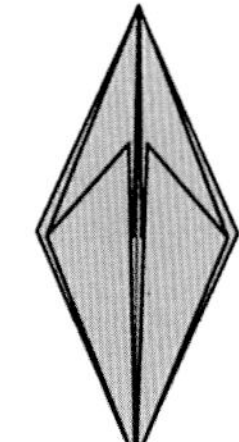

4 The result looks like this on both sides.

PUSH HERE

A small, hollow arrow with a split tail indicates "push here." Usually, that means that rather than being folded toward or away from you, the paper is pushed in symmetrically, or even inverted. For more examples of this, see Reverse Folds (pages 23–25) and the Squash Fold (page 26).

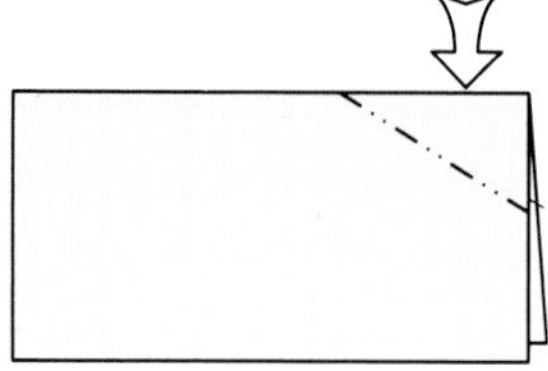

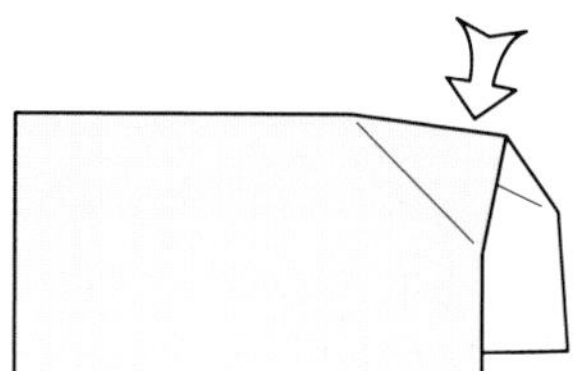

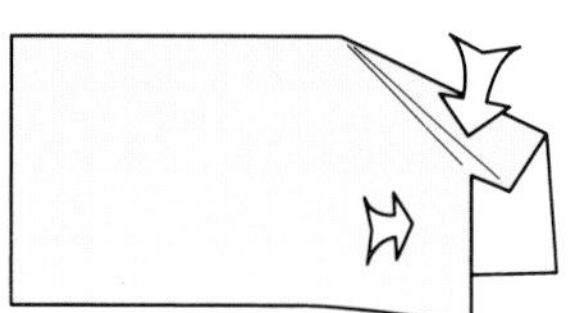

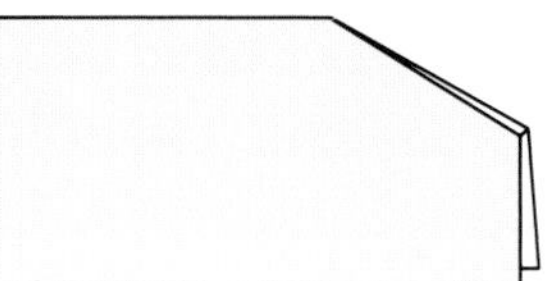

REVERSE FOLDS

Several other combinations of mountain and valley folds occur in origami; they are so common that they have special names. One of these is the "reverse fold," so-called because you turn a portion of the paper inside out. The model shown below is one on which you can practice reverse folds.

Here is a shape you can use to practice making reverse folds.

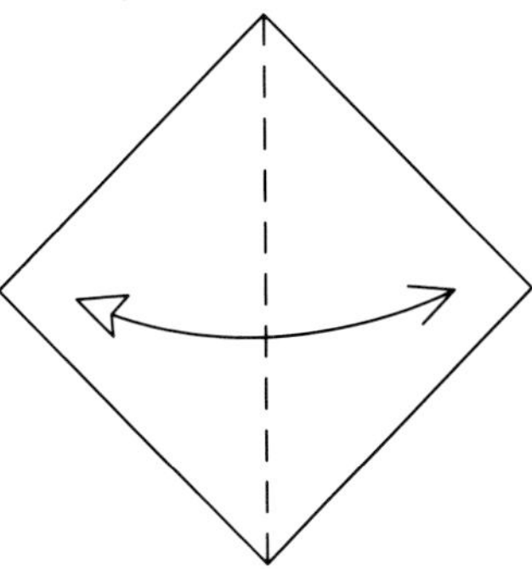

1 Fold the paper in half along the diagonal and unfold.

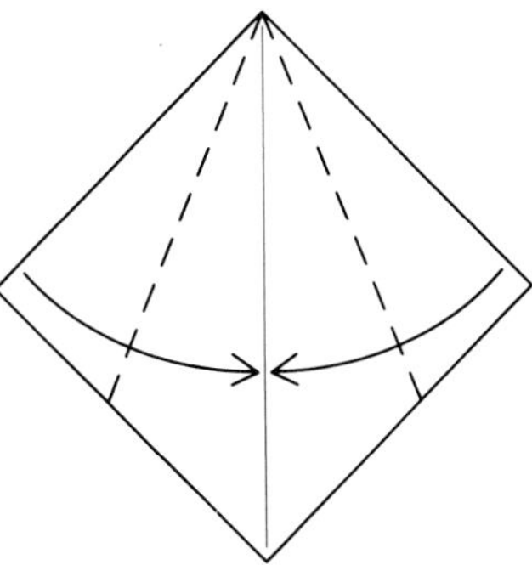

2 Fold the upper sides in to lie along the crease you just made.

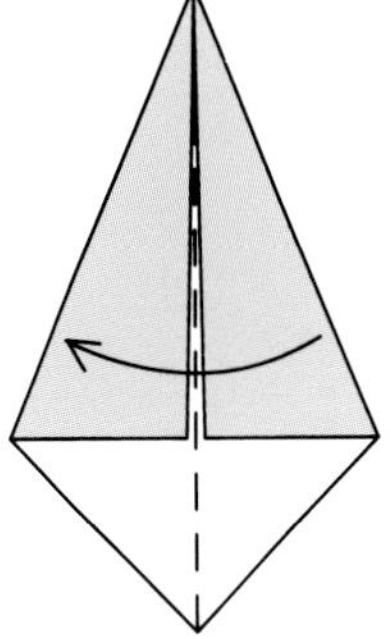

3 Fold the model in half along the vertical crease.

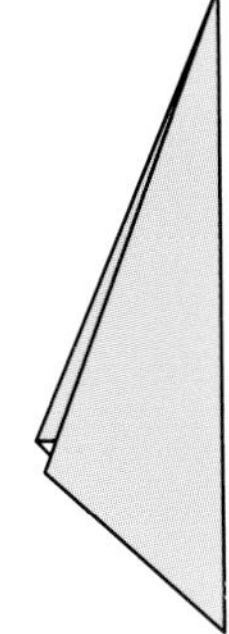

4 This shape is used to illustrate reverse folds.

Inside Reverse Fold

The inside reverse fold is a more permanent way of changing the direction of a flap than by folding it over. It is indicated by a mountain fold line on the near layer of paper and a valley fold line on the far layer if it is visible. There is also a push arrow pointing to the spine of the fold. Inside reverse folds are referred to as "reverse folds" in this section.

To make an inside reverse fold, first fold the flap along the indicated fold line, front and back, and unfold, to weaken the paper. You can do this two or three times in each direction to make sure that the paper is thoroughly weakened along the fold line. Then, spread the near and far layers of paper and push the spine of the moving flap down between them. The flap turns inside-out in the process. Flatten the paper. Be sure that all folding occurs on the existing creases and that you don't add any new ones after the pre-creasing! As you become more experienced in folding origami, you will develop the ability to make reverse folds without precreasing.

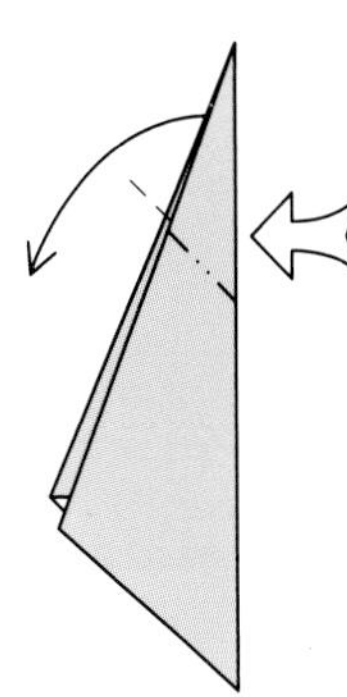

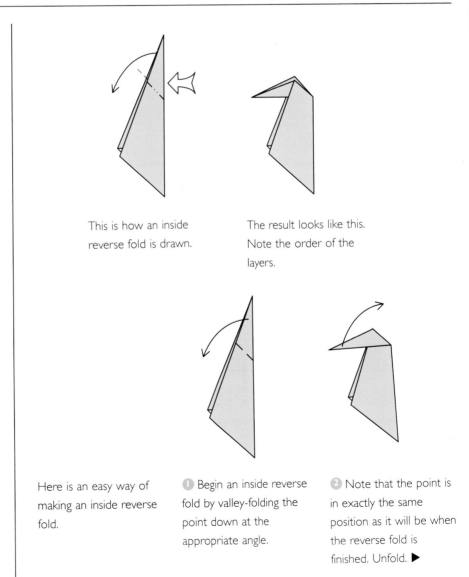

This is how an inside reverse fold is drawn.

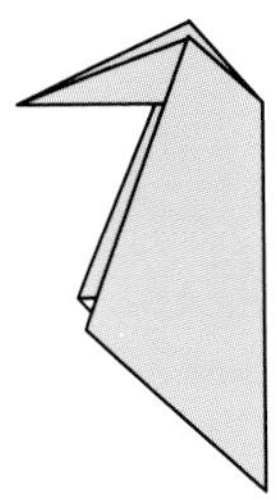

The result looks like this. Note the order of the layers.

Here is an easy way of making an inside reverse fold.

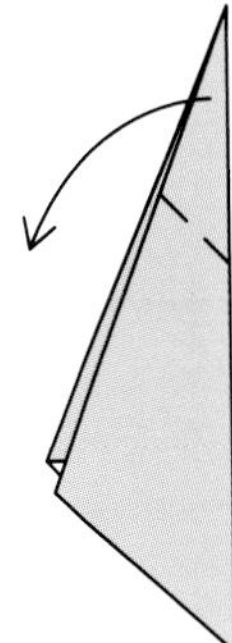

1 Begin an inside reverse fold by valley-folding the point down at the appropriate angle.

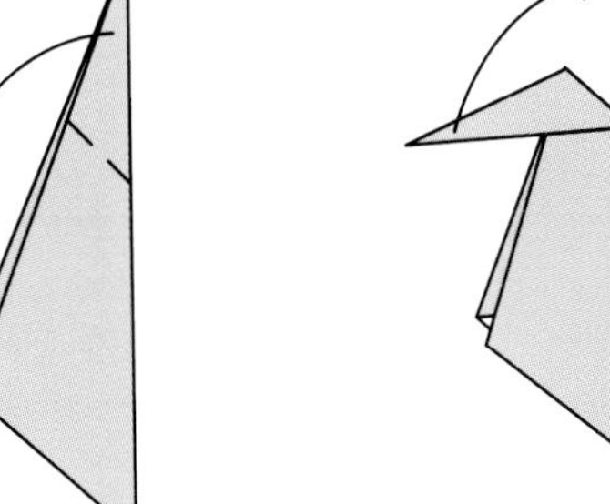

2 Note that the point is in exactly the same position as it will be when the reverse fold is finished. Unfold. ▶

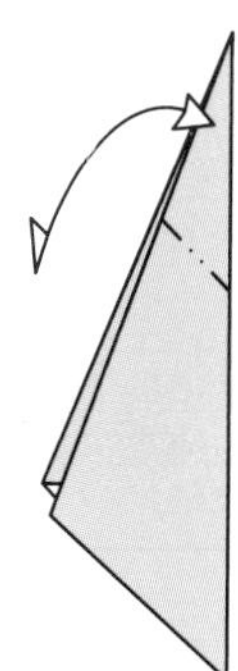

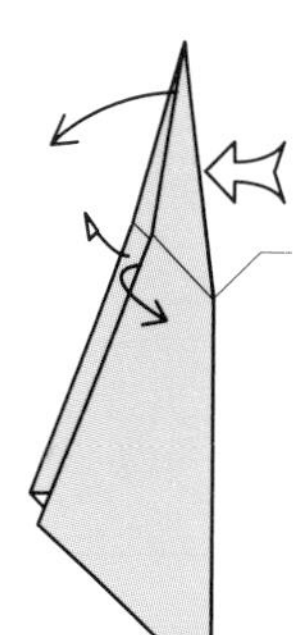

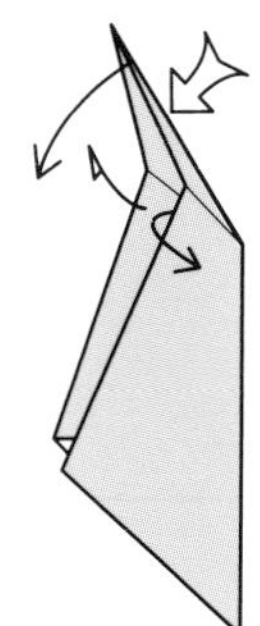

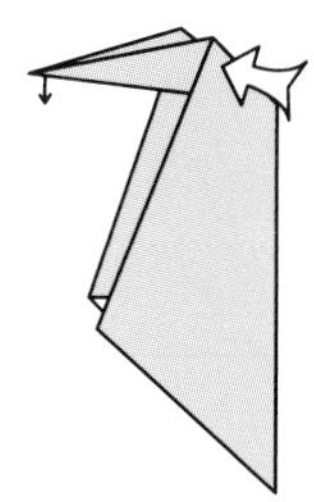

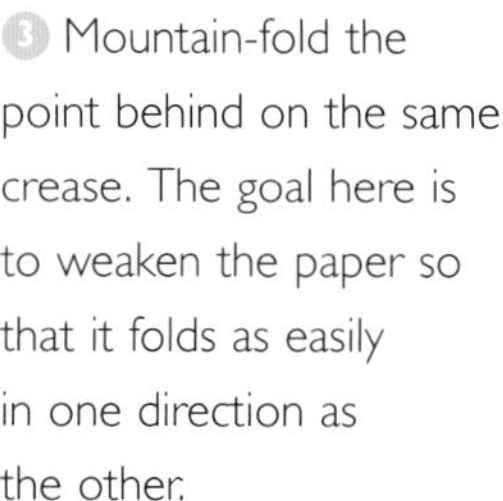

3 Mountain-fold the point behind on the same crease. The goal here is to weaken the paper so that it folds as easily in one direction as the other.

4 Open the edges of the flap apart from each other and push on the spine, so that the top of the flap starts to pivot and flatten.

5 Keep pushing on the spine until the flap goes down between the layers and turns inside-out.

6 When the crease up the spine of the flap has reversed its direction, the model will flatten easily.

Outside Reverse Fold

The outside reverse fold is also a way of changing the direction of a flap. While the inside reverse fold turns a flap toward its open edges, the outside reverse fold turns it in the opposite direction. An outside reverse fold is indicated by a valley fold on the near layer of paper (and a mountain fold on the far layer, if it is visible) and arrows showing the direction of motion of the paper.

To make an outside reverse fold, first fold and unfold the flap along the intended crease line to weaken the paper. Then, spread the layers of the moving flap and wrap them around the rest of the model. Flatten the paper. As with the inside reverse fold, until you become more experienced, you should always precrease the fold.

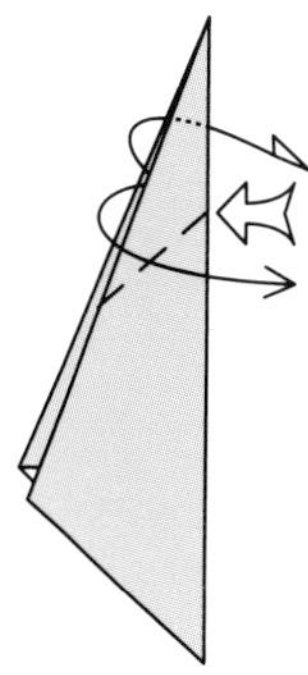

This is how an outside reverse fold is drawn.

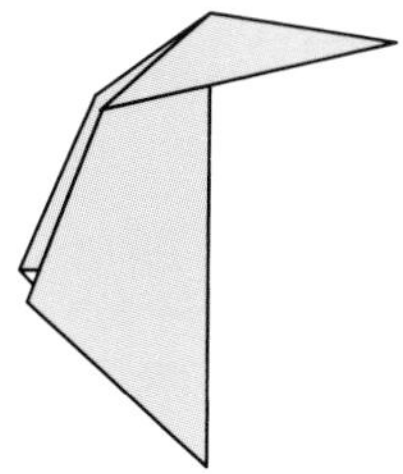

The result looks like this. Note the order of the layers.

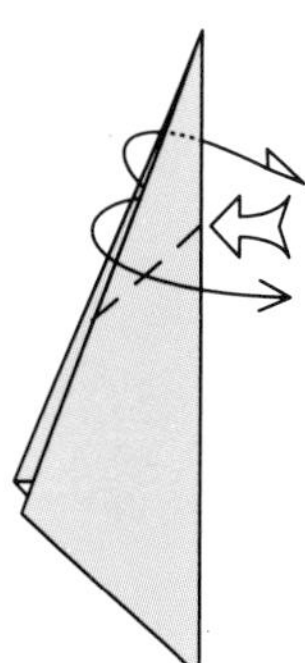

Here is an easy way to make an outside reverse fold.

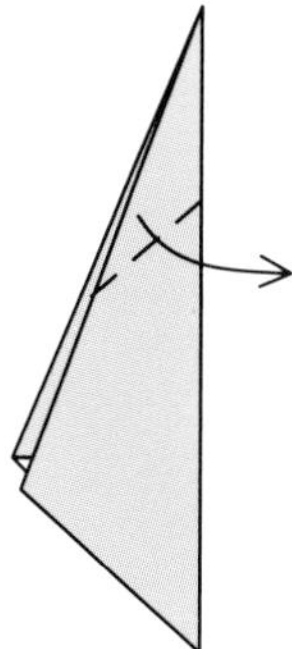

1 As with the inside reverse fold, begin the outside reverse fold by valley-folding the point over at the angle at which you wish the reverse fold to be made.

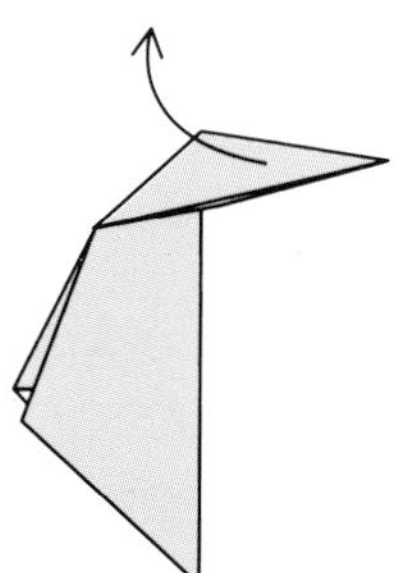

2 Unfold. Repeat in the other direction until the paper folds easily in either direction. ▶

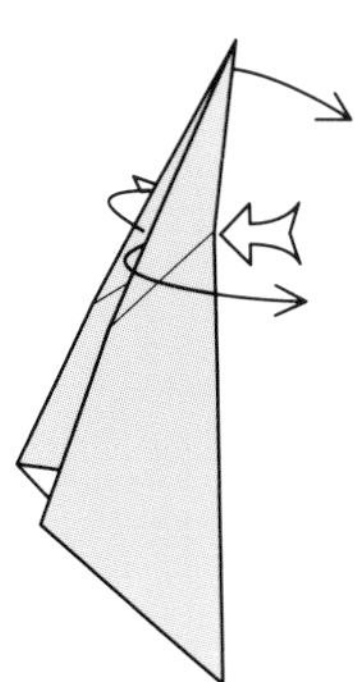

3 Spread the outside edges apart and push in the spine where the crease hits it. You will have to spread the edges more for this fold than for an inside reverse fold.

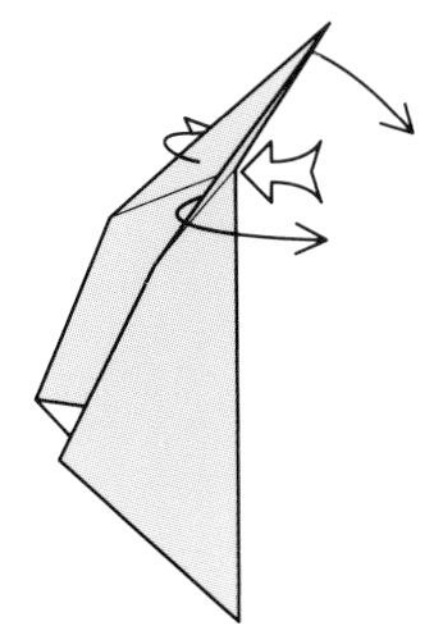

4 As the tip progresses, it will "pop" inside-out.

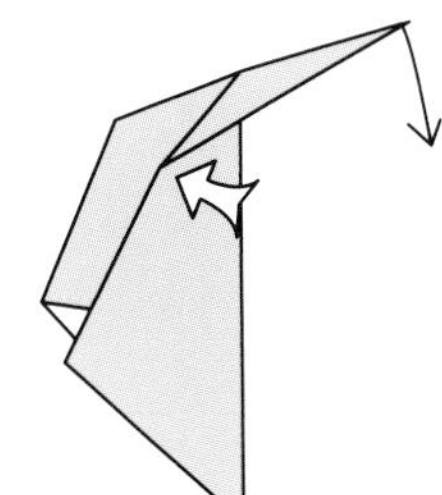

5 Once the crease that runs along the spine has changed its direction, it will flatten easily.

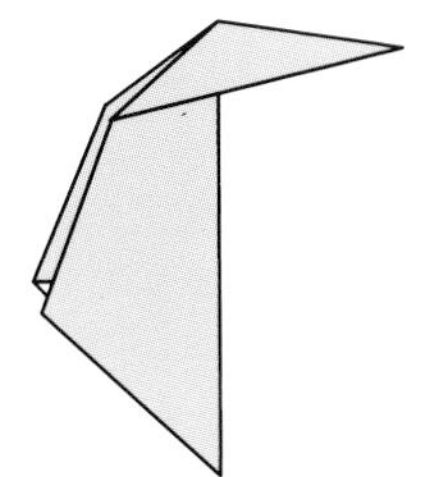

Completed outside reverse fold.

RABBIT EAR

The rabbit ear is a way of narrowing a flap and changing its direction. It is indicated by three valley folds that meet at a point and a fourth mountain fold emanating from that point. Nearly always, the flap is a triangle, and the three valley folds bisect the angles of the triangle. The way to start, therefore, is to crease each of the angle bisectors. Then, bring two sides of the flap together and pinch it in half. Swing the flap down to the side and flatten the paper.

A rabbit ear that uses the same valley folds can go in two different directions. In a model's directions, arrows and the location of the mountain fold will show which way it goes.

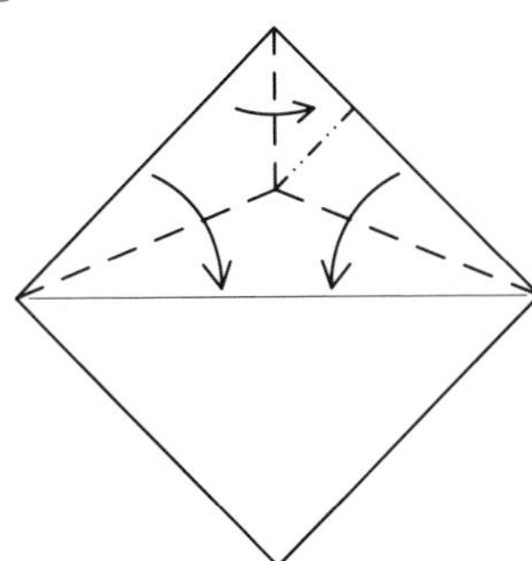

This is how a rabbit ear is diagrammed. Three valley folds and a mountain fold that meet at a point make a rabbit ear.

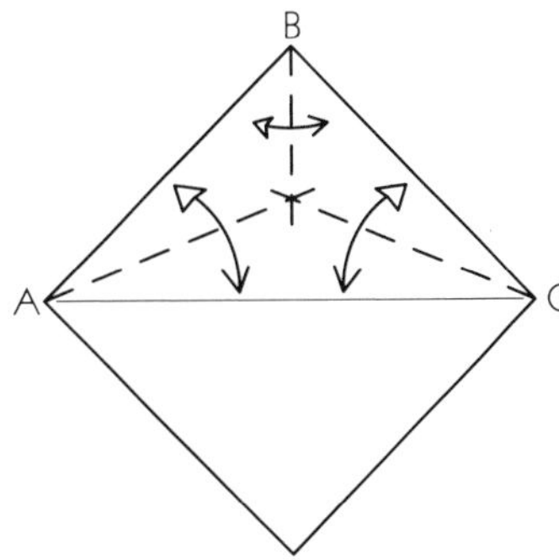

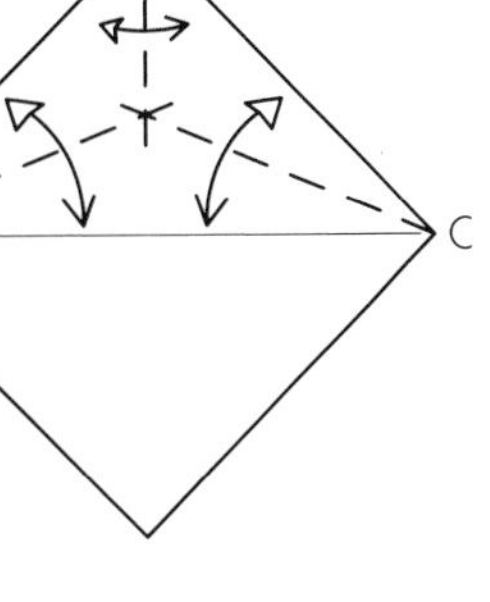

This is how to fold a rabbit ear. The valley folds in a rabbit ear usually connect the corners of a triangle to a central point (in this example, the triangle's three corners are points A, B, and C).

1 Start by folding edge AB to AC; BA to BC; and CA to CB. The three creases you make should all meet at the same point.

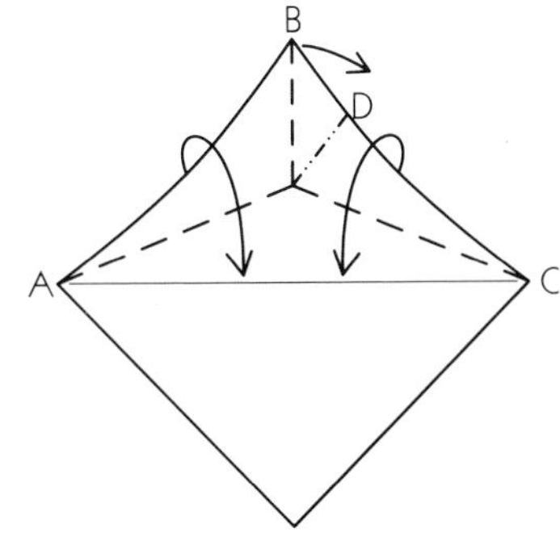

2 Bring edges AB and BC together along line AC; the extra paper goes into a flap that ends in point B. Swing point B toward the side that the mountain fold was on (the right, in this example).

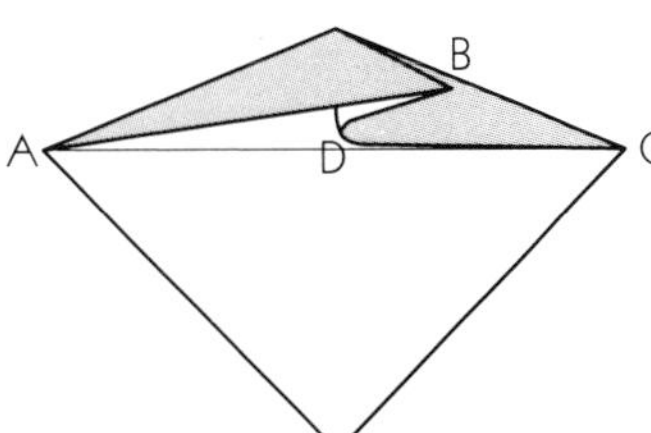

3 Flatten the model. The crease that hits point D forms naturally in the right place.

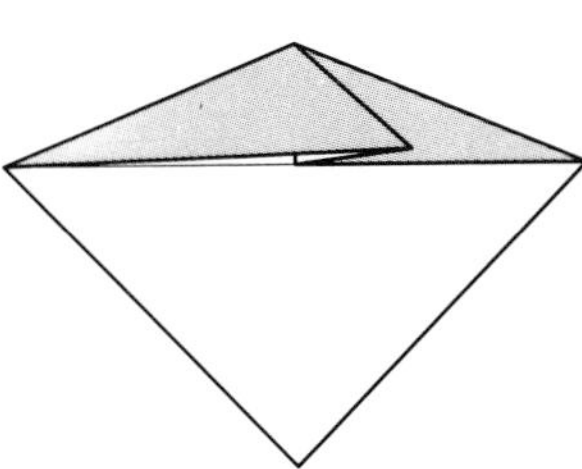

The finished rabbit ear.

SQUASH AND PETAL FOLDS

Squash and petal folds are two types of folds that are somewhat more complicated than inside and outside reverse folds. They are used to create new points and edges in a model.

Squash Fold

The squash fold is a way of converting one folded edge into two. It is indicated by a valley and mountain fold line and a push arrow pointing to the edge to be squashed. To make a squash fold, spread the open layers of the edge to be squashed and flatten them so that the edge ends up on top of the fold line at the base of the flap, as point A does in the example.

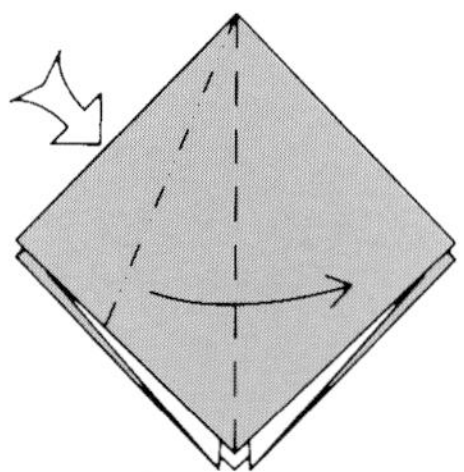

This is how a squash fold is drawn.

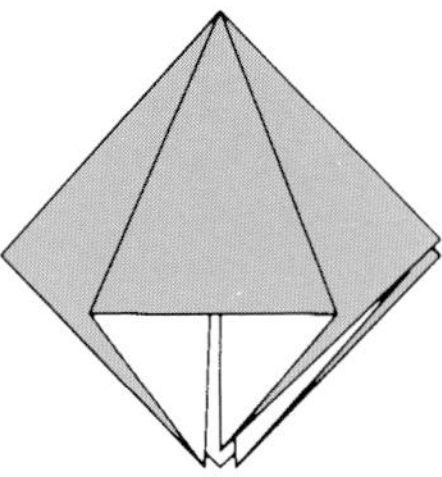

The result looks like this.

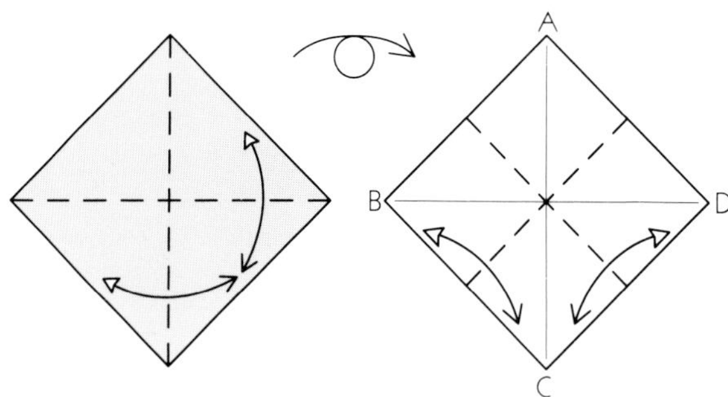

Here is a shape you can practice squash and petal folds upon.

1 Fold the square in half along the diagonals and turn over.

2 Fold edge AB down to CD and unfold. Fold edge AD down to BC and unfold.

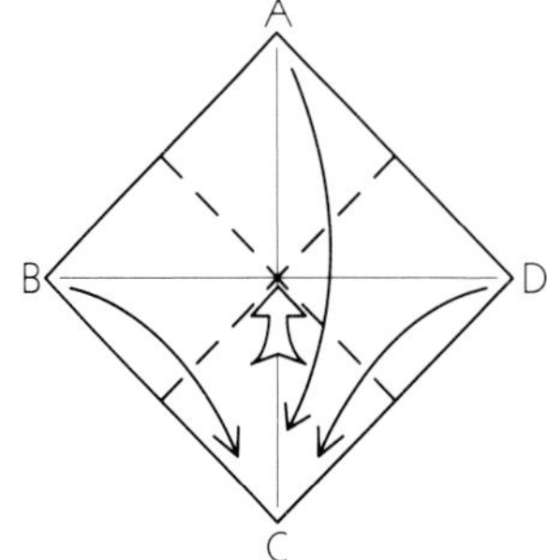

3 Bring all four corners together at the bottom while pushing in the middle.

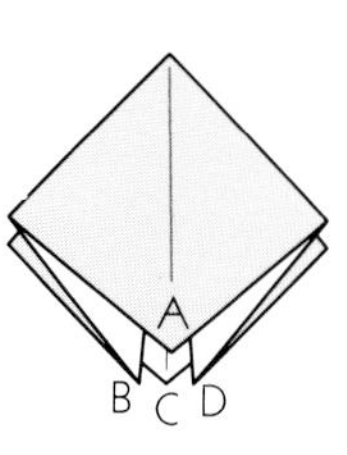

4 Flatten.

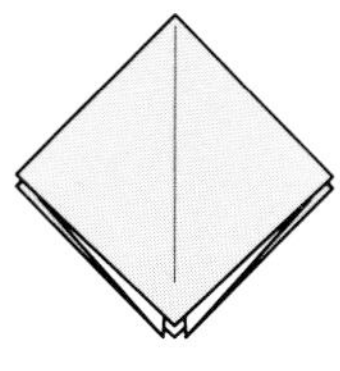

This shape is called the Preliminary Fold.

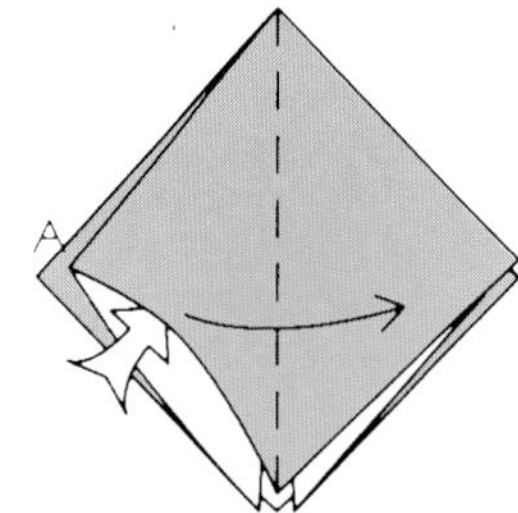

Here is how to make a squash fold.

1 Put your finger inside the pocket and spread its edges apart.

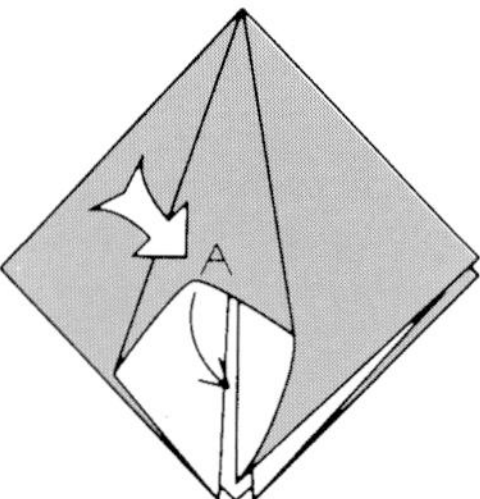

2 Flatten out the flap so that point A hits the folded edges underneath. the remaining folds form automatically.

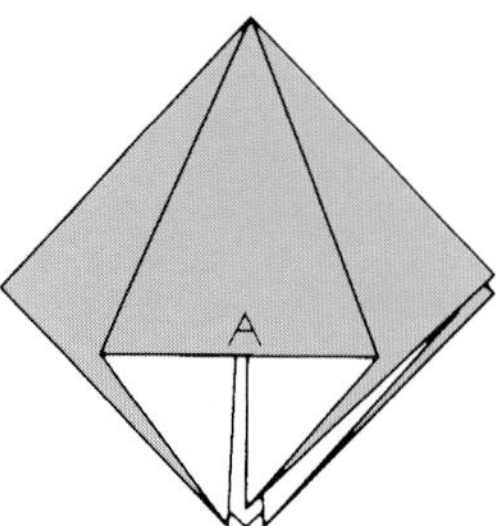

Completed squash fold.

Petal Fold

The petal fold is a means of simultaneously narrowing and lengthening a point. It is indicated by two mountain folds and a valley fold that form a triangle, with a push arrow on each side of the petal fold. The mountain folds are nearly always angle bisectors, and when you precrease (as shown in the example opposite), you should make the creases that become the mountain folds first. Then, make a valley fold to form a crease that connects the mountain folds where they hit the outer edges. Next, lift up the point along the valley fold just made and simultaneously push in the edges on the sides. Watch the two points marked A and C in the example; they end up meeting in the middle when the petal fold is completed.

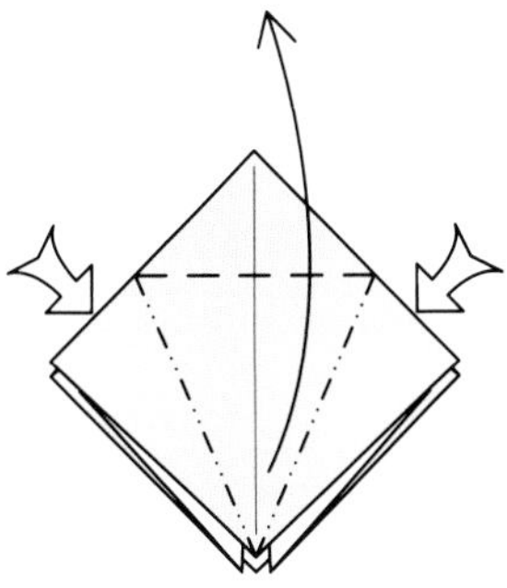

This is how a petal fold is drawn.

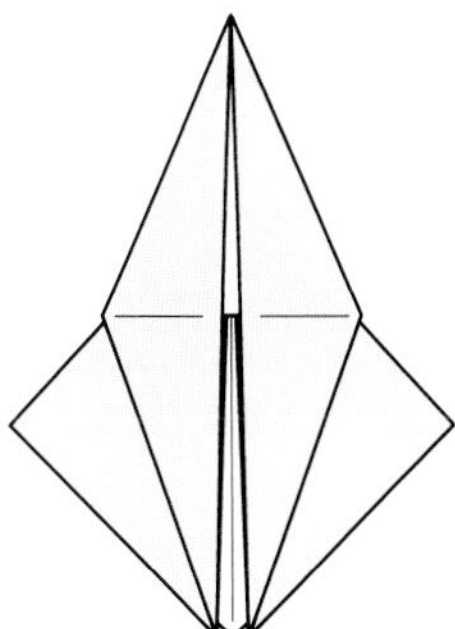

The result looks like this.

Here is how to make a petal fold.

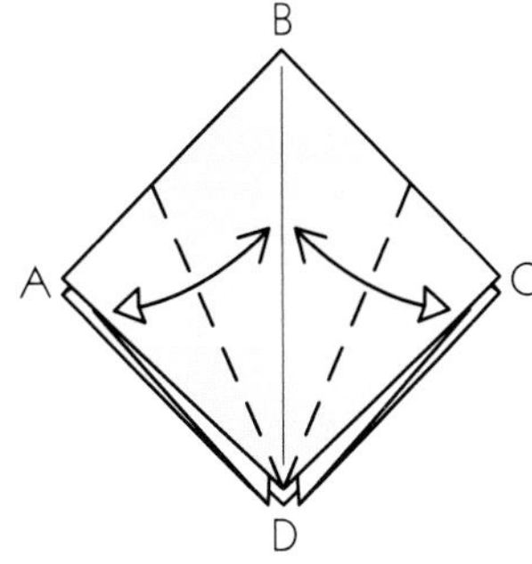

1 Make a Preliminary Fold (see page 26) to practice on. Fold in edges AD and CD to line BD and unfold.

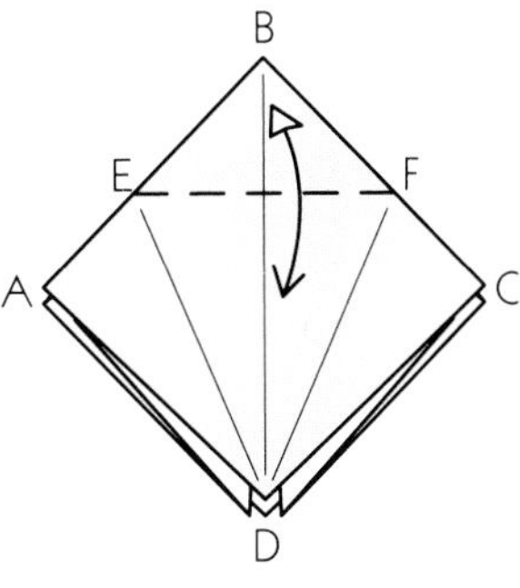

2 Fold down corner B along a crease that runs between points E and F.

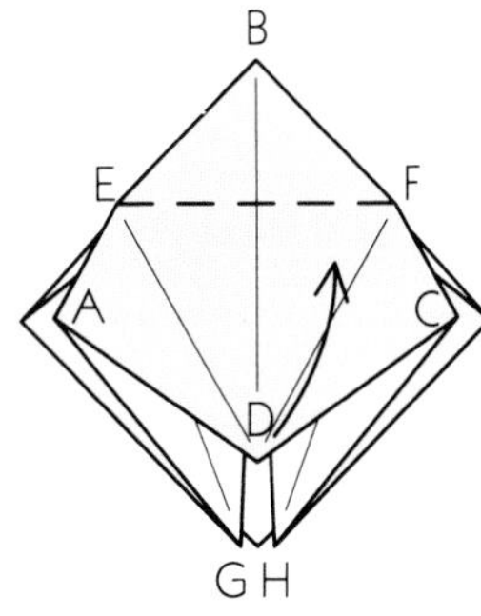

3 Lift corner D upward with one hand while holding points G and H down with the other. Corners A and C will move toward each other.

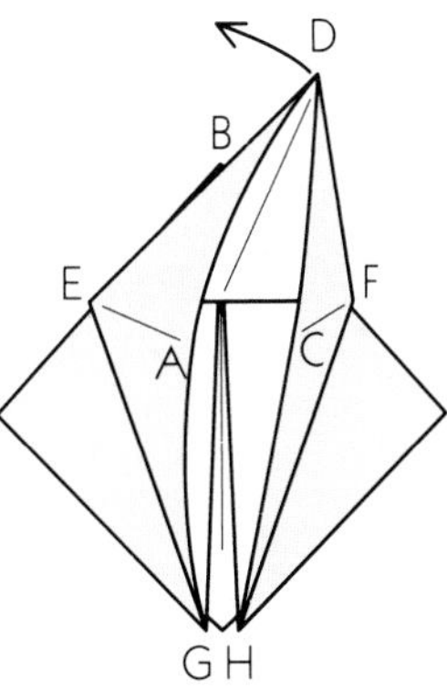

4 As you flatten the point, creases ED and FD change from valley to mountain folds; you might need to change the creases' direction directly. No new creases are added, however.

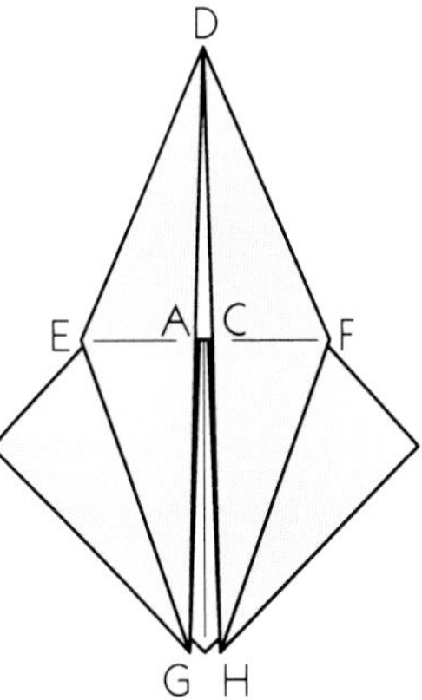

Completed petal fold.

Petal-folding an Edge

It is also possible to create a new point from the middle of an edge with a petal fold, as shown here. To make this kind of petal fold, first crease the angle bisectors at the bottom of the model. Then fold the edge up along a valley fold that connects the top of the first two creases. Push in the sides and flatten the paper; two new valley folds form that converge at a single point in the middle of the edge. Watch the points marked A and B; as the petal fold is made, they move in from the sides and meet in the center of the model.

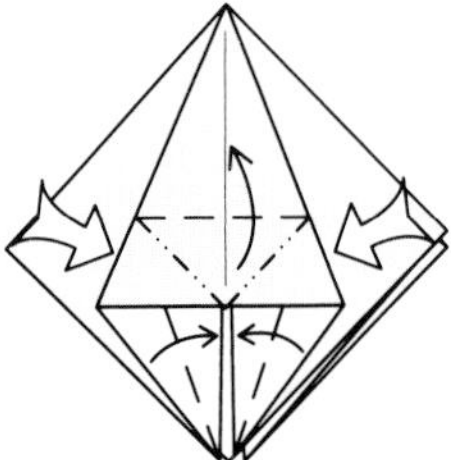

This is how a petal fold is drawn when it is applied to an edge.

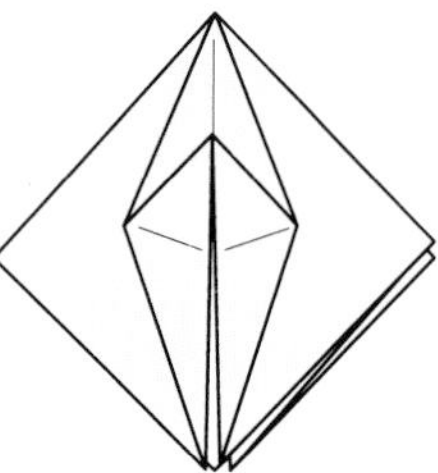

The result looks like this.

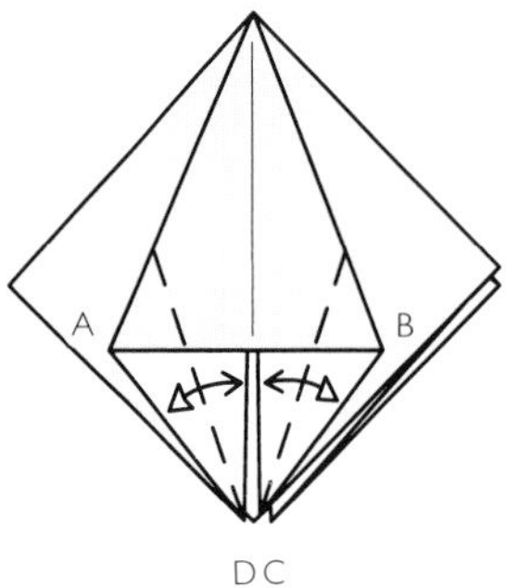

Here is an easy way of petal-folding an edge.

1 Fold in edges AD and BC to the center line and unfold.

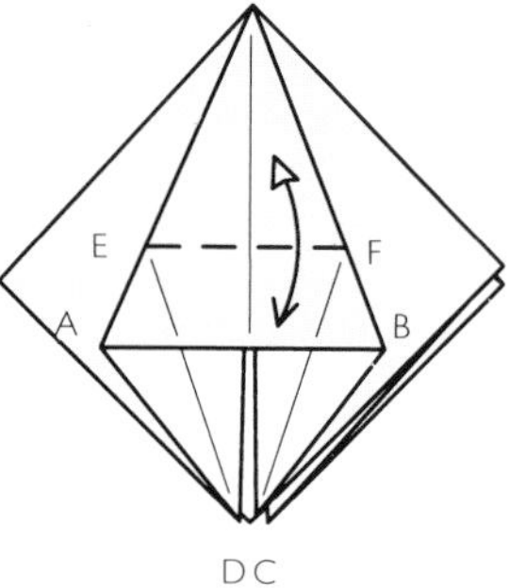

2 Fold down the top part of the model so that the crease connects points E and F; unfold.

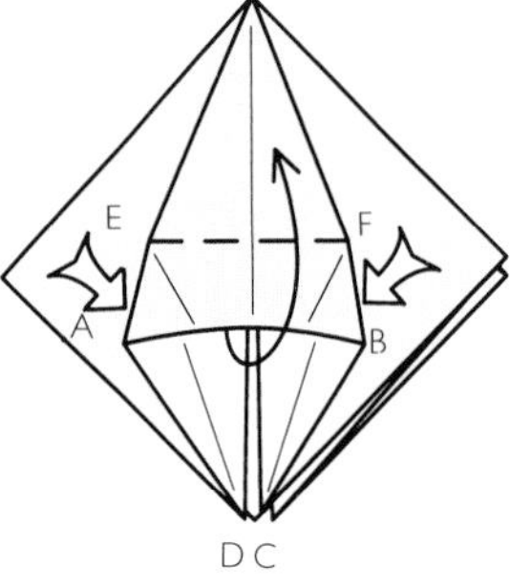

3 Hold down points D and C and lift up the middle of edge AB; corners A and B will move toward each other.

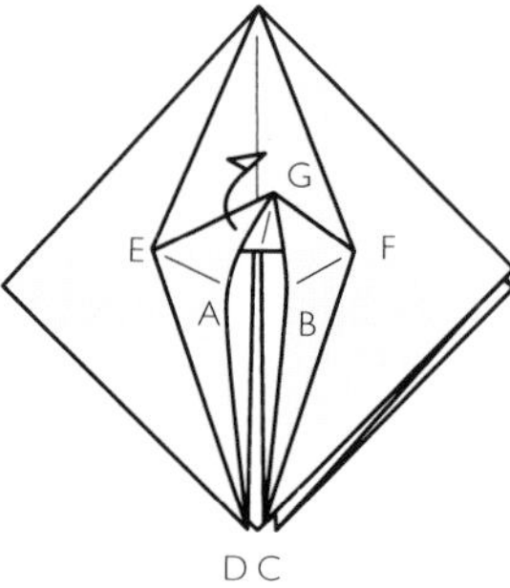

4 Flatten the model. The two creases that create point G from an edge fall naturally into place, but you should adjust them to make the point sharp and even before you make the creases sharp.

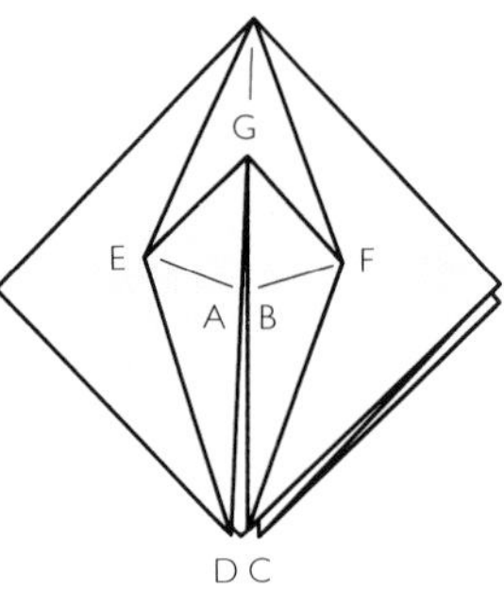

Completed petal fold.

CRIMPS AND PLEATS

When a flap with several layers is folded in a short zigzag, there is more than one way the layers can be folded; the entire flap can be folded back and forth, or it can be folded inside itself and back out. To distinguish these cases, one or more zigzag lines is drawn next to the model as if it were a side view of the edges.

A pleat occurs when the entire flap is folded back and forth, as in the example opposite. Pleats are usually very easy to do, and the only thing that you have to be careful about is whether the valley fold (which is the fold you should make first) is on the right or the left of the mountain fold. A pleat may be made through a single layer of paper or multiple layers of paper.

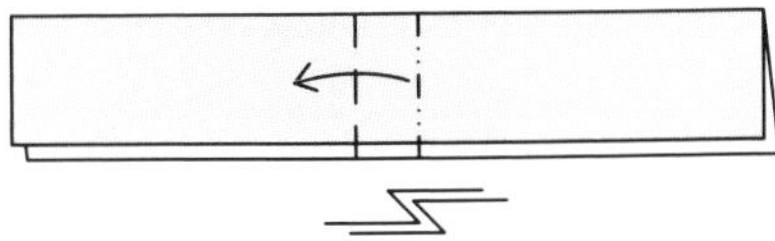

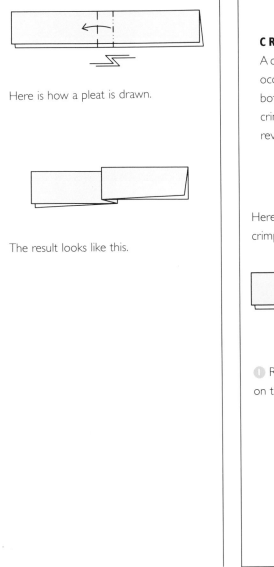

Here is how a pleat is drawn.

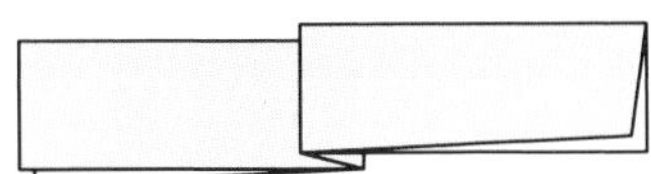

The result looks like this.

Here is an easy way to make a pleat.

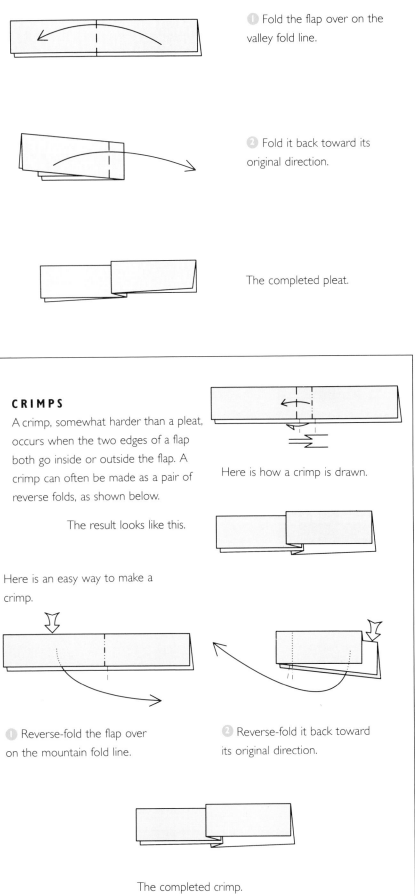

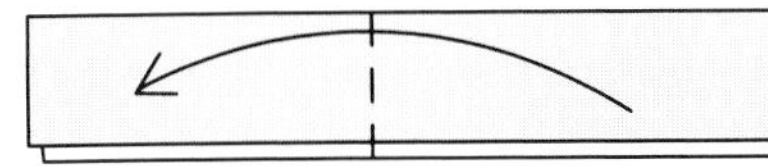

1. Fold the flap over on the valley fold line.

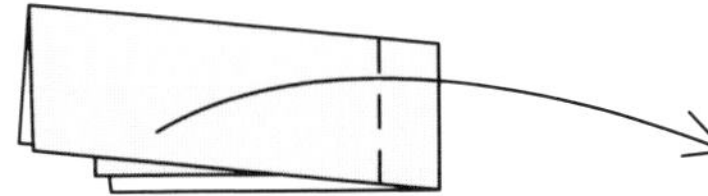

2. Fold it back toward its original direction.

The completed pleat.

CRIMPS

A crimp, somewhat harder than a pleat, occurs when the two edges of a flap both go inside or outside the flap. A crimp can often be made as a pair of reverse folds, as shown below.

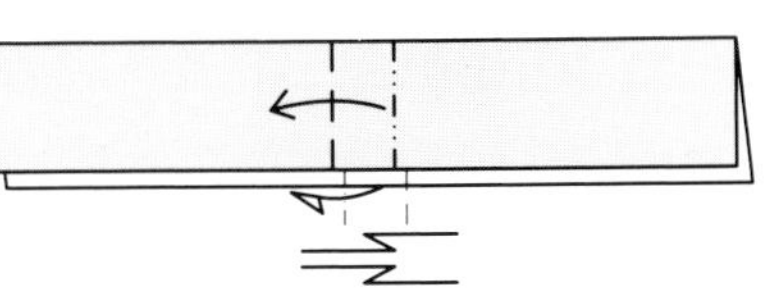

Here is how a crimp is drawn.

The result looks like this.

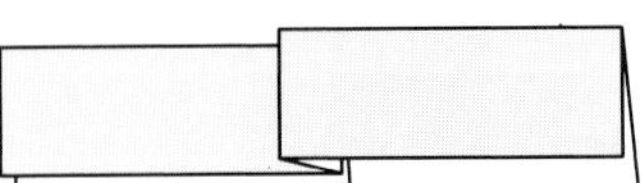

Here is an easy way to make a crimp.

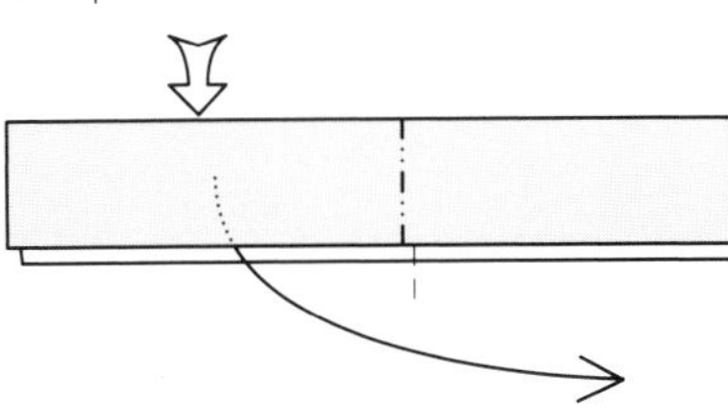

1. Reverse-fold the flap over on the mountain fold line.

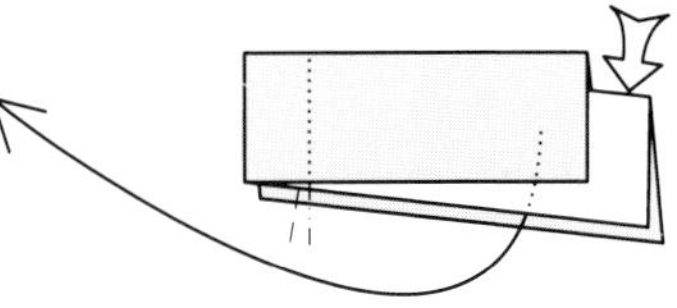

2. Reverse-fold it back toward its original direction.

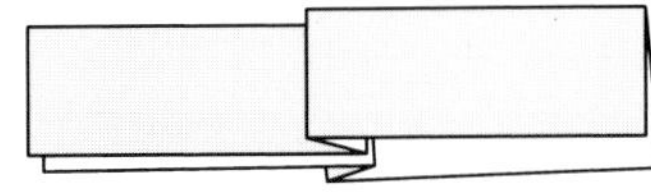

The completed crimp.

BUTTERFLY

★★

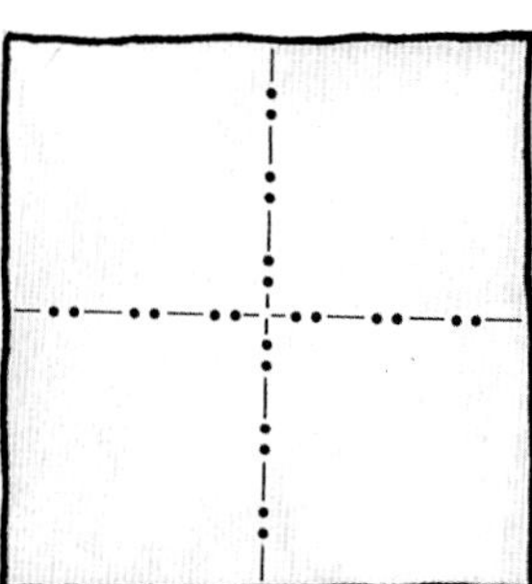

❶ Make horizontal and vertical mountain creases.

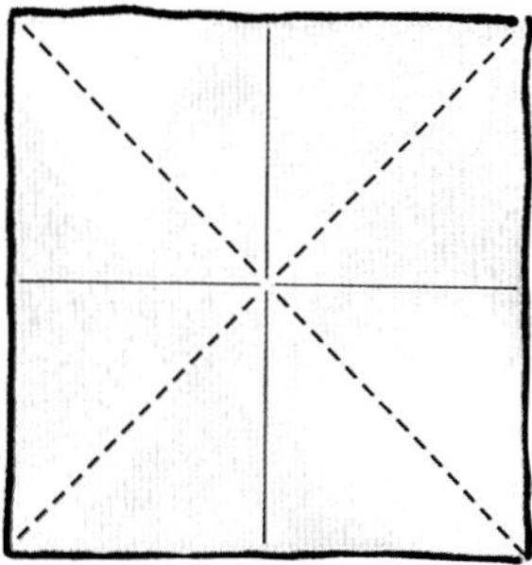

❷ Make diagonal valley folds.

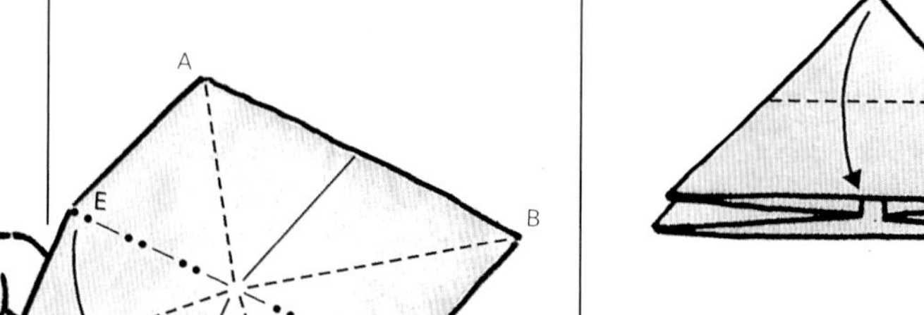

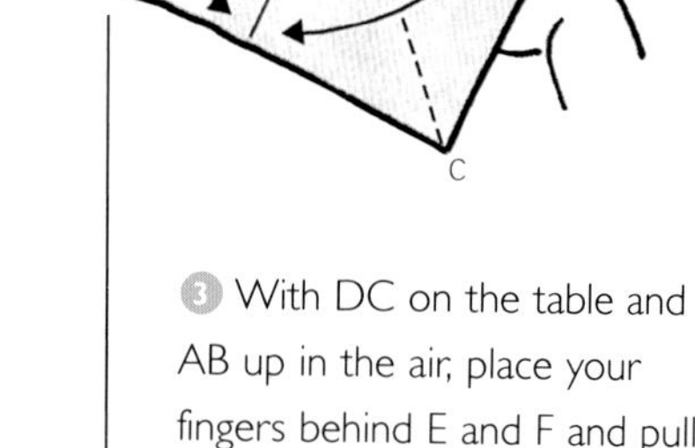

❸ With DC on the table and AB up in the air, place your fingers behind E and F and pull them up and inward . . .

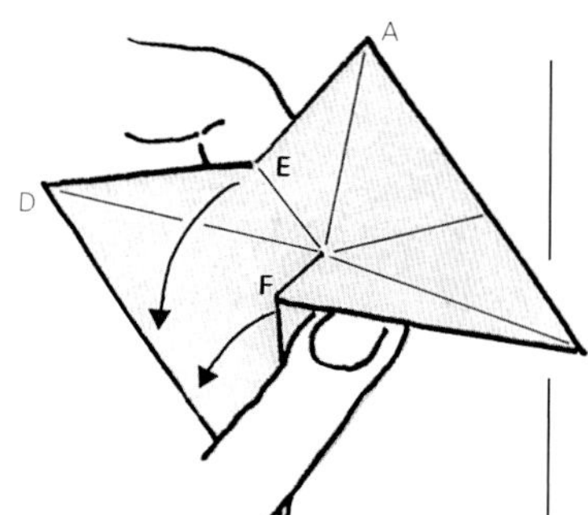

❹ . . . like this, so that they lie together in the middle of edge DC . . .

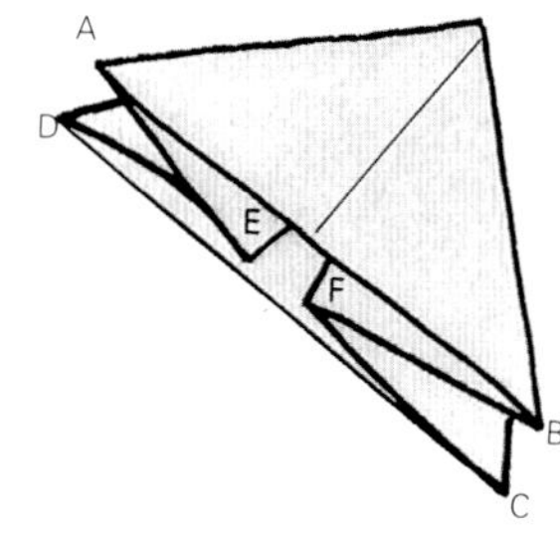

❺ . . . like this. Note how A lies on D and B on C.

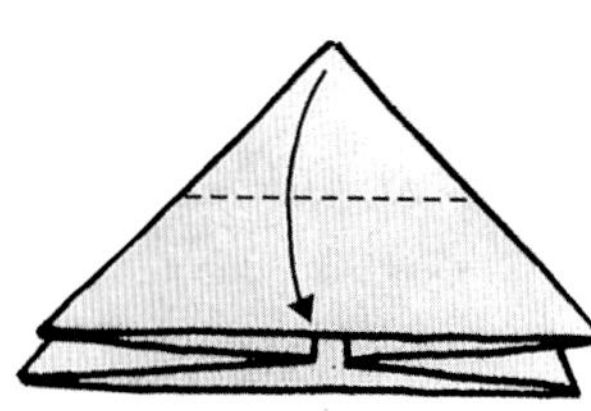

❻ Turn the triangle upside down and fold the bottom corner up to the top edge.

❼ Fold in the bottom corners as shown.

❽ Unfold the corners.

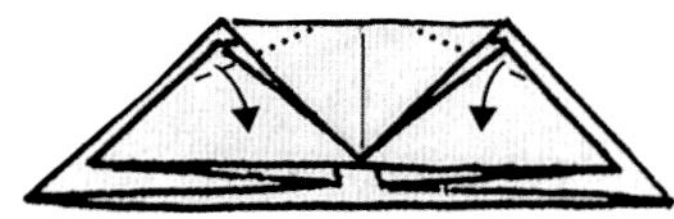

❾ Fold the bottom corners in again, but this time crease only the inner layers. Much of the crease is hidden inside the outer layer. Look at step 10.

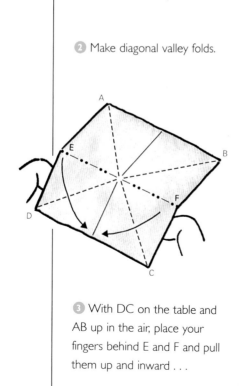

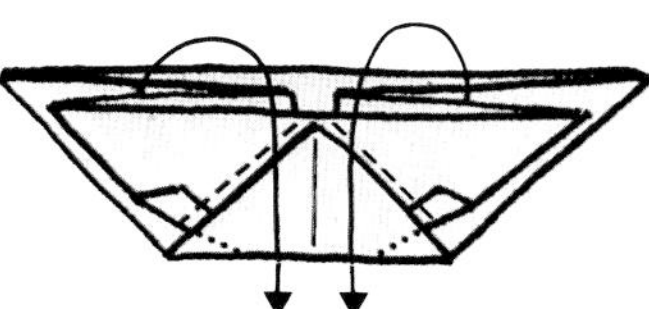

10 Pull down the top layer triangles.

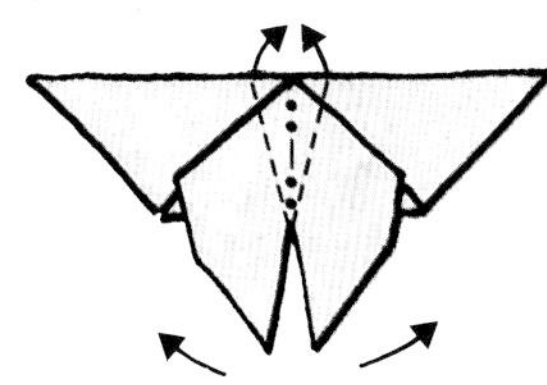

11 Make a central mountain crease, then two valley creases in the shape of a V, one on each side of the mountain. This pinches the center of the butterfly to create a raised body and separates the lower wings.

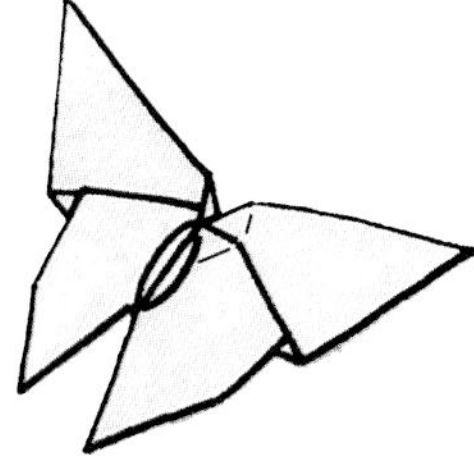

The completed butterfly.

CHATTERBOX

★★

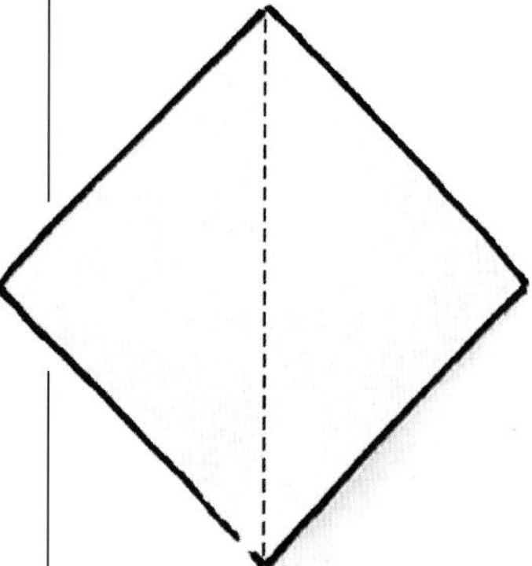

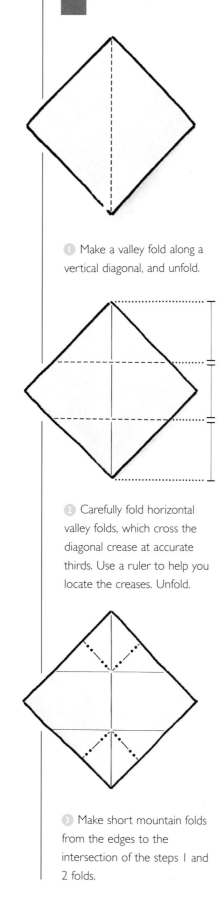

1 Make a valley fold along a vertical diagonal, and unfold.

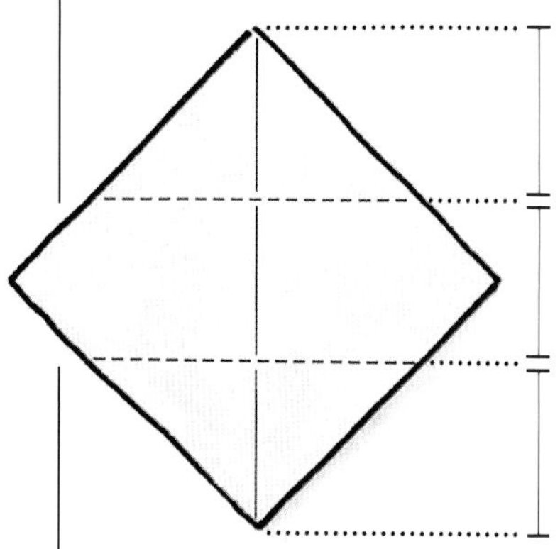

2 Carefully fold horizontal valley folds, which cross the diagonal crease at accurate thirds. Use a ruler to help you locate the creases. Unfold.

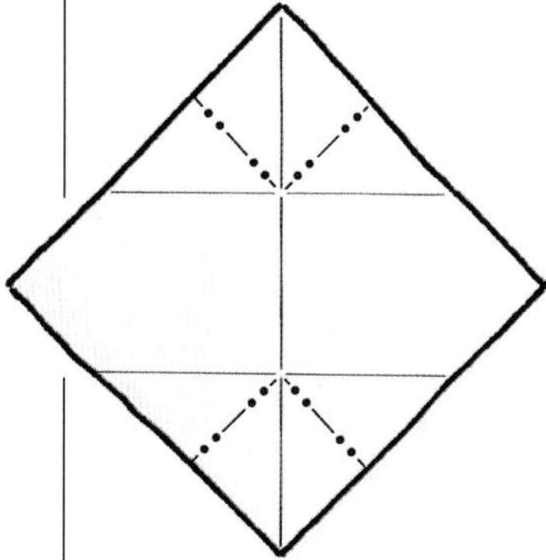

3 Make short mountain folds from the edges to the intersection of the steps 1 and 2 folds.

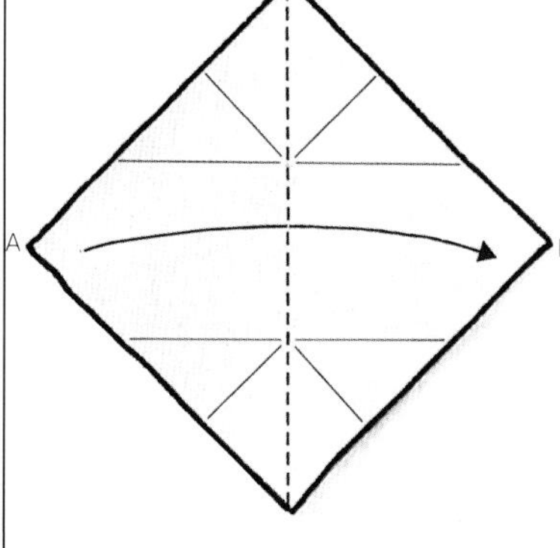

4 Fold the left-hand corner across to the right.

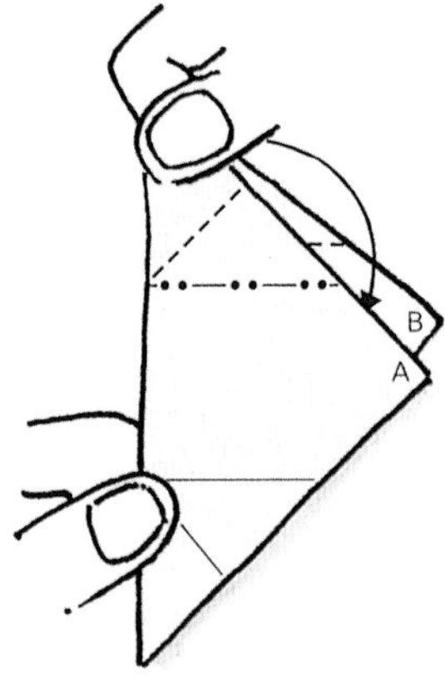

5 Grip the paper as shown. Push the top corner down in between layers A and B . . .

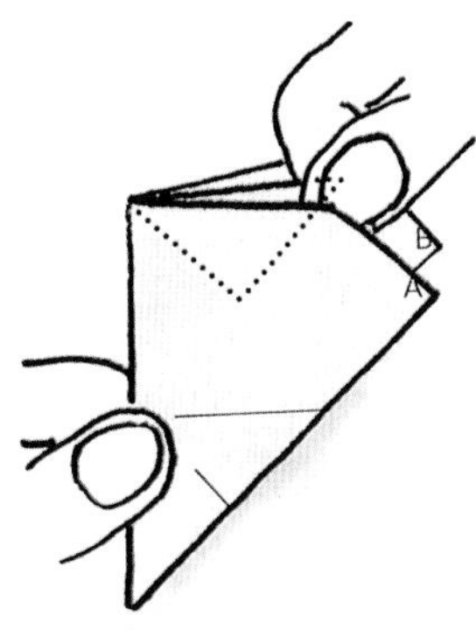

6 . . . like this. Flatten the paper.

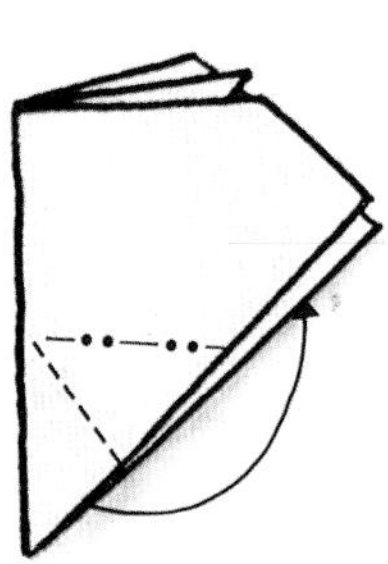

7 Repeat at the bottom.

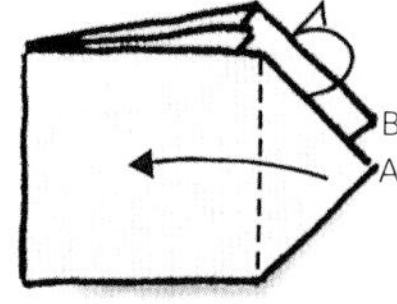

8 Fold A forward to the left, and take B behind to the left.

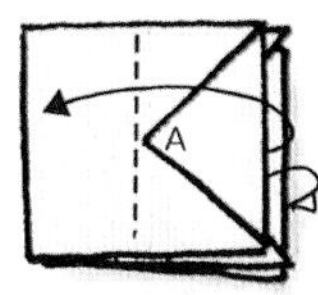

9 Take the upper right edge and fold it forward to the left edge; take the second right edge and fold it behind to the left edge, leaving the central spikes in place.

⑩ Fold the loose triangles in to the middle, two on the front, two on the back.

⑪ Partly unfold step 10, allowing the triangles to stand upright.

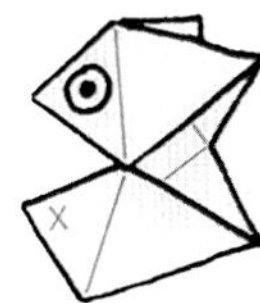

⑫ Draw the eyes. Hold flap X at the front and back, one flap in each hand . . .

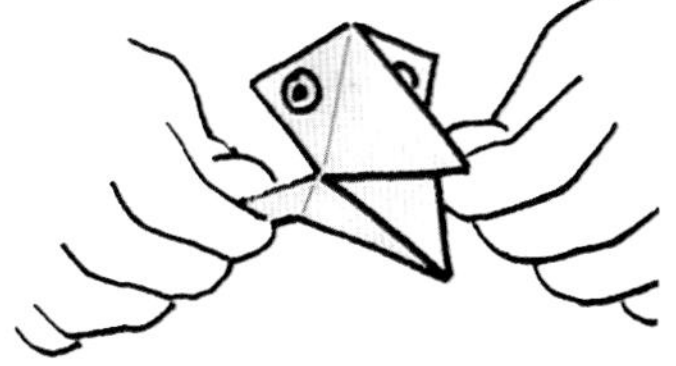

⑬ . . . and chatter away!

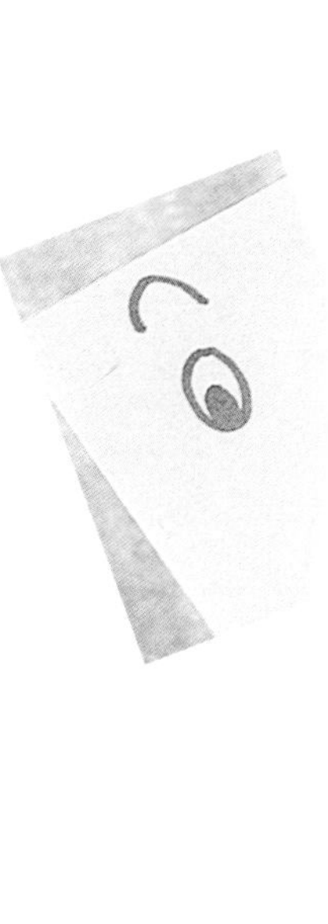

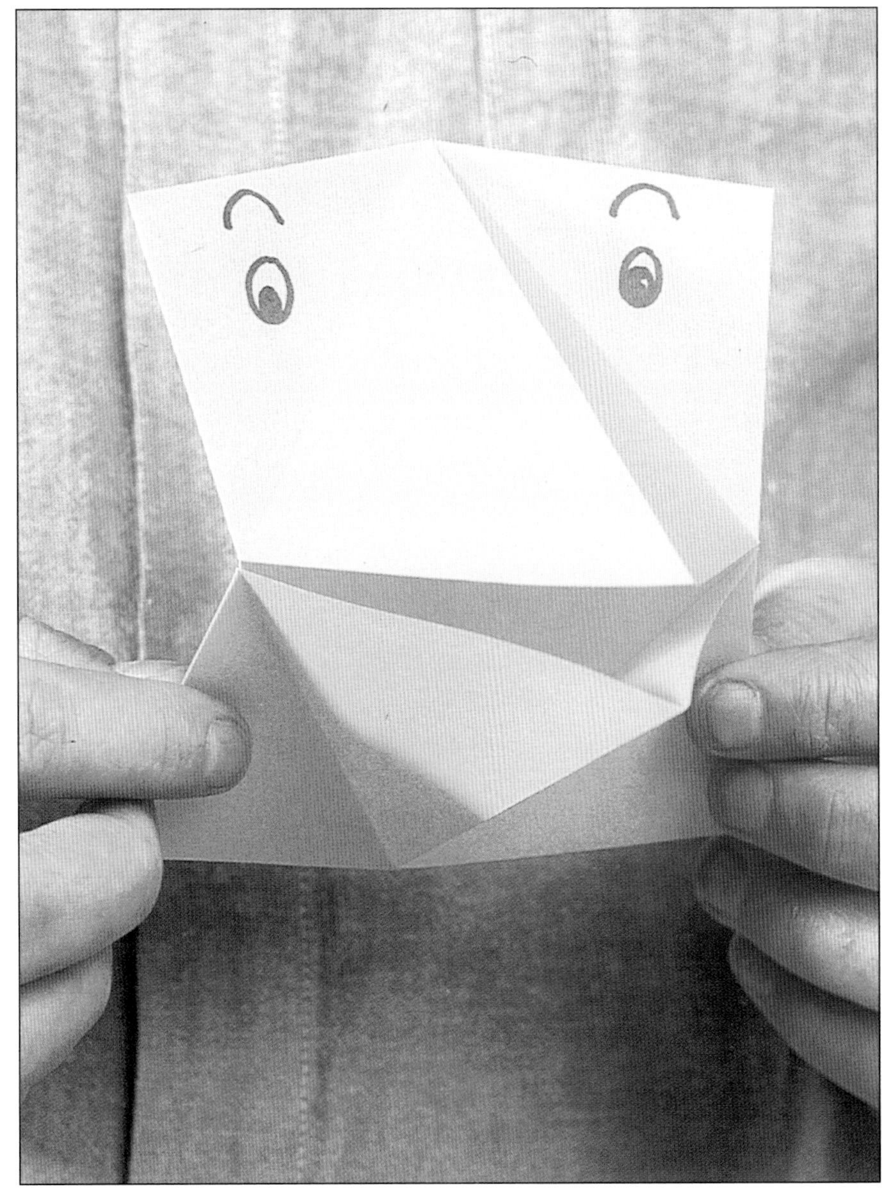

REPEAT PATTERN

★★★

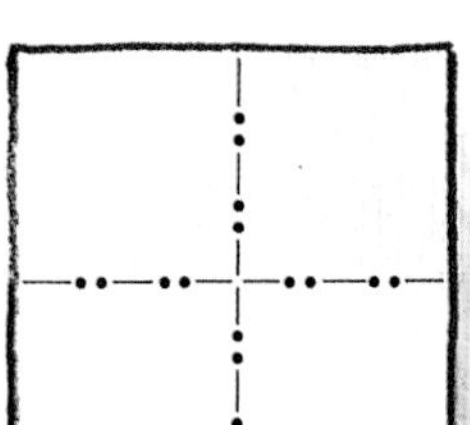

1 Make center mountain creases, horizontally and vertically.

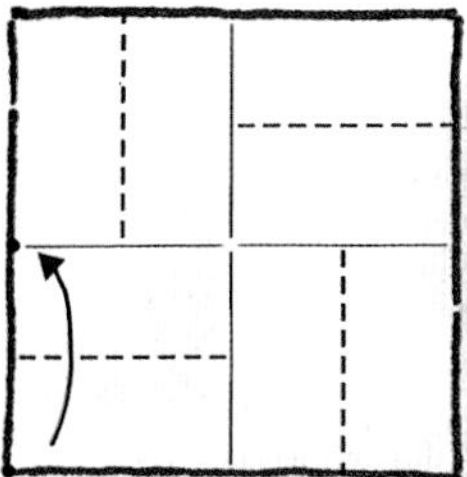

2 Fold the bottom edge of the paper up to the center horizontal crease, but only press flat the left half of the paper, making a crease from the left-hand edge into the center. Do this with all the other edges of the paper.

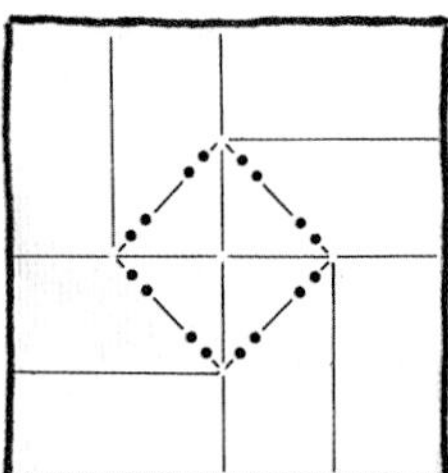

3 Make short diagonal mountain creases (or valley creases if you turn the paper over – this might be easier) connecting the points where steps 1 and 2 creases meet.

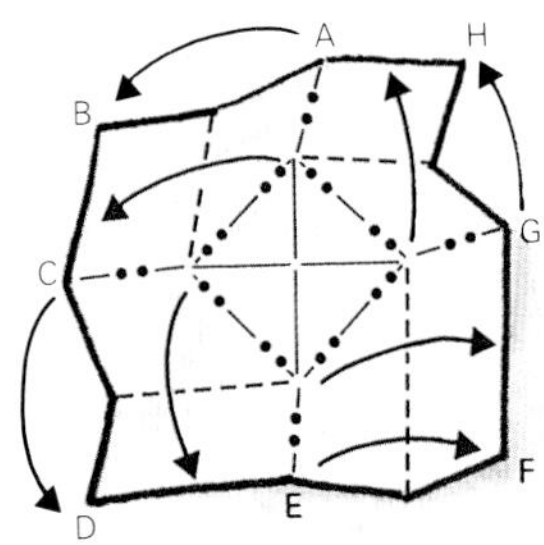

4 This step may be difficult, but persevere! Strengthen all creases. Simultaneously pinch the short mountain creases running into A, C, E, and G and fold them over to corners B, D, F, and H along the step 2 creases. This makes four pleats, contracts the paper, and makes the center diamond shape twist counterclockwise. All the creases move, twist, and collapse together.

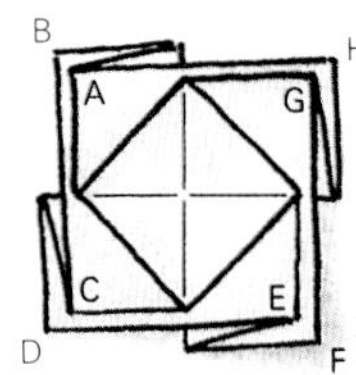

5 The flattened paper looks like this.

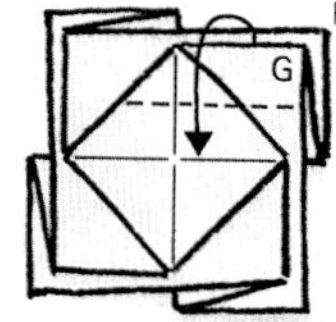

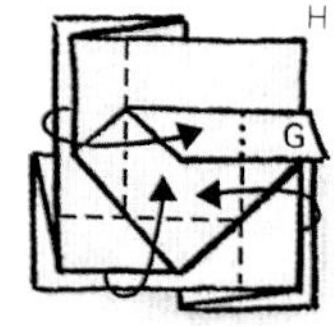

6 Bring the folded edge at the top of the paper (G) down to the center.

7 Repeat with the three other folded edges to make the complete unit.

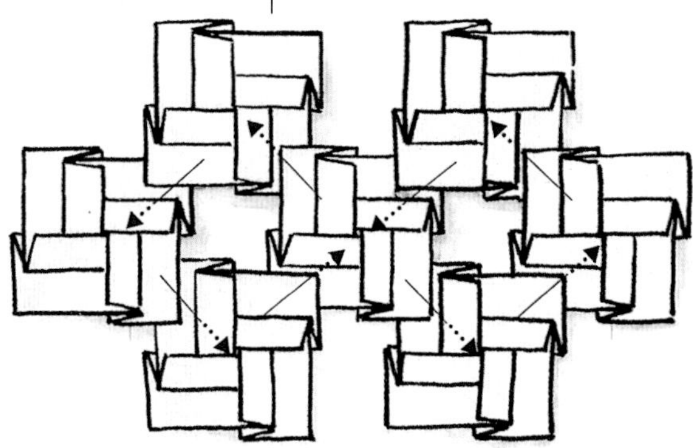

8 Make as many as you need and interlock them as shown, holding them together with glue.

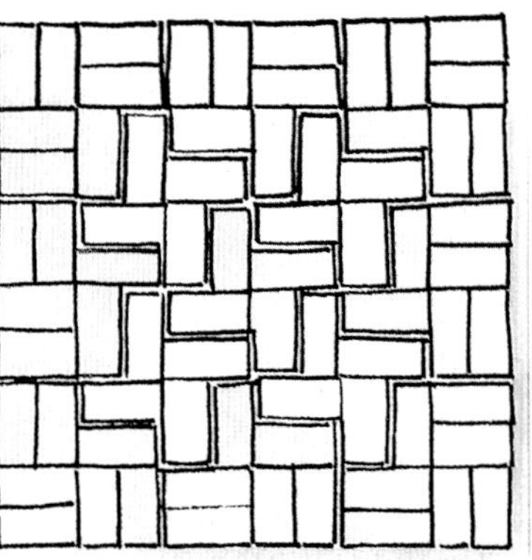

LEFT *This diagram shows 13 units interlocked, four white and nine tinted. Your own patterns need not be so regular.*

FISH №1

★★

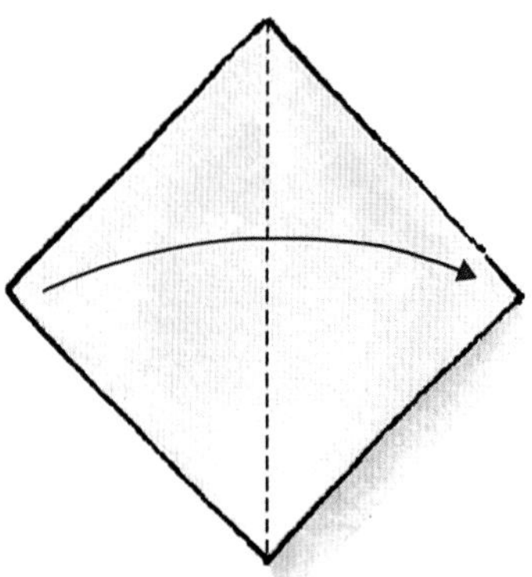

1 Valley fold the sheet in half along the vertical diagonal.

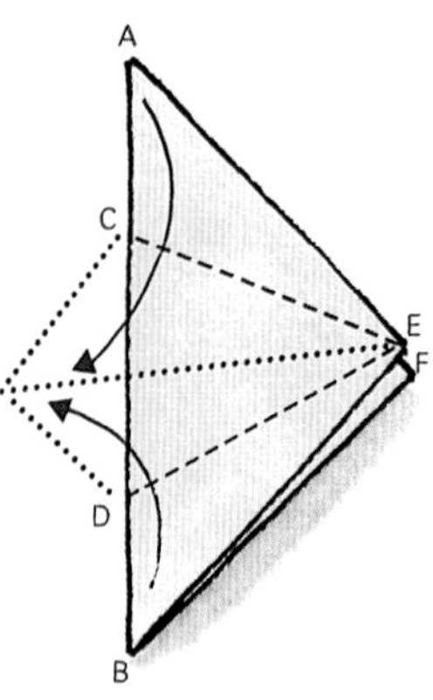

2 Fold corners A and B over to the left so that they touch. (Note that AC is longer than BD.)

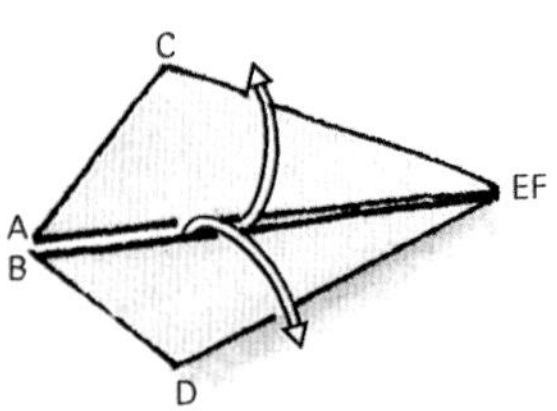

3 Unfold. (Note that triangle ACE is larger than BDE.)

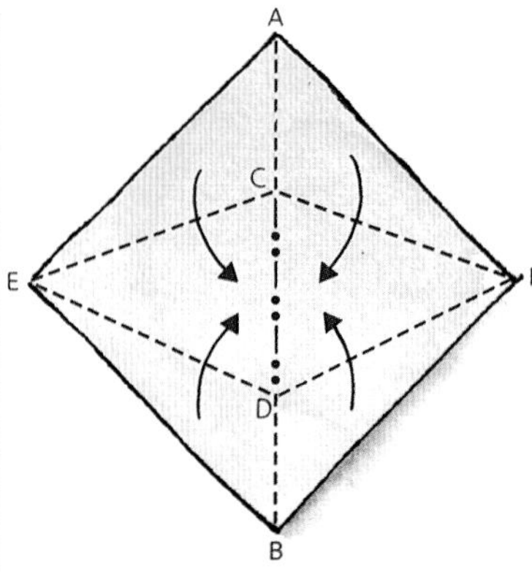

4 Refold all creases exactly as shown. Begin to fold along creases EC, CF, ED, and DF, so that A and B come forward . . .

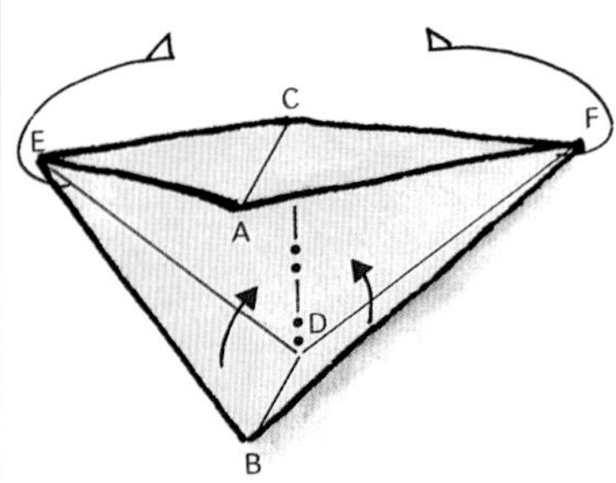

5 . . . like this. Bend E and F backward so that they meet. A and B also meet . . .

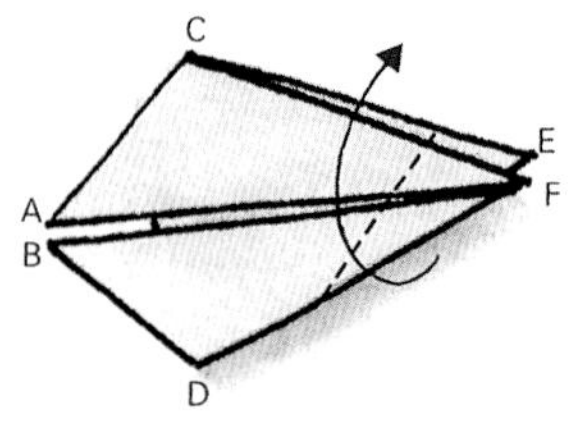

6 . . . like this. Fold up E and F as shown.

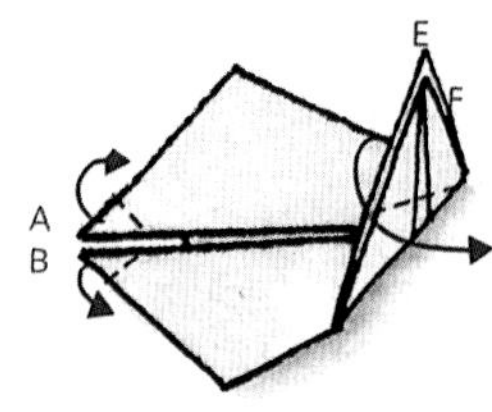

7 Pull down corner F to complete the tail. Turn corners A and B inside out, opening out each to do so.

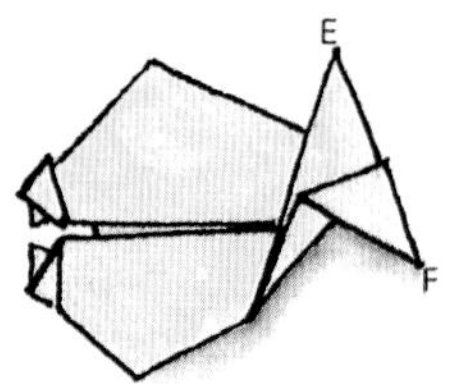

The completed fish . . .

. . . and from the other side.

FISH Nº 2

★★

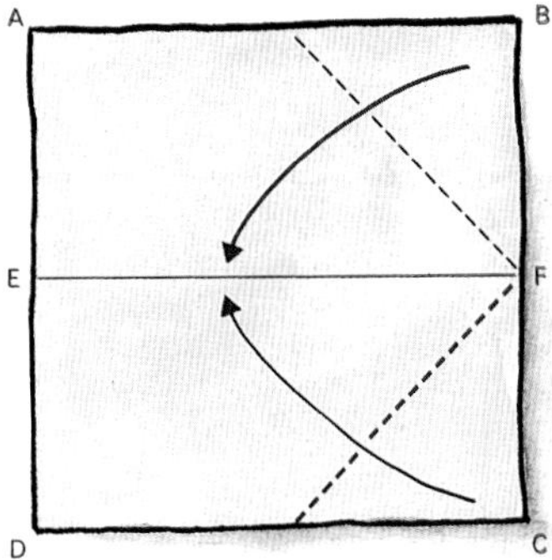

1 Fold a horizontal crease already made and unfold. Fold corners B and C in to the middle.

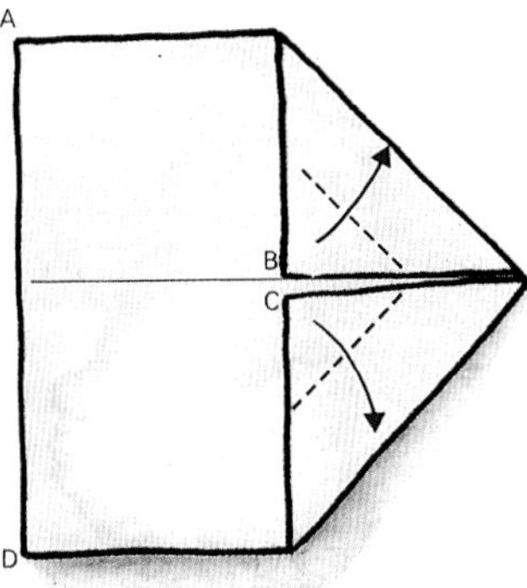

2 Fold B and C back out to the sloping edges.

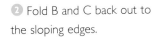

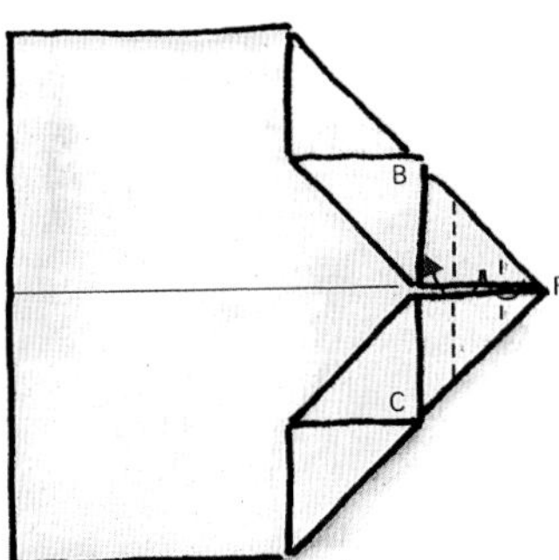

3 Fold corner F over twice to lie next to BC.

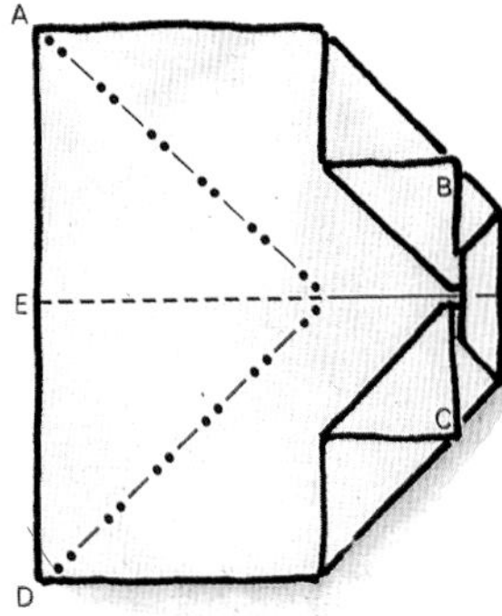

4 Carefully fold diagonal mountain folds, from corners A and D in to the middle and a horizontal valley fold from E to meet them. Begin to fold all three corners at once . . .

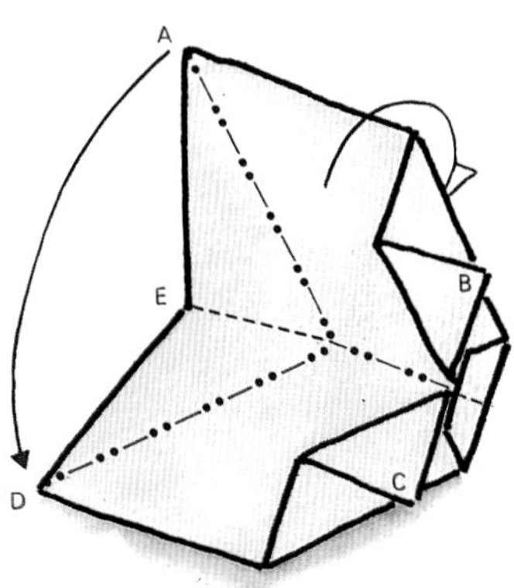

5 . . . so that the paper starts to collapse. A comes toward D. Note the mountain fold between B and C. Let A touch D.

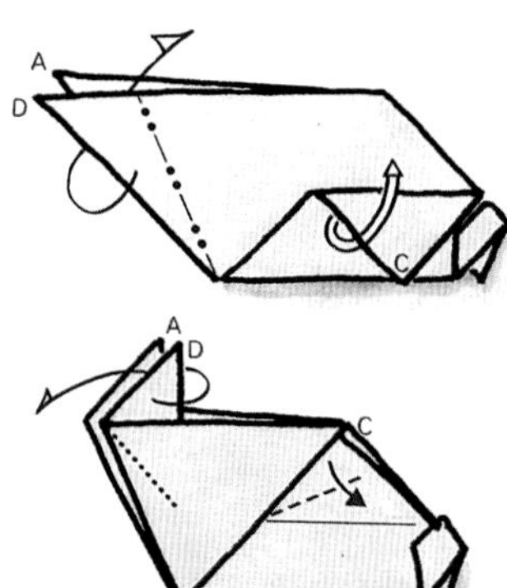

6 Fold D, then A, up through the center. Unfold C (and B behind), (**TOP**). Twist D back out. Fold C forward (and B behind), (**BELOW**).

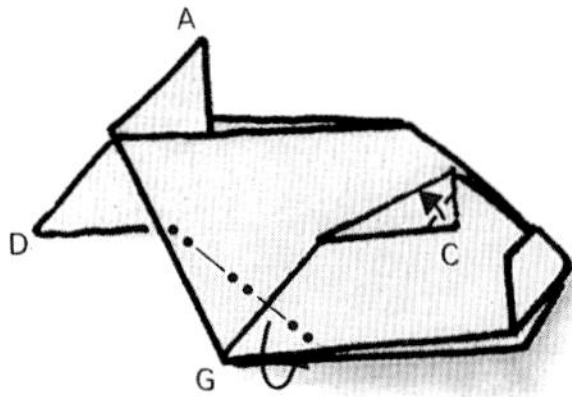

7 Fold back corner C to form an eye (and B behind). Push corner G under to the middle of the fish . . .

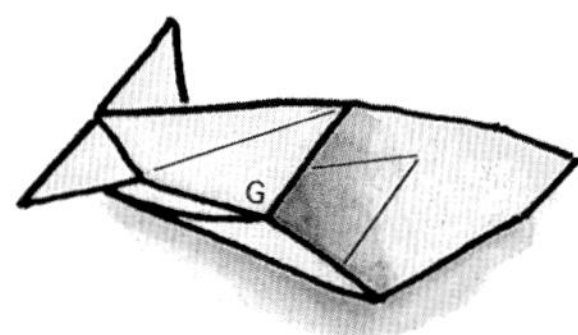

8 . . . to spread open the body, as seen here from underneath.

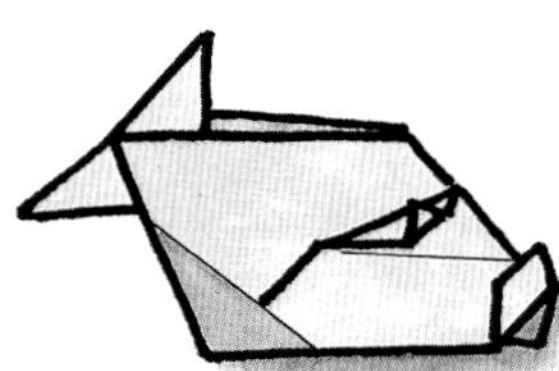

The completed fish.

FISH Nº 3

★★★

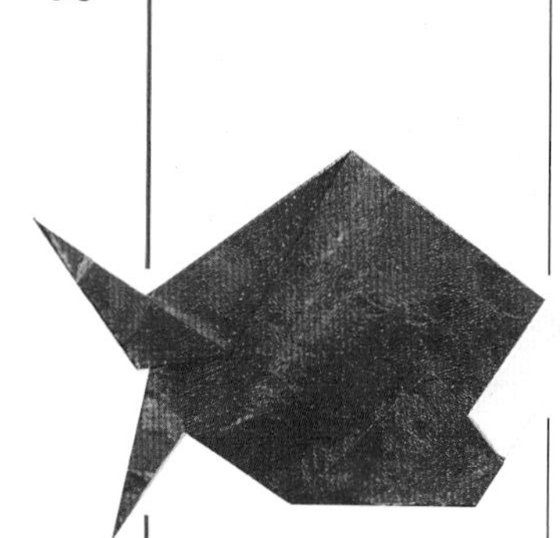

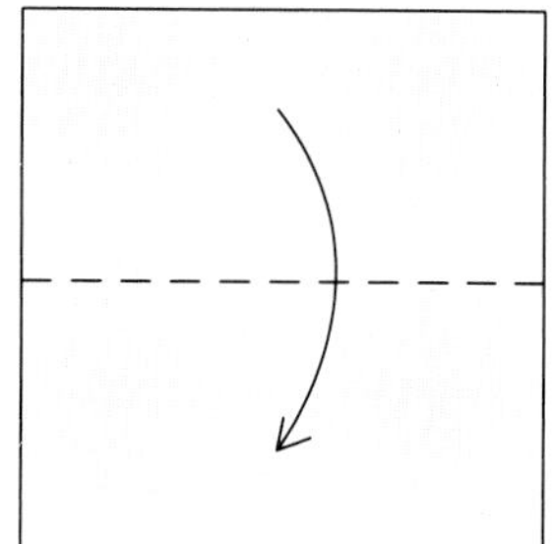

1 Take a 4-inch square of blue paper. Begin with the white side up. Fold the paper in half from top to bottom.

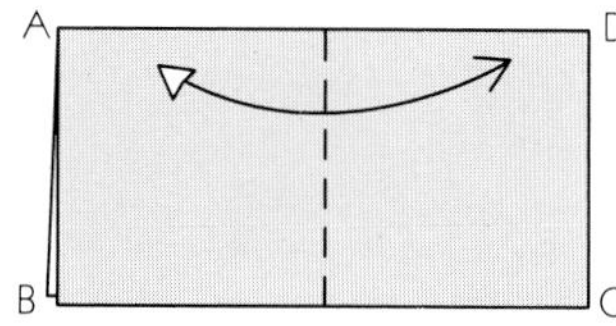

2 Fold edge AB over to edge DC and unfold.

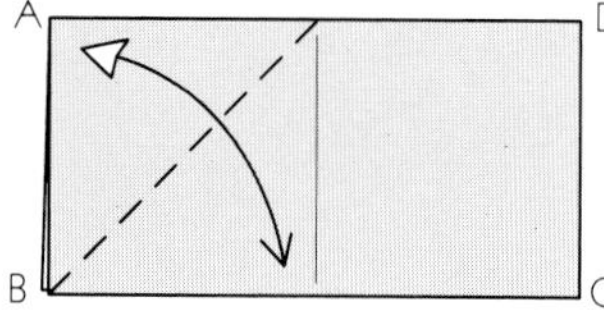

3 Fold down edge AB to edge BC and unfold.

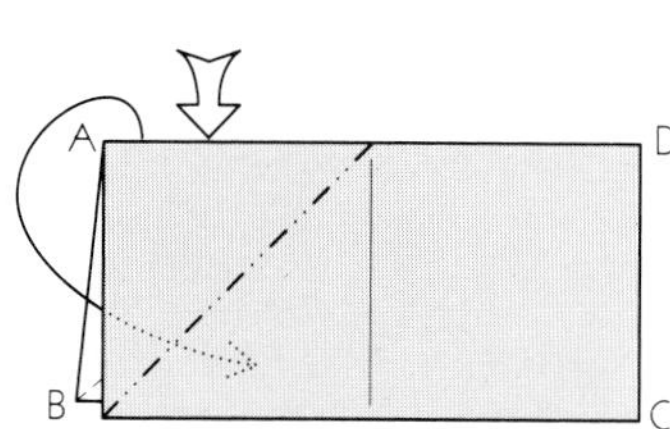

4 Reverse-fold corner A down inside the model on the existing creases.

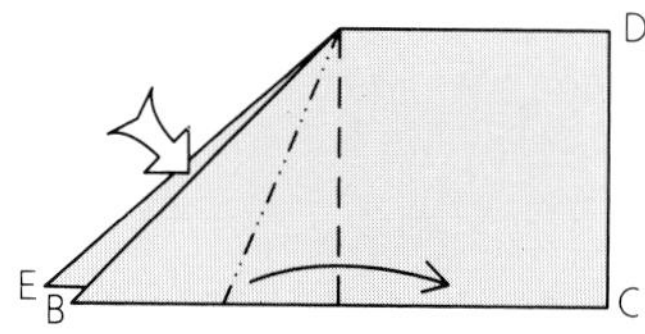

5 Squash-fold corner B symmetrically.

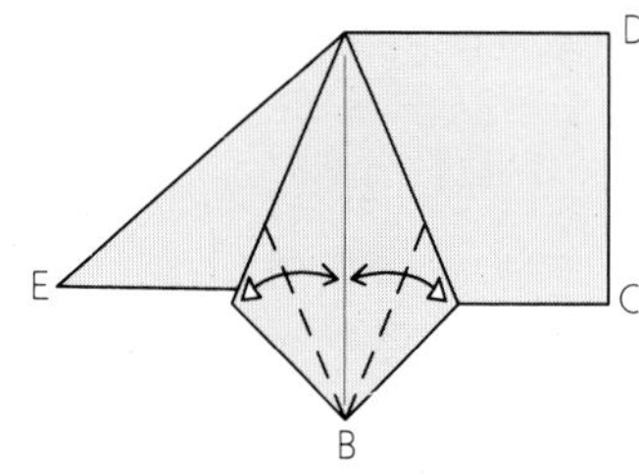

6 Fold the raw edges into the center and unfold.

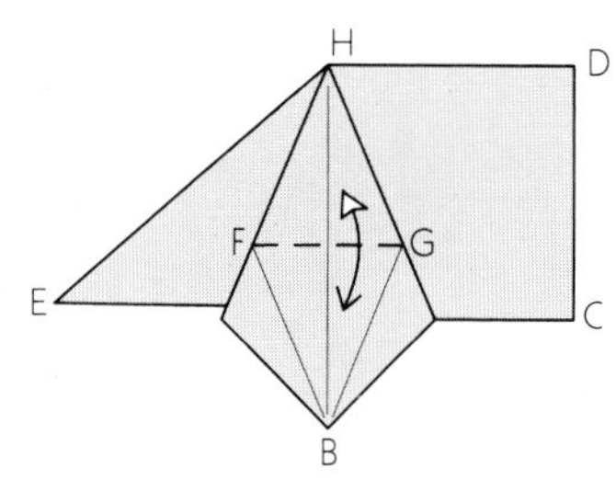

7 Fold down point H to point B along a crease that connects points F and G, folding through all layers of the model. Unfold.

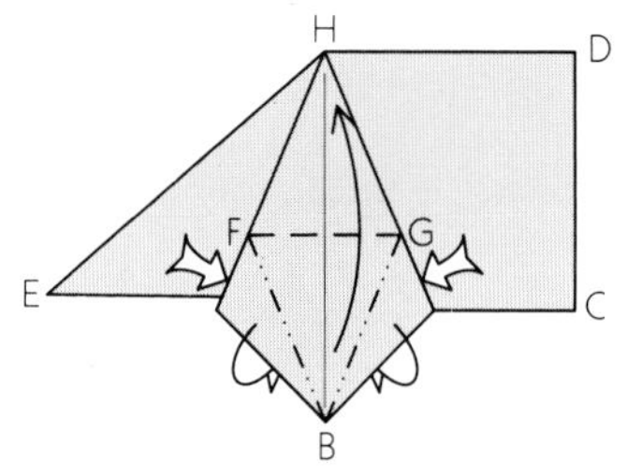

8 Petal-fold point B up to point H, using the existing creases.

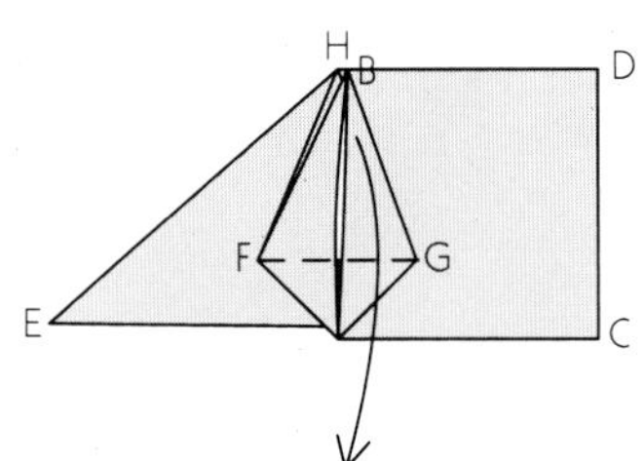

9 Fold point B back down.

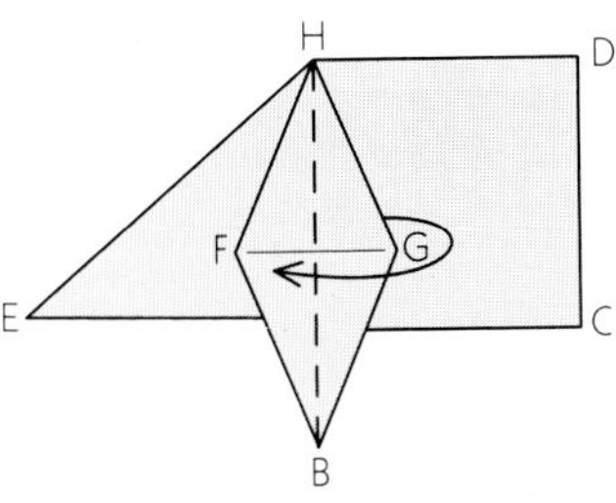

10 Fold corner G to the left.

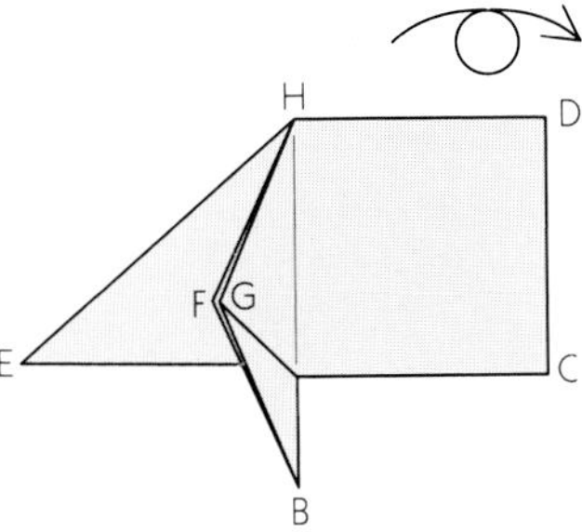

11 Turn the model over.

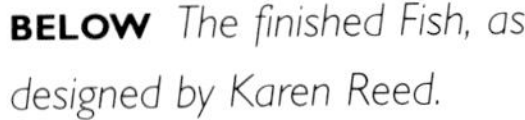

BELOW *The finished Fish, as designed by Karen Reed.*

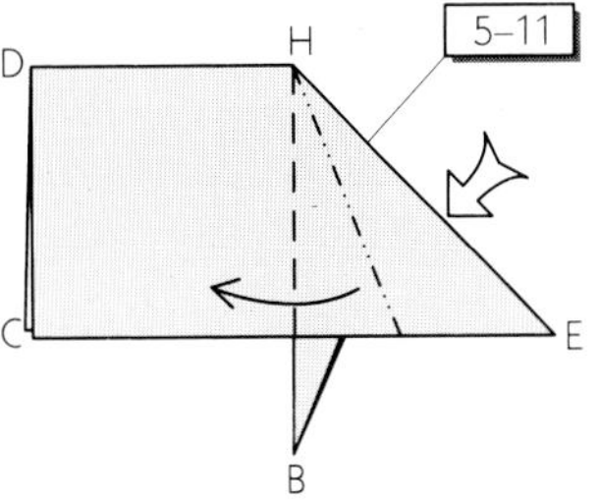

12 Repeat steps 5–11 on flap E (including turning the paper over at the end).

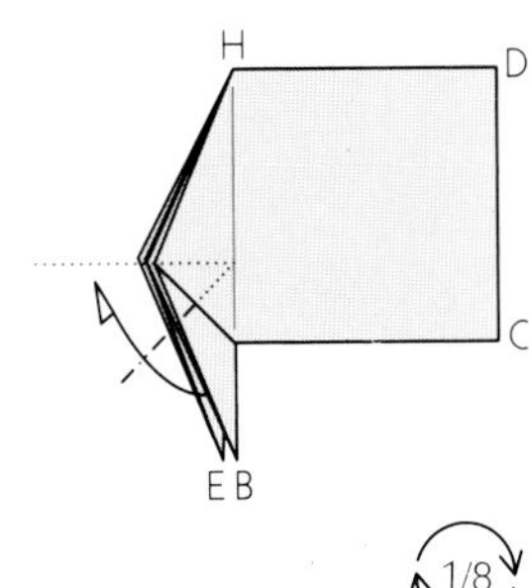

13 Mountain-fold point B underneath and to the left. Rotate the model one-eighth turn clockwise.

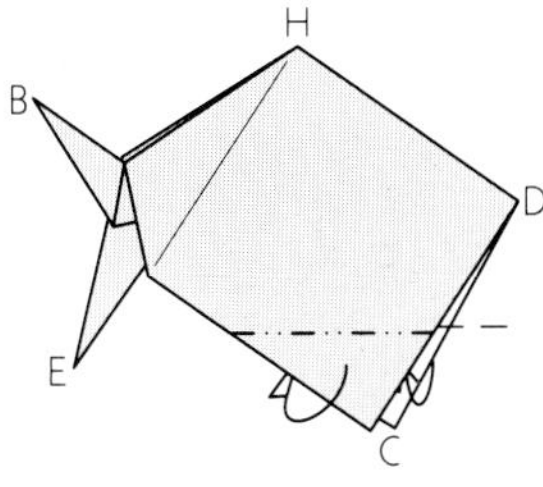

14 Mountain-fold the bottom corners inside. There are no reference points for these folds.

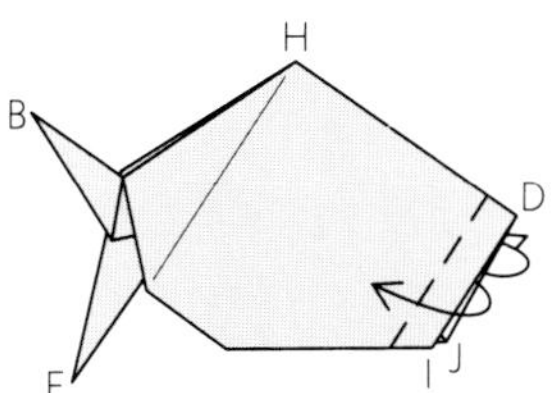

15 Outside-reverse-fold the right edge of the model. (If you spread corners I and J apart, this can be done with a valley fold that runs all the way from I to J.)

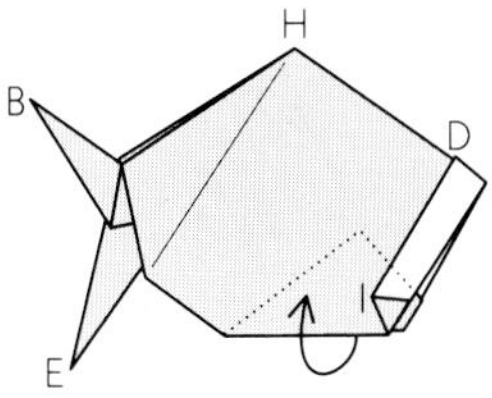

16 Tuck the near layer of the model underneath the colored flap inside.

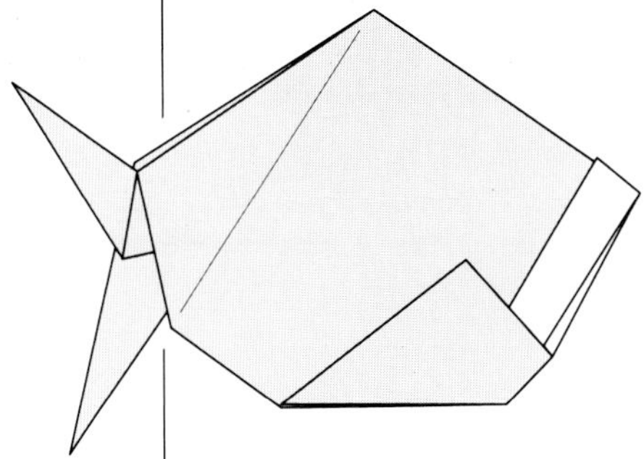

The finished Fish.

VALENTINE'S HEART

★★★

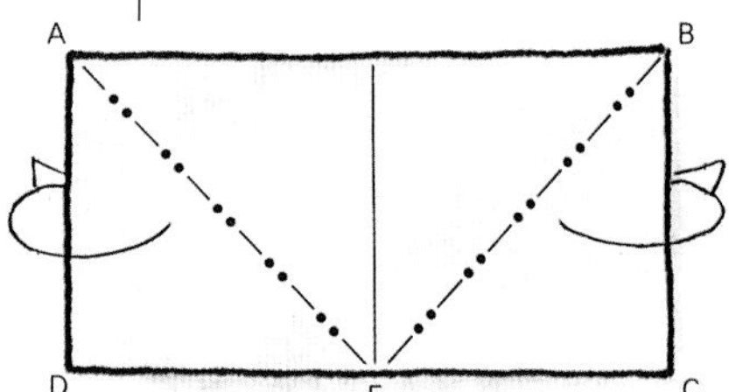

1 Begin with a 2 x 1 rectangle creased down the middle. Mountain fold corners C and D behind.

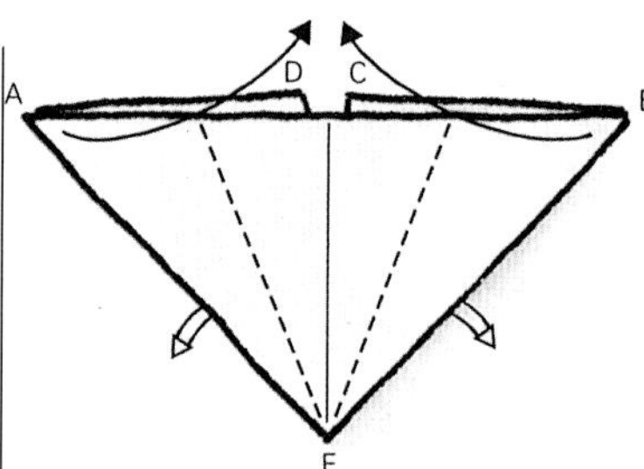

2 Fold edges AE and BE in to the center crease, allowing D and C to swivel downward and to the front . . .

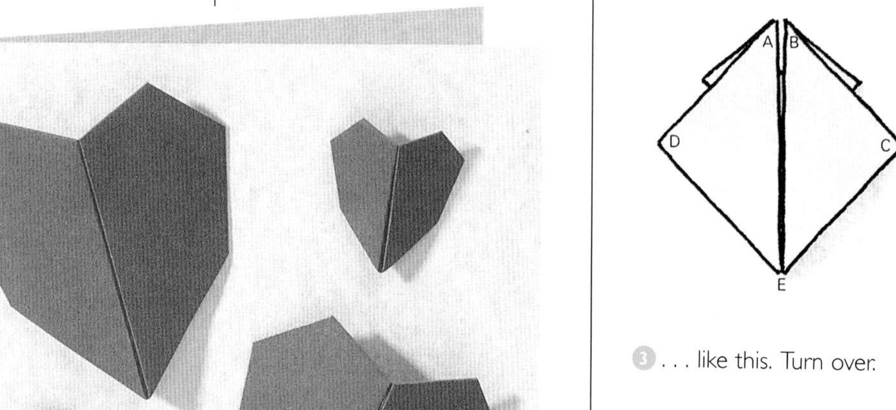

3 . . . like this. Turn over.

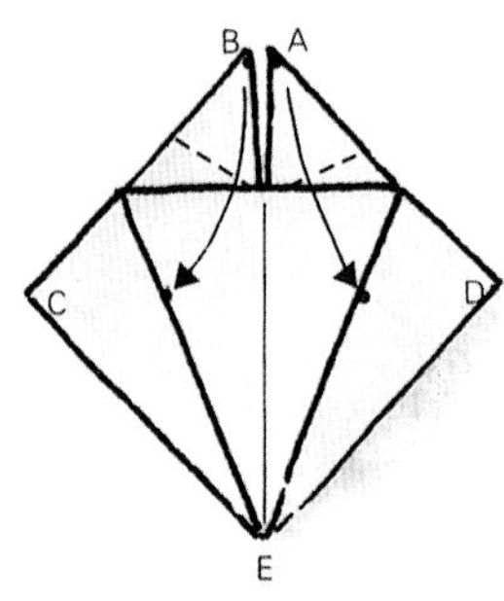

4 Fold B and A downward so that they lie at the folded edges running down to E.

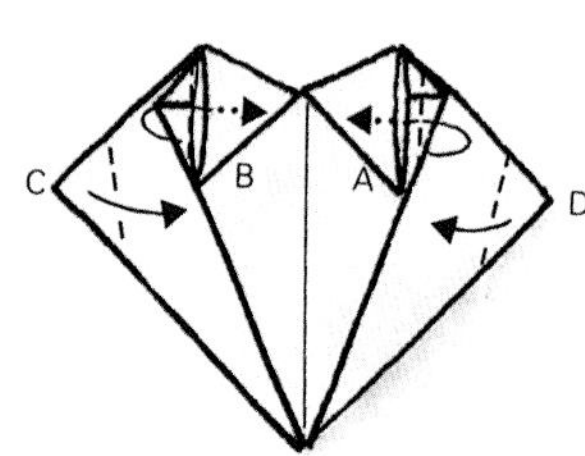

5 Tuck the loose corners into the pockets at B and A, locking B and A to the body of the paper. Fold in C and D as shown.

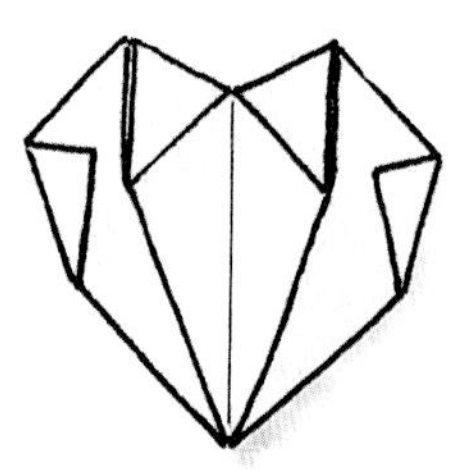

6 Turn over.

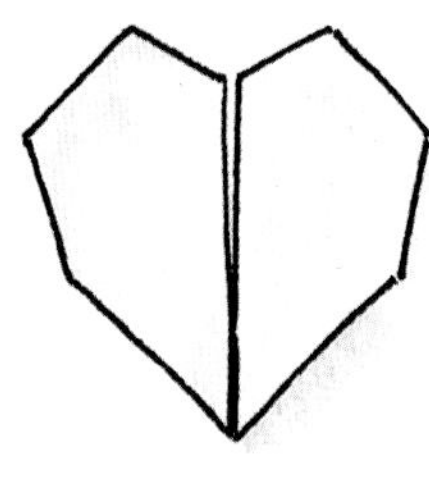

The complete Valentine's Heart.

ORIGAMI MASK

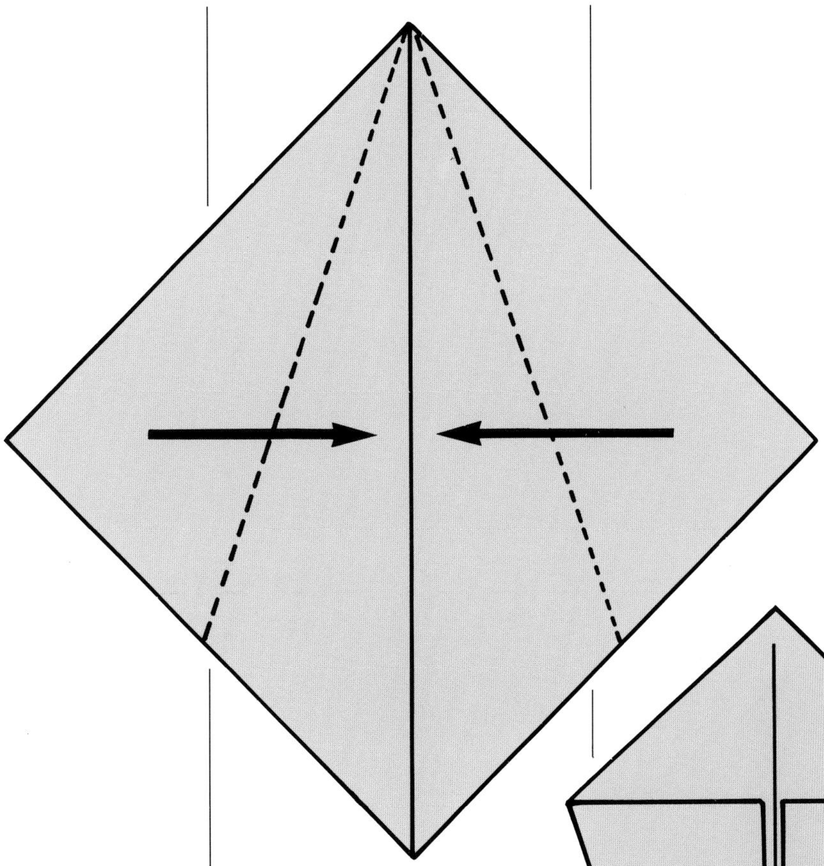

★★

1 Take paper measuring 12 inches square for a child and 14 inches square for an adult. With all masks, these measurements are adjustable for the individual. Fold and crease the paper diagonally and then flatten it before folding the two side corners to the previously creased center line.

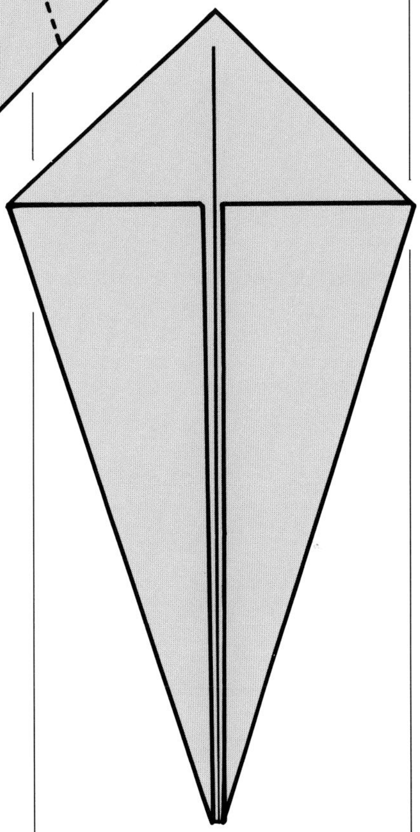

2 The paper now looks like this.

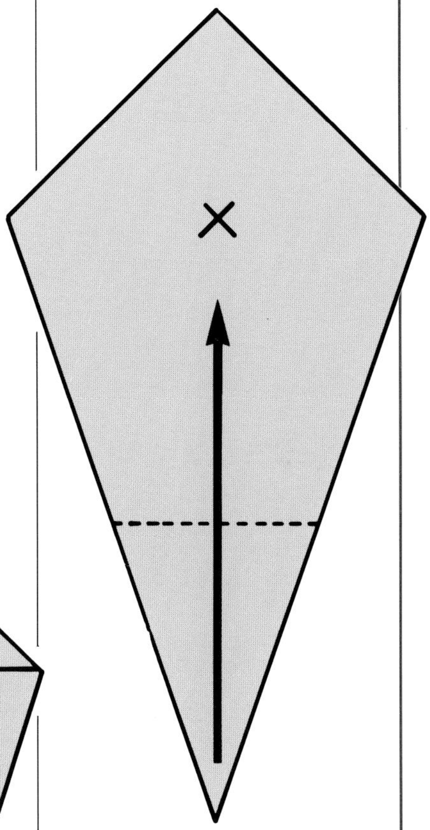

3 Turn the paper over and fold the bottom point up to a point on the center line at the widest part of the folded paper.

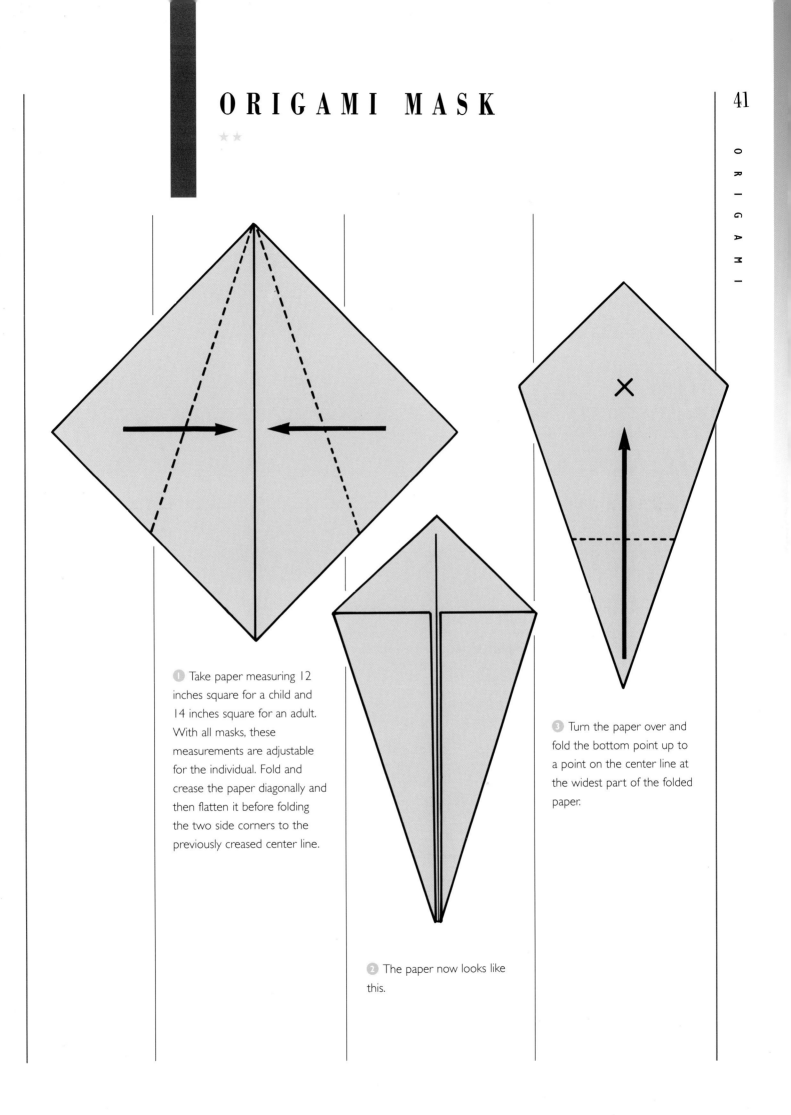

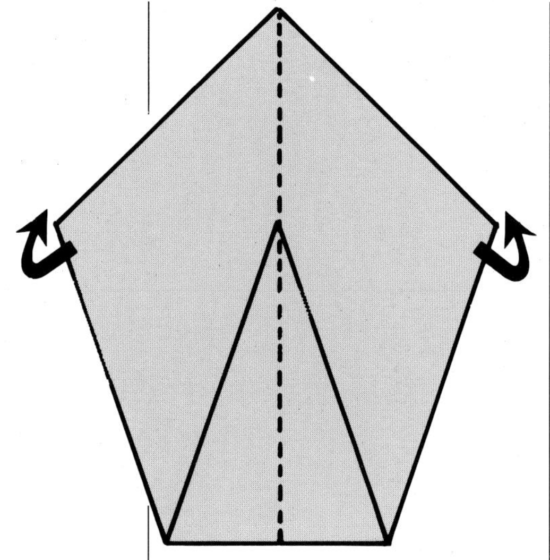

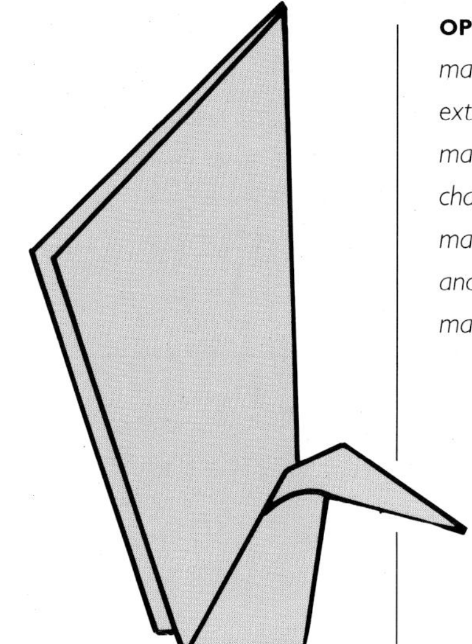

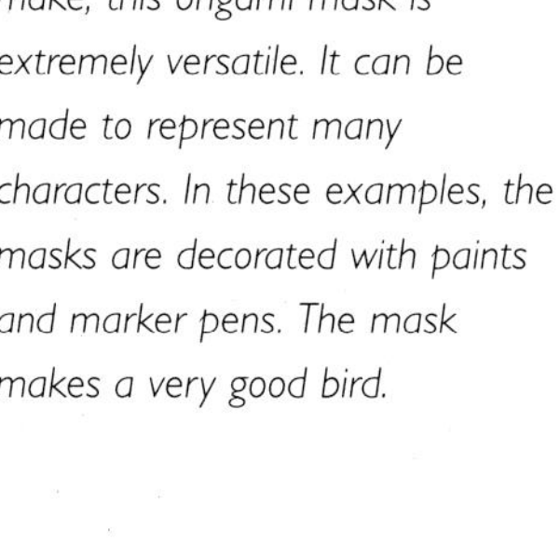

OPPOSITE *Quick and easy to make, this origami mask is extremely versatile. It can be made to represent many characters. In these examples, the masks are decorated with paints and marker pens. The mask makes a very good bird.*

4 Fold the paper (including the point) toward the back along the previously creased center line.

5 Now pull the point forward and crease at a suitable angle to represent a beak or a nose.

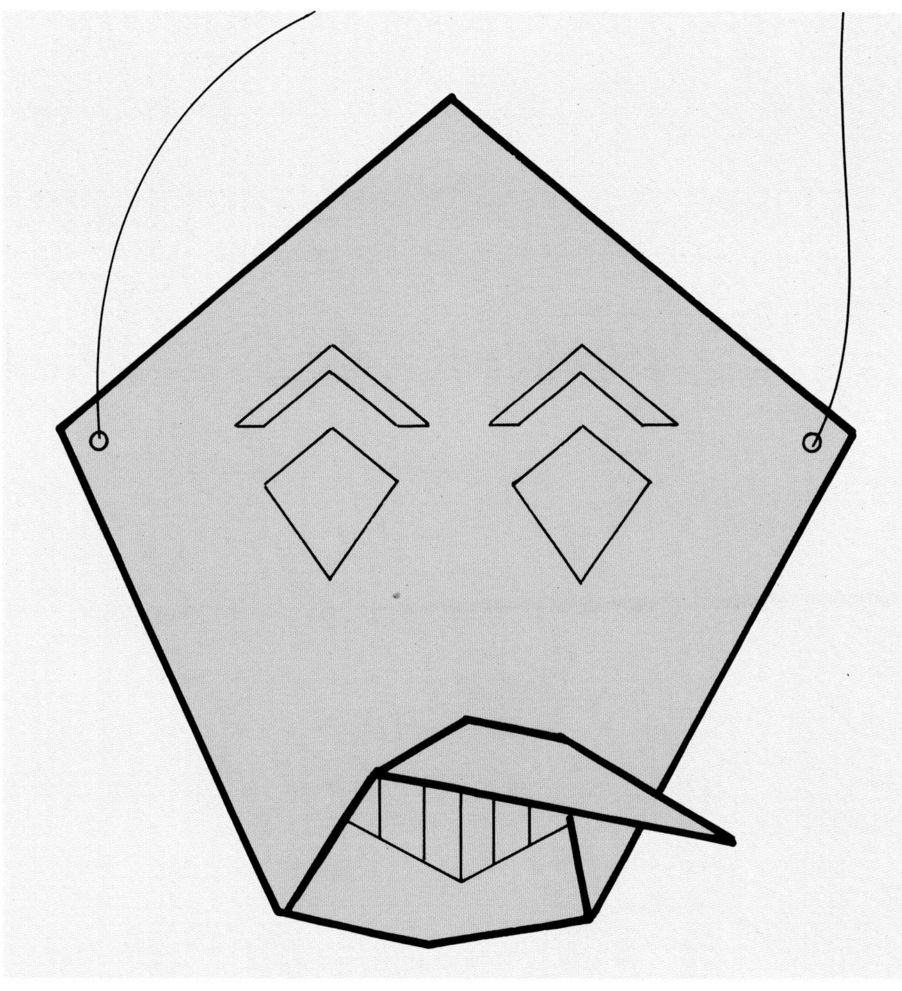

6 Cut out appropriate holes for the eyes and decorate as you like. Make small holes at the widest point and attach string for ties.

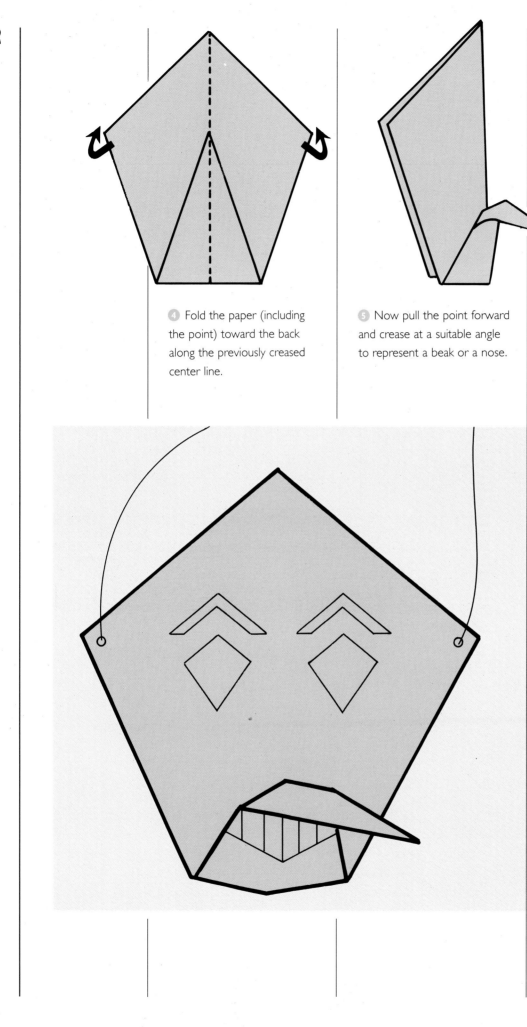

CLASSIC DART

★

This is without doubt the best-known of all paper airplanes, probably because its simplicity and beauty have no equal. If you have never folded paper before, this is the best design to start with since it is almost impossible to get it wrong, provided you take your time. If you know how to make it, try to fold slowly and produce the neatest example you have ever made.

As with all airplanes that have a sharp nose, it is a good idea to cut a small section off to make it safe when throwing. This has a negligible effect on the flight pattern.

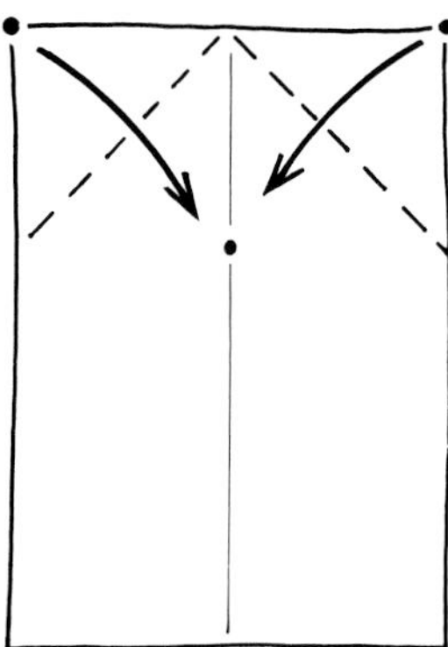

1 Begin with a rectangle, colored side down. Fold in half widthwise and open. Lift each corner and fold it to meet the center crease. Make sure it lines up exactly.

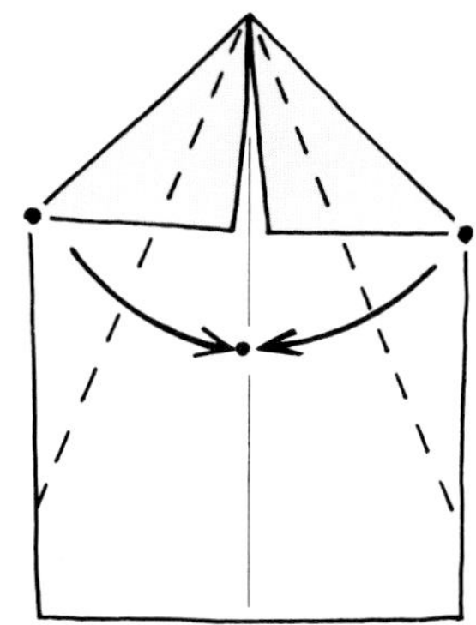

2 Narrow by taking the folded edges (made in step 1) to meet the center crease. Try to keep the upper point sharp.

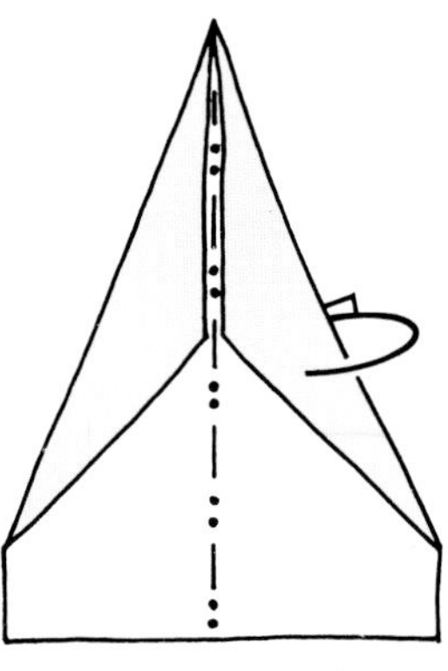

3 Mountain-fold in half. You may find it easier to turn the paper over and make a valley fold.

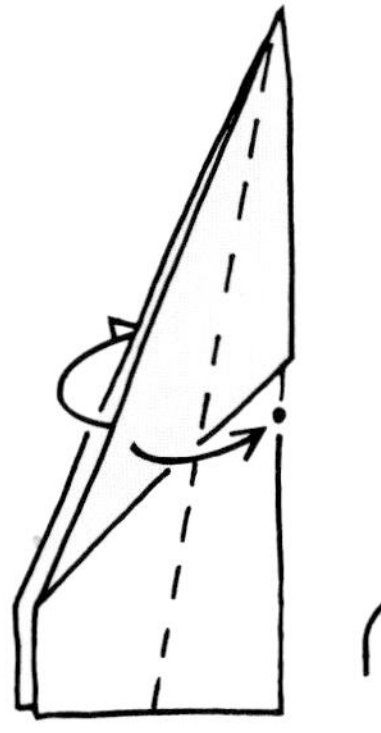

4 Narrow still further by folding each of the two folded edges to the right-hand vertical edge. Turn the paper around so it is horizontal.

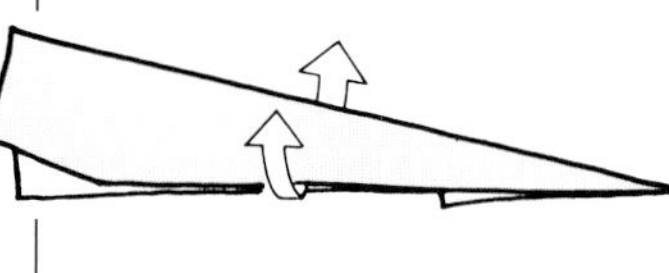

5 Open the wings up to 90 degrees.

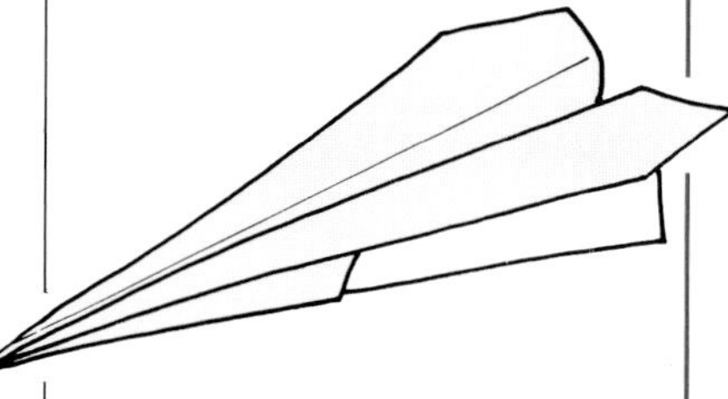

The finished Classic Dart.

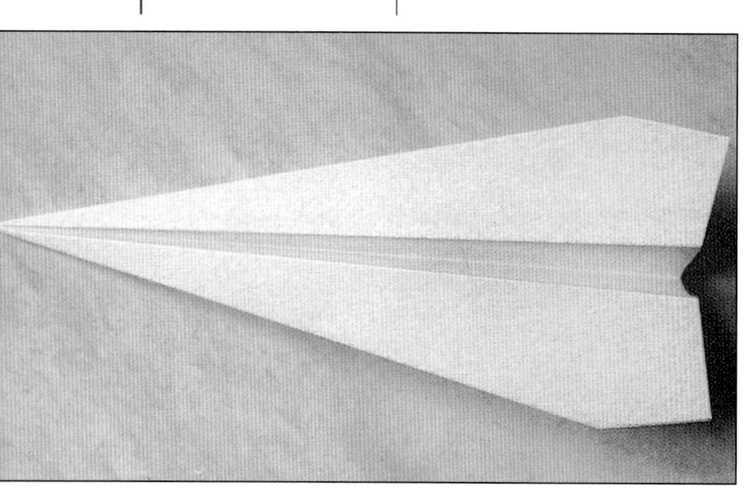

Flying Hints

Launch the dart firmly at a slight upward angle. You may need to adjust the angle of the wings (dihedral) for the best results.

GLIDING TOY

★★

This toy was first published in the 1970s, but nobody knows how old it is, or who invented it. Its beauty is in the simplicity of the design. You can fold it in a matter of seconds, and it glides surprisingly well.

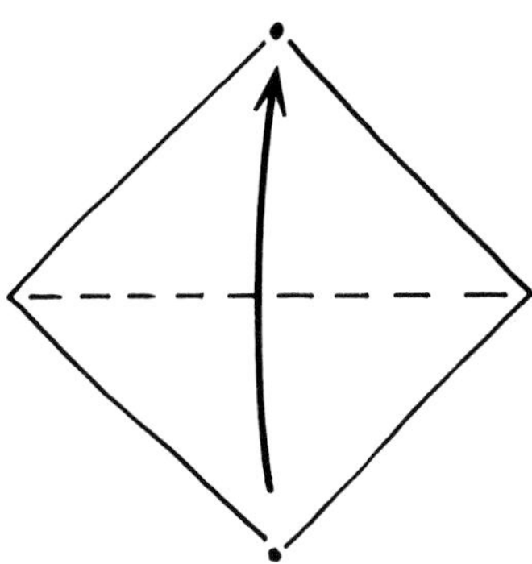

1 Take a small square of lightweight paper. Begin by folding it in half from corner to corner.

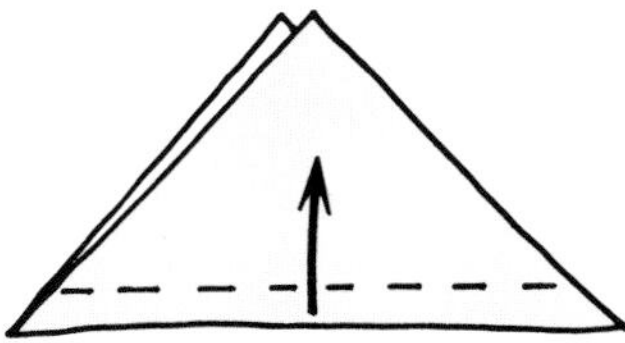

2 Fold a small strip over, try to make the crease parallel to the folded edge.

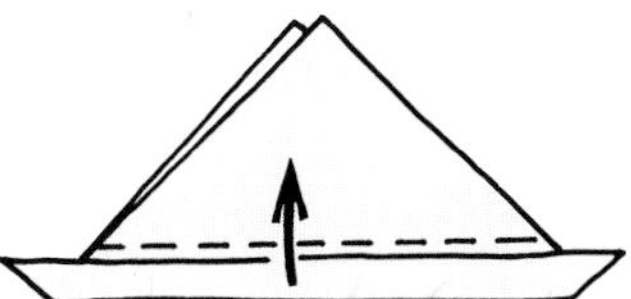

3 Fold the doubled strip over again.

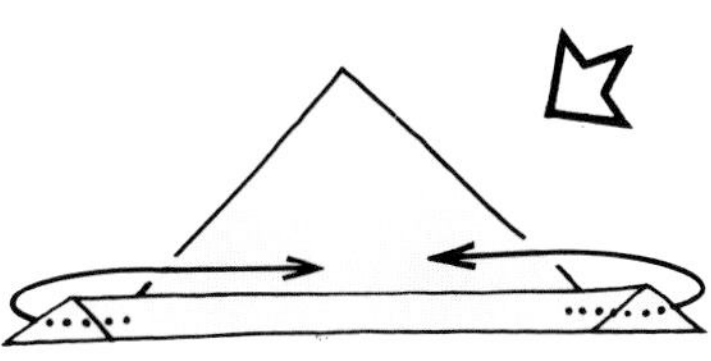

4 Bring the two strips around to meet each other . . .

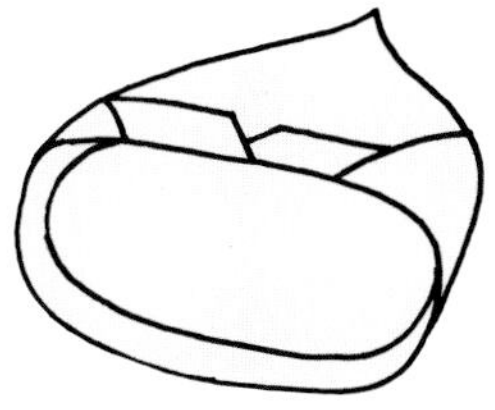

5 . . . and tuck one inside the other. Shape the ring with your fingers to make it as circular as possible.

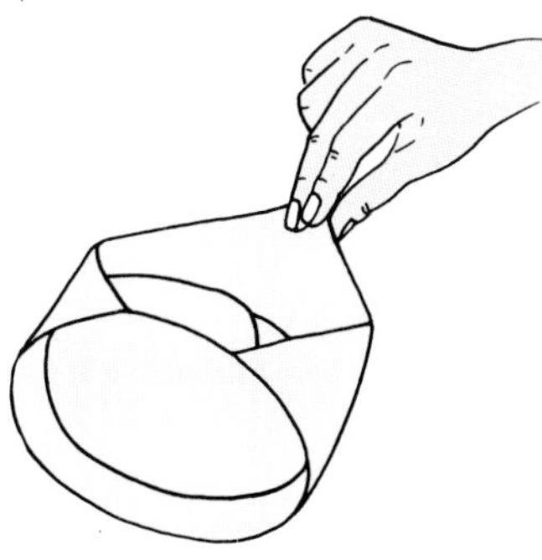

Complete.

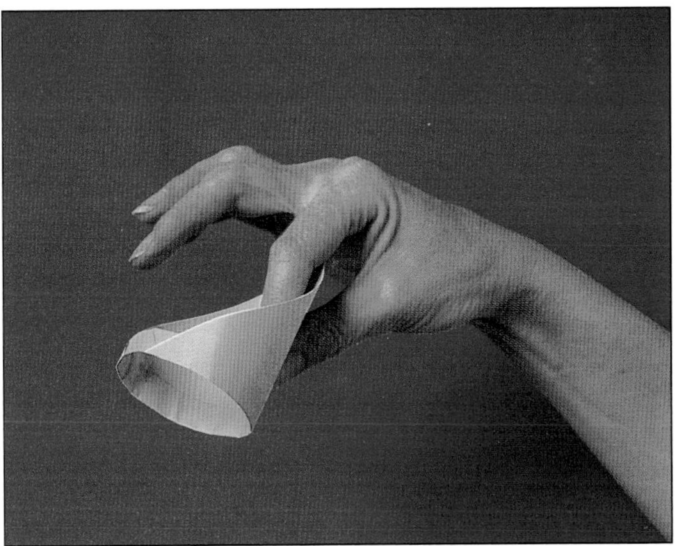

FLYING HINTS

Hold the tip of the tail with the first finger and thumb so that the loop is on top. Launch with a gentle push forward. The higher you are, the farther it will travel.

HARRIER

★ ★ ★

Most paper airplanes depend upon concentrating weight at the front and the challenge is always to achieve this in an unusual and interesting way. This design uses a pleasing sequence of folds to produce a compact "locked" nose section which enables it to fly particularly well. The design isn't based on the British vertical take-off machine, says Michael Weinstein, its designer.

The folding may look involved, but if you fold carefully and keep checking ahead to the next diagram, you will succeed. Make your creases firmly and try not to force the paper. As with all origami, continued folding will make things easier and you will begin to enjoy the moves.

Take a sheet of 8 x 10 paper, colored side up, with the vertical center-crease added.

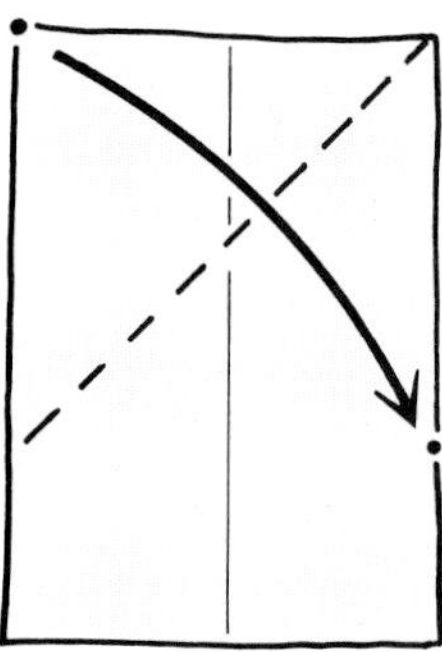

1 Begin by folding the upper short edge to the right-hand long edge.

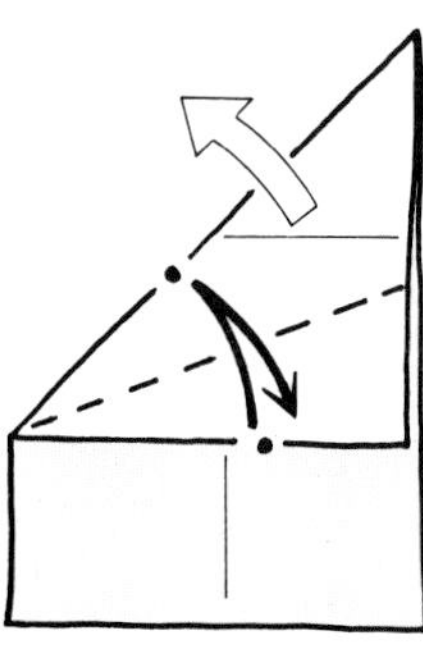

2 Fold the inside raw edge to the upper folded edge and return. Open the paper out again.

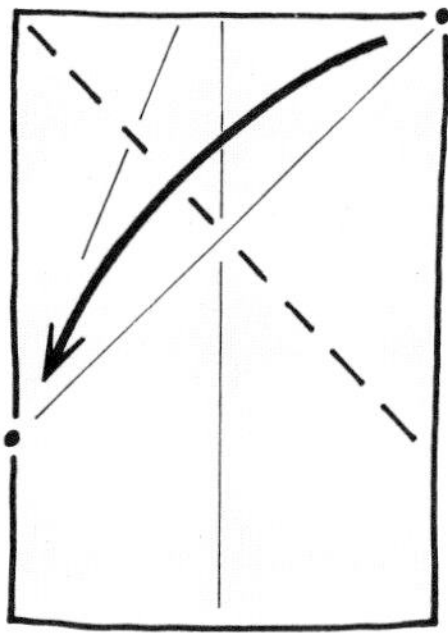

3 Repeat step 1 to the left-hand side.

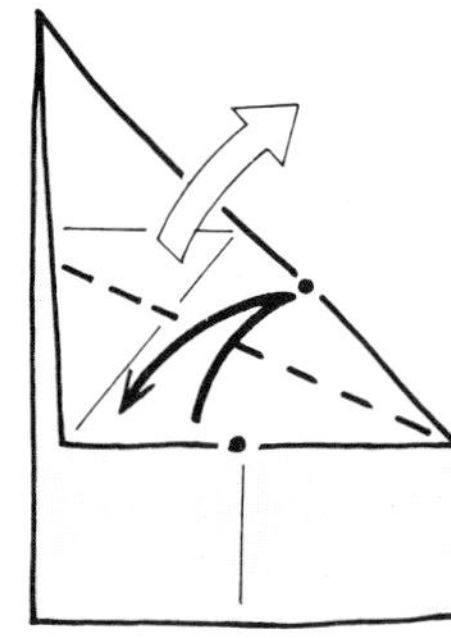

4 Again, crease and return before opening out.

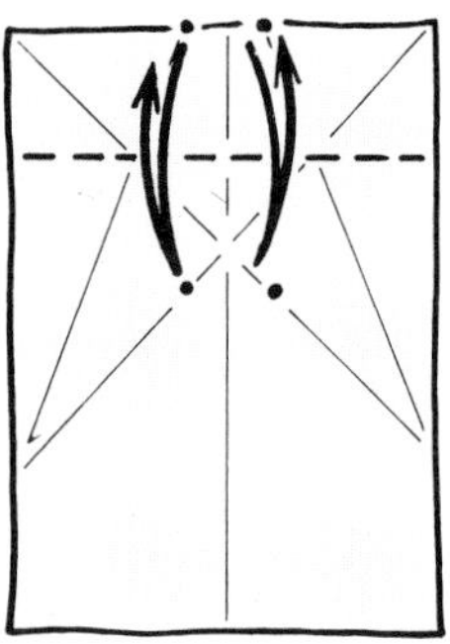

5 Using the location points shown, crease and return.

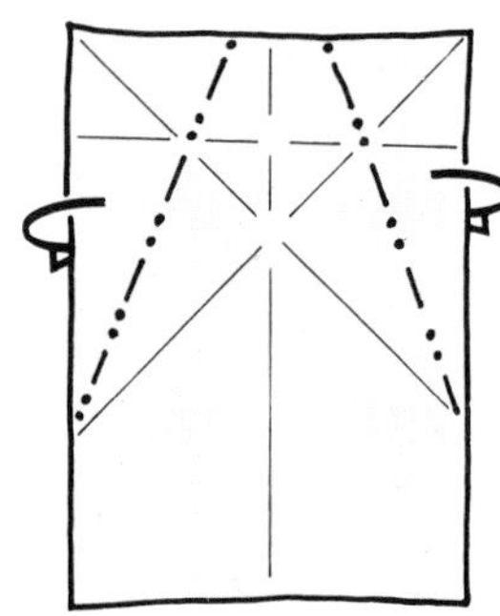

6 Mountain-fold both sides behind on established creases, left corner first.

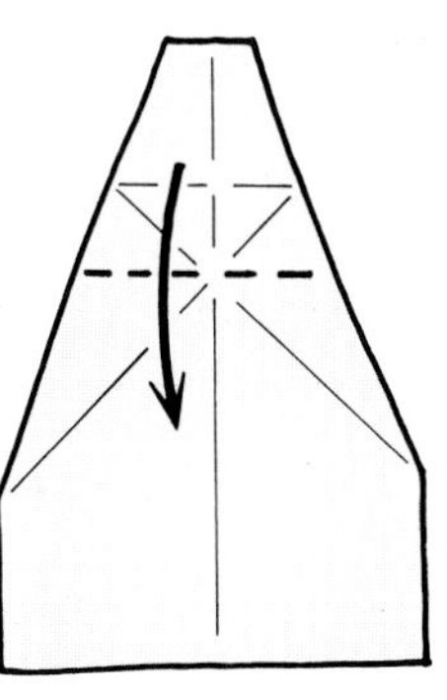

7 Fold the upper section down, making a crease through the intersection point of the three creases.

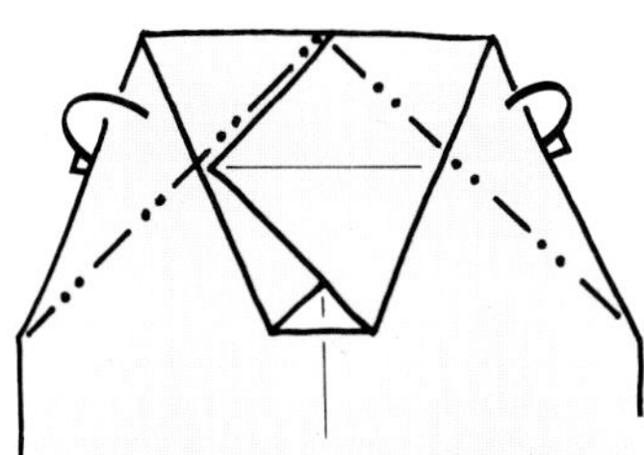

8 Fold the two corners behind.

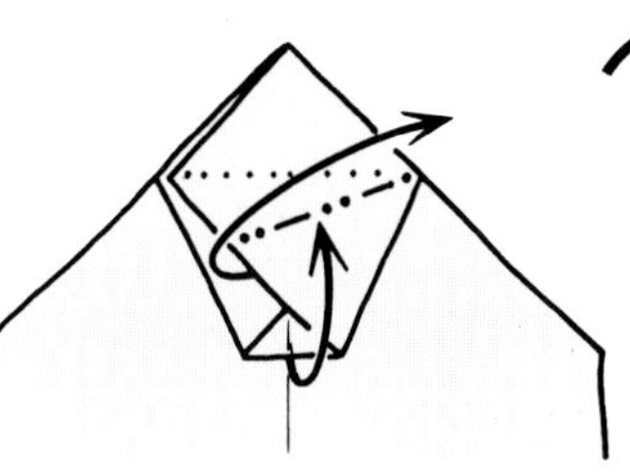

9 Open the pocket, swinging the flap upward. As you fold (slowly), the paper will flatten down naturally to produce the mountain crease. Try it and see! If your paper looks different from the diagram, check the order of the folds in step 6.

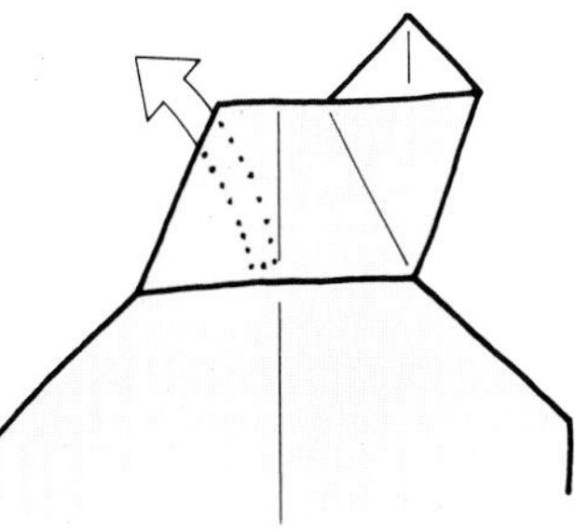

10 Open out the other hidden corner in the same way as the last step.

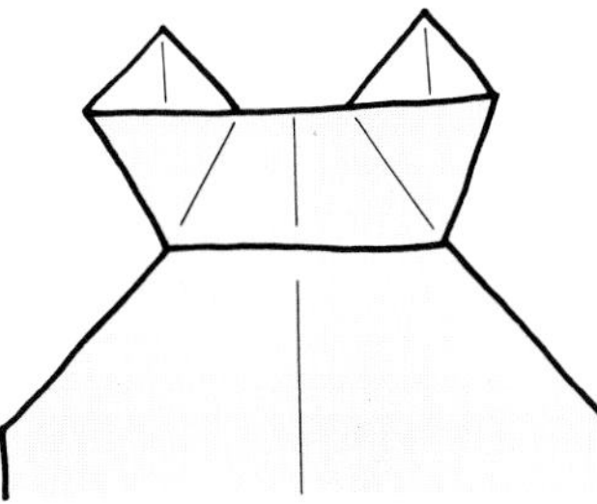

11 This is the result. Flatten the creases firmly and turn the paper over.

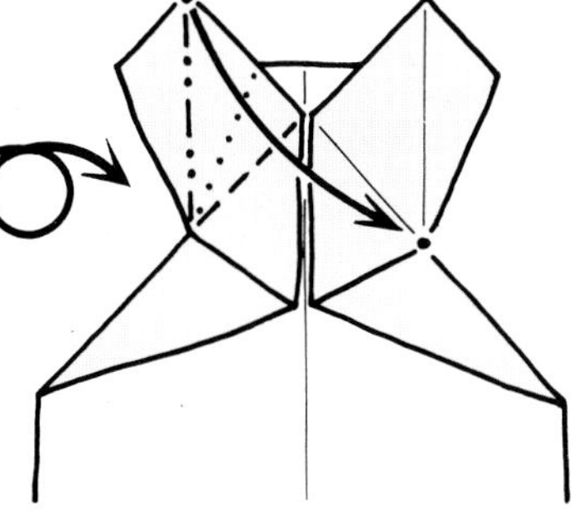

12 Using established creases, flatten the top left corner to the point shown. The dotted line shows the mountain crease that you flatten upon.

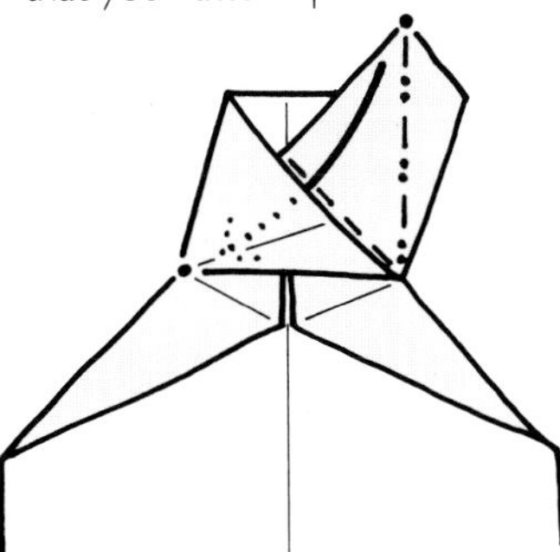

13 Step 12 created a small pocket; repeat the fold on the top right corner, tucking it within the pocket. Neat, isn't it?

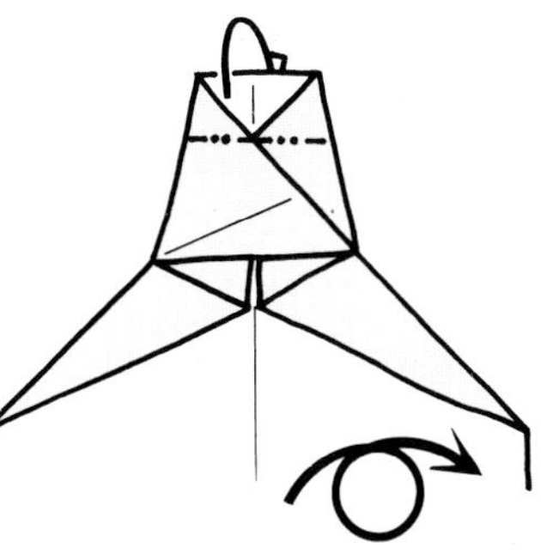

14 Fold the top edge behind, using the inside corner of the small triangle as a guideline. Turn over.

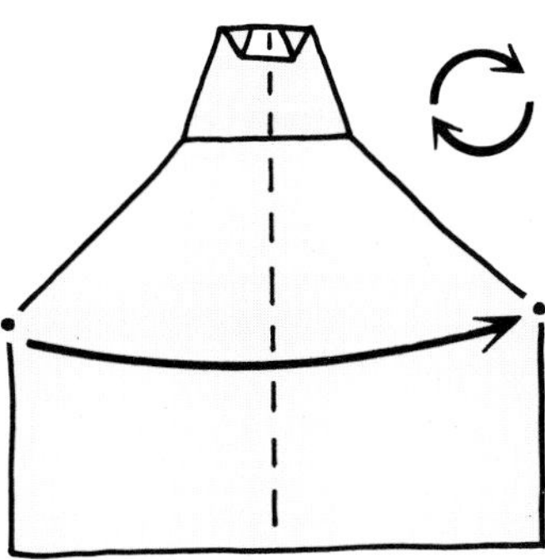

15 This is how the whole sheet looks now. Fold in half along the center crease from right to left.

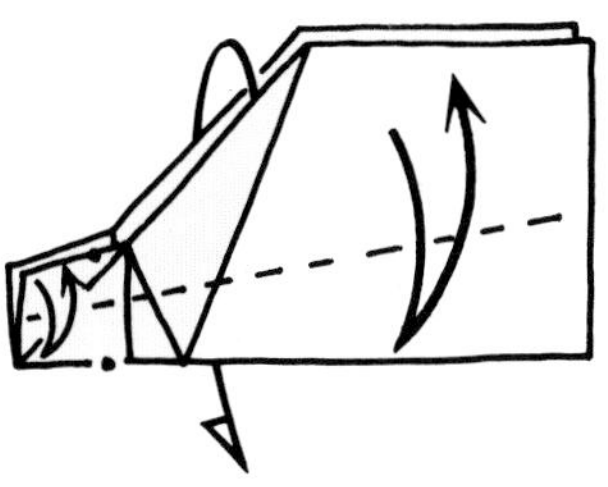

16 Fold the upper side down, lining up the top and bottom edges of the nose section. Unfold this side, then fold down behind and leave it down.

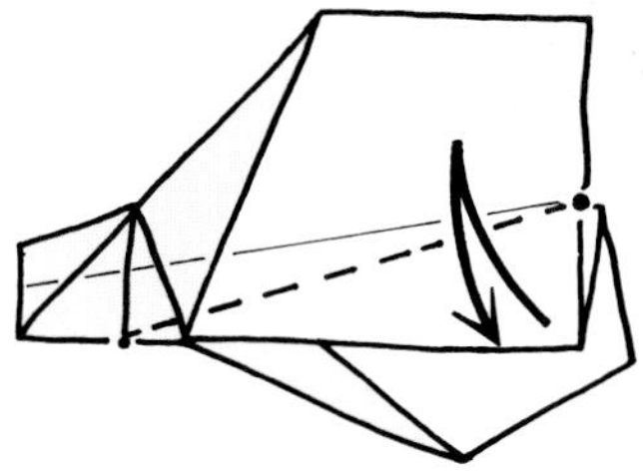

17 Make a crease that joins the right-hand end of the last crease with the lower edge of the nose section. Crease firmly and return.

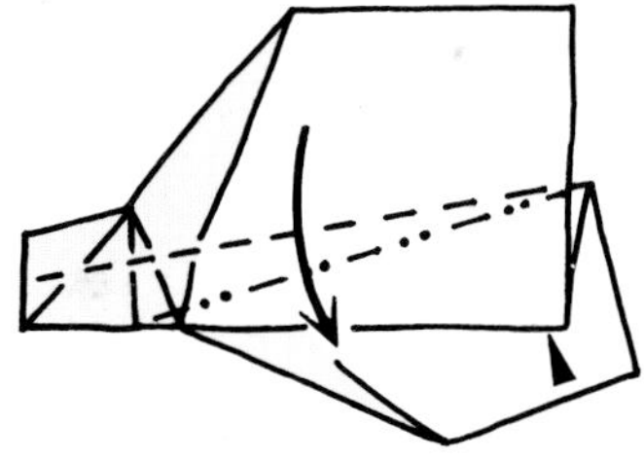

18 Inside reverse fold along the crease made in the last step, then fold the near-side wing down again.

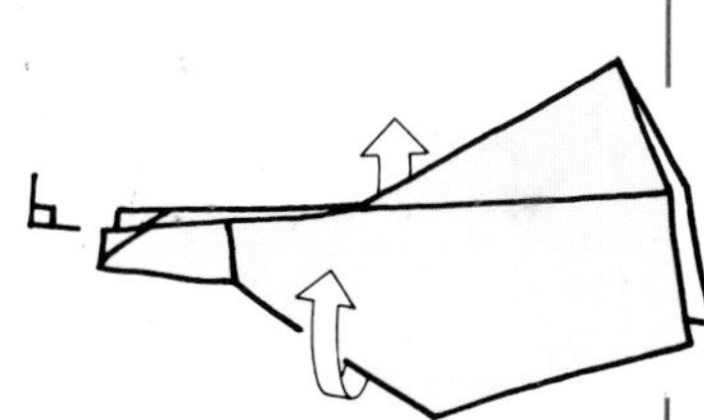

19 Open the wings out to 90 degrees.

20 Ready for flight.

BELOW *The finished Harrier, as designed by Michael Weinstein.*

Launching position.

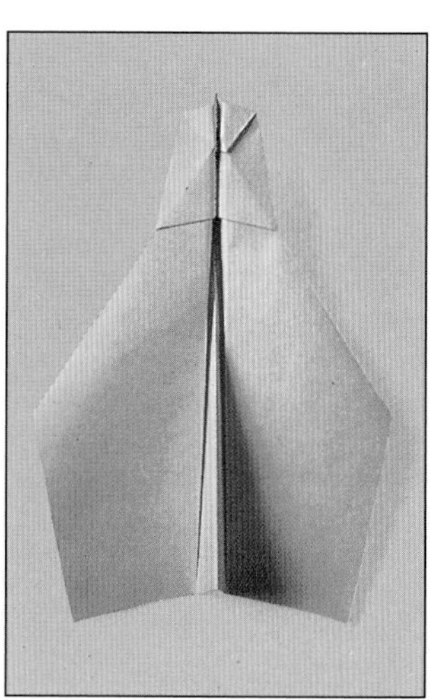

View from below.

Flying Hints

The weight at the nose makes this a stable design that glides very well. Check the dihedral before flying and experiment with different speeds.

BUTTERFLY

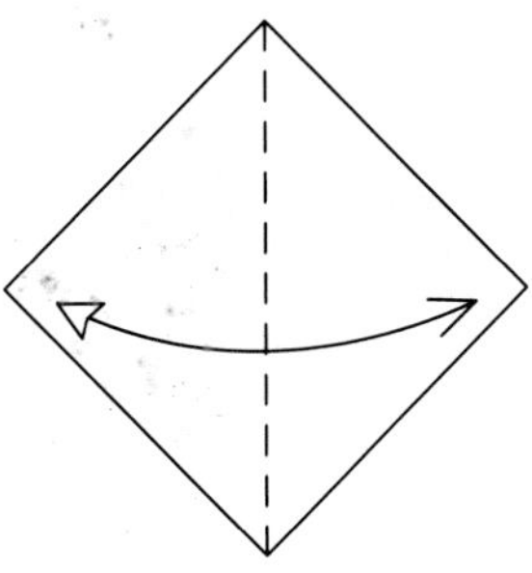

1 Take a 6-inch square of thin, crisp paper. Begin with the white side up. Fold the paper in half along one diagonal and unfold.

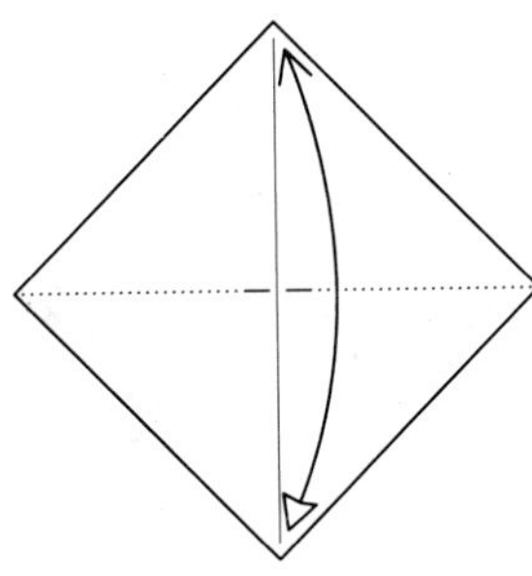

2 Fold the bottom point up to the top point; pinch in the middle and unfold.

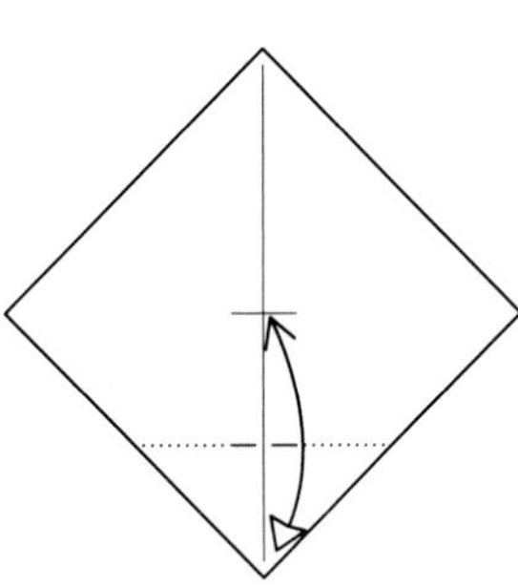

3 Fold the bottom point up to the crease you just made; pinch in the middle and unfold.

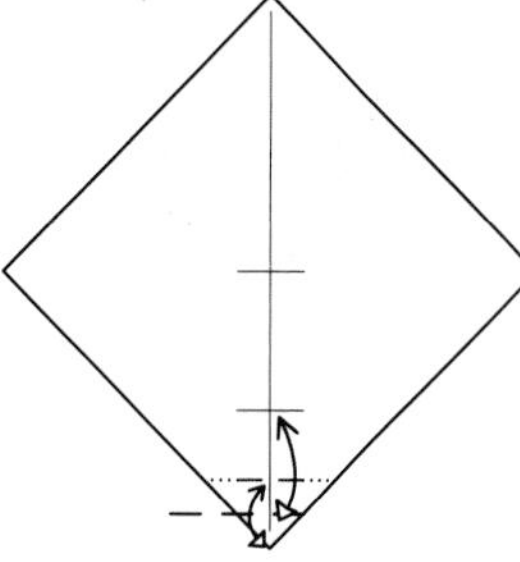

4 Repeat step 3 two more times.

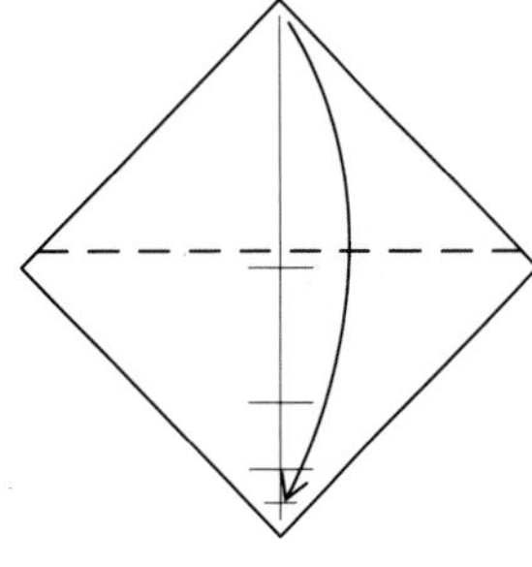

5 Now fold the top point down to the last crease and leave it in place.

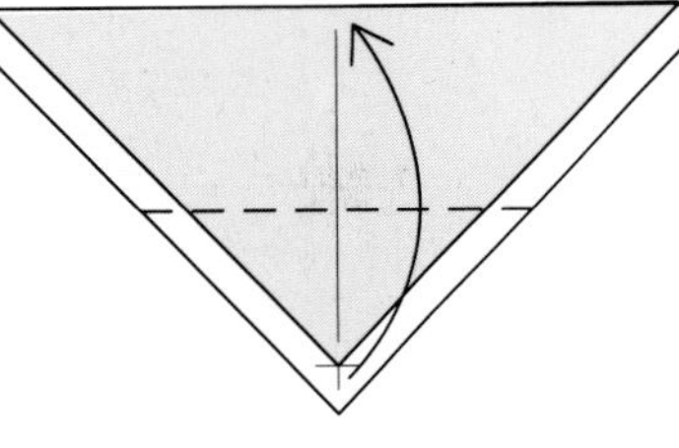

6 Fold both layers together so the bottom point comes up to touch the top edge in the middle.

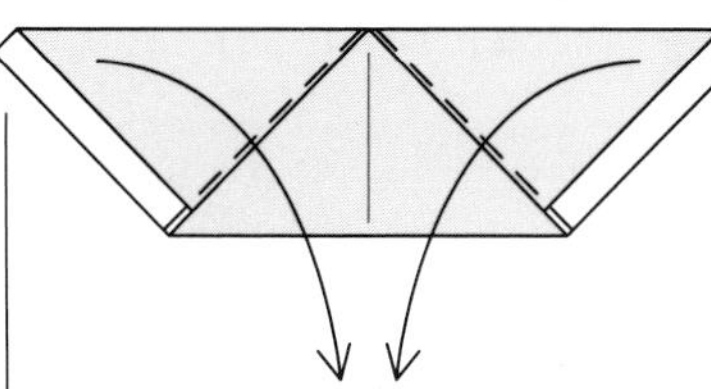

7 Fold the left and right corners down so that their edges meet in the middle.

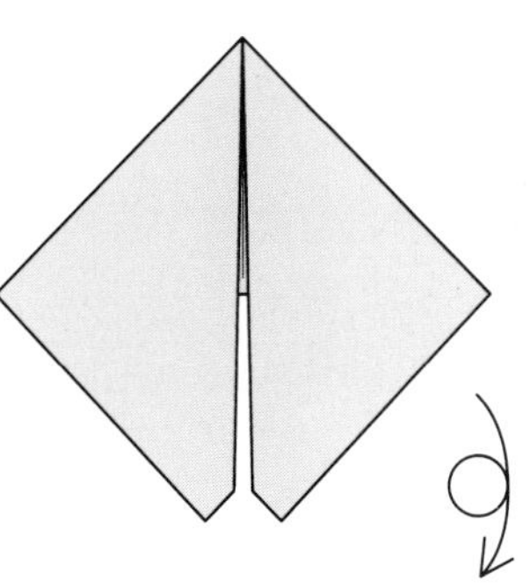

8 Turn the model over from top to bottom.

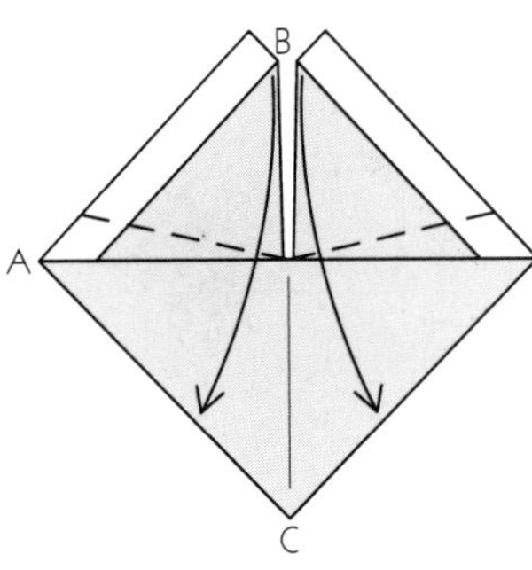

9 Fold down corner B to lie on edge AC. Repeat on the right.

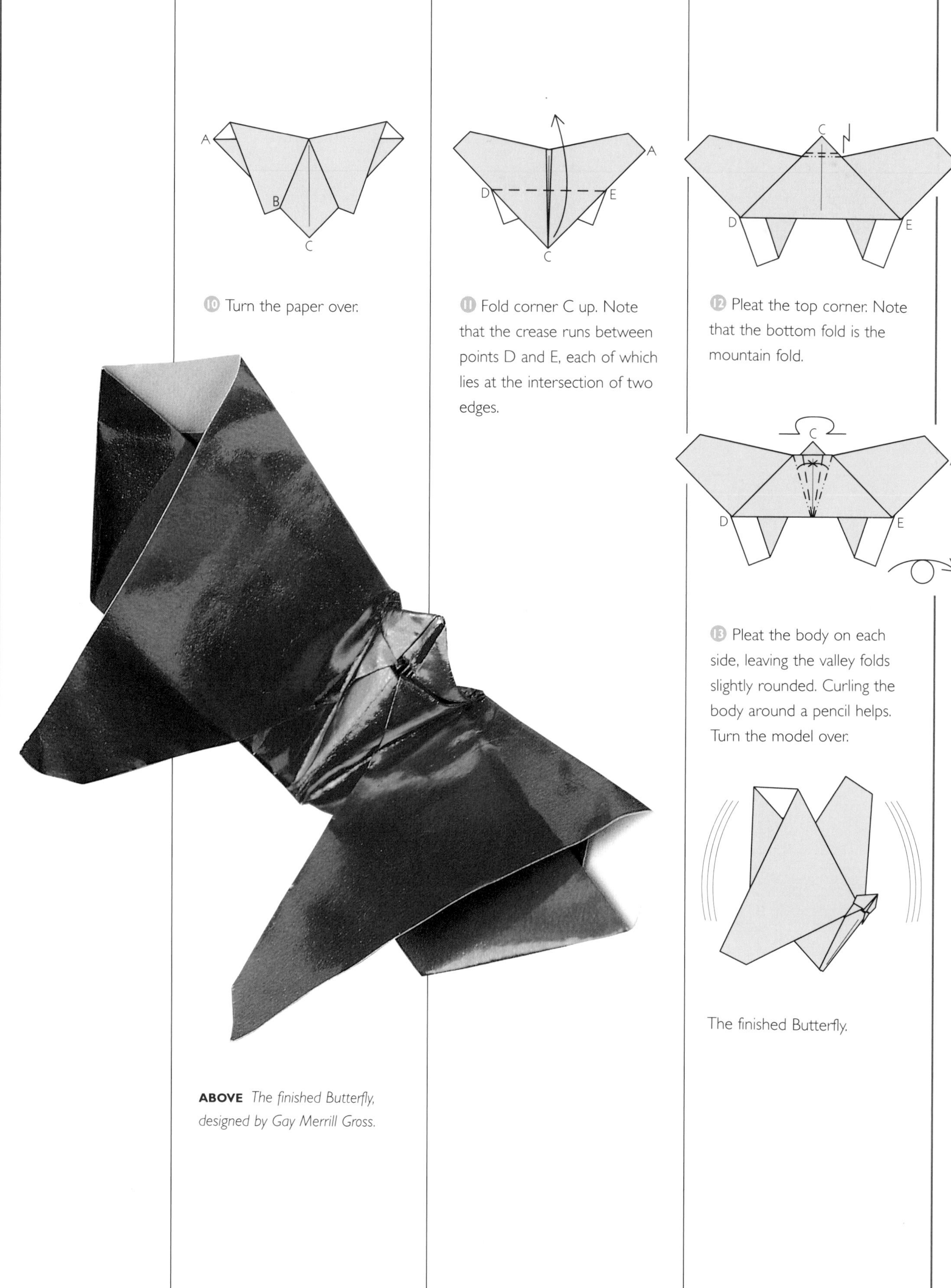

⑩ Turn the paper over.

⑪ Fold corner C up. Note that the crease runs between points D and E, each of which lies at the intersection of two edges.

⑫ Pleat the top corner. Note that the bottom fold is the mountain fold.

⑬ Pleat the body on each side, leaving the valley folds slightly rounded. Curling the body around a pencil helps. Turn the model over.

The finished Butterfly.

ABOVE *The finished Butterfly, designed by Gay Merrill Gross.*

MARMOT

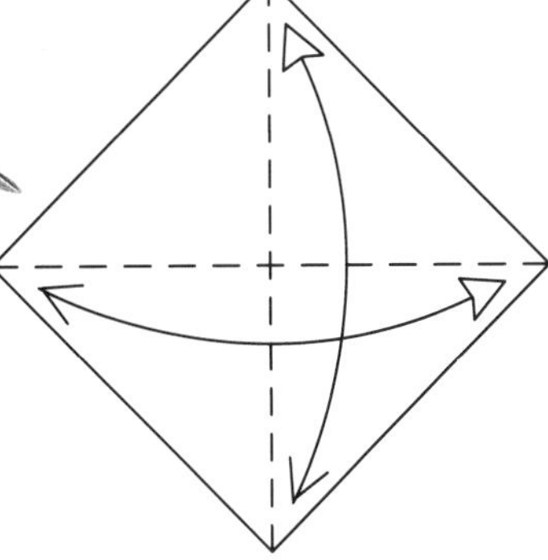

1 Take a 6-inch square of brown paper. Begin with the white side up. Fold the paper in half along the diagonals and unfold.

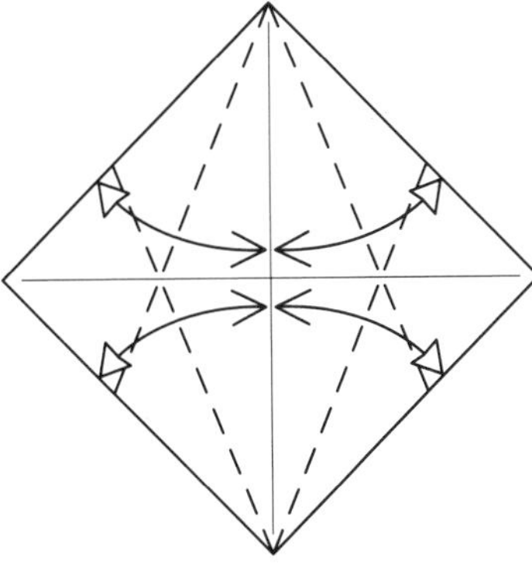

2 Fold in each of the four edges to lie along the center line and unfold.

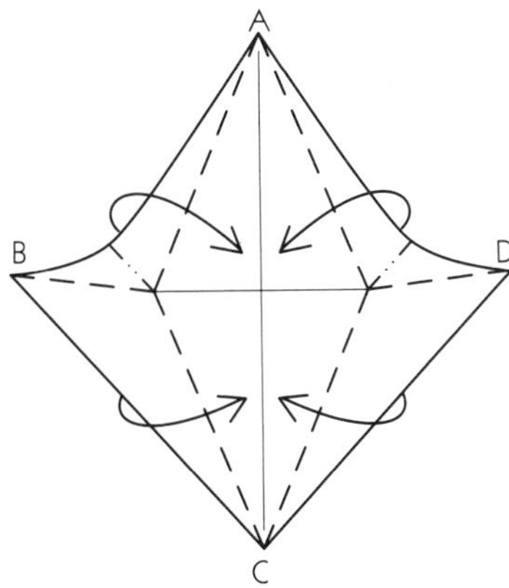

3 Bring all four edges to the center line at once.

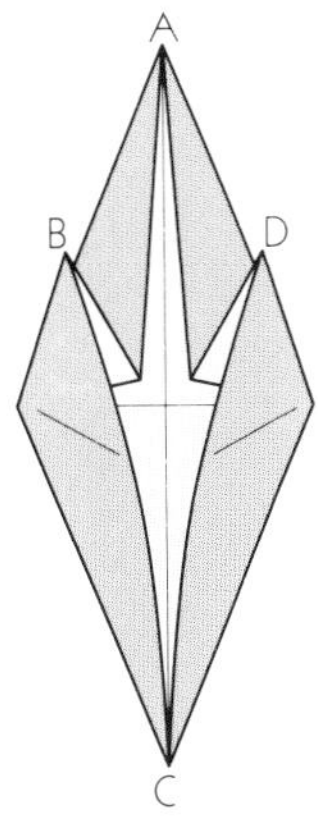

4 Bring corners B and D upward and flatten the model.

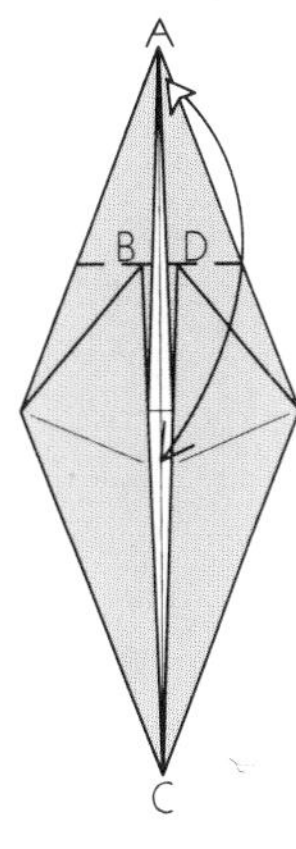

5 Fold point A down to the point where two creases hit the raw edges (the crease runs just under points B and D). Unfold.

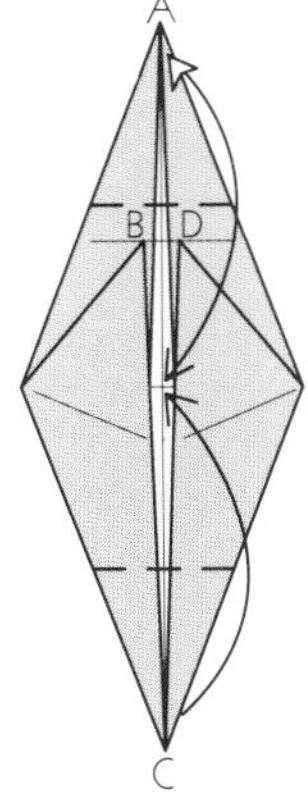

6 Fold points A and C to meet each other in the middle of the model; unfold point A.

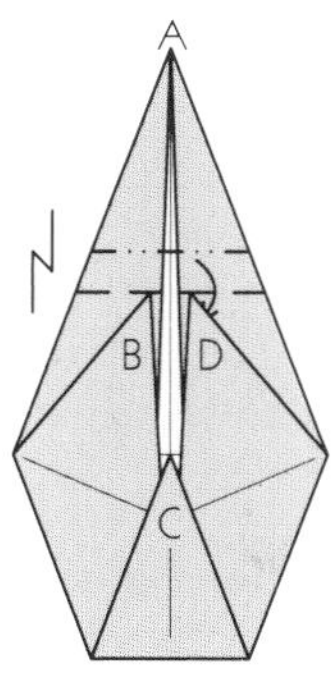

7 Pleat flap A downward behind flaps B and D, using the existing creases.

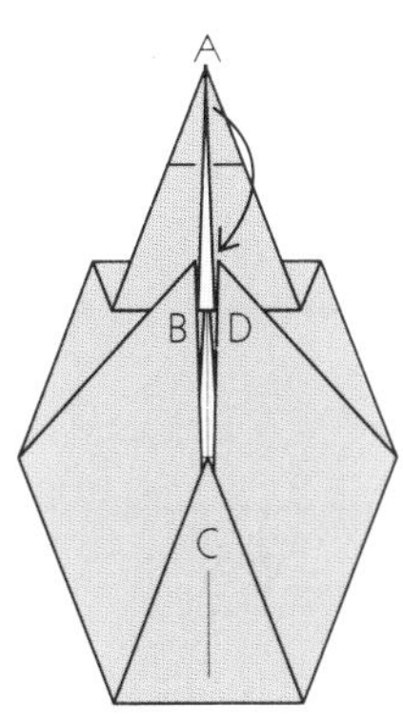

8 Fold down point A to meet corners B and D.

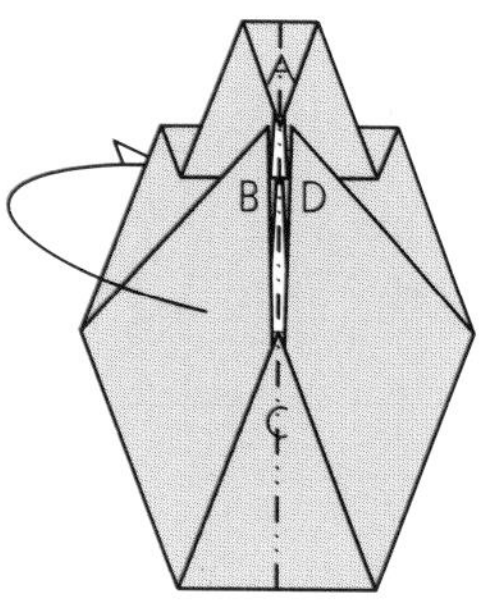

9 Mountain-fold the model in half.

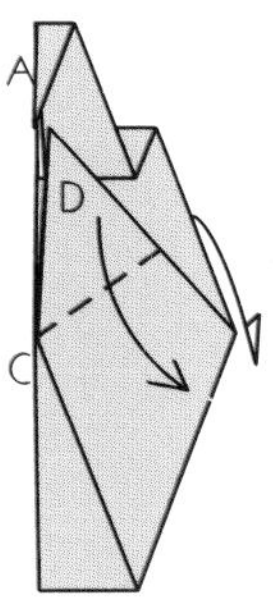

10 Fold corner D down in front. Repeat behind with corner B. There is no reference point for this crease.

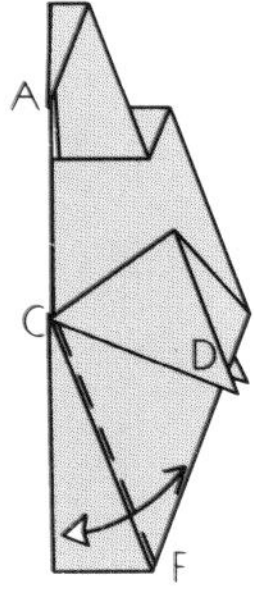

11 Fold the bottom along edge CF and unfold.

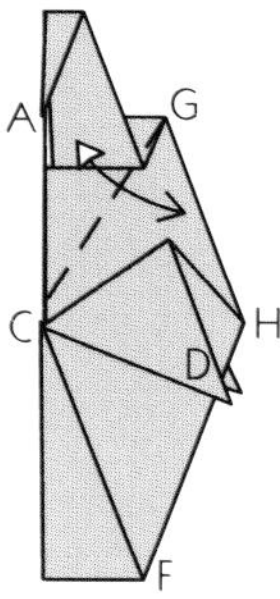

12 Fold the top down so that edge AG lies along edge GH; crease firmly and unfold.

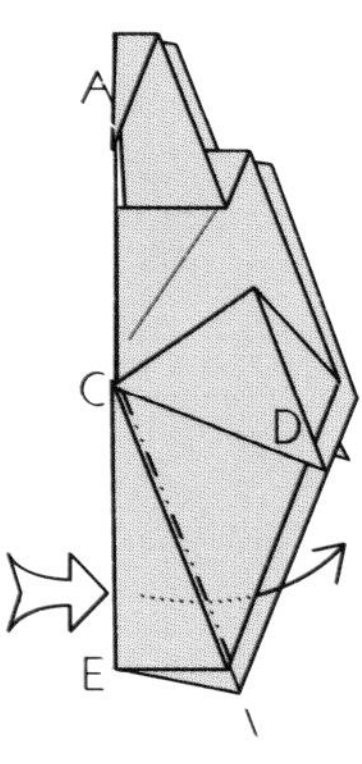

13 Reverse-fold edge CE to the right by pushing it between the layers of the body.

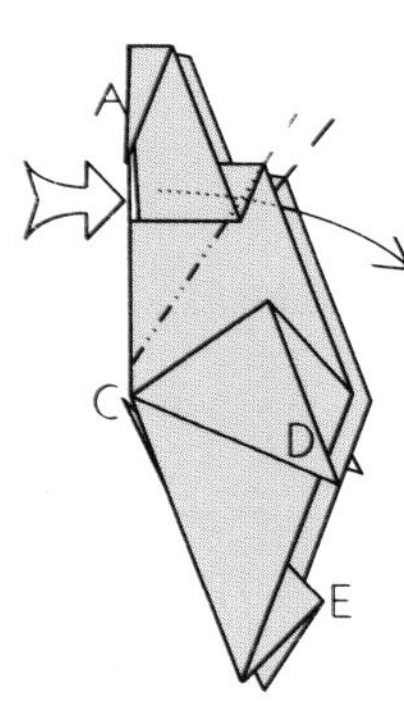

14 Reverse-fold the upper part of the model by pushing on edge CA so that it turns inside-out and goes between the layers of the body.

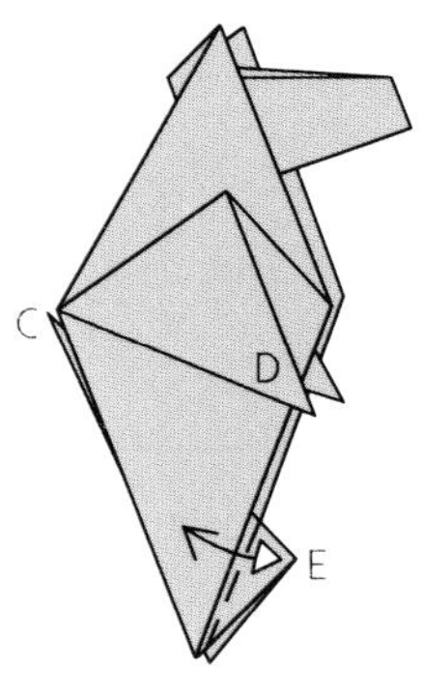

15 Fold and unfold.

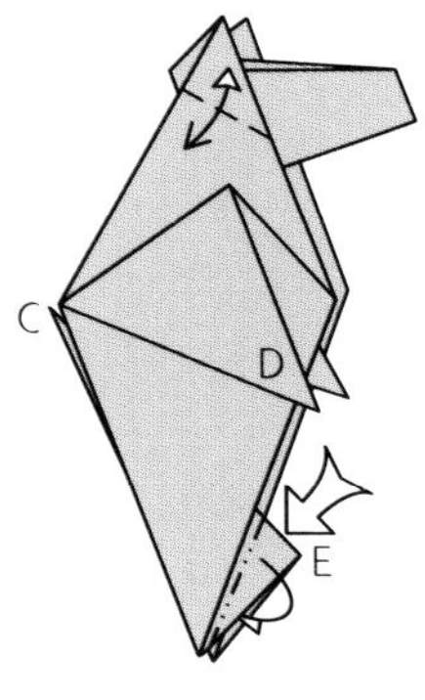

16 Reverse-fold corner E. Fold the ear down and unfold. Repeat behind on the other ear.

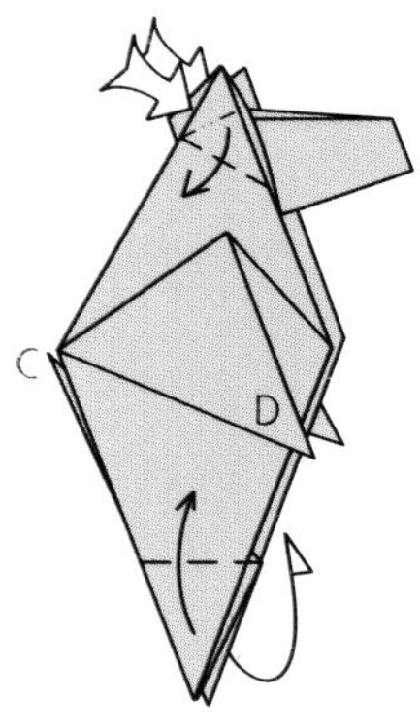

17 Squash-fold the ears. Fold one foot up as far as possible on each side.

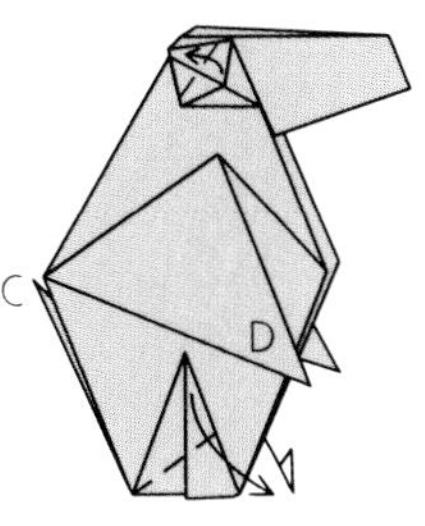

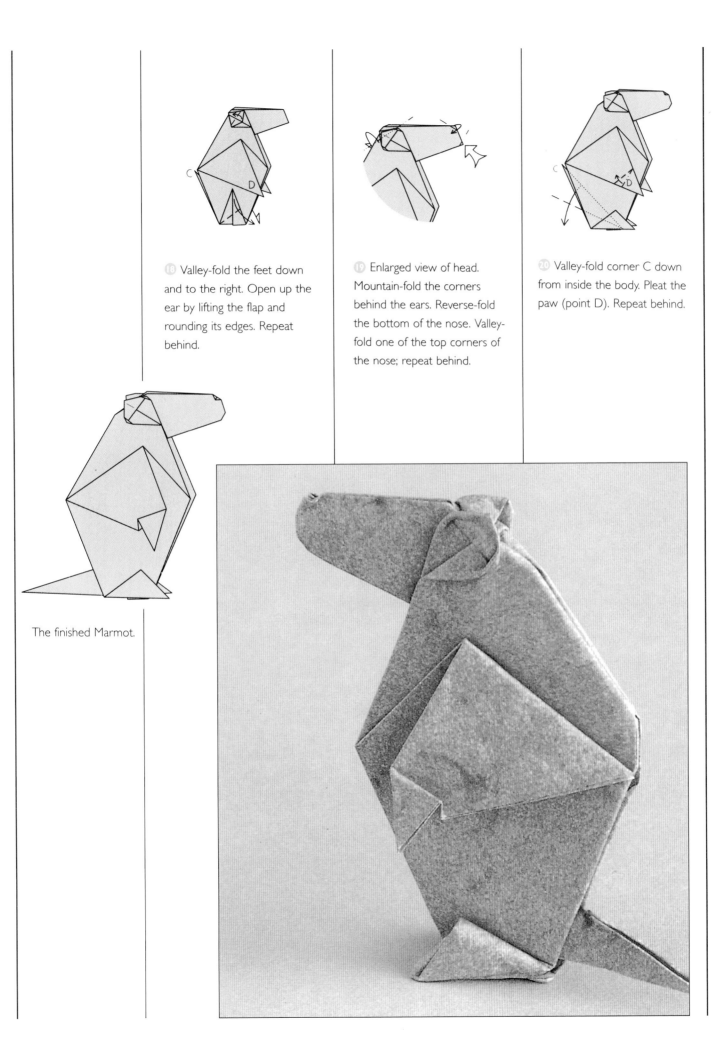

18 Valley-fold the feet down and to the right. Open up the ear by lifting the flap and rounding its edges. Repeat behind.

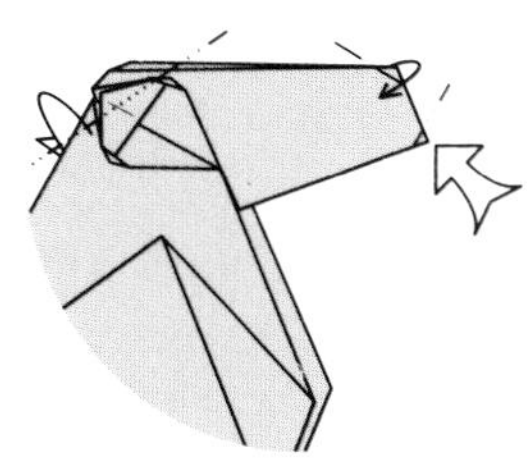

19 Enlarged view of head. Mountain-fold the corners behind the ears. Reverse-fold the bottom of the nose. Valley-fold one of the top corners of the nose; repeat behind.

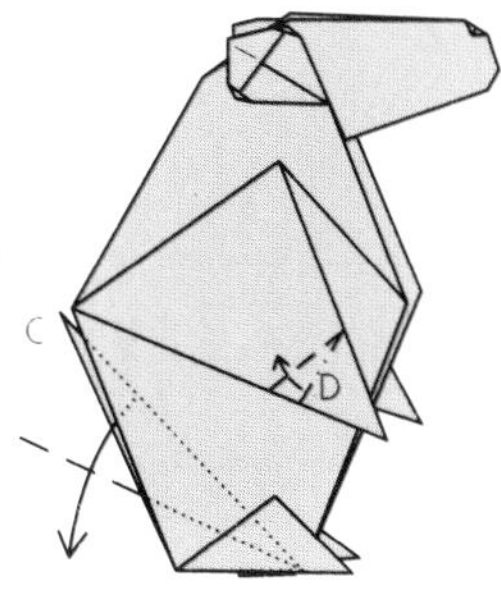

20 Valley-fold corner C down from inside the body. Pleat the paw (point D). Repeat behind.

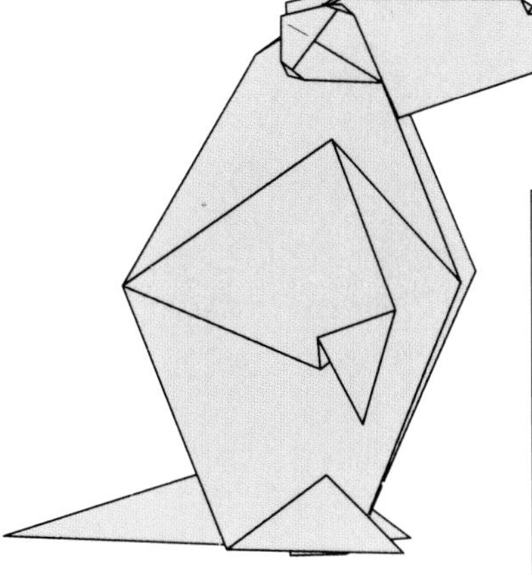

The finished Marmot.

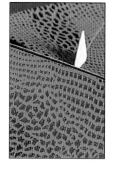

ALLIGATOR

★ ★ ★

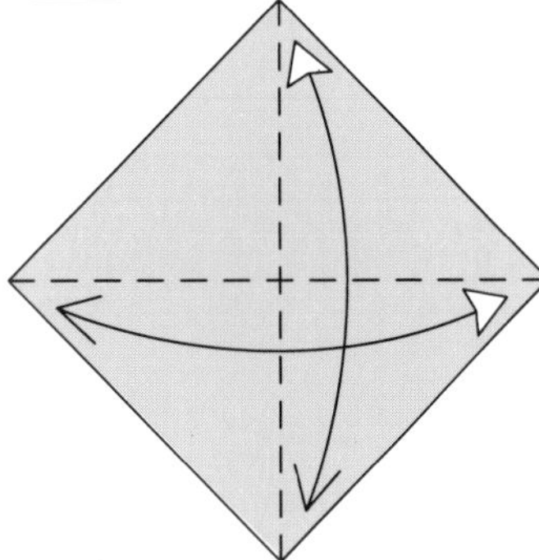

1 Take a 12-inch square of green and yellow paper. Begin with the colored side up. Fold the paper in half along both diagonals and unfold.

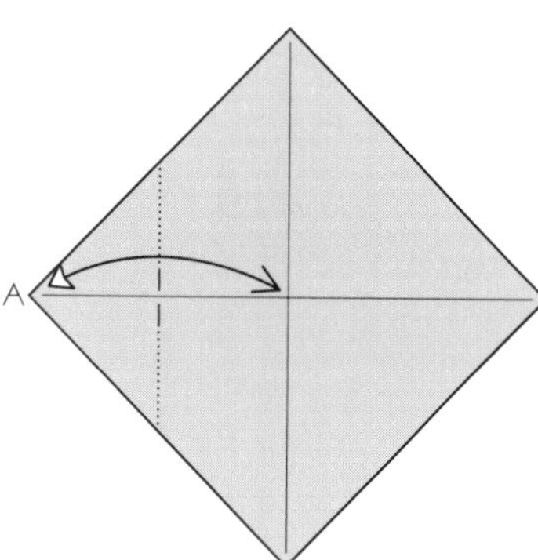

2 Fold point A in to the center and unfold, making the crease sharp only where it crosses the horizontal crease.

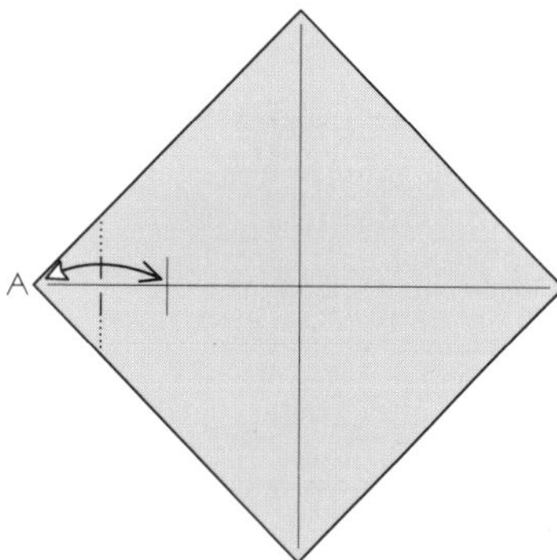

3 Fold point A in to the crease you just made and unfold, making the crease sharp only where it crosses the horizontal crease.

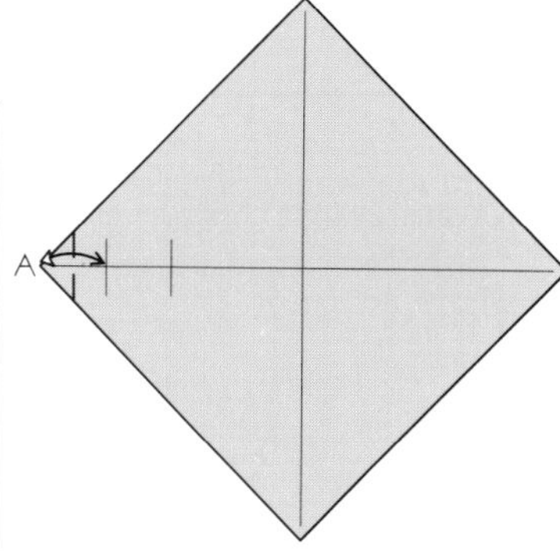

4 Fold point A in to the crease you just made. Unfold. This time, make the crease run all the way across the paper.

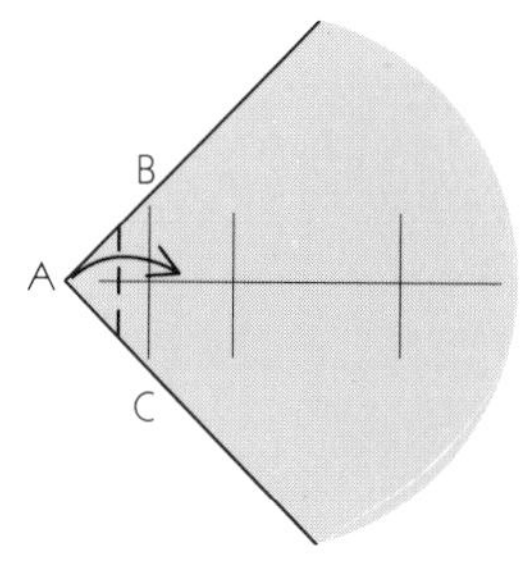

5 This is an enlarged view of the corner. Fold point A in so that crease BC (the crease you just made) cuts across the middle of the white triangle you are making.

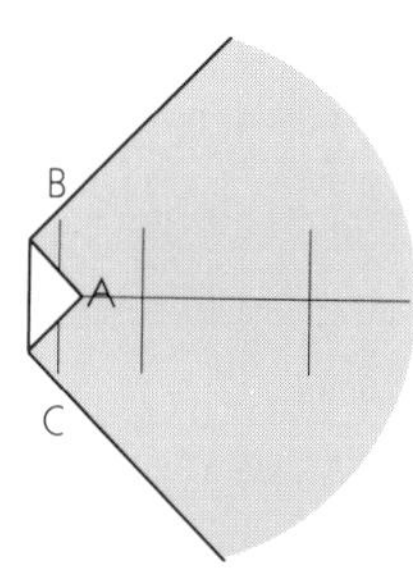

6 This corner is complete. Now repeat steps 3–5 on each of the other three corners.

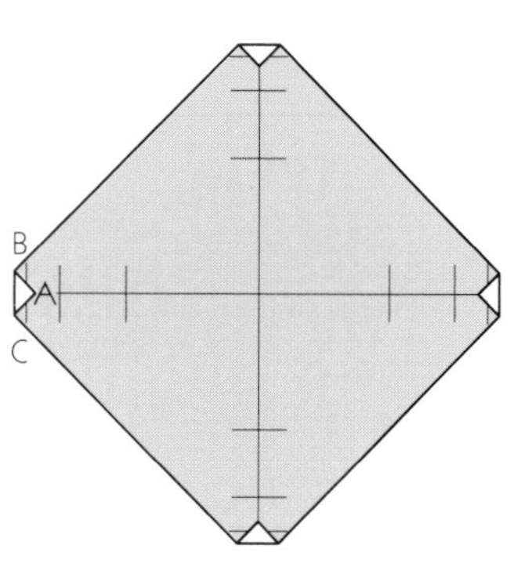

7 Turn the paper over.

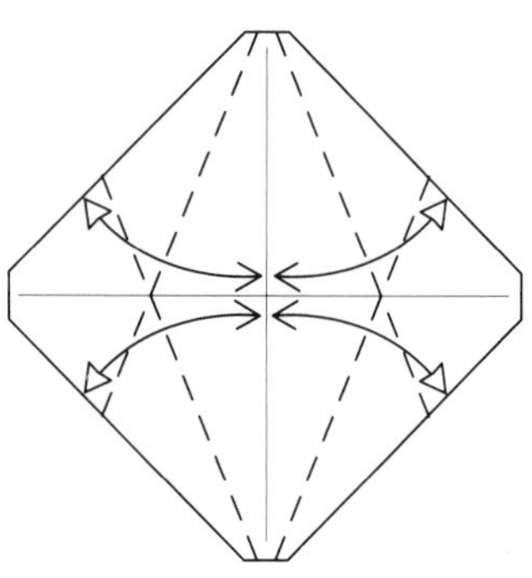

8 Fold each of the four edges in to the center line and unfold.

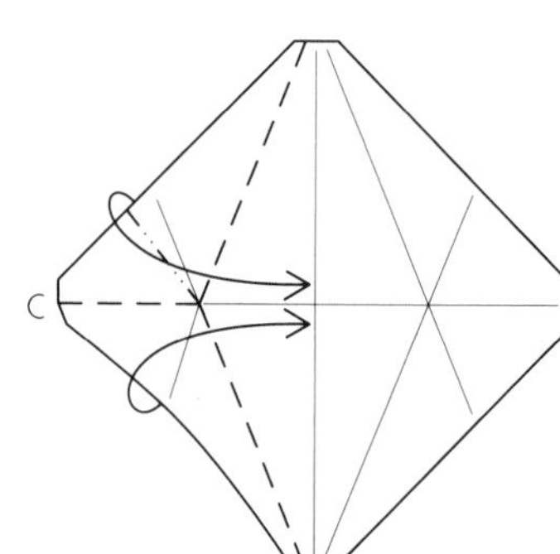

9 Fold the two left edges in to the center together; at the same time, pinch corner D in half. The next step shows this in progress.

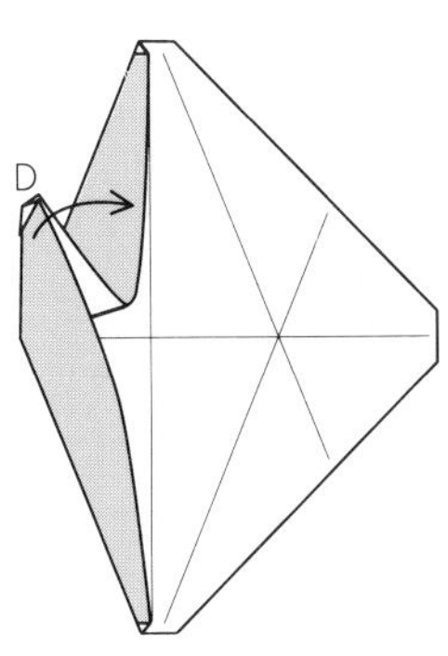

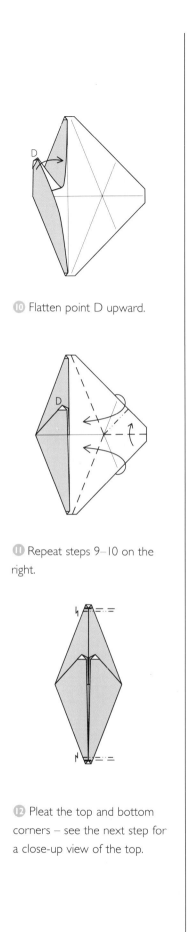

10 Flatten point D upward.

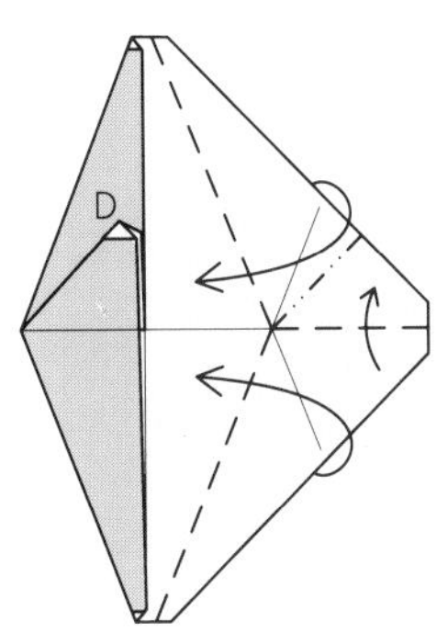

11 Repeat steps 9–10 on the right.

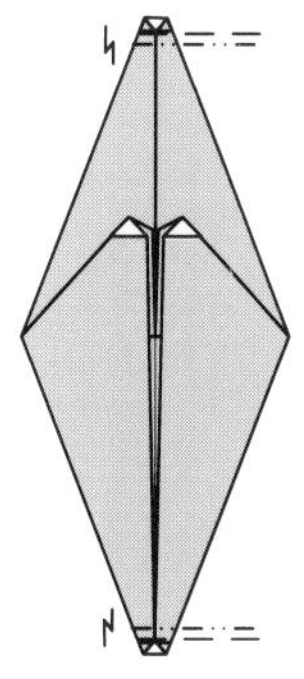

12 Pleat the top and bottom corners – see the next step for a close-up view of the top.

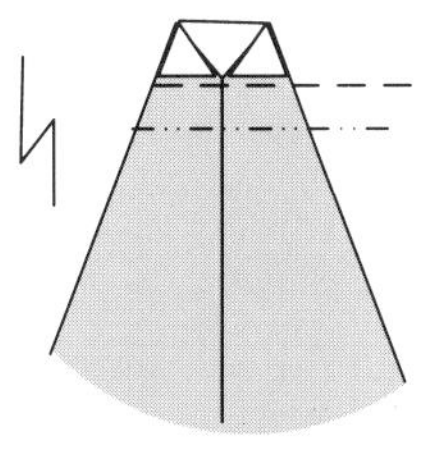

13 Enlarged view of the pleat.

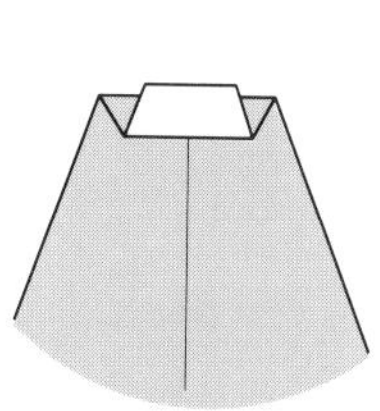

14 This shows the completed pleat at the top; the bottom should look the same.

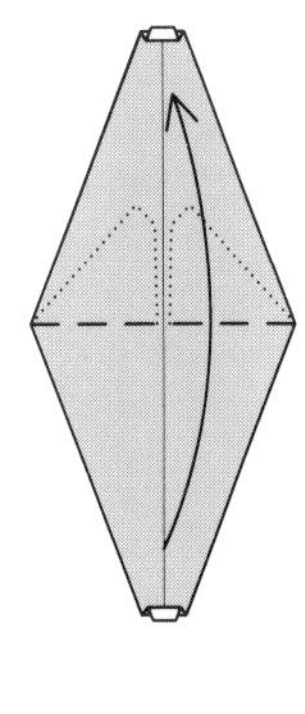

15 Valley-fold the bottom flap upward. The flaps on the back side should be pointing upward. Turn the model over.

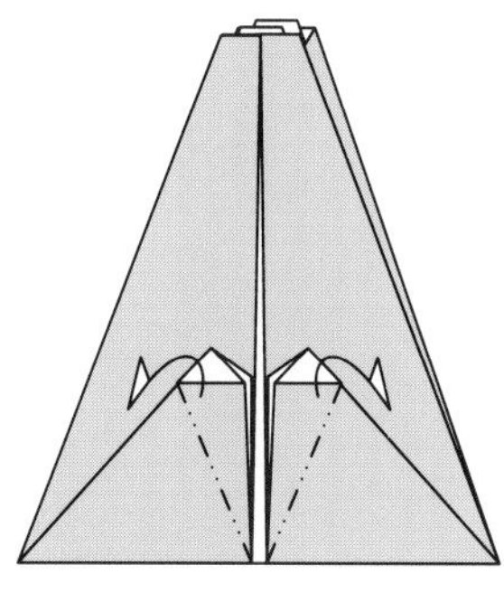

16 Mountain-fold the white corners underneath.

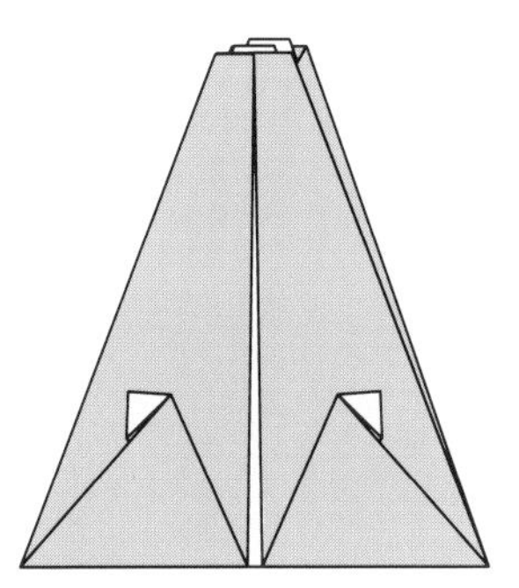

17 Turn the model over.

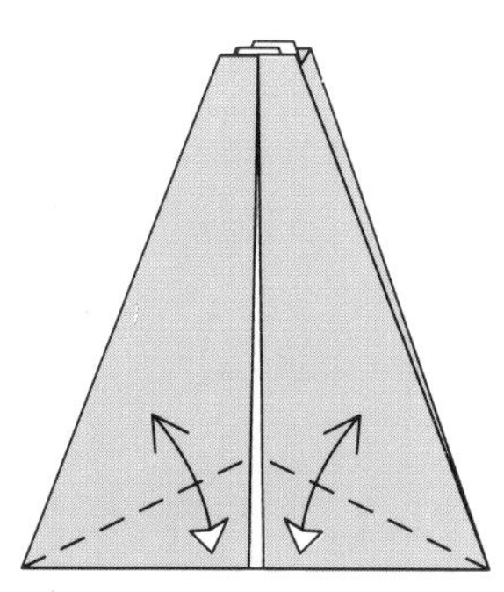

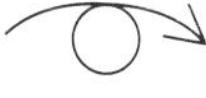

18 Fold and unfold through all layers. Turn the model back over.

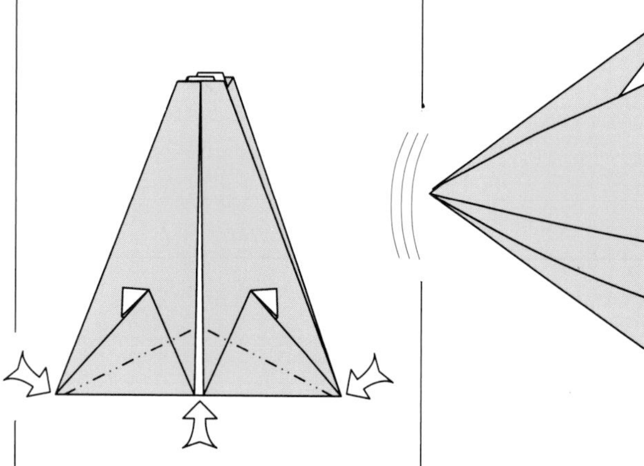

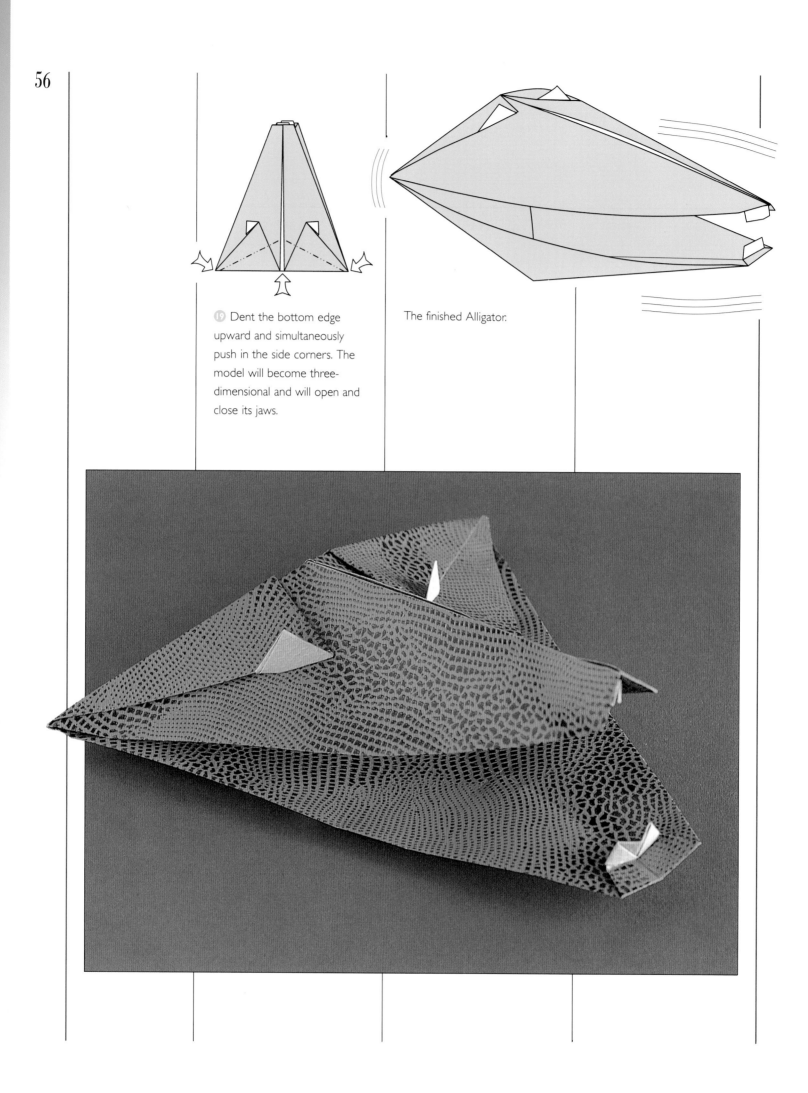

19 Dent the bottom edge upward and simultaneously push in the side corners. The model will become three-dimensional and will open and close its jaws.

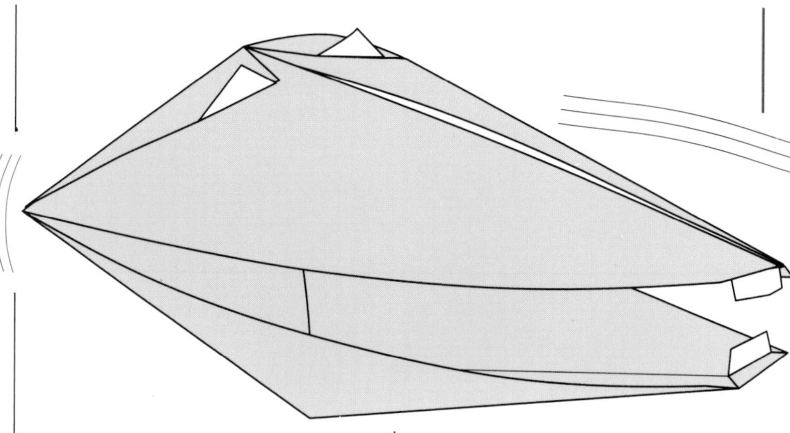

The finished Alligator.

TURTLE

★★★★

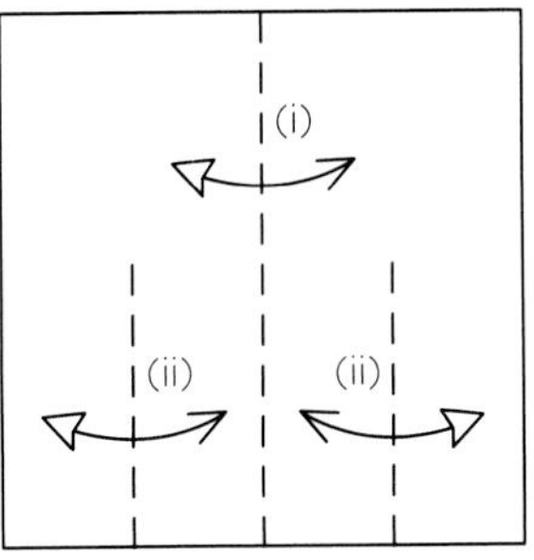

1 Take a 12-inch square of thin green paper. Begin with the white side up. Fold the paper in half vertically and unfold. Then fold the sides in to the center line, crease the lower part, and unfold.

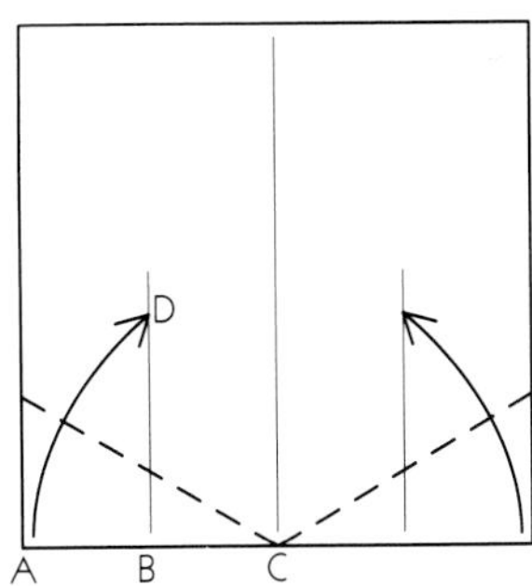

2 Fold corner A up to lie on line BD. Note that the crease hits the bottom edge of the paper at point C, the middle of the bottom edge. Repeat on the right side.

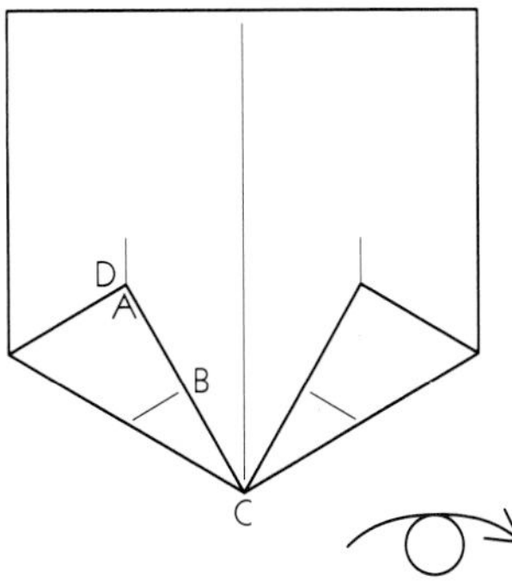

3 Turn the paper over.

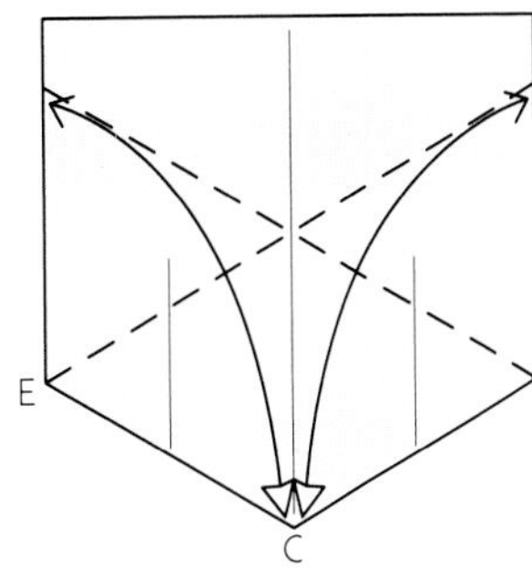

4 Fold corner C up to lie along the left edge – the crease runs through point E. Unfold. Repeat on the right.

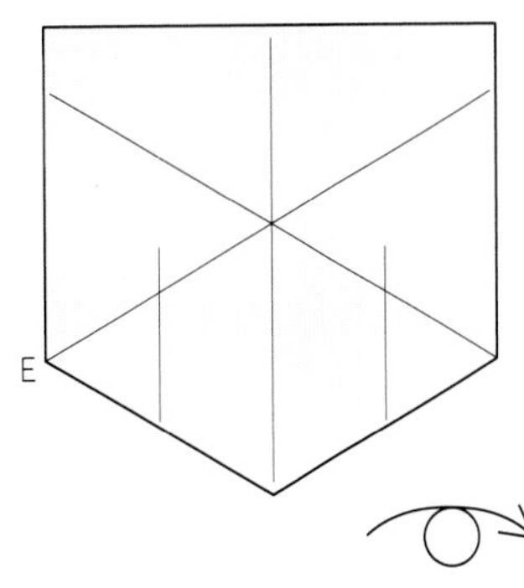

5 Turn the paper over.

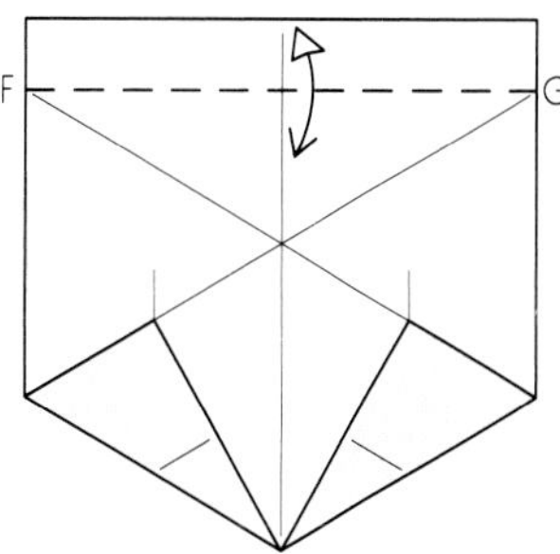

6 Fold down the top edge along a crease running between points F and G (where the two diagonal creases hit the edges). Unfold.

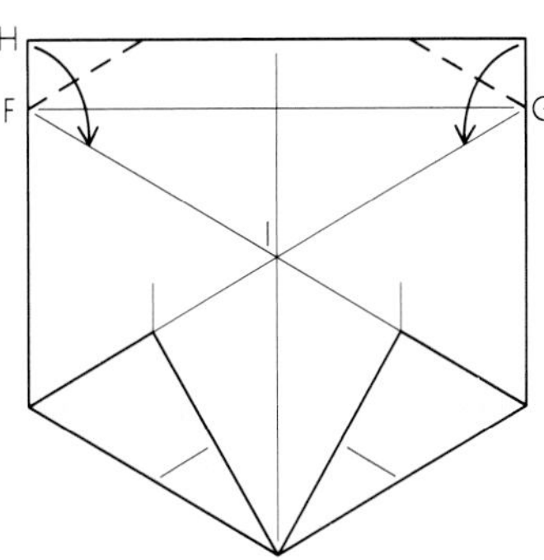

7 Fold down corner H to lie on line FI; the crease hits the edge at point F. Repeat on the right.

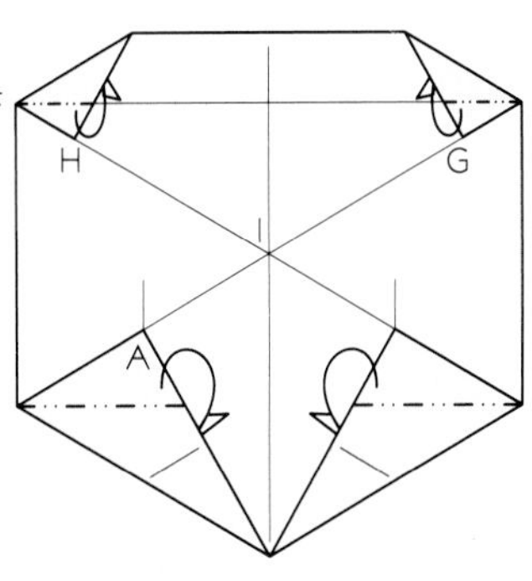

8 Fold corners A and H underneath. Repeat on the right. (This is easily done by unfolding flap A, making the fold, and refolding.)

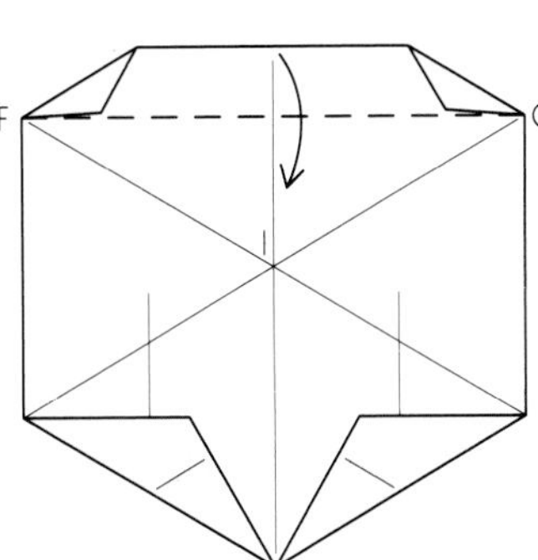

9 Fold the top edge down along the existing crease FG.

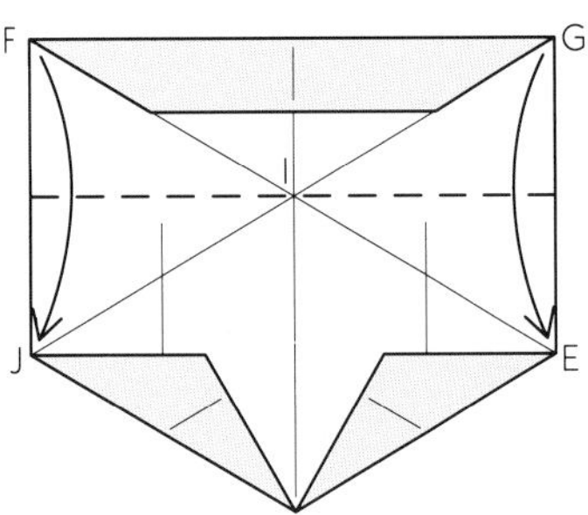

⑩ Fold down corners F and G to meet corners J and E, respectively.

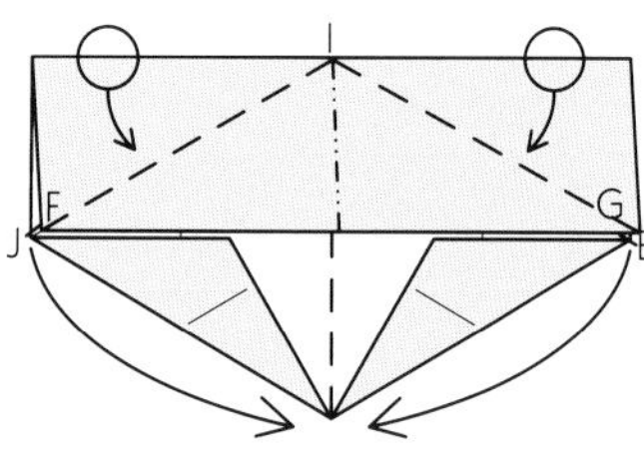

⑪ Bring corners J, F, G, and E together at the bottom of the model (it will not lie flat).

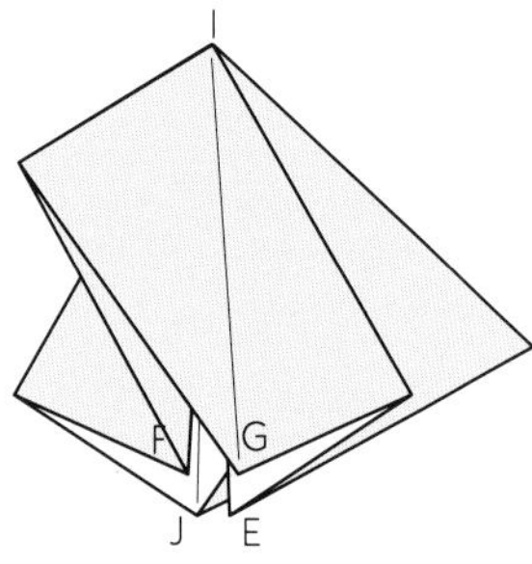

⑫ Flatten the paper out. Note that the top flap swings to the left and the rear flap swings to the right.

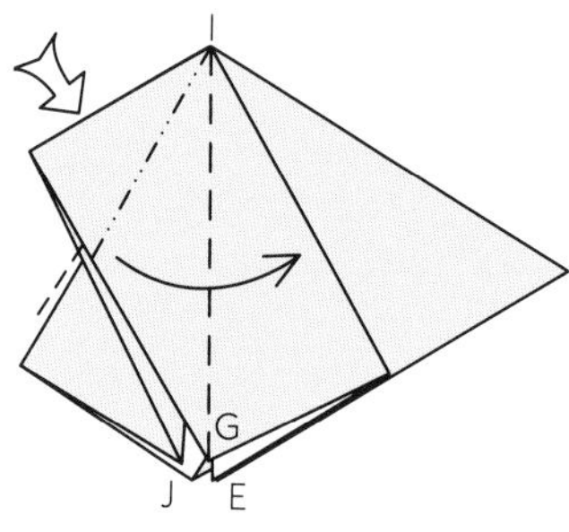

⑬ Squash-fold the top flap.

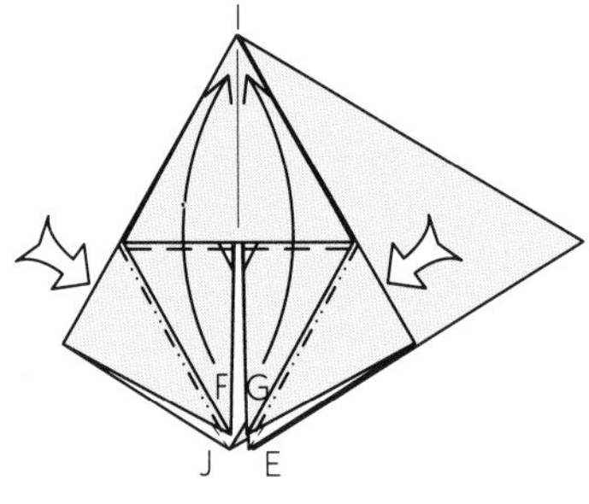

⑭ Squash-fold each side. Corners F and G get folded up to point I.

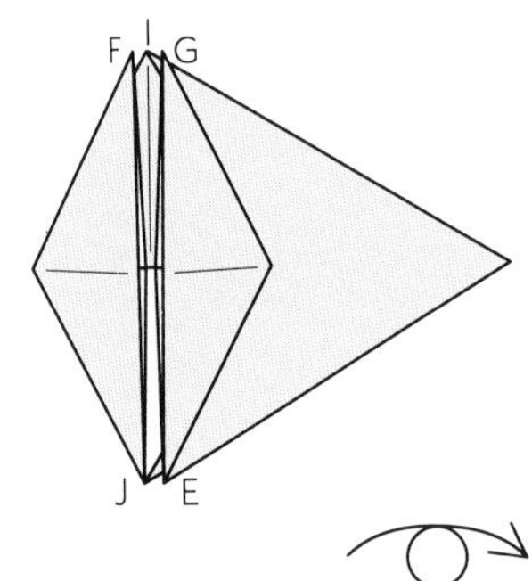

⑮ Turn the model over from side to side.

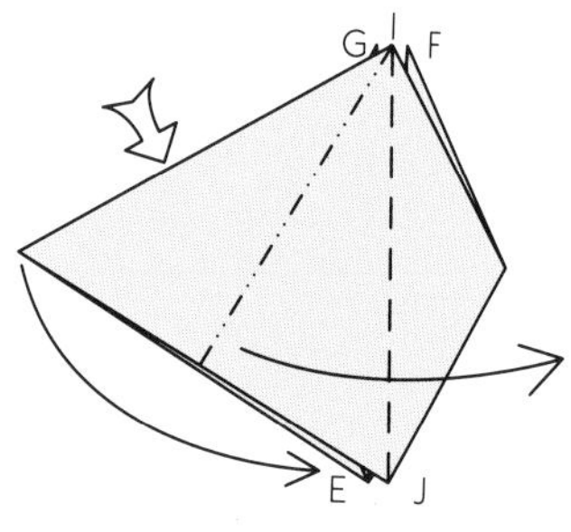

⑯ Squash-fold the large point.

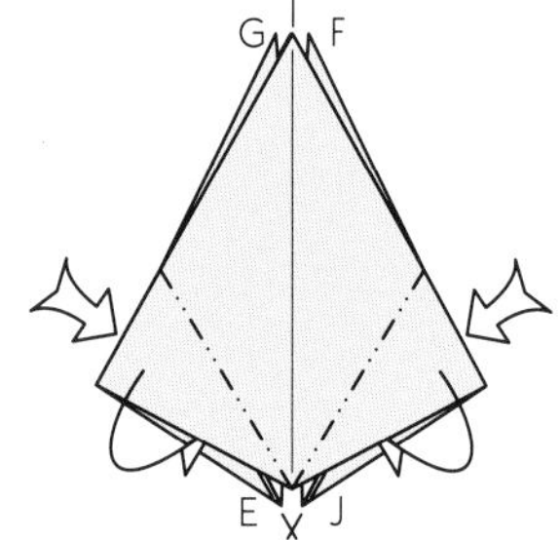

⑰ Reverse-fold the side corners.

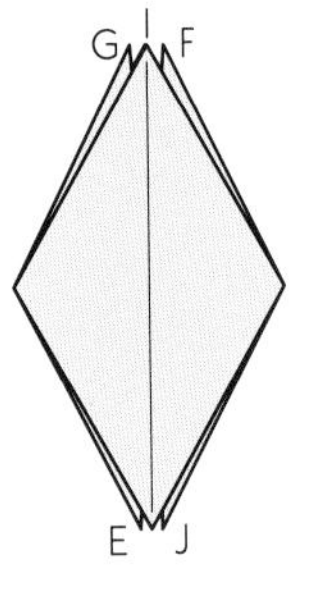

⑱ Turn the model over from side to side.

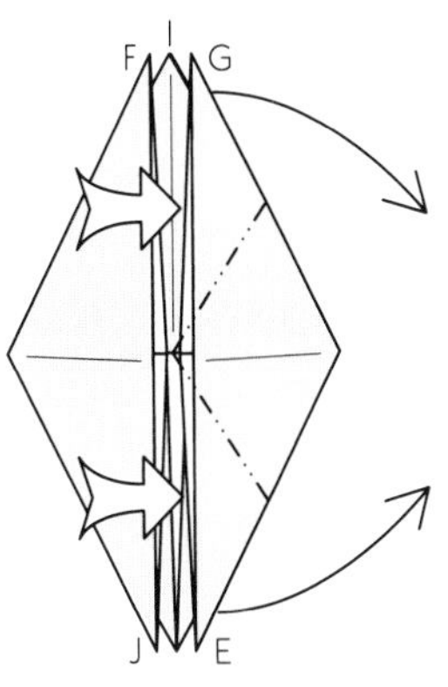

19 Reverse-fold two points to the right.

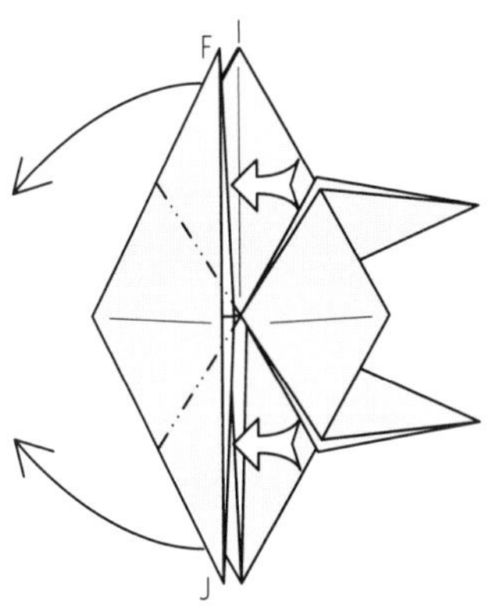

20 Repeat on the left.

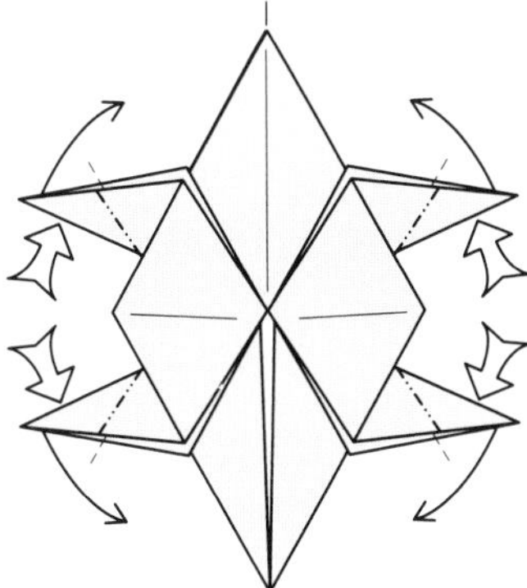

21 Reverse-fold all four points.

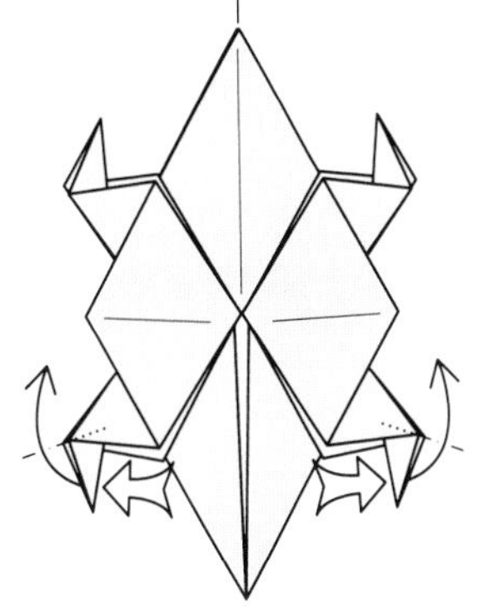

22 Reverse-fold the bottom pair of points upward. Be sure that point I (the thick point) is at the top.

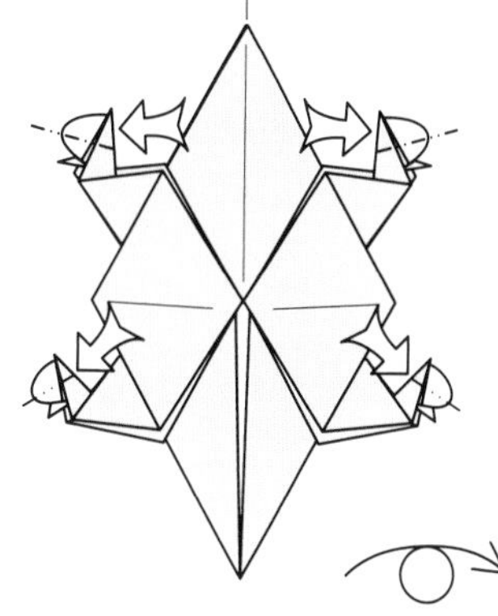

23 Reverse-fold the tips of all four points. Turn the model over.

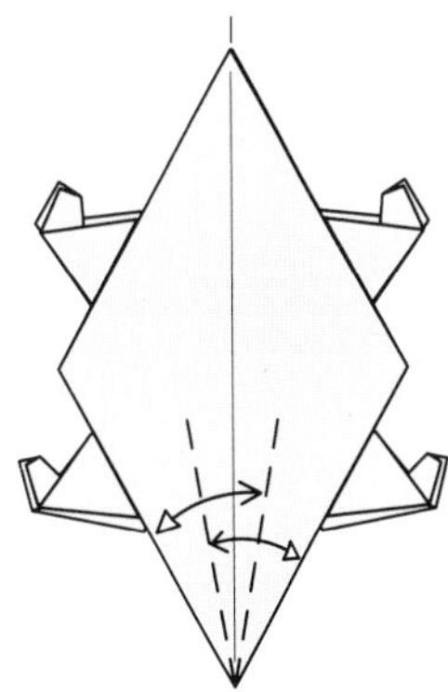

24 Fold the bottom point (the tail) in thirds and unfold. You don't need to make the creases run all the way up.

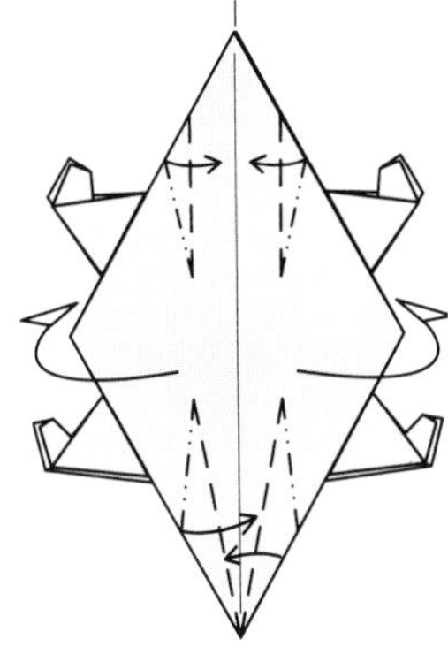

25 Curve the sides of the body away from you; at the same time, crimp the top and bottom of the model. On the bottom, the two edges overlap one another. On the top, they meet in the middle. The shell will bulge upward in the middle.

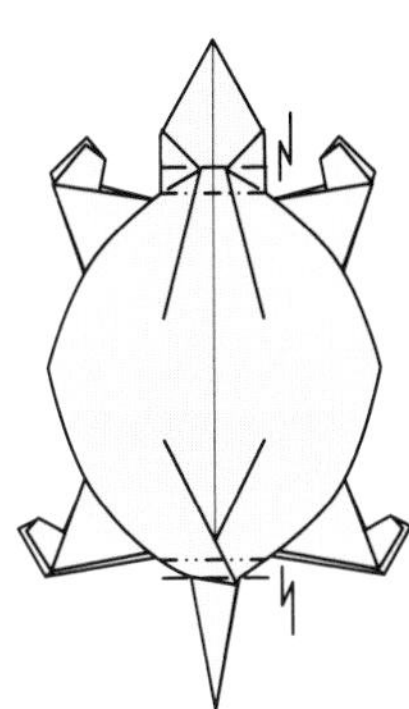

26 Pleat the neck and tail. This locks the crimps from step 25 in place.

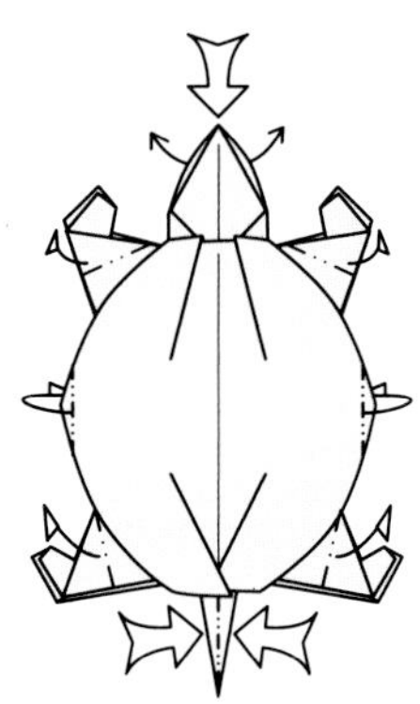

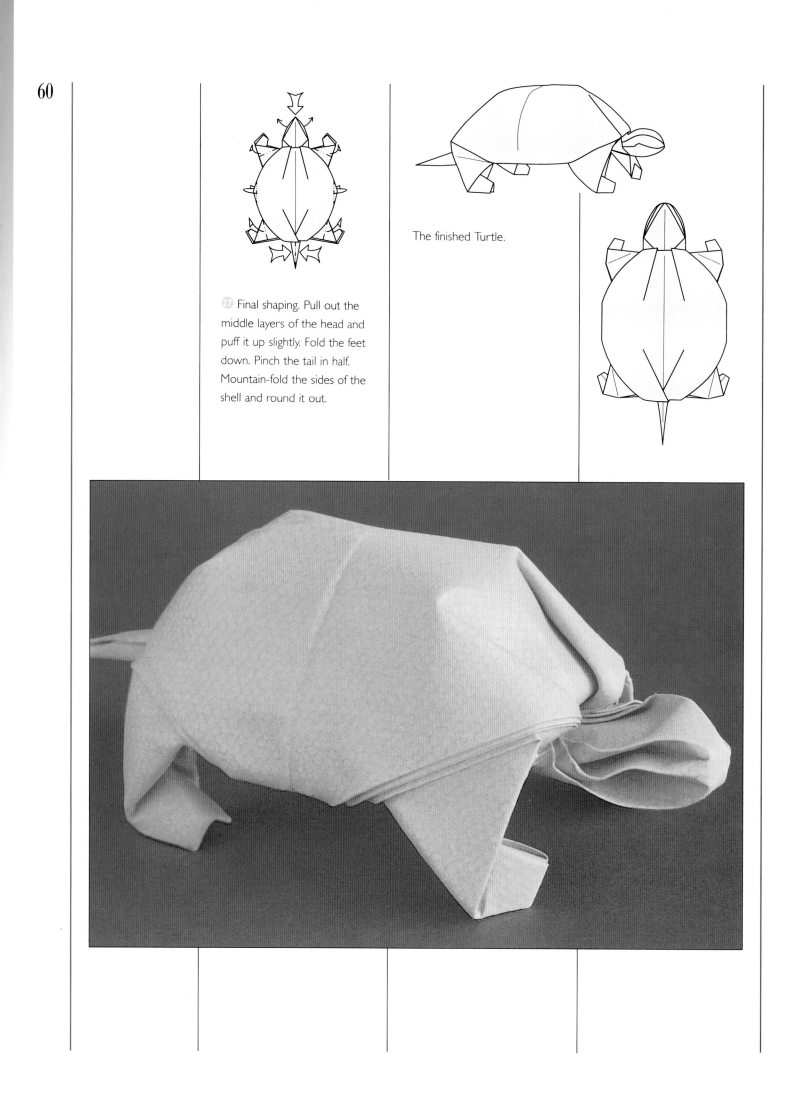

27 Final shaping. Pull out the middle layers of the head and puff it up slightly. Fold the feet down. Pinch the tail in half. Mountain-fold the sides of the shell and round it out.

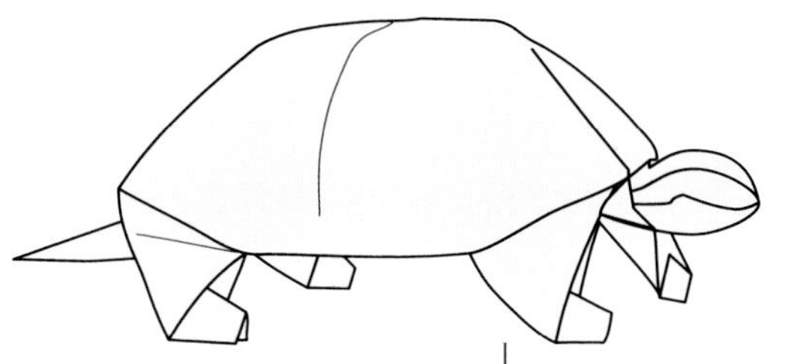

The finished Turtle.

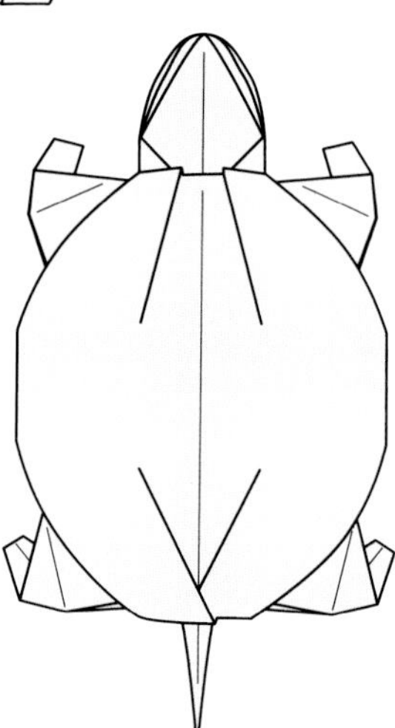

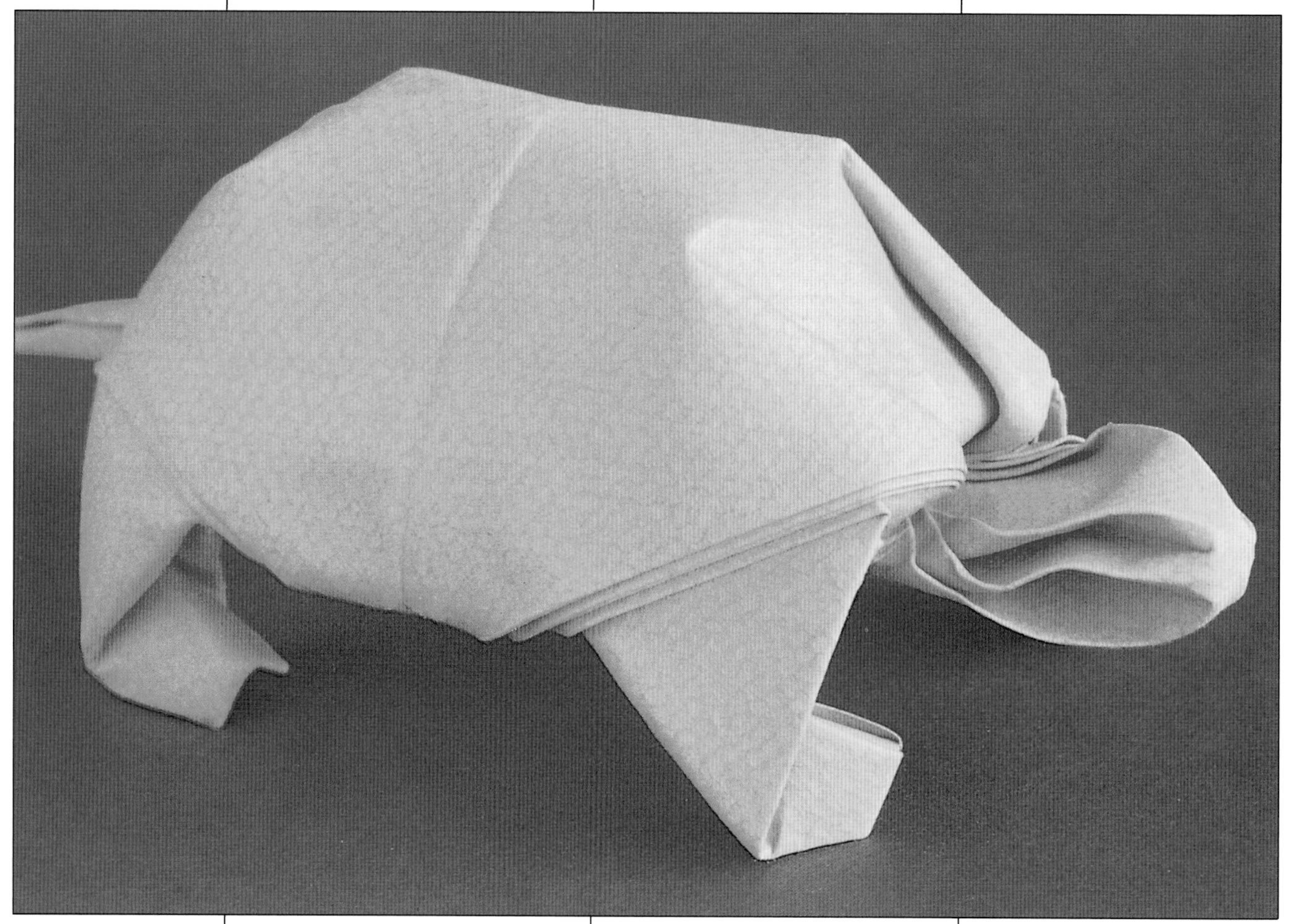

JAPANESE BOX

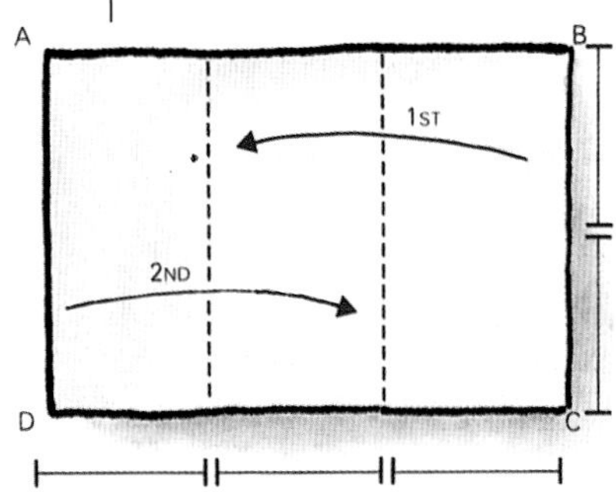

1 Begin with a 3 x 2 rectangle (one that measures three sections along one side to two sections along the adjacent side). Divide it into thirds, first folding BC across to the left, then fold AD across on top to the right.

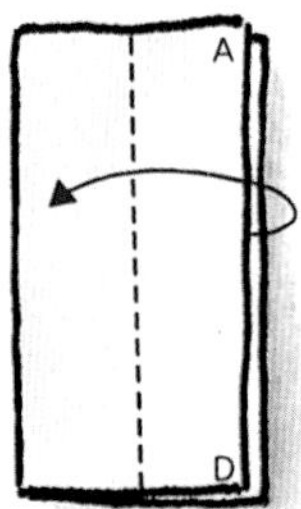

2 Fold AD back to the left edge.

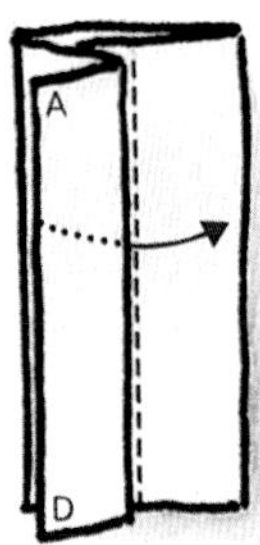

3 Pull out edge BC from under AD and fold it back tc the right.

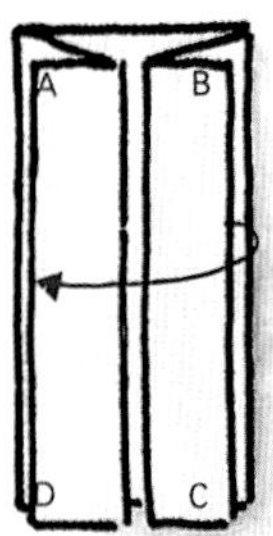

4 Unfold BC so that it meets and covers AD.

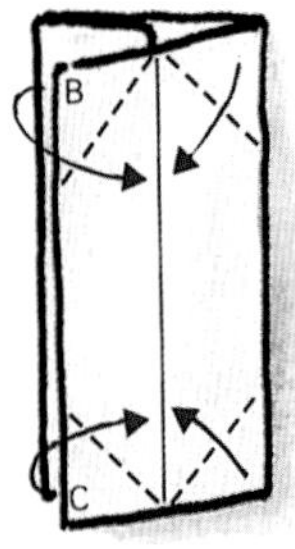

5 Turn in the four corners, the ones at B and C being single layers.

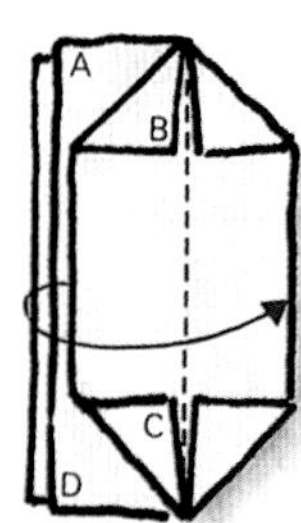

6 Fold BC back over to the right to meet the right-hand edge.

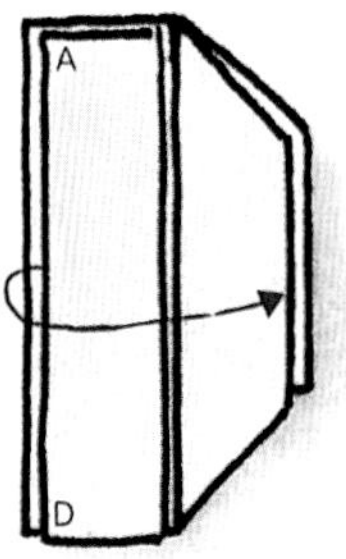

7 Unfold AD over to the right.

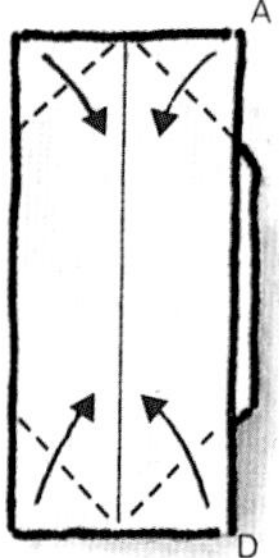

8 Turn in the four corners to meet the center crease.

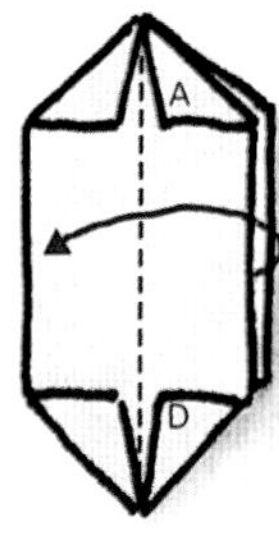

9 Fold AD back over to the left.

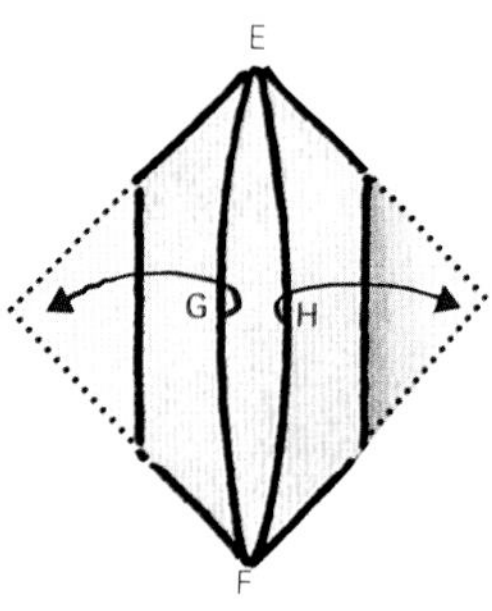

10 The paper is now symmetrical. Pull open the slit at G and H . . .

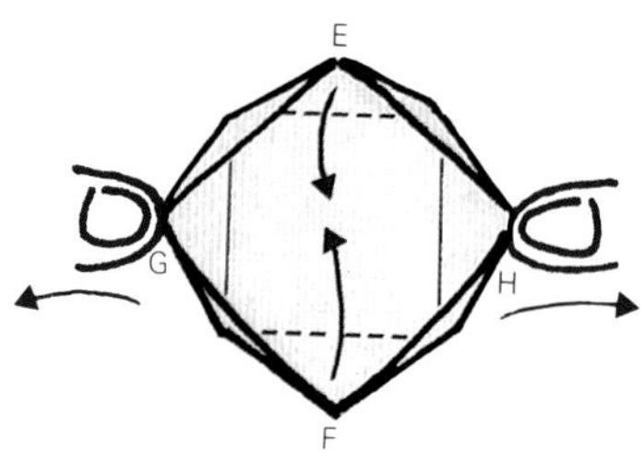

11 . . . opening up the box. Continue to pull so that as G and H separate, E and F come together in the middle . . .

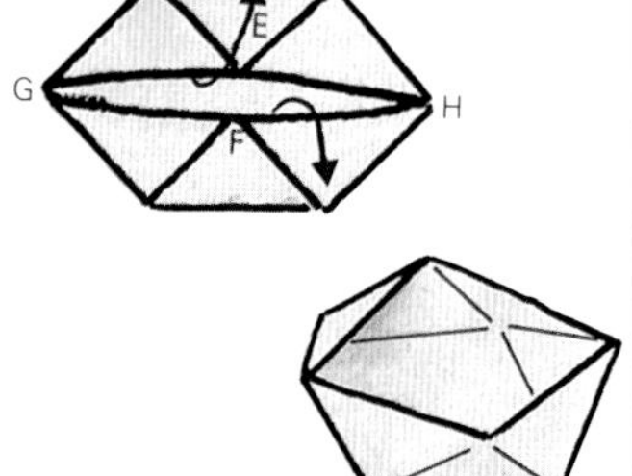

12 . . . like this. Open up EF a little (**TOP**). The Japanese box is now complete (**ABOVE**).

KAYAK

★★★★★

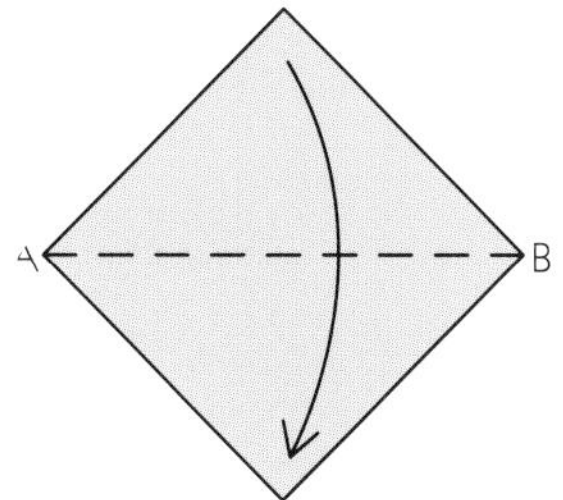

1 Take a 10-inch square of thin brown paper. Begin with the colored side up. Fold down the top corner to the bottom along line AB.

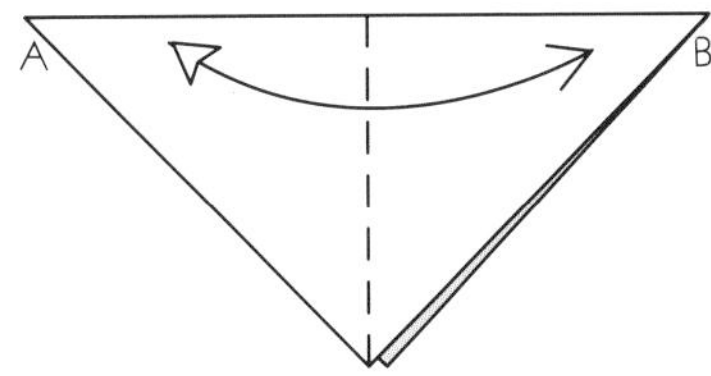

2 Fold the left corner (A) over to the right (B) and unfold.

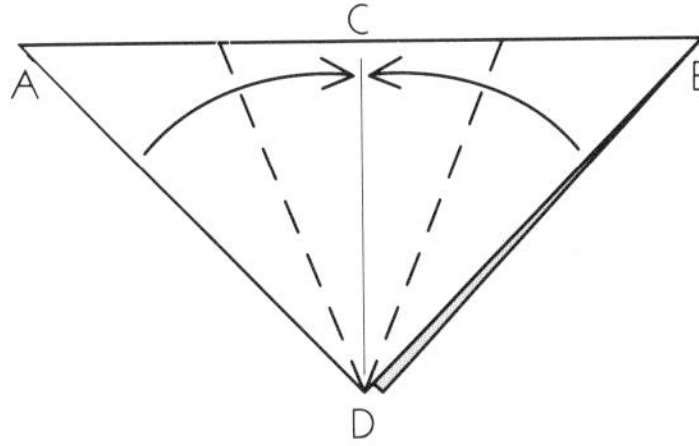

3 Fold in edge AD to lie along the center line CD. Fold edge BD in the same way.

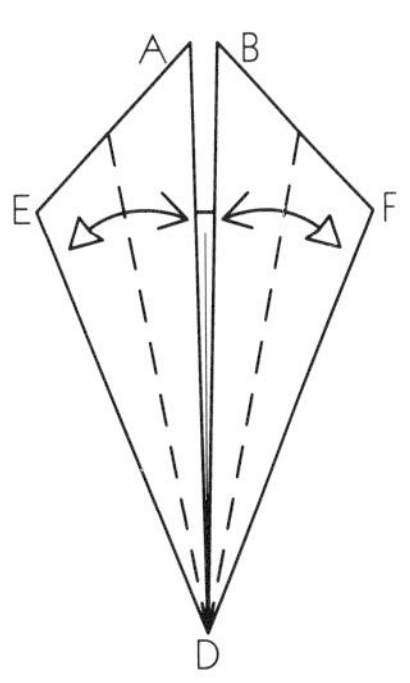

4 Fold in edges ED and FD to meet at the center line; crease firmly and unfold.

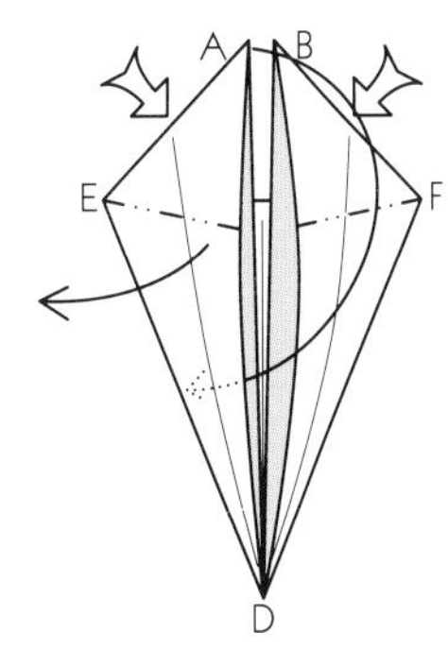

5 Squash-fold point A down to lie on line ED. Repeat on the right on point B.

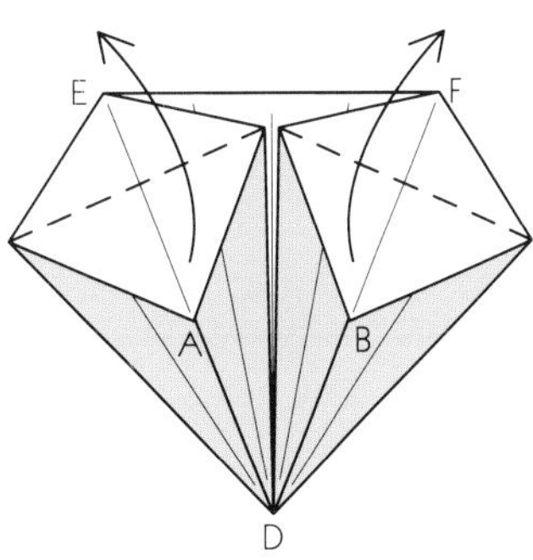

6 Fold corners A and B up as far as possible.

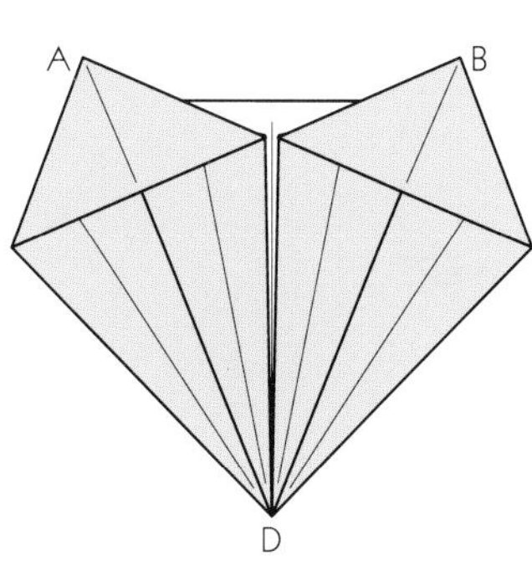

7 Turn the model over.

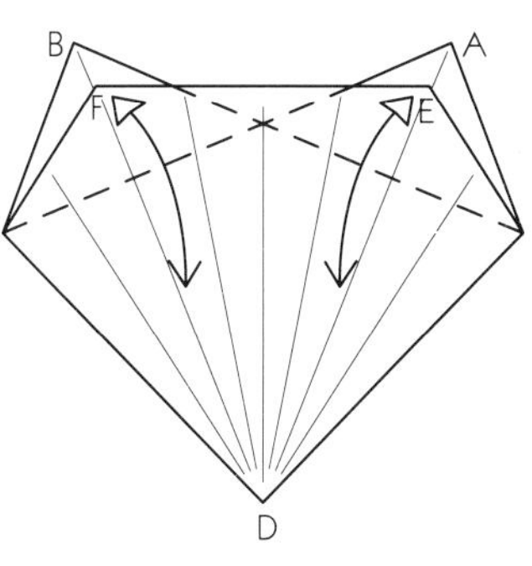

8 Fold down corner F, crease, and unfold. Repeat on the right on corner E.

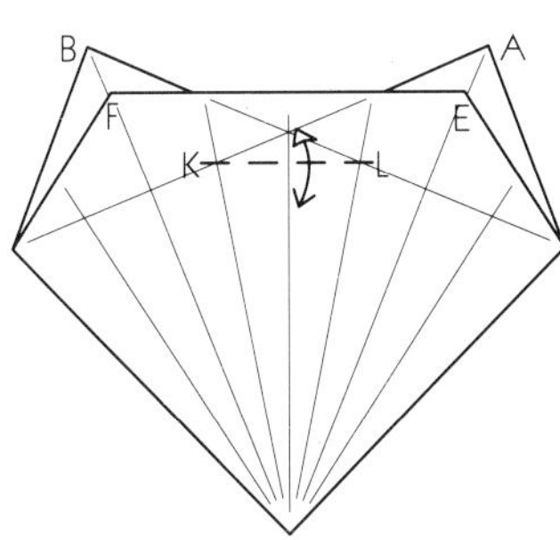

9 Make a crease that connects points K and L. Fold through all layers, crease firmly, and unfold.

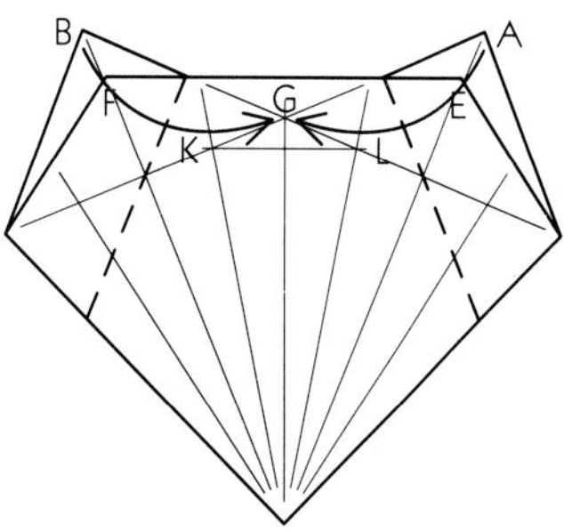

10 Fold point B in to point G, which is the intersection of the two creases you made in step 8. Repeat on the right with point A.

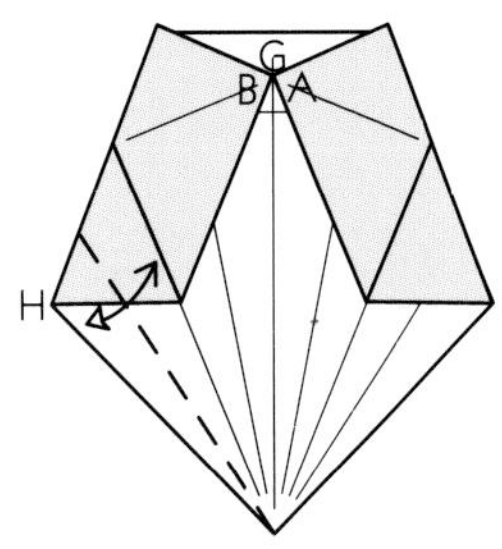

11 Fold corner H in on an existing crease, crease firmly, and unfold.

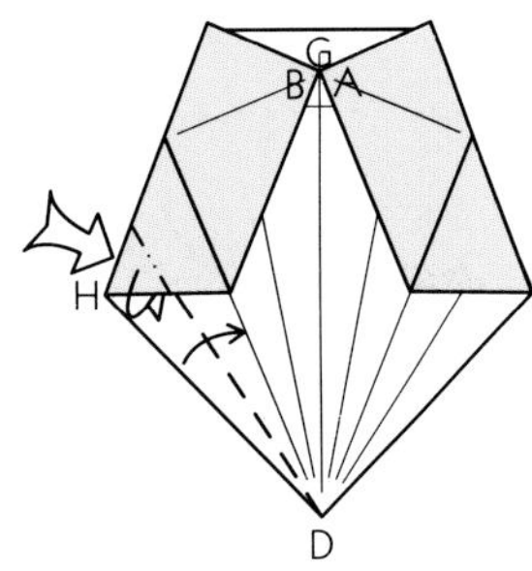

12 Reverse-fold corner H and fold in edge HD on the crease you just made. Do not repeat on the right.

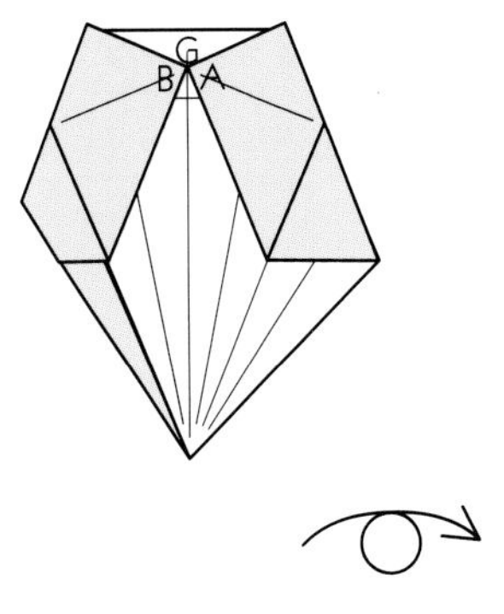

13 Turn over the model.

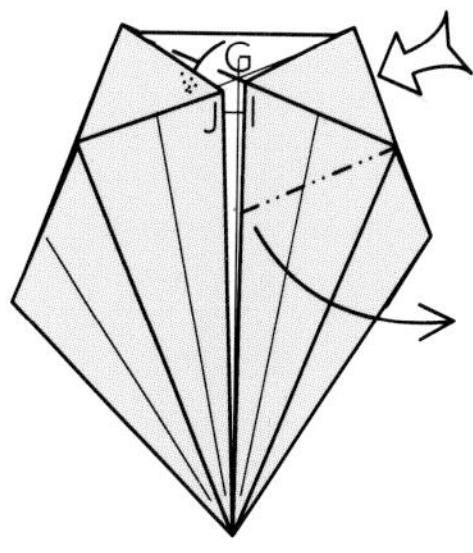

14 Squash-fold the upper right edge. Look at step 15 to see the final position of corner I. Note also that the top edge goes underneath corner J.

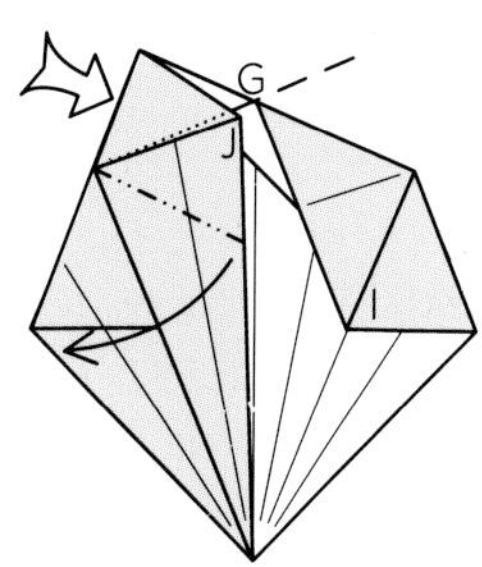

15 Squash-fold the upper left edge in the same way. Note that corner I landed on an existing crease; corner J does the same.

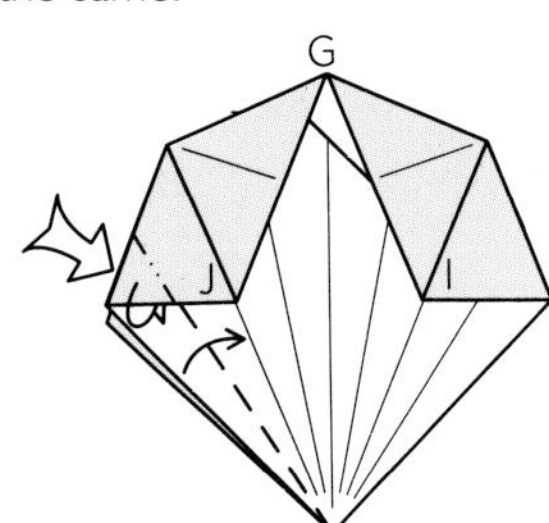

16 Reverse-fold the edge just as you did in steps 11–12. Do not repeat on the right.

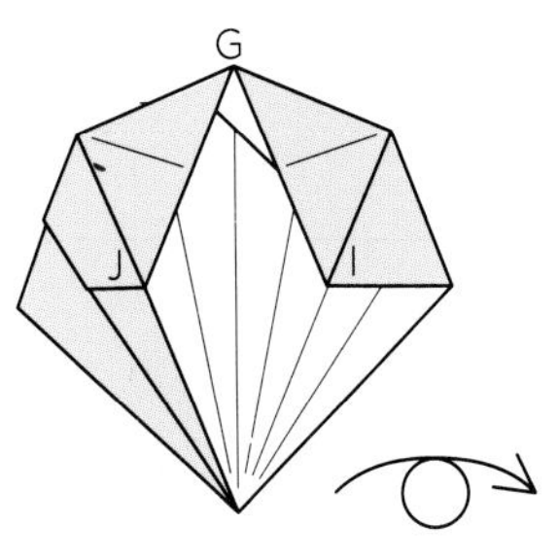

17 Turn the model over.

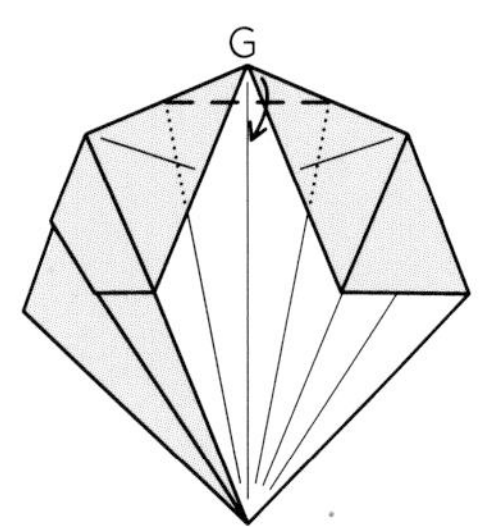

18 Carefully fold down the thick point on the crease you made in step 9.

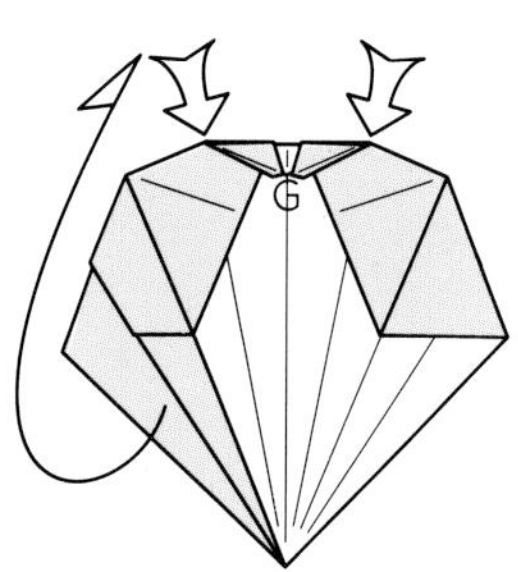

19 Fold the rear layer upward, pushing down on the two corners; the model will not lie flat.

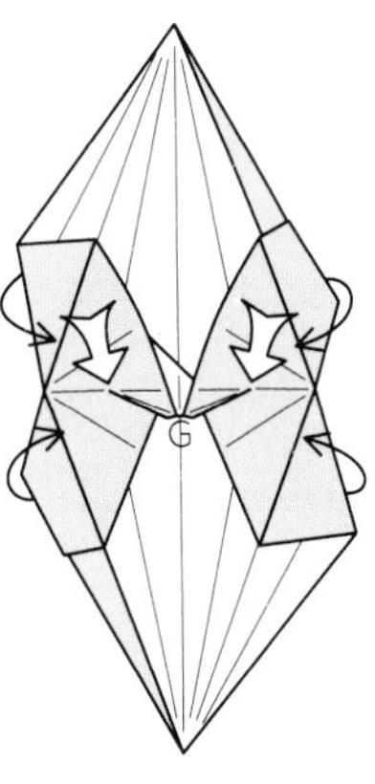

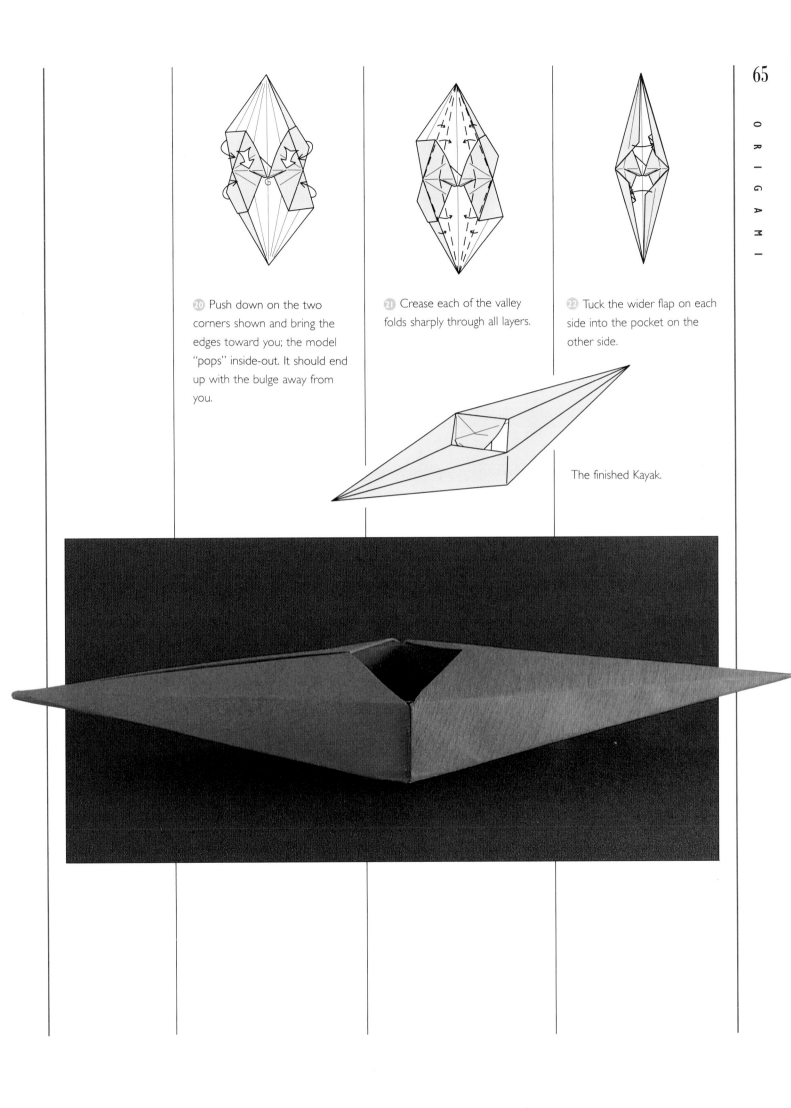

(20) Push down on the two corners shown and bring the edges toward you; the model "pops" inside-out. It should end up with the bulge away from you.

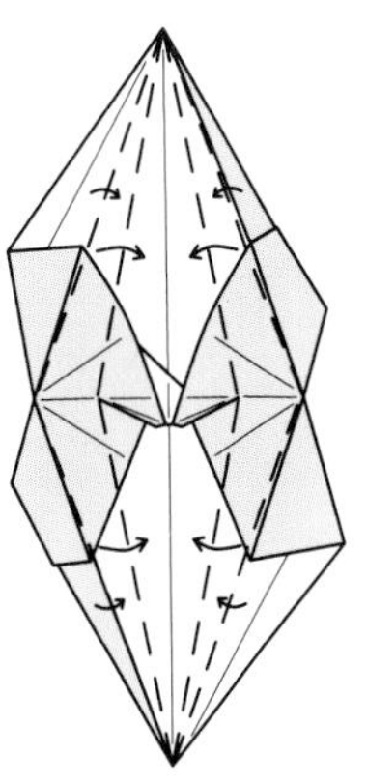

(21) Crease each of the valley folds sharply through all layers.

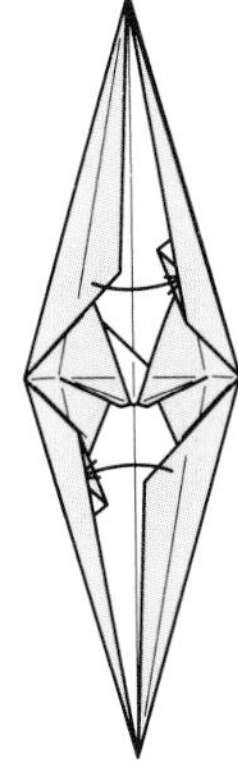

(22) Tuck the wider flap on each side into the pocket on the other side.

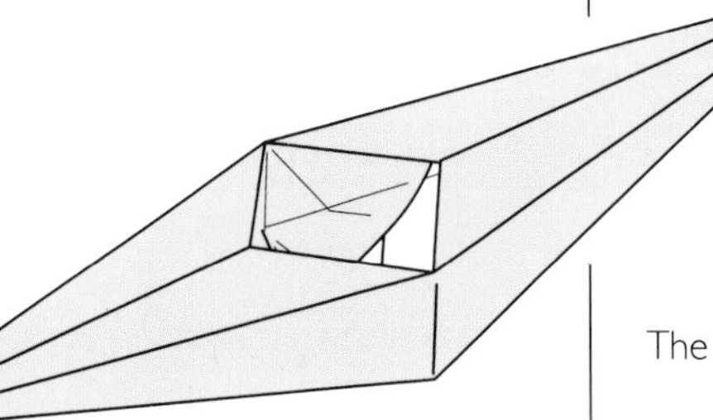

The finished Kayak.

PADDLE

★ ★ ★

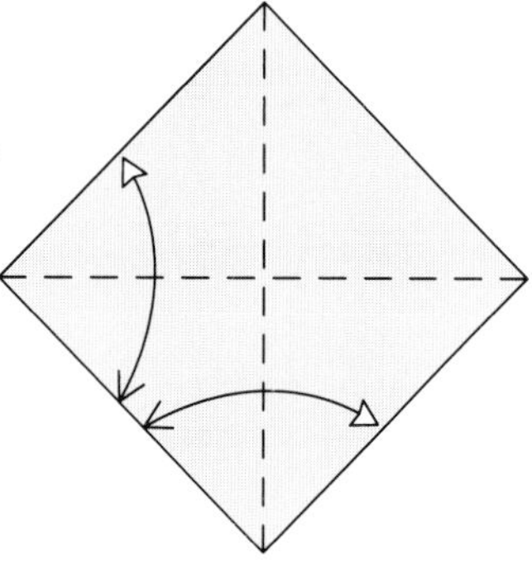

1 Take a 6-inch square of brown paper. Begin with the colored side up. Crease the diagonals.

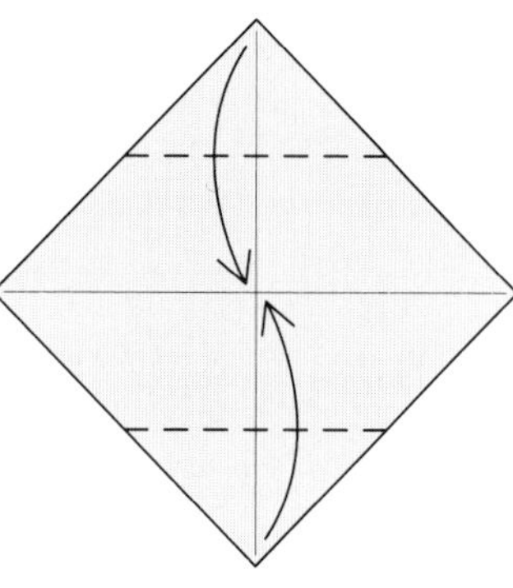

2 Fold the top and bottom corners to the center of the paper.

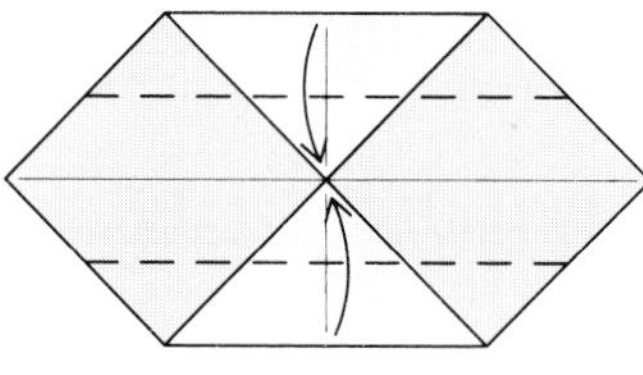

3 Fold the top and bottom edges to the horizontal crease. Be sure that the two corners stay touching in the middle.

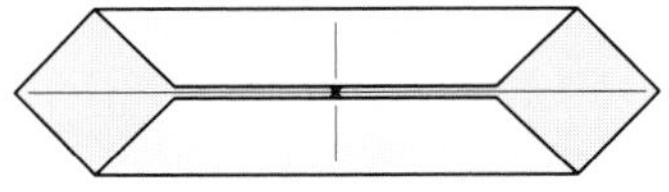

4 Turn the model over.

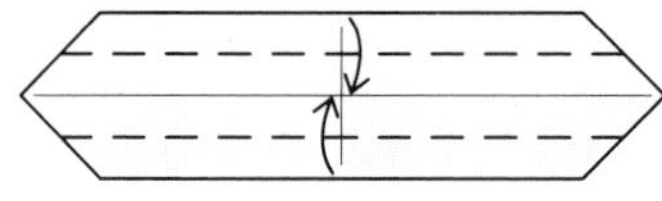

5 Fold the top and bottom edges to the horizontal crease.

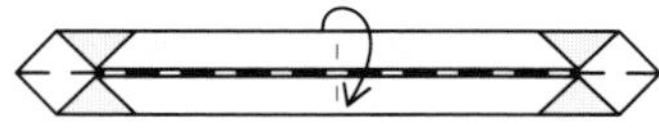

6 Fold down the top half over the bottom.

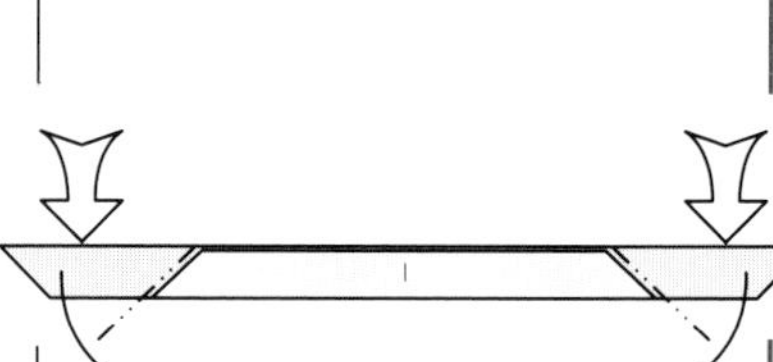

7 Reverse-fold the ends downward on a crease that runs along the border between the white and colored areas.

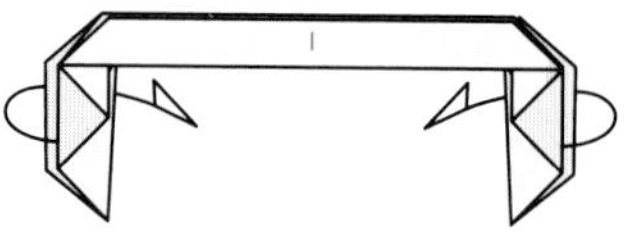

8 Fold the rear layer of each of the downward-pointing flaps behind and toward the center.

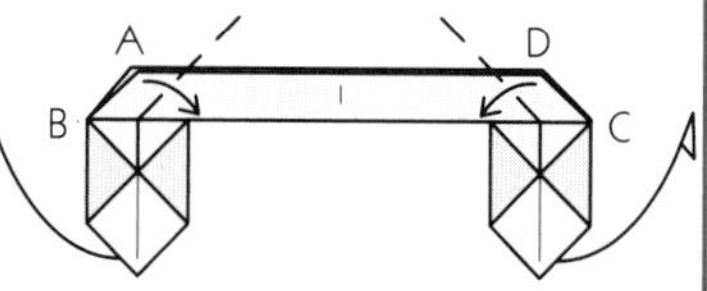

9 Fold down corners A and D to lie on edge BC; the two downward-pointing flaps swing out to the sides.

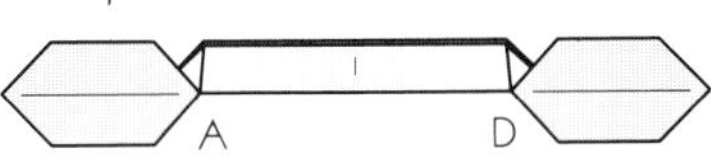

10 Turn the model over.

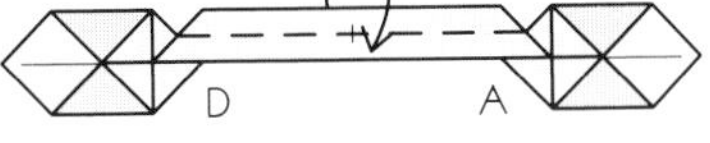

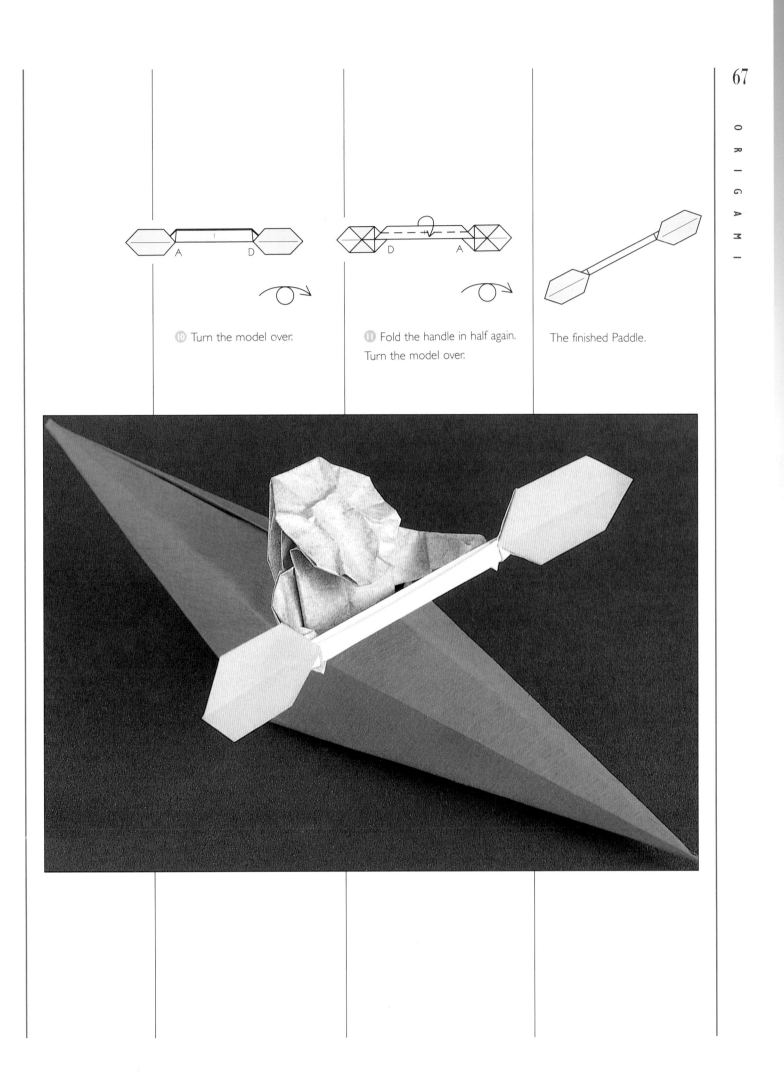

11 Fold the handle in half again. Turn the model over.

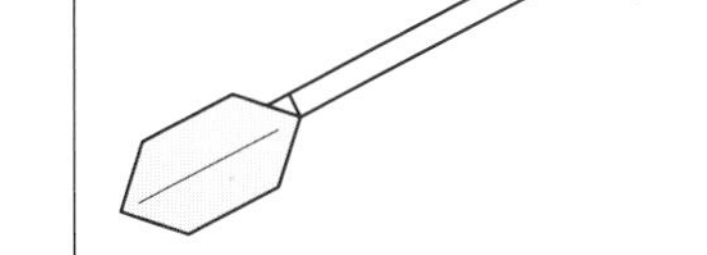

The finished Paddle.

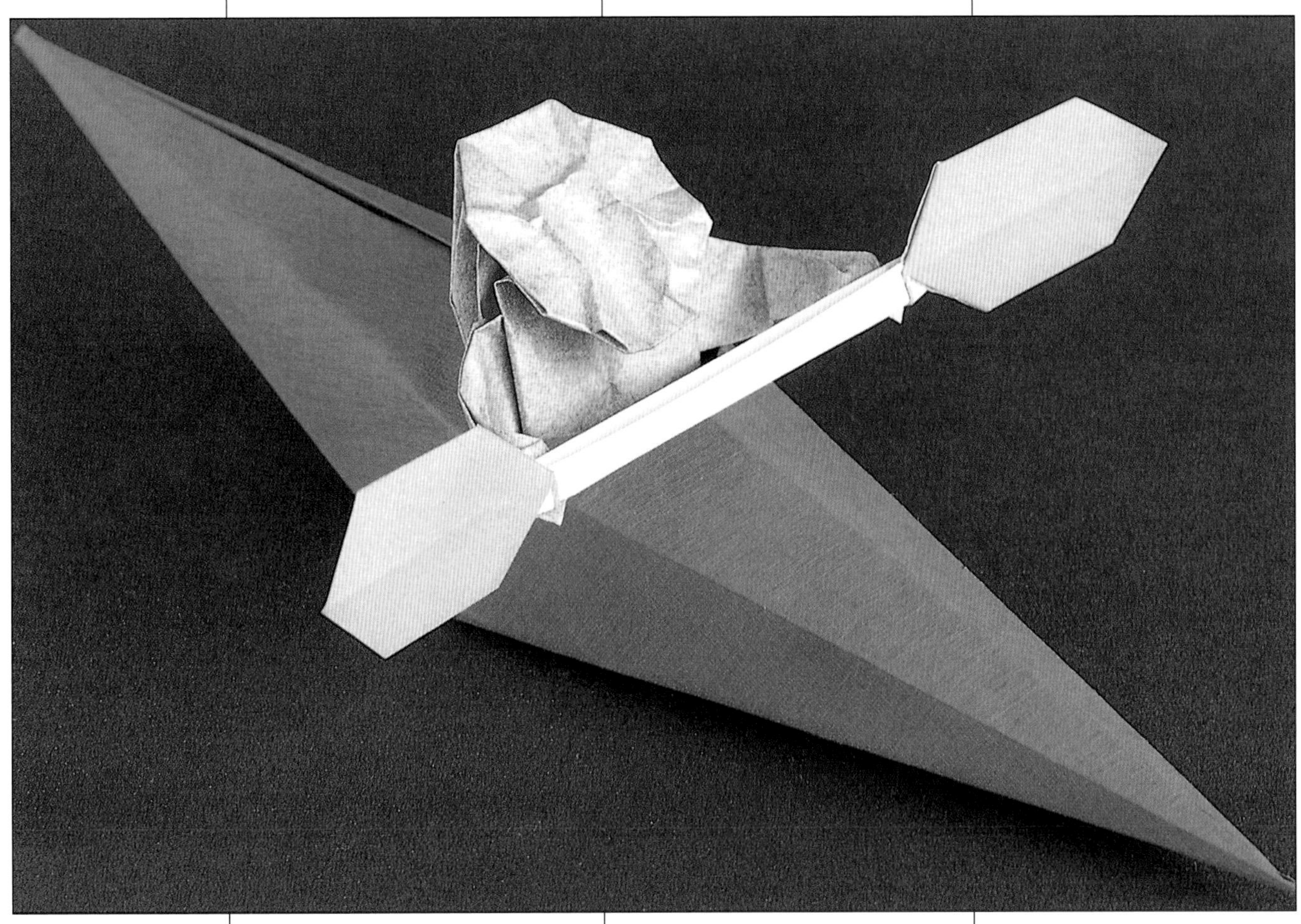

ESKIMO

★★★★★

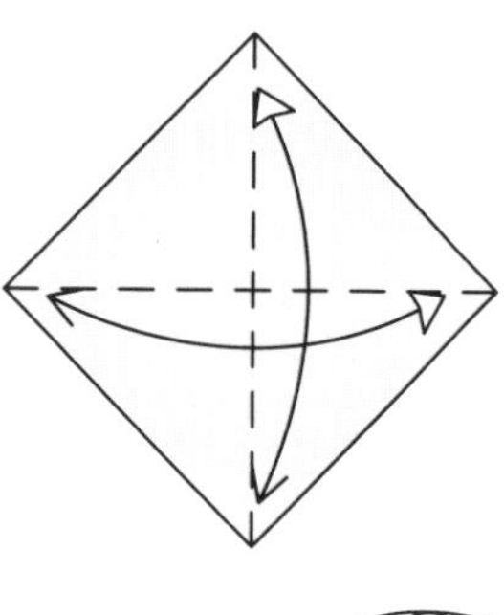

1 Take a 12-inch square of gray paper. Begin with the colored side up. Crease both diagonals. Then turn the paper over.

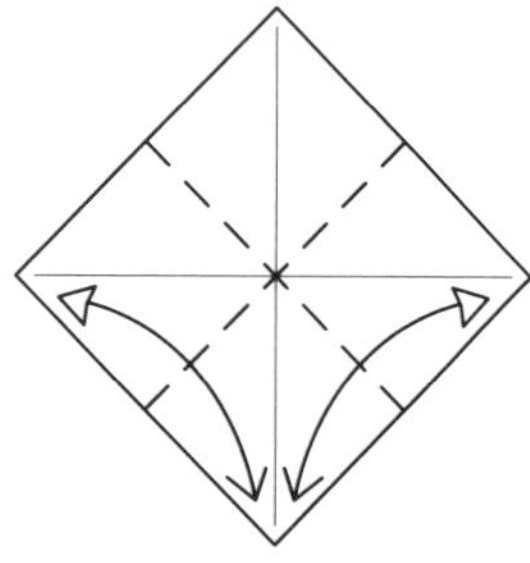

2 Fold the paper in half along the other two directions and unfold.

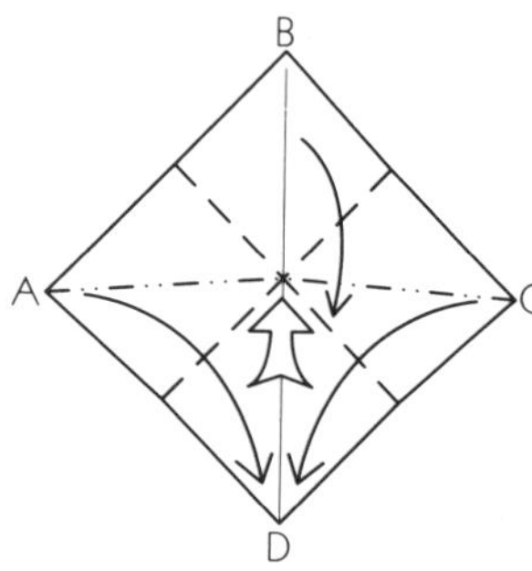

3 Push in the center of the paper and bring corners A, B and C together at the bottom point D.

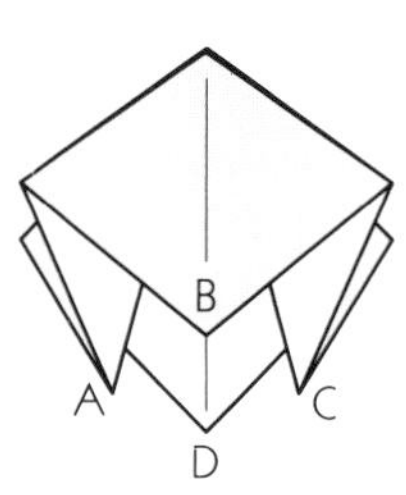

4 Flatten the model.

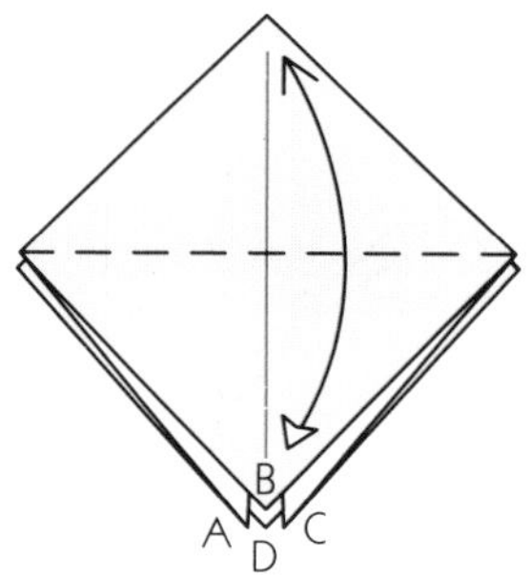

5 Fold point B (single layer only) up to the top and unfold.

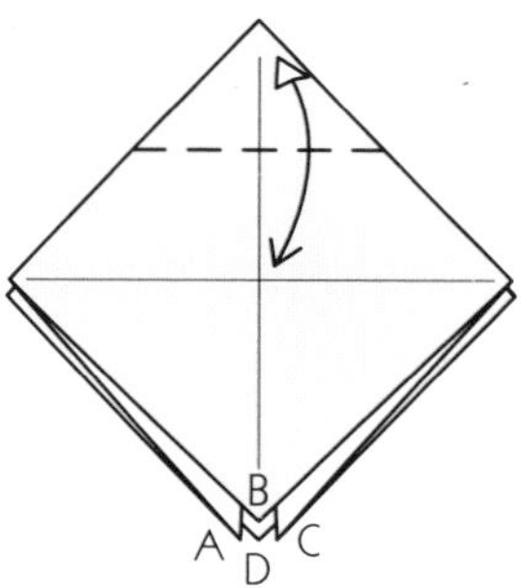

6 Fold the top point down to the crease you just made and unfold.

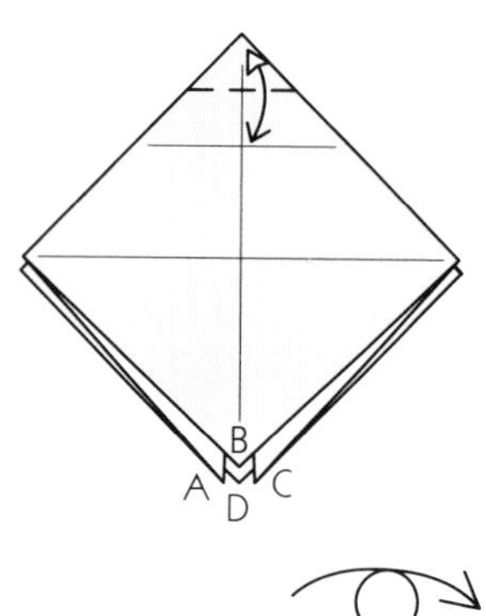

7 Fold the top point down to the crease you just made; crease firmly and unfold. Turn the model over.

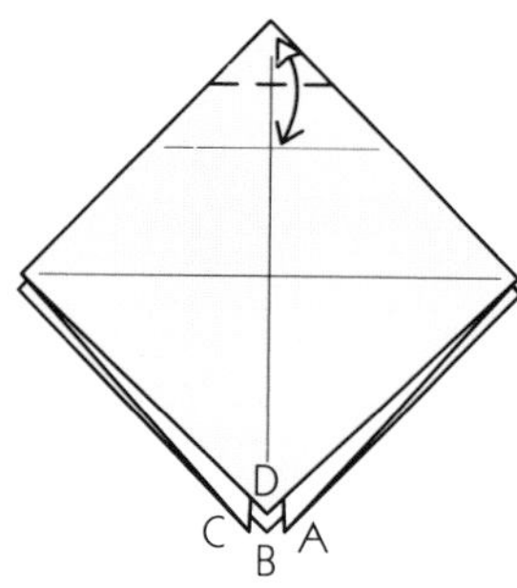

8 Fold the top point down on the same crease; crease firmly and unfold. Do this on both sides of the paper several times until the point folds easily in either direction.

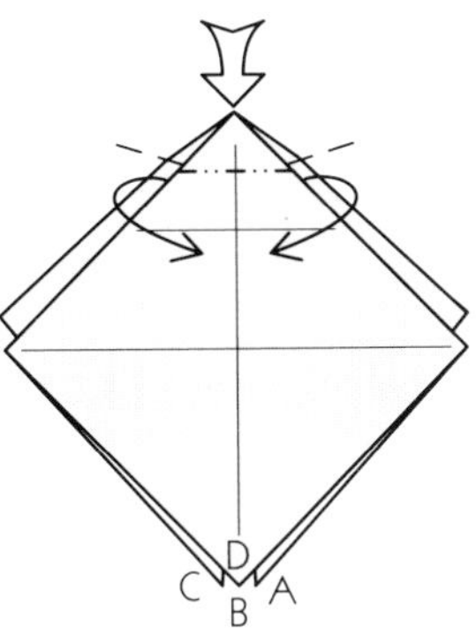

9 Pull the near edges toward you and press down on the top point so that it begins to flatten out. Try to keep points A–D together at the bottom.

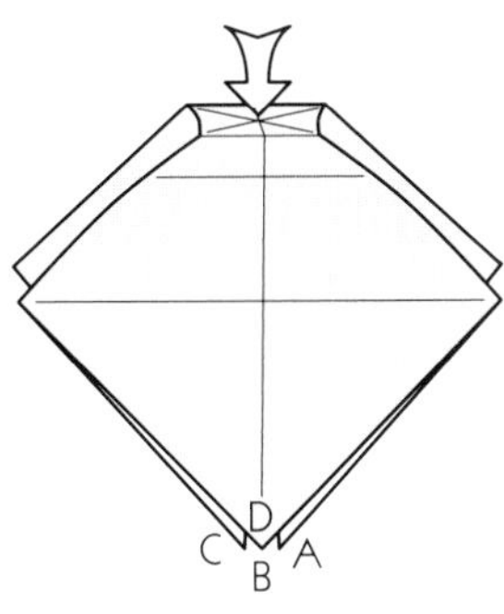

10 Push the flat part down inside the model, changing the direction of some of the creases.

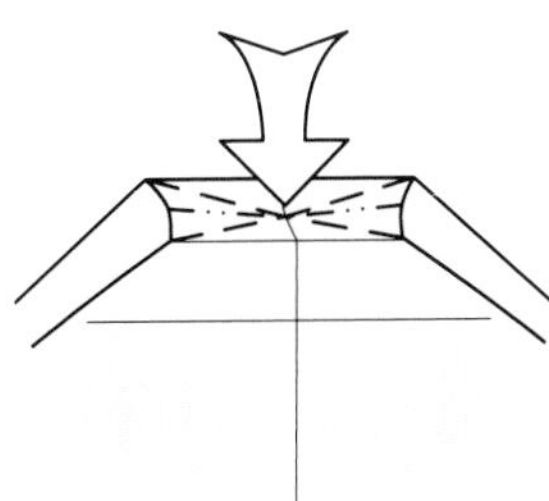

11 Close-up view showing the creases. Push down the middle and flatten the model.

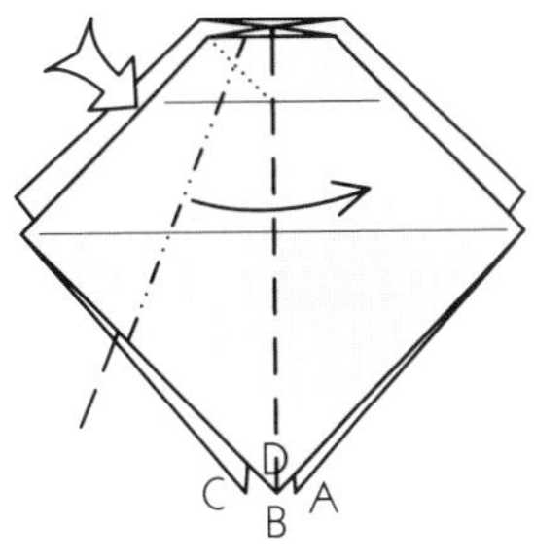

12 Squash-fold the edge by following steps 13–14.

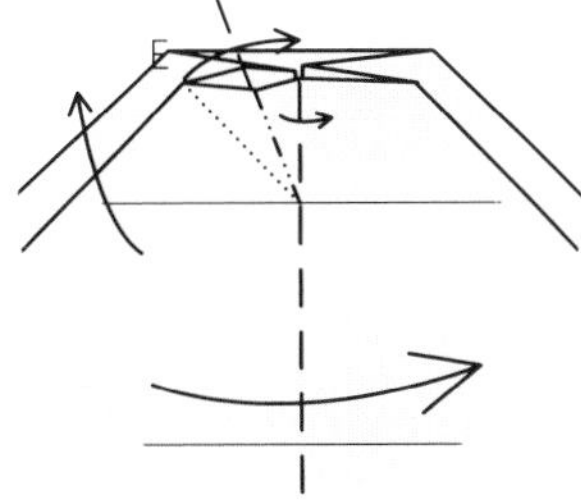

13 First, squash-fold the tiny pocket at the top. It helps to put a pencil or other sharp point inside to spread the layers.

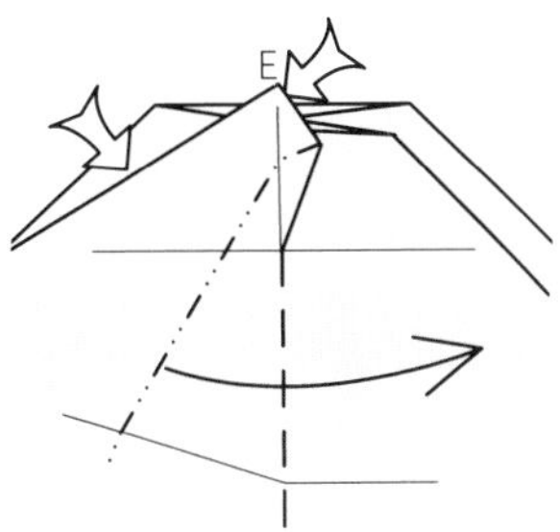

14 Then squash-fold the main edge. Point E disappears in the process. The left flap will come to the center.

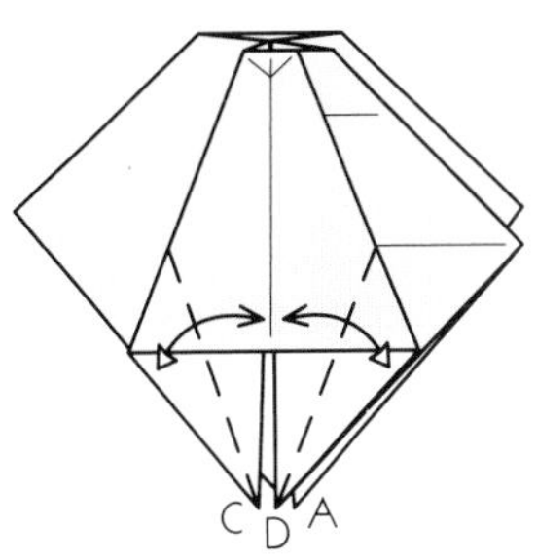

15 Fold a single edge to the center line on each side. Unfold.

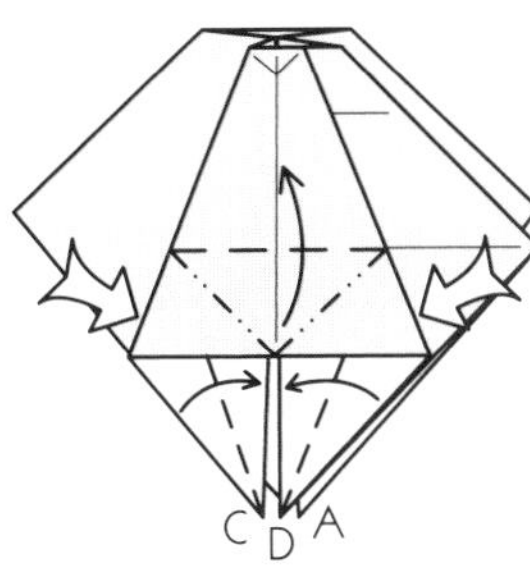

16 Push in the sides and fold the center of the exposed edge up in a petal fold. (It helps to precrease the horizontal valley fold.)

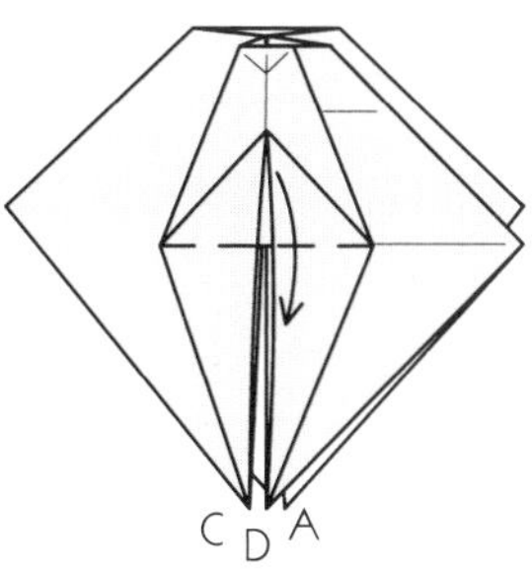

17 Fold the small point back down.

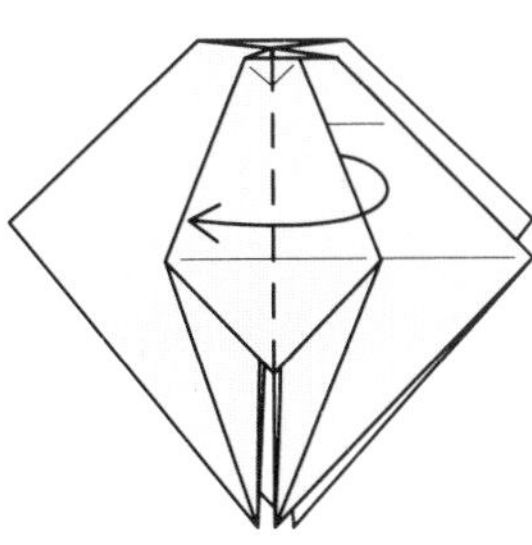

18 Fold one narrow layer to the left.

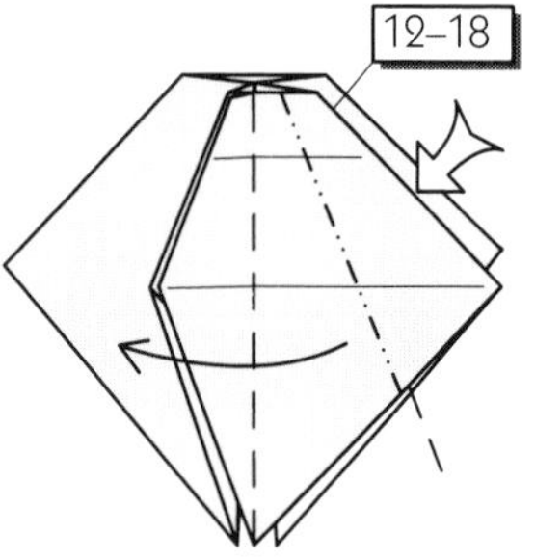

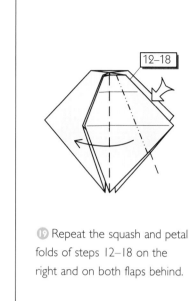

19 Repeat the squash and petal folds of steps 12–18 on the right and on both flaps behind.

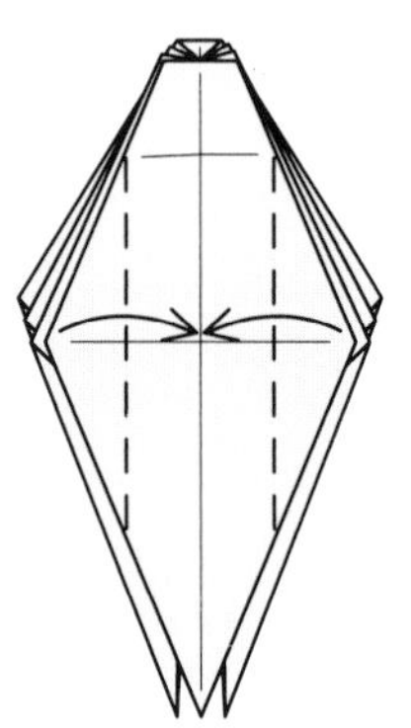

20 Fold in one corner to the center line on each side.

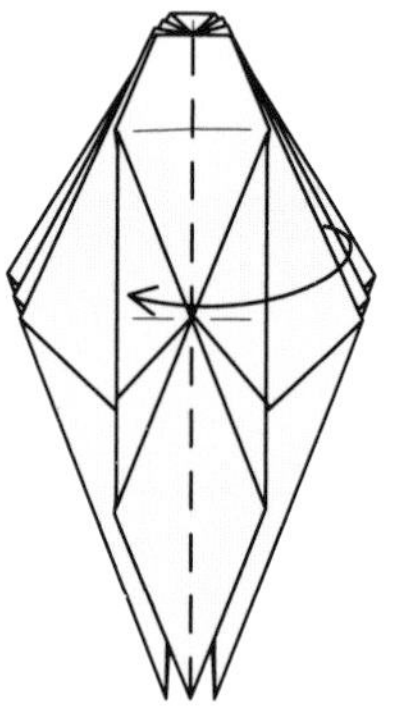

21 Fold one narrow layer and one wide layer to the left.

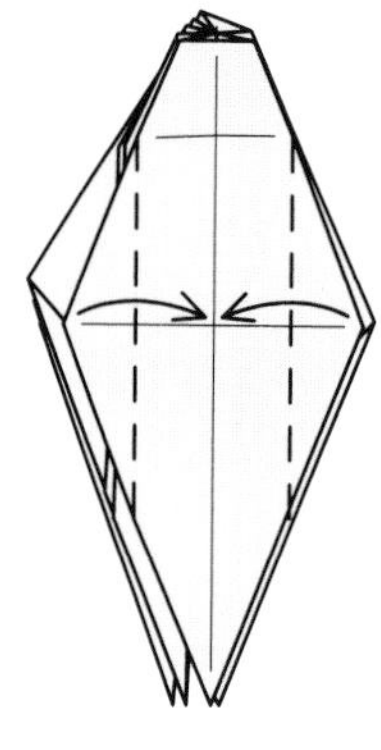

22 Fold in one corner on each side to the center line.

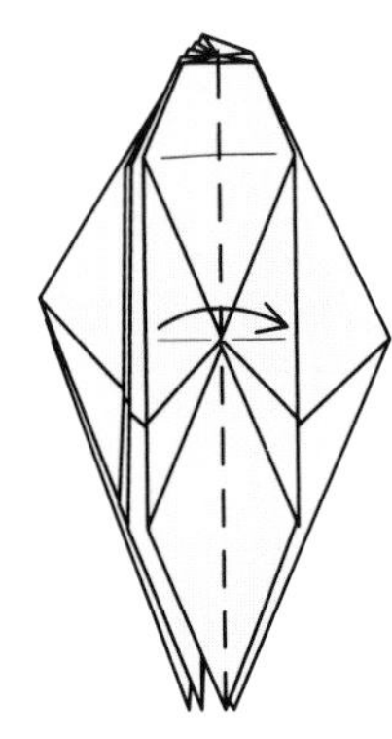

23 Fold one layer to the right.

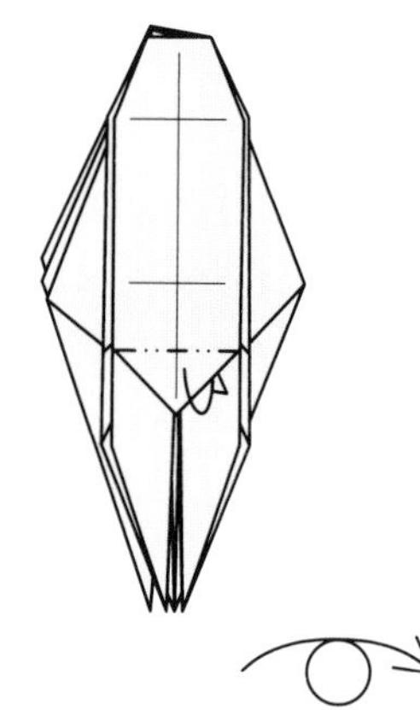

24 Tuck the point underneath and turn the model over.

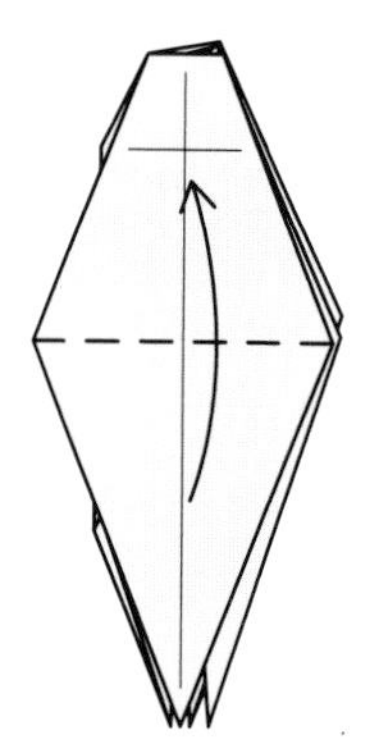

25 Fold one point up.

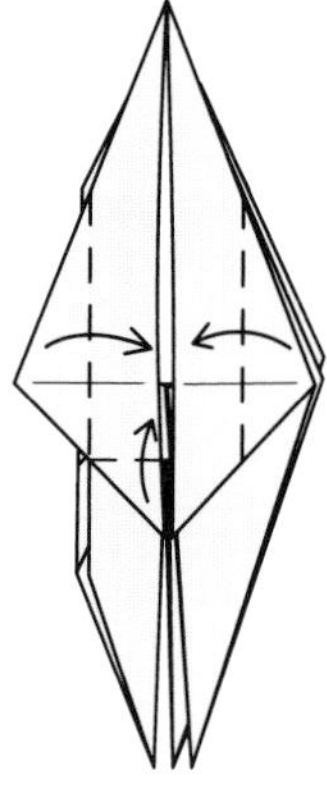

26 Fold in one corner on each side and fold up the left point on the bottom.

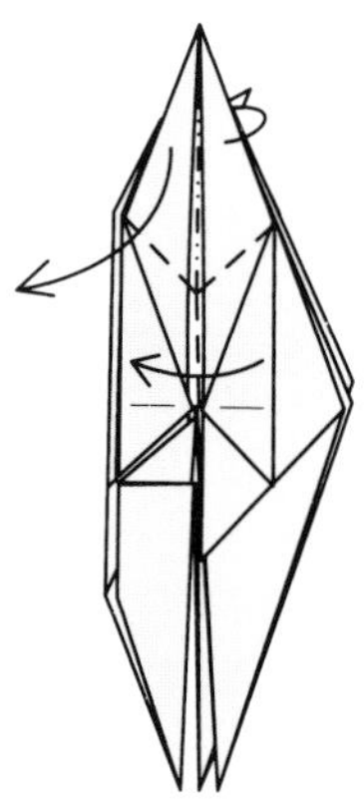

27 Fold one layer to the left while you fold down the top corner and pinch it in half.

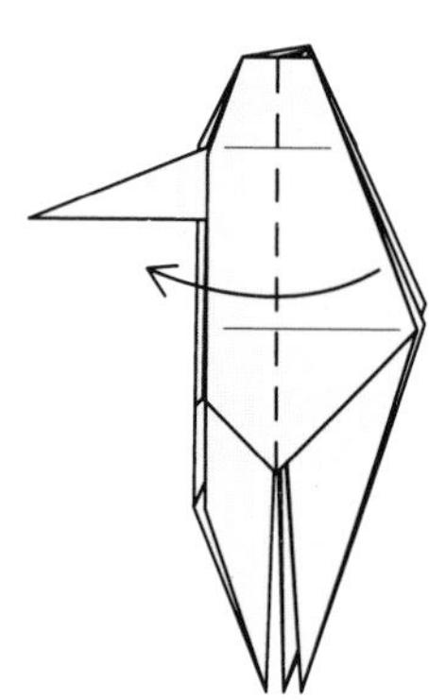

28 Fold one layer to the left.

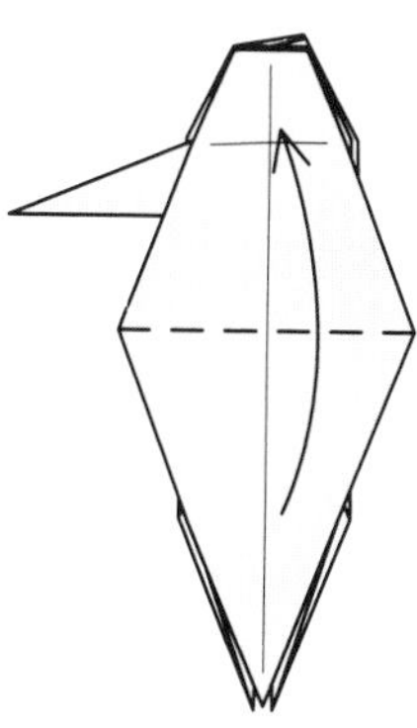

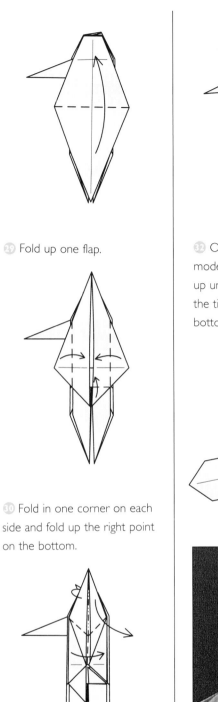

29 Fold up one flap.

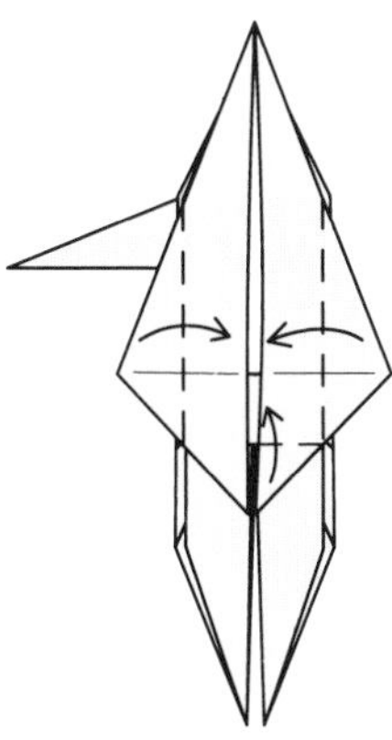

30 Fold in one corner on each side and fold up the right point on the bottom.

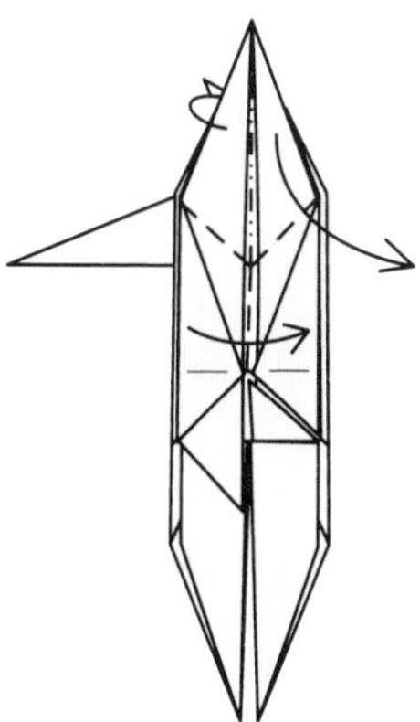

31 Fold one layer to the right while you fold down the top corner and pinch it in half.

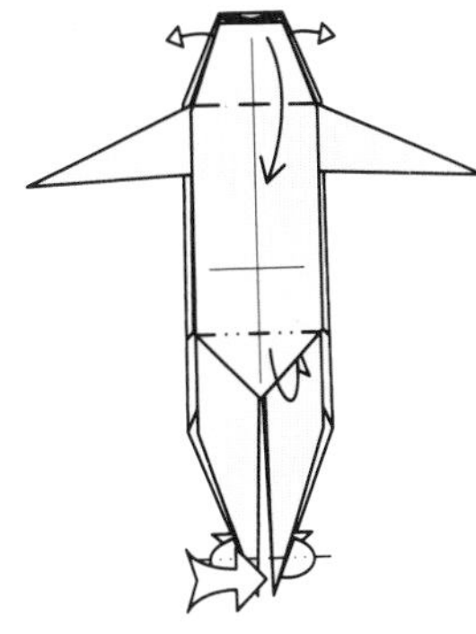

32 Open out the top of the model. Tuck the bottom point up underneath. Reverse-fold the tip of each of the two bottom points.

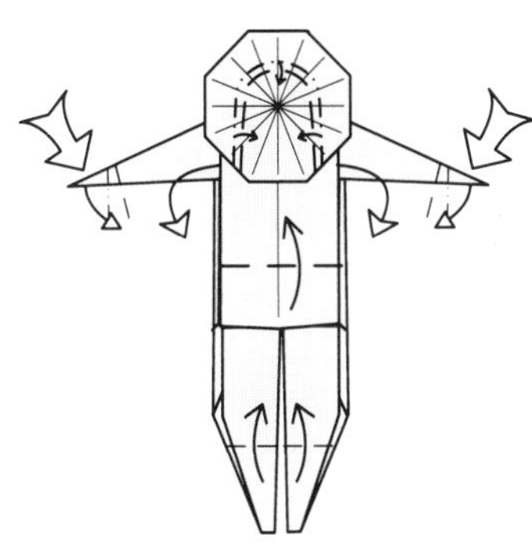

33 Pleat a single layer of paper all the way around the head. Squash-fold the hands and curve the arms around toward the front. Fold the feet up. (If you are putting the Eskimo into a kayak, bend him at the waist.)

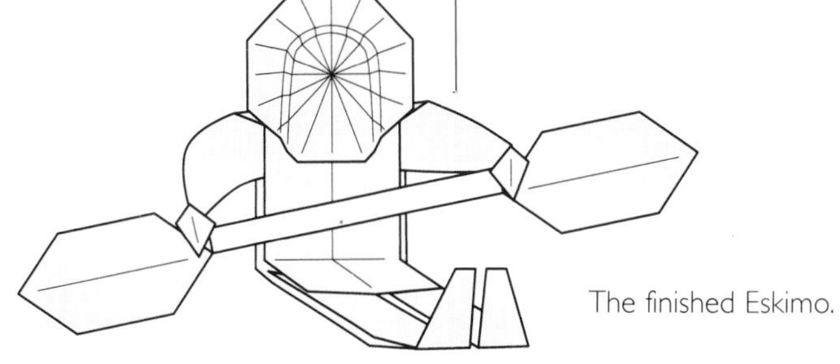

The finished Eskimo.

BELL

★★★

Inflatable origami – blow-ups – are always fun to make, but there are very few such models. Here is one of them.

When folding, leave a small hole at the bottom corner to blow into. Do not close it completely by folding *too* neatly! If the hole *is* too small, snip it open with scissors.

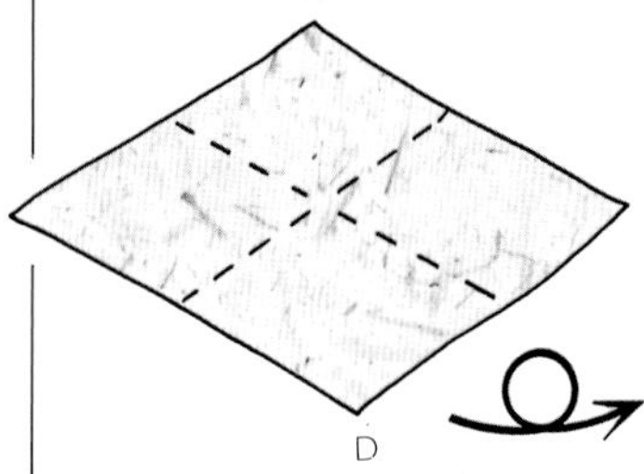

1 Take a 6 to 8-inch square of light- or medium- weight paper or foil. Fold horizontal and vertical valley folds across the paper. Turn over, so that the creases rise toward you.

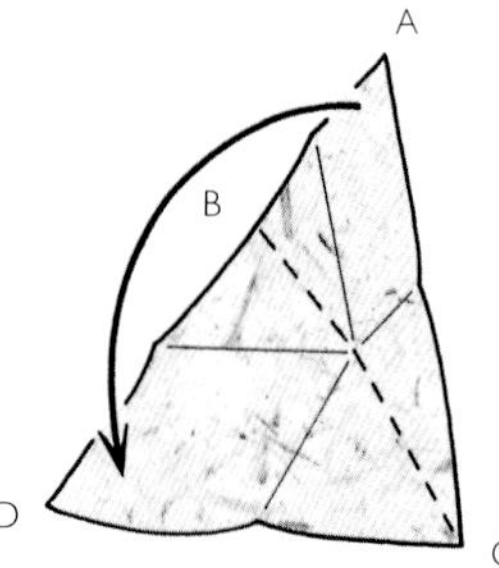

2 Fold A over to D as shown. Unfold. Repeat this move, folding B over to C.

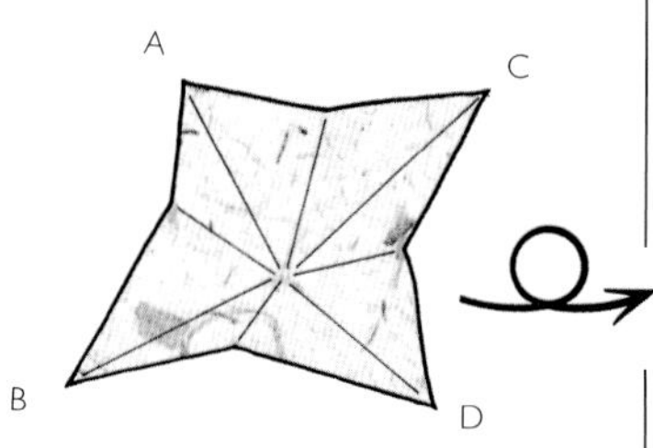

3 The crease pattern should look like this. The paper is three-dimensional. Turn over so that the middle rises up. Push the horizontal and vertical mountain folds toward each other so that the central peak rises up, as shown. Four triangles are formed, meeting at E.

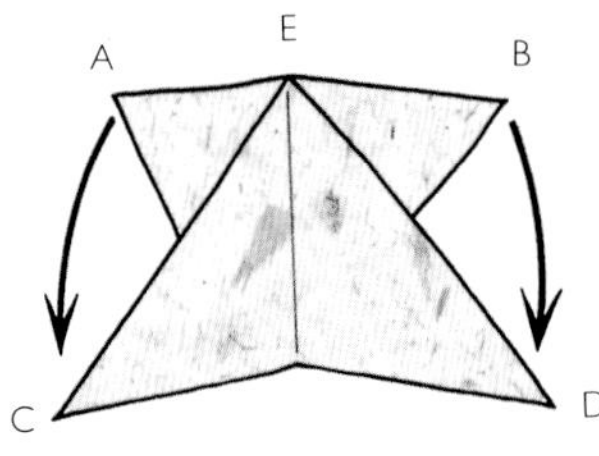

4 Flatten the paper so that two triangles lie on each side of the center.

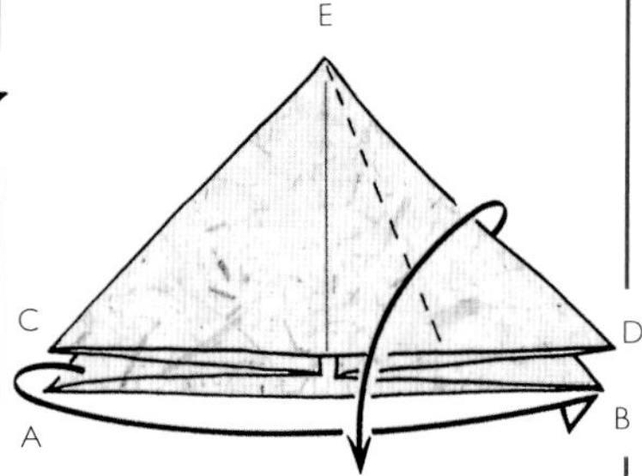

5 Fold D inward so that edge ED lies along the center crease. (It may help to mark ABCD in pencil.) Swing A on the left around the back to the right so that it lies behind B.

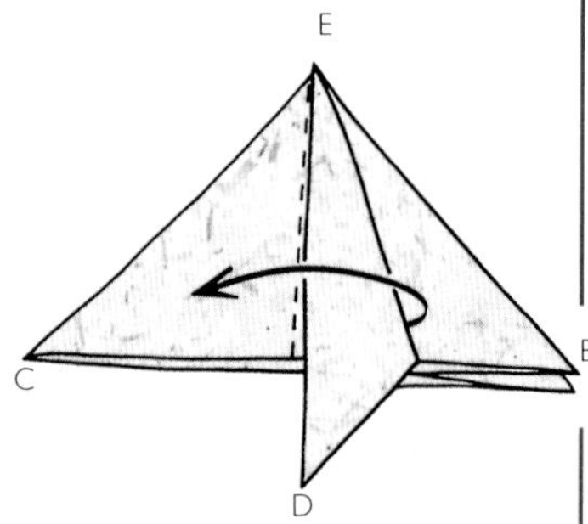

6 Swing D over to the left.

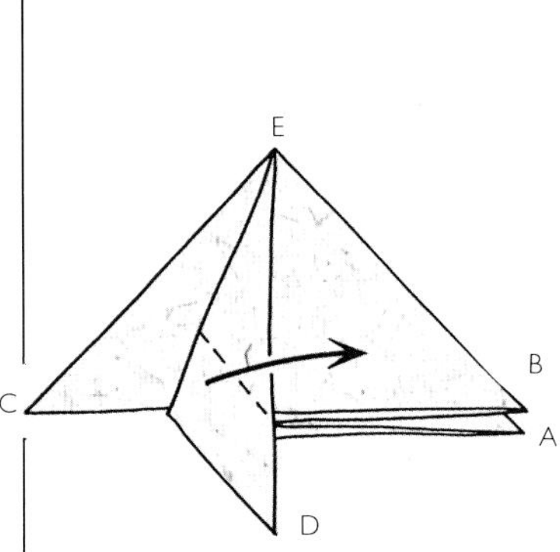

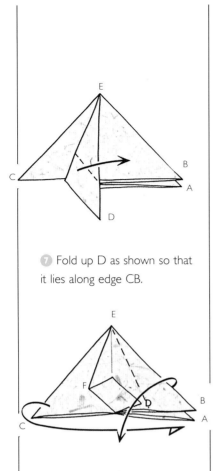

7 Fold up D as shown so that it lies along edge CB.

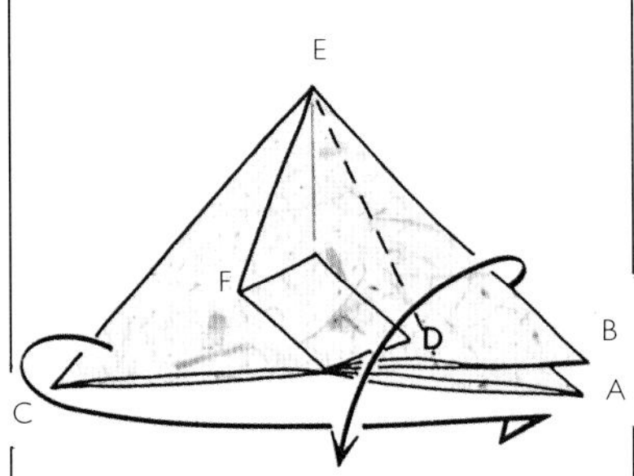

8 The paper now looks like this. The folds in steps 5–7 are now repeated with B, then A, and then C. As in step 5, fold B inward so that edge EB lies along the center crease, covering D. Swing C on the left around the back to lie behind A on the right.

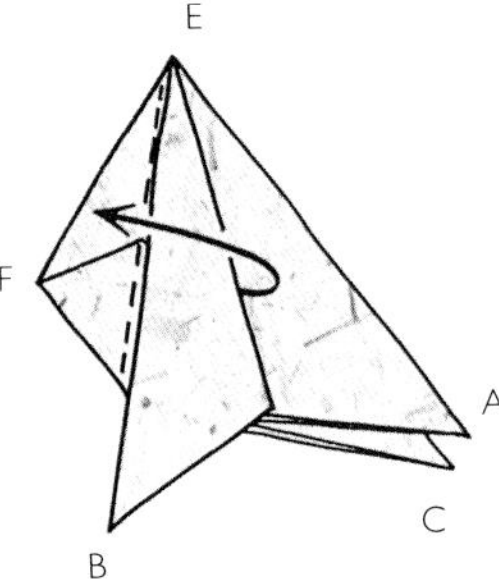

9 Swing B over to the left to lie on top of F. Fold up B like D in step 7.

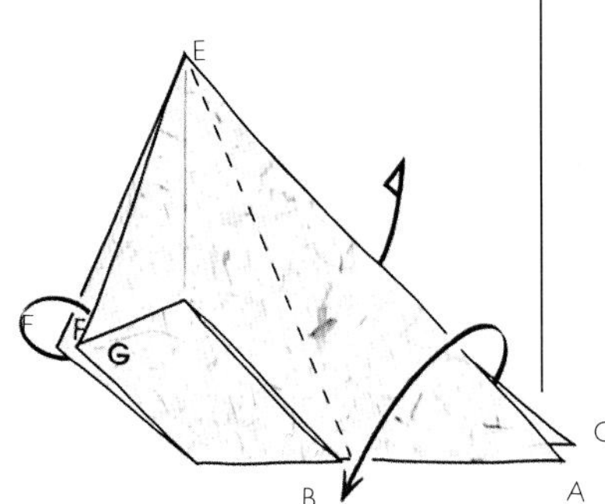

10 As in step 5, fold A inward so that edge EA lies along the center crease, covering B. Swing F on the left around the swing to lie hidden behind C on the right. Swing A over to the left to lie on top of G. Fold up A like D in step 7.

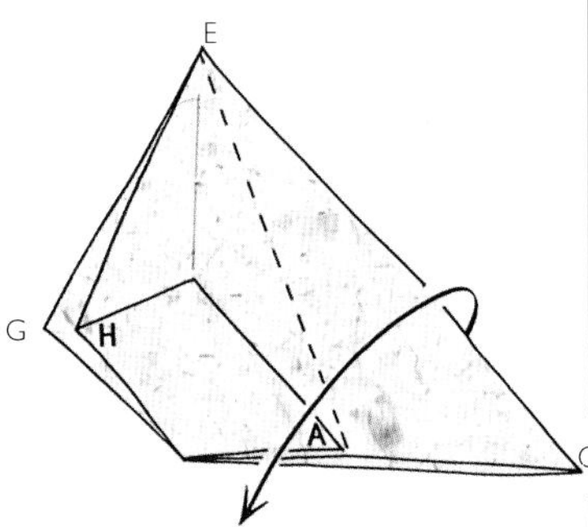

11 As in step 5, fold C inward so that edge EC lies along the center crease, covering A.

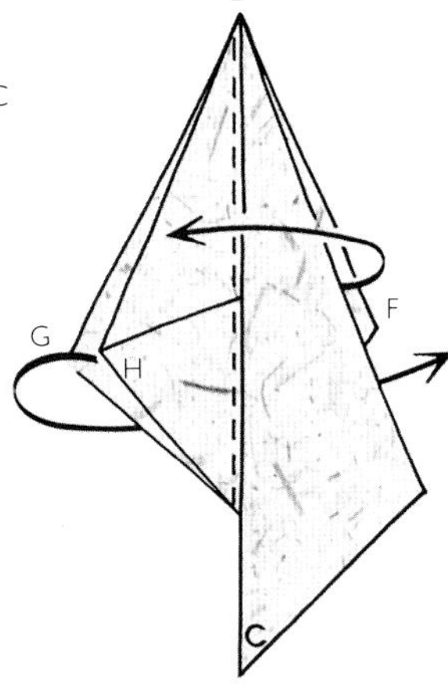

12 Swing G on the left around the back and to the right to lie behind F. Swing C over to the left, to lie on top of H.

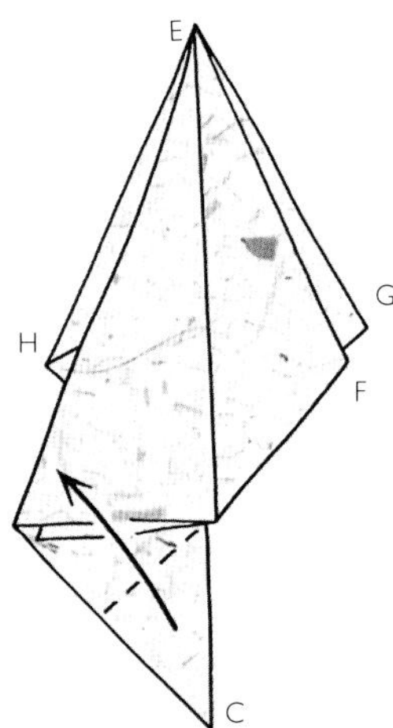

13 Fold up corner C, as shown. Crease flat.

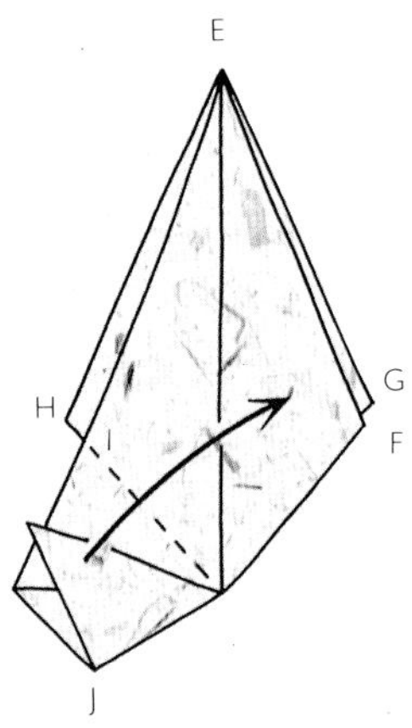

14 Fold the flap up as shown . . .

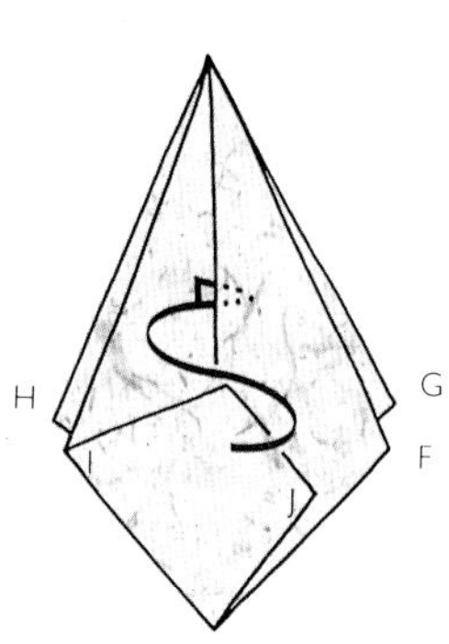

15 . . . and slide J under the edge that runs down the center of the paper, pushing it deep into the pocket.

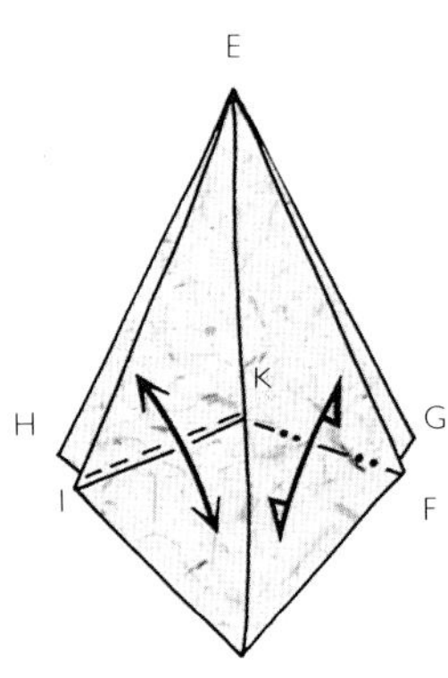

16 The paper is now symmetrical. Carefully form valley creases between I and K, and H and K on the left and mountain creases between F and K, and G and K on the right. Do not crease beyond the center.

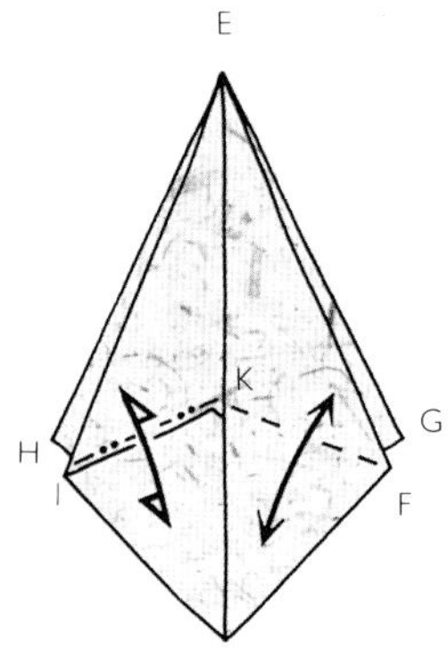

17 Now make mountain creases on the left and valleys on the right, placing these creases on top of the previous ones. This will form creases that can bend backward and forward. Bend them to and fro several times so that they are very flexible.

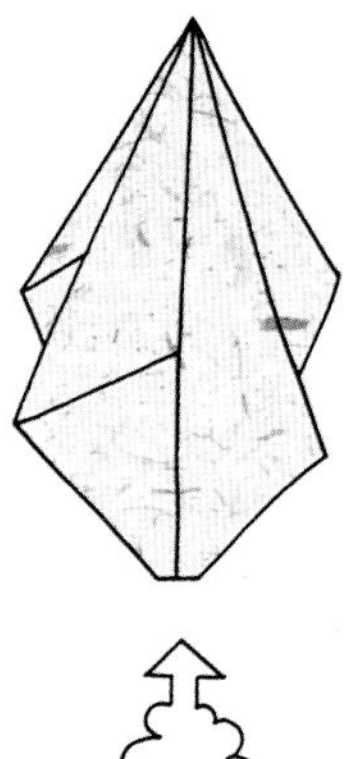

18 At the bottom end, there should be a small hole. Blow into it and the bell should inflate! Inflating it is easier if the four flaps are spread apart and if the hole is clearly visible. The flexible creases just made will form a definite rim to the bell.

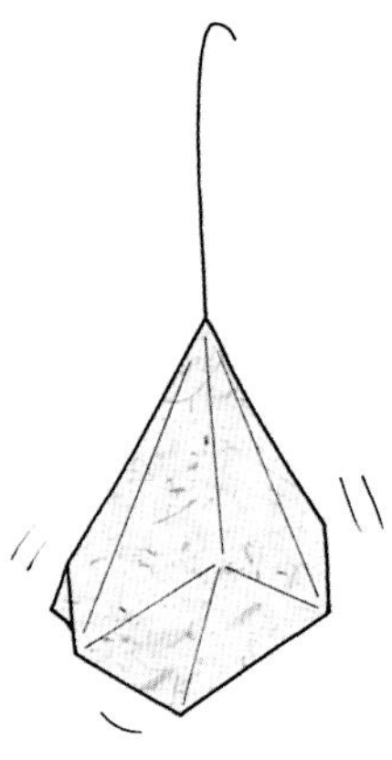

19 The Bell is complete. To suspend, attach a loop to the top of the bell with needle and thread.

OPPOSITE *The finished Bell, designed by Paul Jackson.*

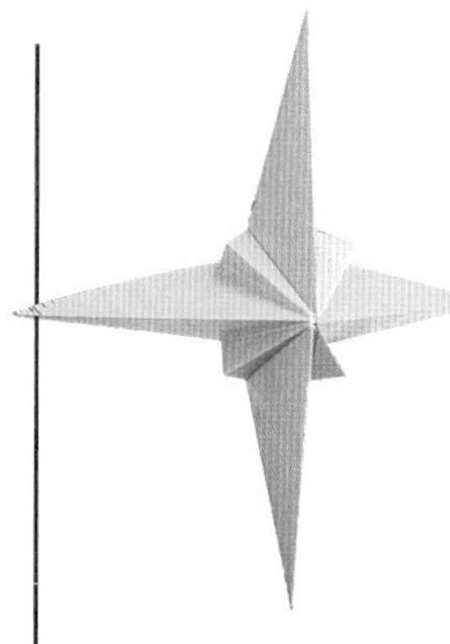

STAR

★★★

A good way to form geometric shapes is to fold a number of simple shapes which can interlock. This is commonly known as "modular origami." The star is a simple example of this kind of folding, and to experiment, try folding six, eight, or more modules to make stars with more than four points.

MATERIALS

Four sheets of lightweight paper or foil about 4 inches square in two colors or textures which work well together. Choosing complementary papers with care always adds to the finished piece.

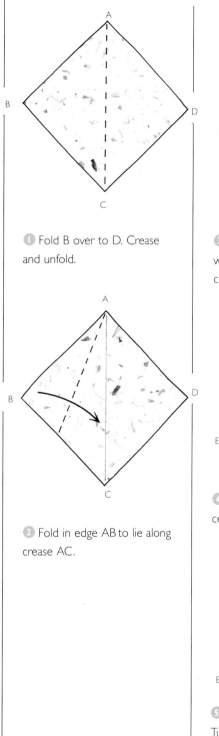

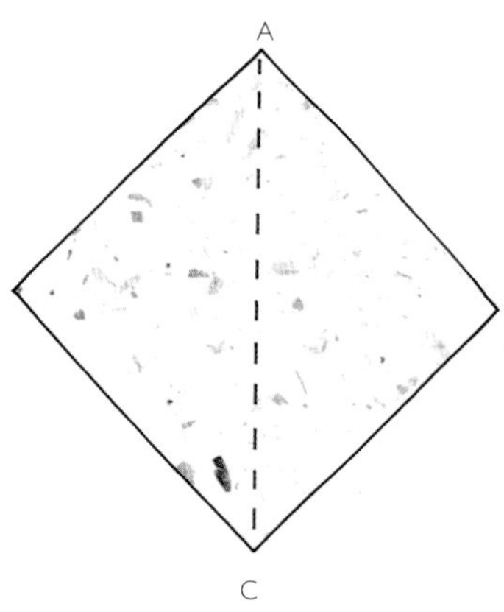

1 Fold B over to D. Crease and unfold.

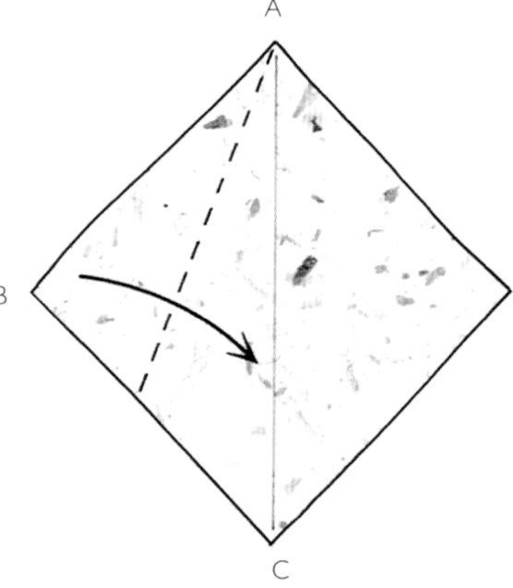

2 Fold in edge AB to lie along crease AC.

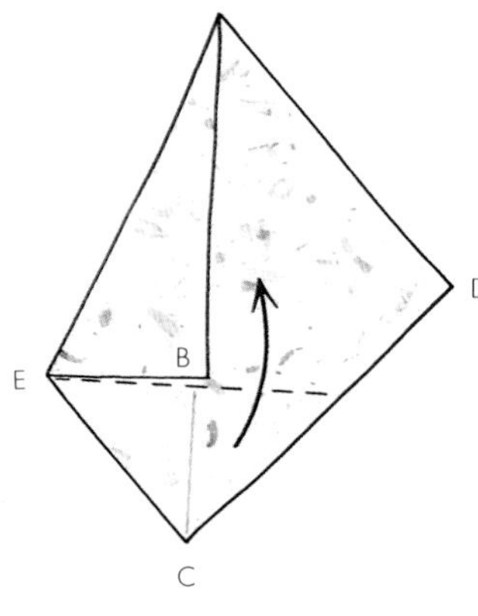

3 Fold up C along a crease which follows edge EB, covering B.

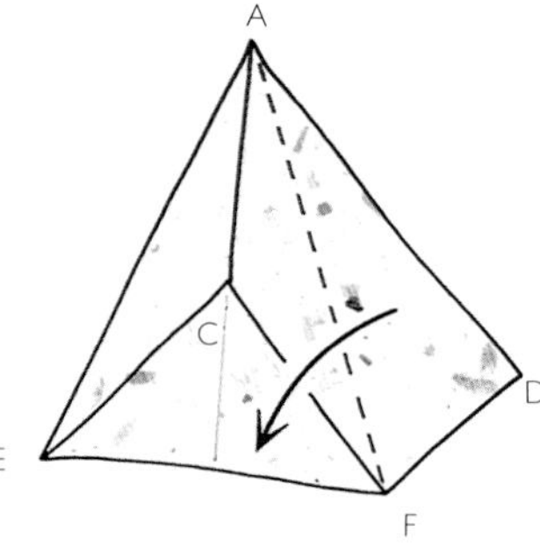

4 Fold in edge AD to the center so that it half-covers C.

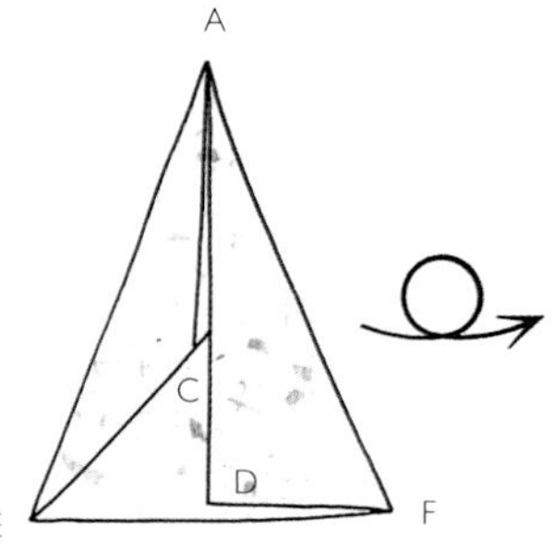

5 The paper looks like this. Turn it over.

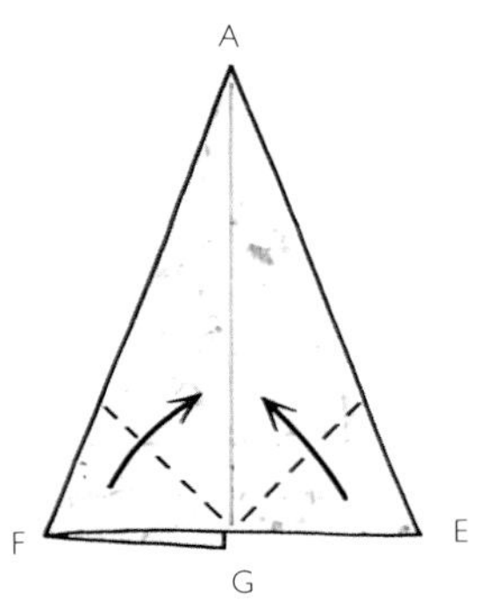

6 Fold in F and E to lie along crease AG.

7 Fold F and E back out to the sloping edges just formed which meet at G. E is shown already folded. Keep the folds neat at G.

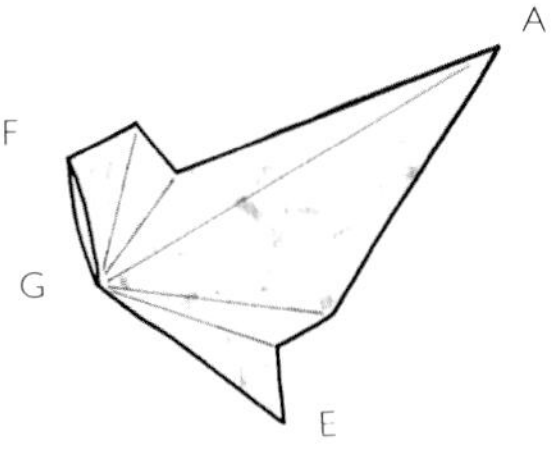

8 Unfold the last two steps so it looks like this. This is one point of the star. Make three more sections just the same as the first, but make two of them in another (maybe patterned) paper.

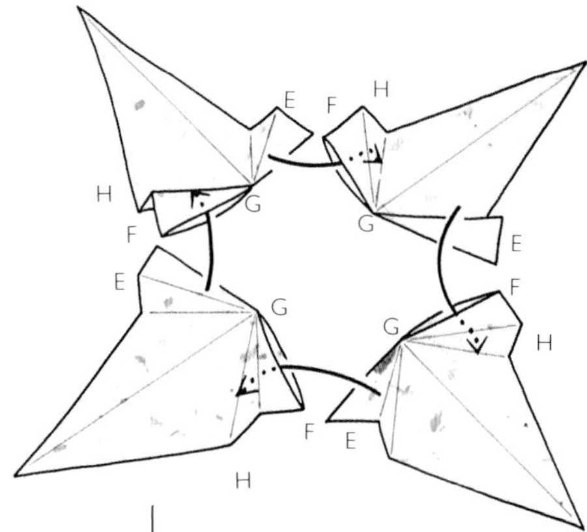

9 Tuck corner E of one section in between the layers of another at F and continue to push it farther in until E touches H and the two Gs touch. The mountain and valley creases should line up where they overlap. In the same way, tuck in the third and fourth sections, alternating the types of paper, and finally locking the first section into the fourth. Strengthen and sharpen all the creases.

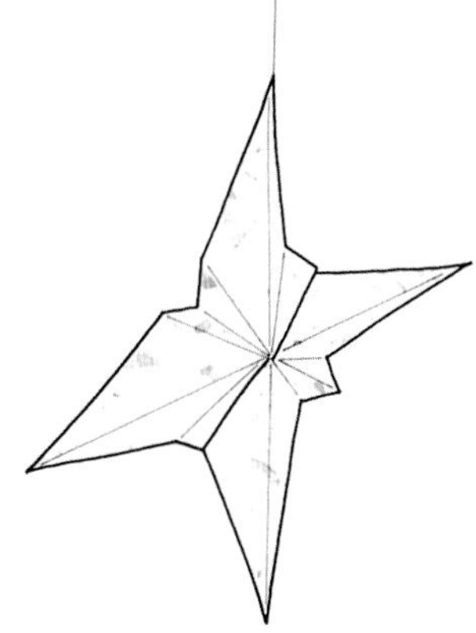

10 The Star is complete. To suspend, attach a loop to one point of the star with needle and thread.

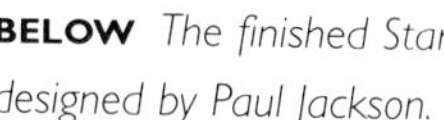
BELOW *The finished Star, designed by Paul Jackson.*

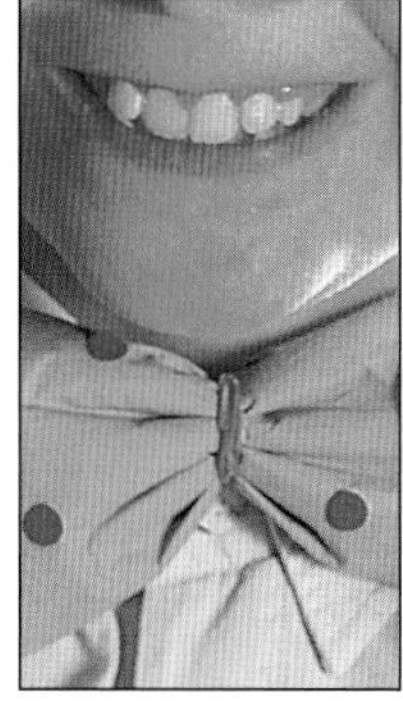

BOW TIE

Simple to make and fun to wear, the Bow Tie is an ideal way of breaking the ice at parties for all age groups!

Decorate the Bow Tie with some self-adhesive colored shapes – dots or squares, for example – for a truly individual effect.

MATERIALS

Use a good-quality 4-ply paper napkin, or fold two 2-ply napkins together. A single 2-ply napkin will make a floppy bow tie.

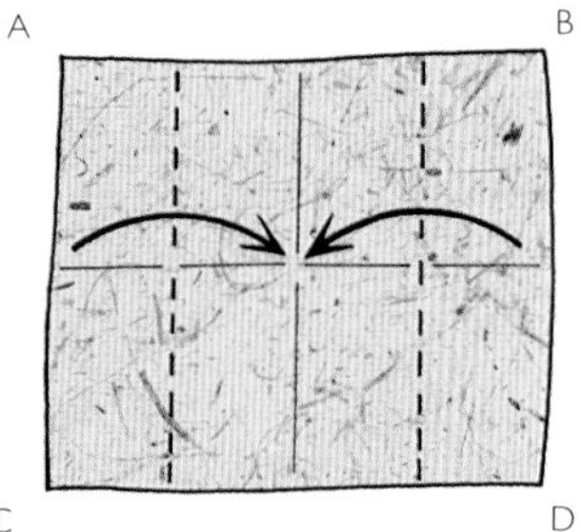

1 Fold the napkin in half horizontally and vertically. Unfold. Fold AC and BD to the central vertical crease.

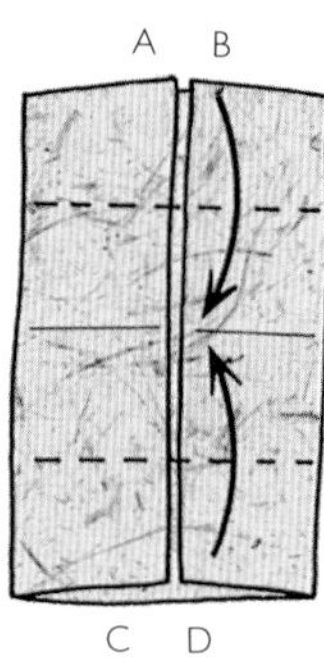

2 Fold AB and CD to the central horizontal crease.

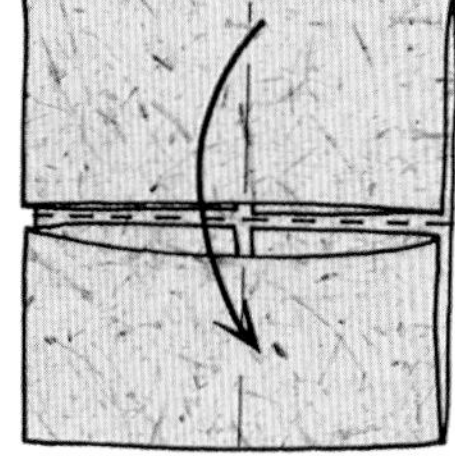

3 Fold in half across the middle.

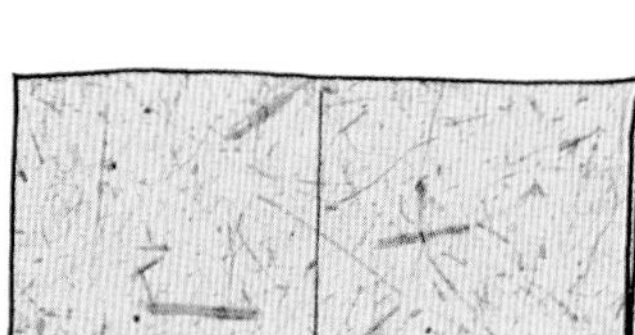

4 The folding is now complete.

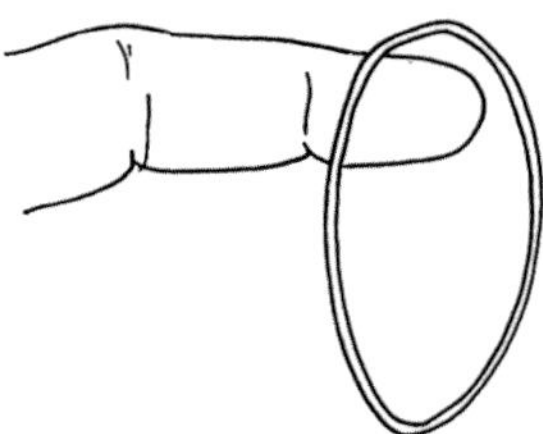

5 Take a rubber band with a diameter of approximately 1½ inches . . .

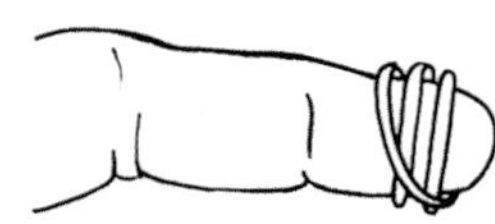

6 . . . and wrap it around a finger three times.

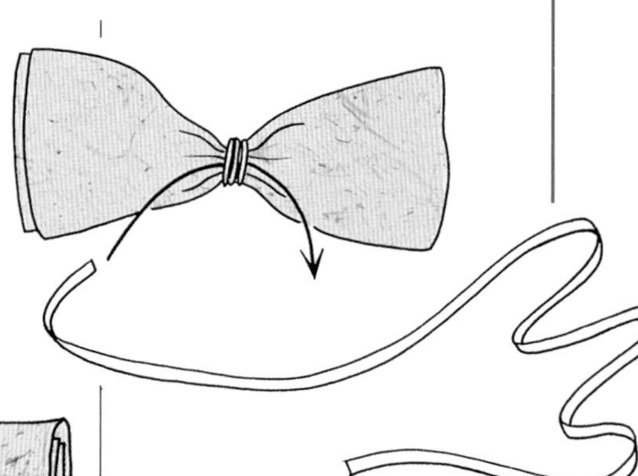

7 Slip the band onto the bow tie, so that the paper bunches neatly in the middle. Take a length of cord elastic and thread it between the rubber band and the bow tie.

8 Tie the ends of the cord elastic together, decorate the front of the bow with self-adhesive colored shapes, if wished, and the Bow Tie is ready to wear.

BELOW *The finished Bow Tie, designed by Paul Jackson.*

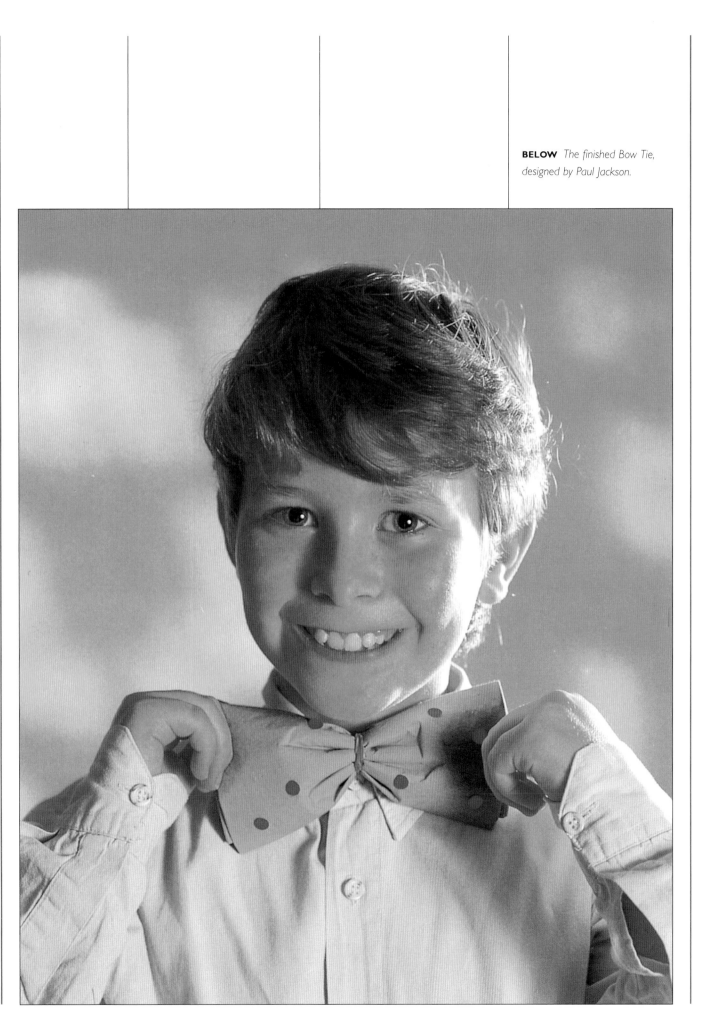

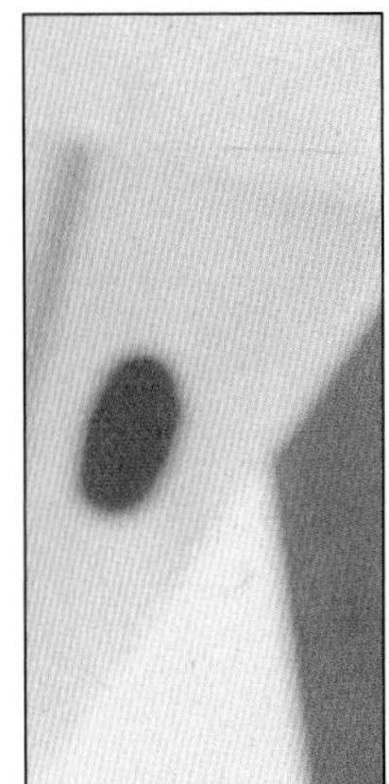

GHOST

★★★

Several Ghosts, of varying sizes, could be suspended on a thread to decorate the house for Halloween, or smaller ones can be used to decorate invitation cards to a "Trick or Treat" party. The drawn eyes are a cheat, perhaps, but they do add a suitably ghoulish effect.

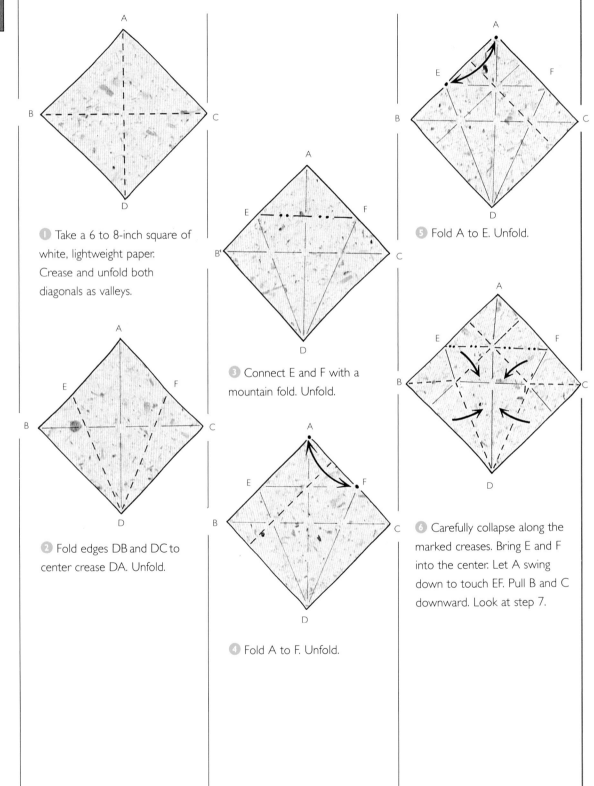

1 Take a 6 to 8-inch square of white, lightweight paper. Crease and unfold both diagonals as valleys.

2 Fold edges DB and DC to center crease DA. Unfold.

3 Connect E and F with a mountain fold. Unfold.

4 Fold A to F. Unfold.

5 Fold A to E. Unfold.

6 Carefully collapse along the marked creases. Bring E and F into the center. Let A swing down to touch EF. Pull B and C downward. Look at step 7.

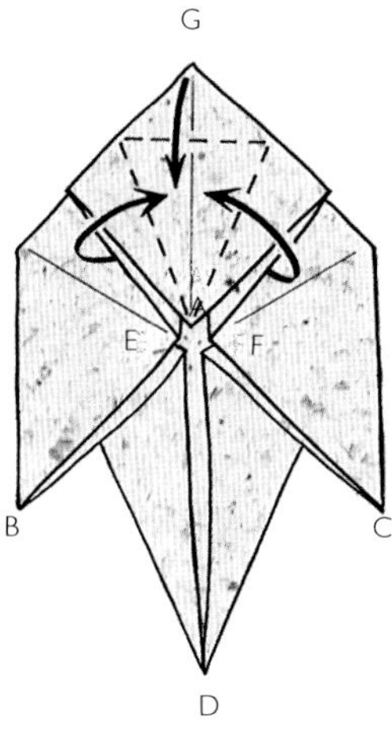

7 Make a petal fold. Fold in the diagonal edges above EF to the center crease, then fold down the top corner G on top.

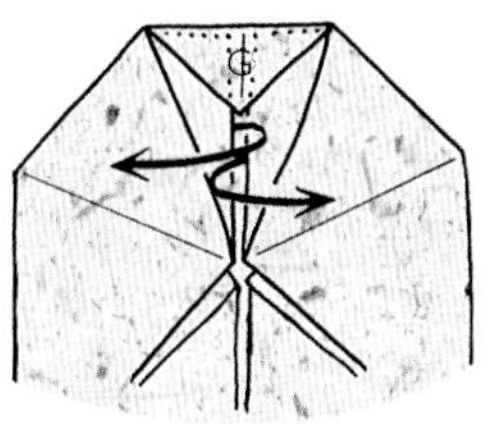

8 Unfold the side triangles, leaving the top corner folded down.

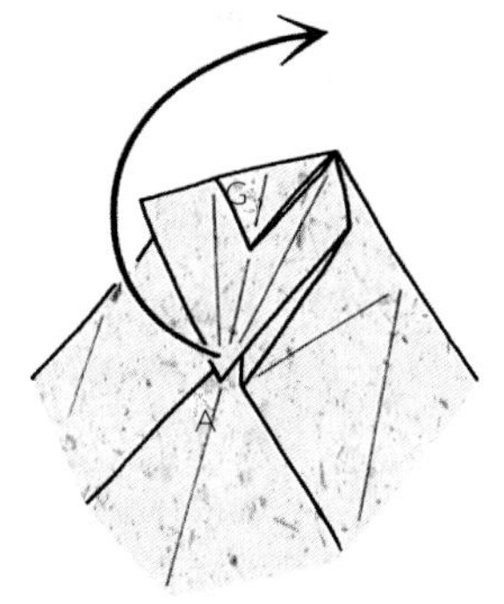

9 Pick up the single layer corner A, and swivel it up and over the top edge of the paper . . .

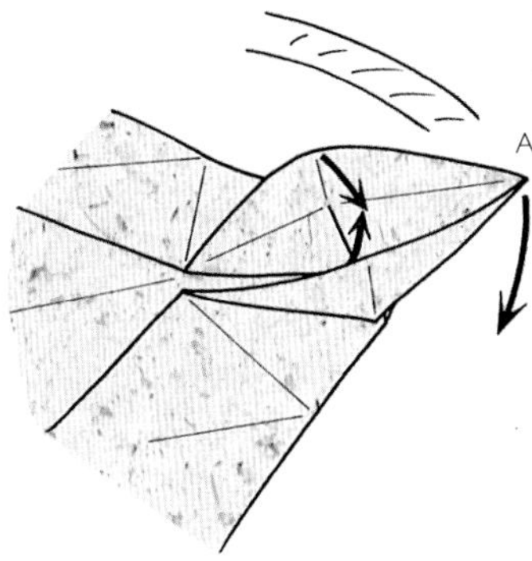

10 . . . like this. The paper becomes three-dimensional. Flatten corner A, allowing the sides to collapse in toward the center crease.

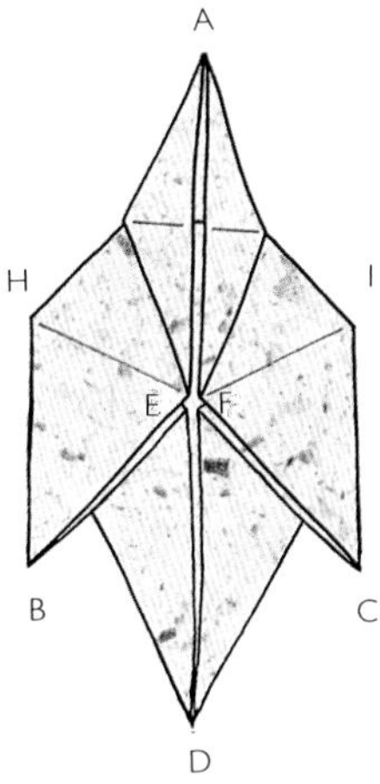

11 The maneuver complete.

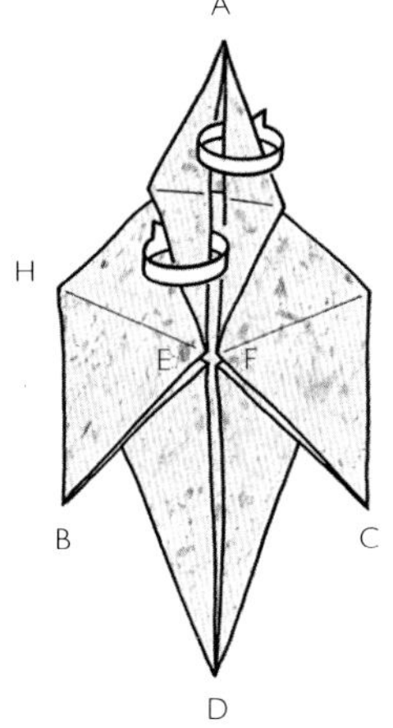

12 Unfold AEF almost to a flat sheet, swinging edges AE and AF behind to touch G . . .

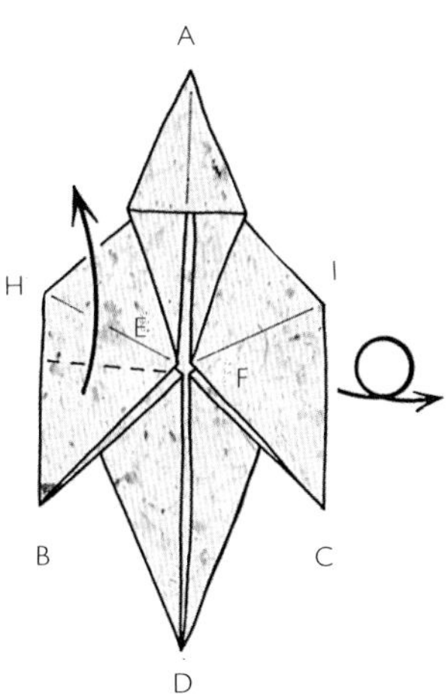

13 . . . like this. Note the large triangle now below A. Fold up corner B. Turn over.

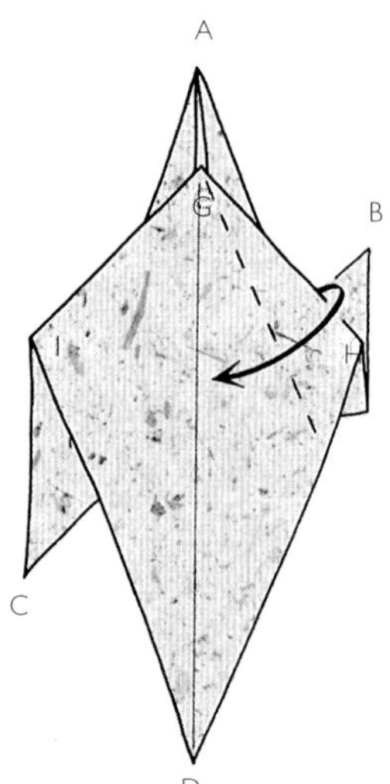

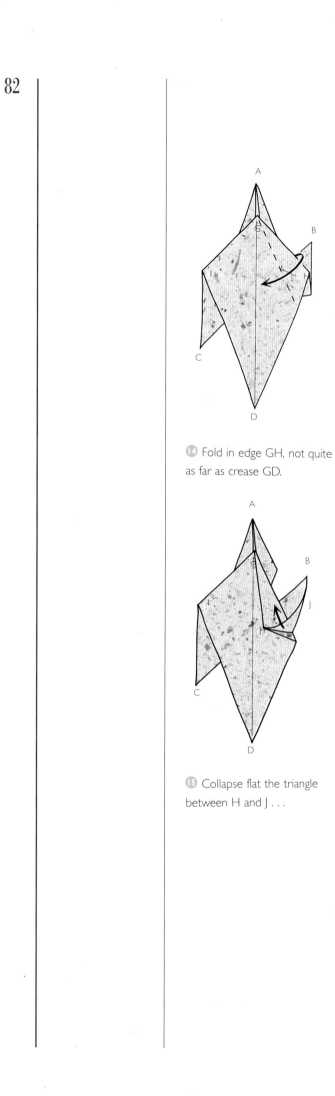

14 Fold in edge GH, not quite as far as crease GD.

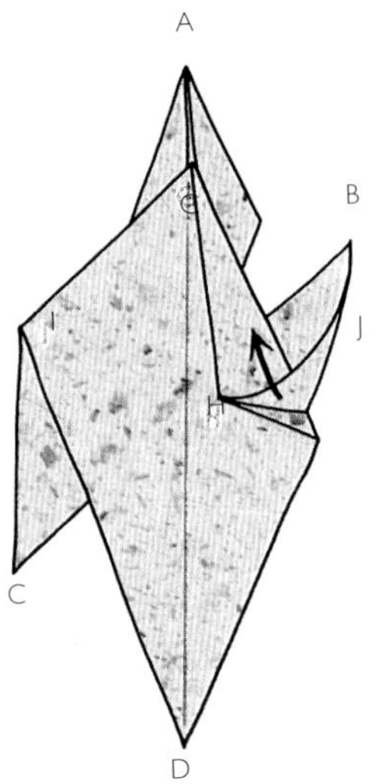

15 Collapse flat the triangle between H and J . . .

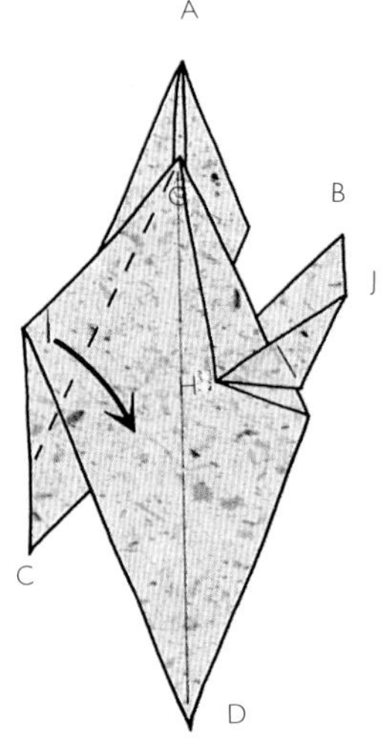

16 . . . like this. Fold in edge GI, as shown.

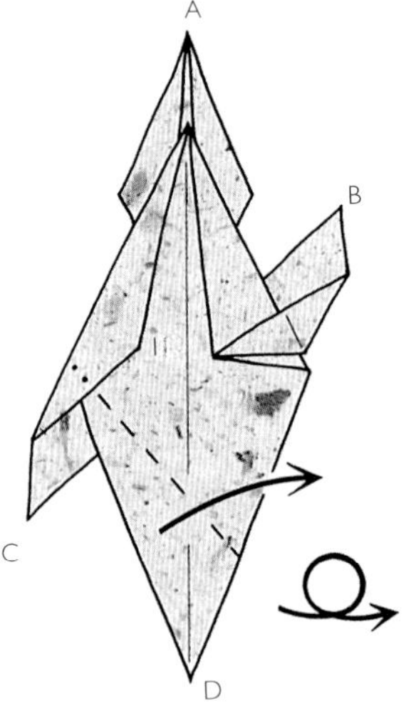

17 Fold out D to the right. Turn over.

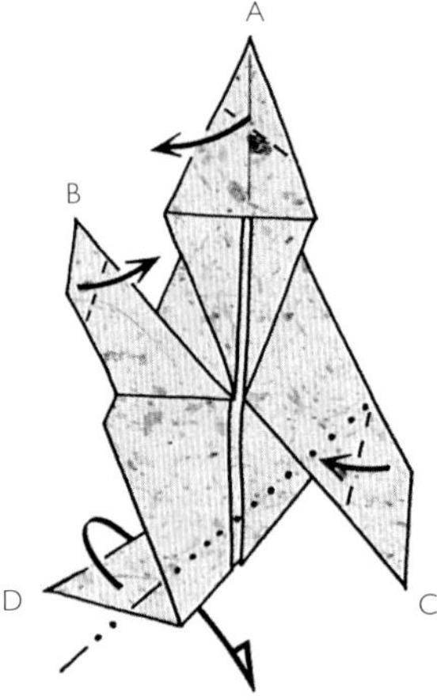

18 Fold A out to the left. Fold in B and C. Pleat D downward.

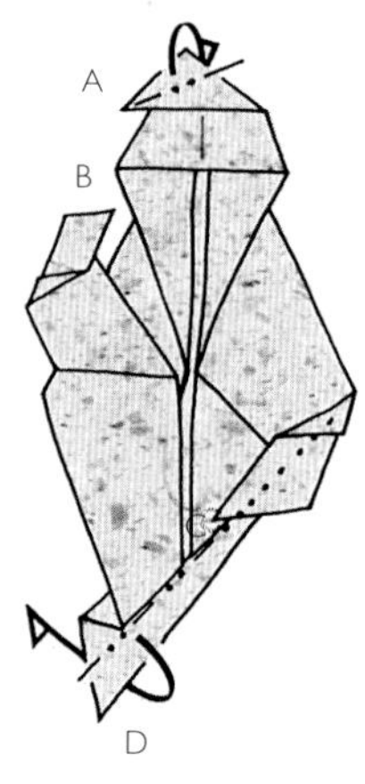

19 Narrow A. Pleat D back up.

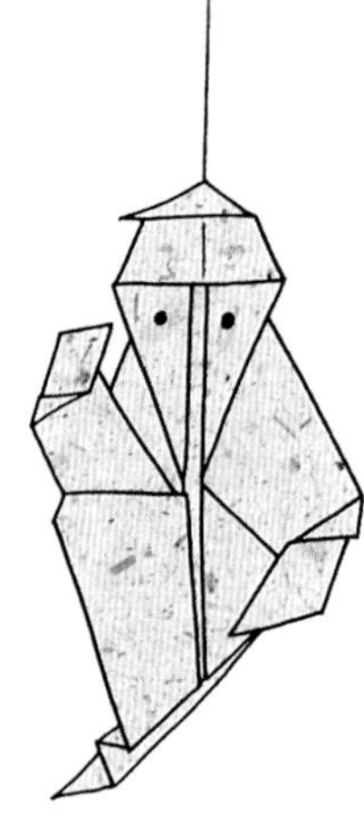

20 Draw the eyes as shown with a marker pen, and suspend using a needle and thread to attach a loop to the ghost's head. The Ghost is complete.

OPPOSITE *The finished Ghost, designed by Paul Jackson.*

MOUNTAIN RANGE

★ ★

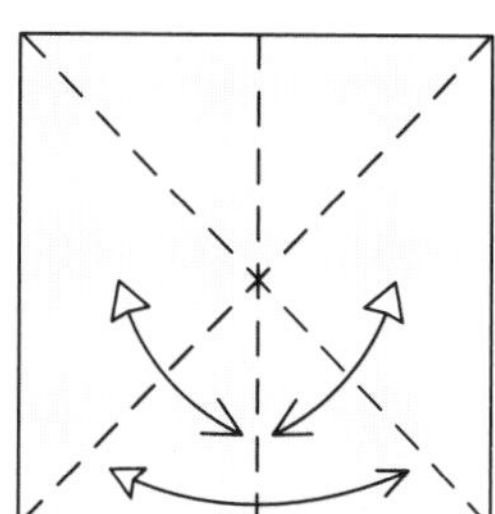

❶ Take a 24-inch square of brown paper, white on one side. Begin with the white side up. Fold and unfold the paper vertically and along the diagonals.

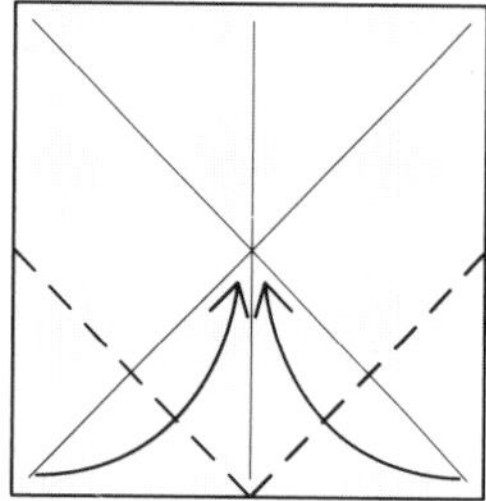

❷ Fold the two bottom corners up to meet in the middle of the paper.

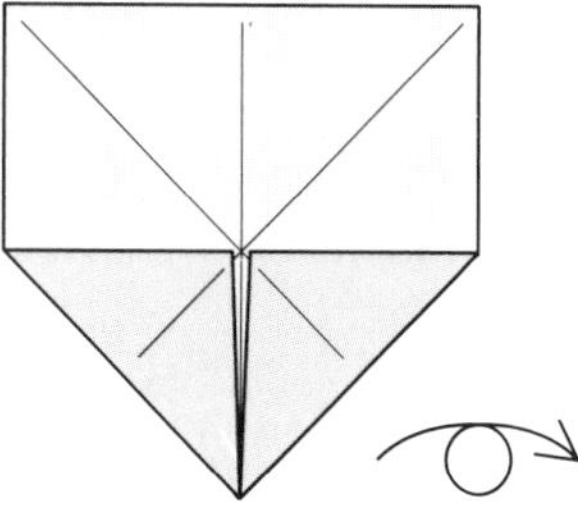

❸ Turn the model over.

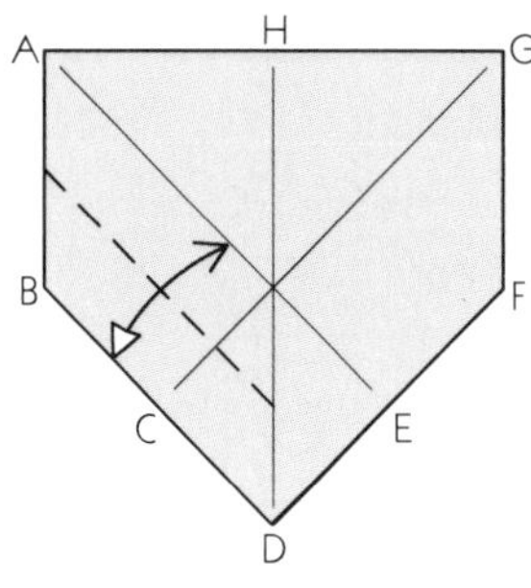

❹ Fold edge BD up to lie along crease AE, making the crease sharp only from side AB to where it hits crease HD. Unfold.

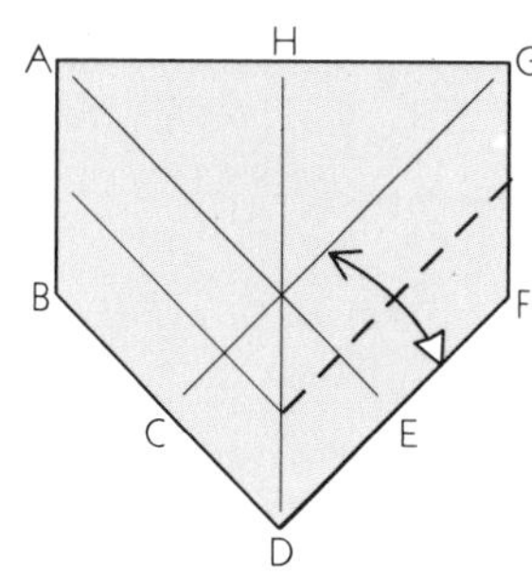

❺ Repeat on the right with edge DF.

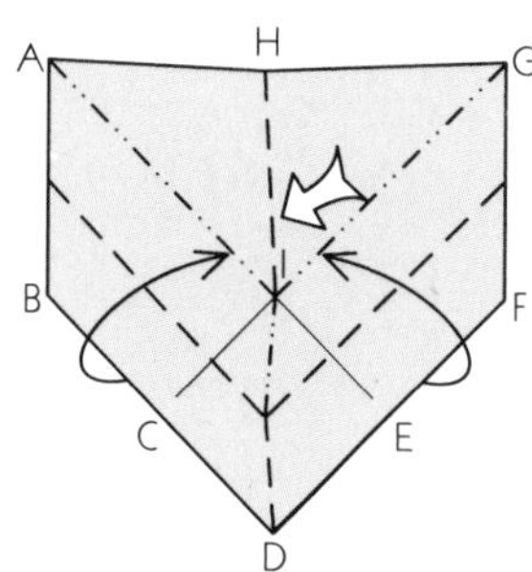

❻ Bring edges BD and DF up and toward each other. At the same time, push down on crease HI. Look ahead to step 7 to see the shape you are trying to make.

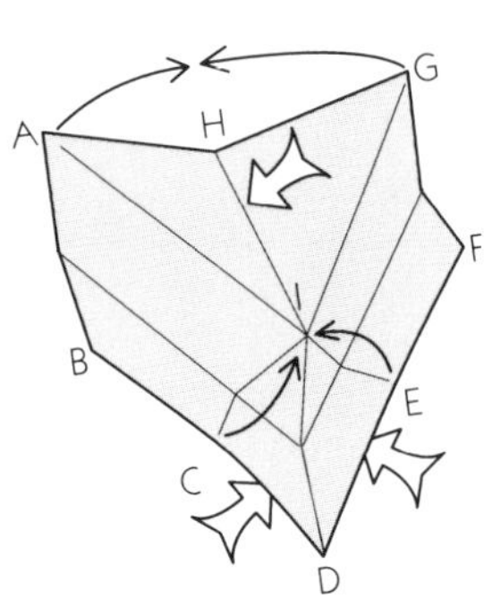

❼ Bring C and E to I and bring corners A and G together.

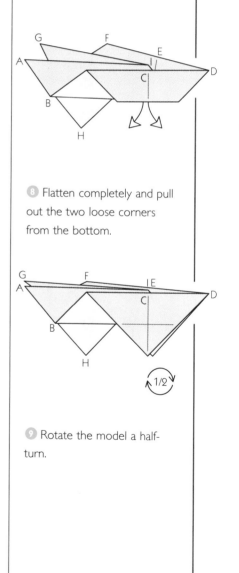

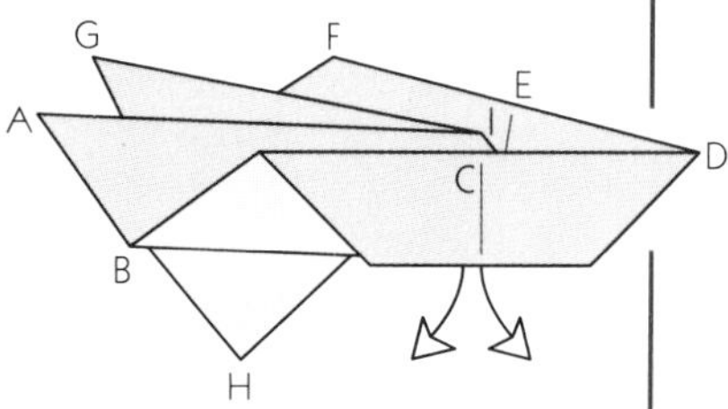

❽ Flatten completely and pull out the two loose corners from the bottom.

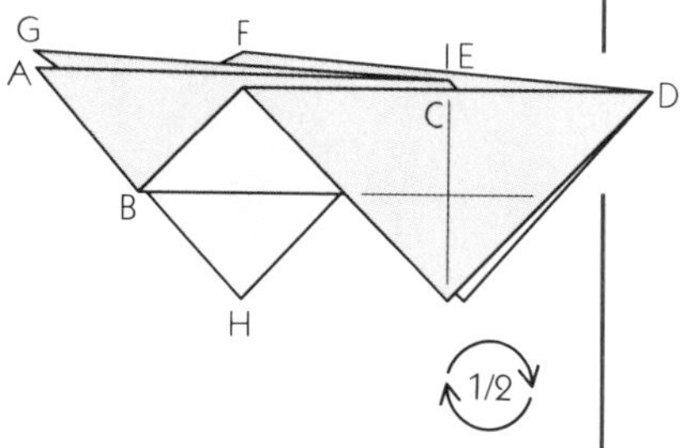

❾ Rotate the model a half-turn.

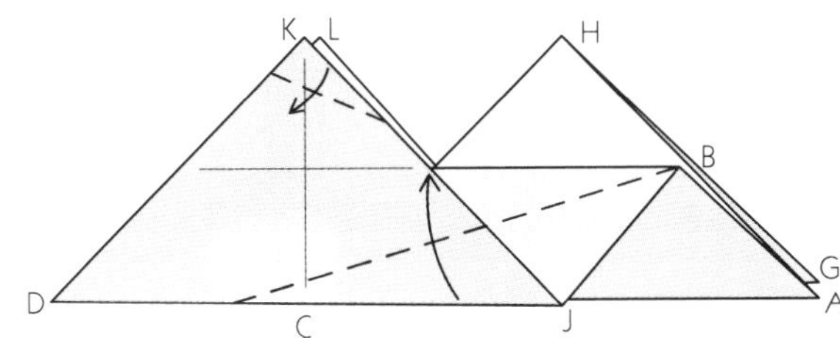

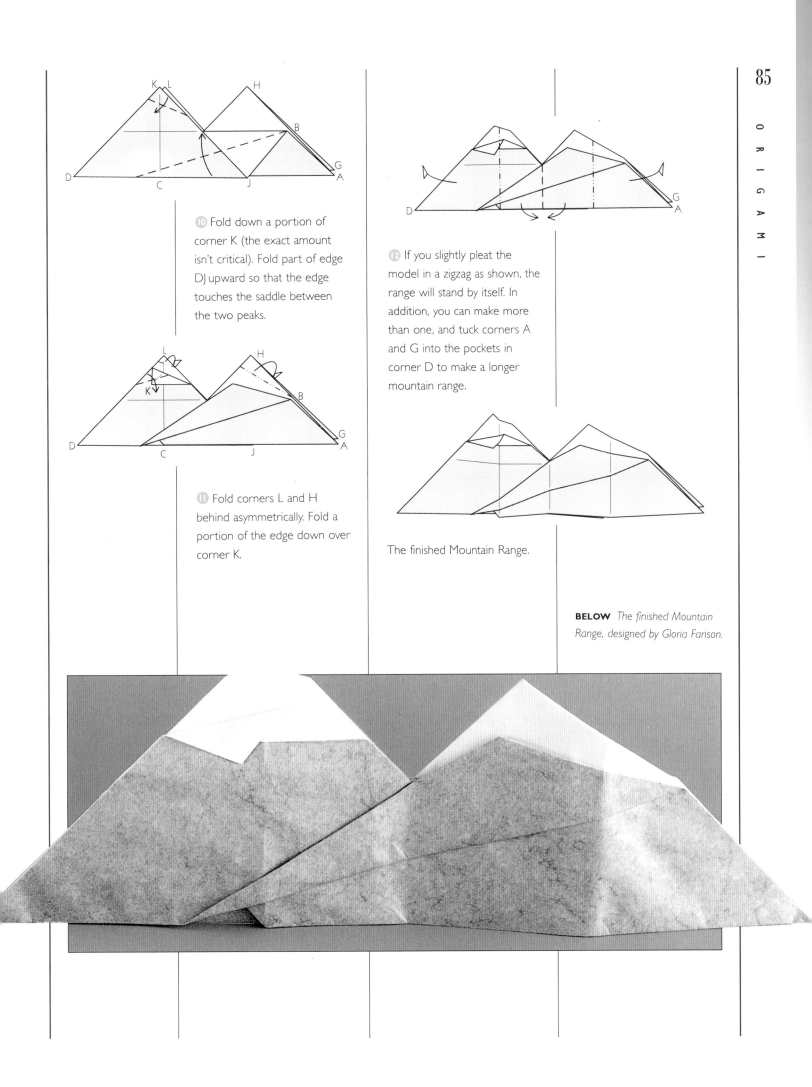

⑩ Fold down a portion of corner K (the exact amount isn't critical). Fold part of edge DJ upward so that the edge touches the saddle between the two peaks.

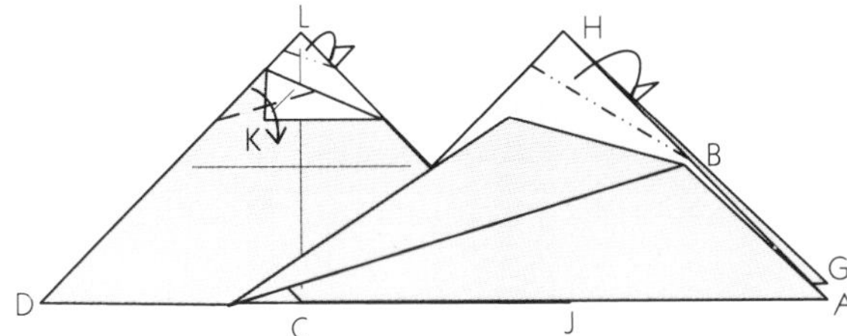

⑪ Fold corners L and H behind asymmetrically. Fold a portion of the edge down over corner K.

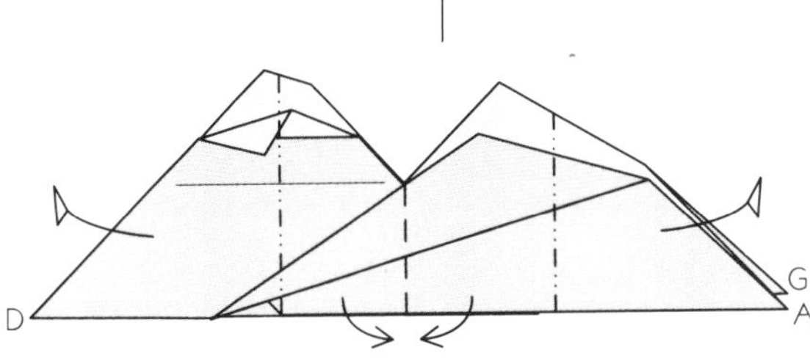

⑫ If you slightly pleat the model in a zigzag as shown, the range will stand by itself. In addition, you can make more than one, and tuck corners A and G into the pockets in corner D to make a longer mountain range.

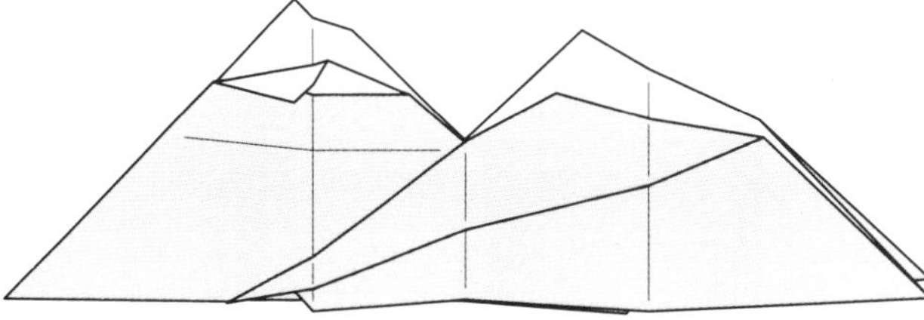

The finished Mountain Range.

BELOW *The finished Mountain Range, designed by Gloria Farison.*

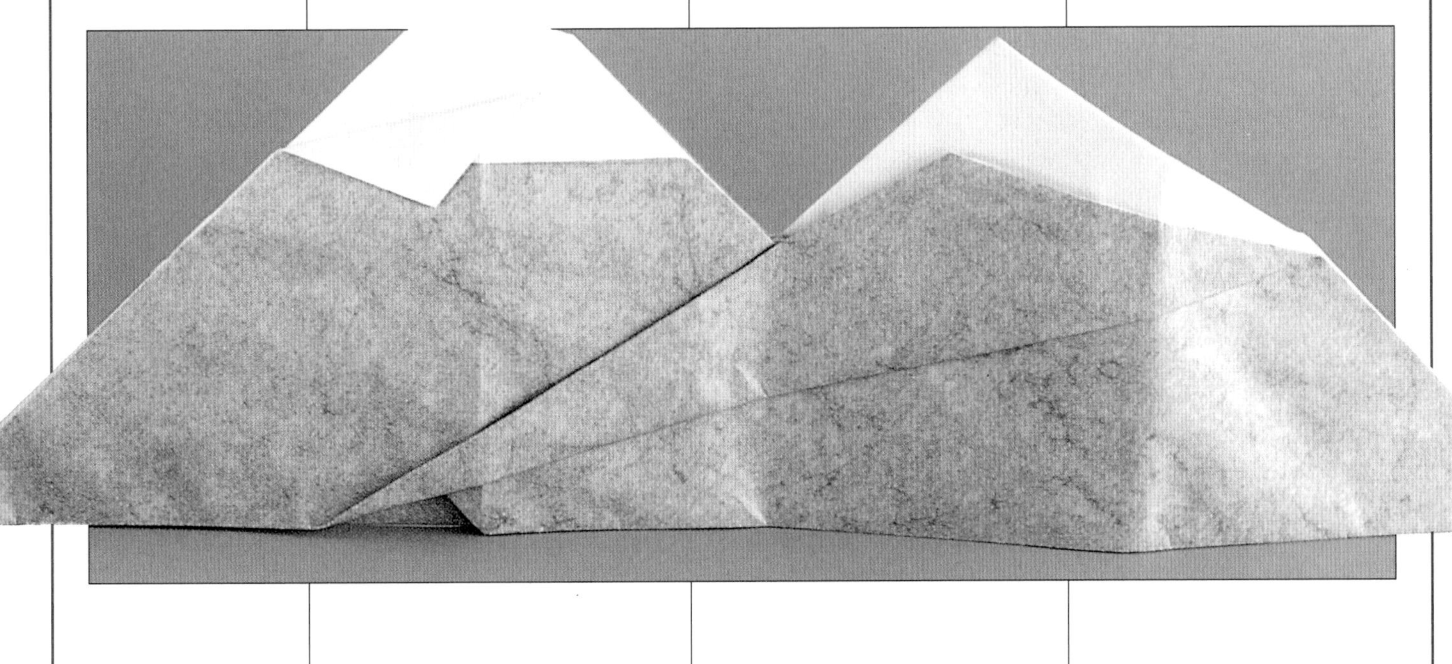

Party Poppers

PART II

POP-UPS

PAPERS AND CARDBOARDS

Papers and cardboards suitable for making pop-up cards can be bought at art and craft suppliers in a surprisingly wide choice of attractive colors and textures. Scrap card from old greetings cards or cereal packets, though, is also useful for making rough practice cards.

If at all possible, store paper or cardboard *flat*. To keep it rolled up for long periods of time will give it a "memory" and nothing is more annoying than trying to work with paper or cardboard that continually wants to curl up! It is also a waste of money. Finding a flat space large enough to store big sheets safely can sometimes by a problem, though, so simply cut the sheets into pieces of a manageable size – pop-up cards are rarely made from large sheets.

CORRECT WEIGHTS TO USE

Choosing the correct paper and cardboard weights for both the backing sheet and the pop-up element itself is important. Please follow this brief guide with care.

The Backing Sheet

The encasing backing sheet on which the pop-up design is built must be strong and thick enough to open without buckling. A backing sheet that does buckle will not fully erect and support the pop-up section inside.

So, for pop-up designs with a lot of stresses and strains, use *mat board* – the thick cardboard used to make picture mats. For those designs with less stress, use thinner board, perhaps the weight of a cereal box.

The Pop-up Design

The pop-up design itself must not be made from board that is too thick, because this will create too much bulk when the design is folded flat, bursting the crease on the backing sheet. Conversely, if it is made from thin paper, the pop-up will not hold its shape when the card is opened.

So, use thick paper or thin board, depending on the size of the design and the weight each piece has to support. The rough pop-up card that you should make before a final card is attempted will guide your choice.

DECORATION IDEAS

The decoration of a pop-up greeting card is an important aspect of the design and must be approached thoughtfully. In particular, the choice of media is crucial, as the incorrect choice can ruin your construction. So . . .

Don't

. . . use water-based paints, such as poster paints, gouache, or watercolor, on ordinary board as the water will make the card "cockle" – wrinkle and warp. If you must use them, an alternative is to use heavy watercolor or etching paper, which are made to hold water without cockling. Even thick markers will cockle most papers and some thin boards, so take care.

Remember, a pop-up piece that has cockled will not lie flat when the greeting card is closed up, preventing the card from shutting. Thus, cockling is not only unsightly, but also affects the pop-up mechanism.

Do

. . . use media such as felt pens, colored pencils and inks (but no washes). Oil pastels, dry pastels, and charcoal may be used, but should be well fixed to avoid them transferring when the card is shut flat. Consider also using other decorative techniques, such as stickers, glitter, collage and colored card. Really, anything is acceptable, so long as it looks good. Remember, though, that too much decoration can distract from the cleverness of your construction and from the three-dimensional shapes that magically appear when the card is opened. Indeed, many pop-up cards look stunning simply left plain!

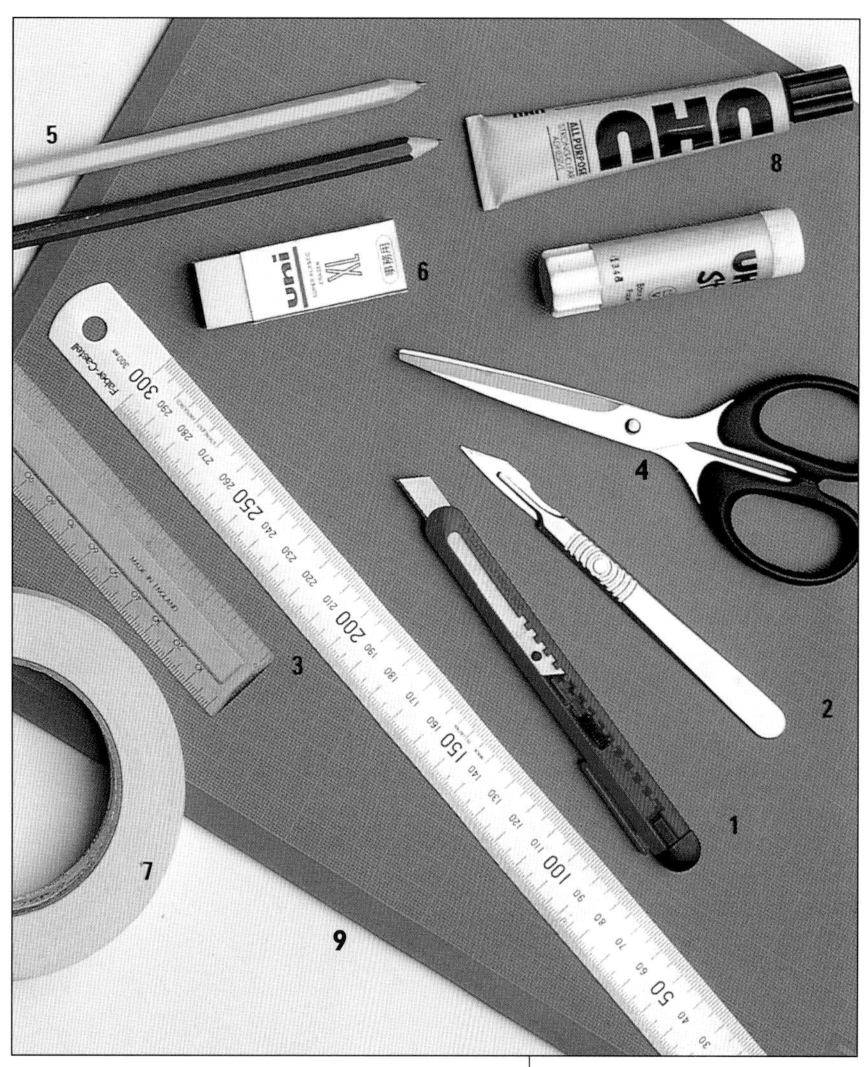

Equipment

The list of essential equipment for making pop-up cards is pleasingly simple and short. Most items can be bought inexpensively at most stationers or art and craft suppliers.

1 craft knife
2 scalpel
3 metal safety ruler or straightedge
4 scissors
5 pencil
6 eraser
7 masking tape
8 glue
9 self-healing cutting mat

BASIC TECHNIQUES FOR MAKING POP-UPS

Throughout this section, two simple pop-up techniques recur many times: the "V" fold and "tab" techniques. The construction procedure for both techniques is explained in the following paragraphs and not repeated in each project, so please refer to these pages when they occur in the projects. The procedures for other techniques are explained as they occur.

"V" Fold

This is a very simple but wonderfully versatile pop-up technique. The two halves of a pop-up form are glued to the backing sheet so that each half falls on each side of a crease, to create the "V" shape. Note the presence of tabs at the bottom.

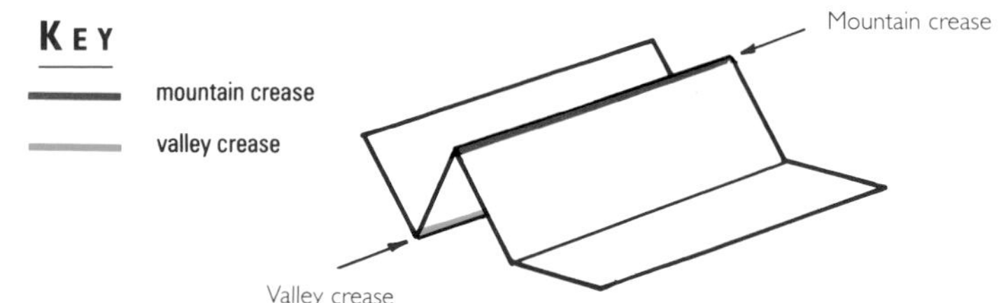

1 This is the basic "V" fold form. The glue tabs fold away from the "V".

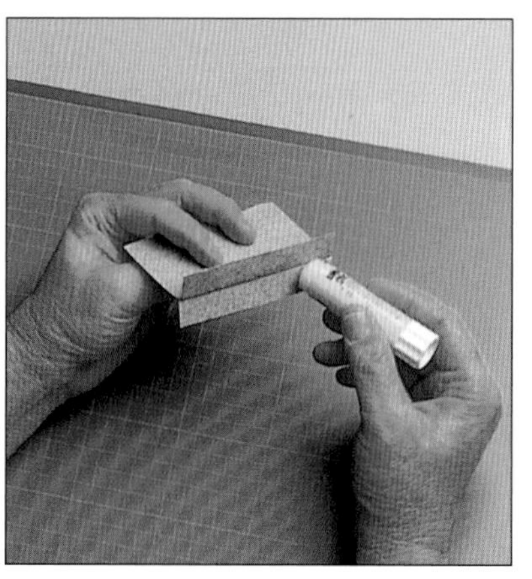

2 Apply glue to the undersides of both tabs.

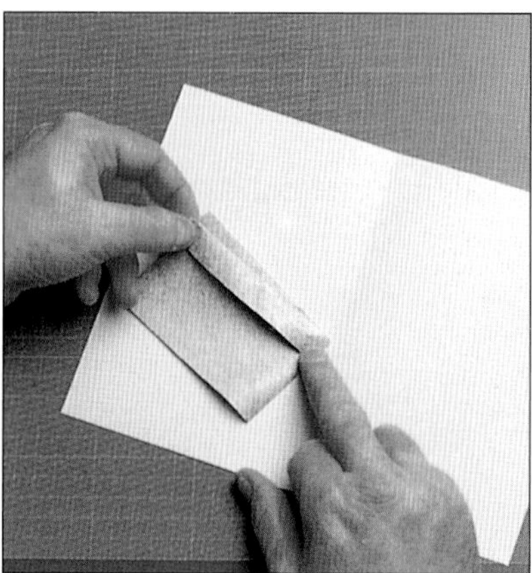

3 Glue one tab to the backing sheet in such a way that the point where the two tabs meet touches the crease on the backing sheet.

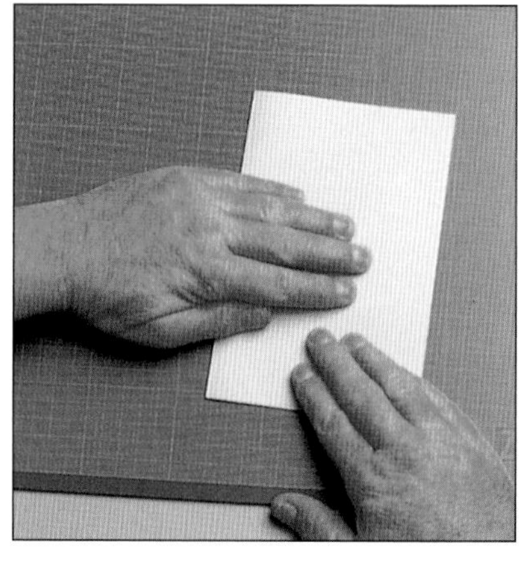

4 Fold the other half of the backing sheet over the top of the "V" fold, to glue itself to the upper tab.

5 Unfold the sheet to see the three-dimensional "V" fold. By following steps 1–4, the "V" fold is guaranteed to lie flat within the pop-up card.

Tab

Unlike the "V" fold technique, the tab *must be measured* before being constructed; otherwise, it will not collapse within the pop-up card when it is closed. Note that the construction technique is the same whether the tab is a separate piece of cardboard that is glued to the backing sheet in the correctly measured position or whether the tab is cut away from the backing sheet, as explained here.

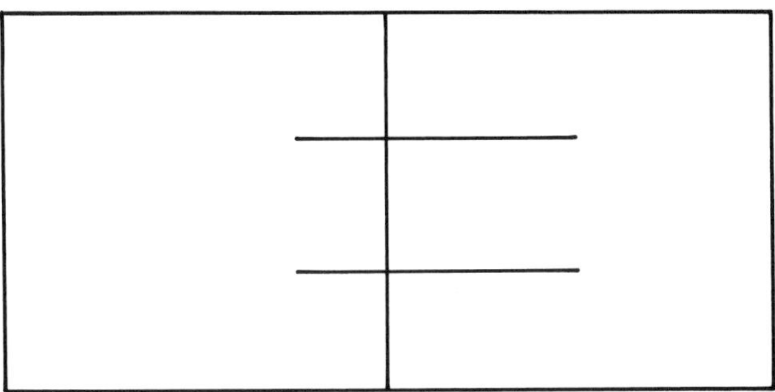

1 Draw the vertical crease on the backing sheet and draw two horizontal cuts (neither crease nor cut yet).

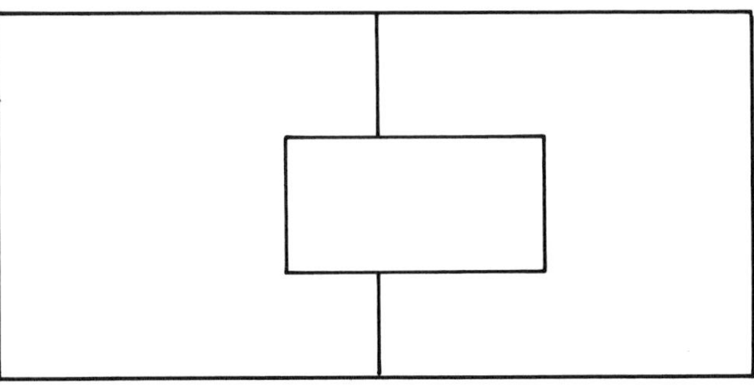

2 Erase the part of the crease between the two cuts. Draw two more vertical creases, parallel to the first (center) crease.

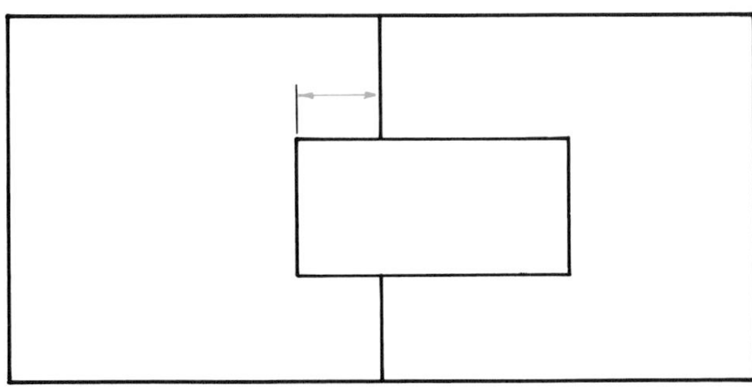

3 Measure AB, the distance between the central crease and the *nearer* end crease, here to the left.

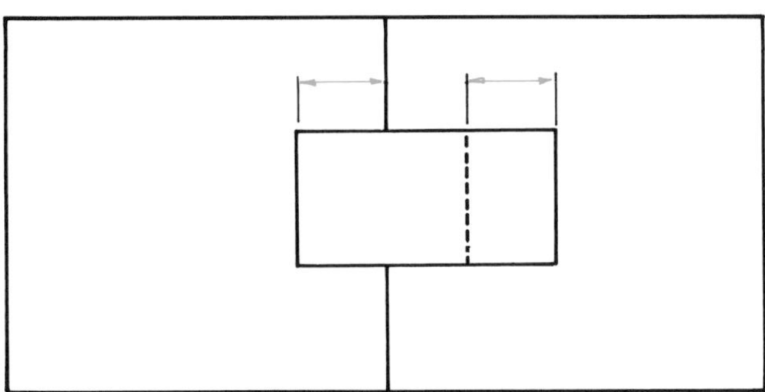

4 Reproduce that distance at the other end. This will locate the position of the mountain crease on the finished pop-up element. Draw in the crease.

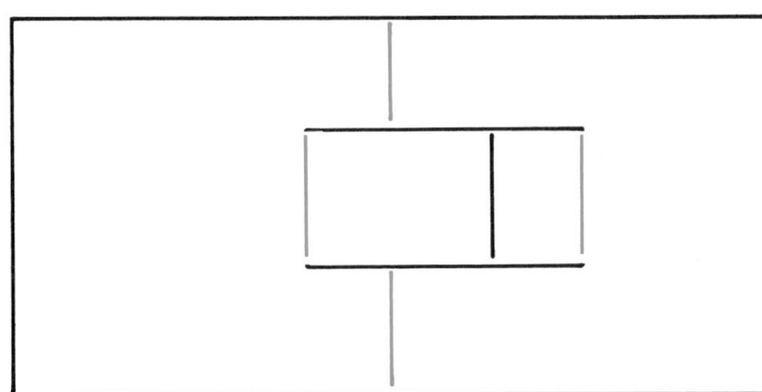

5 Only now, cut and crease your drawing, to create the perfect collapsible tab pop-up mechanism, with all the creases correctly placed.

6 The tab pop-up mechanism is complete. Note how in one the tab is glued to the backing sheet, while in the other, the tab is cut from the backing sheet.

HOW TO MAKE AN ENVELOPE

The pop-up cards in this book conform to no particular proportions when they are folded flat: some are almost square, whereas others are long and thin. All of this means that few will fit snugly into a standard, bought envelope.

One solution is to re-proportion the backing sheet so that the card *will* fit into a standard envelope, but this can pose tricky measurement problems.

Another solution is to make your own envelope. On these pages, two envelopes are suggested: a practical postal envelope and a decorative presentation envelope.

Postal Envelope

This is a version of the classic postal envelope that, carefully made, will hold a pop-up card securely when it is mailed. Use strong, medium-weight paper to make it.

Cut out the shape of the envelope as shown, changing the proportions to suit your card. Pay careful attention to the shapes of the four tabs, making sure that they overlap each other enough to allow adequate gluing. Use strong paper glue.

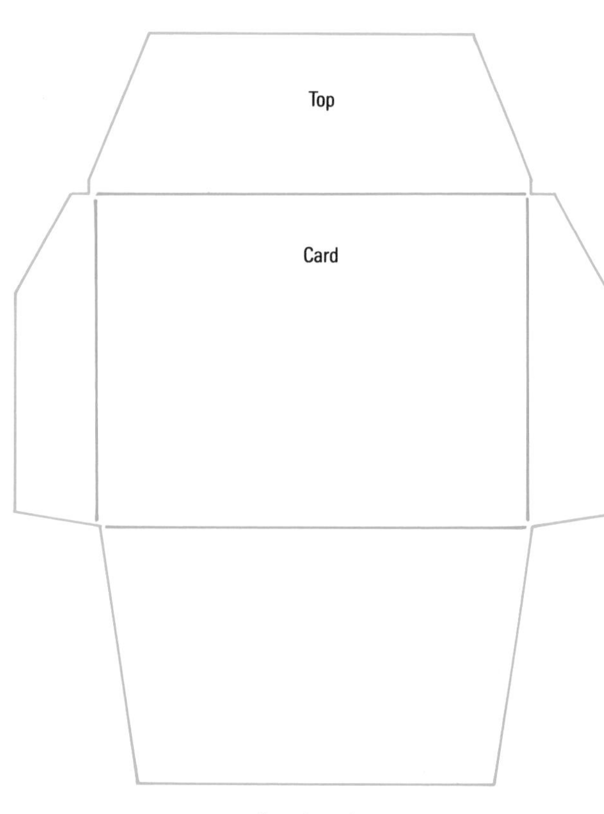

Postal envelope

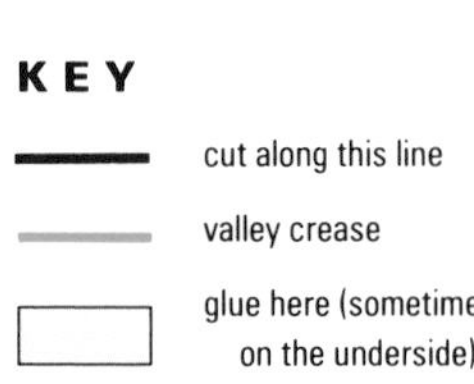

1 Fold in the side flaps.

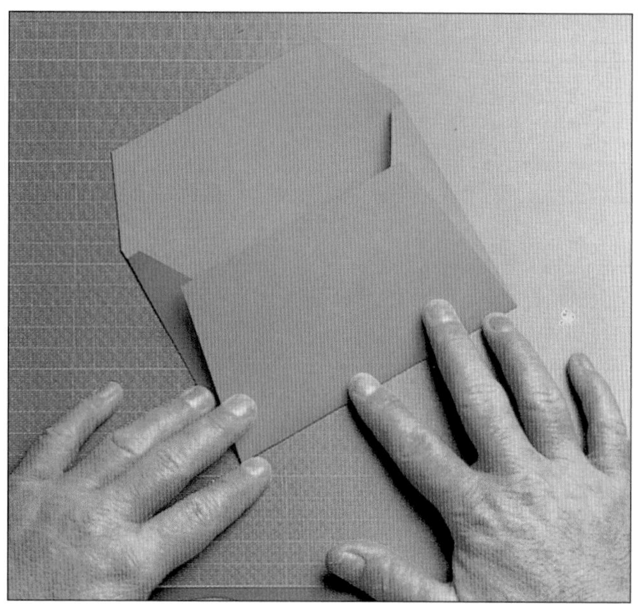

2 Fold up the bottom edge.

3 Open the bottom edge and apply glue to the side flaps underneath, where the bottom edge lies on top.

4 Insert your pop-up card.

5 Before mailing, apply glue to the top flap to close the envelope.

The completed envelope.

Presentation Envelope

How a card is presented is often as important as the card itself. To simply hand it over in a plain envelope can seem a little thoughtless, particularly if the occasion is an important one. So, here is an attractive and versatile way to make a presentation envelope.

1 In the middle of a piece of heavy paper, draw a line around the card, a little distance away from it (to compensate for the card's thickness).

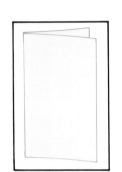

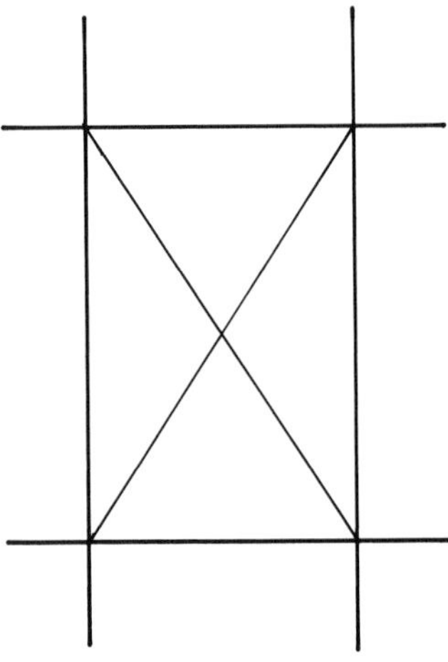

2 Remove the card and extend the horizontal and vertical lines on the inside of the card. Draw the diagonals to locate the center of the card.

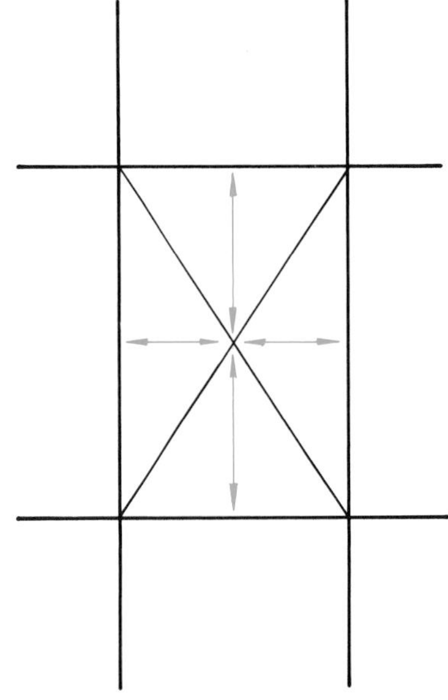

3 Measure the distances from the center point to the edges of the card outline.

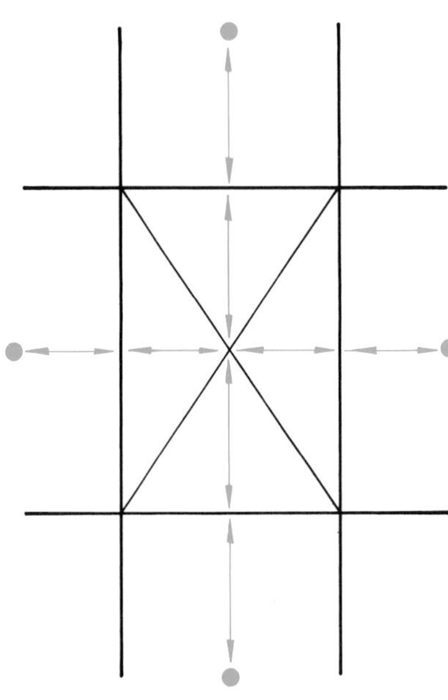

4 Reproduce these distances beyond the central rectangle. Mark the four points with dots. The location of the four outer dots is critical. From this point forward, the shapes of the locking flaps can change. Here is one suggestion.

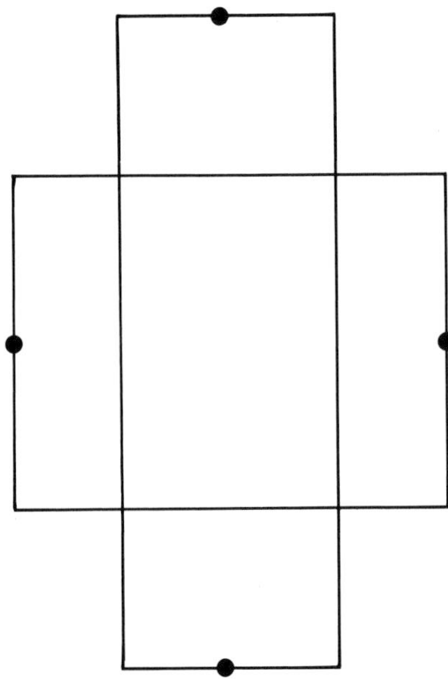

5 Draw rectangles passing through the outer dots. Keep the edges parallel and the corners square.

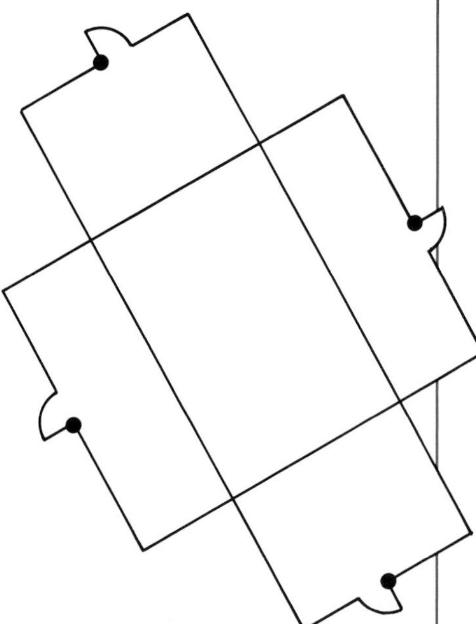

6 With a drawing compass, draw the shape of four quarter-circles, as shown, so that they protrude from the four rectangular flaps. Note that the center of each quarter-circle is one of the dots located in step 4, and that they lie to the *right* of each dot, moving clockwise. Cut out the complete shape.

7 Fold in one edge.

8 Fold in the next edge, moving counterclockwise.

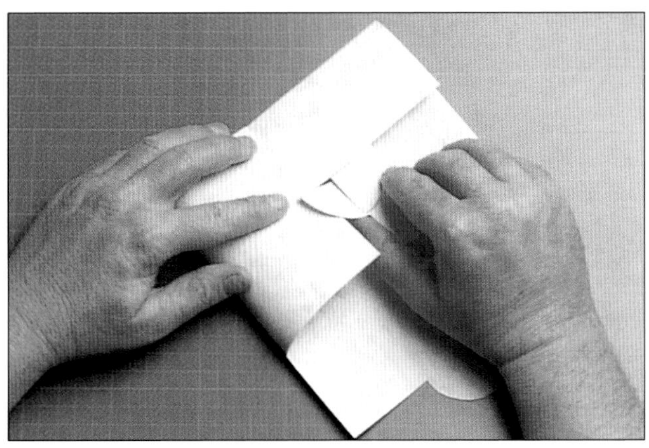

9 Fold in the third edge, tucking it under the quarter-circle opposite the first edge.

10 Fold in the fourth edge, folding it *over* the third and *under* the first.

The completed envelope. Note how the lock is symmetrical, no matter which edge was folded first.

HOW TO CONSTRUCT YOUR POP-UP CARD

The template drawings and the step-by-step photographic instructions for each pop-up project give most of the information you will need successfully to make any design in this section. However, although the designs are different, there are certain procedures that are common to all constructions, so here is a point-by-point check list that takes you through them. Please read it carefully and refer back to it when you are constructing particular projects later on.

The Template Drawings

The drawings of the separate pop-up pieces laid out on the template grids are correctly proportioned, one to another, but will need to be enlarged (unless you want to make a miniature pop-up card, of course!). This can be done in one of two ways. You can draw a grid of squares of the appropriate size on a sheet of scrap cardboard, then transfer the template drawings to it following the lines in each square. Alternatively, photocopy the template drawings from the book and enlarge them with further photocopies, then place a sheet of carbon paper between the photocopy and the cardboard and draw over the lines of the photocopy, carefully holding the paper in position as you do so.

The size of the backing sheet of the cards we made is given on the template grid. The dimensions are of the *open* backing sheet (not folded in half): the first dimension is of the edges bisected by the crease. In addition, an important measurement of a major pop-up piece is given, to relate its size to that of the backing sheet. The sizes of the other pop-up pieces can be gauged from this measurement. If you want to create a card that is larger or smaller than the one shown, the measurements of the backing sheet and the pop-up pieces must be adjusted *in proportion.*

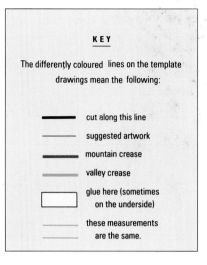

KEY

The differently coloured lines on the template drawings mean the following:

- cut along this line
- suggested artwork
- mountain crease
- valley crease
- glue here (sometimes on the underside)
- these measurements are the same.

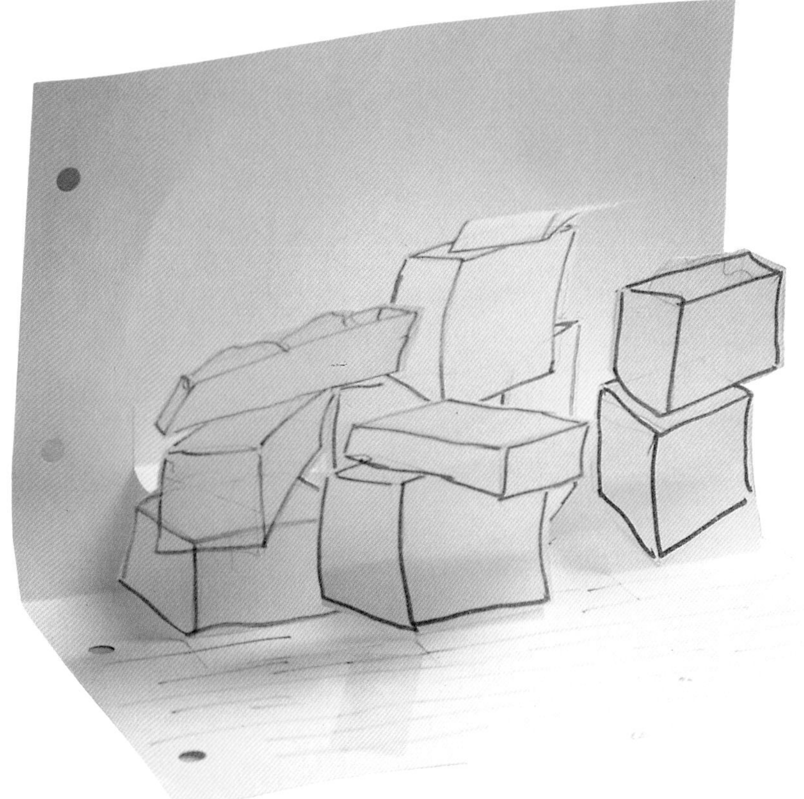

First, make a Rough Card

It is always tempting to rush straight into making a finished pop-up card, but, unless you are experienced and feel that you fully understand the construction techniques, you are *strongly* advised to *first* make a rough card.

Many people – for some reason – become embarrassed at the thought of making a rough, perhaps because it seems a little childish or as though they have failed before they have begun. However, even professionals begin this way. They recognize that, by solving all the problems and understanding the inevitable idiosyncracies of a design before the final version is made, both time and materials are saved.

Your rough can be as rough as you wish – nobody will see it. Make it from scrap paper or cardboard and include only the necessary elements. Practice decoration techniques, too, so you can see what will work and what won't.

Materials
The "Materials" boxes at the beginning of each project show what materials were used in the step-by-step sequences. However, it must be stressed that these materials *are only a suggestion*. In particular, the weights of paper and cardboard may change from those suggested, according to what is on hand. Remember, though, that as a general rule, the backing sheet should be stiff: if a decorative surface is required, attractive paper or thin board can be glued to stiff mat board.

The decorating techniques and media (colored pencils, felt tip pens, etc.) are also only a suggestion. You are strongly encouraged to use media of your own choice.

Decorating the Card
When your rough card has been completed, you can then make your finished version. If the pieces of card are to be decorated, the decoration must be done *before* the pop-up elements are assembled. Whether this is done before or after each piece has been cut away from a larger sheet is a matter of personal choice.

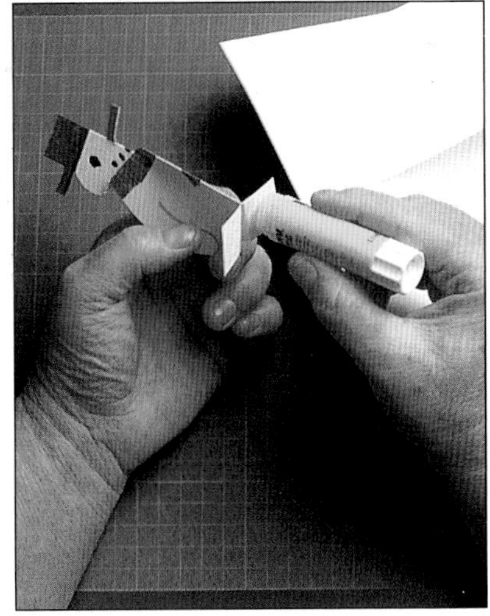

Gluing the Card
Always use glue sparingly. If it seeps out from beneath a tab, the whole pop-up mechanism will stick together when it is folded shut, spoiling all your careful work.

Never use glues that bond instantly or double-sided tape, as you may want to slide the newly glued piece around a little, to enable the card to fold neatly shut. Instead, use a good-quality paper glue, preferably with a nozzle, so that you can direct the flow. Squeeze-out glues are good, but can be messy.

Assembling the Card
Assemble each card piece by piece, in the order suggested by the text. Work carefully: pop-up designs are geometric structures that do not work if they are assembled incorrectly. Test each piece for shape and size before gluing it into position.

Opening a 180° Card Completely Flat
A card that is meant to open completely flat will not do so if the crease on the backing sheet is scored (if the board is heavy) or folded by hand (if the board is light). The card must be cut into two halves along the crease, then the pieces joined back together again so that they will lie flat.

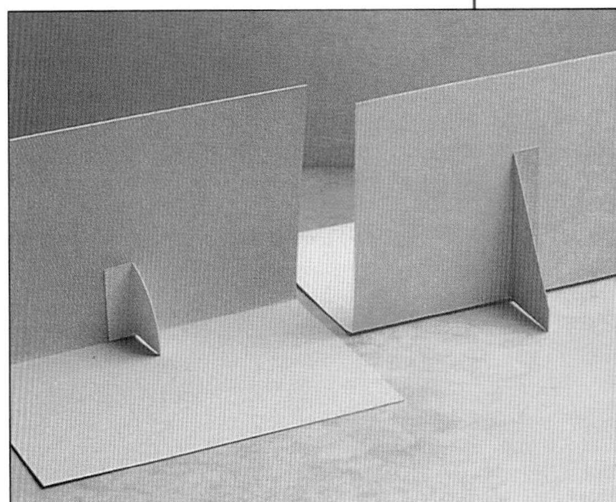

Stabilizing a 90° Card
When complete, some cards that open up to 90° (instead of opening flat to 180°) have the irritating habit of wanting either to close up or open out more than intended, spoiling the design. To stabilize such a card, it may be necessary to add a wing – to the front (if the card wants to close up) or to the back (if the card wants to open out). These wings can be cut from the backing sheet, or separate pieces may be glued on. For symmetrical stability, two wings may be needed near the left and right edges of the card.

FESTIVE FIR

★★★★

The pop-up design here may seem simple, but take care with it as the construction needs to be very precise in order for it to work well. In particular, attention must be paid to how the base of the tree pieces glue to the inside of the tub, as the measurements and creasing need to be done accurately. You will know when you have got it right because the tree will open gracefully.

MATERIALS

Backing sheet: thin orange cardboard glued to mounting mat board

Tree and tub: green and brown thick paper

SIZES

Backing sheet: 14½ x 12¾ inches

Height of tree: 7½ inches

Scale of grid: 1:2.5

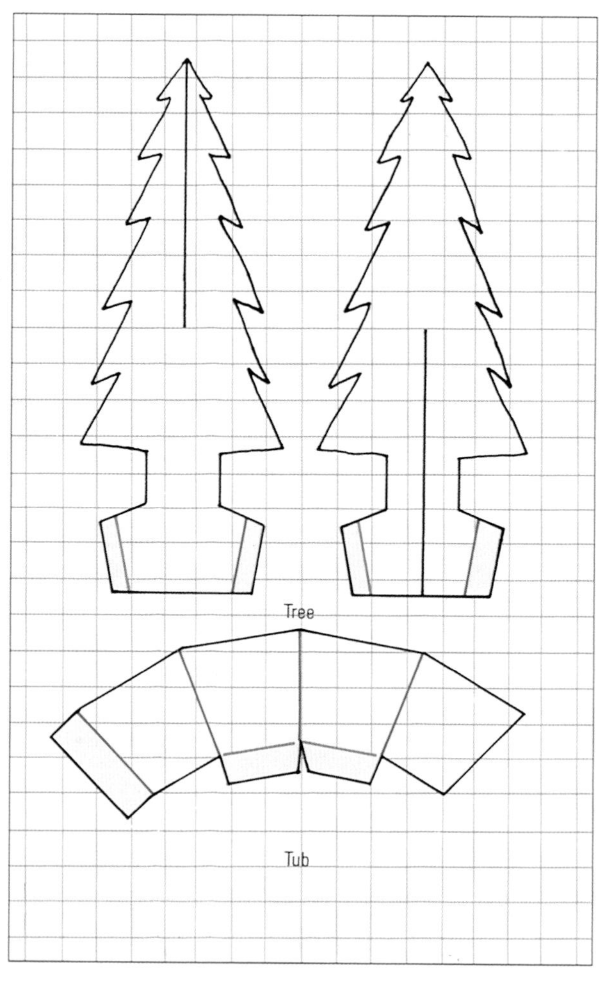

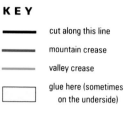

KEY

cut along this line

mountain crease

valley crease

glue here (sometimes on the underside)

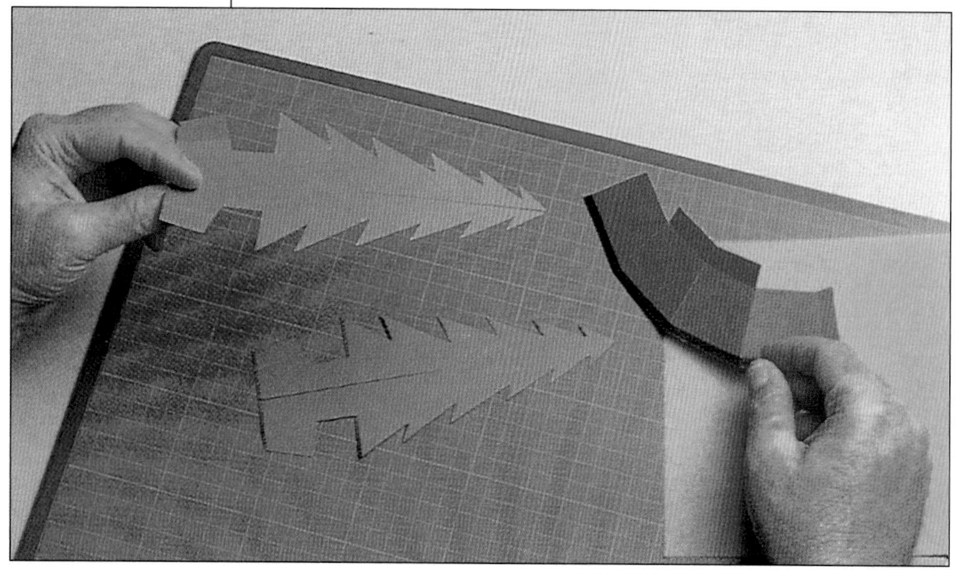

1 Note the differently placed slits on the two tree halves.

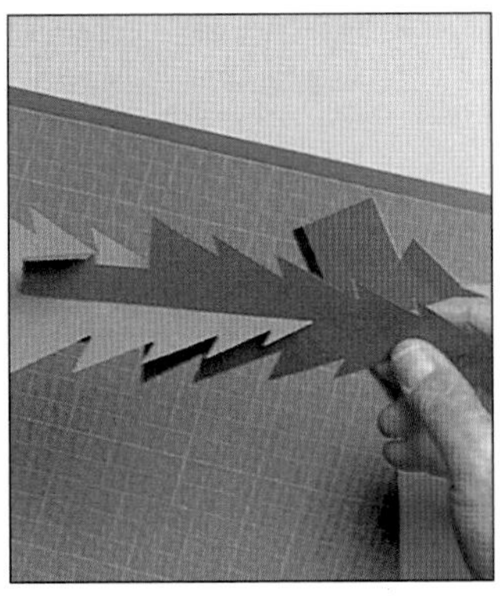

2 Interlock the slits.

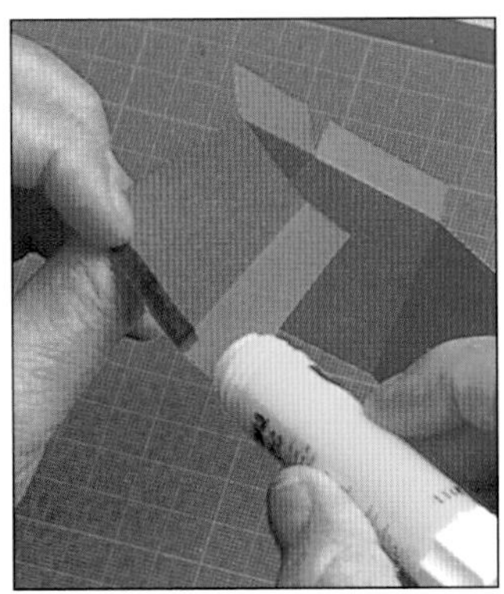

3 Apply glue to the end tab on the tub, then form the square tub.

4 Apply glue to the four tabs at the base of the tree.

5 Glue the tree tabs to the inside of the tub so that the crease on each tree tab lies exactly down the centre of each tub face.

6 Apply glue to the underside of the tub tabs, then glue the tabs to the backing sheet using the "V" fold technique (see page 90).

7 Though very three-dimensional, the tub and tree will easily collapse flat when the card is closed.

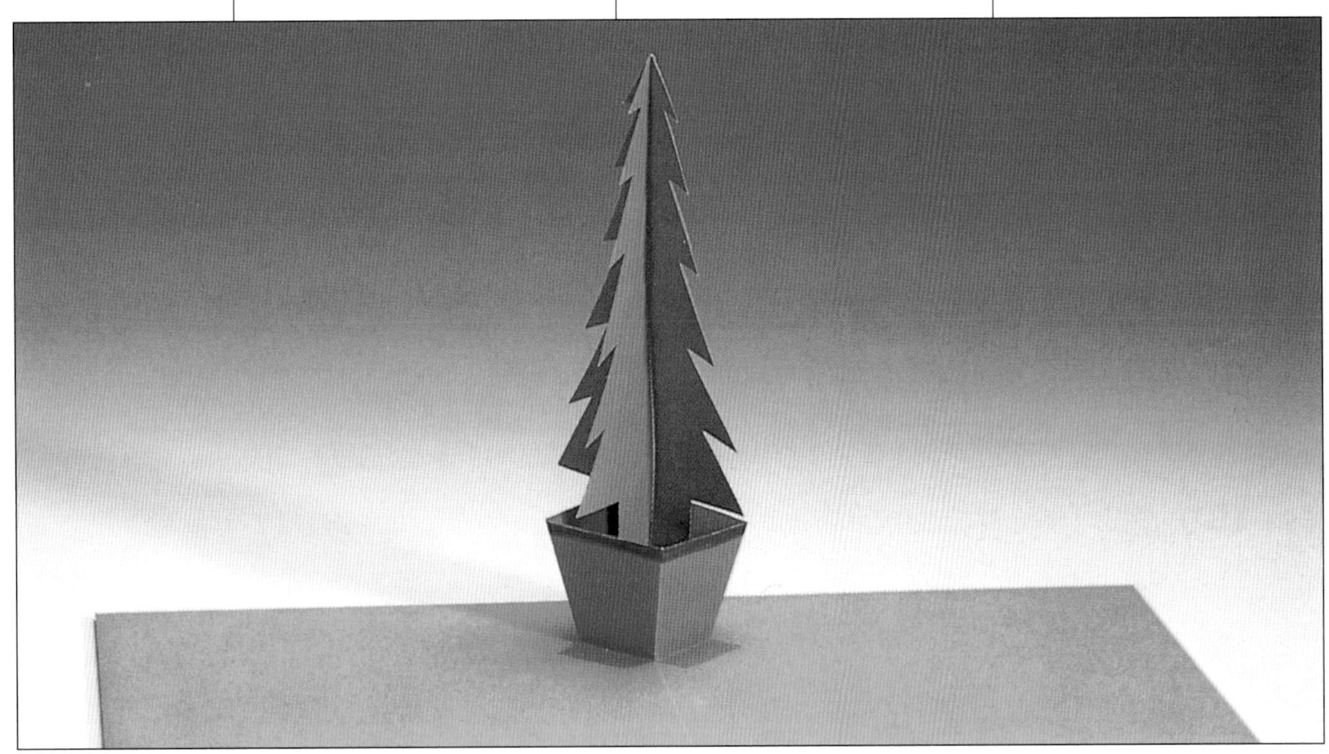

PRESENT PERFECT

★★★

Pop-up boxes are particularly pleasing to make because, unlike other techniques, they fully enclose a space to create a real sense of volume. The lid pieces need to be accurately cut so that the top closes completely.

MATERIALS

Backing sheet: thin textured gray cardboard glued to mat board

Box and ribbons: yellow and red thick paper

SIZES

Backing sheet: 11 x 6½ inches

Length of box: 9½ inches

Scale of grid: 1:2

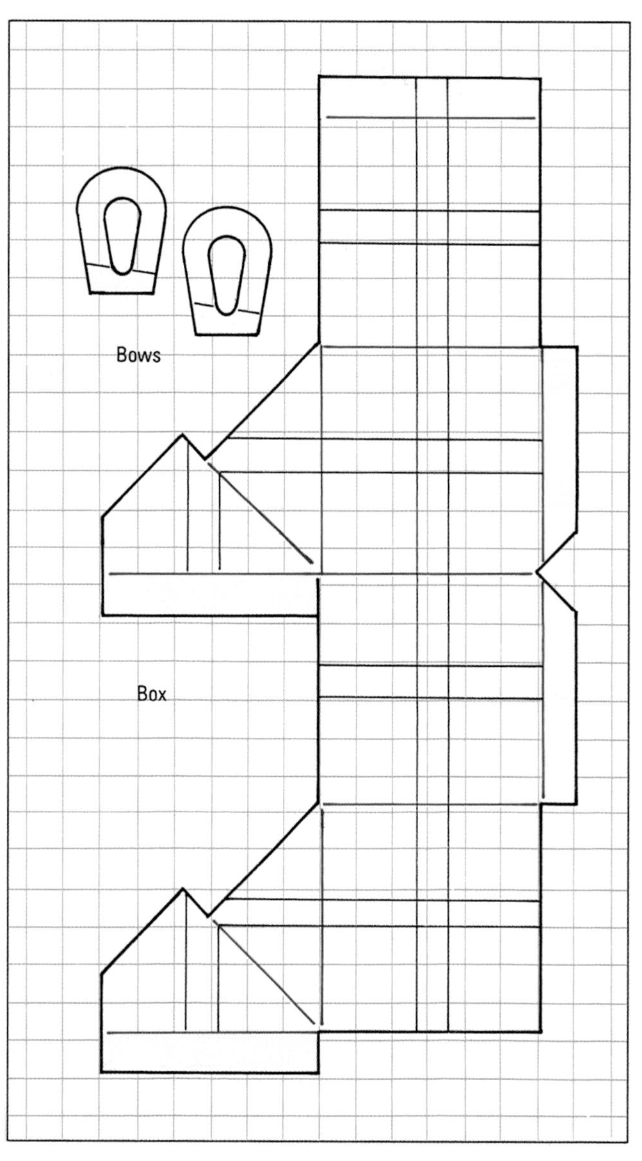

KEY

cut along this line

mountain crease

glue here (sometimes on the underside)

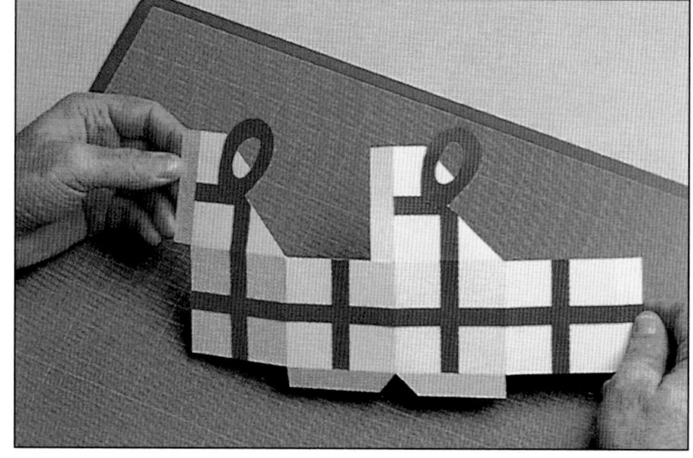

1 Apply glue to the underside of the bows, position on the box, and glue in place. Crease as shown.

2 Apply glue to the end tab.

3 Make a square "tube."

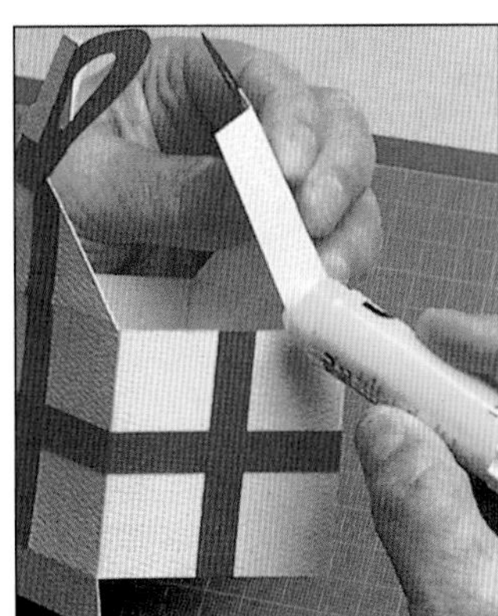

4 Apply glue to each lid tab in turn. The photograph shows the *outer* face of a tab being glued, so that the tab lies inside the box. However, if the *inner* face is glued, so that the tab lies outside the box, the pop-up has more strength and will not burst. the disadvantage, though, is that the tab will be seen, so decide which is best for your card.

5 Glue the underside of the tabs at the base of the box. Note that the tabs are folded inward.

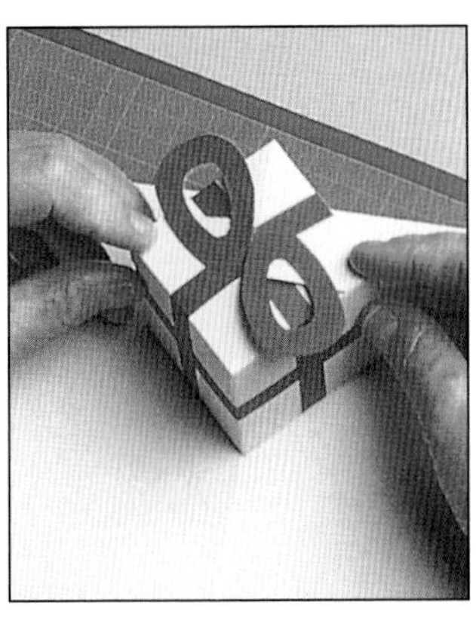

6 Glue the box to the backing sheet, using the "V" fold technique (see page 90).

7 This shows how the pop-up box closes. Note how the lid pieces separate.

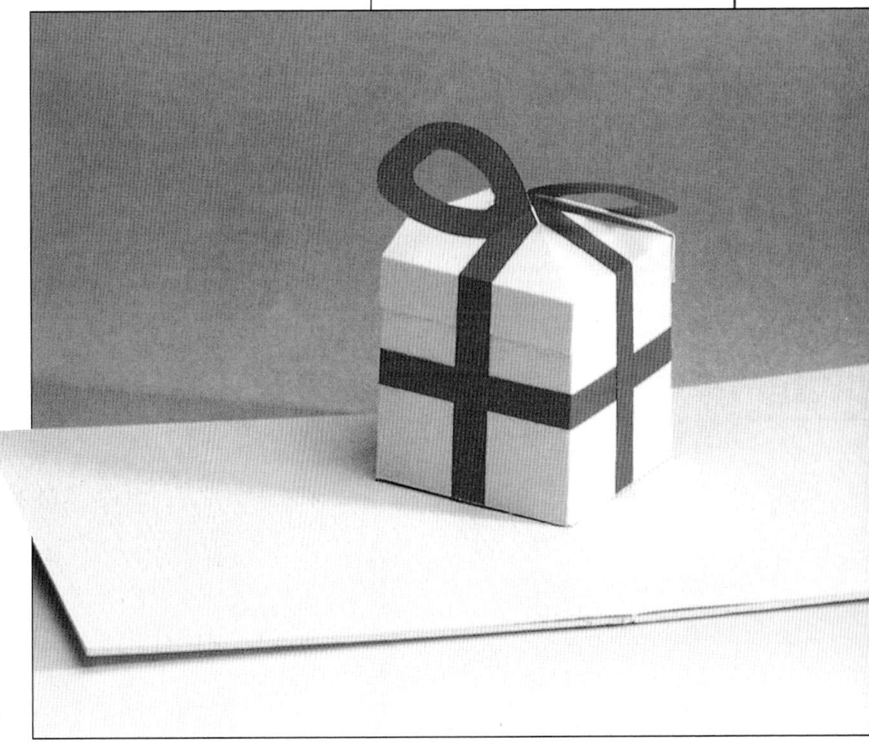

FOR AULD LANG SYNE ...

★★

In this simple but lovely pop-up card, most of the central crease between the two figures has been cut away to create an open construction. Note how a small cut beneath the clock prevents an unsightly crease running through its face and how the feet are cut to point forward.

MATERIALS

Backing sheet: thin red cardboard

Figures and background: thin white cardboard

Felt tip pens

SIZES

Backing sheet: 9 x 6½ inches

Height of background: 5 inches

Scale of grid: 1:2.5

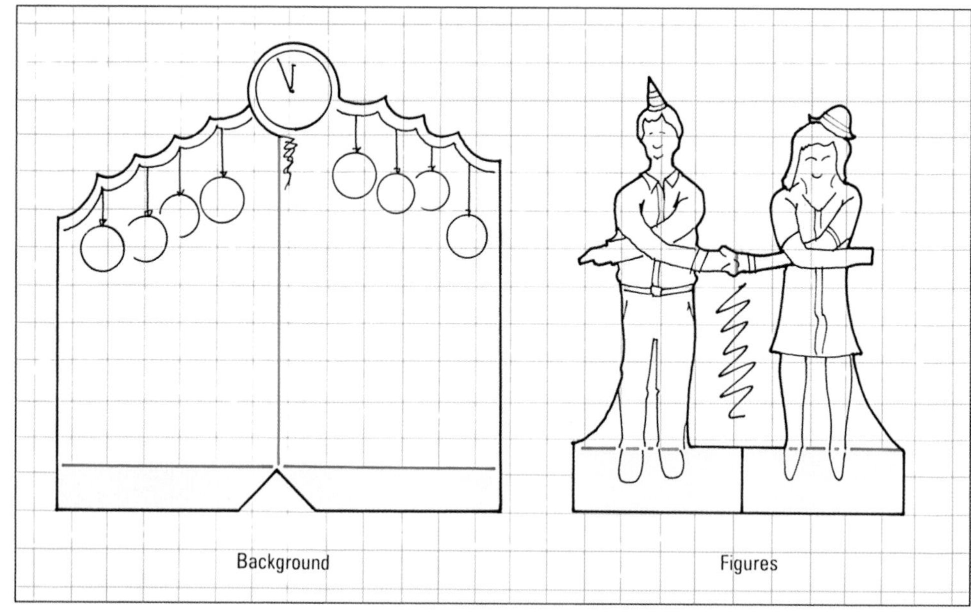

KEY

- cut along this line
- suggested artwork
- mountain crease
- valley crease
- glue here (sometimes on the underside)

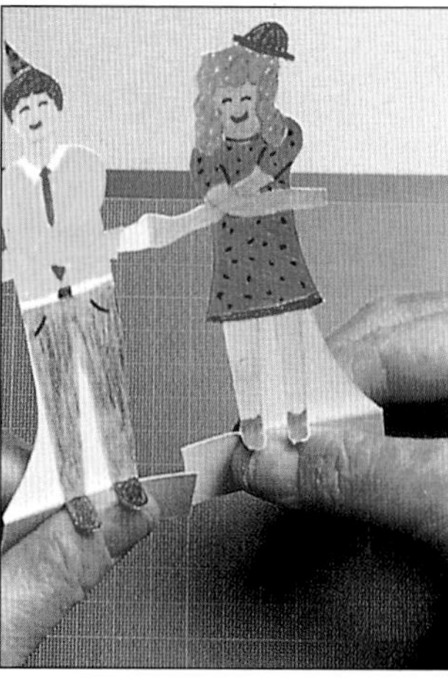

1 Separate the feet from the remainder of the tabs, so that they point in the opposite direction.

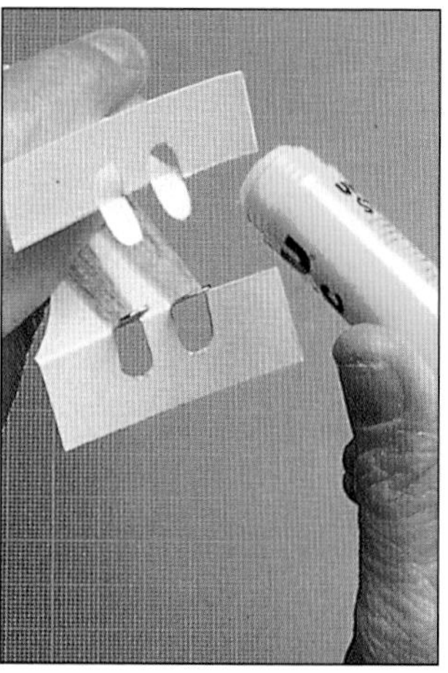

2 Apply glue to the tabs and feet.

Be Creative

Unlike other cards in this section that use the "V" fold technique, this card has the pop-up design falling backward, not forward, when it is closed because the "V" fold crease is at the back of the construction. In display terms, this gives the design a great advantage: the figures are at the front of the card, not the back. When designing your own cards, try to invert the "V" fold as here, so that the pop-up shape does not sit at the back of the card.

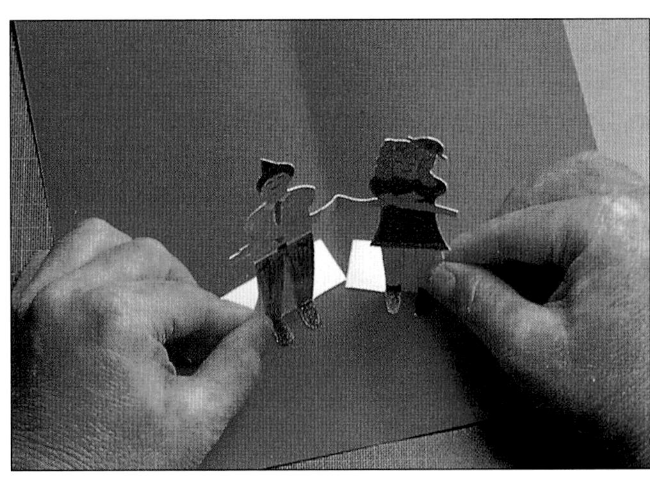

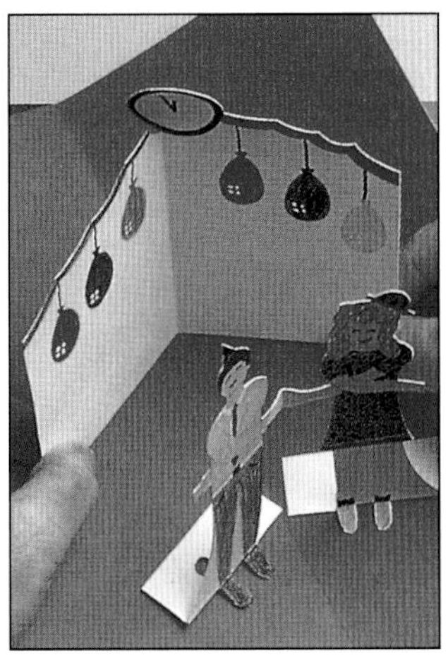

4 Similarly, glue the background to the backing sheet as a negative "V" fold.

3 Glue the feet and tabs to the backing sheet, using the "V" fold technique (see page 90). However, note that the figures form a negative "V" shape, so that they point toward each other across the fold.

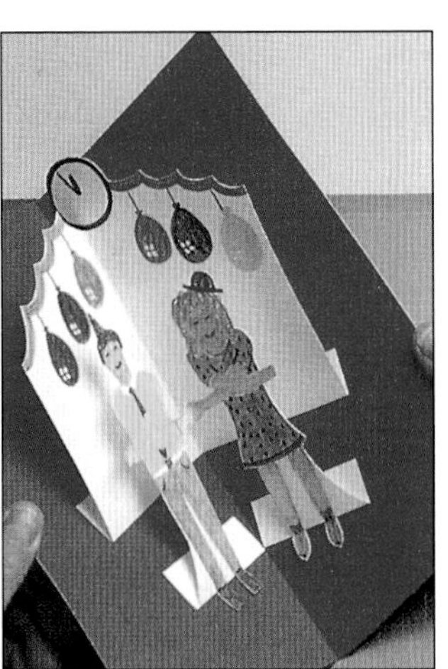

5 Note how when the card is folded shut, the pop-up collapses backward.

TOAST IN THE NEW YEAR

★★

At first glance, this is a simple pop-up of a New Year cocktail. A closer look reveals the slice of lemon to be a clock face with the hands approaching midnight!

MATERIALS

Backing sheet: thick watercolor paper

Cocktail: thick watercolor paper

Colored pencils

SIZES

Backing sheet: 16 x 11½ inches

Height of cocktail: 5½ inches

Scale of grid: 1:2

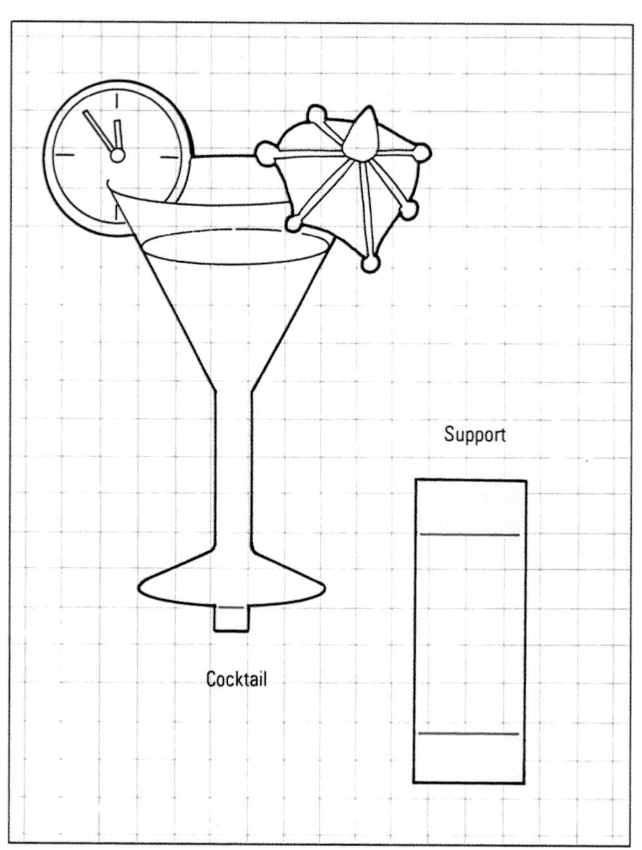

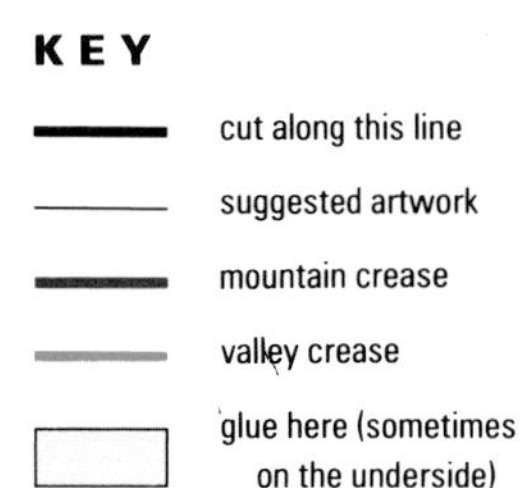

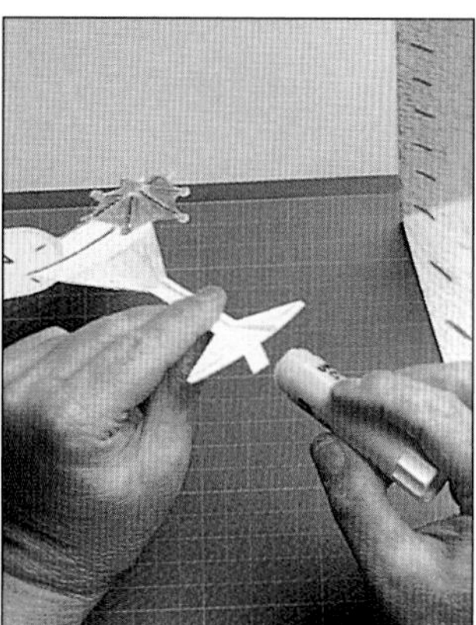

1. Apply glue to the tab at the base of the glass.

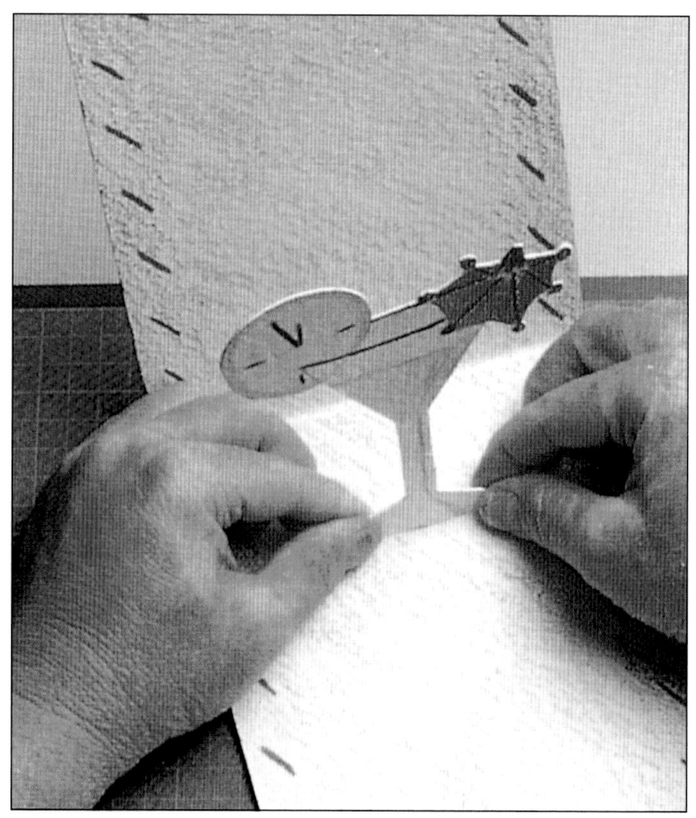

2. Glue the tab to the backing sheet.

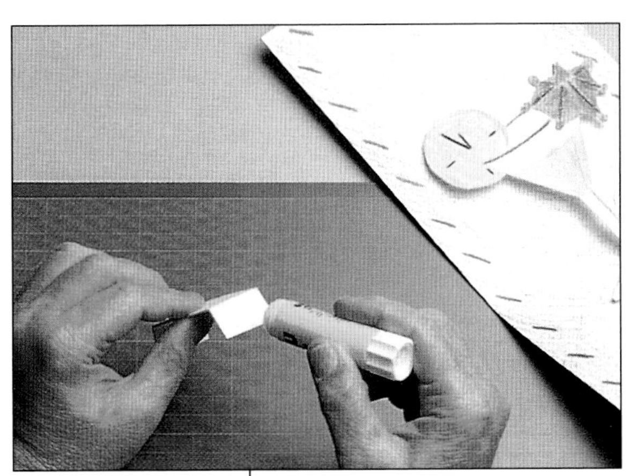

3 Apply glue to both ends of the supporting tab.

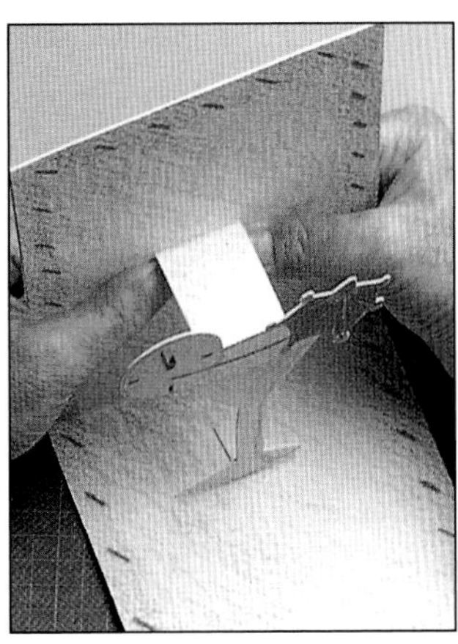

4 Glue the tab to the glass and backing sheet, using the tab technique (see page 91).

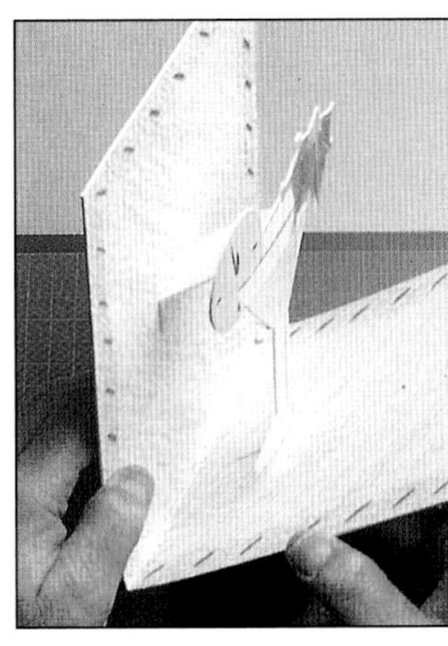

5 The pop-up mechanism is now complete. Note the way that the glass collapses forward when the card is shut.

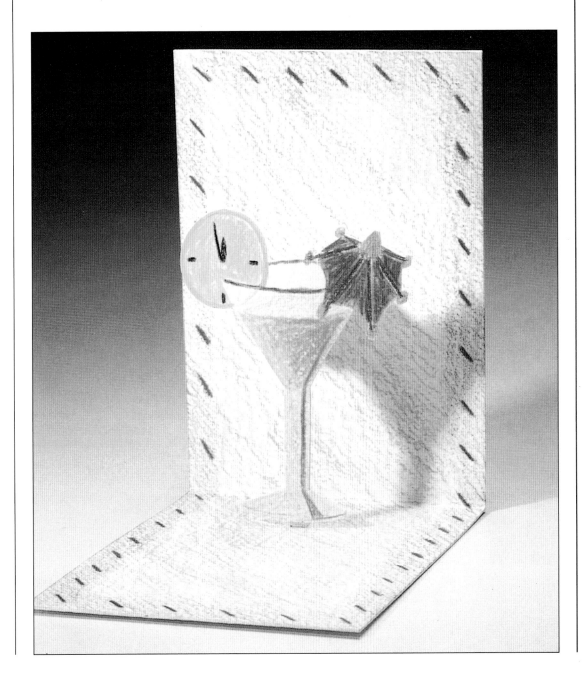

FOR THE UNDER 10s

★★★

Like the Light the Candle card later in this section, the design uses a single piece of cardboard and the same cutaway technique to make part of the pop-up stand freely (in this case, the top half of the number). When making the card, measure the distances carefully so that the number is well proportioned and placed well.

MATERIALS

Medium-weight blue paper

Yellow circle stickers

Colored pencils

SIZES

Sheet size:
12¾ x 6 inches

Scale of grid: 1:2.5

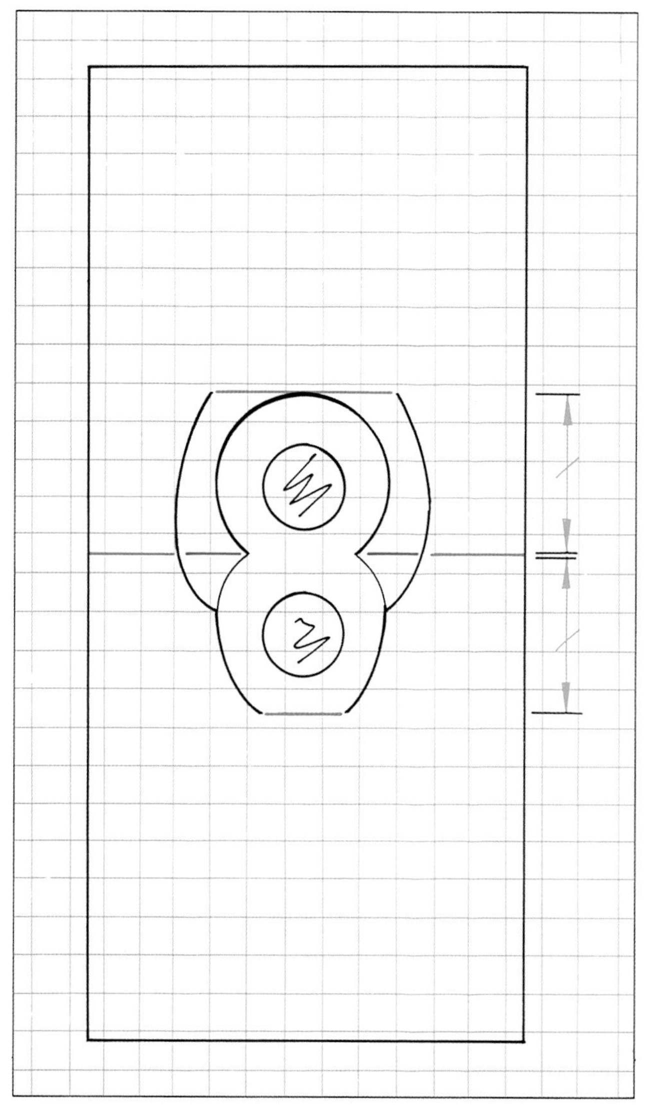

KEY

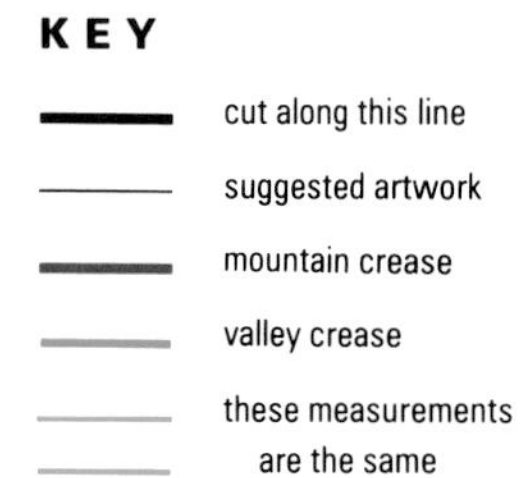

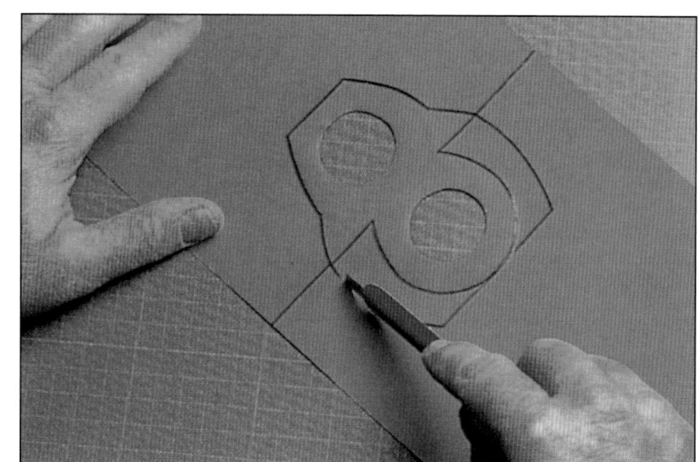

1 Cut along the solid lines shown on the template drawing.

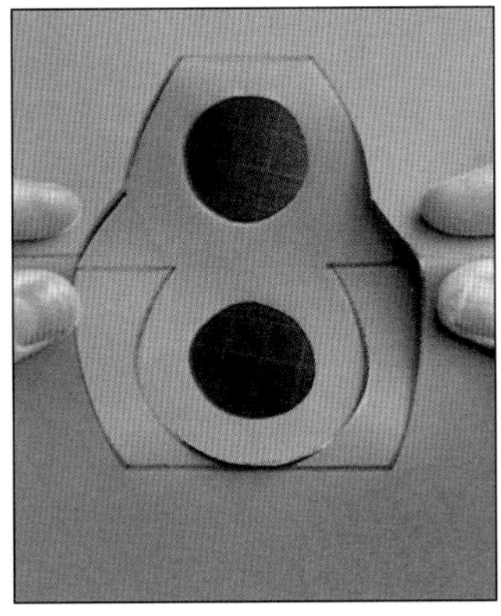

2 Fold the two ends of the central crease.

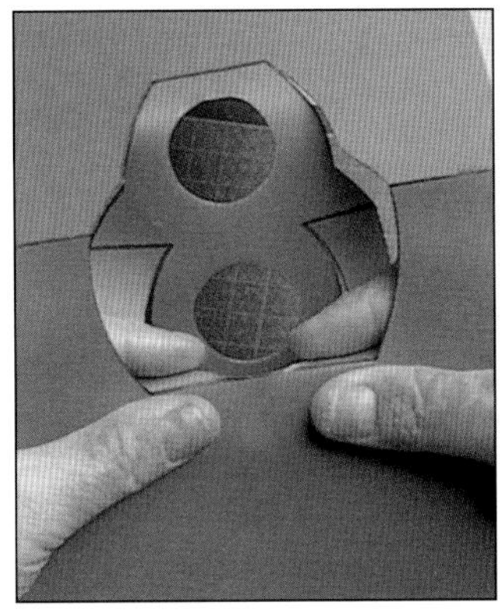

3 Fold the bottom crease.

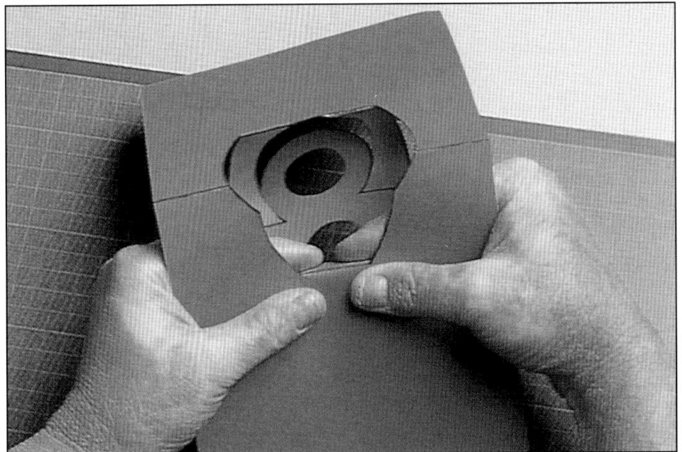

4 Then fold along the top one. Turn the card over.

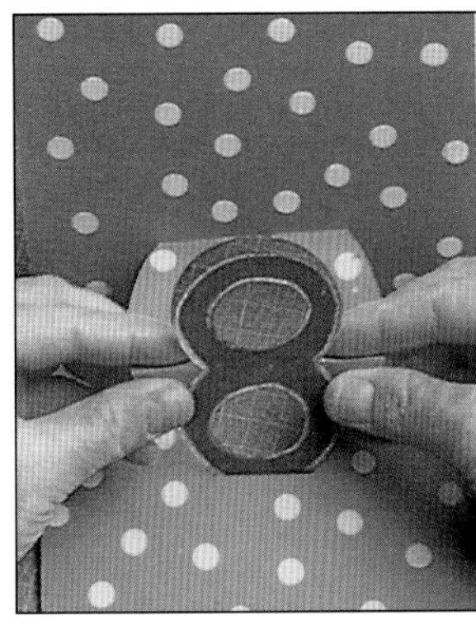

5 Finally, fold the remaining short central creases each side of the number.

6 This is the completed pop-up shape, which will fold flat.

COMING OF AGE

★★

An X shape connects the pop-up numbers to the backing sheet, and it opens and closes with a scissor action. The angle of the X can be altered if you want to present the numbers more closed up or not standing out as far from the backing sheet.

MATERIALS

Backing sheet: pink foil glued to mat board

Supports: thick gold cardboard

Numerals: thin green cardboard

SIZES

Backing sheet: 16¾ x 5 inches

Scale of grid: 1:2

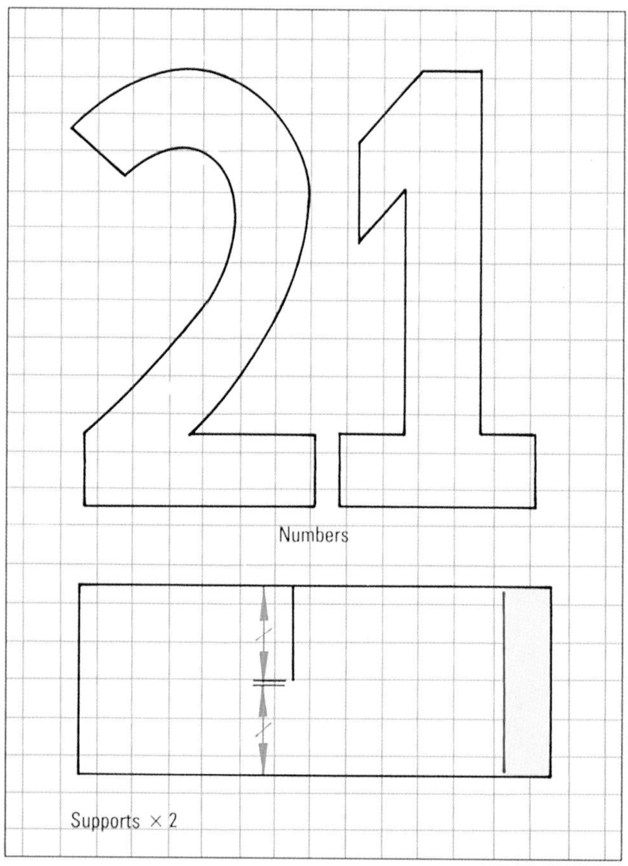

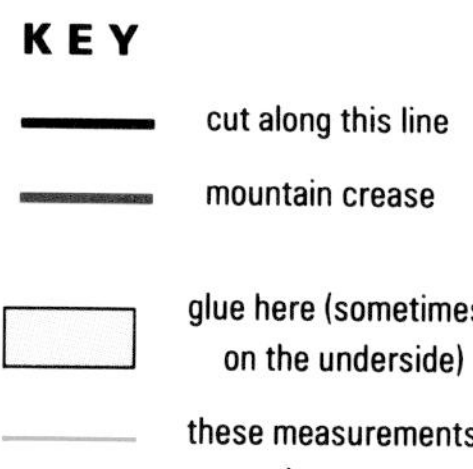

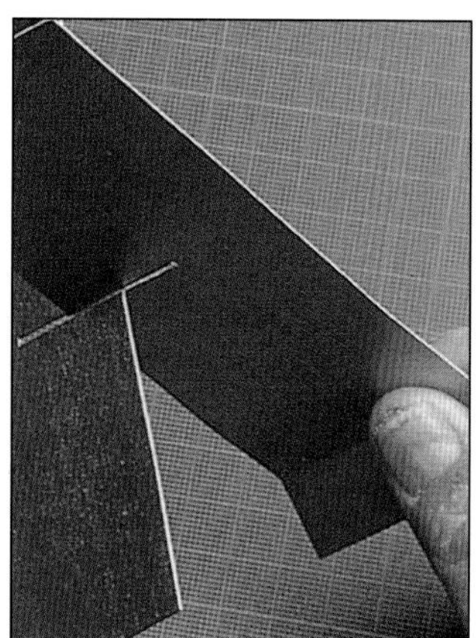

❶ Slot together the two supports.

❷ They will fit together like this.

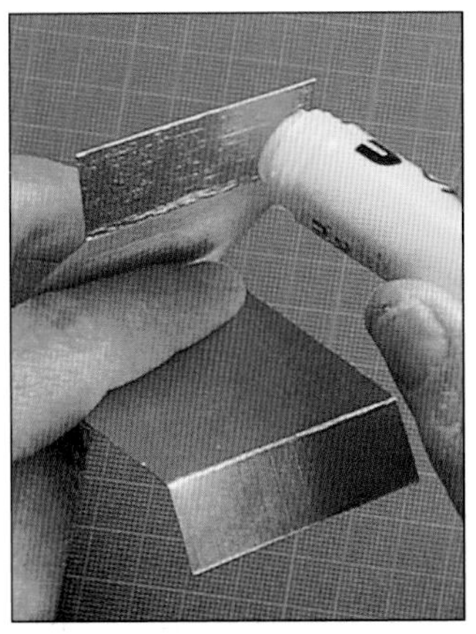

3 Apply glue to the tabs.

4 Glue the tabs to the backing sheet, each the same distance on each side of the central crease.

5 Glue the "2" to the left-hand support.

6 Similarly, glue the "1" to the right-hand support.

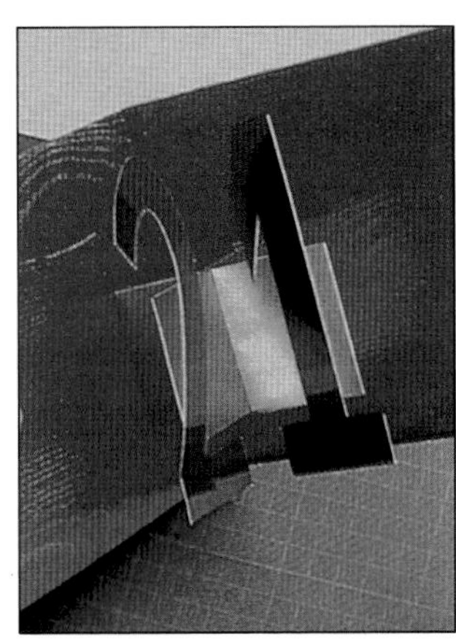

The pop-up element is now complete. Note how the supports display the numbers prominently.

MATERIALS

Backing sheet: thick mirror cardboard

Cake: thin white cardboard

felt tip pens

SIZES

Backing sheet: 10¼ x 6½ inches

Length of cake crease: 4½ inches

Scale of grid: 1:2

★★

This design is really like half of the box used in the Present Perfect card on pages 100–101, or a basic "V" fold with the top lidded over. Although there are seemingly many different pop-up techniques, they are often simply combinations of two or more basic techniques.

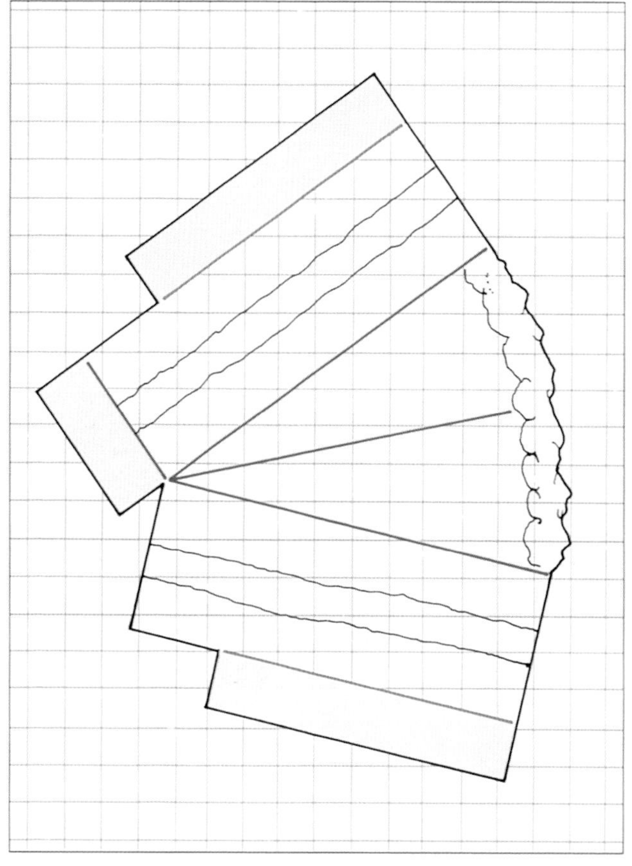

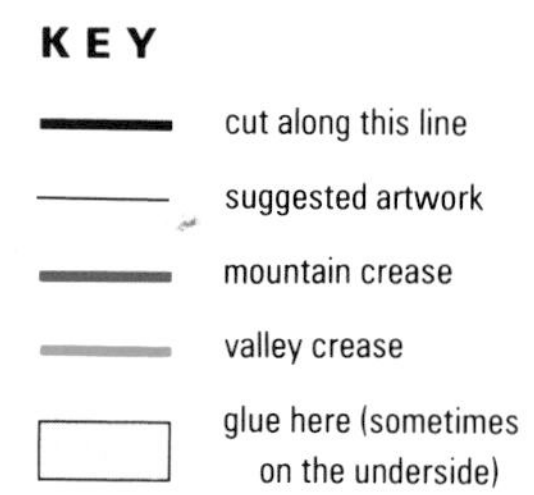

1 Cut the two slits in the backing sheet.

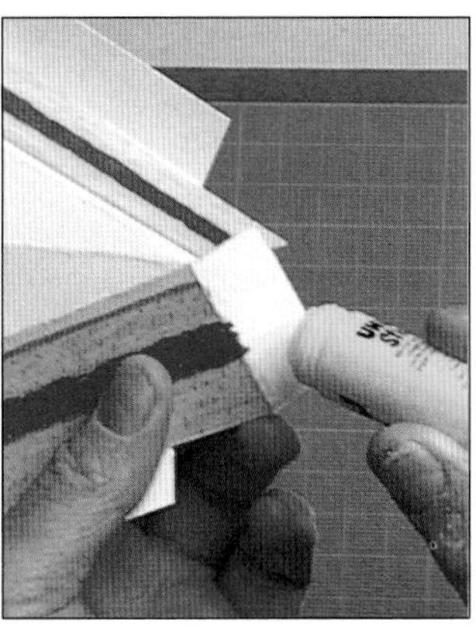

2 Fold the cake along the lines and glue the tab on the point of the cake wedge to make the cake three-dimensional.

3 Push the tabs along the bottom of the cake through the slits.

4 They should fit through them like this.

5 Tape the tabs flat on the reverse of the backing sheet.

The cake complete. Reflective cardboard will make this slice of cake appear to be many!

LIGHT THE CANDLE

★★

One-piece pop-ups are always satisfying to make because you see a three-dimensional shape magically emerge from what was a flat piece of cardboard. The geometry, though, can sometimes be a little mystifying. The key is to measure the placement of all the creases carefully and to understand which distances are equal to other distances. Nothing is arbitrary.

MATERIALS

Thin cardboard

Colored pencils

SIZES

Sheet size:
13½ x 6 inches

Scale of grid: 1:2.5

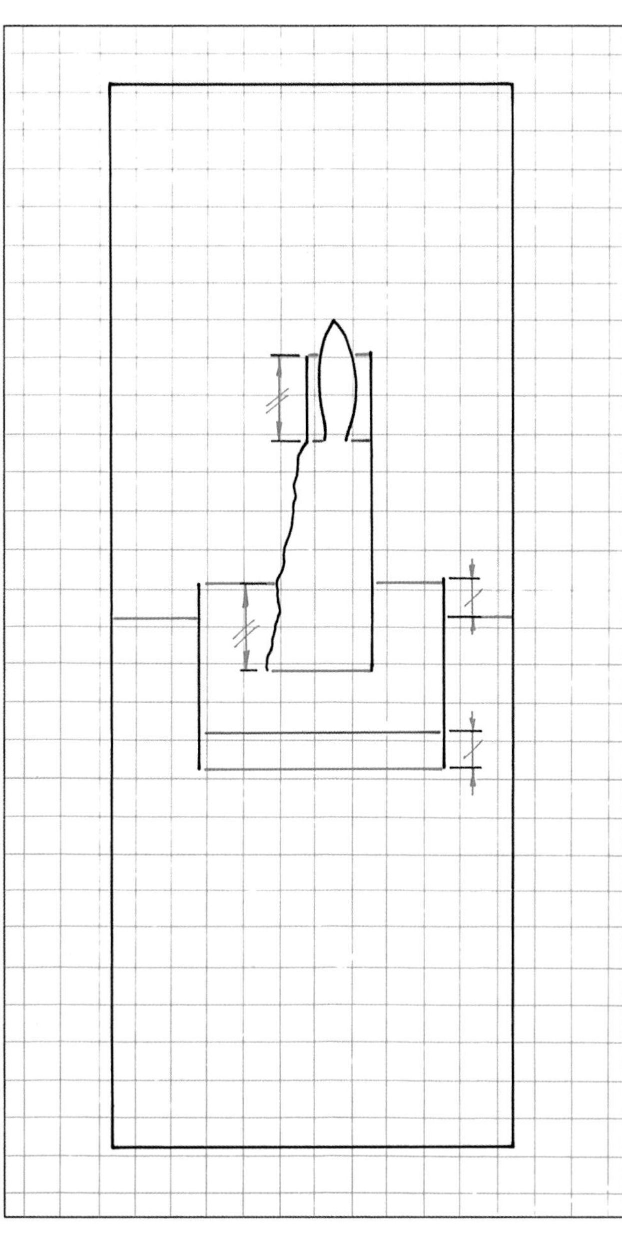

KEY

- cut along this line
- mountain crease
- valley crease
- these measurements are the same

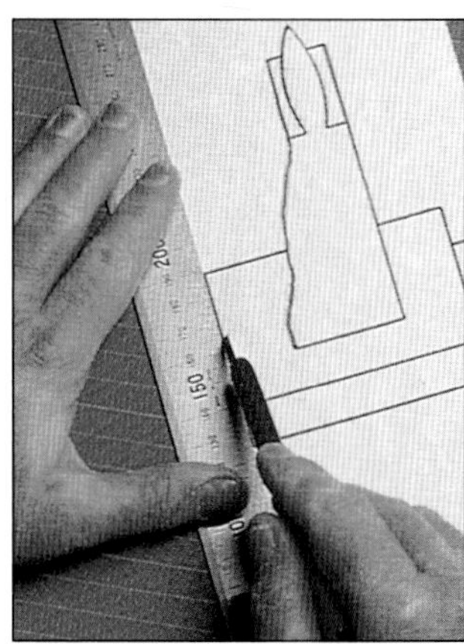

1 Cut along the thick lines shown on the template drawing.

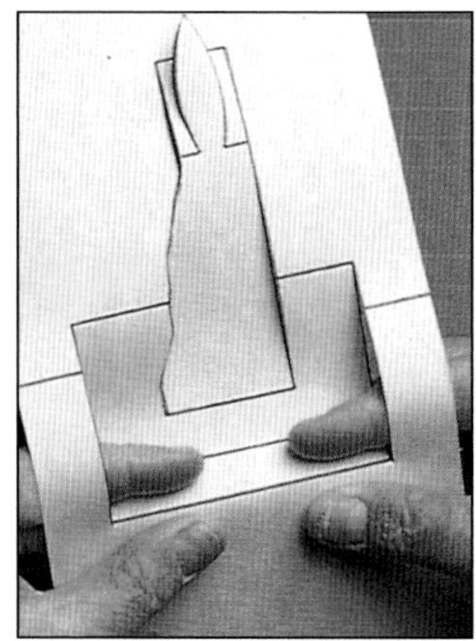

2 Fold the long bottom crease.

For Best Results . . .

Before making a finished card, make a rough card first so you can understand which measurements should be equal.

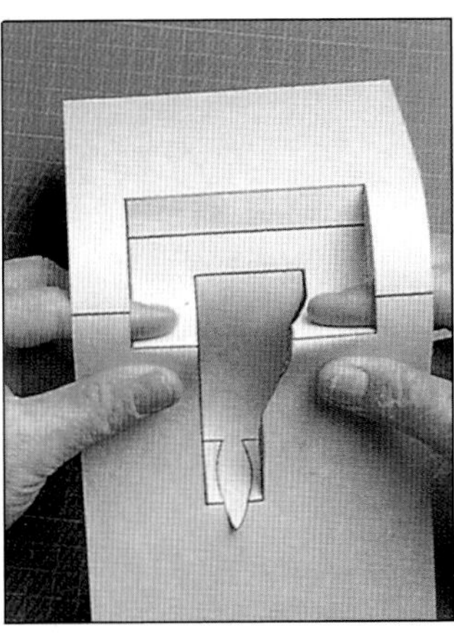

③ Then fold the creases to each side of the candle. Turn over.

④ Fold the creases around the flame.

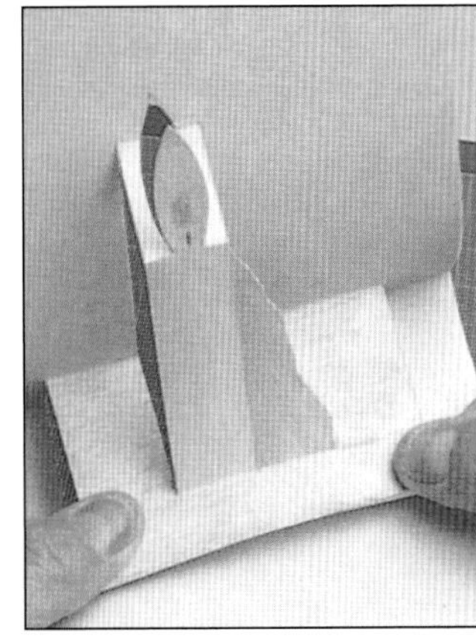

⑤ Fold the front edge of the step.

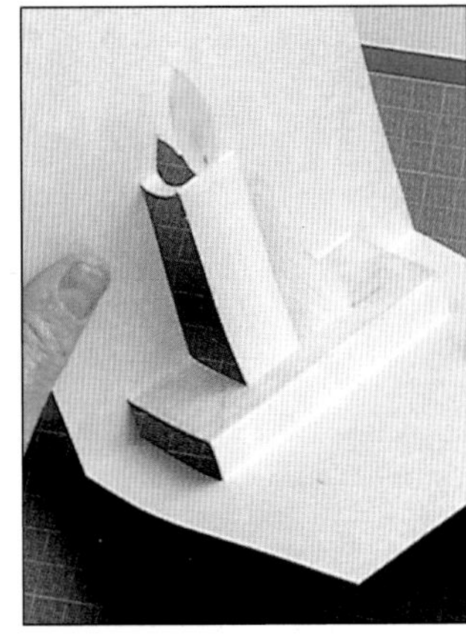

The completed pop-up card. Careful measuring and creasing will permit the candle to fold flat.

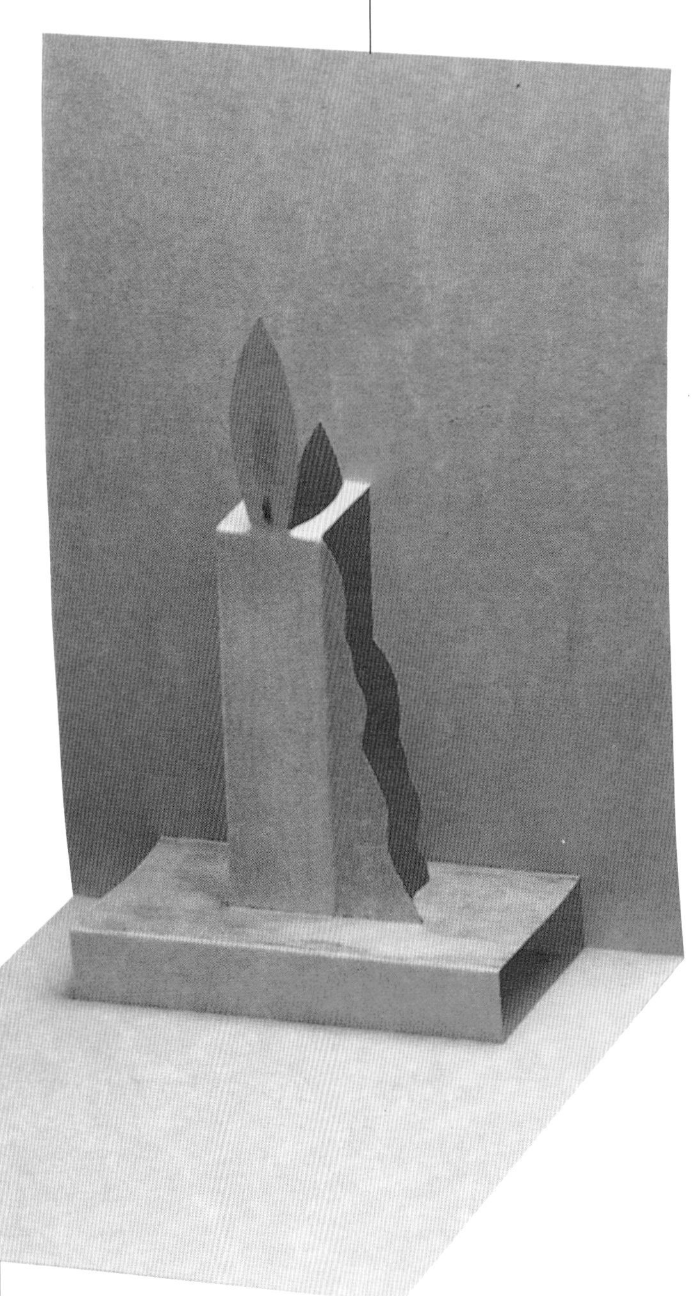

CUPID'S ARROW

★★

There is a certain elegance when a supporting tab becomes part of the design. In this case, the tab that supports the heart has become the arrow. Thus, no part of the design is superfluous. Note also how the arrow slides through the heart when the card is opened – very dramatic.

MATERIALS

Backing sheet: thin glossy yellow cardboard

Heart and arrow: red and blue thin cardboard

SIZES

Backing sheet: 1 x 4½ inches

Height of heart: 4½ inches

Scale of grid: 1:2

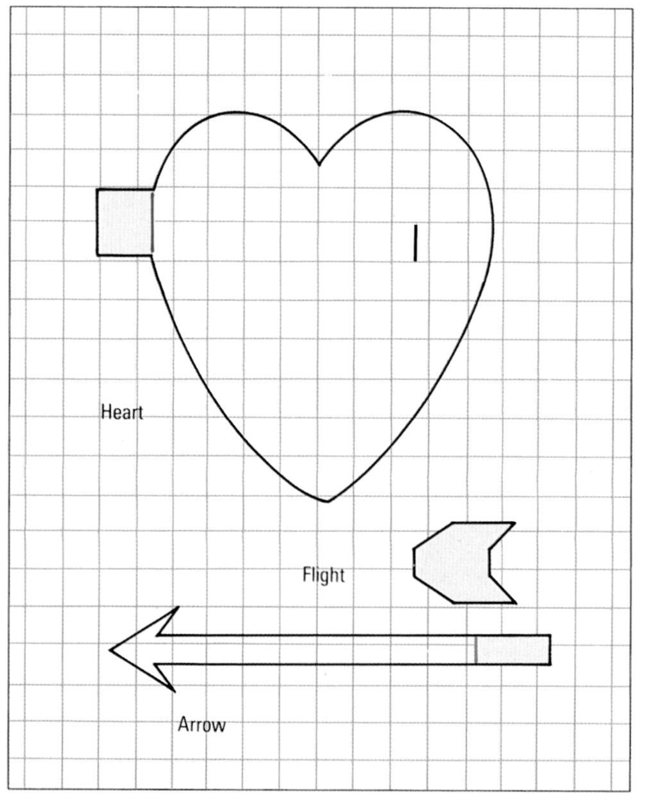

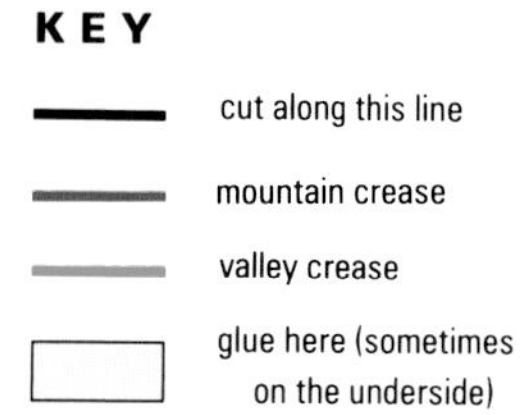

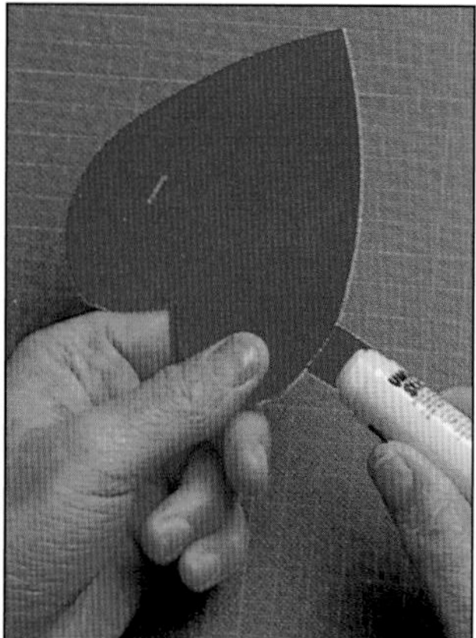

1 Apply glue to the heart tab.

2 Glue the tab to the backing sheet, so that the crease on the backing sheet lies approximately behind the center line of the heart.

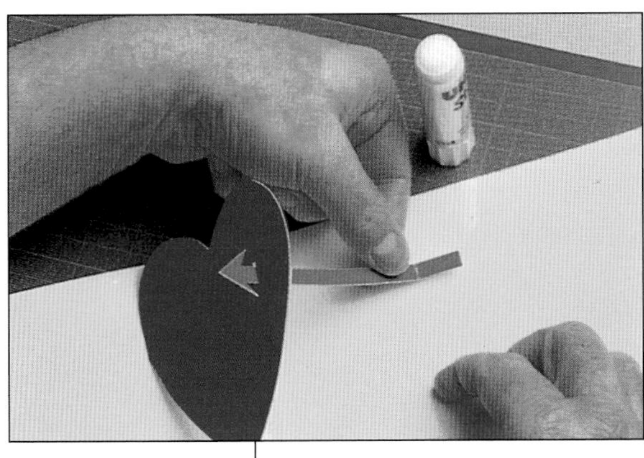

3 Feed the arrow through the slit in the heart from right to left.

4 Glue it to the backing sheet.

5 Glue the flight to the end of the arrow.

BE CREATIVE

The technique of piercing one pop-up shape with another need not be confined to a large shape (the heart) pierced by a thin one (the arrow). Any shape can pierce any other, eliminating the need – as here – for extra supporting tabs.

HEARTS ENTWINED

★★★

This single-piece pop-up mechanism is very satisfying to make. Here, two hearts ingeniously connect, each cut from the other. To achieve this, though, the design *must* be accurately cut. Note that the line that defines each heart forms a single, continuous line from one to the other.

MATERIALS

Thick gray paper

Red felt tip pen

SIZES

Sheet size:
12 x 13¼ inches
(fully opened)

Scale of grid: 1:2

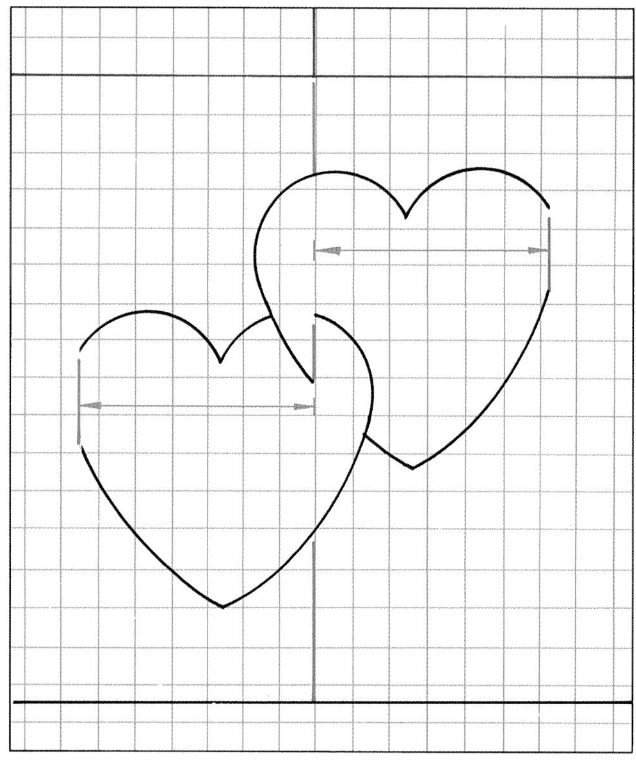

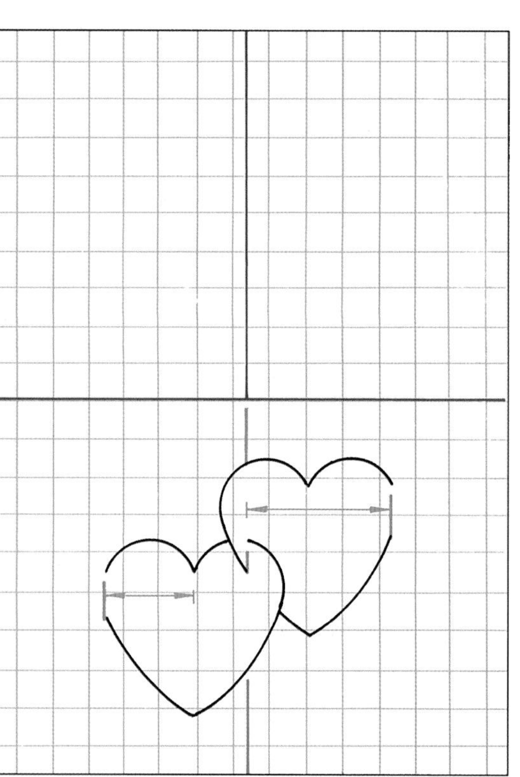

KEY

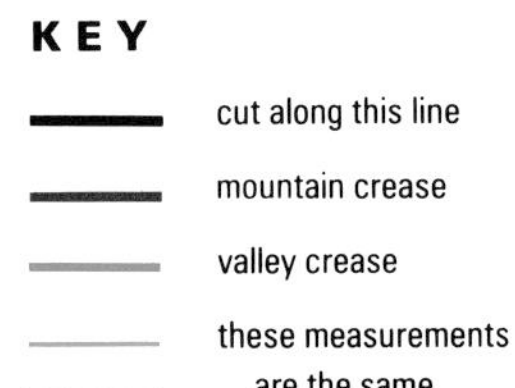

1 Cut the hearts as indicated by the template drawings.

2 Fold the card in half from top to bottom (note that the crease does not go through the hearts themselves).

3 Fold the card in half behind the hearts, allowing the hearts to rise forward.

4 Squeeze the small valley crease that connects the hearts.

5 Strengthen all the creases.

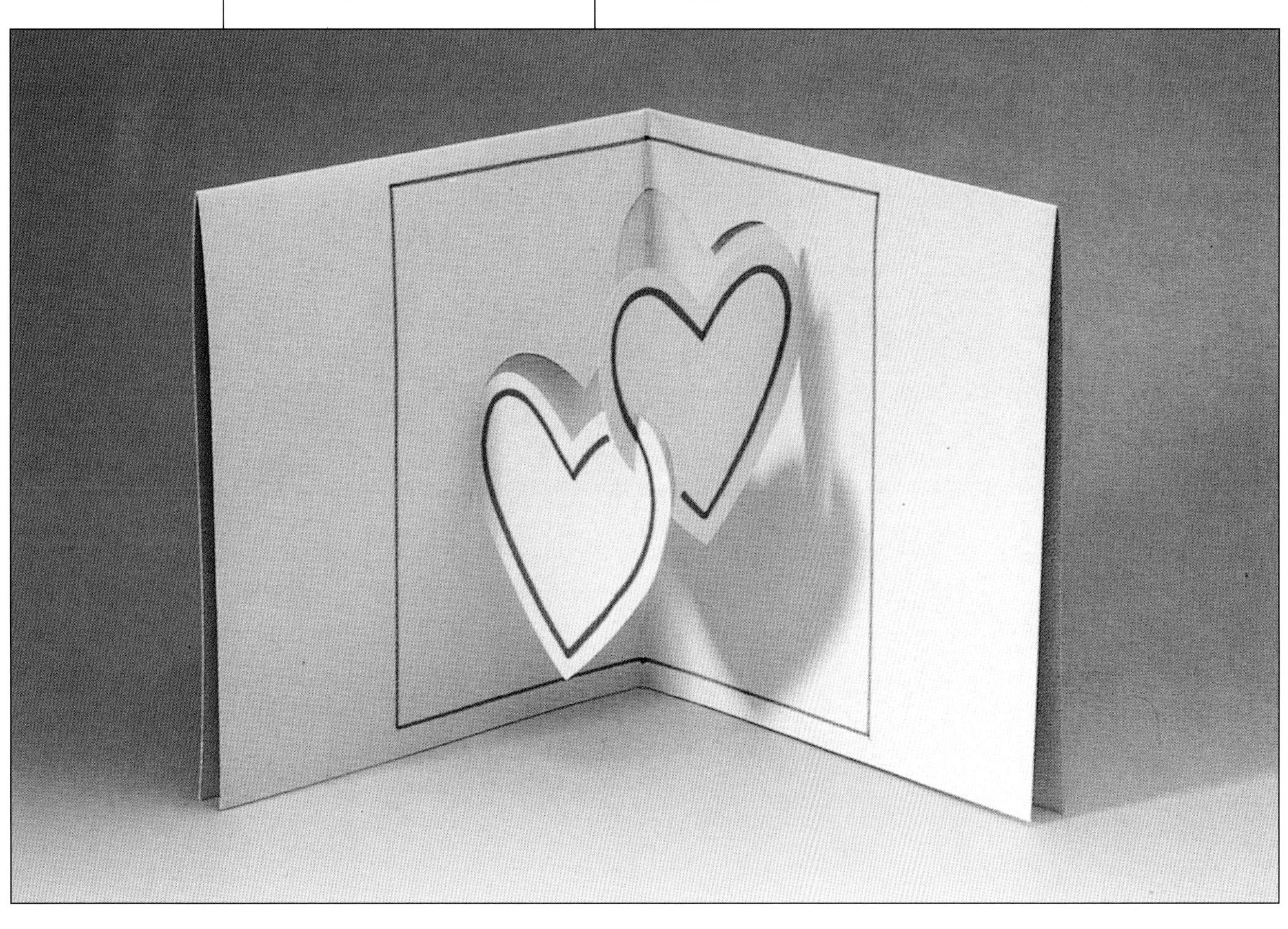

SAY IT WITH FLOWERS

★★

This is a simple design in technical terms, but it is perhaps the most decoratively versatile design in the book. The specific shapes of vase, foliage, and blooms are only a suggestion – try roses, tulips or, more personal, your loved one's favorite flowers.

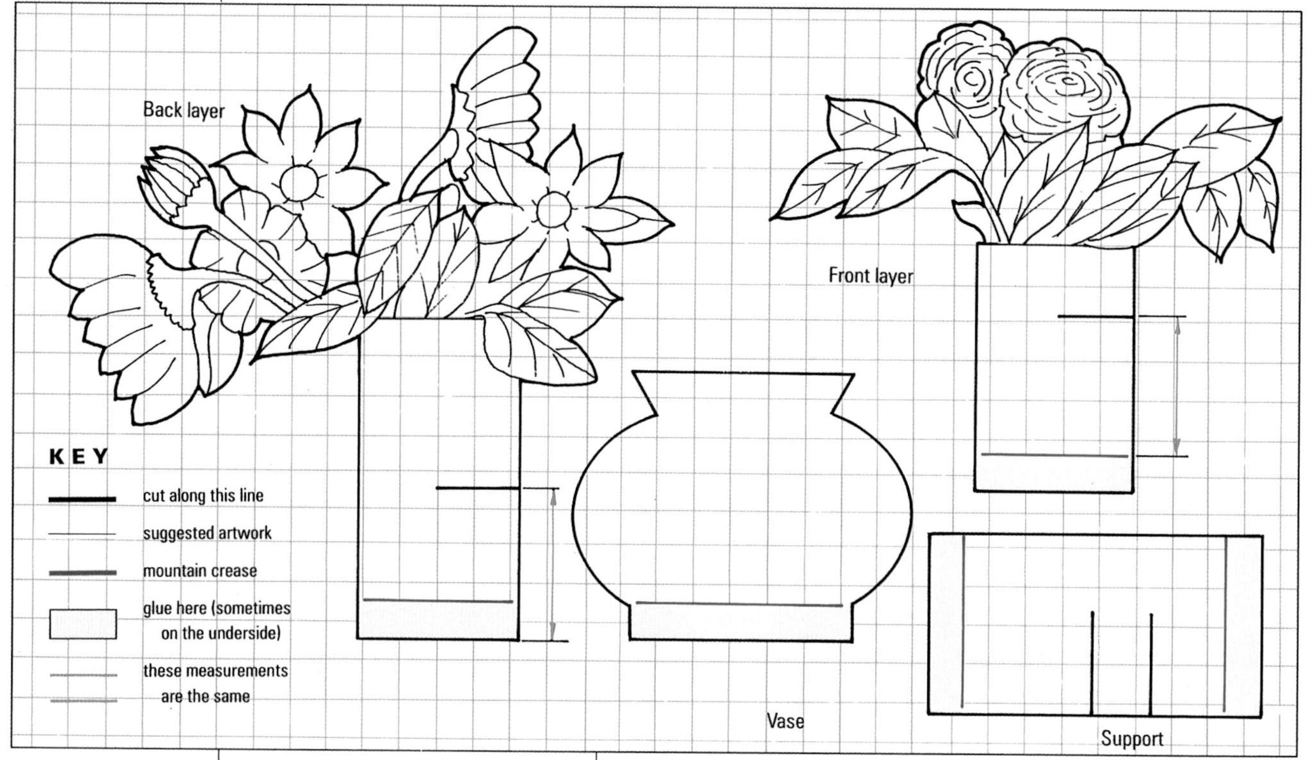

MATERIALS

Backing sheet: white mat board

Flowers and vase: thick watercolor paper

Felt tip pens

SIZES

Backing sheet: 19 x 9 inches

Height of back layer of flowers: 8 inches

Scale of grid: 1:2.5

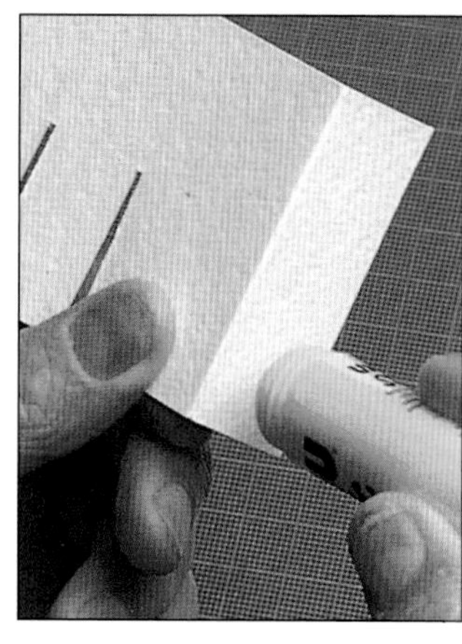

1 Apply glue to the right-hand edge of the support.

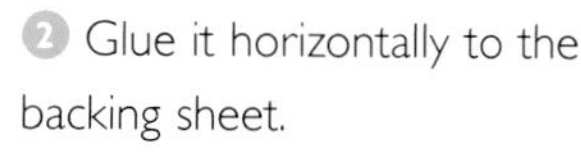

2 Glue it horizontally to the backing sheet.

❸ Apply glue to the base of the back layer of flowers.

❻ Glue the vase to the front of the support to complete the pop-up structure.

❹ Slot it into the first slit in the support (that nearest the backing sheet) and attach the tab to the backing sheet. (This assembly uses the tab technique – see page 91.)

❺ Repeat steps 3 and 4 for the front layer of flowers.

TRUE LOVE

★

This is perhaps the simplest pop-up design in the book. Note how the card is folded behind to create a double thickness that prevents the design from buckling. This also means that the design can be made from paper, rather than cardboard.

MATERIALS

Medium-weight red paper

SIZES

Sheet size:
8 x 10¼ inches
(fully opened)

Scale of grid: 1:2.5

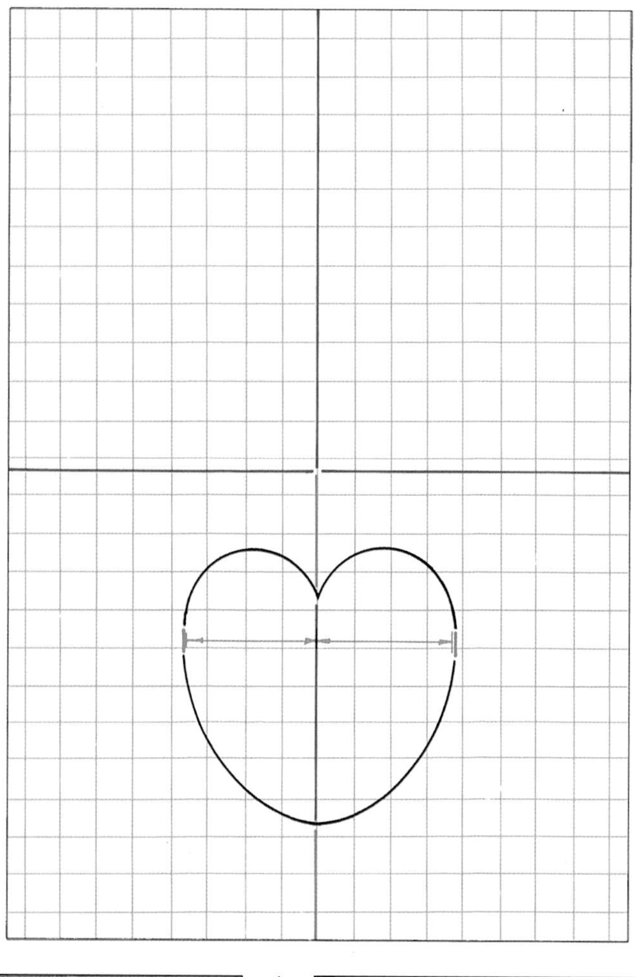

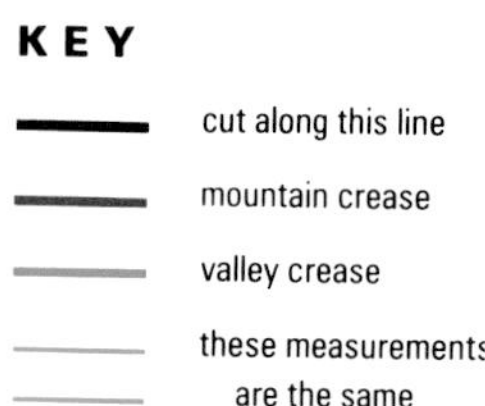

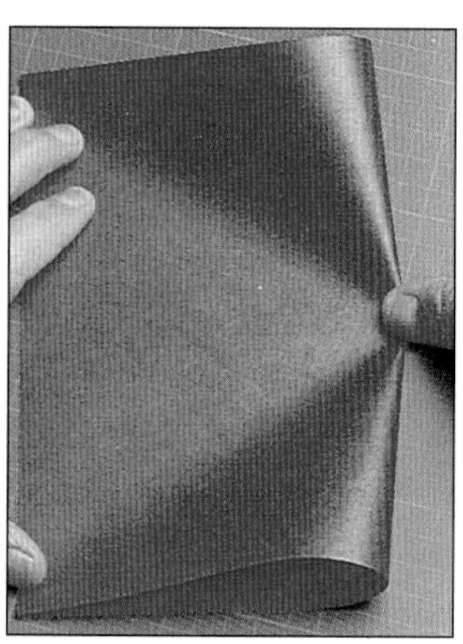

1 Fold the sheet in half (not through the heart). It will look like this.

2 Then fold in half again. It will now look like this.

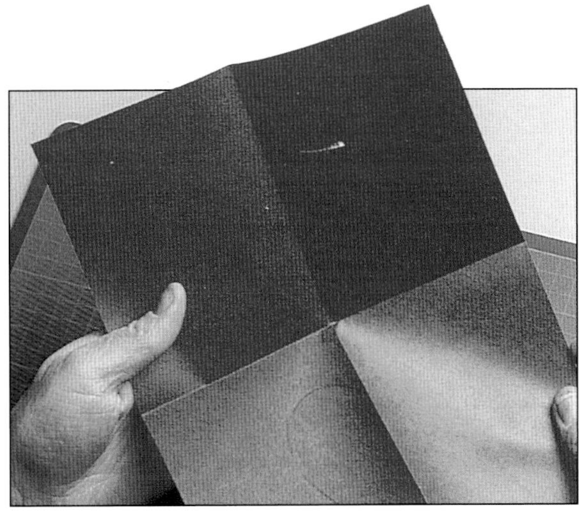

3 Open the sheet out. Note the position of the half-heart drawing.

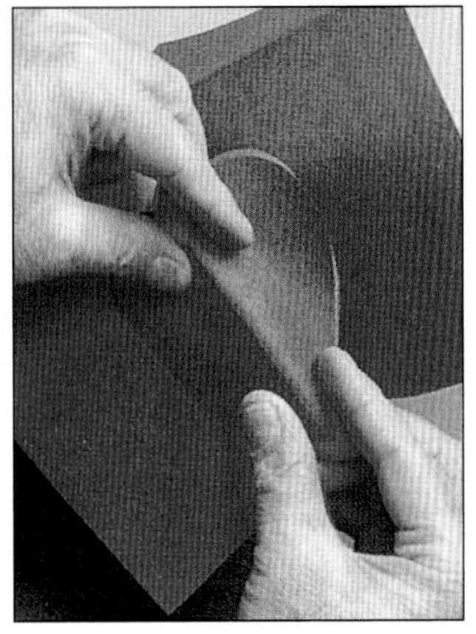

6 Re-form the folds and pull up the heart, creating a mountain fold down the center of the heart.

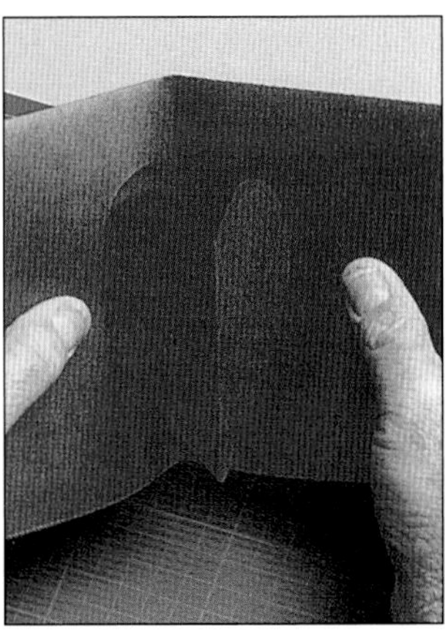

The completed card. Note the crease formation around the heart.

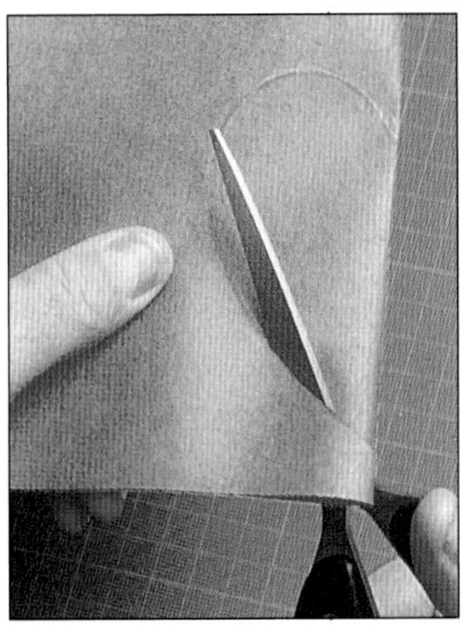

4 Cut out the heart, being careful to leave the small sections uncut that are marked to be creased on the template.

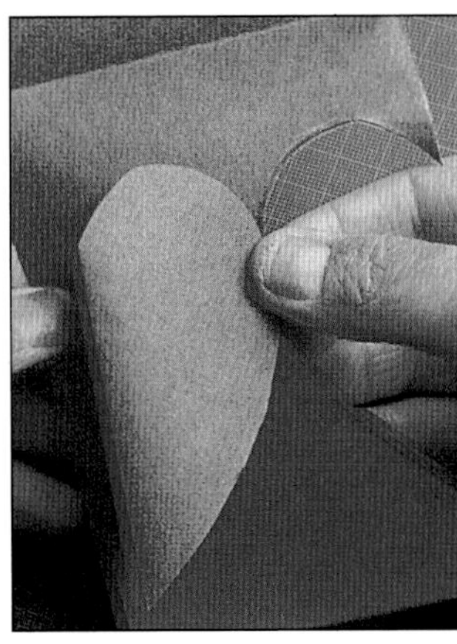

5 Fold back the heart to create these creases.

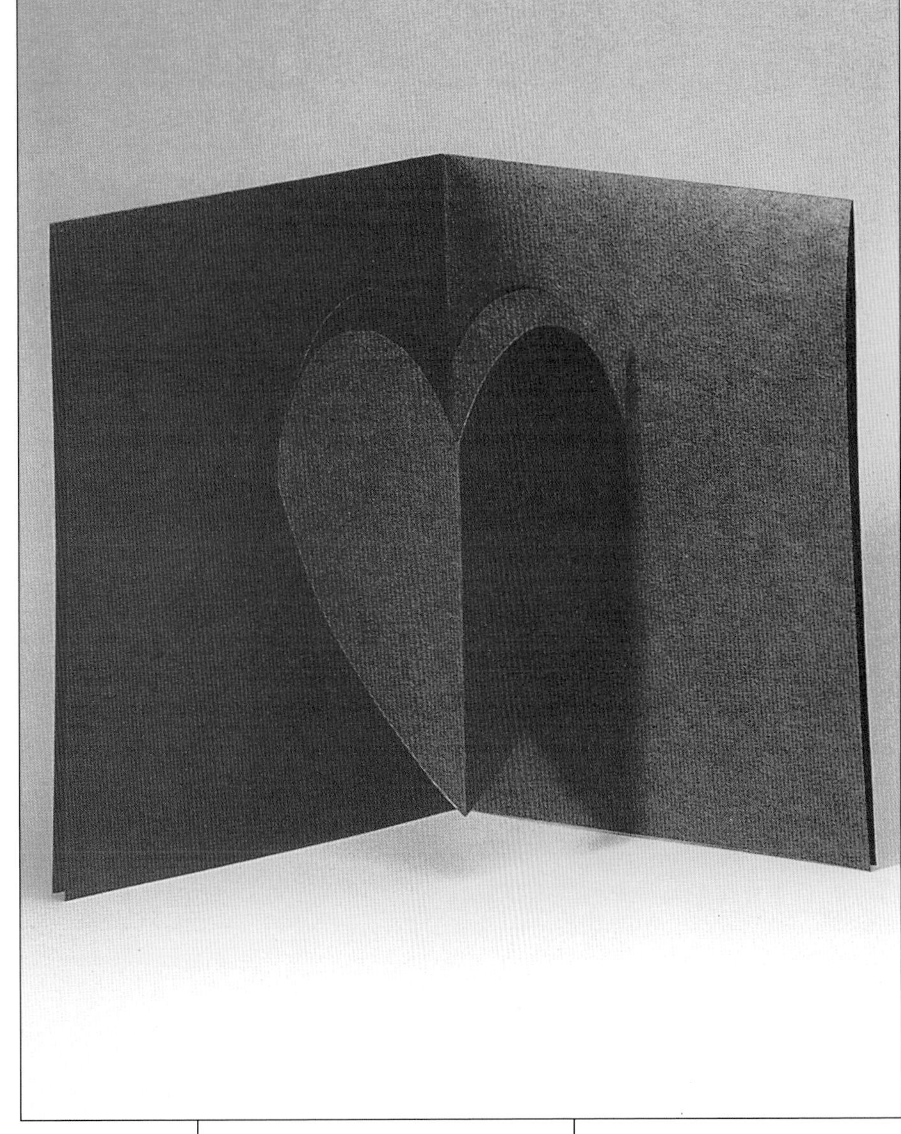

BOO!

★★

Pop-ups that swivel when the card is opened are always fun. The technique used here is common, but also curious, because the ghost will not move quite so effectively unless the restraining wall is placed in front.

MATERIALS

Backing sheet: medium-weight black paper glued to mat board

Restraining wall: medium-weight black paper

Ghost: medium-weight white paper

Gray felt pen

SIZES

Backing sheet: 12 x 8 inches

Height of ghost: 3½ inches

Scale of grid: 1:2.5

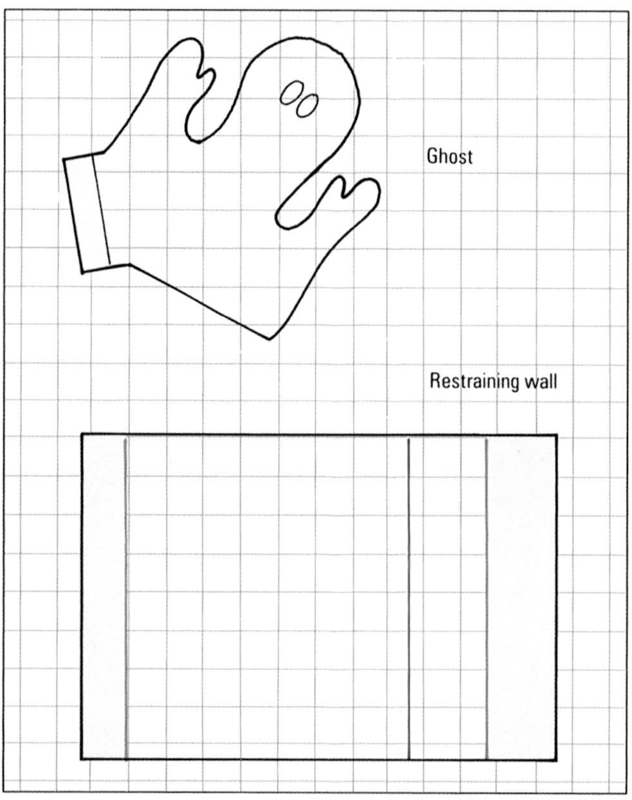

KEY

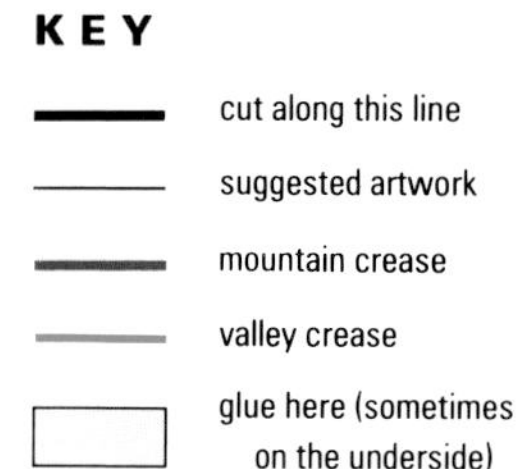

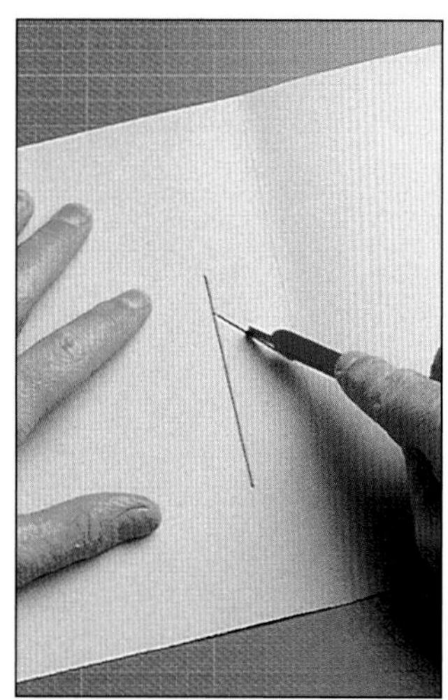

❶ Make the short diagonal slit in the backing sheet (the card should be black, but a paler color has been used here so you can see clearly what you need to do).

❷ Push the tab on the ghost through the slit.

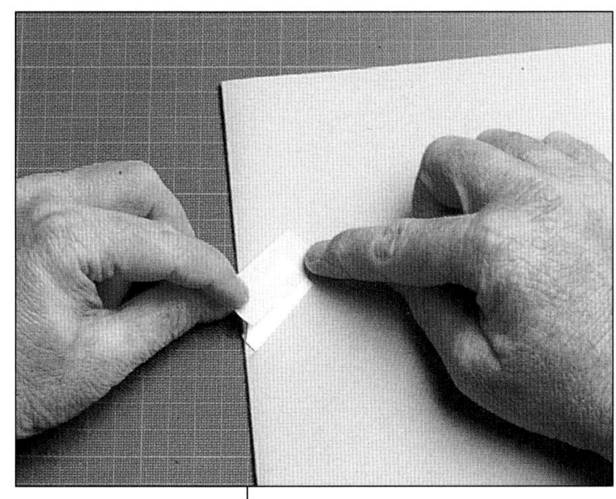

3 Secure the tab on the back with tape.

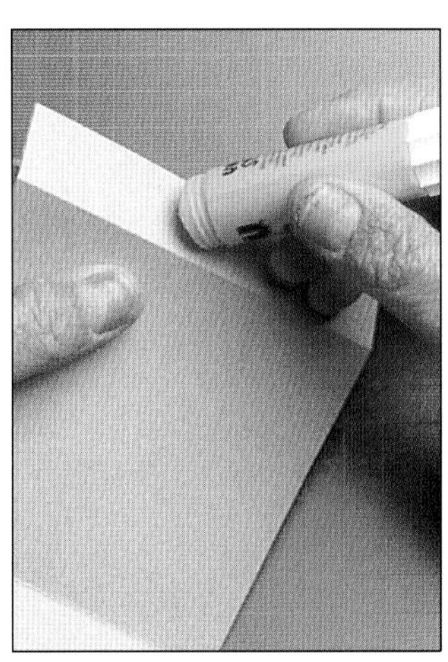

4 Apply glue to each of the end tabs on the restraining wall.

5 Glue the wall to the backing sheet, using the tab technique (see page 91).

The ghost is visible when the card is opened.

Mysteriously, it swivels out of sight when the card is shut.

MAGIC LANTERN

★ ★ ★

Whereas most pop-up designs should be lit from the front, this card should have some light coming through from the back so that the eyes and mouth are illuminated to resemble a real lantern. Unusually for a one-piece pop-up shape, part of the design lies *behind* the plane of the backing sheet. The card can be made from heavy paper, and the illuminated areas are covered from behind with tracing paper.

MATERIALS

Medium-weight black paper

Tracing paper

Orange felt tip pen

SIZES

Sheet size: 15¼ x 8½ inches

Scale of grid: 1:2.5

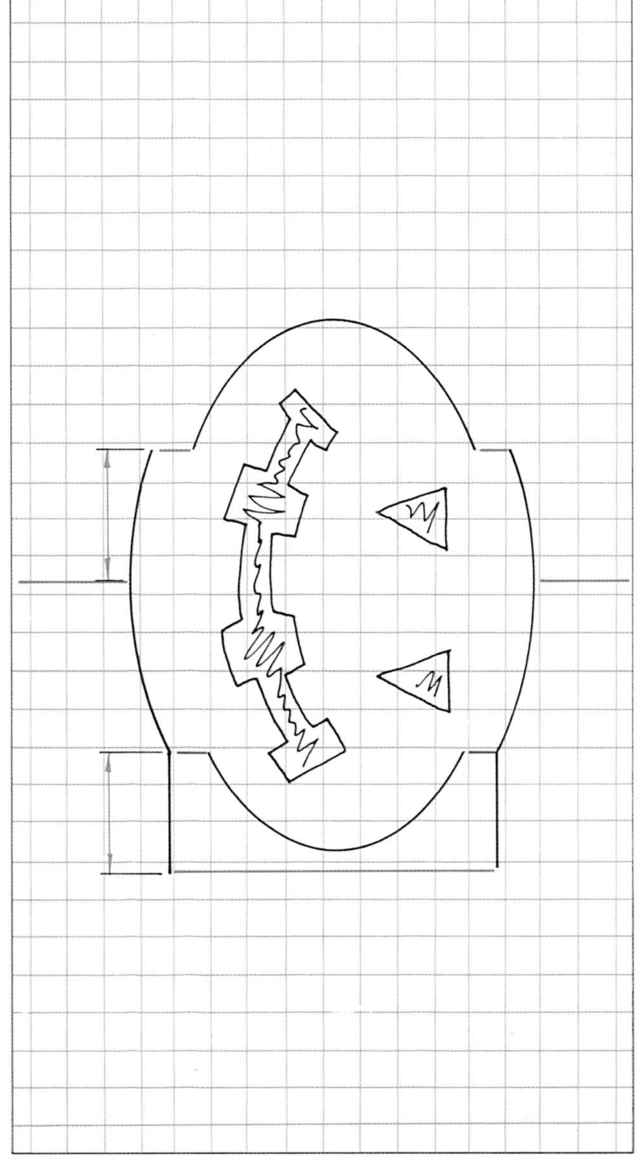

KEY

- cut along this line
- mountain crease
- valley crease
- these measurements are the same

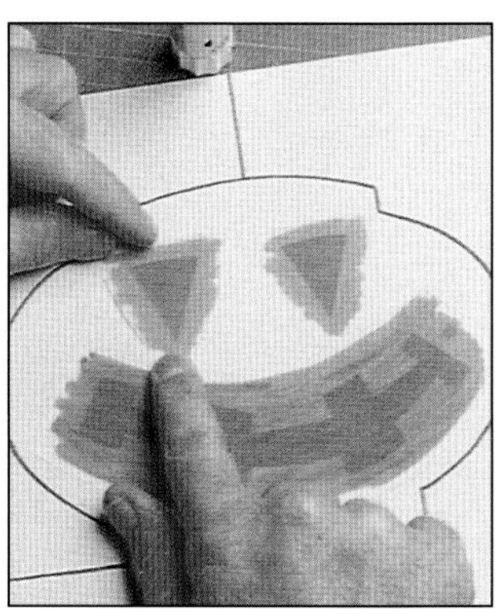

1 Take pieces of tracing paper large enough to cover the mouth and eyes, color them with a felt tip pen, and glue the pieces to the reverse of the card. (The card should be black, but a pale color has been used so you can see clearly what needs to be done.)

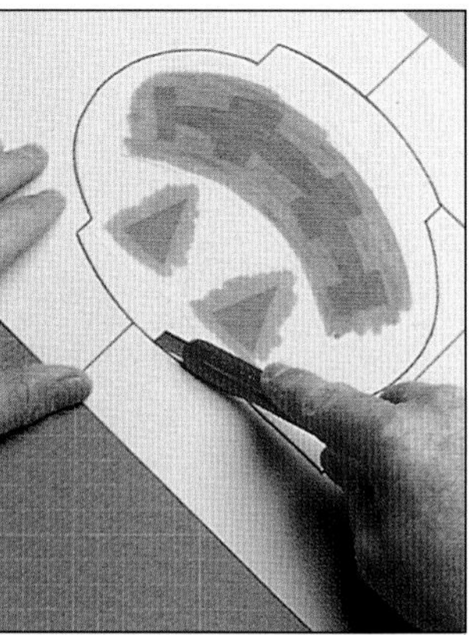

2 Cut along the lines of the pumpkin indicated on the template drawings.

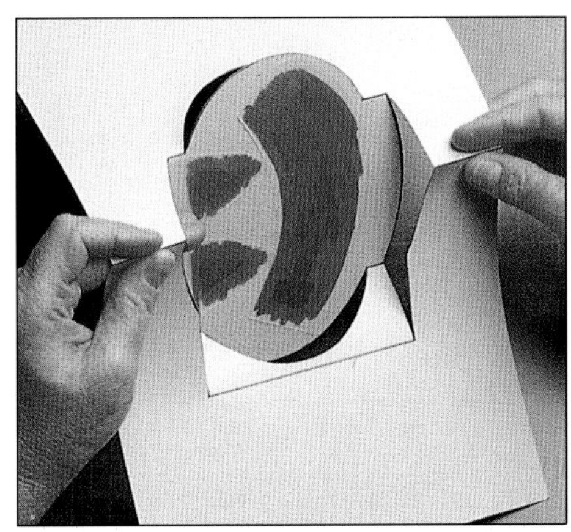

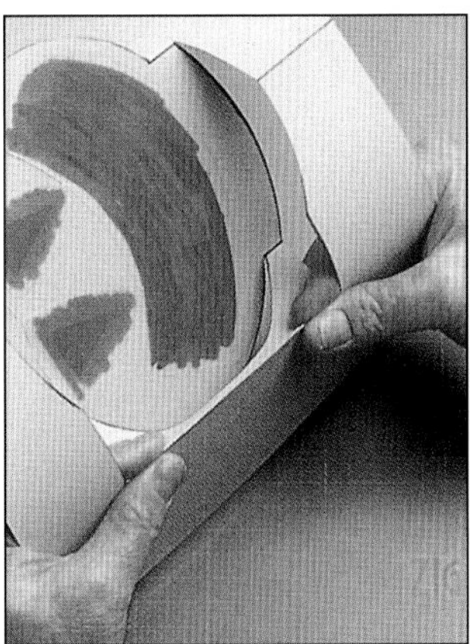

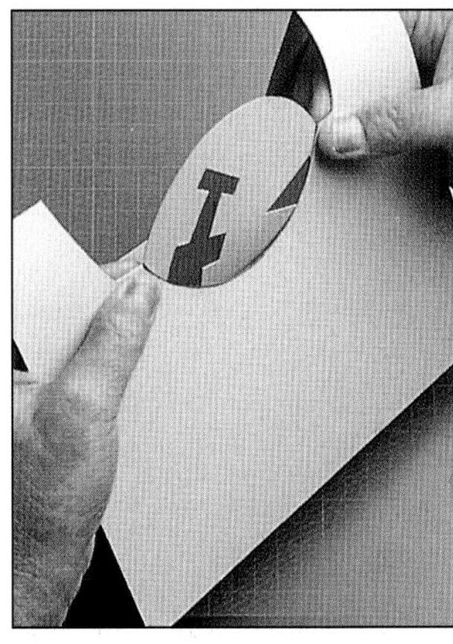

3 Fold the central creases of the card itself.

4 Make the remaining creases.

5 The card will then collapse flat.

For the best effect, the card should be displayed open and lit from behind.

WEDDING BELLS

★★

The design is similar to Hearts Entwined on pages 116–117, but is made from more than one piece of cardboard. To do so allows for a greater freedom in the design or, to put it another way, allows for the design to be made in a less precise way.

MATERIALS

Backing sheet: thick green reflective foil cardboard

Supports: thick green reflective foil cardboard

Bells: thin silver cardboard

Red felt tip pen

SIZES

Backing sheet: 12¾ x 7½ inches

Scale of grid: 1:2

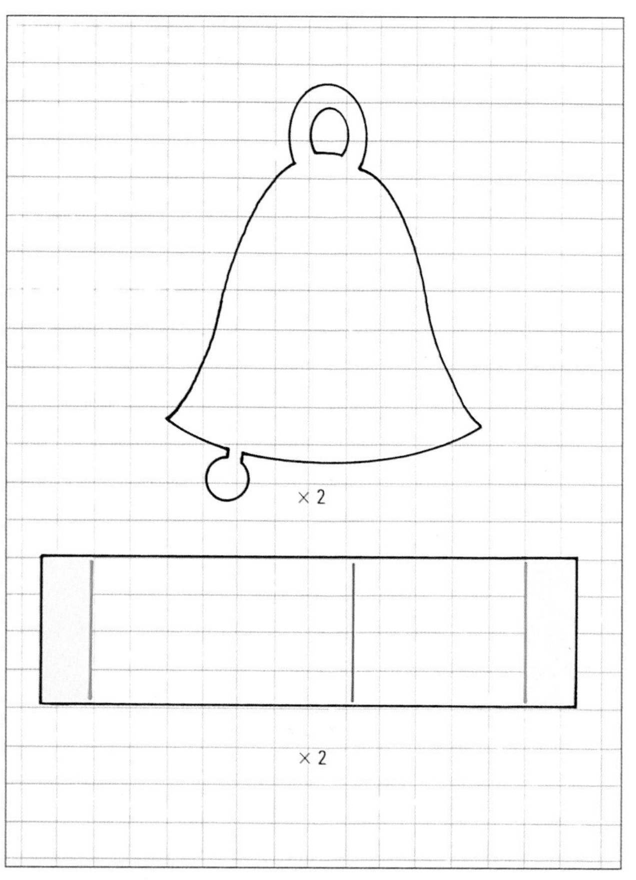

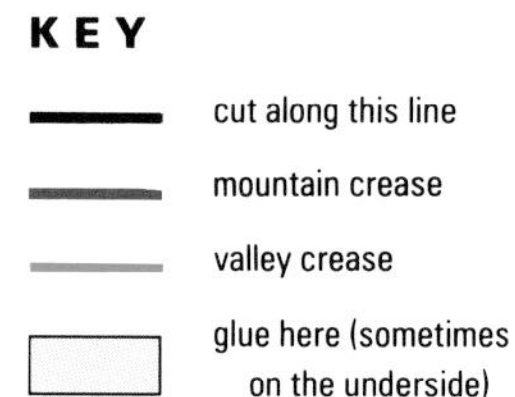

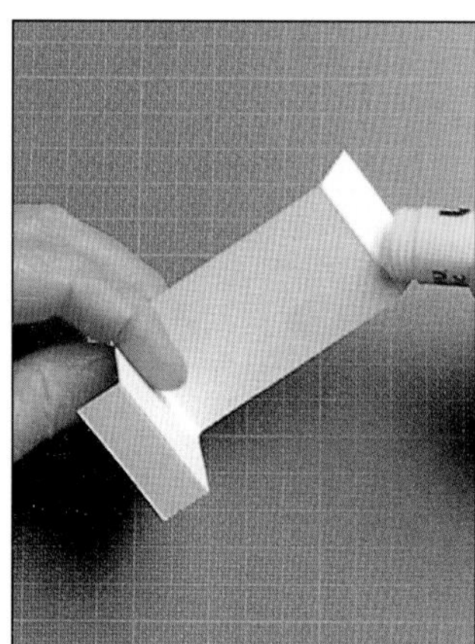

1 Apply glue to the tabs at each end of a support.

2 Attach the support to the backing sheet, using the tab technique (see page 91).

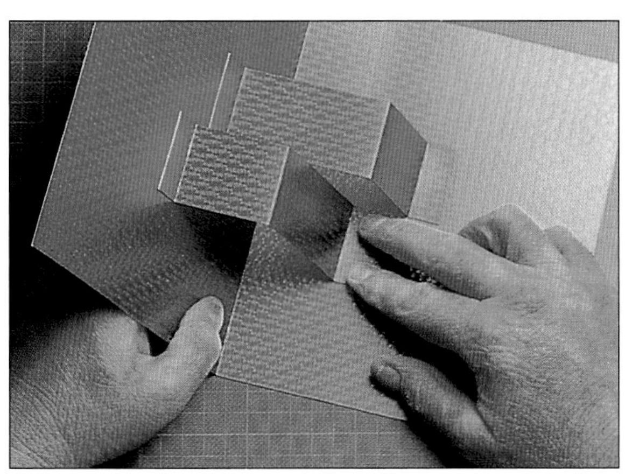

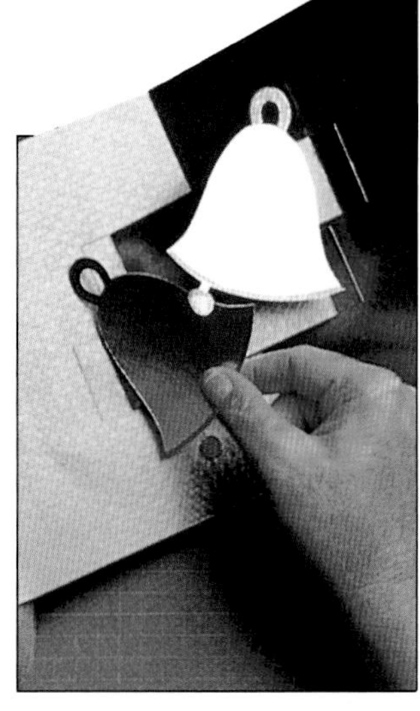

3 Glue the other support to the backing sheet, but reversing the tabs.

4 Glue a bell onto one of the supports.

5 Glue the other bell onto the other support.

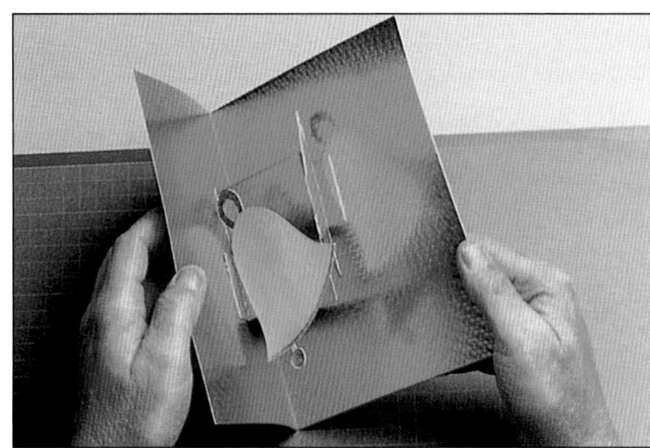

6 The card will close easily if the placement of the supports has been carefully measured.

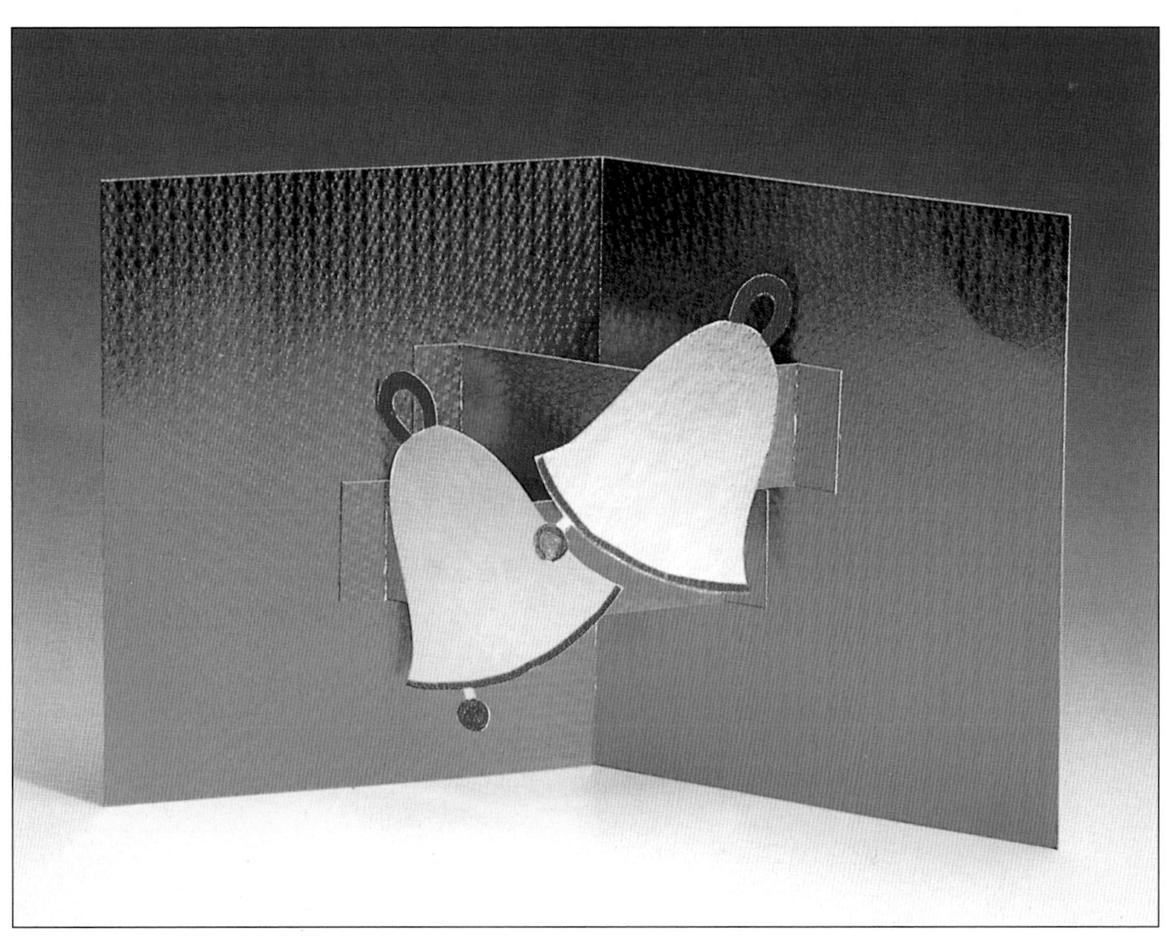

RAINING CONFETTI

★★★

This pop-up design is a pleasant change from the usual designs for weddings. When it is being opened, the hand swivels downward, mimicking the action of showering the happy couple with confetti. Note that when the card is flat, the hand extends beyond the backing sheet.

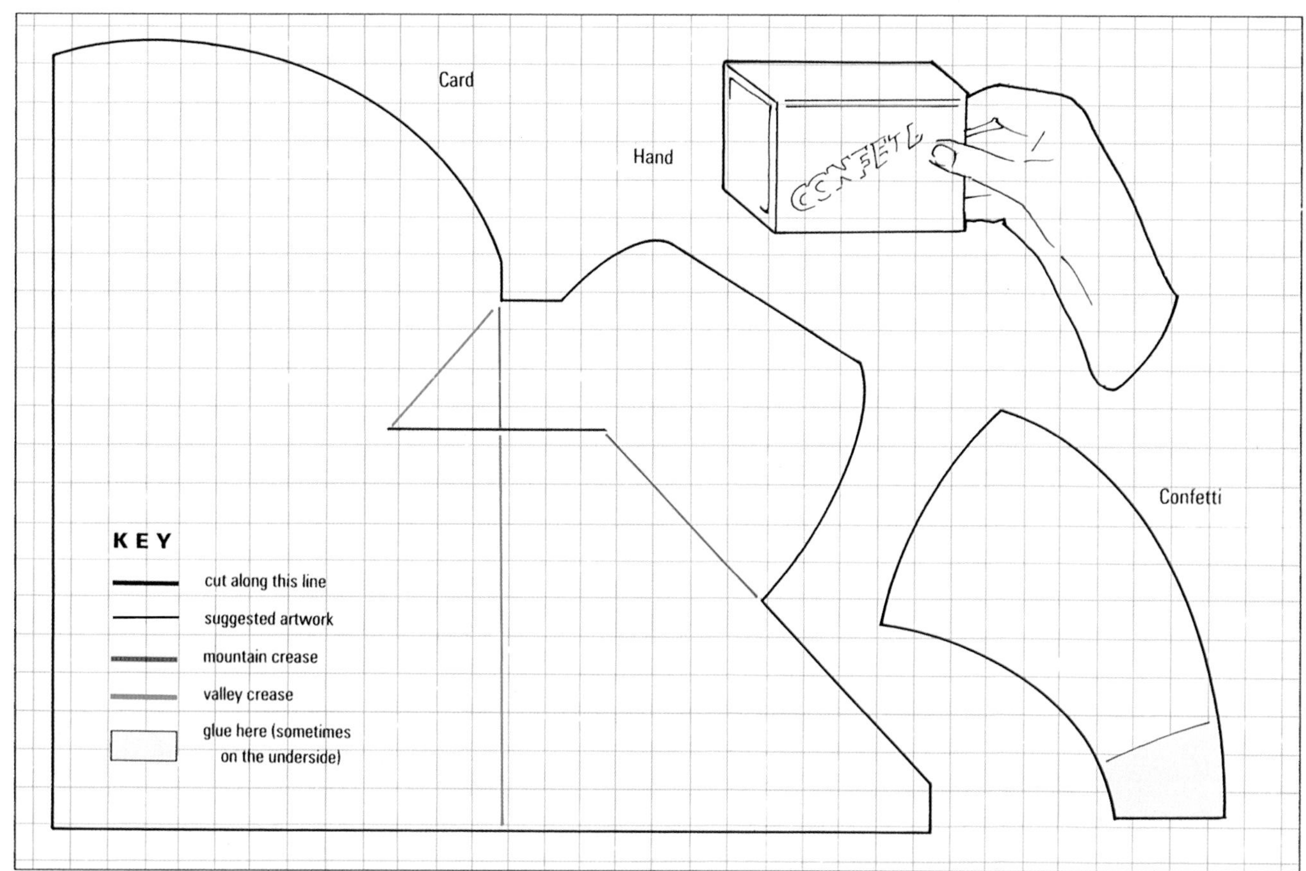

MATERIALS

Backing sheet: thick mottled gray cardboard

Hand and confetti box: thick watercolor paper

Confetti

Felt tip pens

SIZES

Backing sheet: 12 x 10 inches

Length of hand: 4¾ inches

Scale of grid: 1:2.5

1 Cut the backing sheet as indicated by the template drawing.

2 Make the long central creases.

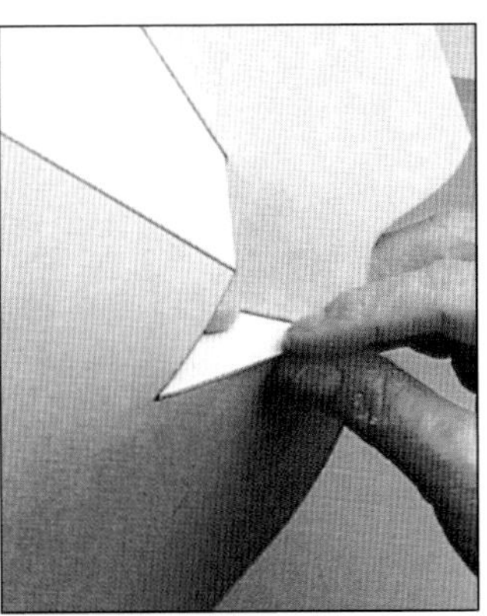

3 Make the smaller folds.

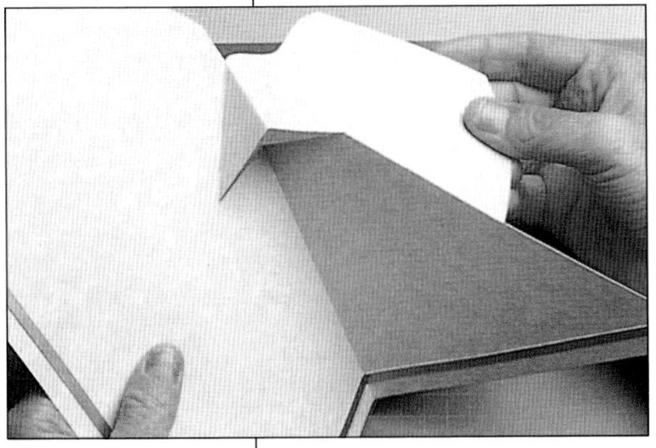

4 You will now have this shape, which will also fold flat again.

5 Attach the hand and confetti pieces to the supporting shelf, passing the confetti pieces through the slot in the confetti box.

6 Your card will now look like this. Adjust the angle of the hand if it does not swivel effectively when the card is opened.

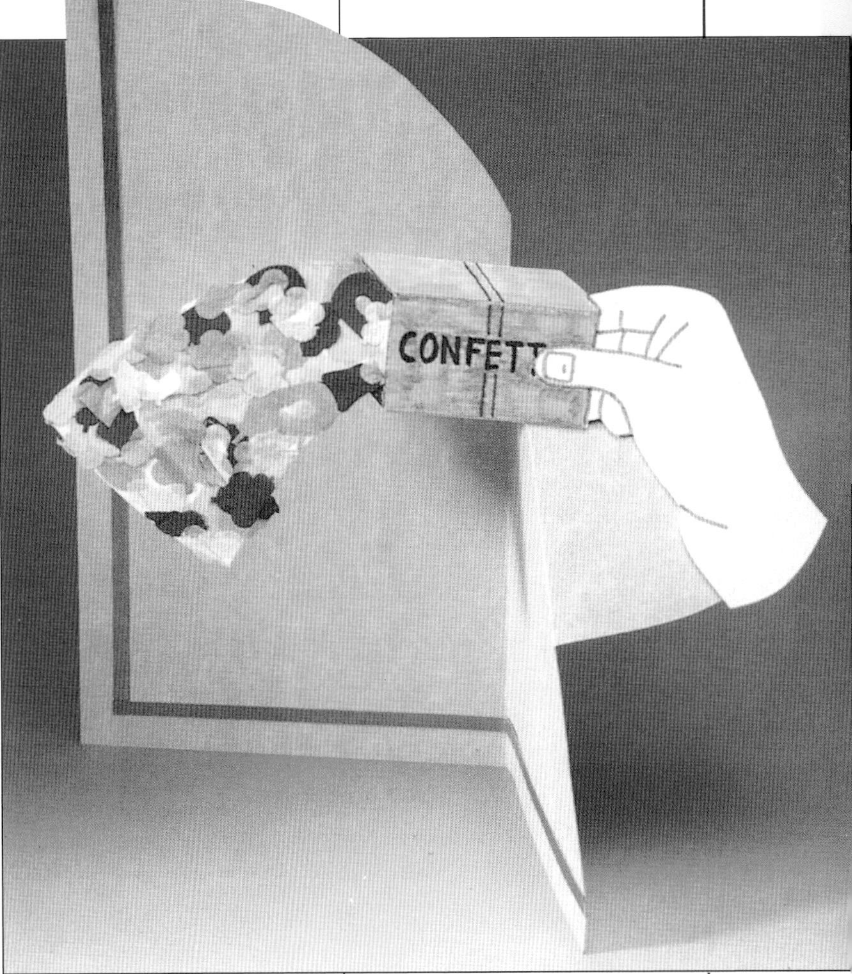

START PACKING

★★

A design such as this can be varied in a great many ways, and you may want to make it suit a particular family you know. For example, you might include a piano, favorite toys of the children, a pet dog, or appropriately humorous box labels. Often, the more a card is personalized (and the less like a bought card it looks), the more it is appreciated.

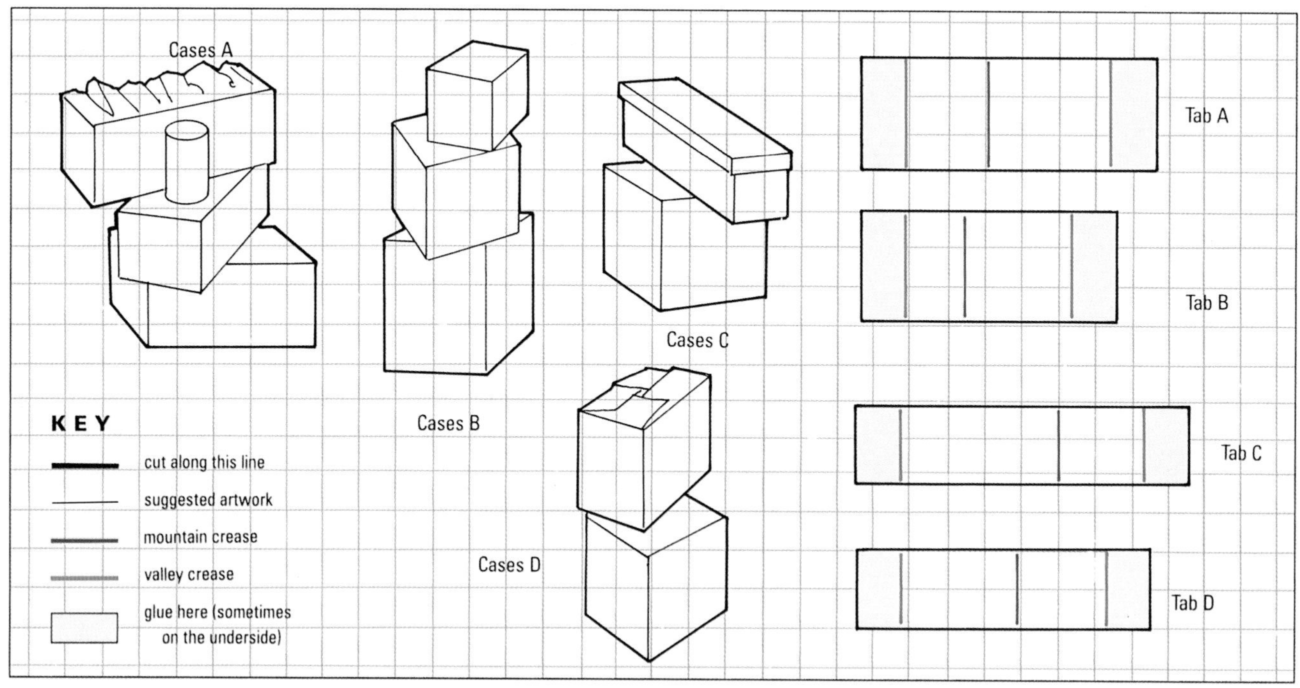

MATERIALS

Backing sheet: thin mottled brown cardboard

Supports and packing cases: thin mottled brown cardboard

Black felt tip pen

SIZES

Backing sheet: 11 x 8¾ inches

Height of packing cases "A": 3½ inches

Scale of grid: 1:2.5

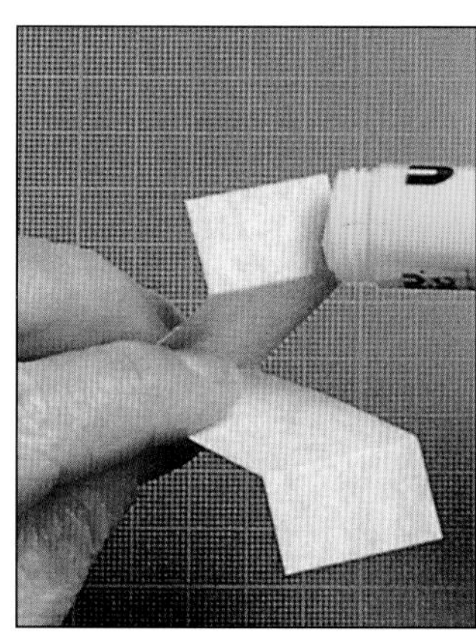

1 Apply glue to both ends of tab A.

2 Position it at the left of the backing sheet, using the tab technique (see page 91).

③ Repeat steps 1 and 2 for the other tabs, each time measuring their placement using the tab technique.

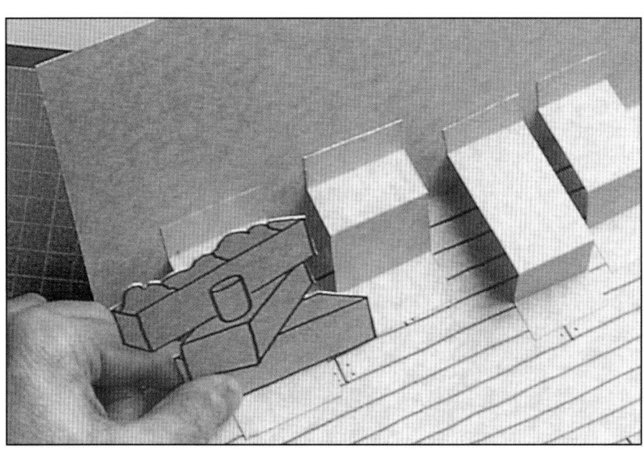

④ Glue cases A onto tab A.

⑤ Repeat step 4 for cases B, C and D.

⑥ Redraw the black lines over the tabs.

FOR BEST RESULTS . . .

Do not overglue the tabs.

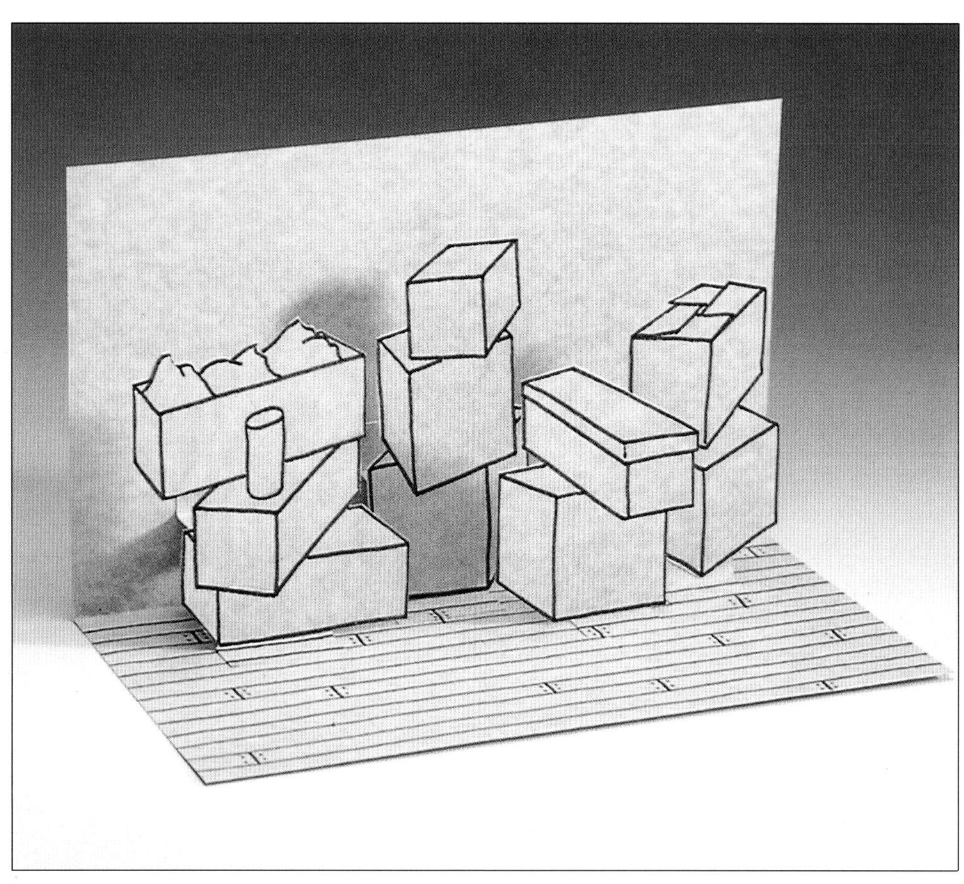

PART III

PAPIER-MÂCHÉ

BASICS

Papier-mâché is a French term meaning "mashed paper." It was first coined, not in France but in eighteenth-century London, by French émigré workers who made papier-mâché objects in small workshops. Only recently have the French themselves recognized the term. In recent years, papier-mâché has undergone a major revival. Its versatility and low-tech method make it the ideal medium for the craftsperson with little space or few facilities.

LAYERING

Layering (or laminating) paper is the more common of the two papier-mâché techniques. It is used to cast from a mold, or former, and involves building up many layers of pasted paper. Although basically a very simple process, it needs to be worked with great care to give a good finish. When using a mold – for example, an existing bowl – this must be well prepared by coating with a layer of releasing agent, such as petroleum jelly or soft soap. This will prevent the first layer of paper from sticking to the mold. It is important to build up the layers of paper, taking care to smooth each piece down with the fingers so that no air or lumps of paste are trapped between the layers of paper to disfigure the final piece when it is dry.

EQUIPMENT AND MATERIALS

Broadsheet (large-format) newspapers are used, as the paper is better quality than tabloid newsprint, and it is much more flexible and adaptable when soaked with paste or glue. The paper must be torn, not cut, into strips along the grain of the newspaper – generally down the columns of type – as this produces smoother and less obvious seams when pasted down.

It is a good idea to use alternate layers of colored newspaper, as this makes the counting of the layers easier. Lay the paper in one direction for one layer, then crosswise for the next. This gives the piece more strength.

When casting from a more complicated form, it is better to use smaller, thinner pieces of newspaper. These will mold themselves to the form without creasing because they can stretch around a curved surface.

An interesting variation would be to layer with different kinds of paper. Fewer layers would be necessary when using thicker, handmade papers (see Papermaking, pages 166–179), although they would need to be torn into smaller pieces to cover a curved surface without creasing. A piece layered in this way need not be painted.

Colored or dyed paper can be used, thus enhancing and revealing the technique of layering, while integrating the decoration of the piece with its construction. Tissue paper will produce a delicate, fragile piece.

The use of different kinds and strengths of paper – making a collage in three dimensions, in fact – is an exciting and worthwhile way to explore the many possibilities of layering.

ADHESIVES

It is equally possible to use a cellulose paste (wallpaper paste) or craft glue. The cellulose is more comfortable to work with, though great care must be taken if using pastes that contain fungicide. Craft glue is very sticky to work with, but will produce a strong finished piece. As a compromise, it is possible to mix the two glues: the consistency should be that of heavy cream. The use of glue or paste is a matter of individual preference, and it is advisable to try both methods.

The glue or paste should be spread onto each side of the strip of paper separately. The paste must be allowed to soak through the paper to render it more flexible, but it should not be wet. It is an idea to paste up a few pieces at a time and lay them around the edge of the paste bowl, so that they are ready to use. They will soon dry and so must be used quickly. Alternatively, a larger piece of paper may be pasted, and strips torn from it to be applied to the mold.

APPLYING THE LAYERS

The number of layers laid down obviously depends on the required thickness of the finished article. About ten would be enough for a bowl, as this would be further strengthened by the use of gesso, paint, and varnish. About eight layers would be enough for a mask.

It is possible to add all the layers in one go, but allowing each layer to dry before applying the next may produce a more reliable and smoother finish, particularly when using cellulose paste. This is a matter of personal preference. There are no absolute rules when using papier-mâché, and each artist discovers and refines her or his own techniques.

DRYING

Drying times vary according to the working environment. It is always best to let the piece dry at an even temperature – a warm place such as a kitchen is ideal. Drying may be speeded up by using an oven on a very low temperature. Rapid drying may cause distortion and would be unwise when casting from a clay mold, because the modeling clay would degenerate.

When the object is dry, the cast should be easy to release and is ready for finishing.

FINISHING

In the case of a bowl, the uneven rim can be trimmed to make a neat edge. Any cut edges should be bound with two layers of pasted paper.

There are many alternative and imaginative ways to treat the rim, which will influence the form and character of the bowl. For example, when layering, allow the torn paper to project from the mold and, when thoroughly dry, tear into a deckle edge. The rim may be cut unevenly, scalloped or zigzagged, or be cut through like latticework. Other possibilities would be to add paper or cardboard to the rim. Pulp (see pages 142–143) may be added to form a softer or more sculpted rim. If the papier-mâché is cut, however, always remember to add two layers to cover the cut.

The form can also be altered by the addition of a foot at the bottom of the bowl, but always cover any introduced material with two layers of paper to unify the whole.

For ideas on decoration, see further on.

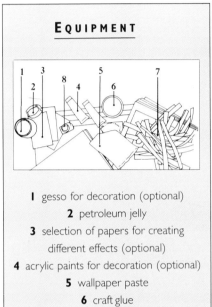

EQUIPMENT

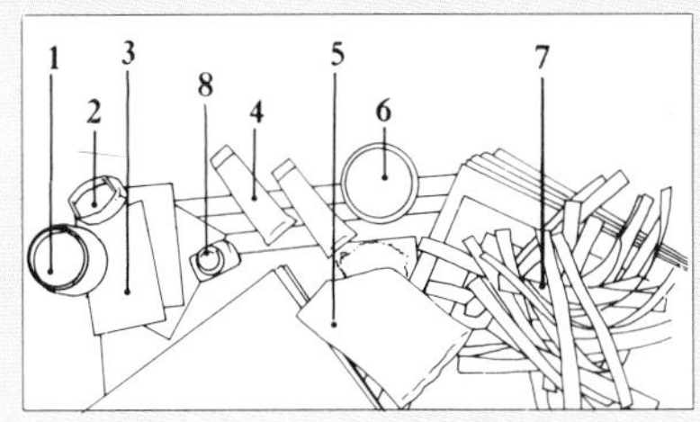

1 gesso for decoration (optional)
2 petroleum jelly
3 selection of papers for creating different effects (optional)
4 acrylic paints for decoration (optional)
5 wallpaper paste
6 craft glue
7 broadsheet newspapers torn into strips
8 varnish

CASTING FROM A MOLD

It is possible to cast from a range of molds, but it's probably easiest to start with a bowl. To get a good finish, the layers need to be worked with care – so don't rush.

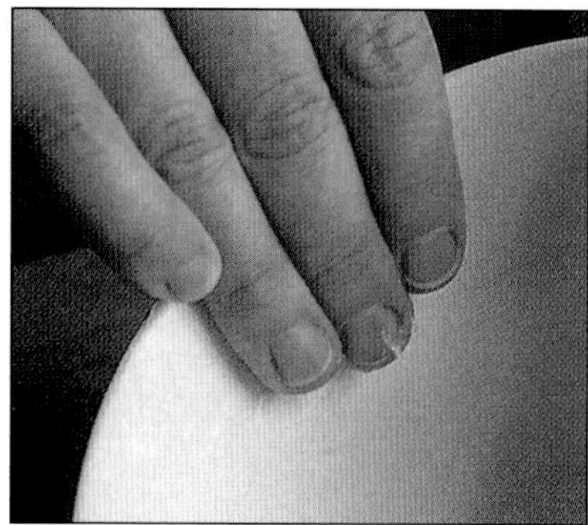

1 In this example, the mold is a bowl – an easy shape to cast from. Cover it with a releasing agent, such as petroleum jelly or soft soap. Take care to include the inside and top of the rim.

2 Tear the newspaper down the grain in strips 1½ inches wide. Tear again into 3-inch lengths.

3 Use a wide bowl to mix the paste, and paste each piece of paper separately with the fingers. Make sure the strips are not soaked and that there are no lumps of paste attached.

4 Lay the strips of paper in the mold, smoothing each piece separately and overlapping each one until the first layer is complete.

5 Lay the second layer of paper over the first, crosswise for strength. Use paper of a different color for each layer if possible. Cover very evenly. Continue with alternating colors until ten layers are finished. Smooth each layer to eliminate any bubbles.

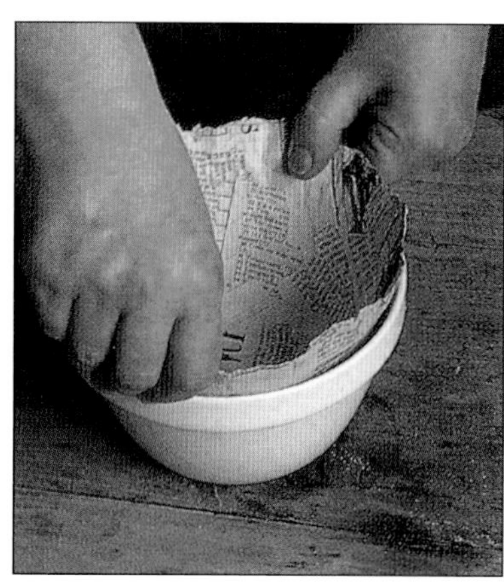

6 When the bowl is completely dry, ease the top of the cast away from the mold.

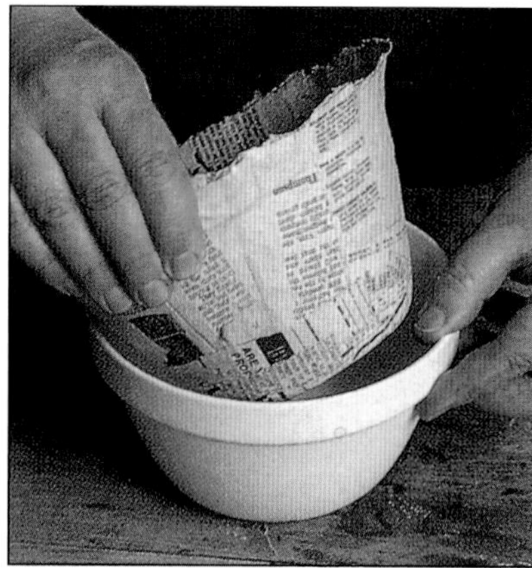

7 Then twist, and the cast bowl will release. If there is any reluctance, or if the first layer seems damp, allow to dry for a little longer.

8 The rim can be cut evenly with a scalpel, if a smooth, neat finish is desired.

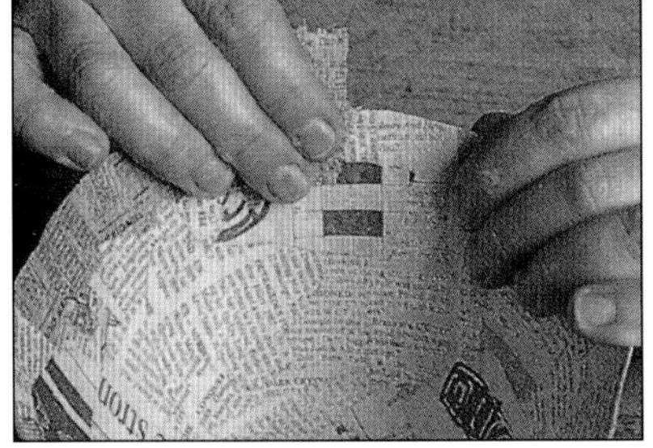

9 Finally, add two layers of pasted paper to disguise the sharp cut edge of the bowl.

ADDING A PAPER RIM

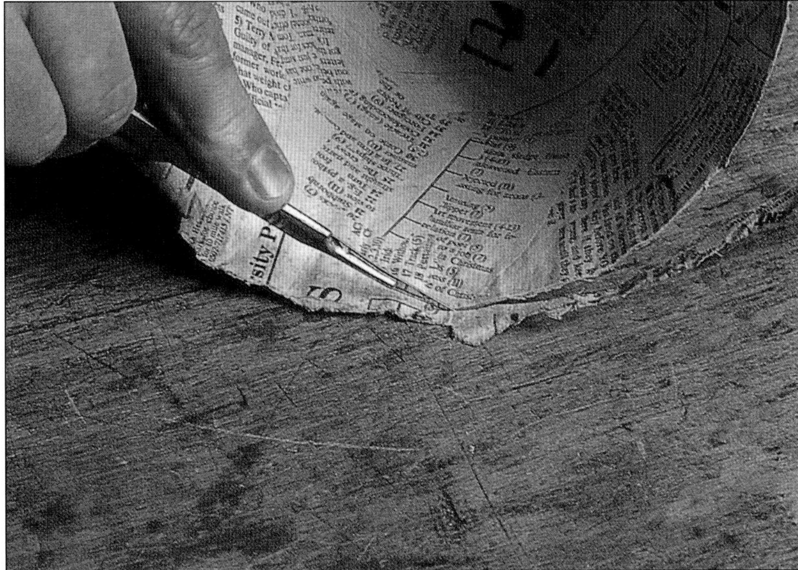

1 Cut the rim evenly with a scalpel.

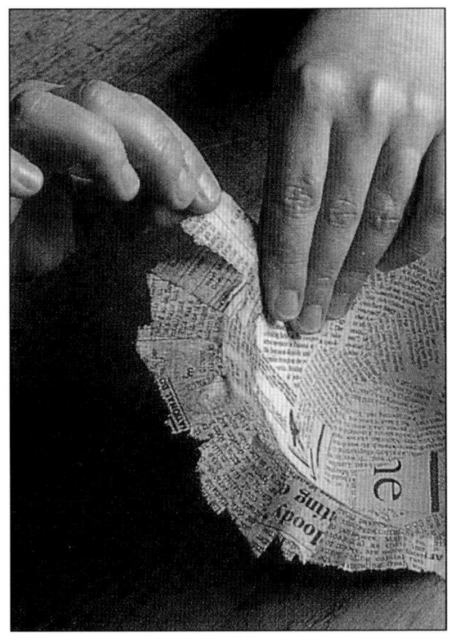

2 Add pasted paper strips to the edge of the rim. Allow each layer to dry before applying the next, in order to prevent any distortion due to the weight of the wet paper, which will tend to sag.

3 Add six layers.

4 Cut the extended rim to shape and cover the cut with two layers of pasted paper.

ADDING A CARD RIM

1 After the rim of the bowl has been evenly cut, turn the bowl upside down on a piece of thin cardboard and trace the circumference onto the cardboard.

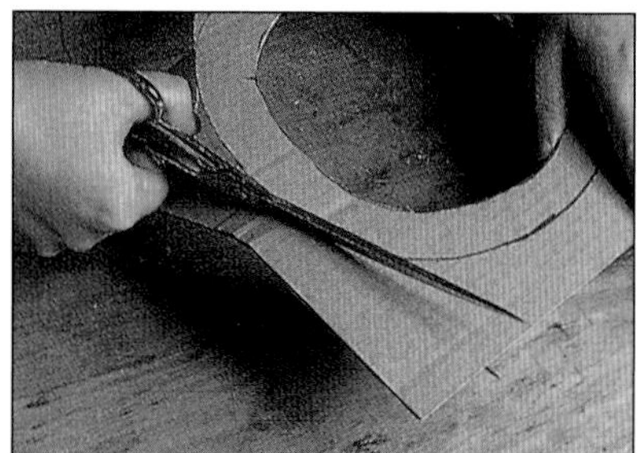

2 Cut the center out of the cardboard, then cut around the outer edge to form a ring.

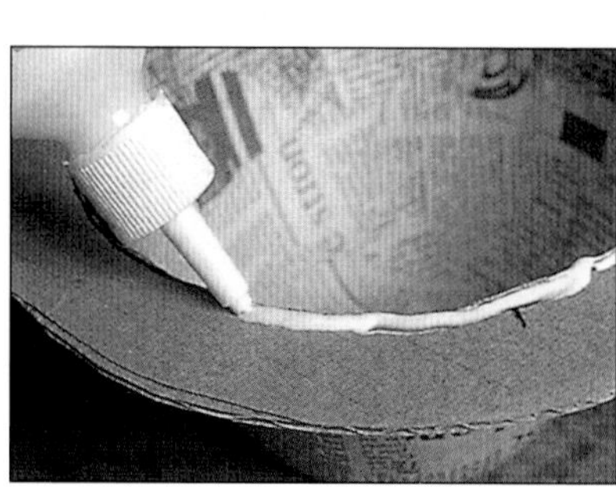

3 Fit the rim onto the bowl. Attach the seam with craft glue.

4 Secure with masking tape until dry.

5 Remove the tape, then cover the two surfaces of the rim and the seam to the bowl with two layers of pasted paper.

ABOVE *Dish. Yanina Temple. The dish has been made by layering paper over a mold. Its finished diameter is 14 inches.*

USING OTHER MOLDS

It is possible to make one-piece casts from a huge range of objects, as long as they are not complicated shapes. For example:

- balls
- balloons
- plates
- flowerpots
- woks.

Always cast from the inside of a bowl or flowerpot in order to release the paper cast in one piece. There is a certain amount of shrinkage of the paper during the drying process, which makes it difficult to release the cast from the outer surface of this kind of mold.

Multi-piece molds

Vases and jugs can be used as molds, but the paper must be cut in order to release it from the mold, to be re-joined afterward.

Such is the versatility of the technique that casts can be taken from anything, from apples to dolls. The more complicated the form, the smaller the pieces of paper should be, in order to cover a variety of curved surfaces without creasing.

When dry, the cast must be cut from the form in two halves with a scalpel. The sections should be released like the two halves of a shell. They must then be glued back together with a small quantity of glue, and the seam held temporarily with masking tape while the glue dries. The seam should then be disguised with two layers of pasted paper torn into thin strips.

Layering a self-made mold

Another approach to the layering method is to construct a self-made mold. This offers numerous possibilities. The simplest is a traditional relief mask (see the following demonstration), but it is entirely possible to make three-dimensional objects, where the paper is layered on all sides of the mold. Although clay is a suitable material for making a mold, the form to be cast can be made from various materials, depending on size. The most important consideration is that the paper can be easily released from the mold.

The methods for three materials are described here: plaster of Paris, wire, and modeling clay.

How to make a plaster mold

A more permanent mold can be made from plaster of Paris. Model the form in clay, then build a retaining wall with wooden boards or clay 1 inch higher than the mold. Build the whole structure on a wooden board and seal the walls to the board to prevent seepage. Mix the plaster according to the instructions. Pour it gently into the mold until it reaches the top of the retaining wall. Bang the work surface to force out any trapped bubbles. The plaster warms as it sets. When set, turn over and remove the clay. When the mold is dry, seal it with a coat of shellac. The mold is a negative. Proceed with the layering technique as described on the previous pages, or the pulp technique featured on pages 141–143.

How to make a mold over a wire armature

To make a larger, free-standing piece, papier-mâché can be layered over a wire armature. Build an armature from aluminum wire or chicken wire on a wooden base. Create a clay form around this armature and proceed with the layering technique as before, remembering to coat the mold first with a releasing agent. When all the layers have thoroughly dried, cut the cast from the mold and reassemble as described for multi-piece molds. The hole at the bottom of the cast where the wire armature was attached to the base can easily be covered by a few layers of paper.

How to make a clay mold

1 Model the shape of the mask on a wooden board. Take care not to allow any part to project too far, as this will cause difficulties when releasing the mask.

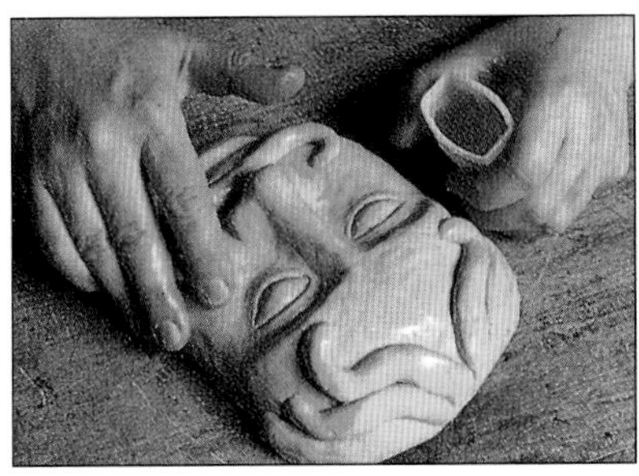

2 Coat the mold with an even layer of petroleum jelly or soft soap.

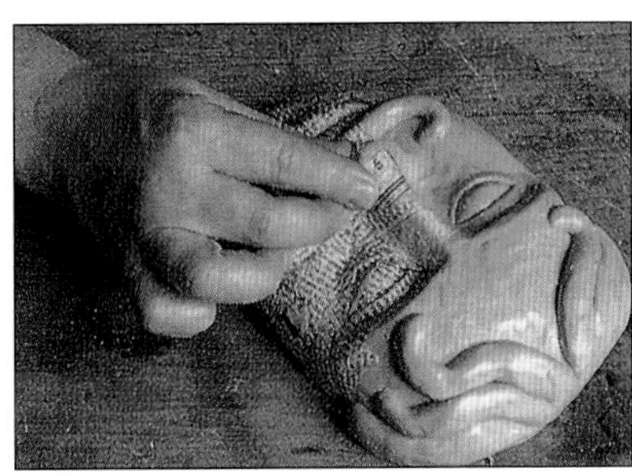

3 Apply the first layer of paper, using very small pieces. Carefully smooth the paper to remove air bubbles and excess paste.

4 Cover with eight layers in alternate colors. Allow to dry very thoroughly before removing from the mold.

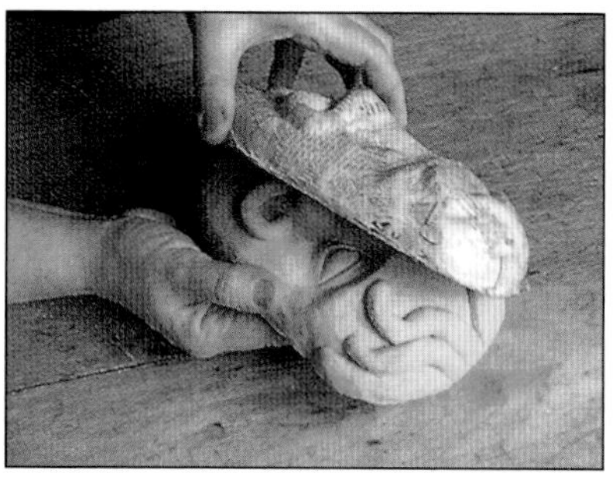

5 Release the cast by prizing the edges away from the clay with fingers or a blunt knife.

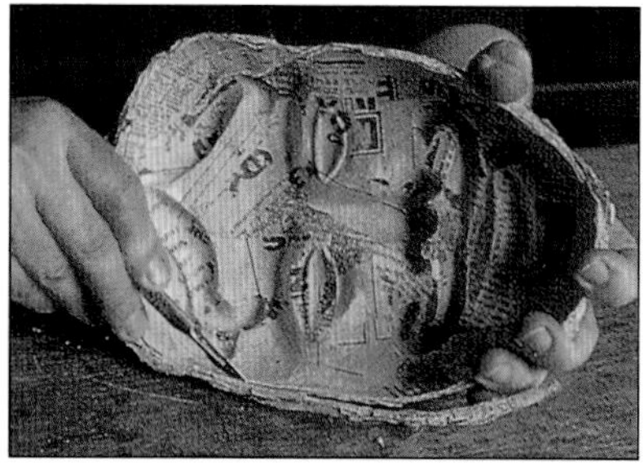

6 Trim the uneven edge of the mask, so that it can lie level.

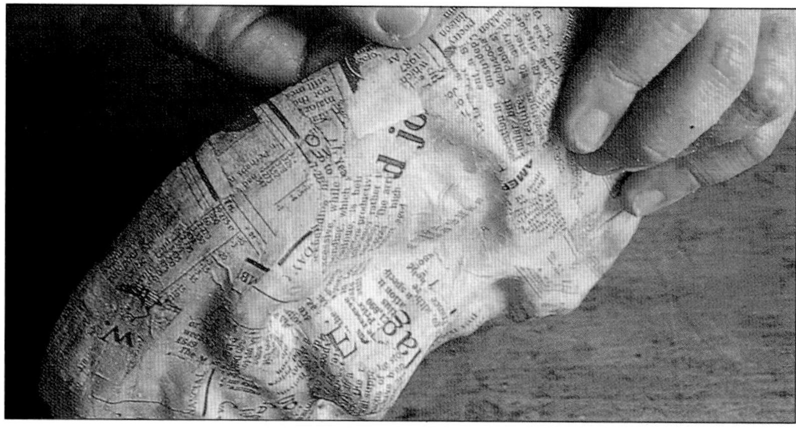

7 Cover the cut edges of the mask with two layers of paper. Allow to dry thoroughly before painting.

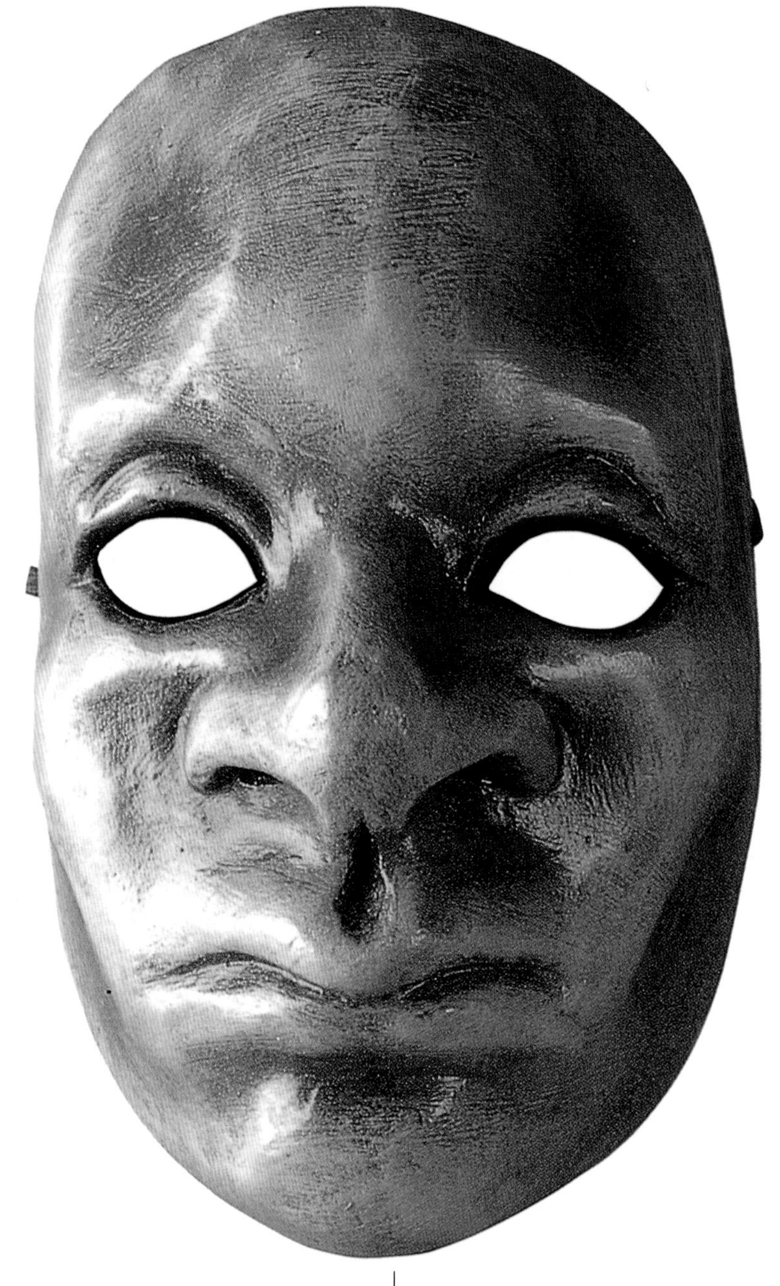

RIGHT *Mask. Mike Chase. The piece is made inside a negative plaster mold, taken from an original clay positive. The papier-mâché is layered, allowed to dry, and any blemishes filled in with modeling paste. Finally, the surface is painted with acrylic. The mask is not decorative, but was made specifically for an actor adopting the persona of a defensive character. It is life-size.*

PULPING

An alternative to the papier-mâché torn-paper method is to make a paper pulp. This can then be pressed into, or shaped over, any of the molds discussed under papier-mâché. It is a much quicker method for building up thickness than layering. Patterns and decoration can be created by using impressions from textured objects. The pulp can also be formed by itself without a mold.

ABOVE *Untitled. Judith Faerber. The piece is made by placing different-colored pulps on a flat bed of white pulp (for added strength). The mushy pulp is flattened under a heavy press, which compresses the fibers and squeezes out the water. Its finished size is 19 x 19 inches.*

How to make the pulp

① Soak a large saucepanful of shredded or torn paper in water overnight.

② Simmer the soaked paper on low for 20 minutes.

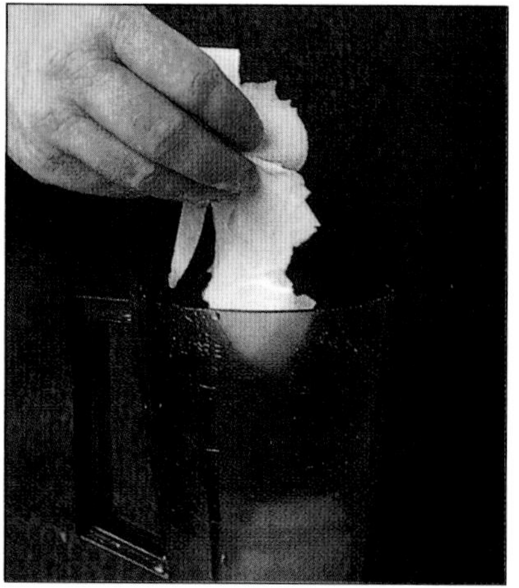

③ If the paper has not been finely shredded, blend or whisk the paper mix to help break it down.

Materials

Try to find shredded paper. Otherwise, any of the papers suggested for the papier-mâché layering method will work. Tear the paper into ½ inch squares.

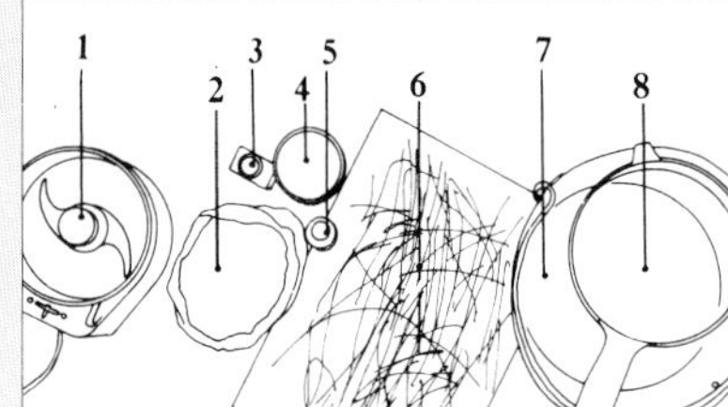

EQUIPMENT

1 kitchen blender or electric beater
2 plaster of Paris (or cellulose filler)
3 linseed oil; a few spoonfuls to help make pulp workable
4 craft glue (and/or wallpaper paste containing fungicide)
5 oil of cloves, a few drops to help prevent mold
6 shredded paper
7 large saucepan (preferably one not used for cooking)
8 strainer (or colander)

4 Strain the mixture through a strainer or colander. Lightly squeeze out excess water, but be careful not to condense the pulp to a hard, waterless mass.

5 Thoroughly mix in 1 cup of craft glue.

6 Sprinkle in enough dry wallpaper paste to give the pulp a workable consistency, mixing it quickly. Fillers and oil can be added if necessary.

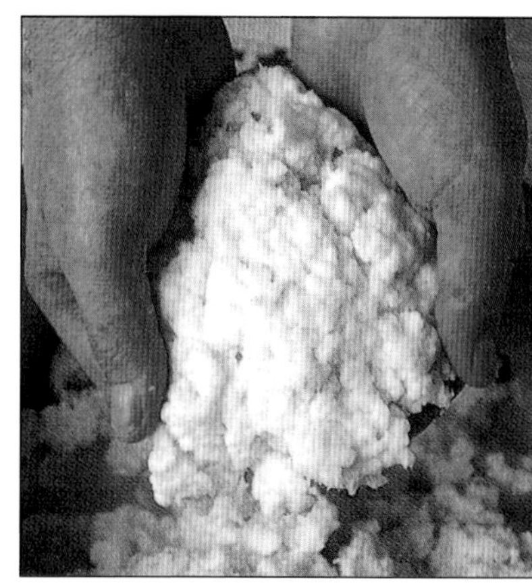

7 Store the pulp in a plastic bag in the refrigerator or use immediately.

AMERICAN INDIAN MASK

★ ★ ★

MATERIALS

Medium-weight cardboard

Balloon and string

Release agent (petroleum jelly)

Old newspapers

Craft glue

Tracing paper and cardboard

Pencil

Craft knife and scissors

Sandpaper

Latex paint

Paint brushes

Paints

Varnish

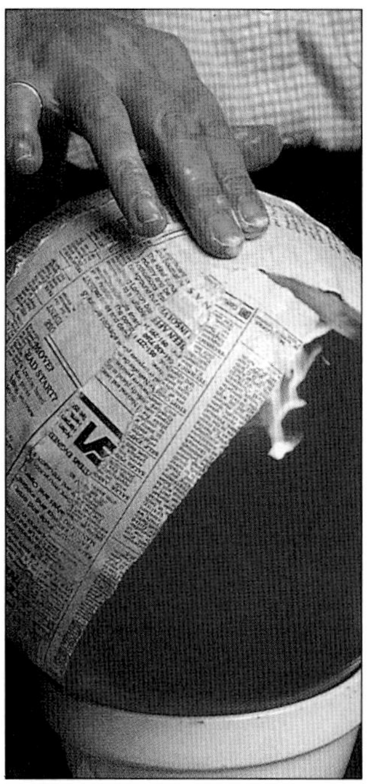

1 Blow up the balloon so that when it is held in front of you it is impossible to see the face. Tie firmly with string and cover with a thin coating of the release agent. One balloon will make two masks. Dilute the glue with water to the consistency of thin cream and tear the newspaper into strips about 1 inch wide. Make sure your working area is protected, as the next stage may be a little messy. Cover the balloon with the first layer of paper. If the balloon jumps around a bit, hold it in place on top of a bowl.

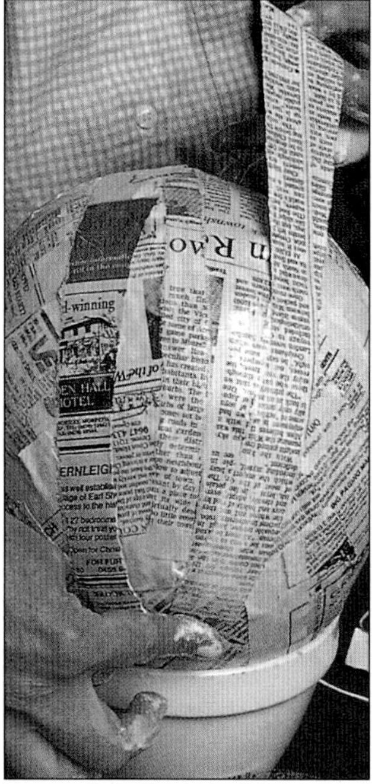

2 Put on a second layer – try to use paper of a different color to make it easier to see what you are doing. Continue in this way until you have completed eight layers. Try to make the last layer especially smooth to save time and work later.

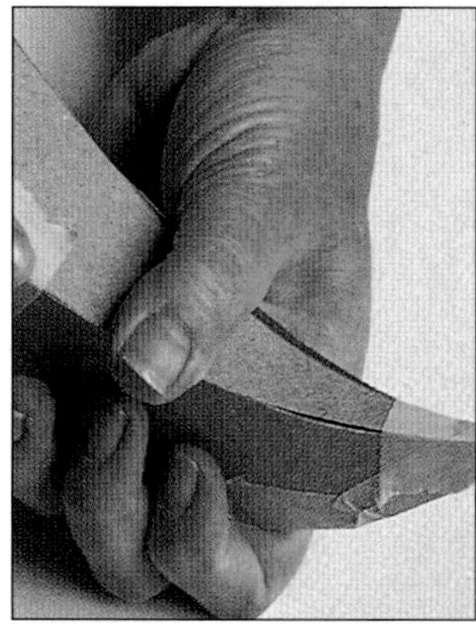

3 Make the beak shape next. Cut two side pieces and one base piece from medium-weight card. Join these pieces together with masking tape and cover with several layers of glue-soaked newspaper strips. It will be necessary to use quite small strips in order to cover the shape smoothly. Leave both balloon and beak to dry for 24 hours.

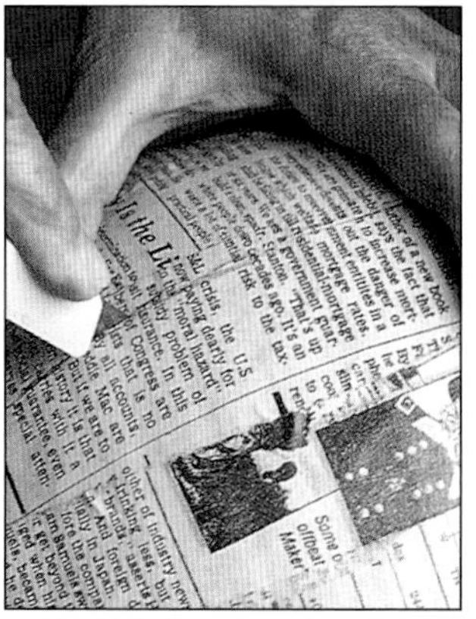

4 Now cut the papier-mâché balloon in half. It is easier if you draw a line around the balloon first and then cut carefully on the line with a craft knife, using a sawing action. The balloon may pop or it may just stick to the inside of the mold, but it will peel away easily.

5 Put on some lipstick and place the mask in front of your face. When it feels as if it is sitting comfortably, press your lips to the inside of the mask so that the lipstick marks the position of the mouth. Draw the required mouth shape on the inside and cut this out. On your own face, measure up from the mouth to the bridge of the nose and mark this distance on the mask. Now measure the distance between the centers of your eyes. Mark the position of the eyes on the papier-mâché. Draw in the shape of the eyes and cut them out carefully.

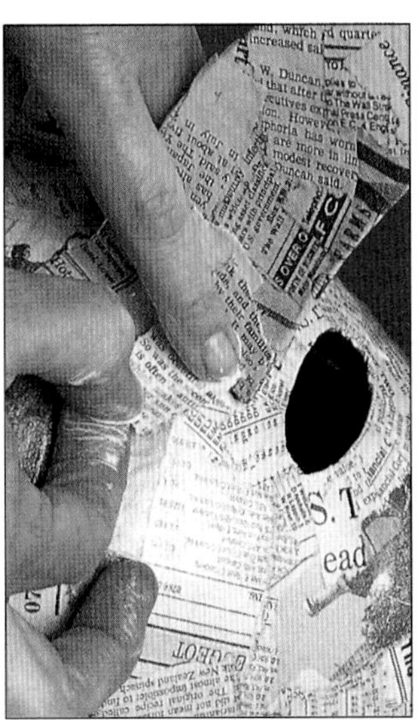

6 Take the beak shape and trim the open edges. Using masking tape, join the beak in position to the mask. Now take some newspaper strips and diluted craft glue and bind the cut edges with two or three layers of paper.

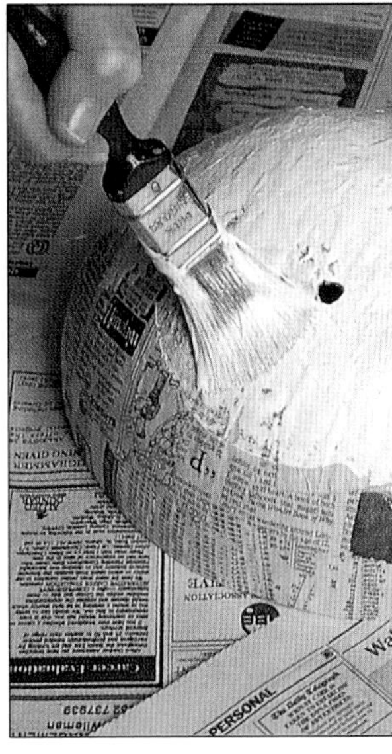

7 Trim the edge of the mask and then bind all the cut edges – outer, mouth, and eyes – with small pieces of newspaper. Leave to dry again. Paint the whole mask white.

8 Next draw the outline of the final design onto the surface of the mask. Mix the colored paints to a smooth consistency and paint carefully. Let the paint dry overnight and then varnish. Make holes in the sides of the mask slightly above eye level and thread string or ribbon through the holes so that the mask can be tied in place.

BELOW *This style lends itself very nicely to the shape created by a papier-mâché balloon mask. Traditionally carved from wood, the mask images are usually taken from animal forms. American Indians lived in harmony with nature, and their folklore gave equality to all living things. Although they recognized that their physical appearances differed from animals, they felt they were descended from them, and each tribe had a special affinity with a particular animal such as a bear, a wolf, or an eagle. It is for this reason that many of their carvings take on the appearance of half animal, half man.*

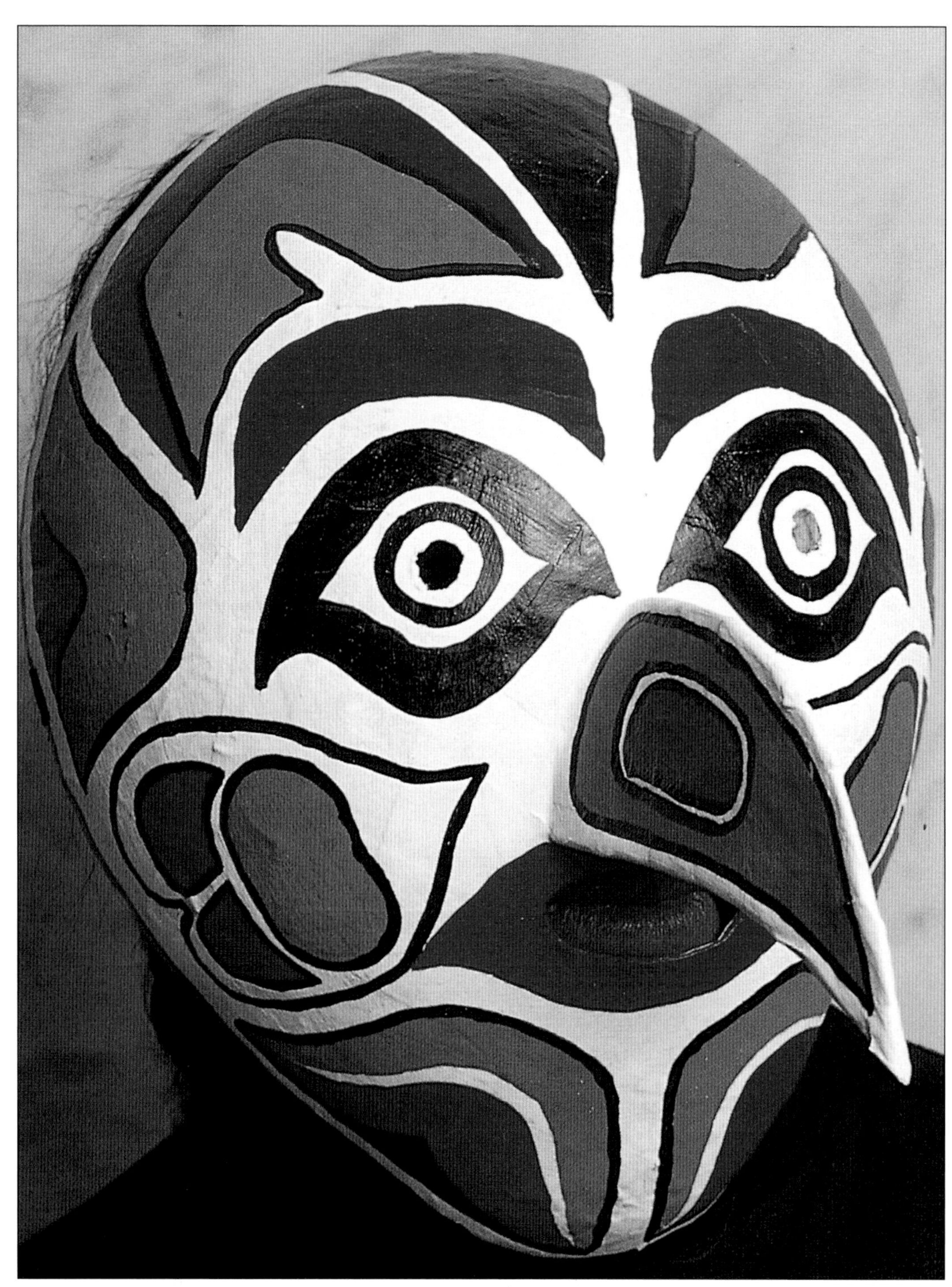

ASTRONAUT MASK

★★★

The mould has been made by piling screwed-up newspaper onto a flat plastic-covered board and taping the pieces so that they stay in position. The shape into which the newspaper pieces are placed is decided by taking a few basic measurements – overall height, width and depth. If there are any curves, look carefully where these occur and use the tape to create the right shape.

When you are satisfied that the overall appearance is correct, cover the mould with polythene – this will provide a smooth surface on which to lay the strips. Put a thin layer of petroleum jelly over the surface, then you are ready to start putting on the newspaper strips. The first layer may be a little awkward but if you use long strips it will help. Making the second layer go in the opposite direction will help you to keep the layers even and will add to the strength.

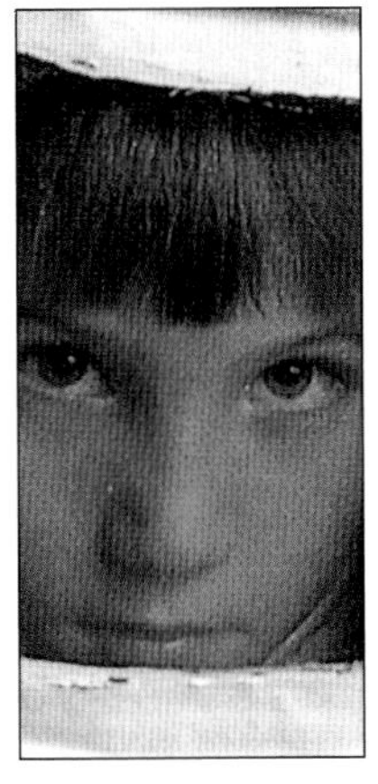

MATERIALS

- Plastic-covered base board for the mold
- Old newspapers
- Sheet of thin plastic
- Masking tape
- Petroleum jelly or similar for release agent
- Craft glue
- Thick string
- Pencil
- Sheet of thin acetate for visor
- Sandpaper
- White paint

1 As the mask sits on the shoulders, it will be necessary to measure from the shoulder to the top of the head to ascertain the height measurement. The width is measured across from ear to ear. When working out the depth measurement, be sure to remember that you should halve it, as the mask is made in two halves. The depth is measured from the back of the head to the front. All the measurements should be generous, as the finished mask has no openings and simply slips over the head of the wearer.

Roughly mark out the dimensions on the board and start piling up the newspapers. Do not try to make a cube – the head is rounded! As the pile grows, it may be necessary to tape it down as you go along. When you are satisfied with the shape, cover it with plastic – some old shopping bags will serve the purpose.

2 Using long strips of newspaper, cover the mold right down onto the base board. Continue to build up the layers until eight layers have been completed. Leave in a warm place to dry out thoroughly.

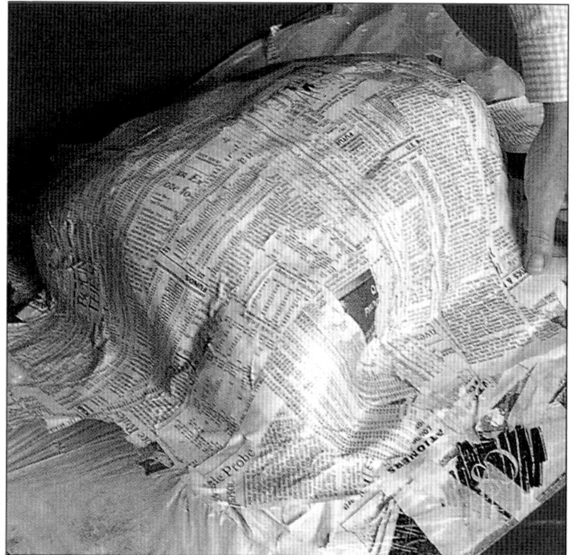

3 Carefully lift the half-mask off the mold and set aside until you have completed the second half. Do not worry if the two halves are not absolutely identical.

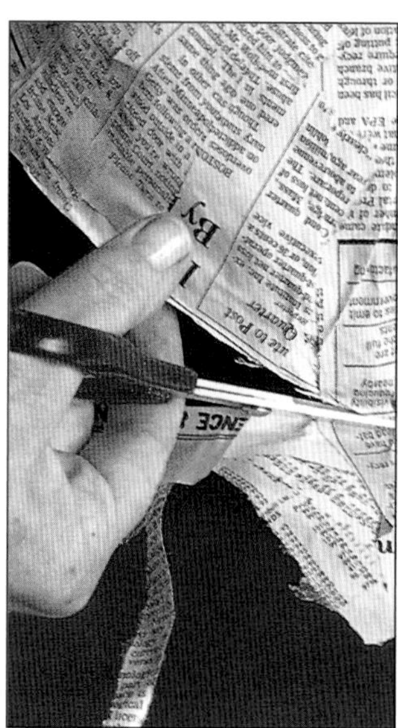

4 Cut away the edge of the mask which was on the base board, including the neck area, and then hold the two halves together to see how well they fit. If necessary, trim away extra bits until the halves touch all around as much as possible. Small gaps can be covered when the two pieces of the mask are joined.

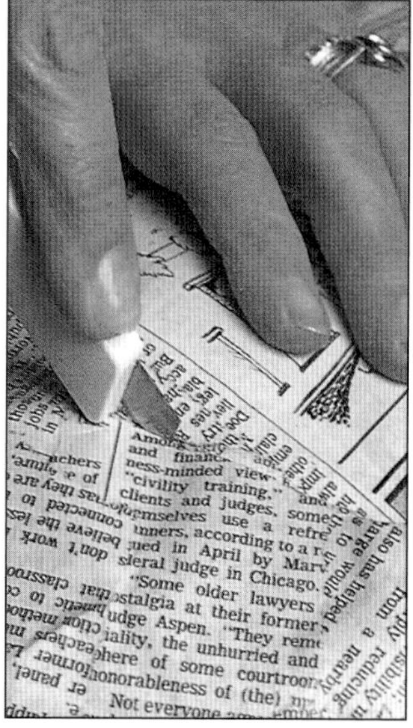

5 Now cut out the window for the visor in one of the halves. This should be almost as wide as the face and from mid-forehead to mid-chin.

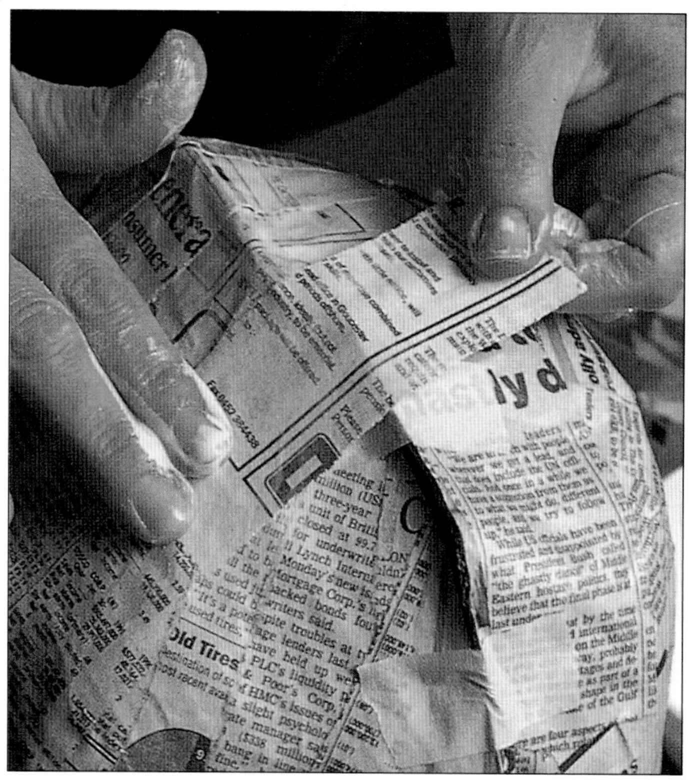

6 Tape the two halves together and carefully try on the mask. Join with three or four layers of newspaper strips. At the same time, bind all the cut edges. Leave to dry.

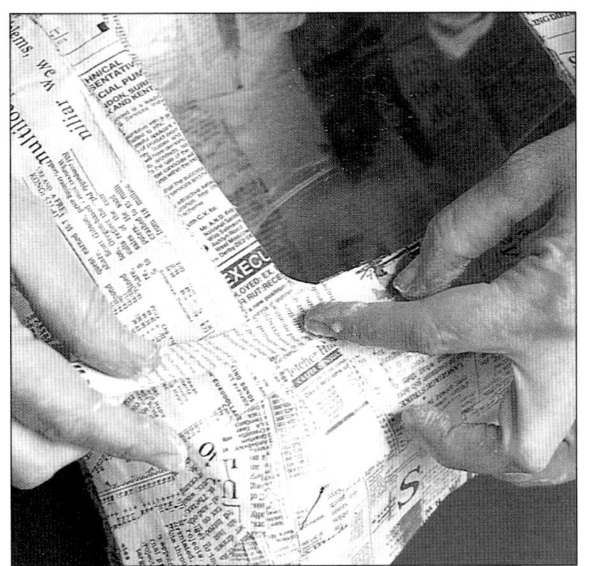

⑦ Cut the acetate so that it overlaps the window by ½ inch and anchor it in place with small pieces of masking tape and newspaper.

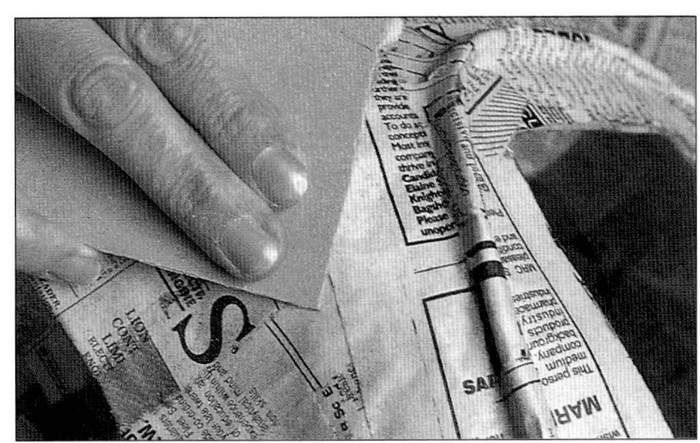

⑨ Use sandpaper to smooth away any noticeable bumps, which may have occurred particularly around the seam.

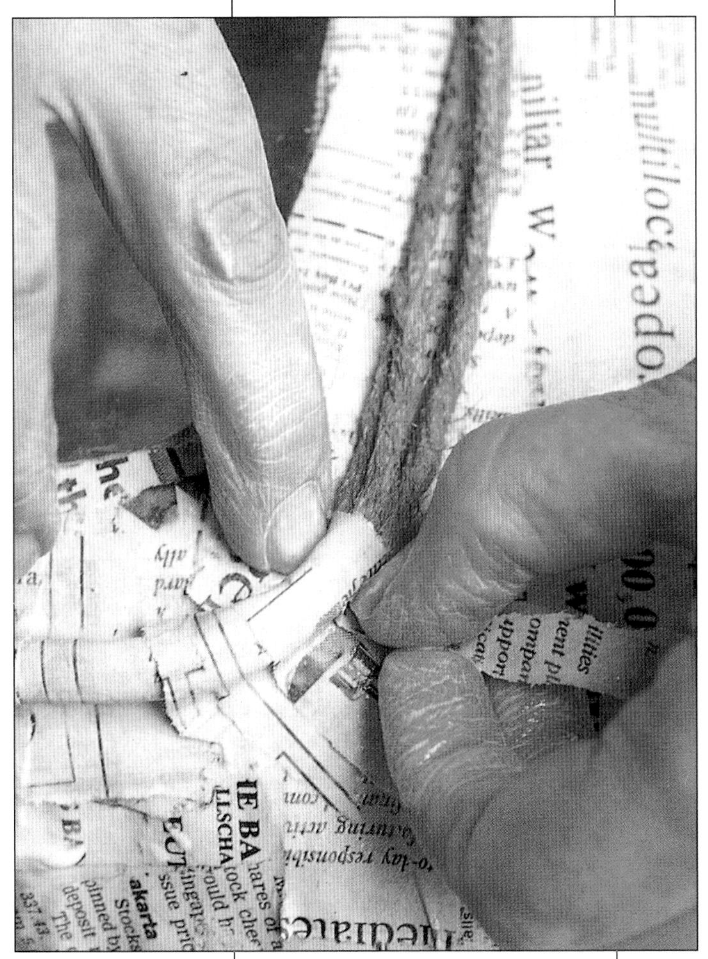

⑧ Make a border around the window with string covered by two or three layers of papier-mâché.

⑩ Paint with two coats of latex, carefully avoiding the visor area.

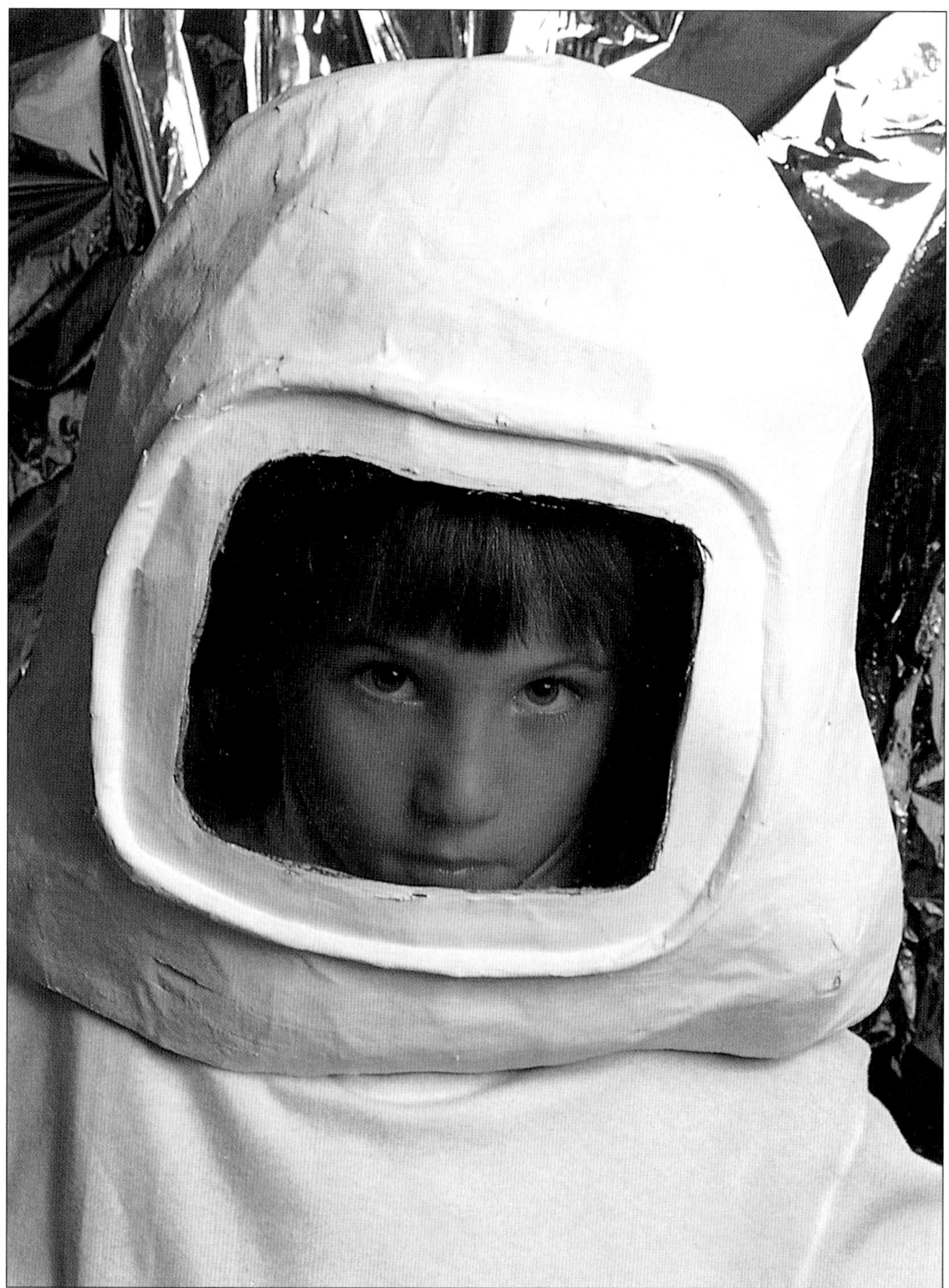

ABOVE *This mask has a very simple shape, but takes quite a long time to make as it is constructed in two halves. The decoration is quite straightforward, and the materials required are readily obtainable.*

THE BIG BREAKFAST

★★

Cook up this mouthwatering big breakfast mobile using papier-mâché and cardboard. The glossy finish is achieved by applying a coat of clear polyurethane varnish.

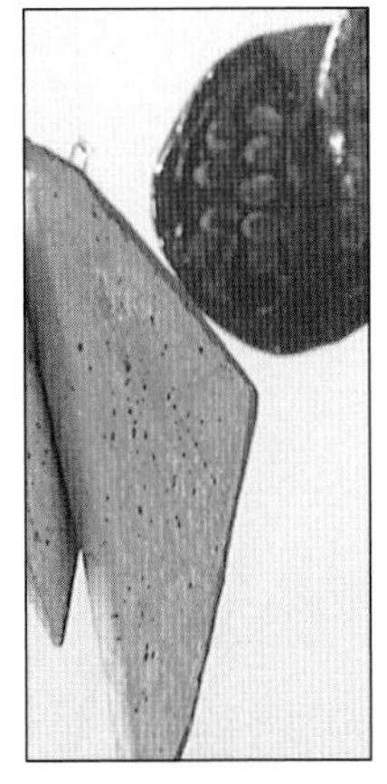

MATERIALS

- Tracing paper
- Pencil
- 11 x 16-inch sheet of corrugated cardboard
- Scissors
- Craft glue
- Flour and water
- Bowl
- Newspaper
- Fine-grit sandpaper
- White latex paint
- Mixing palette
- Paintbrushes in several sizes
- Poster paints
- Clear gloss polyurethane varnish
- Paper clips
- Long-nosed pliers
- Needle
- About 3 feet galvanized wire, 1/25-inch in diameter
- Colored cotton thread

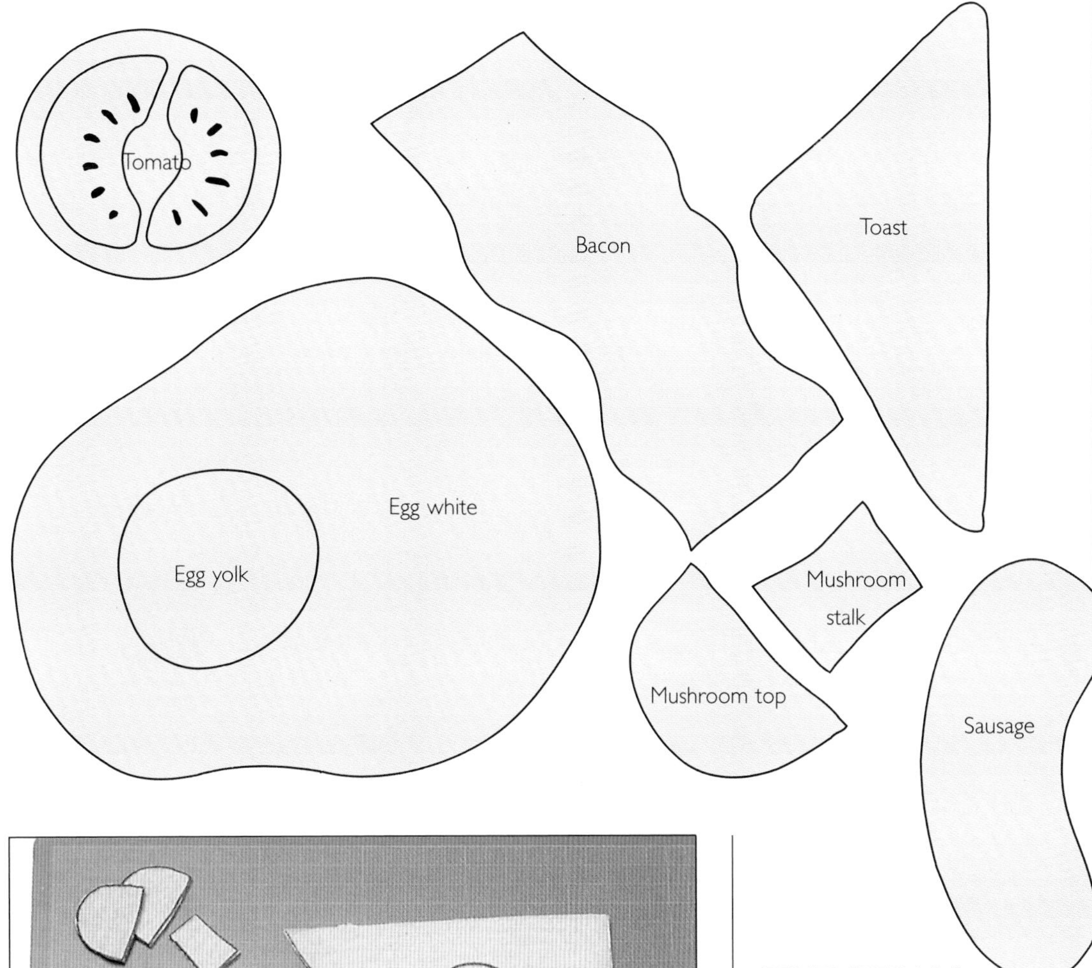

TEMPLATES 1:1.5

1. Trace the templates of the food shapes from this book, cut them out and use them as guides to draw the shapes on corrugated cardboard. Cut out the cardboard shapes – here we are showing the egg and mushroom, which are three-dimensional. You will need two sausages, two slices of toast, two tomatoes, four mushroom tops, and two mushroom stalks.

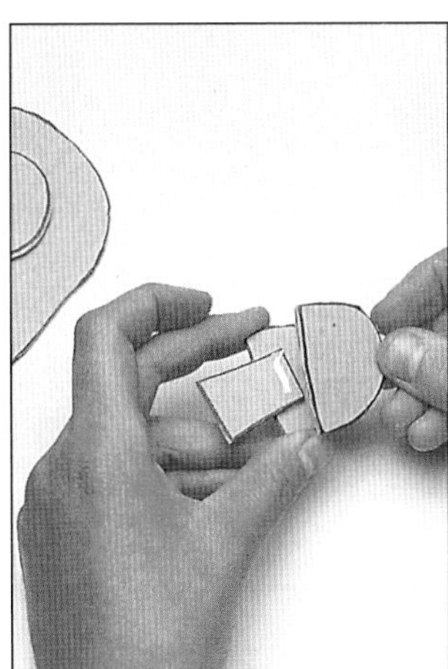

2. Some of the shapes require extra details, such as the egg yolk, also made of cardboard. Glue these on. Glue the mushroom top pieces on each side of the stalk.

3 Mix a flour and water paste in a bowl; it should have the consistency of thick batter. Tear up strips of newspaper, dip them in the paste, and use them to cover the cardboard food shapes – about two or three layers should do. Leave in a warm place to dry.

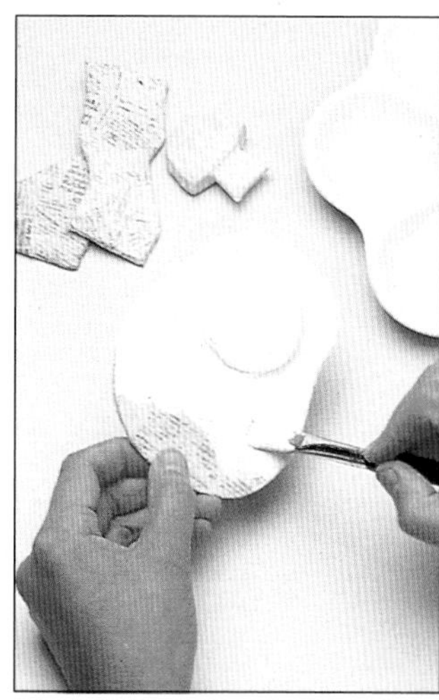

4 Once the papier-mâché shapes have dried, smooth down the surface and edges with fine sandpaper. Paint with a base coat of white latex paint.

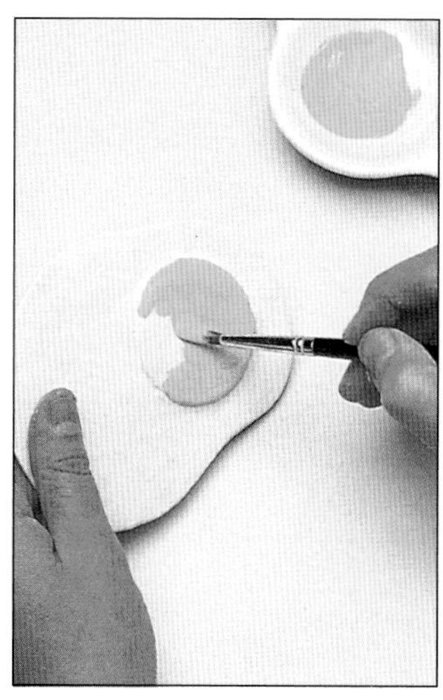

5 When the base coat has dried, paint the shapes in the appropriate poster colors (for instance, yellow for the egg yolk) and paint in details (such as seeds on the tomato slices).

6 Once the shapes are all dry, apply a coat of clear gloss varnish to both sides.

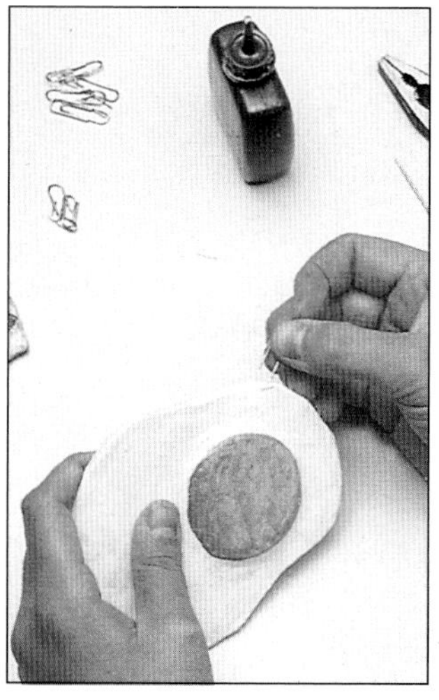

7 Cut three paper clips in half, using pliers, to make hooks. Use a needle to pierce two holes in the edge of each food shape ¼ inch apart. Place a drop of glue on each end of the hooks and insert them into the shapes. Allow to dry.

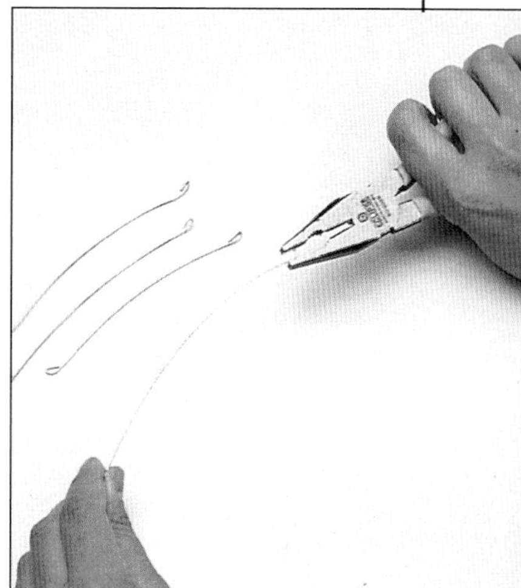

8 From the wire cut three struts measuring 6 inches and one measuring 11 inches. Use pliers to make a hook at each end of each strut.

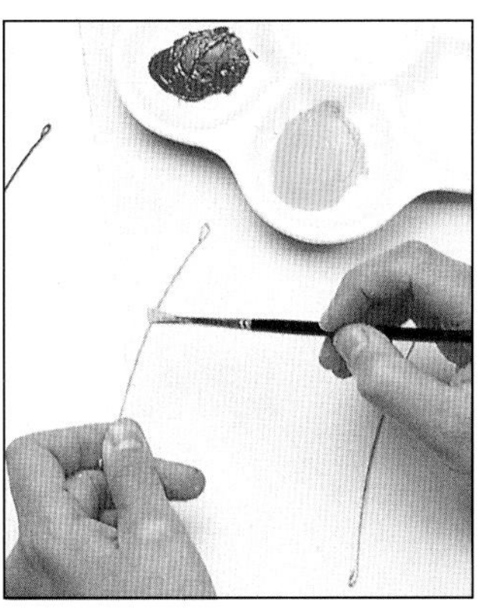

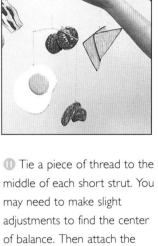

9 Paint these struts in colors that go with those of the food shapes – yellow and red.

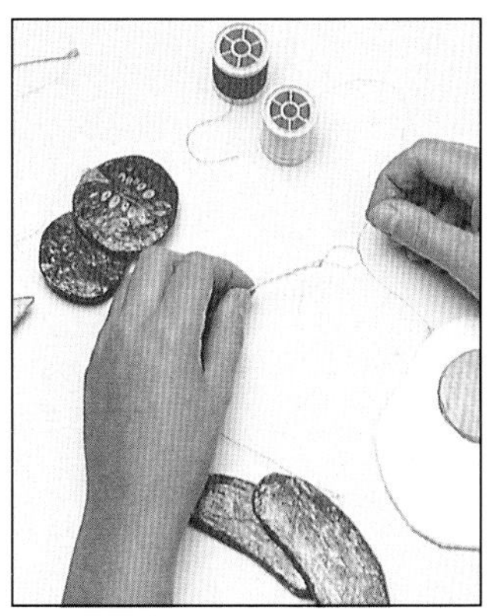

10 Using different lengths of thread, attach a piece of food to each end of each short strut.

11 Tie a piece of thread to the middle of each short strut. You may need to make slight adjustments to find the center of balance. Then attach the three short struts to the long strut, one at each end and one in the middle. To achieve a visually satisfactory mobile, you may need to adjust the lengths of the threads from which the food hangs.

MATERIALS

Balloon

Flour and water

Bowl

Newspaper

Dressmaker's pin

Fine-grit sandpaper

White latex paint

Mixing palette

Paint brushes in several sizes

Poster paints

Silver spray paint

11 x 16 sheet of white thin cardboard

11 x 16 sheet of white mat board

Tracing paper

Pencil

Scissors

Craft knife

Craft glue

About 12 flat beads

Needle

Silver thread

Assortment of sparkling beads

About 3 feet of galvanized wire, 1/16 inch in diameter

Masking tape

About 6 feet of galvanized wire, 1/25 inch in diameter

UNDERWATER WORLD

★★★

Create a magical ocean world of shells and sea creatures. Sparkling beads and silver spray paint are used in this mixed-media project to complete a marine-inspired mobile.

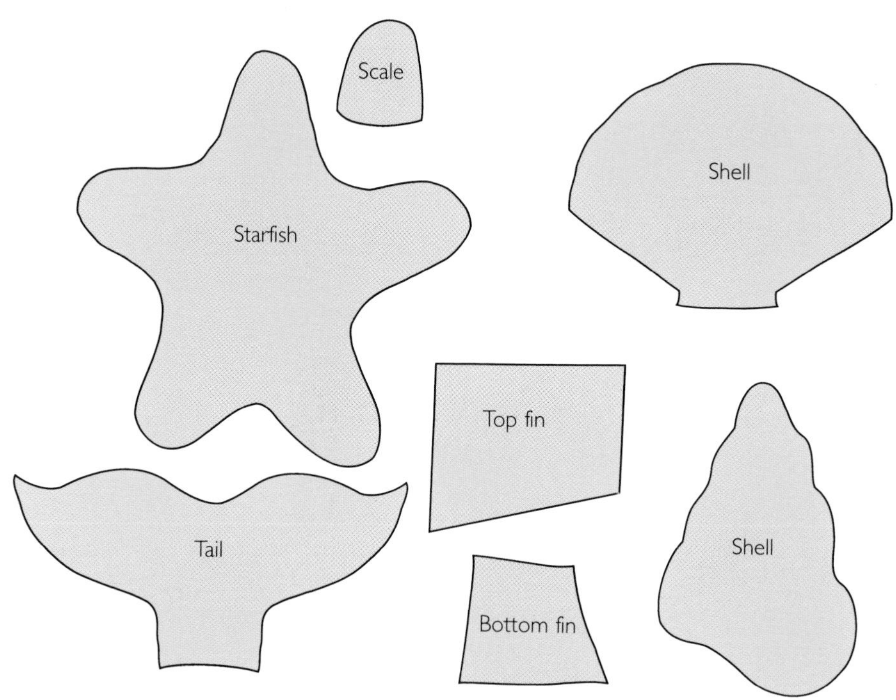

TEMPLATES 1:1.5

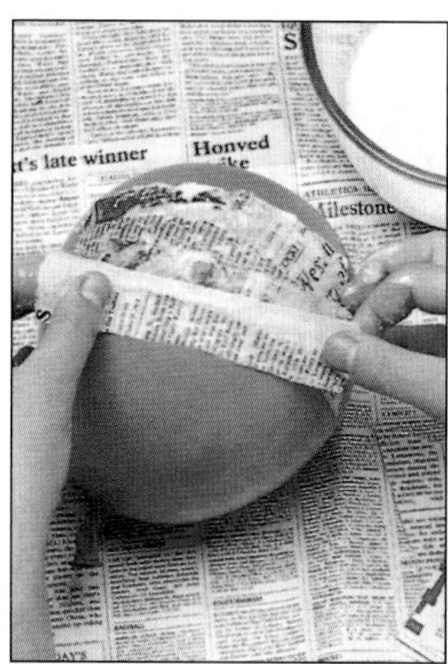

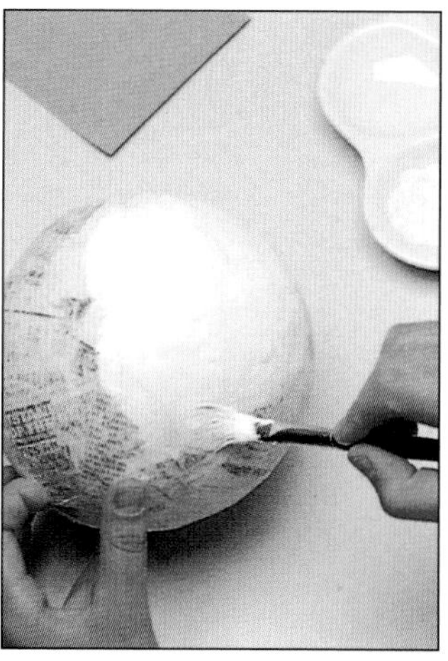

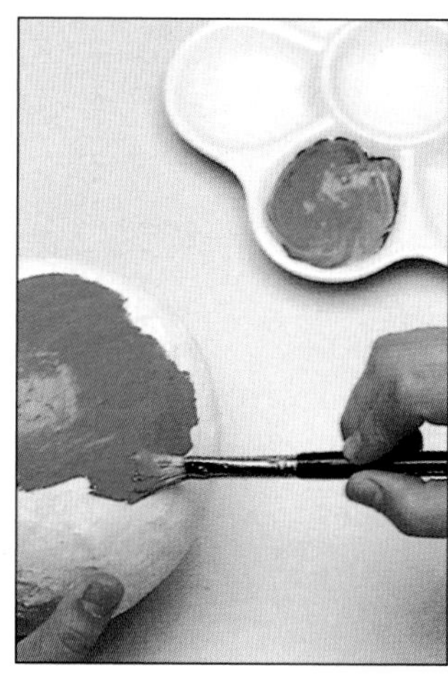

1 Blow up a balloon, but not fully – just enough to achieve a round shape. Mix some flour and water into a paste in a bowl; the mixture should resemble thick batter. Tear up the newspaper into small strips, dip these into the paste and use them to cover the balloon with two or three layers of papier-mâché. Leave in a warm place to dry, perhaps overnight.

2 When the balloon is dry, pop it with a pin and gently smooth down the ball shape with fine sandpaper. Apply a coat of white latex paint. Allow to dry.

3 Apply a poster color to the ball shape – we have chosen purple. Allow to dry.

4 Spray the ball with silver spray paint. When this is dry, splatter it with paint of another color. Hold the brush of water paint about 1 inch away, bend back the bristles with your fingertip, then let them spring back. Lay a sheet of thin cardboard and a sheet of mat board on newspaper and spray them lightly with the silver spray paint.

5 Trace the templates for the fish's tail and fins from this book and cut them out. Use them as a guide to draw the shapes on the silver-sprayed mat board, then cut these out with scissors. Cut about thirty scales from the silver-sprayed thin cardboard.

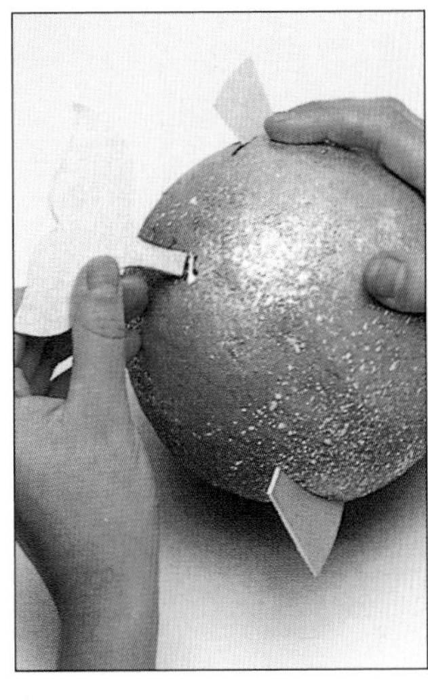

6 Use a pencil to mark on the fish the positions of the fins and tail. Cut slits of the appropriate size using a craft knife. Place glue in the slits and insert the fins and tail. Allow to dry.

7 Attach the scales in clusters on the body of the fish by applying glue to the narrower end of each one. Bend them slightly before you attach them and make sure that they overlap.

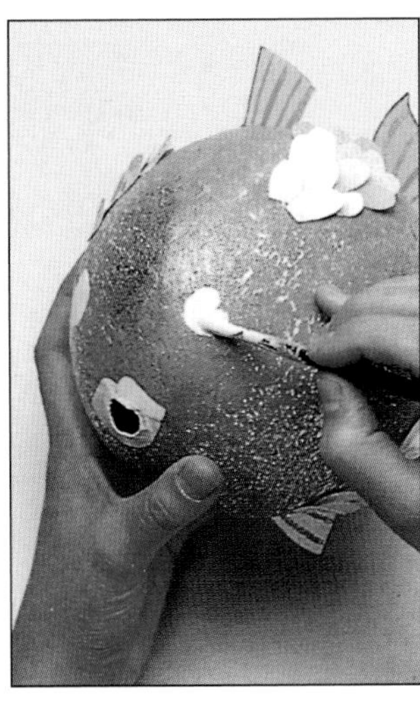

8 Paint stripes on the fins and tail of the fish. Make a small hole for the mouth using a craft knife and paint lips around it. Paint the eyes.

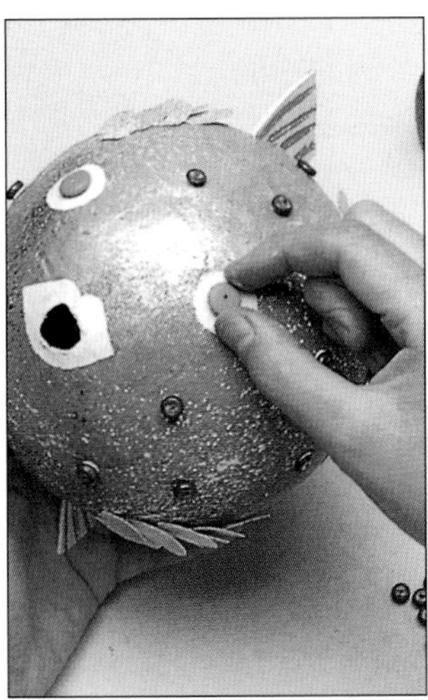

9 Use glue to attach flat beads or any other decoration you may want to add. Glue larger beads to the eyes, too.

10 Trace the templates for the shells and starfish from this book and cut them out. Use them as a guide to draw and cut out a total of eight shapes.

11 Paint the shapes in a variety of poster colors – we have chosen pastels.

12 Add more detail to the shapes to bring out their shell-like qualities. Splattering is a useful technique at this stage, too.

13 Thread a needle with silver thread and use it to pierce a hole in each shape. Knot the thread to secure it. Now thread some sparkling beads at intervals along each thread: do this by taking the needle through each bead twice.

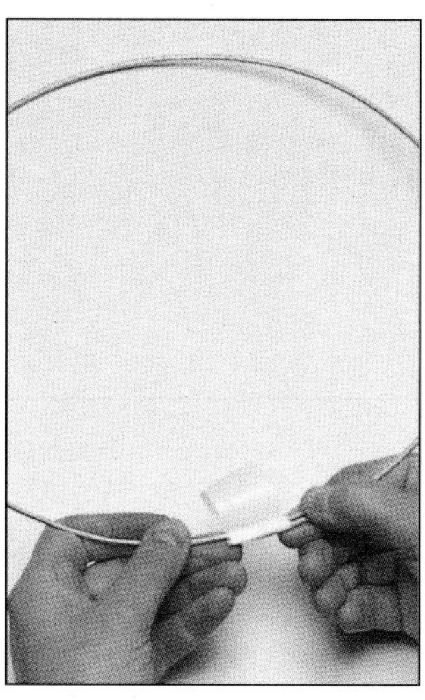

14 Use pliers to cut a piece of the thicker wire 27 inches long and bend it into a circle with a diameter of about 8 inches. Secure the two ends together with a small strip of masking tape. Spray or paint the masking tape silver to match the wire.

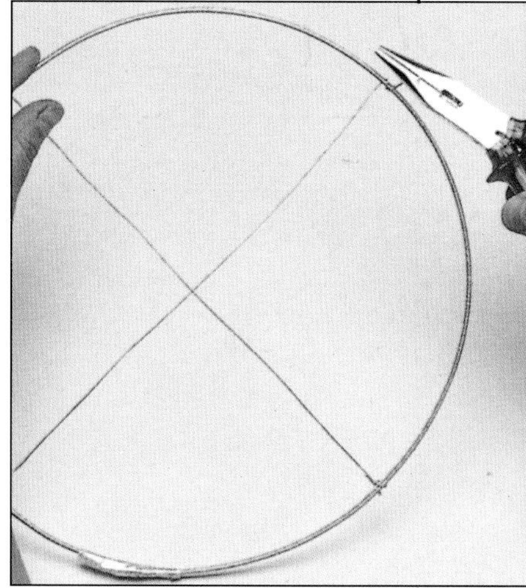

15 Cut two pieces of the thinner wire about 10 inches long. Use pliers to bend the ends of these two pieces of wire around the circle so that they cross over one another, dividing the circle into quarters. The wires should be taut and rigid.

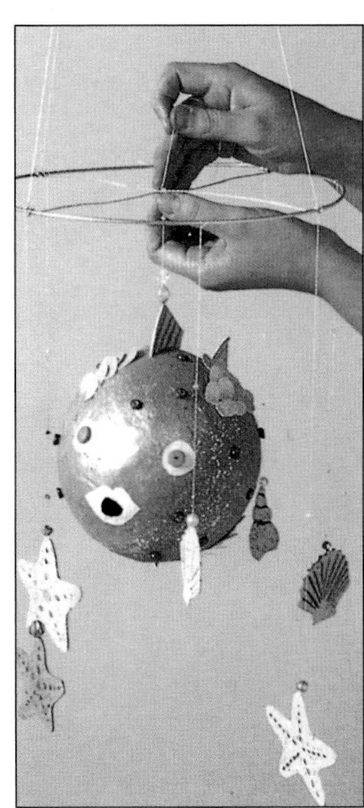

16 Cut four pieces of silver thread 20 inches long and attach each one to the wire circle at the point where a thinner wire meets it. Draw all the threads up above the wire frame and play around with the balance until the frame is level, then tie the threads together in a knot. Attach the shells and starfish to the frame so that they are equal distances apart. Pierce the top of the round fish's fin with needle threaded with silver thread, add a couple of beads, and tie it to the circular frame at the point where the wires cross in the middle.

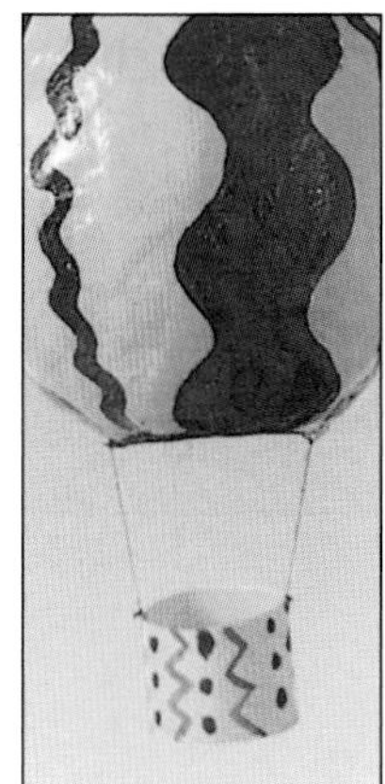

MATERIALS

3 balloons

Flour and water

Bowl

Newspaper

Dressmaker's pin

Fine-grit sandpaper

Drawing compass

Craft knife

White latex paint

Mixing palette

Paint brushes in several sizes

Pencil

Poster paints

Clear gloss polyurethane varnish

3 sheets of thin 10 x 8 cardboard in different colors

Craft glue

Needle

Colored cotton thread

Long-nosed pliers

Paper clips

1 wooden skewer

HOT-AIR BALLOONS

★ ★ ★

One of the most basic techniques in papier-mâché involves molding paper around a balloon, and what could be more appropriate than to use this process to create this stunning trio of hot-air balloons?

1 Blow up three balloons to slightly different sizes. Mix a paste of flour and water in a bowl; it should be the consistency of thick batter. Rip up newspaper into strips roughly 1 x 4 inches, dip these in the paste, and use them to cover the balloons with three or four layers of papier-mâché. Try to avoid air bubbles and lumps forming as you go. Leave in a warm place to dry, possibly overnight.

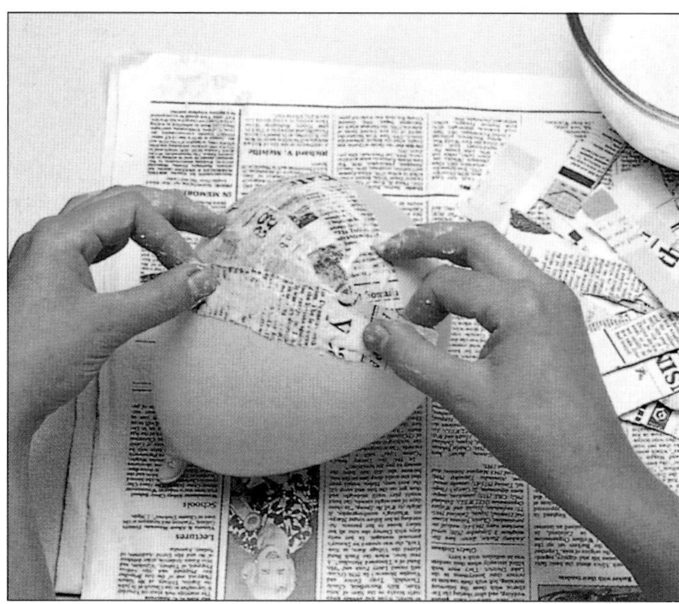

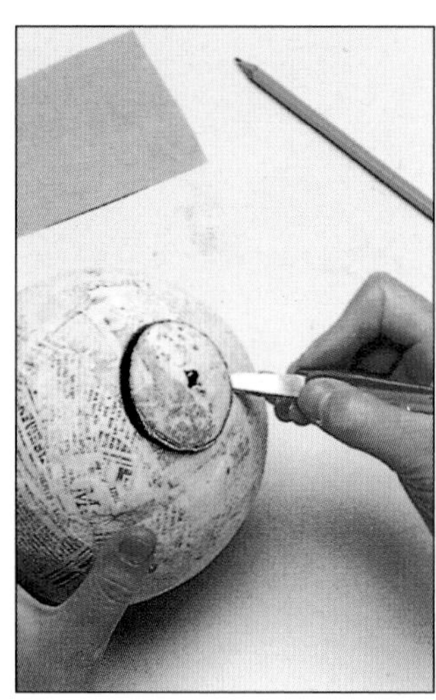

2 Once they are fully dry, burst the balloons with a pin, then gently sand the shapes using fine sandpaper. Draw a circle with a diameter of 2 to 3 inches on the base of each balloon and cut it out with a craft knife. Smooth off any rough edges using the sandpaper.

3 Paint the balloons with a coat of white latex paint and allow to dry thoroughly.

4 Using a pencil, lightly draw designs on the balloons. Paint with poster paints.

5 Once the paint is dry, apply a coat of clear gloss varnish.

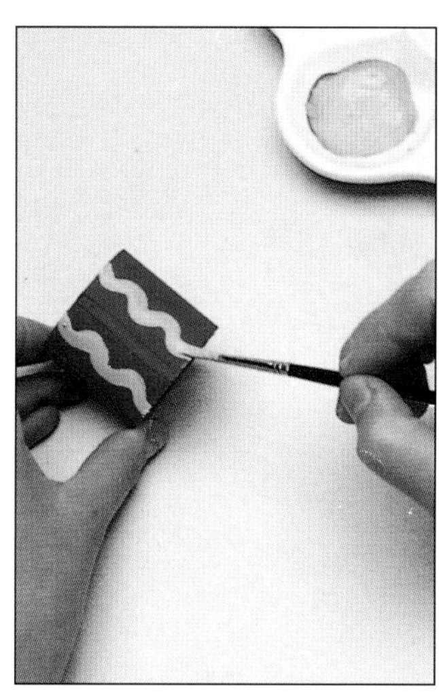

6 To make a basket, cut out a strip of colored cardboard about 2 x 7 inches. Glue the two ends together, slightly overlapping them to form a cylinder, and decorate with paint.

7 Place the cylinder on a piece of the same color cardboard, draw around it, cut this out and glue it to the base of the basket. Repeat this step for the other two baskets, but make them all different colors.

8 Use pliers to cut two paper clips in half, creating four hooks (only three of which you will need). Using a large needle, pierce two holes ¼ inch apart at the top of each balloon. Place a drop of glue on each end of each hook and insert them into the holes.

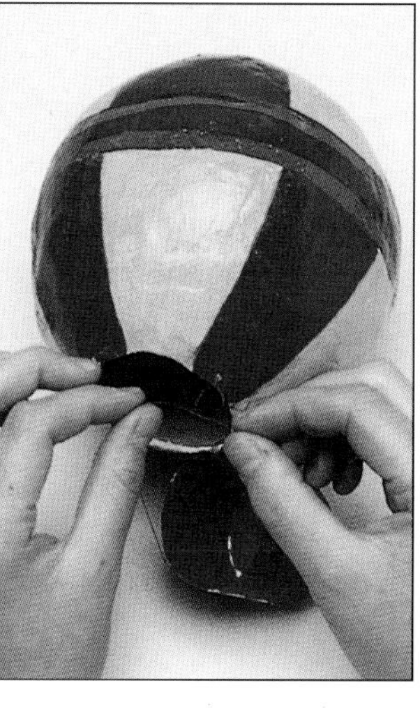

9 Thread a needle with thread in a color that matches the balloons. Make a knot in the end. Pierce the needle through the top edge of one of the baskets. Take the needle through the hole twice to make it secure. Now pierce the needle through the matching balloon's base at the edge of the circle. Allow 2 to 3 inches of thread between the basket and the balloon, and secure it by taking the needle through the hole once more and knotting it. Repeat this on the other side and on the other two baskets and their balloons.

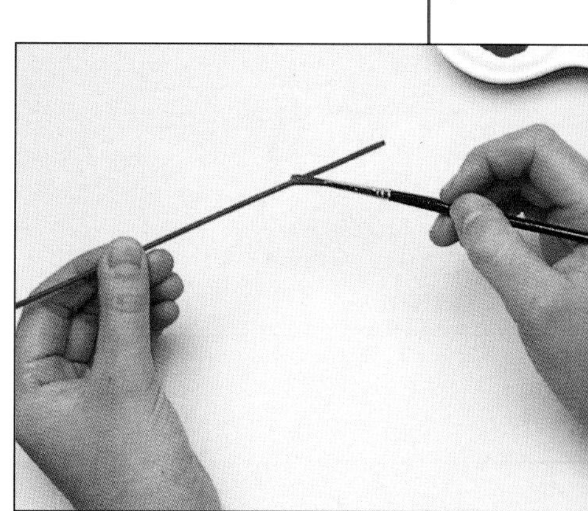

10 Cut off and discard the sharp end of a wooden skewer. Paint it a color to match the balloons: this will form the strut from which the mobile will hang.

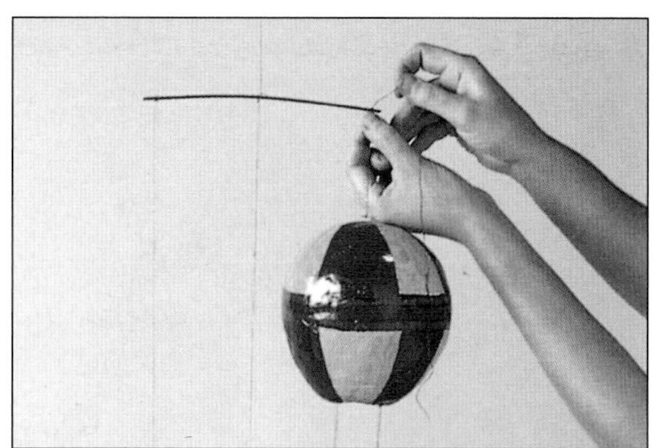

11 Attach a double-thickness of thread to the middle of the strut to hang the mobile from. Now tie one end of a length of thread to each balloon hook and the other end to the strut, attaching one balloon in the middle and one at each end. Suspend the balloons at different lengths.

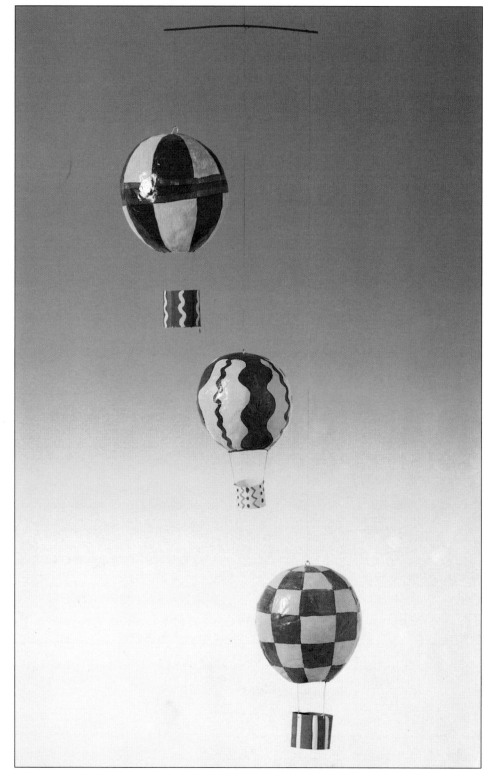

FEATHERED FRIENDS

This richly decorated flock of exotic papier-mâché birds combines an interesting "layered" paint technique using sandpaper with bright feathers, sequins, and glitter pens, resulting in a dazzling mobile.

MATERIALS

Tracing paper

Pencil

Scissors

11 x 16 sheet of corrugated cardboard

Craft knife and cutting mat

Flour and water

Bowl

Newspaper

Fine-grit sandpaper

White latex paint

Mixing palette

Paint brushes in several sizes

Bright poster paints

Assortment of sequins

Craft glue

Glitter pens

Needle or pin

Bright-colored feathers

Long-nosed pliers

Paper clips

2½ feet of galvanized wire, 1/16 inch in diameter

Masking tape

Silver spray paint

20 inches of galvanized wire, 1/25 inch in diameter

Gold thread

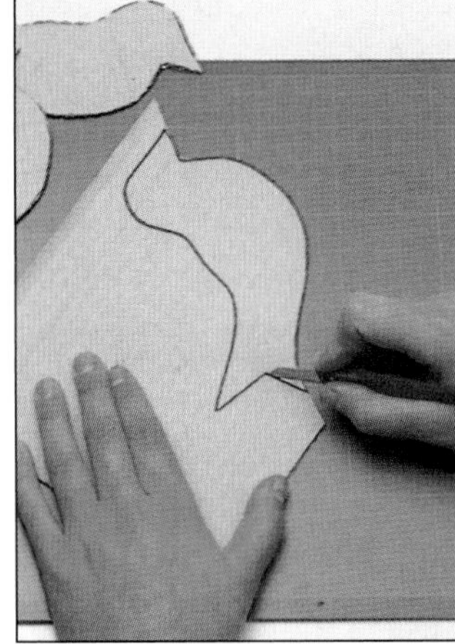

1 Trace the bird template from this book and cut it out. Use it as a guide to draw five bird shapes on corrugated cardboard and cut these out using a craft knife and cutting mat.

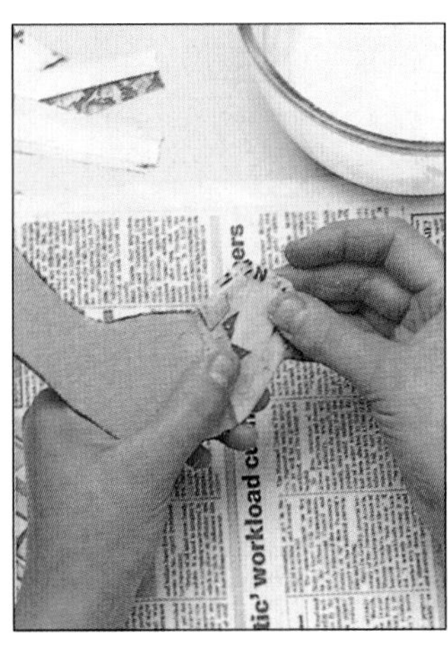

2 Mix a flour and water paste in a bowl; it should be the consistency of thick batter. Tear up newspaper into small strips, dip these in the paste, and use them to cover the bird shapes with two or three layers of papier-mâché. Leave in a warm place to dry.

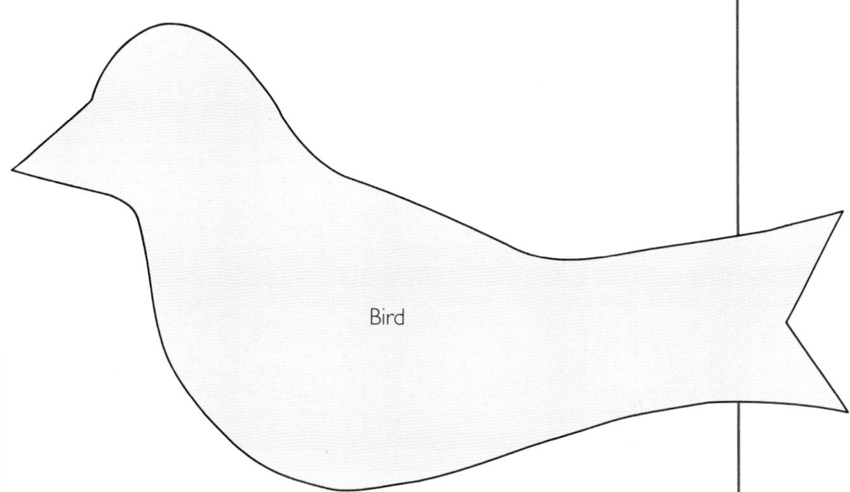

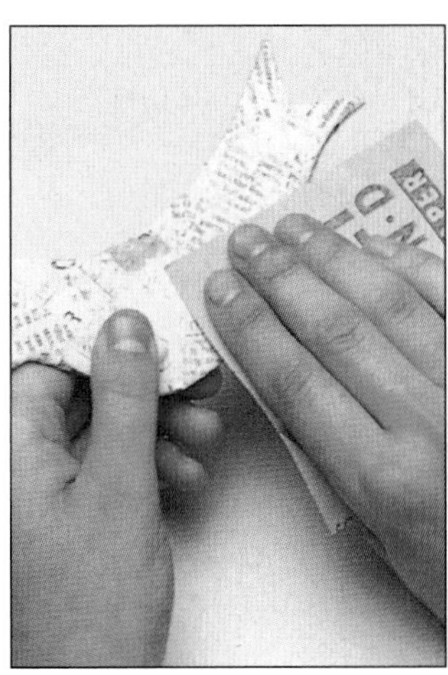

3 Once the shapes are completely dry, smooth them down using fine sandpaper.

4 Paint the birds with a coat of white latex paint. Allow to dry, then apply an even, thick coat of a bright, strongly-colored poster paint – we have used a vibrant pink.

5 When the paint is dry, apply another coat of white paint. Once this has dried, coat with a further strong color, which will contrast well with the earlier one – we have chosen a bright blue.

6 When the paint is completely dry, gently rub the surface of the bird shapes with sandpaper. You will notice how the first color soon begins to show through the final coat to create a mottled appearance. When you are happy with the effect you have achieved, you can think about adding other details.

7 Paint the beaks yellow, glue on sequins, and decorate with glitter pens and more paint if desired.

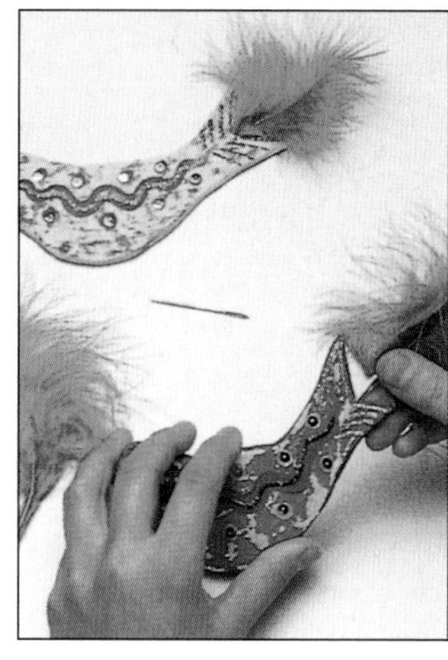

8 Use a needle or pin to make a hole in the tail of each bird at the point of the V and enlarge it if necessary with a piece of wire. Select a feather for each bird, trim it to the required length if it is too long, put a drop of glue on the end, and insert it into the hole.

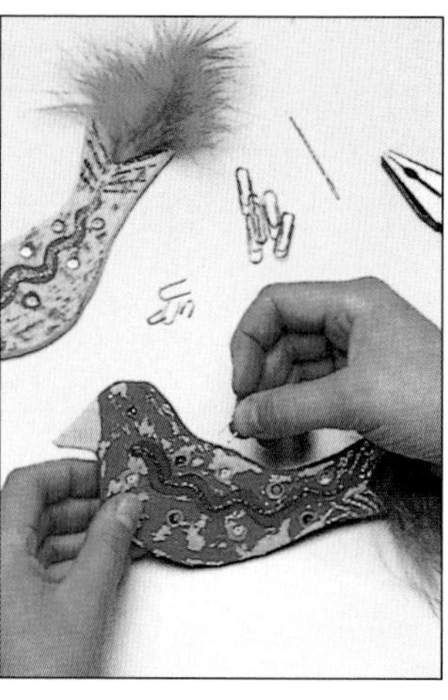

9 Using pliers, cut three paper clips in half to make hooks to attach to the birds. Make two holes ¼ inch apart in the top edge of each bird, place a drop of glue on both ends of each hook, and insert them into the holes.

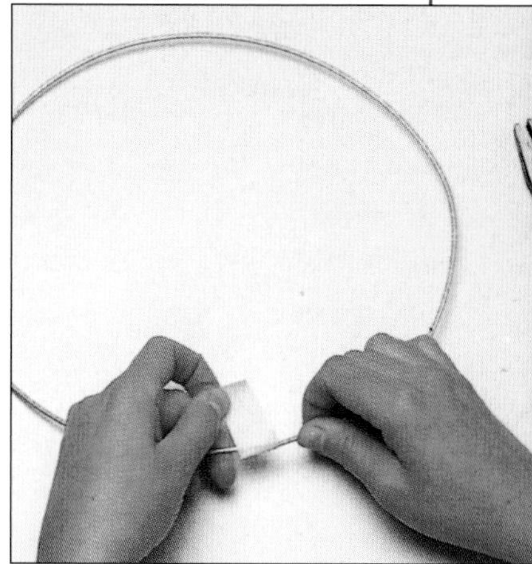

10 Using pliers, cut a piece of the thicker wire about 2½ feet long and bend it into a circle with a diameter of about 9 inches. Overlap the edges slightly and use a strip of masking tape to secure the joint, then paint or spray the joint silver.

11 Using pliers, cut two pieces of thinner wire about 10 inches long. Attach these across the wire circle, so that they divide it into quarters. Use pliers to wind the ends of the cross-wires around the outer wire circle until they are taut and secure.

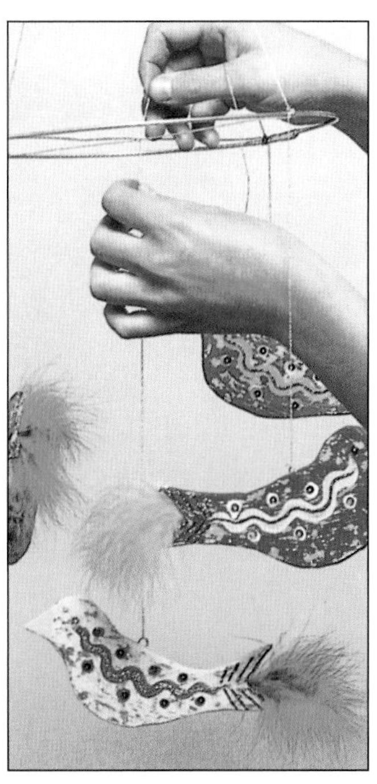

12 Cut four lengths of gold thread, each about 2 feet long, and tie each one to the point on the circle where the cross-wires are attached. Gather them together at the top and suspend the circle by them. When it hangs evenly, tie the threads into a knot at the top. Attach a length of gold thread to the hook on each bird. Now attach four of the birds to the wire frame and suspend the fifth bird from the middle of the circle, where the wires cross.

PART IV

PAPERMAKING AND DECORATING

For most of its 2,000-year history, paper has been made by hand. Only since the Industrial Revolution has the process become mechanized. The technology of modern papermaking is very complex, yet the basic process remains so simple that even a child can make paper.

Papermaking is spontaneous, open-ended, and decorative, and it is also highly satisfying. A little time must be spent beforehand to prepare molds and deckles and to gather equipment, but once everything is assembled, paper can be made time and again.

EQUIPMENT AND MATERIALS

We waste an enormous amount of paper, much of which could be recycled, such as photocopy, computer, or typing paper, and many more. It is worth approaching local printers, colleges, and offices who might be able to provide good-quality waste paper and would be pleased to see it going to good use.

Avoid using paper that has a lot of black type on it: the plainer the better. Newspaper, being highly acidic, will turn yellow and brittle too quickly. Slick magazines are also best avoided. If in doubt, test a small amount to see if it gives the desired result. The following pages show you how to make a sheet of paper very simply (by the Western method). Handmade paper made by skilled papermakers uses practically the same method, the only difference being the quality of materials and equipment.

Paper should be presoaked, preferably overnight or at least a couple of hours beforehand.

You will need:

- Paper, presoaked overnight or a couple of hours beforehand.
- Plastic sheets. Papermaking is a wet business, so all surfaces will need to be covered, including yourself.
- Plastic tub should be large enough to accommodate the mold and deckle with your hands on each side.
- Kitchen blender (1 quart capacity).
- Boards (approximately 13 x 15 inches) should be rigid and non-absorbent; if wood is used, prime it first. Two boards needed.
- Curtain netting should have a close enough weave to prevent pulp escaping.
- Interfacing is an excellent support material for the freshly made sheets. It is available from the dressmaking department of large stores. Buy 4 yards of the sew-in variety, medium-weight; the iron-on type has undesirable chemicals in it. Less expensive and good for beginners are handwipes or non-woven household cloths, but these do contain chemicals that may eventually harm your paper. It is also important not to choose a material

with too much texture, as this will imprint itself on your sheets. Cut the material into 10½ x 13-inch pieces.

- Felts. A local secondhand shop will usually be able to supply wool blankets, which make a perfect substitute for the felts used in papermaking mills. They should be cut into 12 x 14-inch pieces.
- Mold and deckle, bought or made.

OPTIONAL EXTRAS

Additional items include: Formica (as a surface to dry sheets on). A 3-inch paint brush (only needed if transferring damp sheets to a board for drying).

CARE OF EQUIPMENT

Wash interfacings after use and hang out to dry. The felts should also be hung out to dry. Rinse off the mold and deckle at the end of a session. Keep everything as clean as possible and in a dry place.

STORING PULP

Pulp can be stored for a few days, but it will eventually start to rot and smell. To store the pulp temporarily, strain it through a strainer and netting. Keep it in an airtight container. A preservative (oil of cloves or thymol) can be added to give it a slightly longer life.

Alternatively, squeeze out as much water as possible from the pulp while it is in the netting, then lay it out to air-dry. Once dry, store it in plastic bags and reuse when needed. Never pour pulp mixture down the kitchen sink; it will cause a blockage.

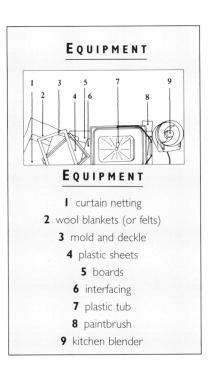

EQUIPMENT

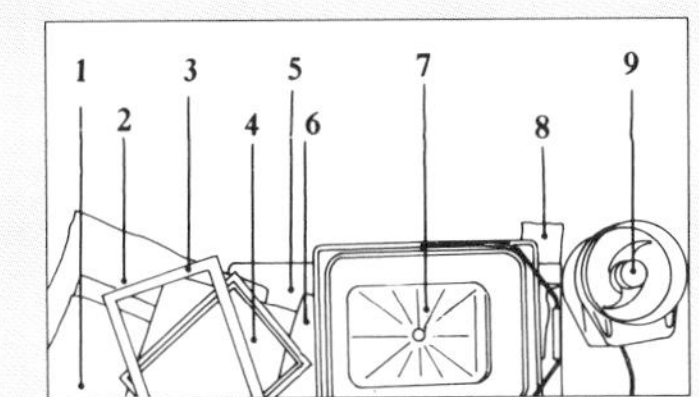

EQUIPMENT

1 curtain netting
2 wool blankets (or felts)
3 mold and deckle
4 plastic sheets
5 boards
6 interfacing
7 plastic tub
8 paintbrush
9 kitchen blender

MAKING A MOLD AND DECKLE

A mold and deckle is the piece of equipment used for actually forming a sheet of paper. The mold is a frame with mesh stretched over it; the deckle is the frame that fits on top. A mold and deckle can be bought from a craft shop, or you can make your own. You will need:

- 6-foot length of ¾-inch square lumber.
- Glass curtain material or nylon/metal mesh.
- Staple gun or thumbtacks (avoid materials that rust).
- L-shaped brass plates with screws less deep than the wood.
- Screwdriver.
- Scissors.
- Saw.
- Clear varnish.
- Wood glue.
- Insulating tape.
- Draft-stopper tape.
- Sandpaper.

1 The best wood to use is a hardwood, such as mahogany. Cut the wood into four 8-inch lengths and four 9-inch lengths. Place them together to make two separate frames of identical size. Glue the corners and screw a brass plate in each corner on one side. If you have the tools and skill, make more secure mitered or lap joints using wood glue and screws. Sandpaper any sharp edges. Varnishing the wood will make it tougher.

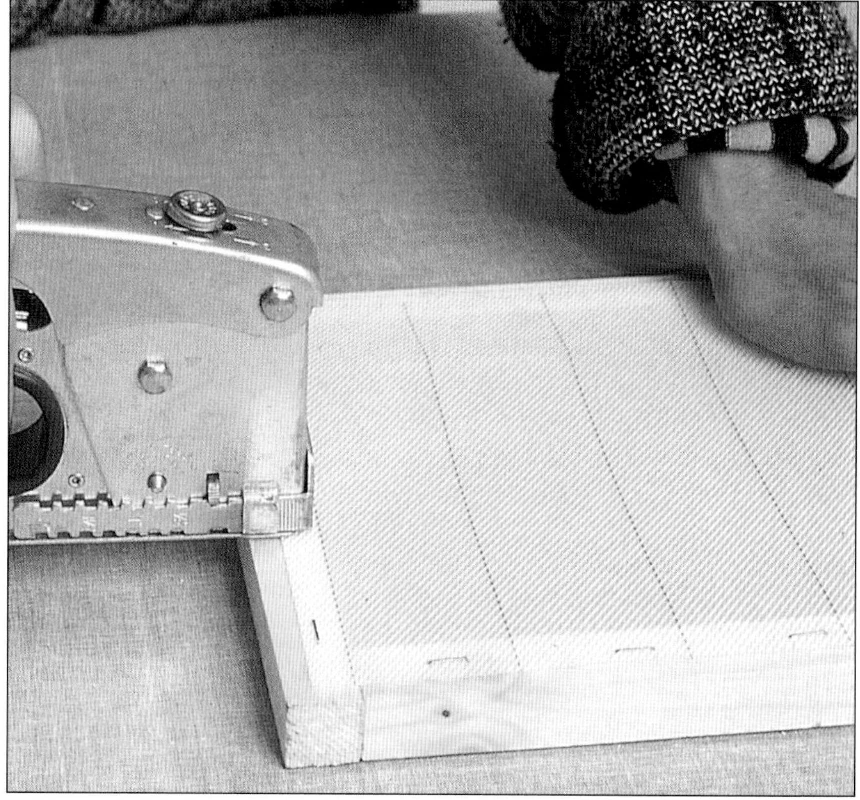

2 The mesh has to be stretched tensely and evenly over one frame to make the mold. Place the mesh over the frame (on the opposite side from the brass plates), leaving at least a ¾ inch overhang. Stiff mesh should be cut to the right size before stretching. Staple from the middle of each side and work out toward the corners.

3 Trim the mesh in line with the outside edge or just within it. Then place tape over mesh and wood to seal messy raveling or sharp edges.

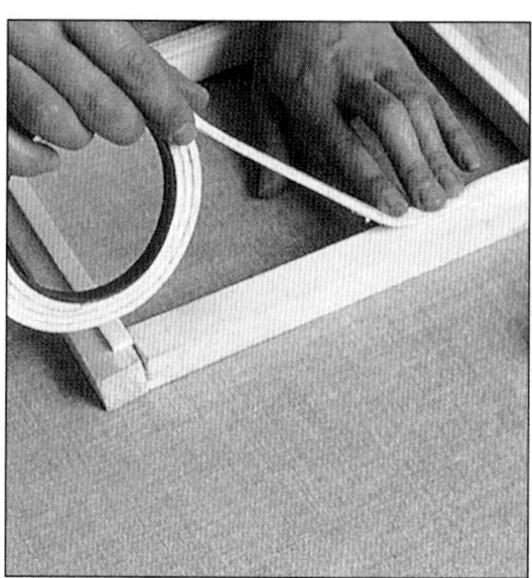

4 The deckle – the other identical frame – is made exactly like the mold, but without the mesh. Draft-stopper tape placed along the edge of the deckle that will be placed together with the mold will help the mold and deckle fit snugly.

MAKING PULP

Ideally the paper to be used for recycling should be soaked overnight, having first been torn into 2-inch squares. Using a paper shredder is a big timesaver.

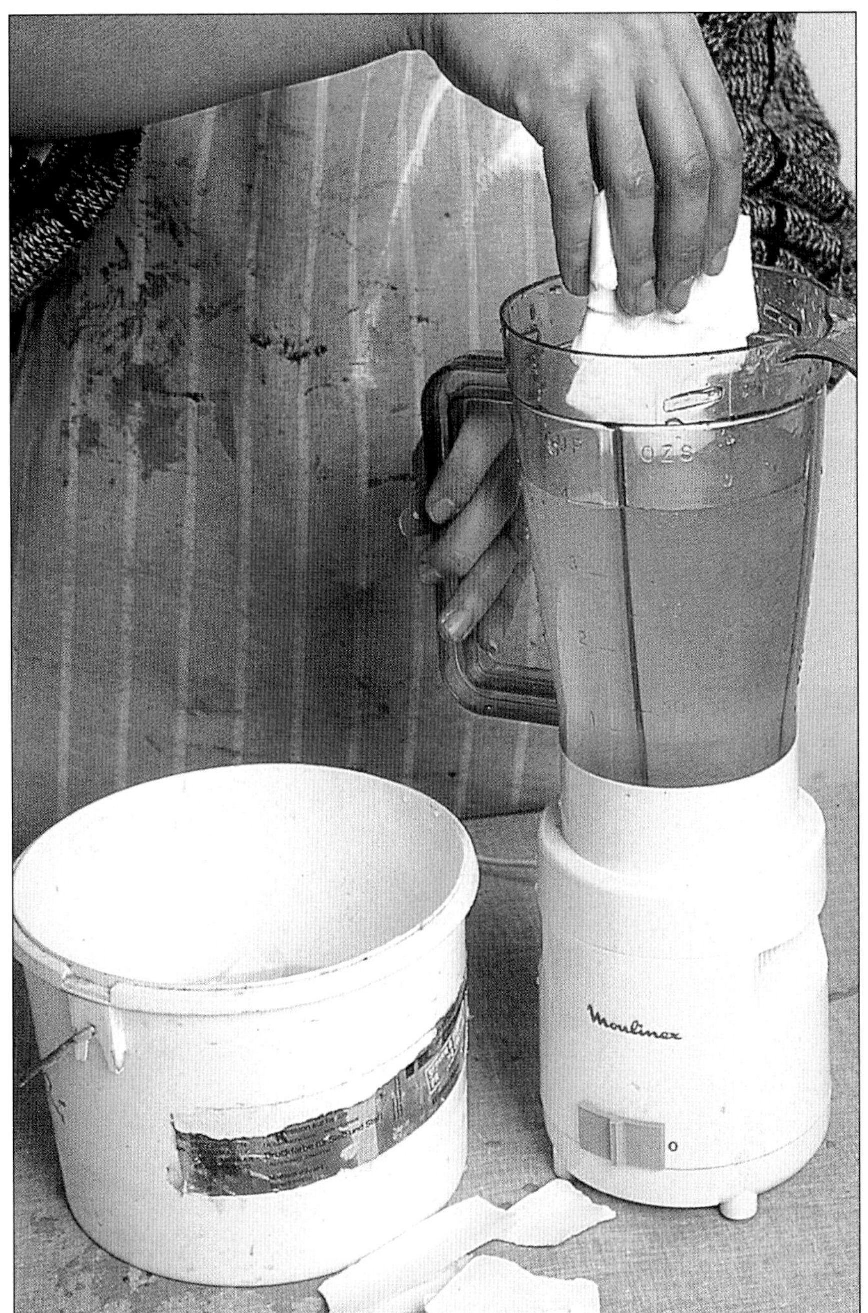

1 Fill the blender no more than three-quarters full with warm water; then take a small fistful of paper and blend. The blender should not be overstrained. If it sounds overloaded, take out some pulp and top up with water. Short bursts on the blender are best to prevent the motor from burning out. For soft paper, a 10-second run should be enough. Use several bursts for tougher paper.

2 Pour the pulp into a clean tub. Carry on pulping and filling until the tub is half-full. Then top up to three-quarters full with warm water.

MAKING PAPER

The pulp and water mixture in the tub needs agitating gently before beginning each sheet as pulp tends to settle at the bottom. Try to develop the steps listed below into a smooth, continuous action.

1 Place deckle (taped edge down) on top of the mold.

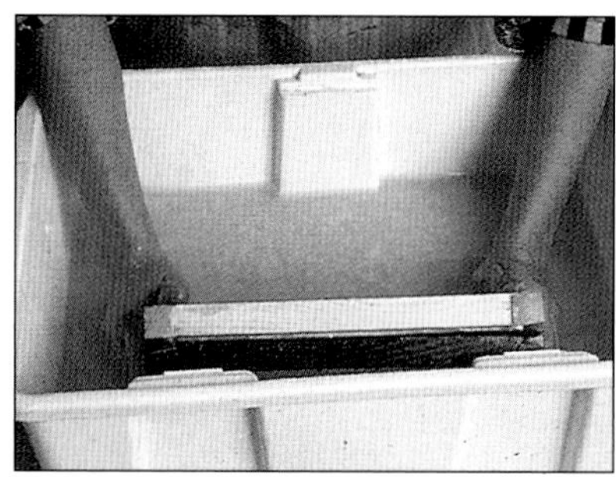

2 Hold the two firmly together with the deckle uppermost. Move hands to the back edge of the tub, holding the mold and deckle vertically, and with arms outstretched. Dip the mold and deckle into tub and scoop up the pulp by quickly moving the mold and deckle toward the body and simultaneously changing to a horizontal angle.

3 Lift the mold and deckle out of the mixture and let the water drain back into the tub. Gently shake the mold and deckle from side to side and back and forth to distribute the fibers of the pulp evenly.

4 When most of the water has drained back into the tub, continue draining by tipping from one corner.

5 After a few seconds, rest the mold and deckle on the edge of the tub and carefully remove the deckle without dripping onto your freshly made sheet. The sheet is ready for the next stage, couching. If the sheet is unsatisfactory, place the mold face down on the surface of the mixture in the tub and start again.

COUCHING

Couching is the action of transferring the wet layer of pulp on the mold to the support material (interfacing or cloth). One layer of cut-up blanket should be placed underneath the interfacing, and beneath this a board. Wet both the interfacing and the blanket, as this greatly helps the couching process. Place them directly one beneath the other, making sure that there are no creases. Steps 1, 2, and 3 should be done in a continuous, firm movement.

You may find when couching that the pulp refuses to come off the mold. This could be because the sheet is too thin, in which case you need to put more pulp in the tub. Alternatively, the sheet might be too dry. Gently wet it again by placing the mold flat, pulp side up, just touching the surface of the water. This allows the pulp to soak up more water. Then try couching again.

The felt and support material might also be too dry, or you may not be exerting enough pressure during the couching action. It can help to use fingers to press down the back of the mold while it is flat on the supporting material.

1 With the longest edge of the mold vertically in front, place the freshly drained mold on the right side of the support material.

2 Firmly lower the upper edge of the mold. The sheet should be pulp face down in the middle of the support material.

3 Raise the right side of the mold with the right hand and then remove the left edge of the mold. The wet sheet is now resting centrally on the support material.

4 To keep making more sheets, simply cover the first one with a piece of interfacing placed centrally on top. Place the next sheet to lie on top of the one below. If you have plenty of blanket pieces, place them between interfacings to soak up the water. The pile, or post as it is known in the trade, can consist of as many as 12 to 15 sheets or just one. Complete the pile with a blanket topped by the second board. It is now ready for pressing.

PRESSING, DRYING, SIZING

The more water that is pressed out the better. there are several ways of doing this. The one described on this page is the most basic. Take the pile of papers with the boards at each end. Place some newspaper on top of this. Now go to an area where wetness doesn't matter, like the back yard. Step onto the pile and move gently around to press all areas. Enlist a few more people to add weight.

Drying

There are two main ways of drying: first on boards of Formica, plastic, or wood (be careful that the wood does not stain the paper). (See page 173.)

The second method of drying is air drying. Simply separate the interfacings with the damp papers on them and lay them out to dry, one beside the other on a clean, flat surface like a carpet. This is very space-consuming. Alternatively, remove the sheets onto dry interfacing or a sheet of ready-made paper. This is done by placing the interfacing with the wet sheet face down on the dry interfacing and pressing firmly with the back of the hand. Then gently peel back the wet interfacing, leaving the paper transferred. Gently remove the paper when thoroughly dry.

Sizing

Once the paper is dry, it will be as absorbent as blotting paper. This is called "waterleaf" paper. In order for the paper to have the necessary strength, say for painting, calligraphy, or printing, it will have to be sized. The amount of size added will vary according to intended use: writing paper needs to be more heavily sized than watercolor paper, for example.

There are two ways to size:

- Starch size. Simply add a tablespoonful of laundry starch to your tub and follow directions on the packet.
- Gelatine, size (see page 173).

Pressing

The key to this technique is to make sure that as much water as possible is squeezed out. Find an area where wetness doesn't matter, such as the back yard or patio. Take the pile of papers with the boards at each end. Place newspapers on top of this. Stand on the pile and move gently around to press all areas.

Board drying

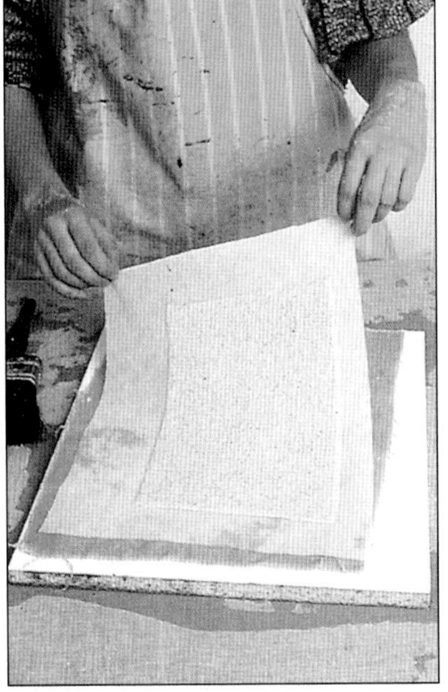

1 After pressing, take off the top board and felt. Carefully pick up the first interfacing with the damp paper on it.

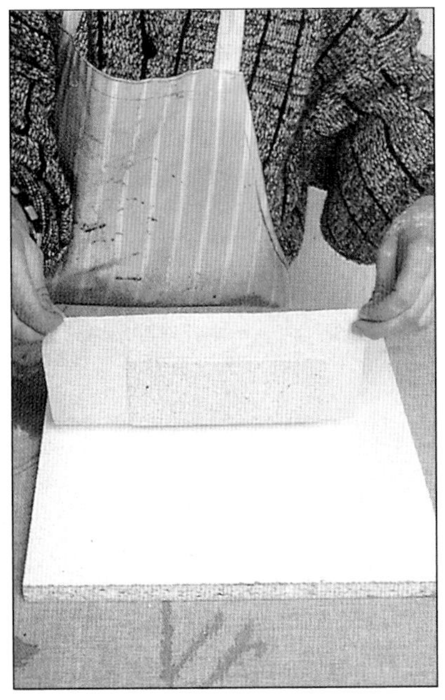

2 Place this interfacing paper face down on a clean board and press gently down.

3 With a brush, firmly brush the back of the interfacing and paper, using both horizontal and vertical strokes.

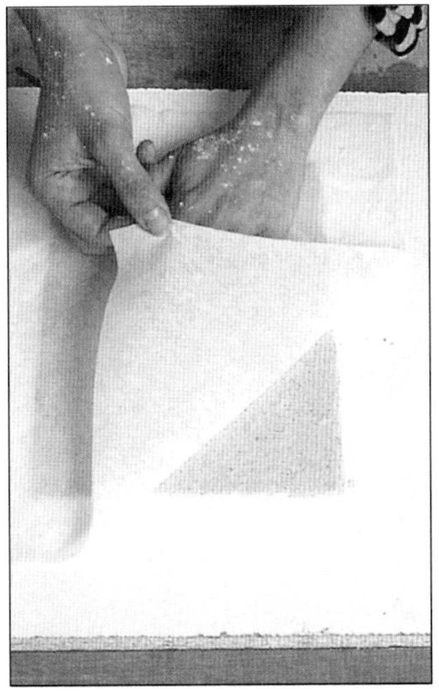

4 Carefully peel off the interfacing, leaving the paper on the board. Double check that all sides are flat on the board; if not, gently press with your fingertips.

Sizing

Dissolve 1tsp of gelatine in a cup of boiled water, add to tray, and top up with warm water till it is 1 inch deep. Place one sheet in the tray, and it will absorb the gelatine liquid.

Place one hand, with fingers spread, underneath the sheet, then lift it out and drain it from one corner. Place the sheet on blotting paper to dry.

MAKING PULP FROM FIBERS

Papers made from fibers contain beautiful effects. A wonderful sense of achievement can be felt at having not only made a sheet of paper, but having picked and processed the fibers as well.

Fibers

The cellulose in plant fibers is the important element in papermaking. Many plants are suitable; each gives its own special characteristics. Some produce very little usable fiber for papermaking, whereas others, such as the New Zealand flax plant, give a high percentage. Large quantities are needed, as most of the plant breaks down during processing, and at least a bucketful should be gathered.

In cities, a farmer's market is an excellent place for picking up the right plant fibers. Pineapple leaves, corn husks, gladioli, iris and daffodil leaves are all suitable. In the countryside there is a greater choice: pampas grass, stems of weeds, rush, straw, and wild lilies, to name but a few. To recognize suitable plants for papermaking, observe the leaf structure: long, tough vertical strands of fiber are ideal.

Preparation

To prepare the plant fibers, follow the instructions on page 176.

Beating

After preparing the plant fibers, place a handful of rinsed fibers on the board and add some water. Beat with the mallet or flat side of the stone. The fibers will separate and feather out slightly. If making sheets from fibers only, beat until well disintegrated. Put beaten fibers in the tub and proceed to make paper as previously described. Adding a capful of fabric conditioner to the tub of fibers aids couching, which can be difficult with long, tangly strands of fiber. A blender can be used to break down fibers instead of the mallet or stone. However, the blender cuts the fibers rather than feathering them out in the way preferred for papermaking.

Bleaching

The natural color of fibers is not always desirable. Bleaching can lighten them, and this is best done when the rinsing is partially finished.

Safety

Always wear gloves and an apron when using chemicals such as bleach and caustic soda. Work outside or in a well-ventilated room and immediately wash off any drops that fall on your skin. Always add caustic soda carefully to water – never pour water on it.

EQUIPMENT

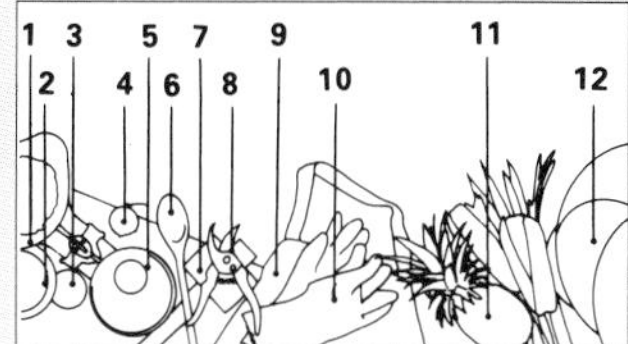

1 caustic soda or soda ash (sodium carbonate) crystals
2 bleach
3 wooden board (or formica)
4 pH strip, available from a drugstore
5 scales
6 wooden spoon
7 wooden mallet (or flat stone)
8 pruning shears (or scissors)
9 apron
10 rubber gloves
11 plant fibers
12 stainless steel bucket with lid

Also needed:
kitchen blender, electric hot plate or camping stove, strainer, and net.

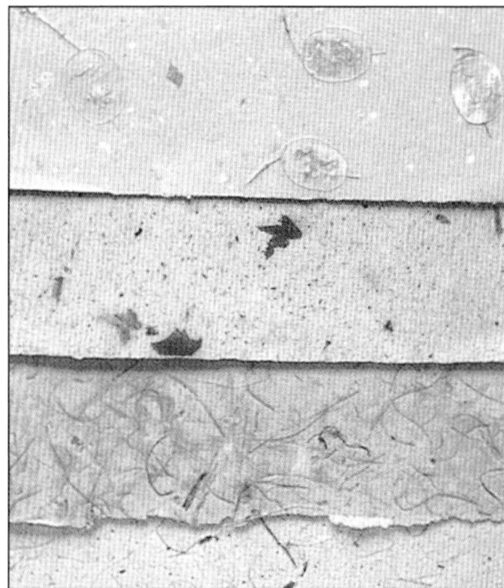

ABOVE *Examples of papers made using pulp containing fibers.*

Preparation

Don't rush the fiber preparation process – chemicals are dangerous and need to be handled with care. Work in a well-ventilated room to disperse the fumes, or outdoors, simmering the fibers on a portable electric hot plate or camping stove.

To prepare the fibers for the process below, cut them into 1-inch strips and weigh them.

1 Place fibers (see above) in stainless steel bucket. Cover with cold water.

2 Add 2 percent caustic soda to the dry weight of the fibers or 15 percent if using soda crystals. Mix with the spoon.

3 Bring to a boil and simmer, with the lid on, for two hours.

Key to Papers

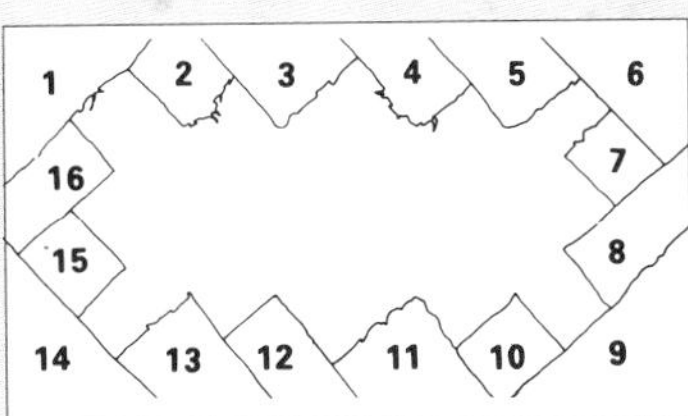

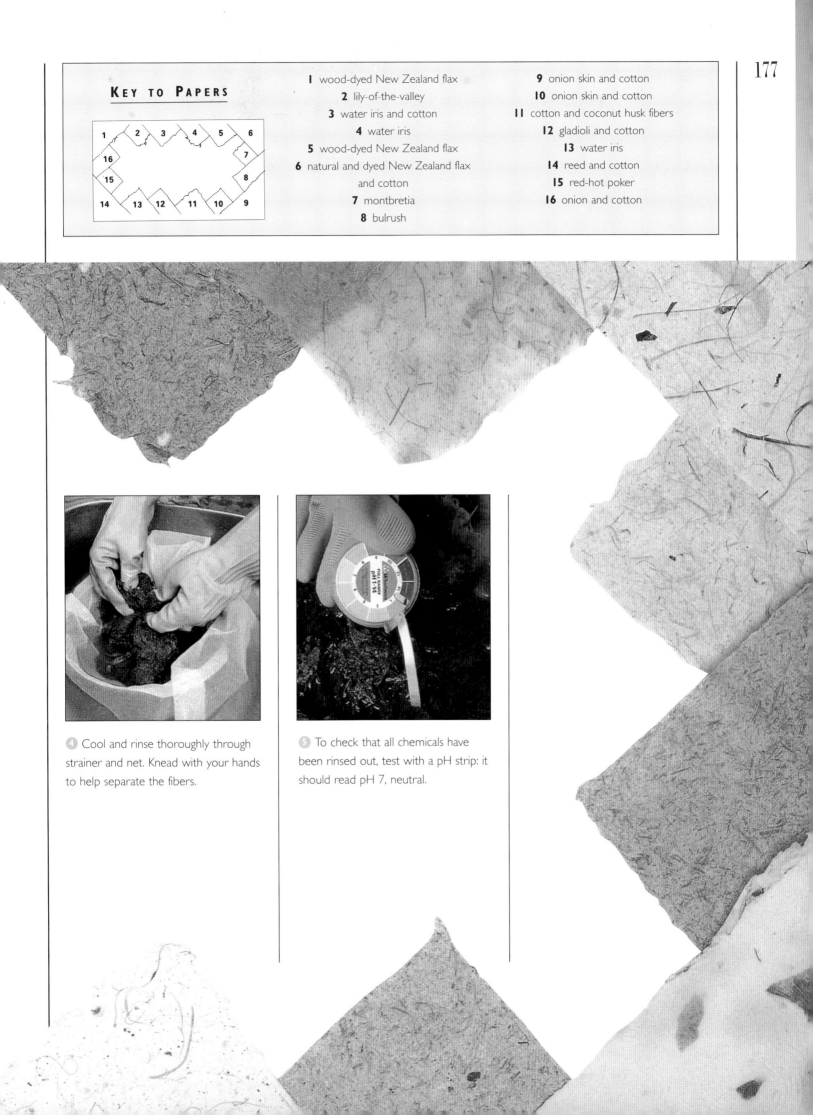

1 wood-dyed New Zealand flax
2 lily-of-the-valley
3 water iris and cotton
4 water iris
5 wood-dyed New Zealand flax
6 natural and dyed New Zealand flax and cotton
7 montbretia
8 bulrush
9 onion skin and cotton
10 onion skin and cotton
11 cotton and coconut husk fibers
12 gladioli and cotton
13 water iris
14 reed and cotton
15 red-hot poker
16 onion and cotton

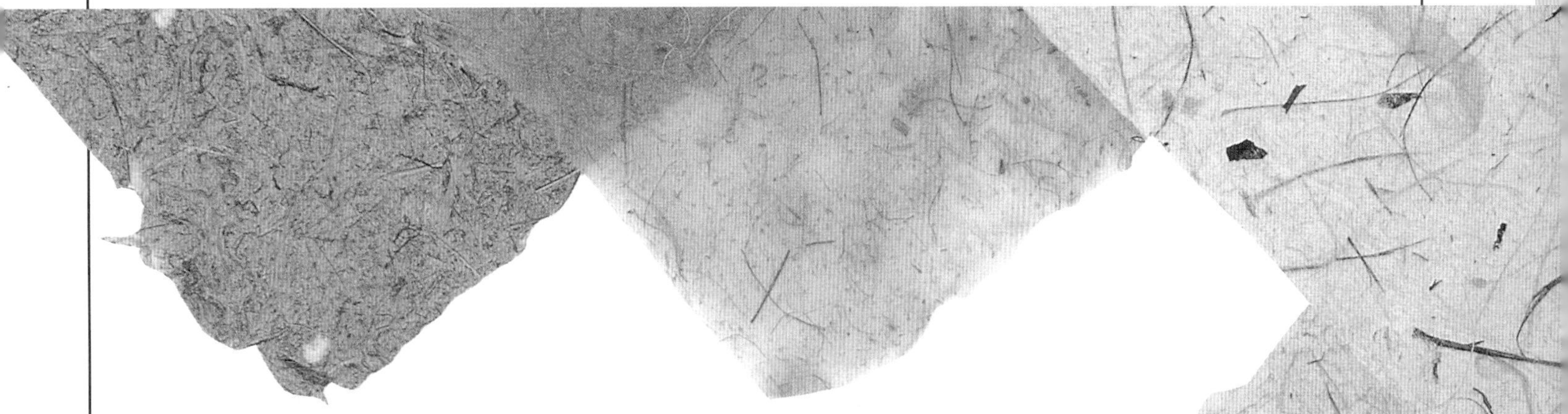

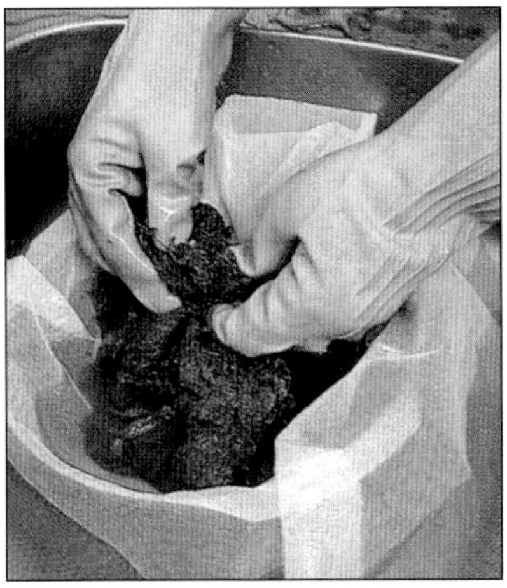

4 Cool and rinse thoroughly through strainer and net. Knead with your hands to help separate the fibers.

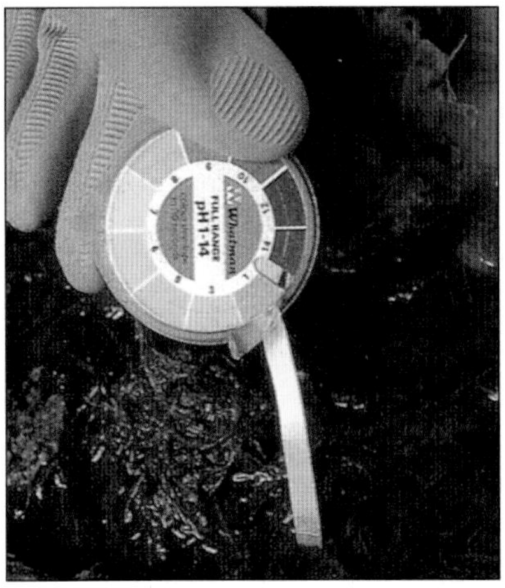

5 To check that all chemicals have been rinsed out, test with a pH strip: it should read pH 7, neutral.

CREATIVE PAPERMAKING

Creative papermaking is a comparatively new art form and is still developing, reaching into many other areas of art. With the revival of papermaking in recent decades, some papermakers have specialized in high-quality papers for artists, printers, and bookbinders. Others make papers that are beautiful objects in themselves, richly textured and sometimes shaped.

Coloring pulp

Pulp can be colored with textile dyes. Cold-water dyes need a week for the color to be fully absorbed. Remember to rinse thoroughly. A simpler way to make colored pulp is to recycle colored papers.

Porridge technique

This is great fun and is best done with several colors. Strain off colored, porridge-textured pulp. Using your hands, place the pulp directly on a rigid clean surface, such as Formica or sheet plastic. Place colored pulps down next to one another. Colors can be put down in any order and not necessarily in a rectangular format. When the image is ready, place a sheet of interfacing on top and gently press out excess water with a sponge. This helps bonding and speeds drying. Leave to dry naturally.

Two-colored sheet

Make two tubs of pulp, one of each color. Couch a sheet from one color. Partially dip the mold into the other tub and couch this on top of the base sheet.

Encapsulation

Pulp can act as a glue. By laying flat objects onto a base sheet and then partially or totally covering them with pulp from the turkey baster, they are held in place.

Pressed flowers and leaves

Pressed flowers and leaves can look very attractive in a sheet. First seal with artist's fixative, so that the color does not run onto the sheet.

Pastry cutters

Pulp can be poured through a pastry cutter to make a definite shape. This is best done on the mold or interfacing before couching or transferring onto the base sheet.

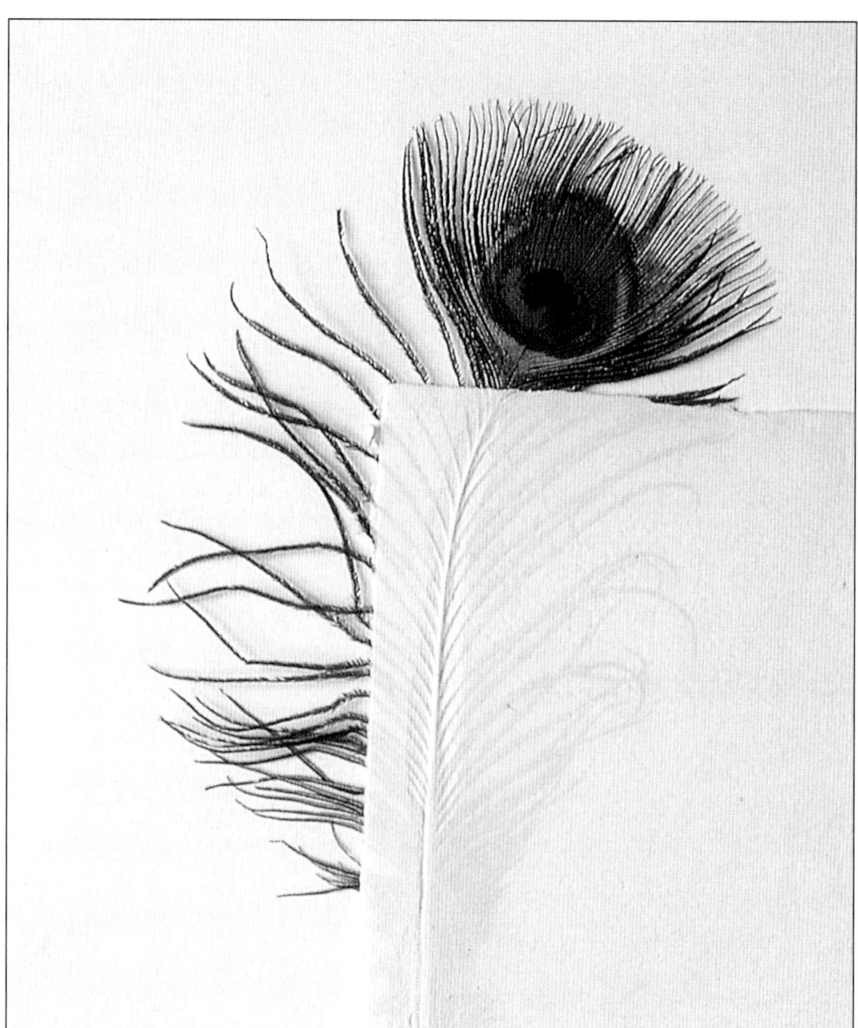

Sandwich method

Couch a base sheet. Lay threads, feathers, or any relatively flat objects on top. Couch a second sheet on top of this, thereby making a "sandwich" of the objects. This can be left as it is, or some of the pulp from the top sheet can be gently taken off to expose the middle layer.

Pouring pulp

Different colored pulps can be separated into plastic containers and used like an artist's palette. In place of a brush, a turkey baster makes it easier to suck up pulp and deposit it on a base sheet (a freshly made sheet of paper). The pouring can be done directly onto the base sheet or couched off the mold. Poured pulp can be built up in several layers, which will magically stick together during the pressing.

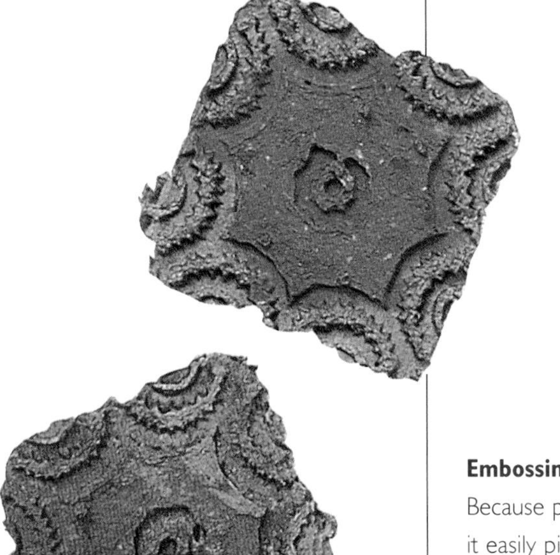

Embossing

Because pulp is a malleable substance, it easily picks up textures when pressed. Lay a textured piece of lace on a freshly made sheet, and cover with interfacing and felt for padding. Press. Leave the sheet to dry with or without the lace on.

WEAVING

★

Paper weaving can be extremely challenging, but can also be very simple. It can be used in a purely decorative way to make a picture or in a more practical way to form a box. The pleasure comes in the many exciting types and colors of paper you choose to use for your efforts. The main thing to remember is that there are no rules, and the experimenting is all part of the fun. The paper used can be colored, patterned, or textured, and even illustrations from magazines.

MATERIALS

- Various medium-weight papers
- Cellophane tape
- Glue stick
- Scissors or craft knife
- Metal ruler
- Pencil

1 Using a metal ruler and a craft knife, cut strips of paper. These will provide straight edges in the pattern. Use a variety of colors, if desired.

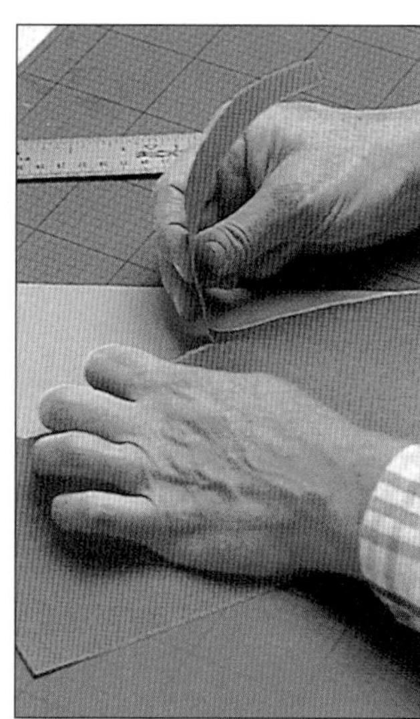

2 Alternatively, tear strips to create a looser-edged pattern. Use different colors for greater effect.

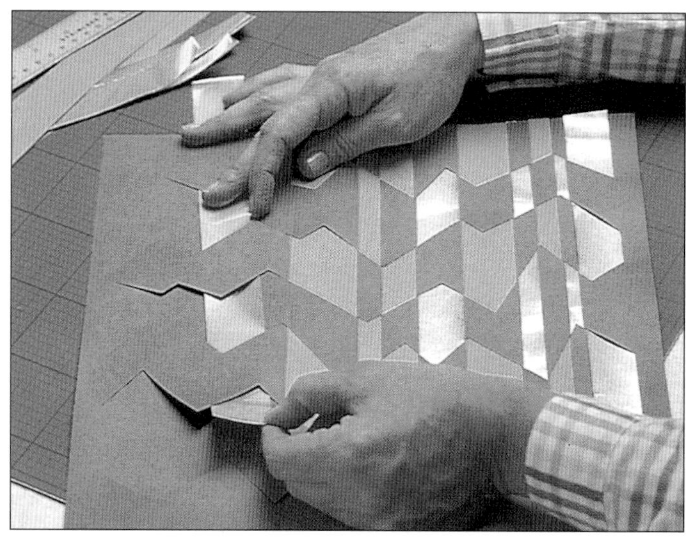

3 When you are combining strips of paper in a woven design, the vertical strips represent the warp threads and the horizontal strips the weft threads, as in any form of weaving. Cut the warp into zigzags and thread different colored and textured strips through it.

4 Alternatively, cut the warp into curves for a wavy pattern and thread different-colored weft strips through it.

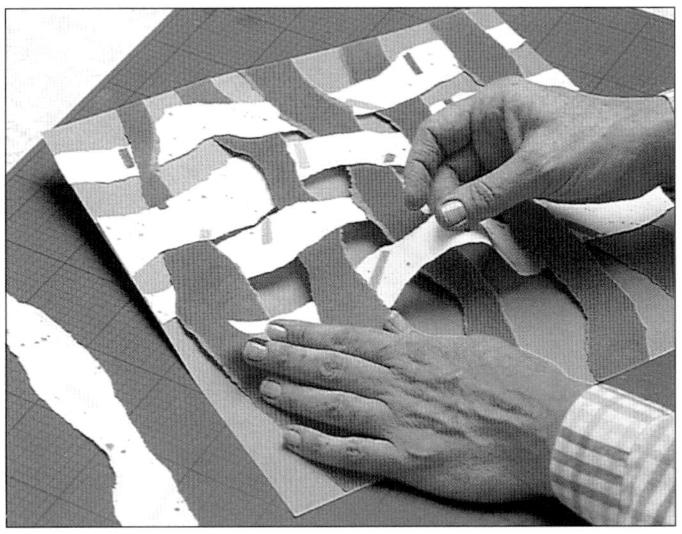

5 For a more random effect, tear the strips and lay them across and through each other. The warp can be spread out and the weft can be woven irregularly so that spaces show between the strips.

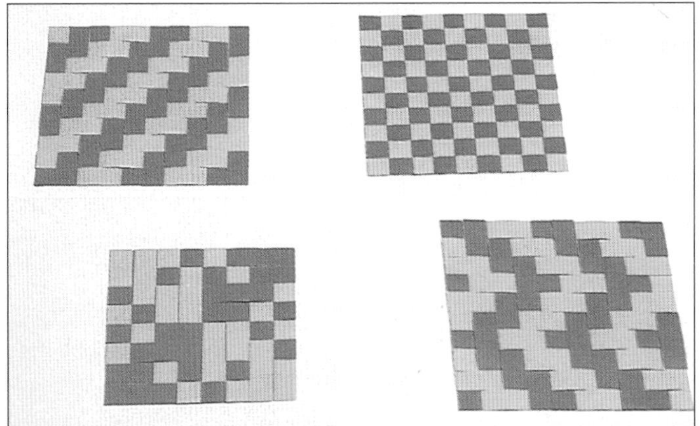

ABOVE *Rigid, geometric patterns are produced with straight-edged strips.*

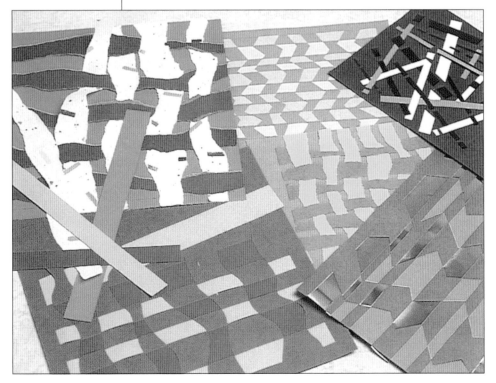

LEFT *Create interesting patterns with irregular warp and weft strips.*

COLLAGE

★

The word collage comes from the French verb "*coller*," meaning "to stick." Collage is regarded as an art form, and the examples shown here can be developed further.

MATERIALS

Light- to medium-weight paper

Colored tissue paper

Japanese papers

Glue stick or spray adhesive

Gummed papers

Foil papers

Decorated tape

Self-adhesive stickers

TIPS

Although expensive, decorative Japanese papers can also be used to great effect.

If time is short or you do not feel very creative, make decorative patterns by covering plain papers with bought stickers or patterned tapes, or with your own shapes cut out from gummed papers.

1 Tear up small pieces of tissue paper and place on glued lightweight paper, using spray adhesive or a glue stick.

2 Leave some edges of the tissue paper unattached and allow them to overlap a little. Finished sheets can be cut up and used on the front of a greeting card, for example.

RIGHT *These finished examples can be used for many of the projects covered later in the book.*

CAUTION!!

Remember that the dyes used in tissue paper are not usually colorfast, so take this into account when you are using different colors: yellow and purple may look nice next to each other, but mixed together the result will be a murky brown!!

STENCILING

★★

Stenciling can be messy, so it is advisable to protect the working area and surrounding surfaces with newspaper to avoid accidents. The patterns in this section are mostly created by blocking out an area of paper and coloring the remaining part. The blocking out can be done using several kinds of stencils.

MATERIALS

Medium-weight paper

Stencil paper

Self-adhesive shapes

Foil

Spray diffuser

Toothbrush

Stencil brush

Sponge

Paintbrush

Paints and paint palette

Colored inks, felt-tip pens, and colored pencils

Cut shapes out from stencil paper. Both the negative and positive parts of the stencil can be used.

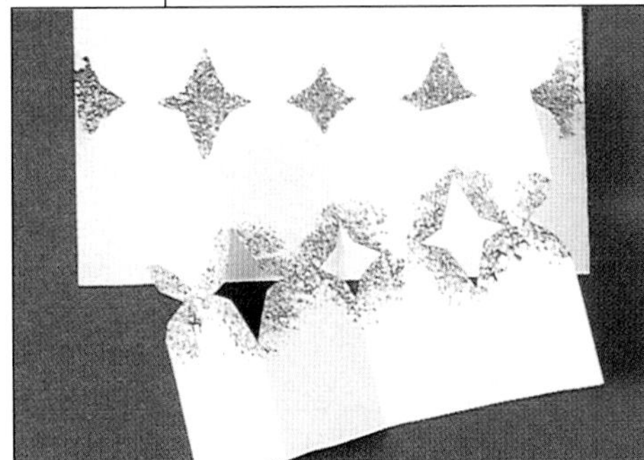

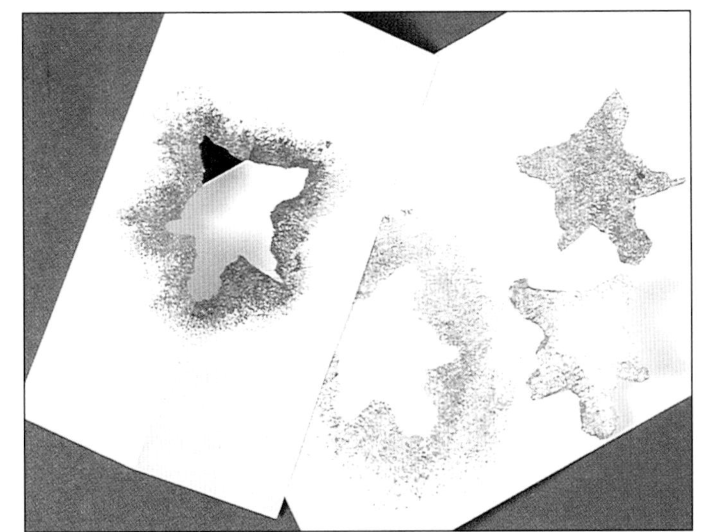

Fold a sheet of paper and cut or tear shapes out of the folded edges (above). Color through or round the shapes onto another piece of paper (right).

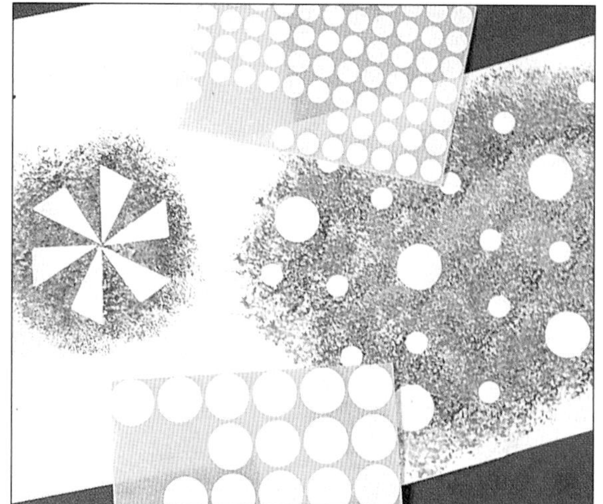

Try using self-adhesive shapes as stencils. Paint over them and then remove them when dry.

Cut shapes out of a folded sheet of foil. Unfold the shape and brush one color through it. Swivel the stencil around slightly and paint through it with another color to create an attractive kaleidoscopic effect.

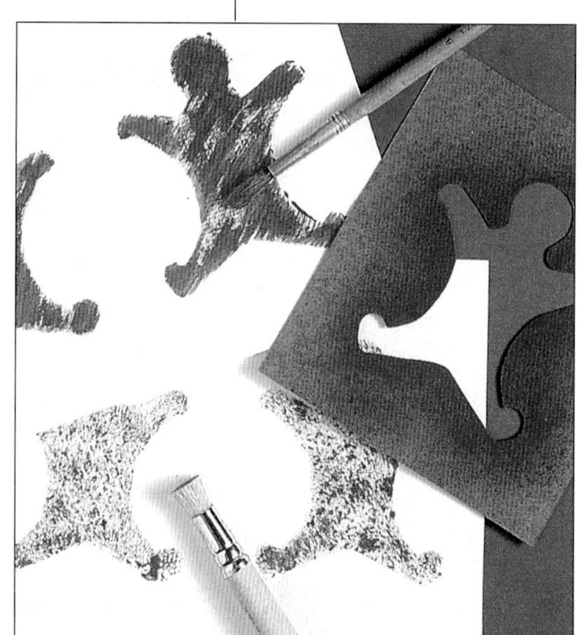

You can apply color in a number of ways. Try brushing the color on with an ordinary paint brush, or for a more stippled textured, use a stencil brush.

If you apply the color with a sponge, some of the cellular texture of the sponge will transfer onto the paper. For an even effect, use a spray can or airbrush. For a fine stippled effect, spatter the paint onto the paper from a toothbrush or a larger brush. Dip the brush in the liquid paint and shake off the excess before pulling a finger or ruler across the bristles. Keep the bristles facing down!

1 Using a leaf-shaped positive stencil, paint is applied to a colored background with a sponge.

2 Using the cutout leaf shape as a negative stencil, paint around the shape with a stencil brush.

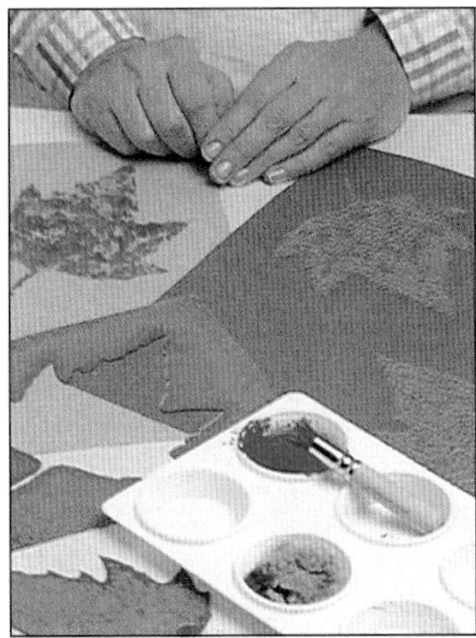

3 You can have great fun experimenting with these methods. Try using several colors in one design, or use colored paper as the background, as this will add to the design.

Tips

- **Spray the paper with water first before you stencil onto it to increase it absorbency; the colors will spread more when you apply the paint.**
- **Do not make the paint too wet, or it will run under the edge of the stencil.**
- **Do not load too much coloring medium on the brush or sponge, or the texture of the mark will be lost.**
- **Folded paper stencils cannot be used too often because they absorb the paint and become too sodden to be used cleanly.**
- **When using self-adhesive shapes, allow them to dry before you remove them to make sure that you do not smudge any part of the design.**
- **Try using acetate as a stencil material, and cut it with a scalpel or craft knife. As it does not tear, this material allows for quite a lot of detail and also has the advantage of being transparent so it can be positioned exactly with ease.**
- **Try tearing a large shape from a piece of paper and place it on another sheet; paint over the edges all around the shape. Lift off and tear off the painted edge, making the shape smaller and changing it slightly. Reposition it within the painted area and, perhaps with another color, paint over the new edge. Repeat the same process as many times as possible.**

ABOVE *These examples were all created using the methods explained in this section.*

RESIST METHODS

★★★

These methods can be tightly controlled or very random. They can be done with wax crayons and paint, wax rubbings and paint, paste and paint, or wax crayons and ink. Wax crayons and paint and wax rubbings and paint are very similar in application, although the final result is very different in that the first can be used to create a picture, whereas the second produces a pattern. Paste and paint is not strictly a resist method, but the end results look similar to other resist methods. It is a good way of making textured patterns on paper.

MATERIALS

Wax crayons
Wallpaper paste
Wax candles
Poster (alkyd) paints
Bowl
Wide brush
Black drawing ink
Medium- to heavyweight paper

WAX RUBBINGS AND PAINT

1 Cover a textured surface, such as a strip of plastic netting, with a piece of white or colored medium-weight paper and rub a candle or colored wax crayon over the paper. Remove it from the textured surface.

2 Next, brush some thin water-based paint over the entire sheet. The paint can be one color or can be brushed on in stripes of different colors.

3 Make sure that you brush the paint right over the edges of the paper, and protect the surrounding area with waste paper. Allow the paper to dry naturally.

TIPS

Mix the paint wash thinly and always mix enough to cover the whole sheet to give an even tone of color.

Use a wide brush to cover large areas: this will save time and effort.

It is possible to use thin paper for this method. If you mount it onto another sheet of lightweight paper, it will be strong enough to make a box or bag (see pages 202–211).

ABOVE *These examples show a variety of rubbings on papers of different textures. Look around you for different materials which can be used for rubbings: cane chair seats, tennis racquets, brick walls, tree bark – the list is endless.*

1 Mix wallpaper paste to the directions on the box – it should be reasonably thick, but not lumpy. Add water-based paint to this mixture. Test the intensity of the color on a piece of paper (top). Using a broad brush, spread the paste mixture across the whole sheet as evenly as possible (above).

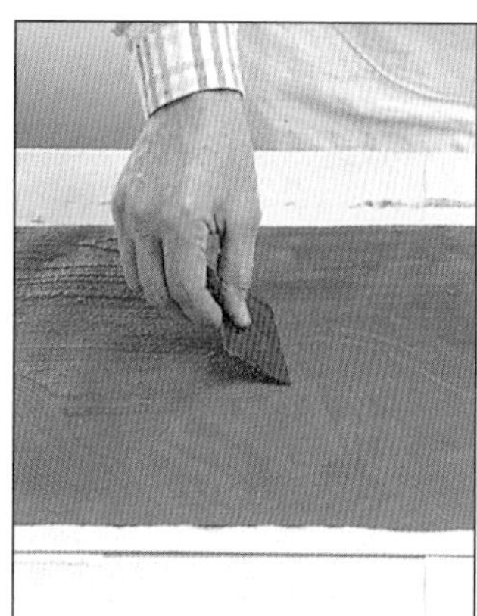

2 Now let your imagination take over. Using a finger, the handle of a paint brush or an improvised comb, draw patterns in the paste and paint mixture.

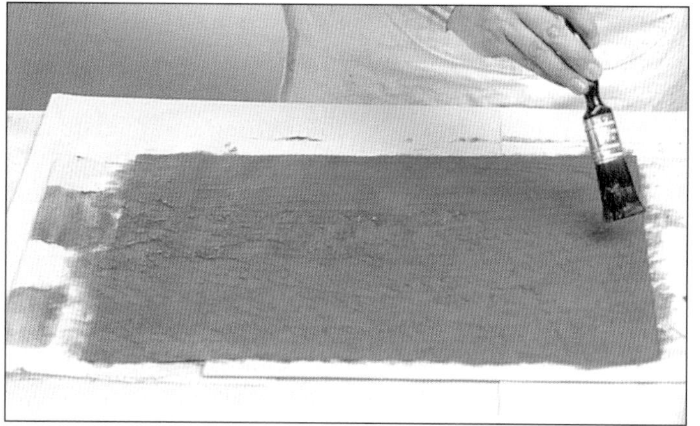

3 If you do not like the design, simply brush over it and start again! Depending on the amount of paste you use, the patterned paper will take quite a while to dry. To create a lighter appearance, when the paper is almost dry, lay a piece of thin paper (newsprint or similar) on top of the pasted paper and rub evenly over it, or use a roller, and then peel it off.

ABOVE *An infinite range of attractive designs can be created using different implements to pattern the paste mixture.*

1 Using the crayons, draw bands or areas of color onto heavyweight paper. If you would prefer a black and white design, use white candle wax on white paper. Now, paint over the entire area with black drawing ink. It may be necessary to repeat this step in order to cover the wax crayon completely.

BELOW *The two finished examples here show both random and controlled techniques.*

2 When the ink is dry, take any improvised drawing tool – the handle of a paint brush, the end of a pencil, an empty ballpoint pen, or the end of a ruler – and scratch through the ink to reveal the colors of the crayons. Either draw a picture or make a pattern; whichever you choose, the results will be stunning.

TIP

This process can be reversed – paint an area with black paint, and when it is dry, color in areas over it with the wax crayons, pressing firmly onto the paint. Then scratch through the wax areas to reveal black lines or shapes, giving more detail to the crayoned design. This method creates a more individual design than the wax band of color painted with ink.

DIPPING AND FOLDING

★★

MATERIALS

Thin absorbent paper

Paper towels

Small dishes

Colored ink, food coloring or watercolor paint

Stiff brush

Large paper clamps

Roller

This method is simple, quick, colorful and very exciting. It involves folding paper in various ways and then dipping it into a colored liquid.

It is essential that you use very lightweight paper for this process, but you will have to experiment with different brands to discover which papers work best. For the photographed examples here, colored tissue paper and large sheets of lens tissue, available in some specialist paper shops, have been used. Many of the tissue papers sold in packs are not colorfast, and when they are wet, their color may run. This can add to the design, but you should be aware of this possibility. It may be advisable to wear surgical rubber gloves while working with your chosen coloring medium (household gloves are too cumbersome to allow you to unfold the wet tissue without tearing it).

All designs start with some form of accordion pleat (see Fig. 1). For dip-dyeing, fold the pleat into smaller shapes (see Figs. 2, 3, and 4 for some of the possibilities). The broken lines represent valley folds, or creases which recede, and the dot-and-dash lines represent mountain folds, which come forward.

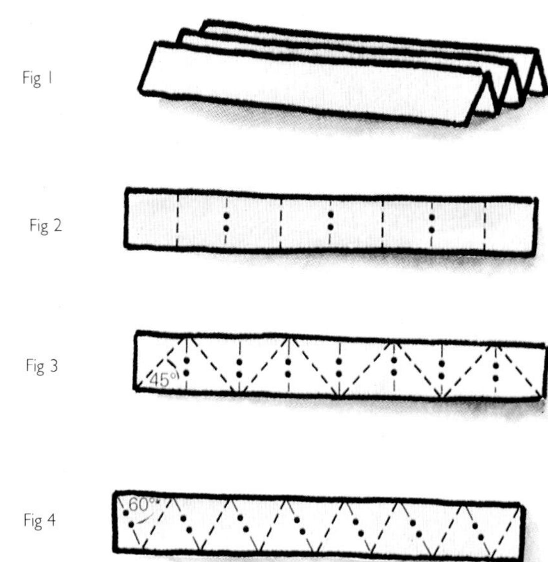

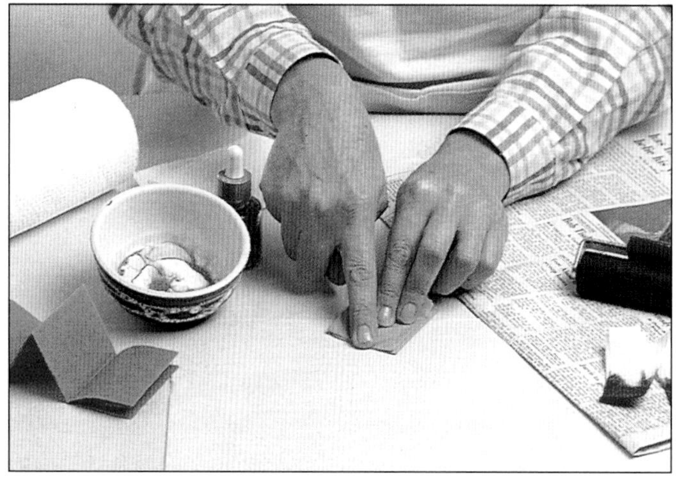

❶ Make an accordion pleat (see Fig. 1) with your chosen lightweight paper – colored tissue paper is ideal. Now fold as in Fig. 2, 3, or 4, or experiment with your own folding ideas.

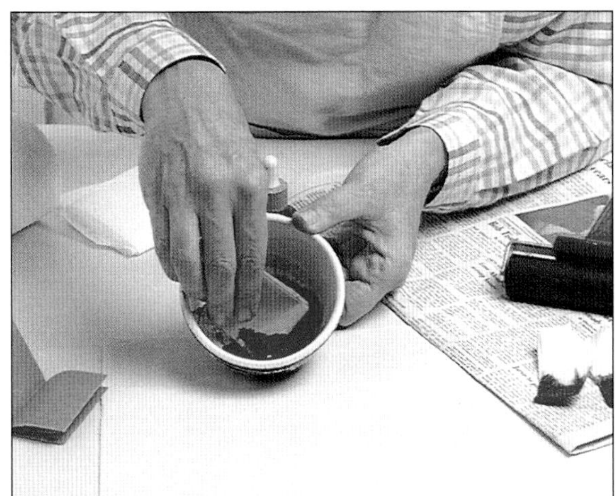

2 Pour some coloring – liquid watercolor, colored ink, food coloring, or similar – into a shallow container (preferably one that will not stain) and dip either a corner or an edge of the folded paper into it. Allow the paper to absorb the color and let it spread a little.

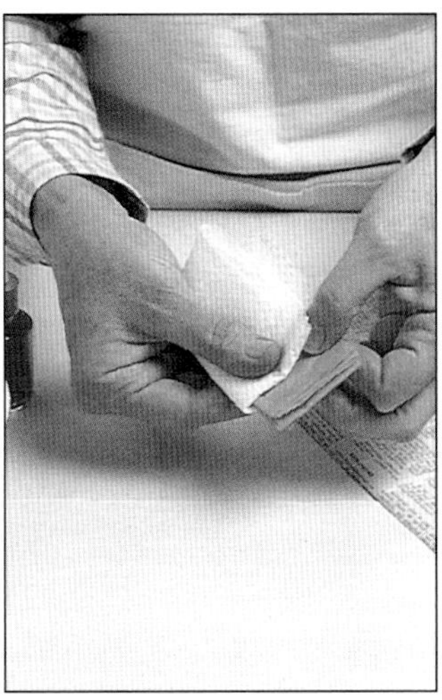

3 Squeeze the excess liquid from the paper between paper towels or newsprint. Continue to color the folded paper as much as you desire. At this stage, the wet tissue is very fragile.

4 Unfold the paper so that it forms a long pleated strip. Place this strip on some waste paper, cover it with more waste paper, and either rub hard all along the strip or, preferably, use a roller. This removes a great deal of the excess moisture.

5 Now unfold the paper completely. Take care not to tear the tissue. Move the paper as little as possible at this stage and allow it to dry. When it is dry, it can be ironed to remove some of the crease marks.

Tips

For softer-edged effects, first dip the paper into water and squeeze it out before coloring it.

Be careful not to transfer any color to the base of the iron; this is more likely to happen if the paper is still wet.

ALTERNATIVES

★★

It is also possible to draw patterns into the folded shapes using felt-tipped pens. When the paper has been folded, dip it in water and squeeze it gently so that it is damp, not dripping. The felt pens will now easily penetrate several layers of paper. Open the folds partially to check how far through the layers the color has seeped, and rework the pattern from the faintest layer out. Broad felt tips give bold results, whereas fine felt tips give delicate and more detailed patterns. Dry as for the basic method already described.

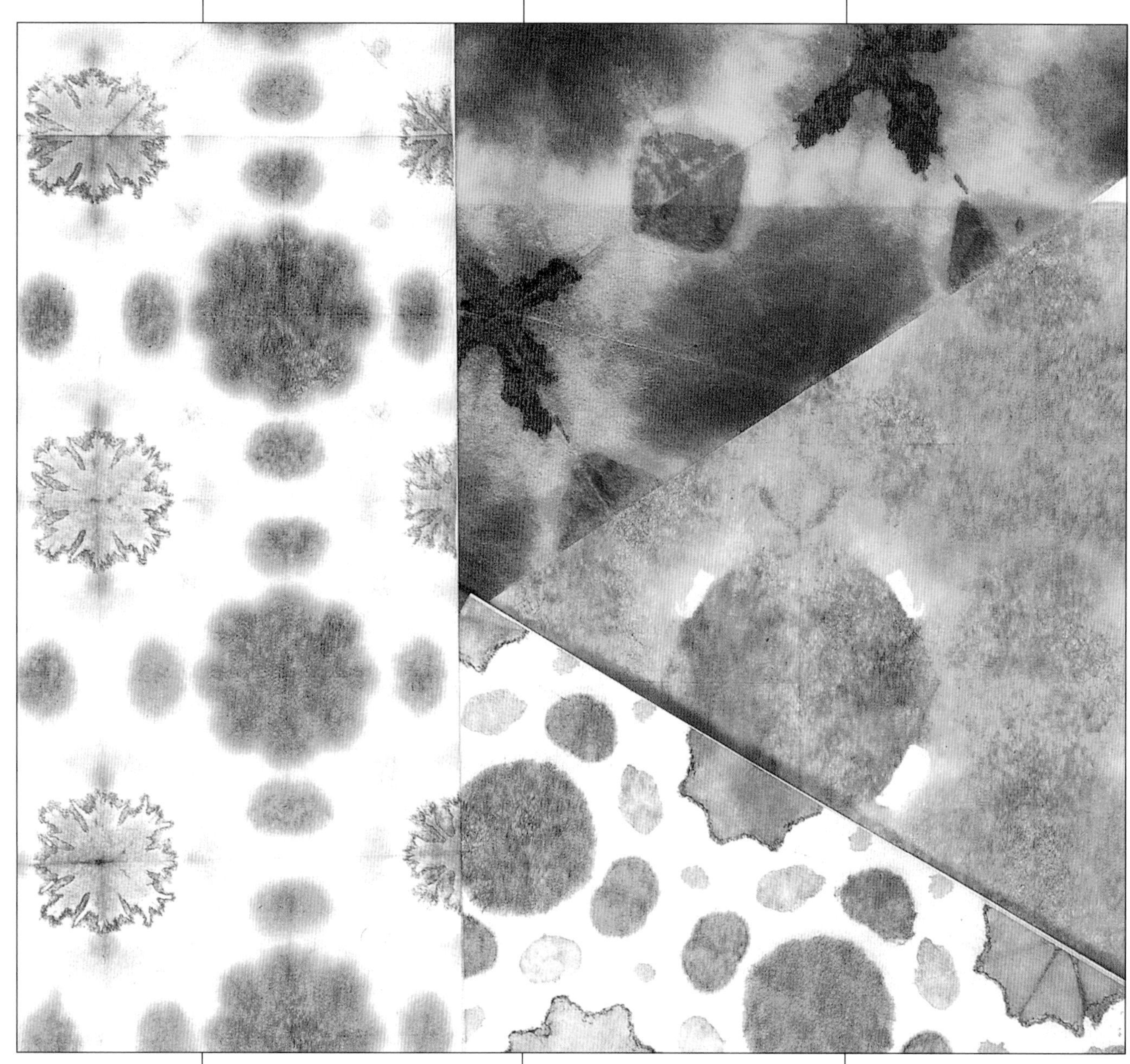

ABOVE *These dip-dyed examples show a variety of methods: use of wetted paper (left); felt pen technique (top right); wetted paper completely dyed (right); and use of dry paper (bottom right).*

PLEATING

★ ★

A method related to folding and dyeing is pleating and painting. There are many ways to pleat a piece of paper (see Figs. 5–8 for some ideas). When the paper is pleated, hold the edges together on one side with paper clamps, and paint the edges on the other side (see Fig. 9). Repeat the process for the opposite edges. Dry as for the basic method. It is possible to re-pleat another design – checks or chevrons, for example – when the paper has dried, and to paint it again.

The finished papers are extremely decorative and can be used for many other projects: such as greeting cards and papier-mâché decoration. The tissue paper can be mounted onto other sheets of paper using spray adhesive.

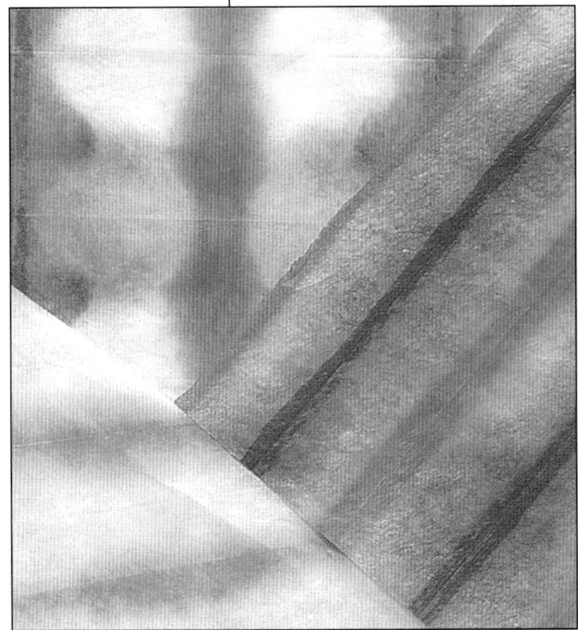

ABOVE *These finished examples show different ways of pleating: straight pleating of colored tissue paper (right); diagonal pleating (bottom left); and re-pleating (top left).*

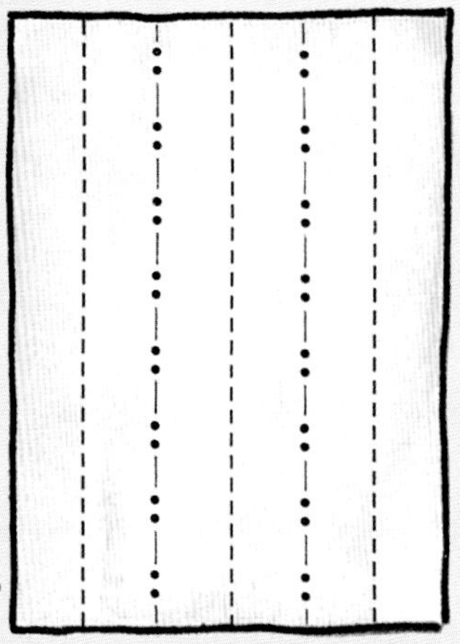

Fig 5

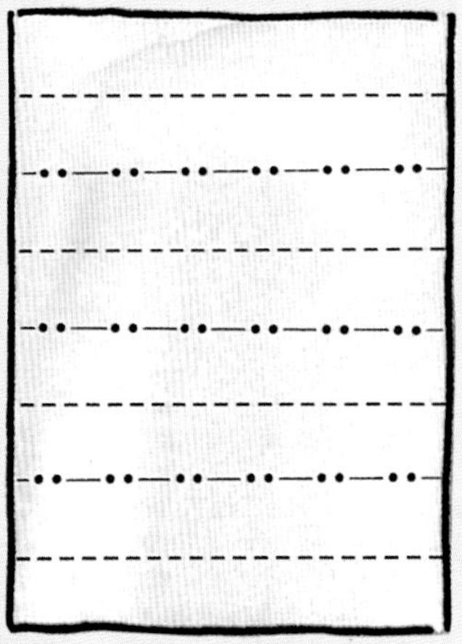

Fig 6

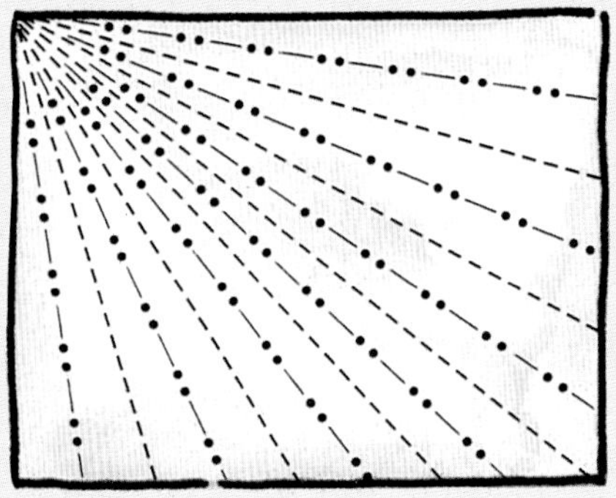

Fig 7

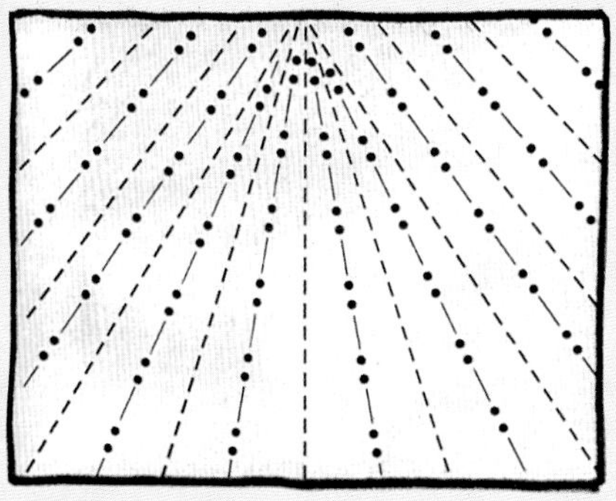

Fig 8

Fig 9

MARBLING

★★★

MATERIALS

Shallow tray (photographer's tray or baking pan)

Wallpaper paste and mixing bowl

Oil paints

Turpentine or mineral spirit

Ox-gall (available from artists' supply stores)

Jars for paints

Old newspapers

Sticks or knitting needles, for stirring

Medicine dropper or pipette

Cardboard

Double-sided tape

Ruler

Pencil

Pins

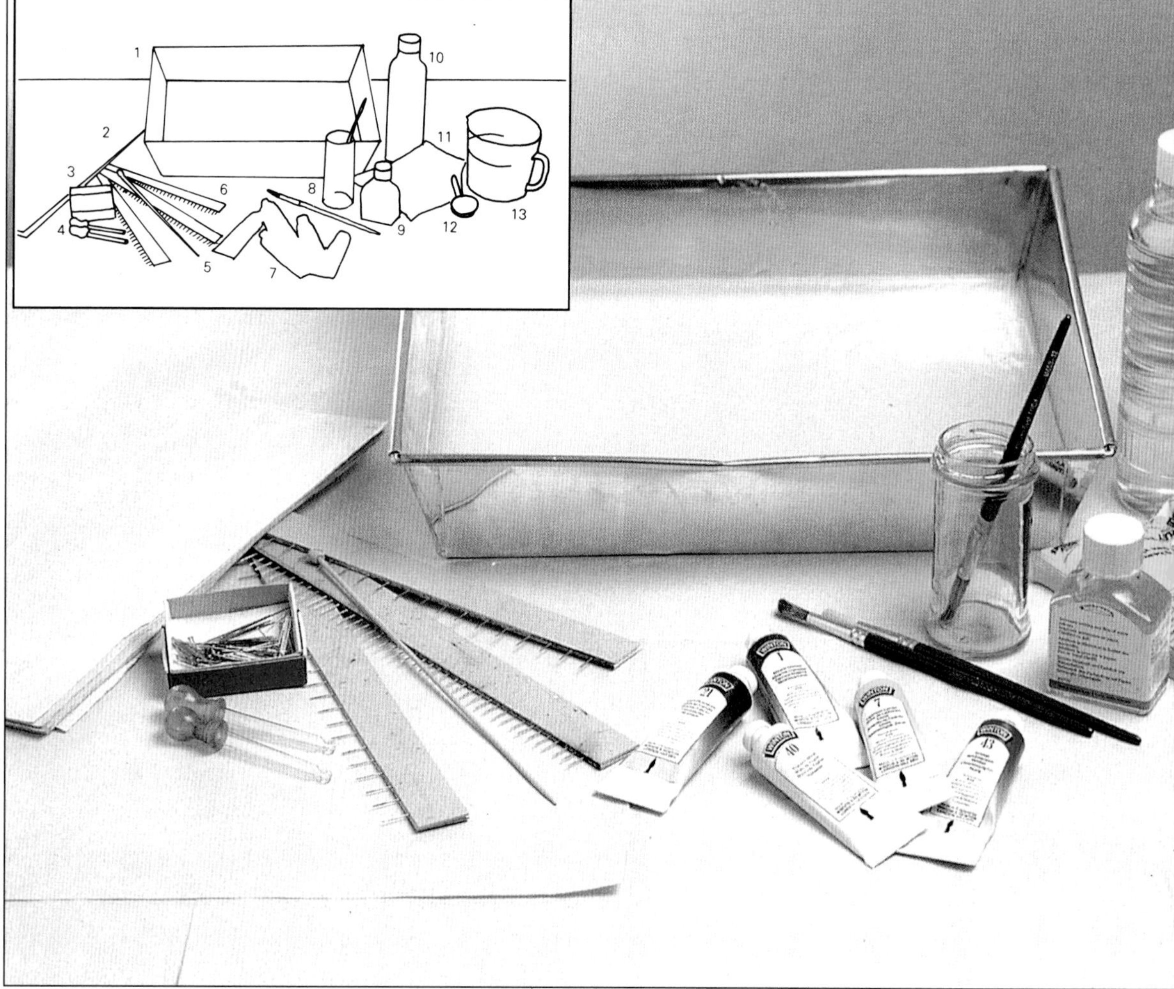

The technique of marbling, by which paper is given a marbled pattern, is thought to have been invented in eastern Europe in the sixteenth century. The process relies on the fact that oil and water do not mix. Oil colors are floated on size or water, the paper is laid on the surface of the liquid, and when it is lifted off, picks up the pattern of the colors. It is a simple technique, but needs practice to achieve consistent patterns. However, do not be deterred because it is a most enjoyable craft to practice, and even your first experiments will be presentable.

Marbled papers are mainly associated with bookbinding, but these days they appear on many household accessories: lamps and lampshades, candlesticks, wastebaskets, stationery holders and boxes, etc. Some marbled papers are now printed, but these do not usually have the quality – both visually and textually – of handmade ones.

PREPARING THE BATH

Using approximately one heaped tablespoon to 1 pint of hand-hot water, mix about one-quarter of the water with the paste (also known as size) in the tray until the paste is smooth. Then add the rest of the water, stirring well so that the size is free of lumps. Allow the mixture to stand for a while and prepare the colors.

Marbling can be done with a single color, particularly if you are using colored paper, but two or three colors can also

be used. Squeeze out some oil paint onto a saucer or a palette. Add some turpentine or mineral spirits and stir continuously until the colors are thinned to a runny consistency. Then transfer the colors to individual jars.

The next step is the most uncertain part of the process and will probably need several attempts. Add ox-gall to the colors in order to reduce the surface tension and to allow the colors to spread on the size. Ox-gall reacts differently with each color, depending on factors such as the temperature of the room and the size, the consistency of the colors, etc. Start by adding five drops of ox-gall to two teaspoons of each color. If colors are being placed on top of each other, the second color will need additional ox-gall. However, you can make these adjustments during the marbling session.

Make sure that you have plenty of strips of newspaper or newsprint prepared for skimming excess color from the surface of the size. The strips should be slightly narrower than the tray and 3 inches wide.

Having completed these basic preparations, it is now time to start experimenting with the consistencies and temperatures of the size and the oil colors. Test each color individually (see chart) before attempting to use two colors or more together.

BELOW *Some decorative examples using these marbling techniques on colored as well as white paper.*

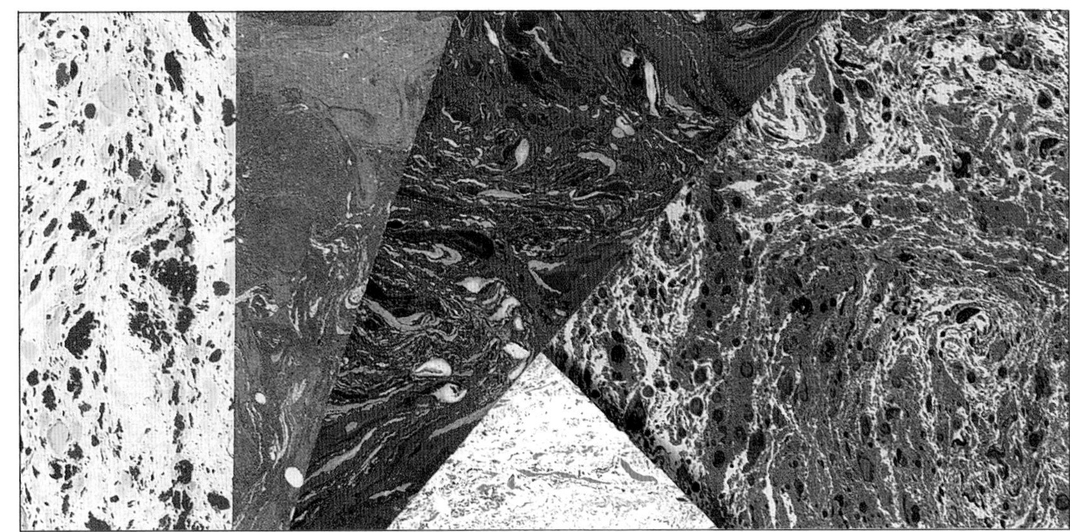

Equipment

1 Shallow tray
2 Medium-weight paper
3 Pins
4 Medicine droppers
5 Knitting needle
6 Marbling combs (see page 197)
7 Oil colors
8 Mixing jar
9 Ox-gall
10 Mmineral spirits
11 Wallpaper paste
12 Measuring spoons
13 Measuring cup

Test Chart

CAUTION It is essential that you skim the surface of the size with the strips of paper between each trial so that you can see clearly how the oil colors are reacting and also to get into the habit of skimming the surface between patterns.

If the color disperses too thinly, there is too much ox-gall and you need to add more thinned color.

If the color does not spread, there is not enough ox-gall – add more, drop by drop. If this does not work, it is possible that the size is too thick and more water should be stirred in carefully.

If the color sinks through the size, it usually means that the size is too thick and should therefore be thinned.

If the color still sinks, the temperature of the size may not be right. If the size feels warmer than room temperature, then add cold water to it, and if it feels colder, add warm water.

BASIC METHOD

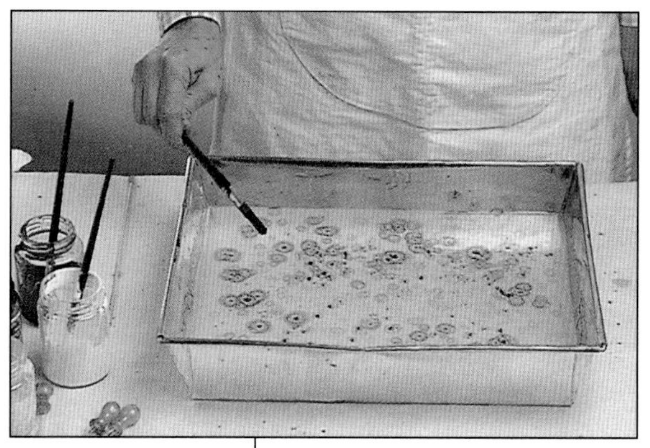

1 Having achieved all the right consistencies, it is time to make a pattern. Drop color randomly from a brush, loaded with color, tapped against the side of the tray. Repeat with more colors, if desired.

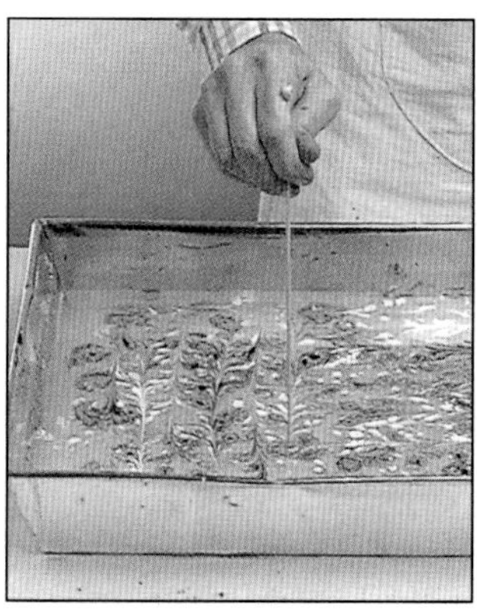

2 Using a stick or knitting needle, draw patterns in the size by dragging the implement through the oil colors. Take care to work only on the surface of the size and move the pattern-making implement gently and fairly slowly so that you disturb the bath as little as possible.

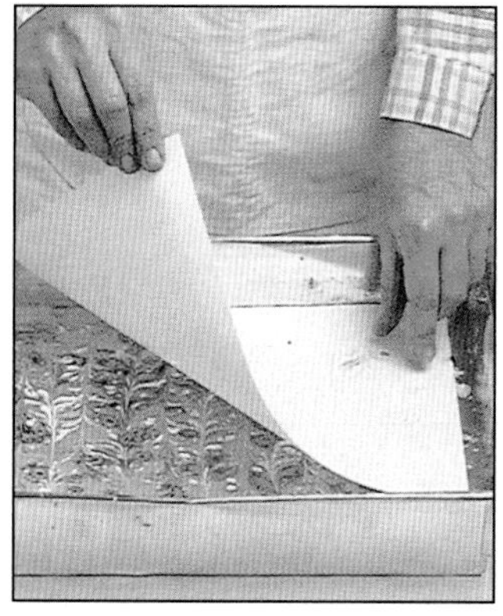

3 When the pattern looks satisfactory, take a piece of light- to medium-weight paper by the opposite corners and lay it onto the size carefully, with a rolling movement. Do this fairly slowly or air bubbles will become trapped beneath the paper, forming unintended white spaces in the pattern.

4 Lift off the paper almost immediately by picking up two adjacent corners and peeling it off the surface of the size.

5 Let it drain on the side of the tray for a minute or so and then lay it on some newspaper to dry. You can rinse the paper very gently to remove the excess size, but this can affect the color and is not really necessary. You can also hang the paper on a line to dry.

DESIGN VARIATIONS

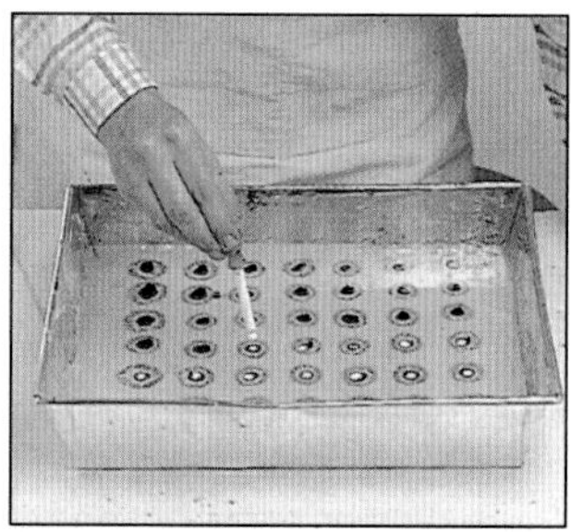

1 **a** Drop color onto the size with a pipette. Continue by dropping further colors onto the first color.

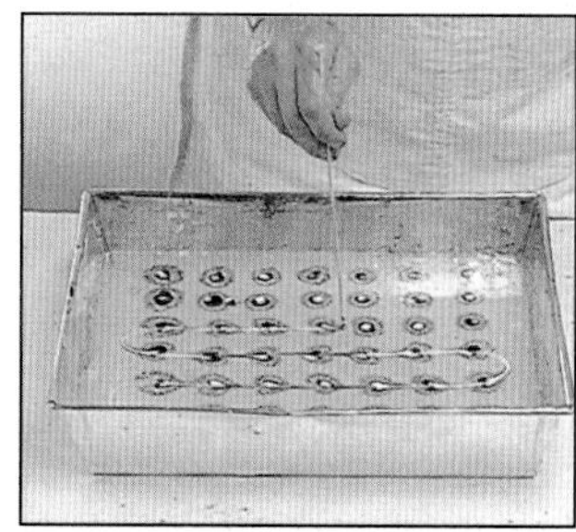

1 **b** With a knitting needle, draw through the center of the dots to make a continuous thread.

CAUTION!!

Remember to clean the excess color from the surface of the size before you start to create the next pattern. Lay a sheet of clean paper onto the paste mixture to soak up any remaining color.

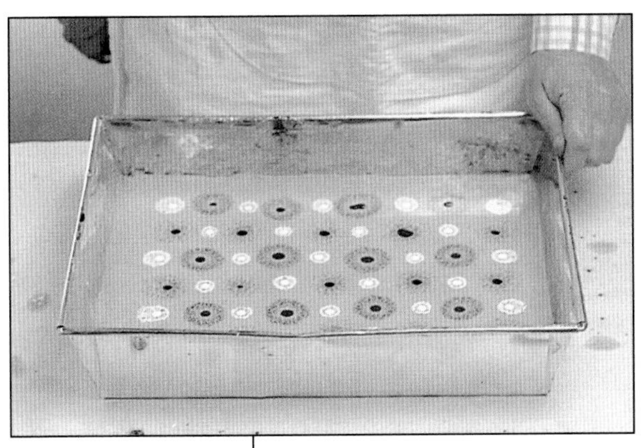

2 **a** Alternatively, intersperse different-colored drops of paint on the size.

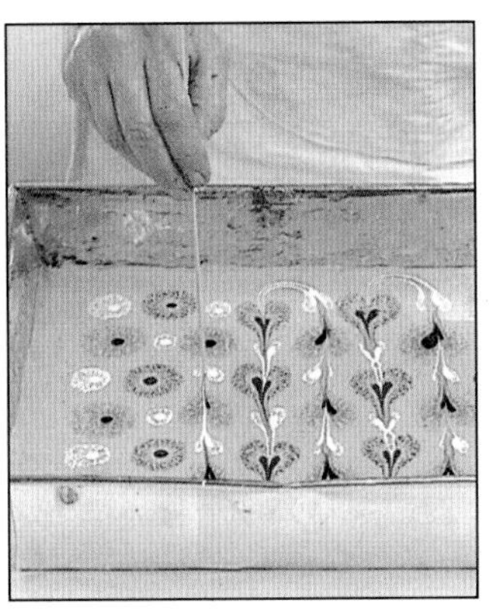

2 **b** Draw down through the rows of dots to feather the colors and create a design.

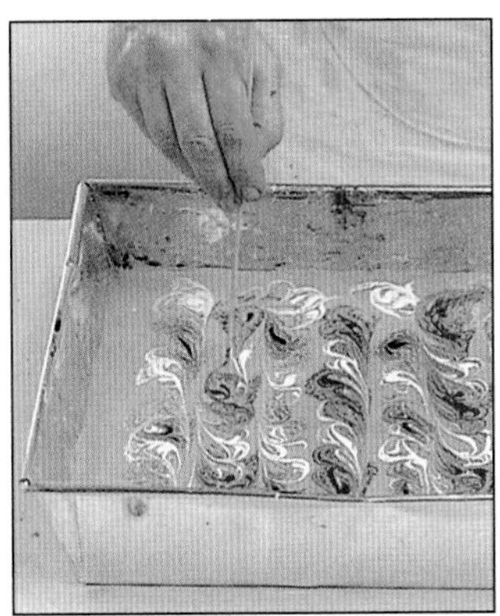

2 **c** Agitate the surface slightly with the needle to make the lines of color wavy.

2 **d** Lay the paper slowly down onto the size.

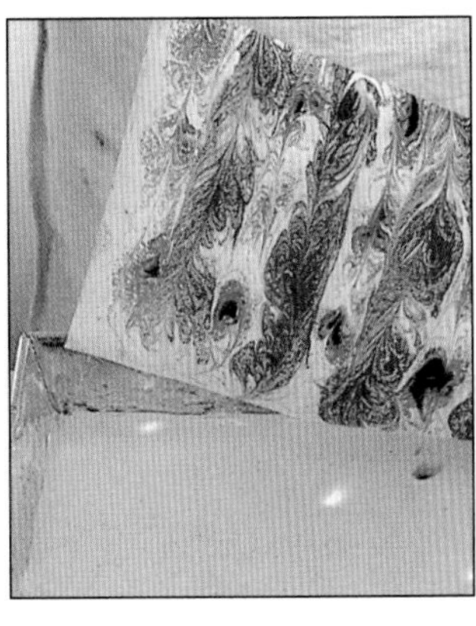

2 **e** Quickly lift the paper off.

3 **a** Alternatively, use larger movements to swirl the colors.

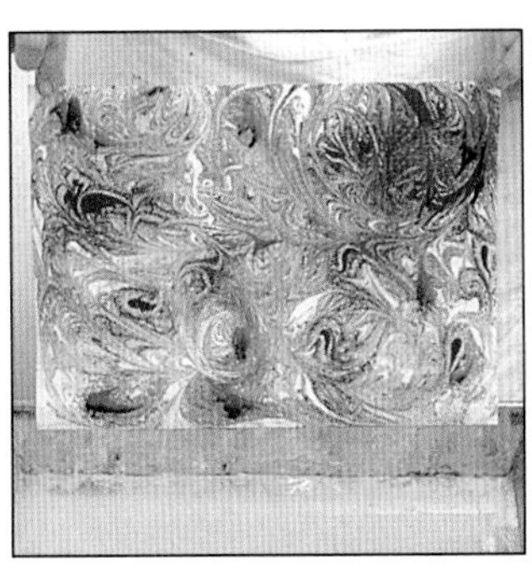

3 **b** This produces a bolder, spiral design.

HOW TO MAKE A MARBLING COMB

1 Take 2 strips of cardboard ½ inch shorter than the width and/or length of the tray, and about 2 inches wide. Mark ½-inch spaces on 1 strip.

2 Cover the strip with double-sided tape.

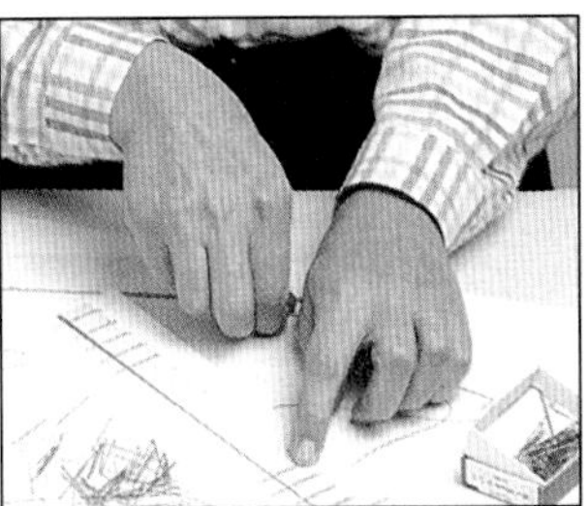

3 Position long pins on the tape at the marked points. Stick more tape to the other piece of cardboard and stick the two boards together carefully.

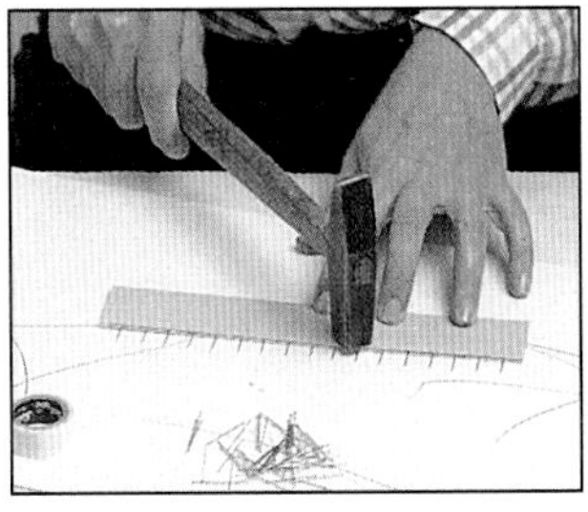

4 Bang the 2 pieces firmly together with a hammer. Additional combs can be made, setting different spaces for the "teeth".

PART V

CUTTING, FOLDING, AND STICKING

BASICS

BASIC EQUIPMENT

There are numerous ways of attaching pieces of paper, cardboard, and fabric together. Some of these ways are listed here, but you will probably think of other methods. Some of the methods are suitable only as a temporary measure, but they are still important, particularly when an extra pair of hands is unavailable!

EQUIPMENT

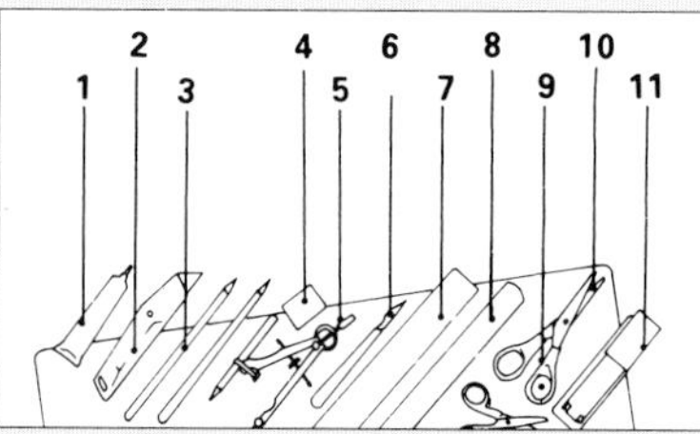

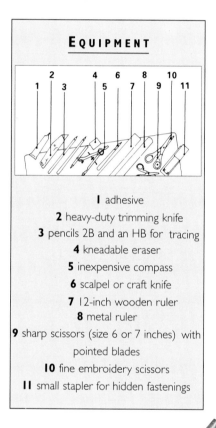

1 adhesive
2 heavy-duty trimming knife
3 pencils 2B and an HB for tracing
4 kneadable eraser
5 inexpensive compass
6 scalpel or craft knife
7 12-inch wooden ruler
8 metal ruler
9 sharp scissors (size 6 or 7 inches) with pointed blades
10 fine embroidery scissors
11 small stapler for hidden fastenings

Tape

There are three main types of tape – masking tape, which has low tack and is extremely useful for temporary fixing and usually does not mark the material which is being held; normal cellophane tape, which is usually sold under a brand name; and double-sided tape, which is excellent for creating invisible bonding.

Adhesives

There are many types of glue available and each person has his or her own favorite brand. In this book we have used mainly craft, sometimes called white glue or school glue. This glue is clean to use, dries transparent, and allows the user time to position the parts being attached. Sometimes a quick-drying glue is required, and for this purpose, one of the brands of clear glue is suggested.

Stapler and staples

These are very useful for joining parts together quickly, but be sure to cover the open ends with tape if they are anywhere near the face.

Slots and tabs

These are methods of creative fixings without using any other material. A slot is cut into one piece of material, and a tab is added to the other piece of material. This tab is then pushed through the slot. Sometimes glue or tape can also be used to create a more permanent fixing. If the board is thick, it may actually be necessary to cut out a sliver of cardboard from the slot to accommodate the tab.

TEMPLATES

As every face is different, it is not possible to give a universal pattern for every style of mask, so you will have to tailor the mask to fit your needs.

In the first instance, it is suggested that you trace the pattern onto paper or thin cardboard and try it on. Cut or extend this basic shape where necessary; this way you will be able to personalize the patterns. You will soon become accomplished at altering where necessary.

Some of the templates are not shown full size. Any alterations to these will need to be made after the pattern has been enlarged.

DECORATIVE TECHNIQUES

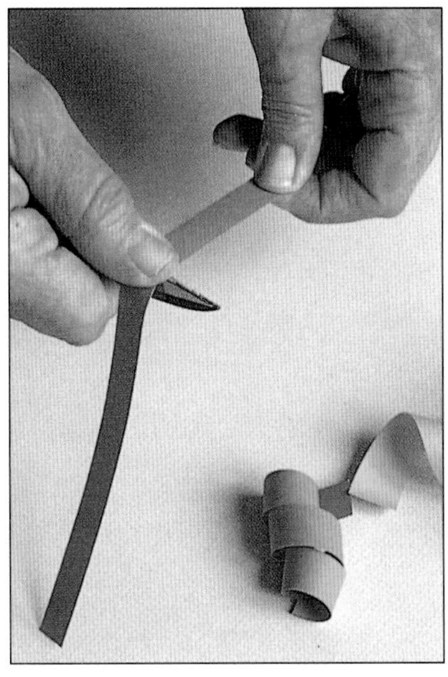

Curling

To make paper curls, cut the paper against the grain and then pull the strips, one by one, across the back of a knife, scissors blade, or ruler – this causes the paper to stretch on one side and thus curl. Practice with different weights of paper to discover what works best for your purpose.

Rolling

Paper can be rolled around various objects and held in place with some form of adhesive, depending on the final use of the roll. Rolls can vary from pencil size to large cylinders. As with the previous method, the roll will be best achieved if created with the grain.

Scrunching

This method is fun, but is best suited to very lightweight papers. Cut or tear the paper into squares or triangles and crumple up the pieces. This can be done tightly or loosely, and the resulting shape can be glued in position where required – sometimes a little glue may be added to the shape.

Pleating

Pleating is a good way of using paper for decorative purposes. The folds will crease more crisply if they are made with the grain, where possible.

BASIC BOX

★

When drawing a plan for a basic box, work out the dimensions; and whatever the size, make sure that all angles are 90° (see Fig. 1). The larger the box, the thicker the cardboard should be.

The number of flaps should equal the number of cut edges.

Use a sharp knife to cut out the shape, and cut away from the work – it would be infuriating to cut into the shape accidentally, having spent time carefully drawing it out.

Check the fit of the box, and stick the sides together, using clear, all-purpose adhesive, rather than a glue stick. Next, stick the base in position. The box is now complete.

If you are using plain cardboard, you could decorate the outside, or cover it with gift-wrap paper. It is best to decorate or cover the cardboard before assembling the box.

It is possible to make the basic box collapsible. Add the glue flaps to the base instead of the bottom of the sides, and then stick only the side glue flap in position. The box can now be flattened and assembled when required, but remember that the box will not be as strong as a rigid one, and do not forget to stick the base in place so that the bottom does not fall out of the box at the wrong moment!

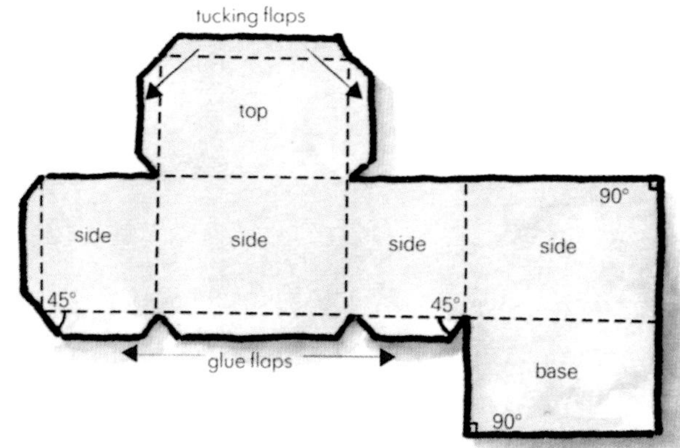

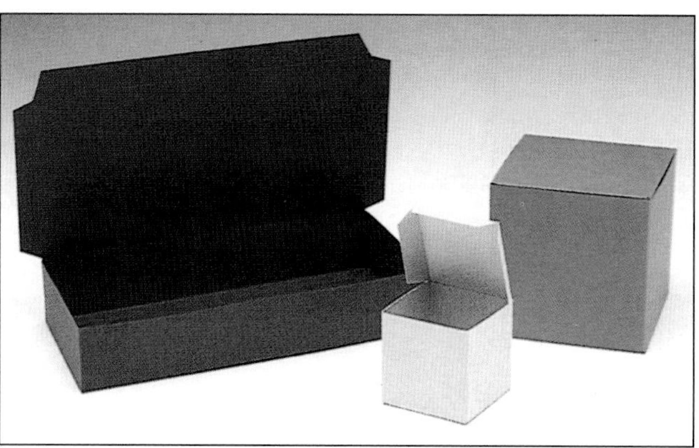

ABOVE *These three boxes were made from solid-colored cardboard with different dimensions using the basic method.*

TWO-PIECE BOX

★★

A two-piece box can be as simple as the silver box in the photograph overleaf, or more complicated, like the red one with the star shape. A two-piece box is more economical to make than the basic box, but cannot be collapsed.

SILVER BOX

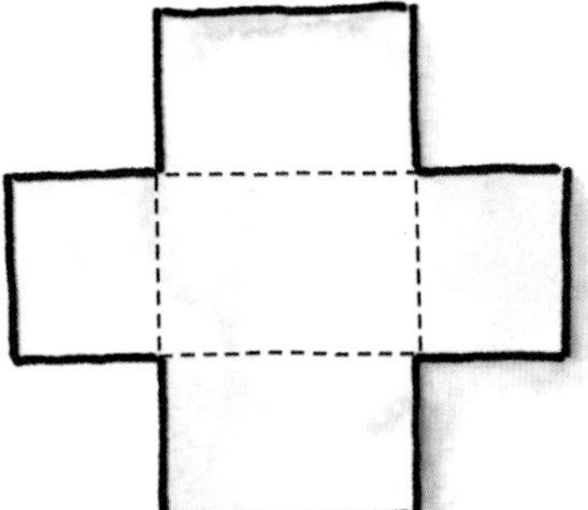

1 The easiest way to make a box with a separate lid is to cut out the box shape to the required size and stick the sides together using decorated tape.

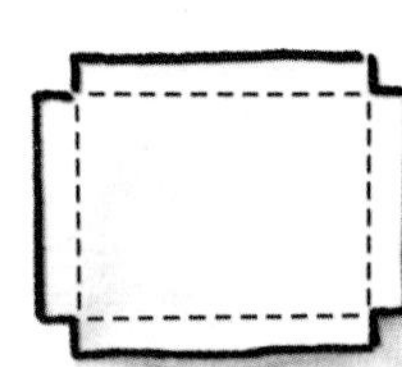

2 Make the lid in exactly the same way, but make the sides very short; the dimensions of the rectangle should be ⅟₁₆ inch larger in both directions.

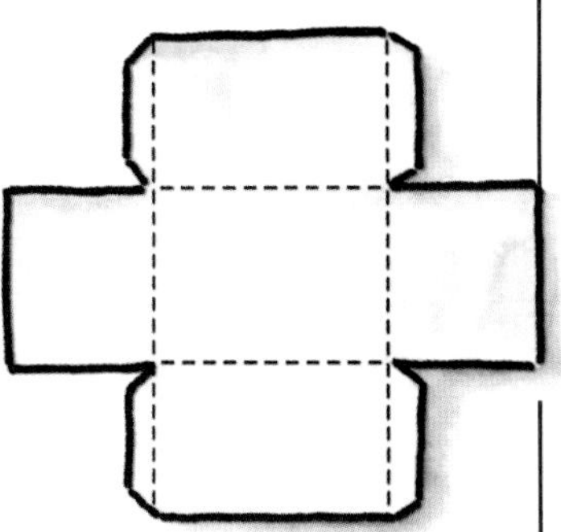

The same result can be achieved by adding glue flaps. Make generous allowance for the cardboard's thickness when making the lid, because the glue flaps will increase the thickness.

BLUE BOX

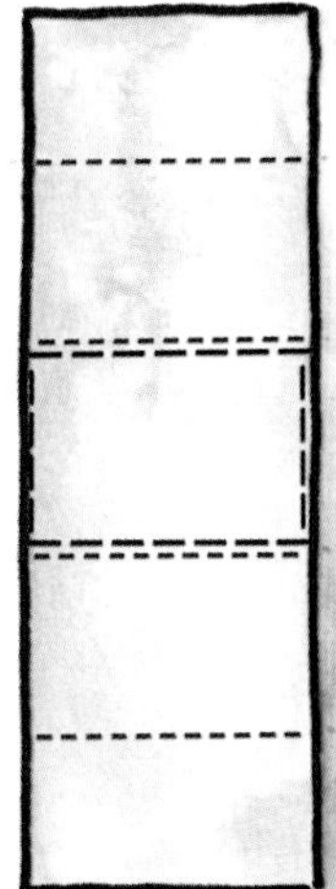

1 Mark a strip of cardboard which is equal in length to twice the length and twice the width of the gift plus a glue flap, and equal to the height of the gift plus a glue flap. The strip can be joined if necessary. Cut out, score the folds, and glue to form a box.

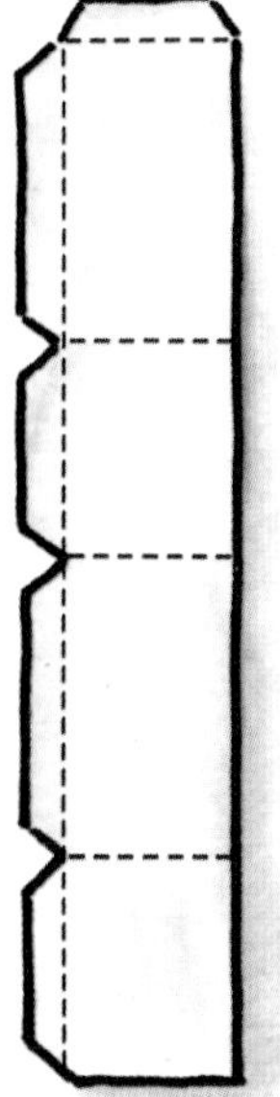

2 For the wraparound lid, mark a piece of cardboard measuring the length of the gift by twice the width and twice the height plus an overlap. Cut out and score the folds.

3 Glue the center section of the lid to the glue flaps at the base of the box. Fold the side and top pieces around the box, enclosing the gift. Either tie it to close or seal with a sticker.

STAR-SHAPED BOX

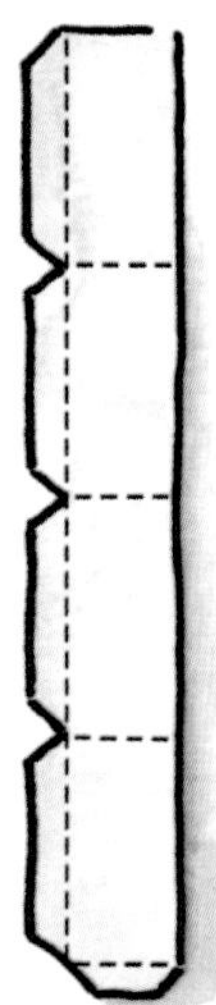

1 Mark a strip of cardboard (see Blue Box, step 1), but with the sides of equal measure to form a square box. Make the lid in the same way, but slightly larger.

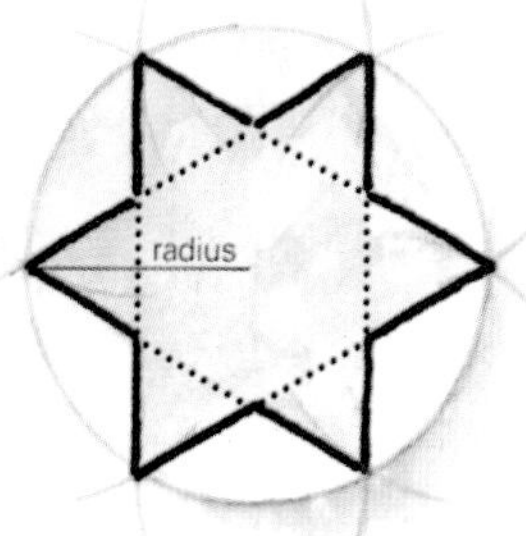

2 To construct the star, measure the length of one side of the box with the compass. This is the radius of the circle. Draw the circle. Keeping the same radius setting, place the point of the compass on the circumference of the circle and mark the point it crosses on the curve. Move the compass to this point and repeat the process until you have six points around the circumference. Join alternate points with a pencil and ruler.

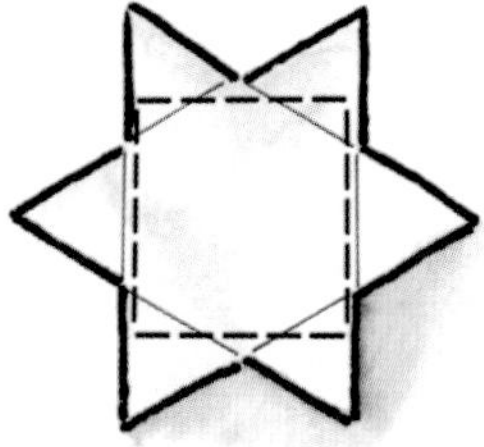

3 Cut out two star shapes and glue one to the flaps at the base of the box and the others to the flaps at the top of the lid. The box is now complete.

BELOW *The possibilities for decorating homemade boxes are endless. Decorated tape, stickers, and attractive ties all add a professional finishing touch. The basket-type box was made using strips of metallic cardboard woven together, see pages 180–181, with a simple strip attached to act as a handle.*

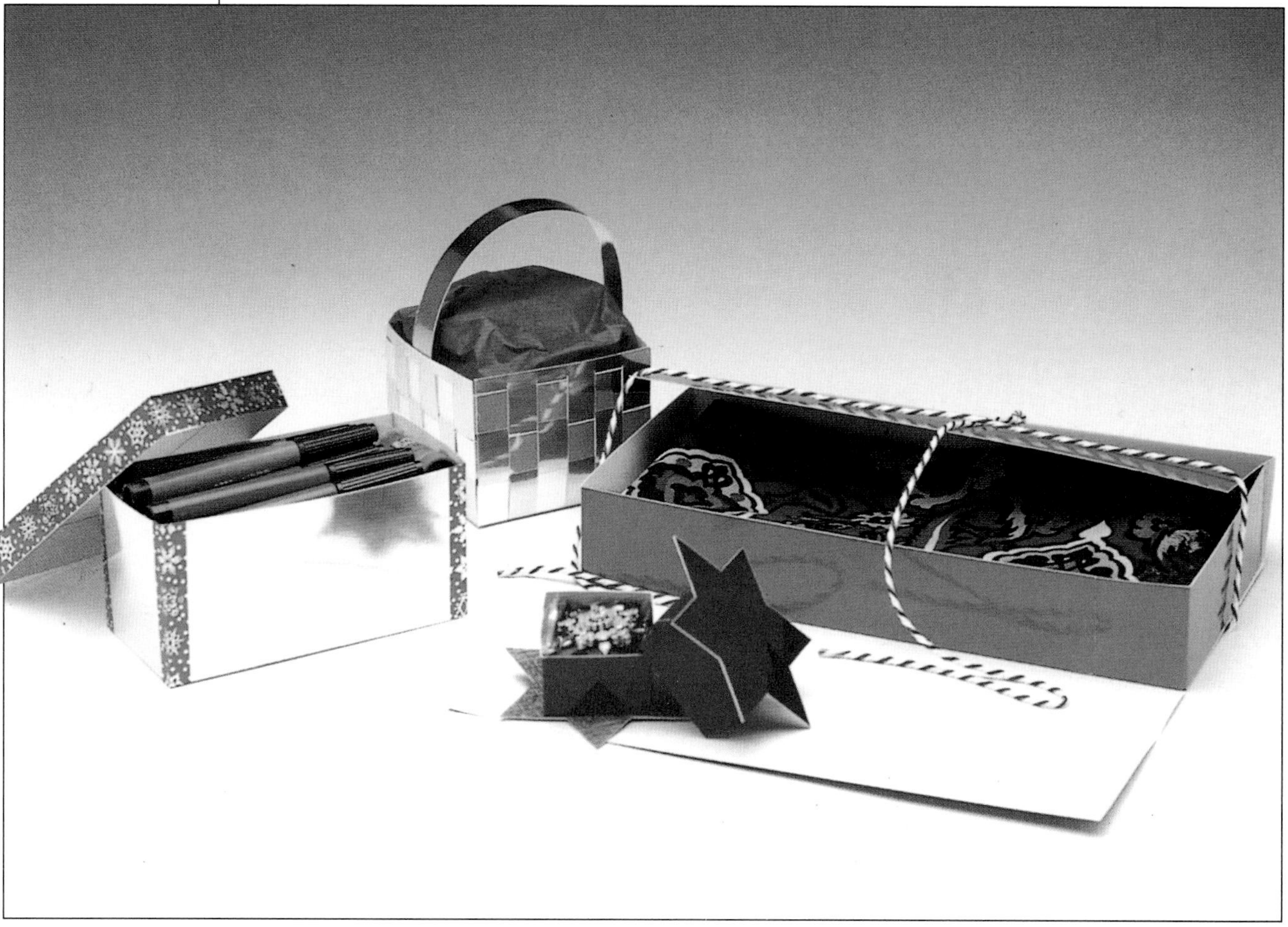

COVERING BOXES

★★

Boxes can be re-used; chocolate and soap boxes particularly are often a suitable size for other gifts. There are two ways of disguising their previous uses. Often it is necessary only to re-cover the lid, but the method is the same if the bottom is also being re-covered.

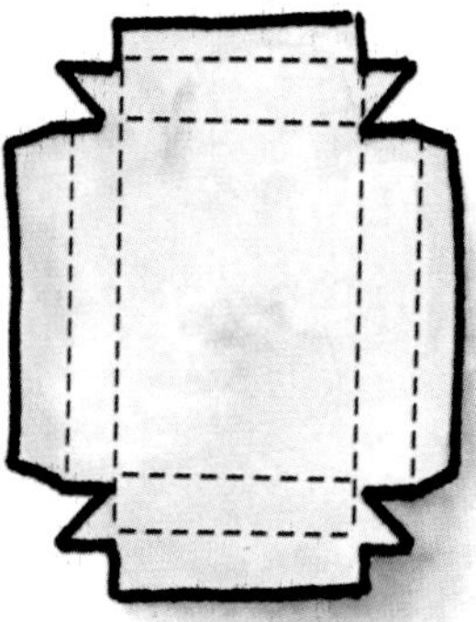

1 Measure the width and length of the box lid and the height of the box sides. The piece of paper will need to be big enough for the lid measurement plus four times the sides. Draw the rectangle in the center of a piece of lightweight paper; add sides all around and then add another set of sides to turn in. Draw "ears" as in the diagram.

2 Cut out, score, and fold the whole shape. Position the box on the drawn rectangle, turn the "ears" inward.

3 Glue the "ears" and the turn-in allowance down.

4 Then glue the opposite sides.

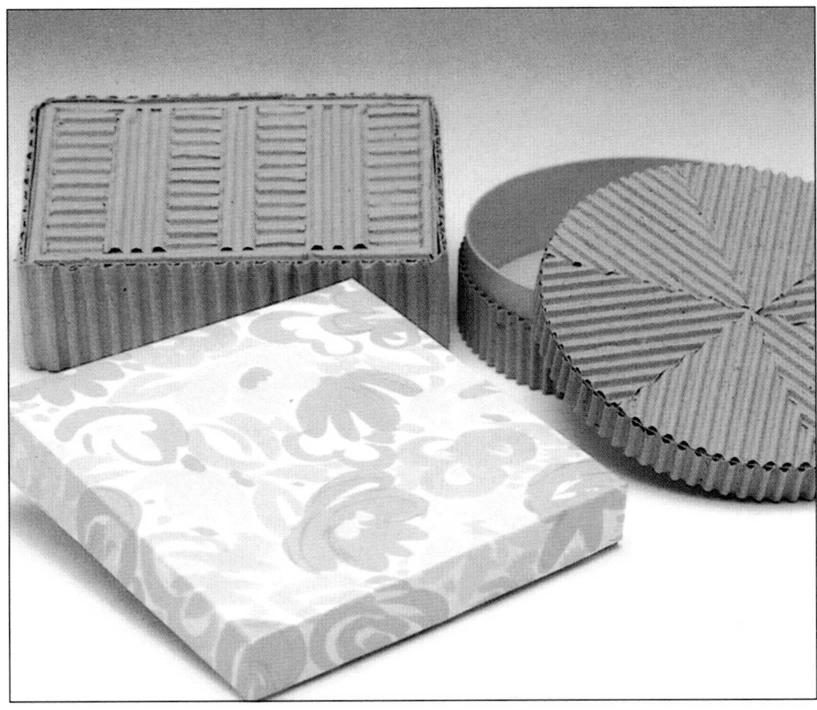

VARIATIONS

Many interesting patterns can be made using corrugated paper; the photograph (RIGHT) shows two such designs. Always cut the corrugated paper with a sharp knife on the wrong (flat) side without pressing hard, because this would flatten the "ribs." Use a fairly strong adhesive. Cover the top first and then, with the covered top downward, wrap a strip of corrugated paper around the sides.

COMPLEX BOXES

★★★★

FLAT GIFT HOLDER

This type of box is most suitable for flat gifts, such as scarves and ties. Measure the gift and then make the gift holder the length of the gift, and the width plus the height of the gift (if the gift is solid, allow a little extra). At its deepest point, the curves at the top and bottom of the holder should measure approximately twice the height of the gift.

With these measurements, it is now possible to draw the plan of the gift holder (see diagram). The curve can either be drawn with the compass, placed on the center line, or using a plate. Join two sides with one curve and trace this onto a piece of scrap cardboard and use this as a template to draw the other curves. Cut out and score. Stick the glue flap to the side. Place the gift in the holder and close by turning in the curves.

To make the gift holder extra-special, a shape – a butterfly for example – can be cut and folded from the right side; glue a piece of decorative paper underneath and lift the cutout.

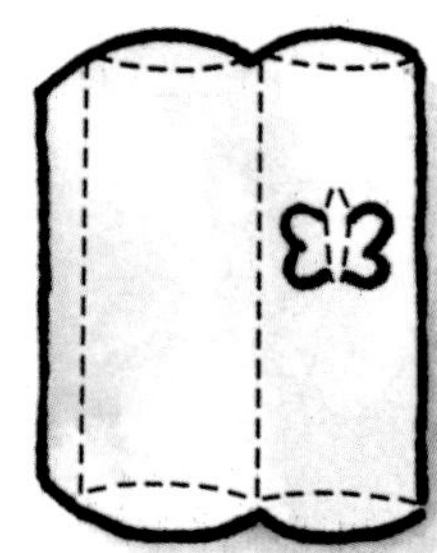

ABOVE *Basic plan for the flat gift holder.*

BELOW *The blue gift holder is decorated with a butterfly-shaped cutout (see main text). The green one was made with lightweight cardboard that had been decorated with a stenciled design (see pages 183–185).*

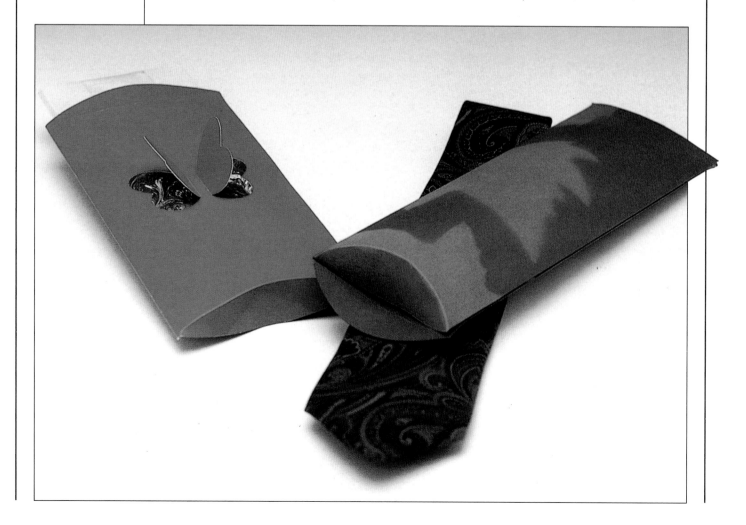

PYRAMID BOX

This little box can either be used as a box or as a decoration. The size is variable. Start by drawing a line and draw a semicircle on this line. Place the compass point, with the same radius, at one end of the semicircle and mark the center and the point it crosses on the curve. Repeat from the other end. With the same radius setting, draw another semicircle so that it joins the first. Put the compass point on the join and mark the point it crosses on this curve. Join all the marks, and four equilateral triangles will emerge. Add one glue flap to the base of the first triangle, two tucking flaps with slits, and two tabs to correspond with the slits (see diagram). Cut out the basic shape and score all the other lines. Stick the glue flap and place the gift inside and close the box tightly with the tabs – it is quite tricky to tuck in the tabs, but provides a very secure closure.

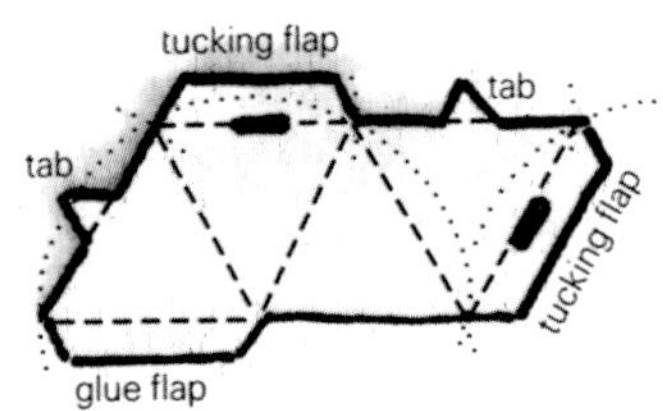

ABOVE *Basic plan for the pyramid box.*

BELOW *You can make your pyramid box to any size. Use plain or foil light cardboard, or decorate using the techniques described on pages 182–197.*

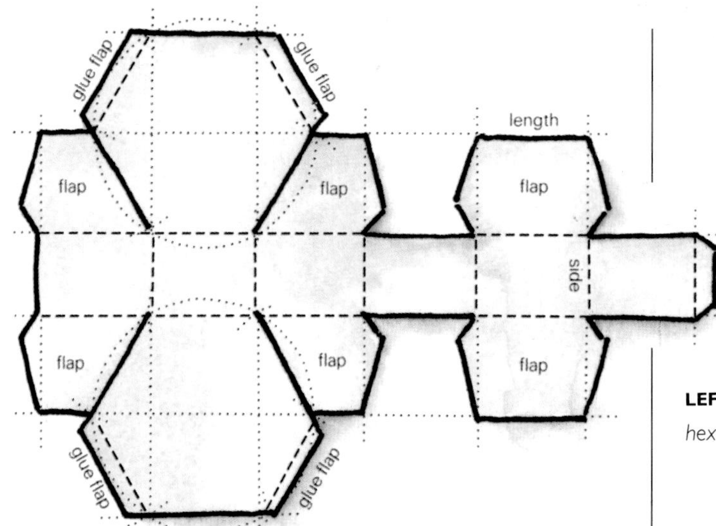

LEFT *The basic plan for the hexagonal box.*

HEXAGONAL BOX

This box looks most impressive and is not as complicated as it appears. Once the size of the hexagon has been worked out, it is quite easy to construct. If the box is being used for a circular gift, this must fit *within* the hexagon; work this out using scrap paper.

Draw a circle larger than the gift. Draw a horizontal line through the middle of the circle. Using the same radius setting, place the compass point on one of the intersections and mark the point it crosses on the curve. Move the compass to this point and repeat until you have six points around the circumference. Join these points and check whether the gift will fit into this hexagon – if not try again. Once this is correct, draw a plan following the diagram. The sides of the box are equal to the height of the gift and one side of the hexagon in length. The three flaps, top and bottom, are half the height of the hexagon. Cut out, score, and fold. Check the angles of the flaps before gluing, in case any adjustments need to be made. Stick the glue flap and assemble the box. If necessary, glue down the tucking flaps on the base so that the box does not fall apart if the gift is heavy.

LEFT *This hexagonal box has been made using embossed foil cardboard. Filled with chocolates, it makes an inexpensive yet impressive gift.*

PAPER GIFT BAGS

★

BASIC BAG

These bags are easy to make and can look extremely decorative. They can be made in many different sizes, and matching gift tags can be added. Unusual handles can be made from harmonizing or contrasting materials, such as plaited yarn or ribbons.

There are a few basic rules: all angles should be right angles (90°), so that the bag stands square when finished; the bottom flaps should be about ½ inch less than the width of the sides; score the fold lines to give a crisper crease; this is essential on thicker paper and cardboard.

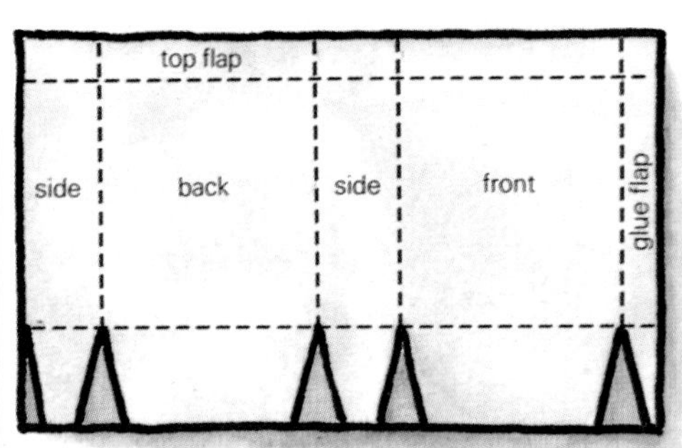

BELOW *For the handles, punch holes in the top edge and thread ribbon, cord, or braid through them. The holes can act as closures or can be simply decorative.*

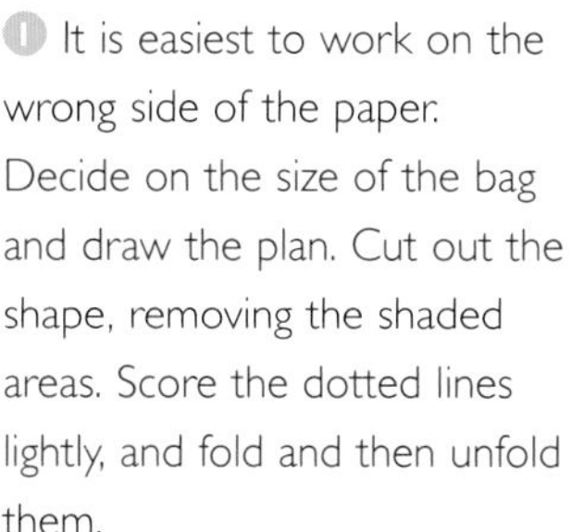

1 It is easiest to work on the wrong side of the paper. Decide on the size of the bag and draw the plan. Cut out the shape, removing the shaded areas. Score the dotted lines lightly, and fold and then unfold them.

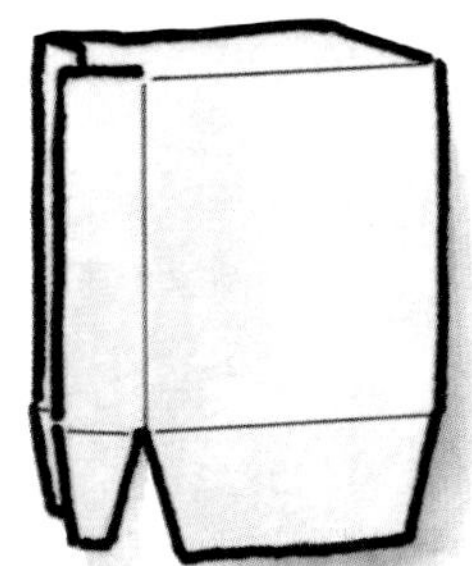

2 Glue down the top flap, which adds strength and looks neater. Next glue the front flap to the side.

3 Finally, glue the bottom flaps to each other – the side flaps to the back flap and the front flap on top of the side flaps.

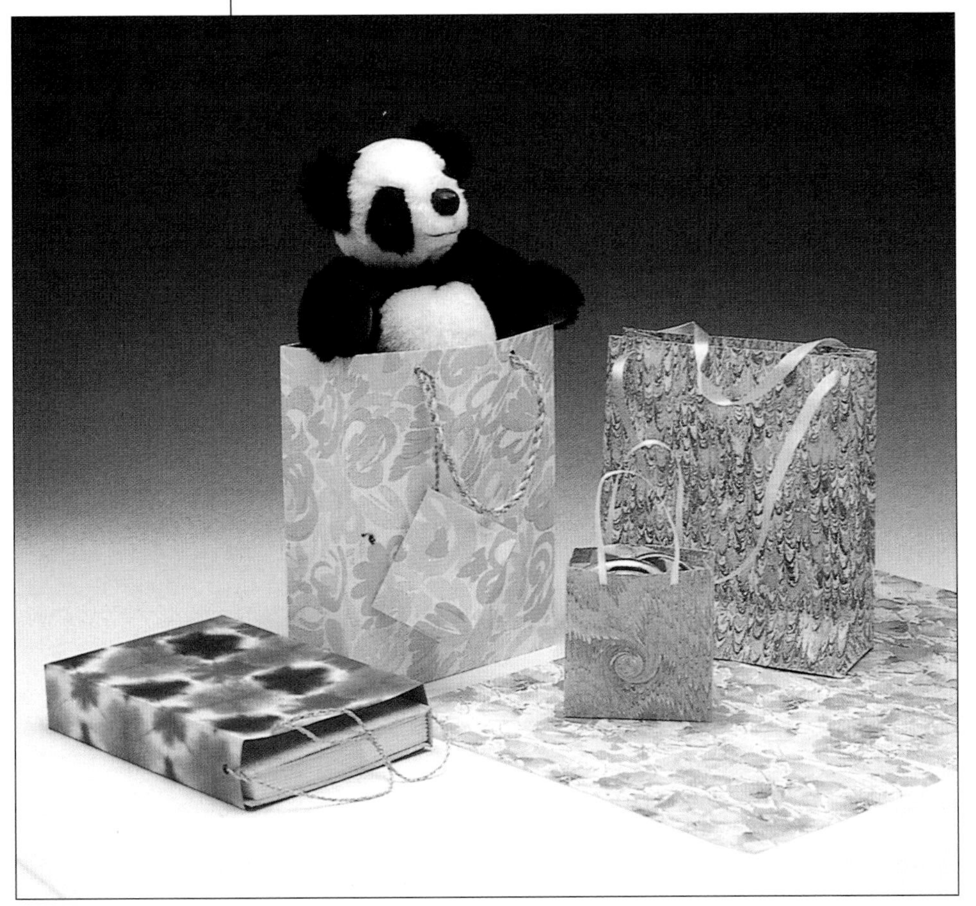

STRONG PAPER BAG

Making a bag which will carry a bottle or a heavy or large gift poses a few problems, but these can easily be overcome.

If a bottle or heavy gift is to be placed in the bag, it is advisable to glue a piece of cardboard inside the base of the bag. To strengthen the top of the bag, add an extra strip of paper under the top flap. The basic plan is the same as for the ordinary bag, page 209, except that the measurements for all the sides will be identical and should be the diameter of the bottle plus ¼ inch. The height of the bag should be 2½ inches more than the height of the bottle, so that the top edges can be pulled together.

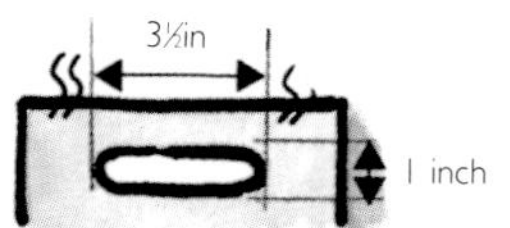

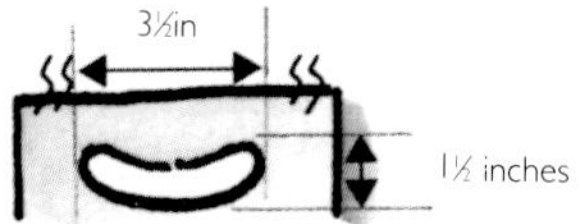

When making a large bag, it is quite simple to add a strong handle. Cut a piece of plain lightweight cardboard the width of the bag and at least 3 inches deep. Cut the hand shape out of the center of the cardboard and mark this hole on the bag plan. Cut these holes out of the paper on the bag and top flap, and glue the cardboard stiffener in position. Continue as for the basic bag.

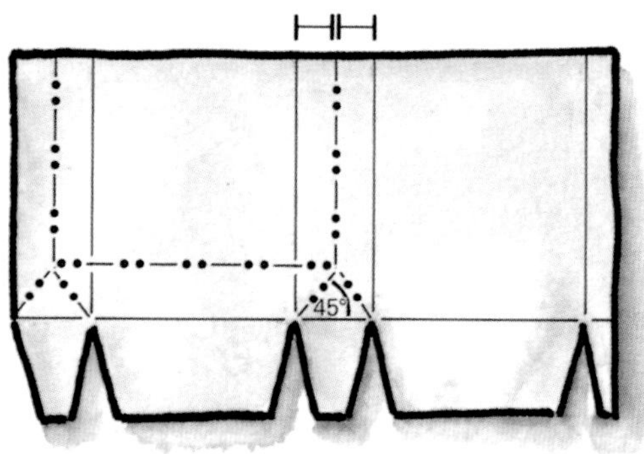

It is possible to fold the bag flat by scoring lines in addition to the ones on the basic plan. Practice with some scrap paper – this is not as complicated as it looks.

BELOW *Strengthening the basic paper bag for heavy or large gifts can be achieved easily by reinforcing the base or handles with extra cardboard.*

HEART-SHAPED BAG

The decorative heart-shaped bag shown on this page is deceptively simple. The design is based on a semicircle and can be made from many different types of paper or cardboard. It is easy to alter the size by following the directions.

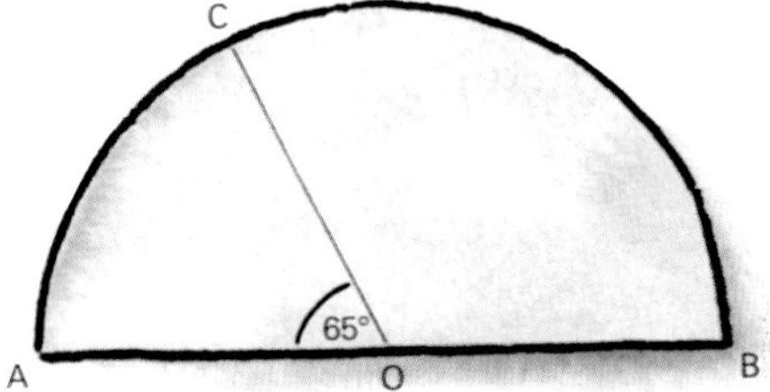

❶ Draw a semicircle and mark a point about 65° from one edge, at C.

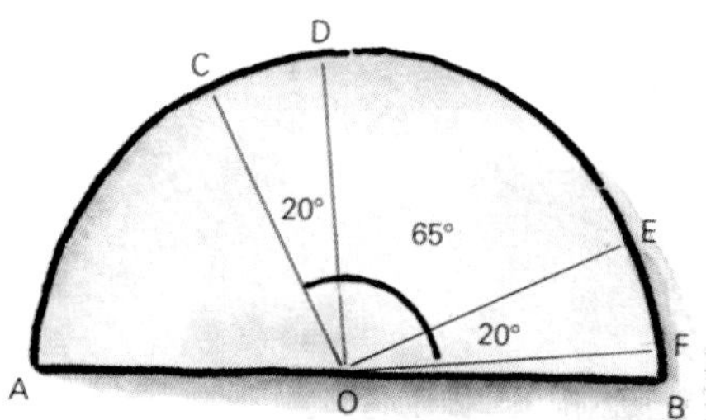

❷ Mark another point 20° from C, then another at 65° and another at 20°. Join all these points to the center.

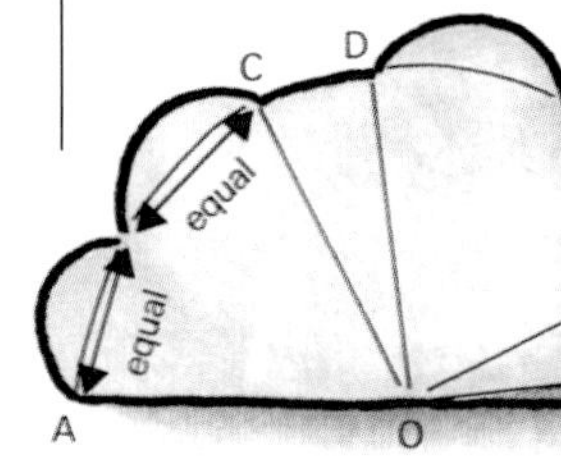

❸ Now divide both of the largest arcs in half, either by measuring or using a protractor. Draw semicircles on each half.

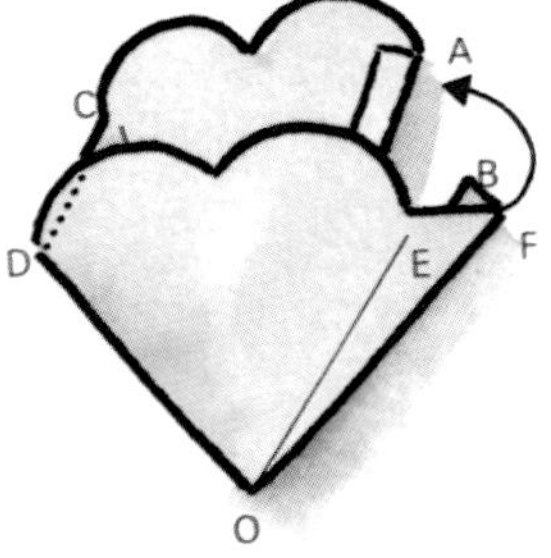

❹ Cut out the whole shape and score all lines from the center out to the edge and fold. Glue the shaded area to the heart shape.

BELOW *Holes can be punched in the side panels to make handles. Decorate the bag if you wish.*

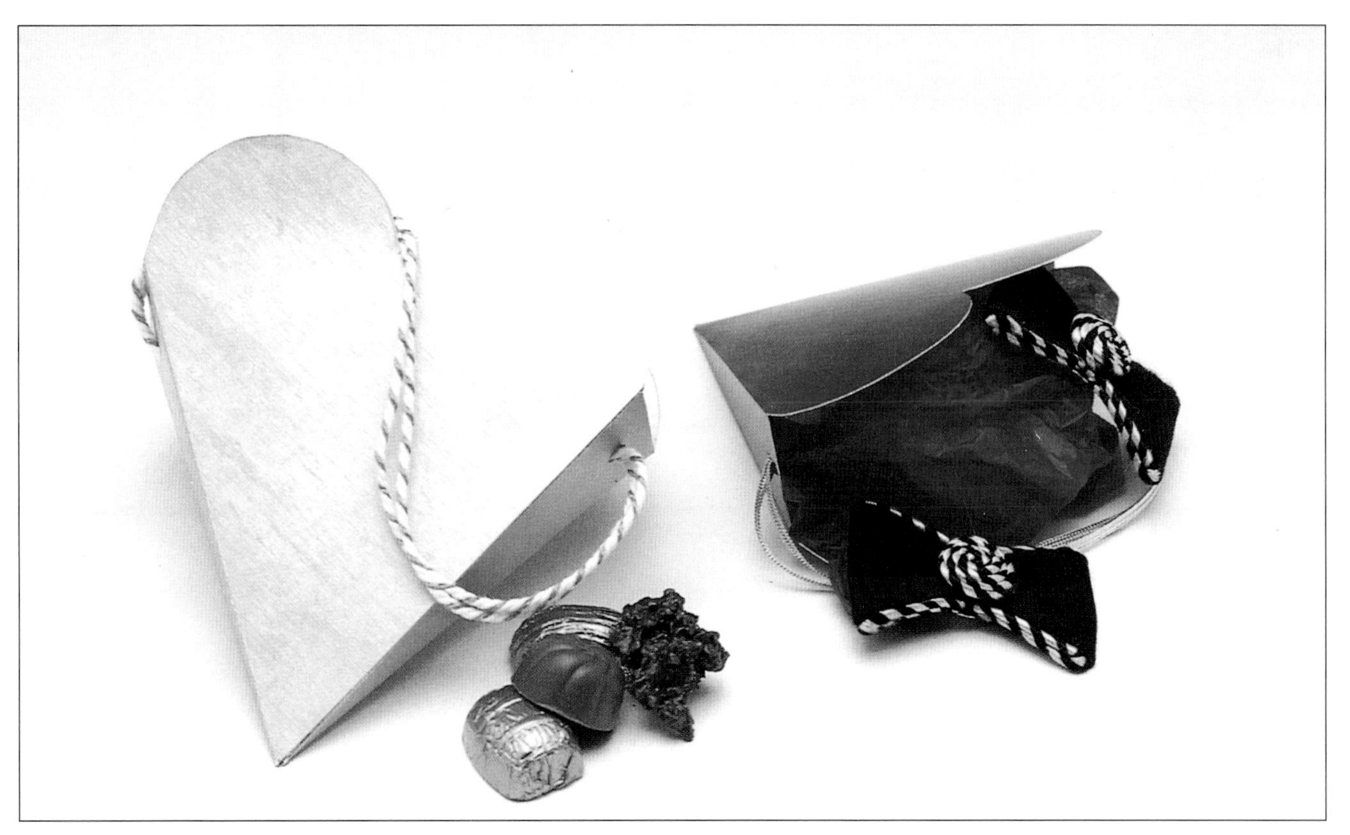

A SIMPLE SHADOW PUPPET

★★★

Shadow puppets are normally flat, cutout figures held by a rod or wire and illuminated against a translucent screen, hence their name. Traditionally made of parchment or hide, now they are usually made from cardboard.

For a simple silhouette, black cardboard is ideal, but not essential. Any fairly strong board, such as that from a cereal box, will make a good puppet. Think about the size of your puppets in relation to the size of the screen, leaving space for all planned actions.

MATERIALS

Black cardboard

Scissors

Craft glue

Glue brush

12-inch length of ⅜-inch diameter softwood dowel

Thumbtack

1 Transfer the design from paper onto cardboard. For a screen that is 28 inches high, make puppets up to 12 inches high.

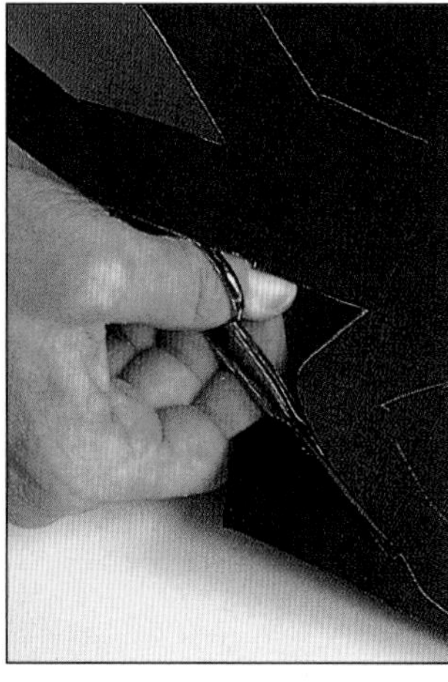

2 Cut out the shape with sharp scissors for a clean outline. If you wish, you can stiffen the cardboard by coating it with white glue.

3 Hold the puppet gently between your thumb and index finger, adjusting the position to find the point of balance. Attach the dowel control rod slightly above this point, so that there is just a little more weight below the control rod than above. This is to make sure that the puppet remains naturally upright, rather than tending to somersault as you operate it.

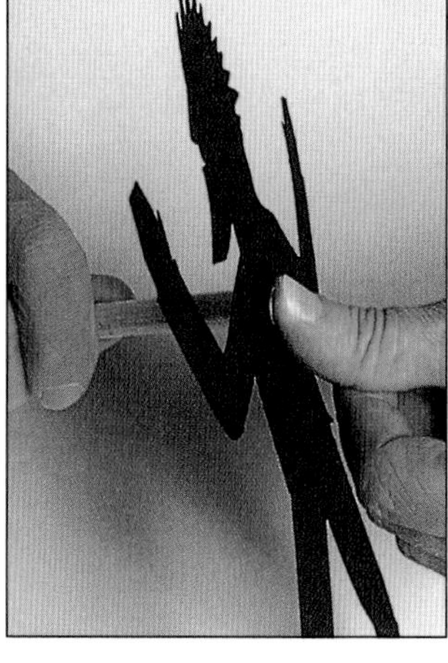

4 Secure the rod to the puppet with the thumbtack, just above the point of balance. You will need to tap the thumbtack in securely to make sure that the puppet turns with the rod and does not swing uncontrolled. With this type of control rod, the puppet cannot turn around, but it is very easy to make a duplicate facing in the opposite direction.

Tips for Strengthening a Puppet

If part of a puppet needs strengthening, glue a piece of clear acetate over the weak part. Then cut the acetate to follow the outline of the part. Alternatively, it is possible to feed the puppet parts through a laminating machine.

DECORATION

You can add to the design of your shadow puppets by cutting out decorative or key shapes within the outline using a sharp craft knife or small, pointed scissors or by punching holes. You will find it helpful to study Javanese *wayang kulit* shadow puppets and Chinese figures, as they use cutout decoration to superb effect. Remember that these figures are made of leather that can hold its shape even when much of it has been removed, but do not cut away too much of your cardboard figures or they will be too weak to withstand a performance!

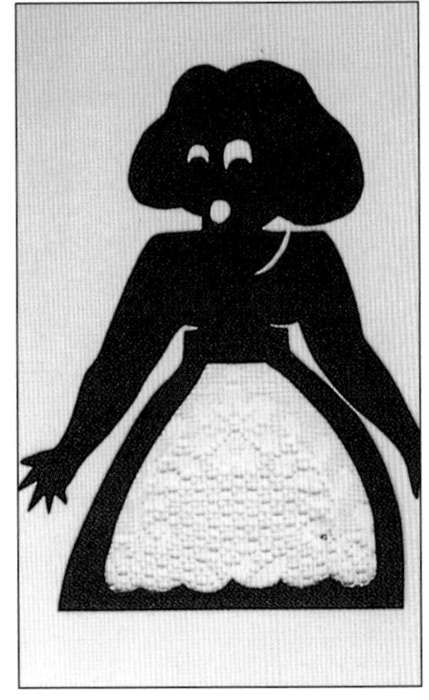

As an alternative to cutting out intricate decorations, you can cut away larger areas and cover the exposed sections with suitably textured materials that allow light to show through the design – for example, nets, lace, or paper doilies.

LEFT *Here lace has been used to add detail to the skirt.*

ABOVE *Colored translucent acetate adds to the effect of this puppet.*

A JOINTED SHADOW PUPPET

★★★★

Jointed shadow puppets are very effective, but do keep them simple. By all means articulate parts that can achieve their effect by swinging freely to where you can effect some degree of influence over their movement through the operation of the main control rod. However, it is a mistake to make a jointed puppet that needs a lot of control wires.

MATERIALS

Heavy smooth cardboard

Scissors

Paper hole punch

Thread or brad fasteners

12-inch length of ⅜-inch diameter softwood dowel

Thumbtack

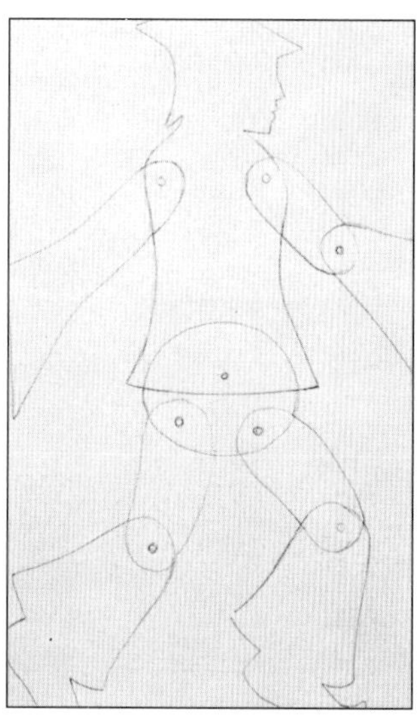

1 Draw the silhouette figure on paper. Draw clearly the overlapping parts where you want to make a joint.

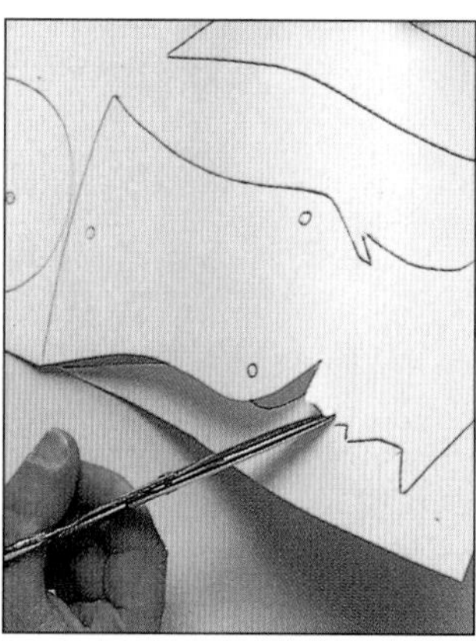

2 Copy the design to another sheet of paper with all the parts drawn in full without overlapping so that you can cut out a pattern for each part.

3 Draw around your templates onto the cardboard. Cut out the separate parts.

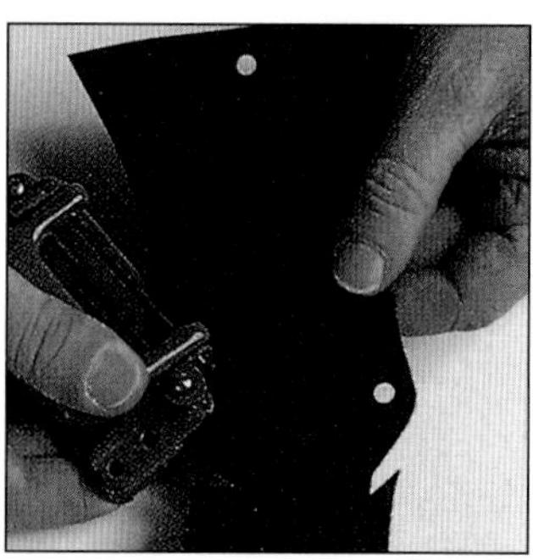

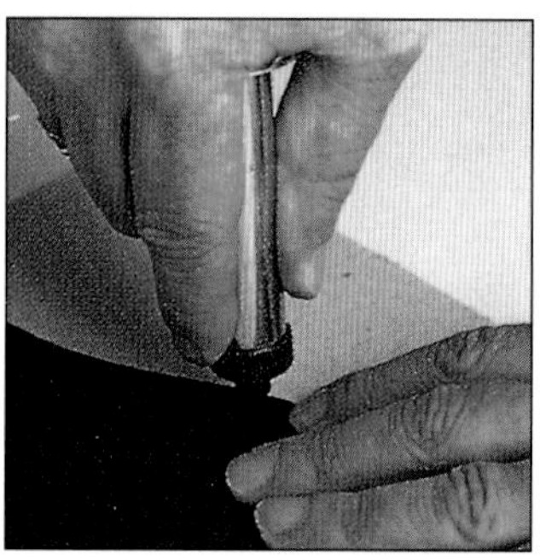

4 Use the paper punch to make clean holes at the center point of the overlapping parts. A simple stationery punch is suitable for use near the edge of the cardboard, but further in you might need a single hole punch, as illustrated.

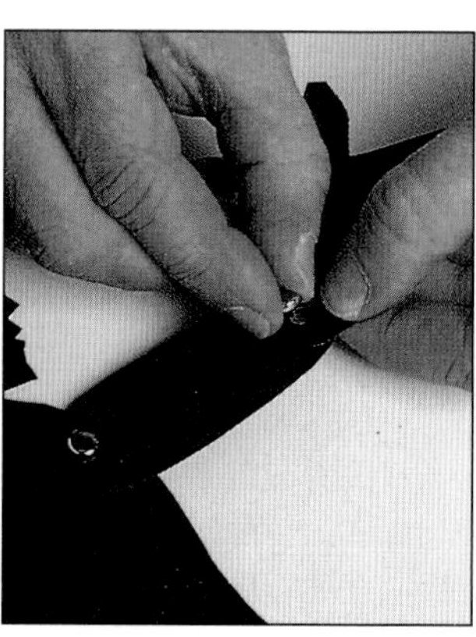

5 Lay the overlapping parts on top of each other. Do not join them in a fashion that will permit them to catch in position. For the joint, use either knotted thread or rivet-type brads. If the puppet is normally to be used facing in one direction, make the joints with the head of the fastener on the screen-side of the puppet. Press the ends as flat as possible against the cardboard without restricting movement.

6 If the fasteners have long, split ends, bend the points back in toward the center as shown in order to reduce the possibility of their snagging.

7 Secure the dowel control rod with the thumbtack (see page 212). Attach it to the body if there is no neck joint, or to the head if the neck is jointed.

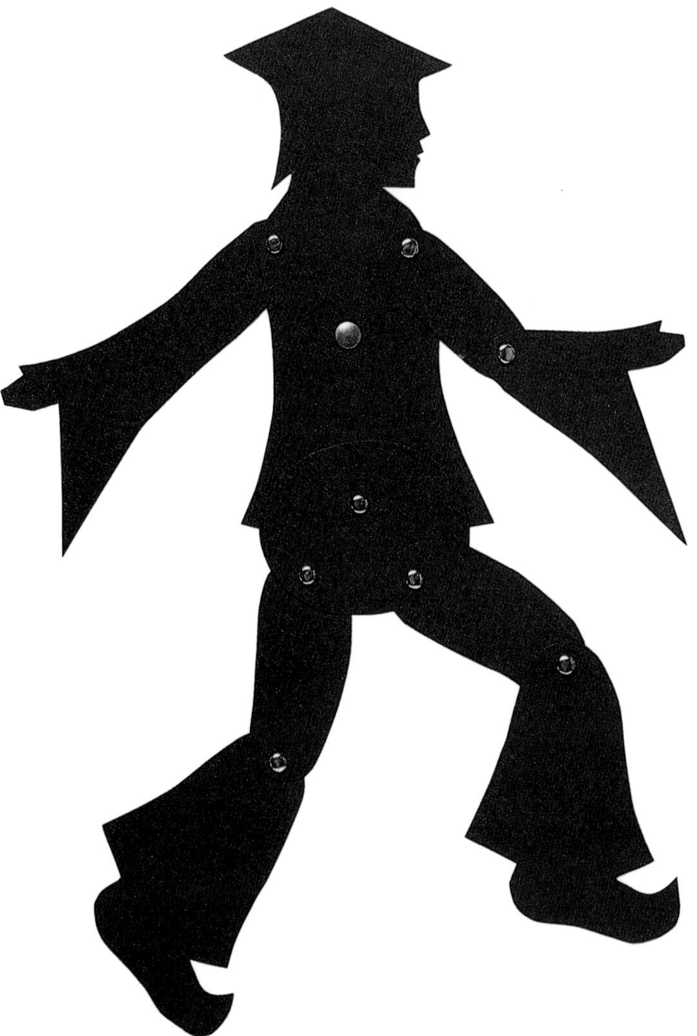

Knotted Thread Joint

Dacron braided nylon fishing line makes an excellent alternative to brad fasteners. It is best if pulled over beeswax before use as this prevents it from fraying. Using a large-eyed needle, push the thread through the center point of the overlapping parts and knot it on each side of the joint, make sure that the knots are close enough to the surface of the cardboard for the joint to be reasonably tight, but not too tight – it should move freely and smoothly. Seal the knots with clear contact glue.

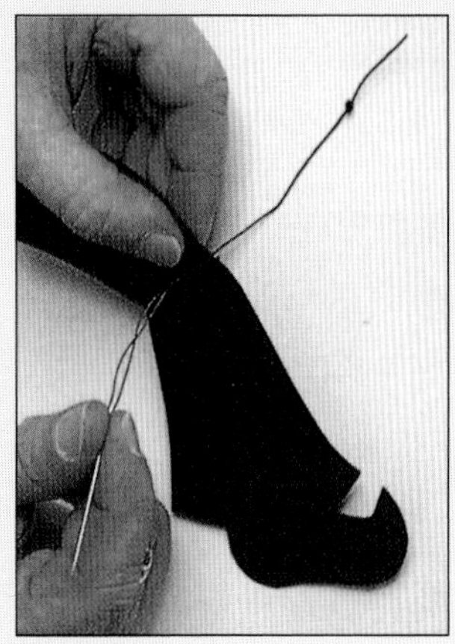

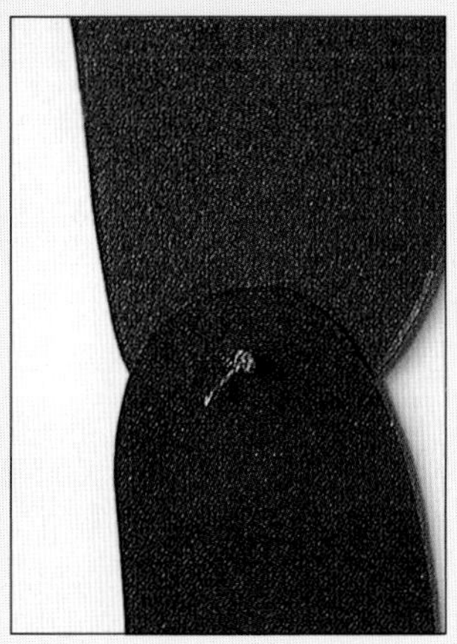

A WIRE CONTROL ROD

Instead of using a dowel control rod on shadow puppets, you can use a control wire, which gives good control and can be raised or lowered as necessary to permit operation from behind or below, making rear projection lighting techniques possible.

For this method use a piece of glavanized wire (coathanger wire) and a length of dowel for a handle. The control rod is usually attached to the body, but if the puppet has a neck joint, the control must be attached to the head; generally having head *and* body controls makes the puppet too difficult to handle.

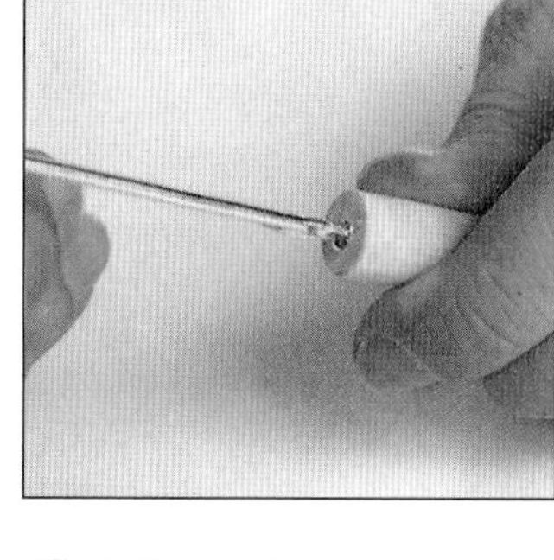

1 Drill a small hole into a piece of dowel approximately 3 inches long. Glue one end of the wire securely into the hole.

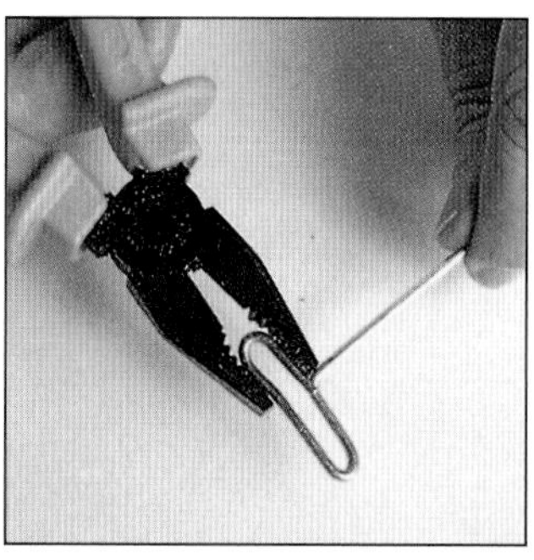

2 Bend the other end of the wire into an elongated loop.

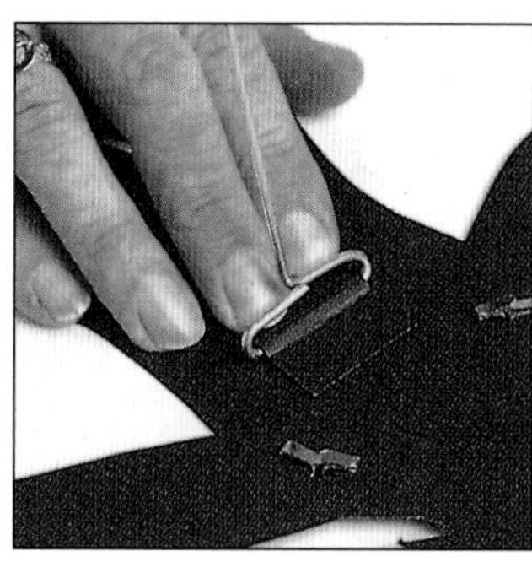

3 Secure the loop to the puppet with a piece of cardboard, stepped as shown, gluing it to the puppet.

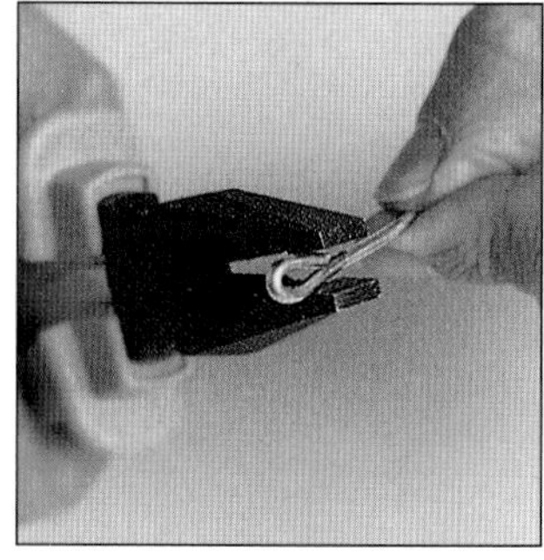

4 If additional controls are needed, for example for a hand, use a piece of galvanized wire, make a small loop in the end and seal the closure with glue.

5 Knot one end of a piece of thread, use a needle to take the other end through the cardboard, from the side facing the screen, and attach this end to the loop of wire.

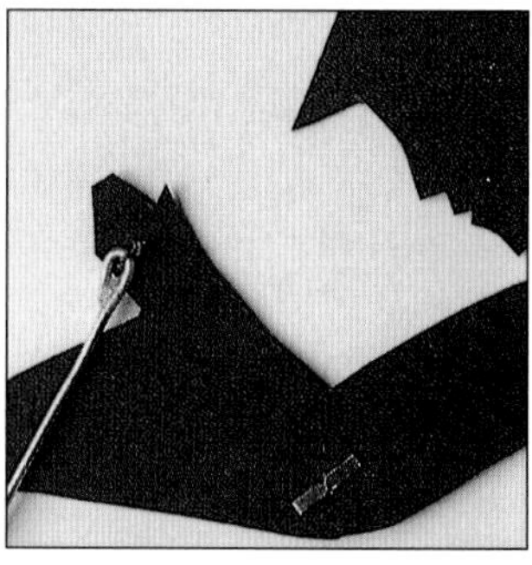

6 With large puppets, you can use the traditional technique of actually picking up the hand and holding it against the screen.

TIP

If you need to restrict movement of the joints – for example, to prevent double-jointed movement – link the moving parts with thread, which limits the degree of movement possible.

COLOR

Color can be introduced to the shadow puppets and scenery by covering cutout designs with pieces of colored acetate, cellophane (such as candy wrappers), or tissue paper. Simply glue them to the surrounding area of the back of the puppet. This can produce wonderful results in enhancing the appearance of clothing.

Particularly effective is a combination of translucent color and textured materials, such as lace or gauze.

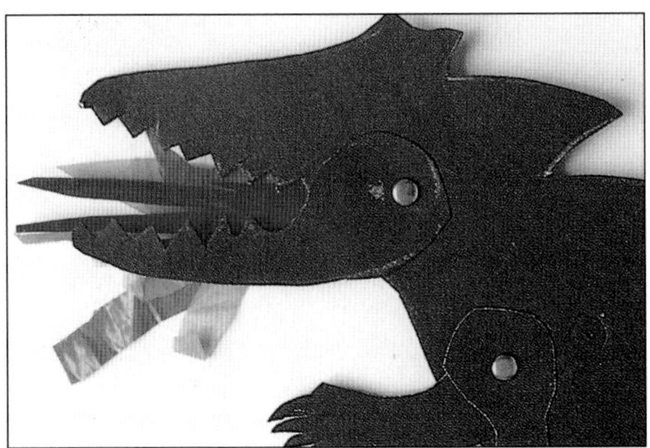

SCENERY

Keep scenery simple: unless it is translucent, every piece of scenery cuts down on the acting area for the puppets. Make black scenery with shapes cut from cardboard.

Moving parts of sets such as doors can be secured with a hinge of fabric glued in place. Tape a piece of wire to the moving part for easy operation. If the puppet needs to walk on the scenery, glue small strips of wood onto the back of the set for the puppet to walk on.

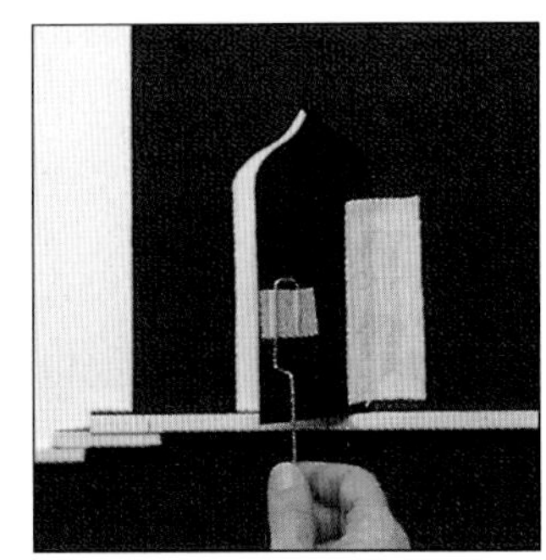

A TRANSLUCENT PUPPET

★★★★

MATERIALS

Plain white cardboard

Felt pens or radiant concentrated watercolous

Paper towels

Cooking oil or clear liquid paraffin

Scissors

It is possible to use modern materials in ways akin to the traditional oriental methods applied to leather, treating it to make it translucent and coloring it with dyes. For some time, puppeteers have imitated the traditional puppets using lampshade parchment tinted with inks to very good effect, but more recently another technique has become very popular for producing full-color translucent puppets. Plain white cardboard is first colored, then treated with oil to make it translucent.

To achieve this effect yourself, use good-quality cardboard – Ivory Board is recommended and the best weight is 335g/m². If your cardboard is too thin, the puppet will be too floppy; if it is too thick, it will not be translucent enough.

1 First, draw the design on paper, then draw it lightly on the white cardboard (remember that, if it is to be jointed, you must draw all the parts separately, allowing for the overlaps). Do not cut out the parts at this stage.

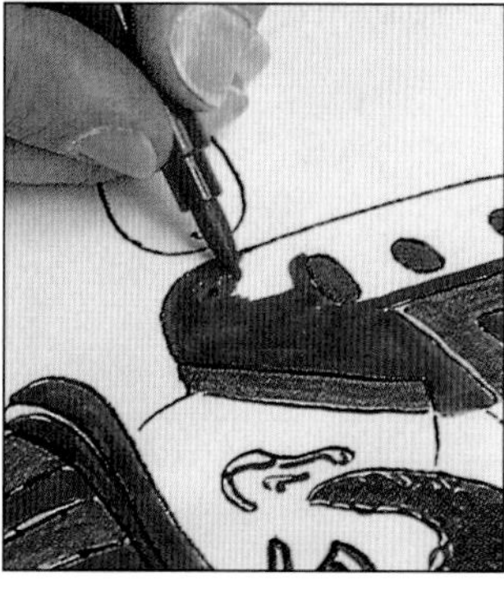

2 Color the puppet with the felt pens or radiant concentrated watercolors as described on page 219.

3 Make sure that your work surface has protective covering if needed. To make the cardboard translucent, rub it with paper towels soaked in either cooking oil or preferably, because it is cleaner, clear liquid paraffin (available from drugstores). First, treat the colored side, rubbing the oil right in. The board will tend to curl up very slightly at the edges on the side you oil first; if you oil the colored side first, as suggested, it means that the edges of the puppet will remain flat against the screen when held by the control rod.

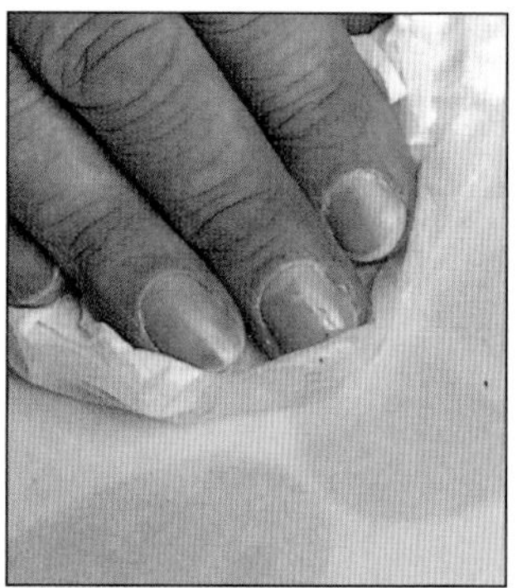

4 Turn the cardboard over and rub oil into the other side. In a very short time, the color will appear on this side, too. When all the color shows through and the card is fully translucent, wipe away any excess oil using a clean paper towel. It is easy to see if any parts have been missed, but if you are in any doubt, hold the board up to the light and you will see darker, rather gray patches if you have missed an area.

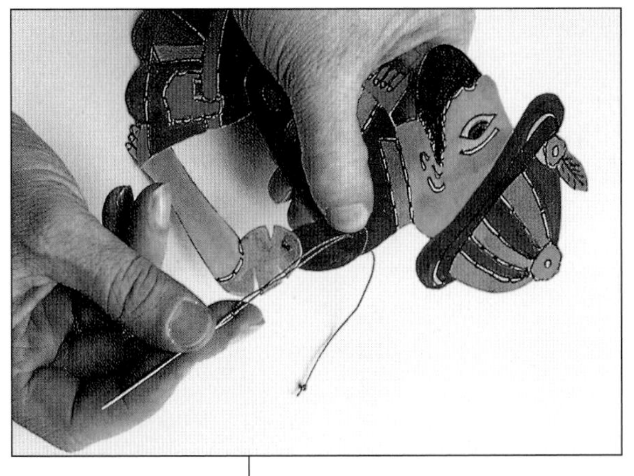

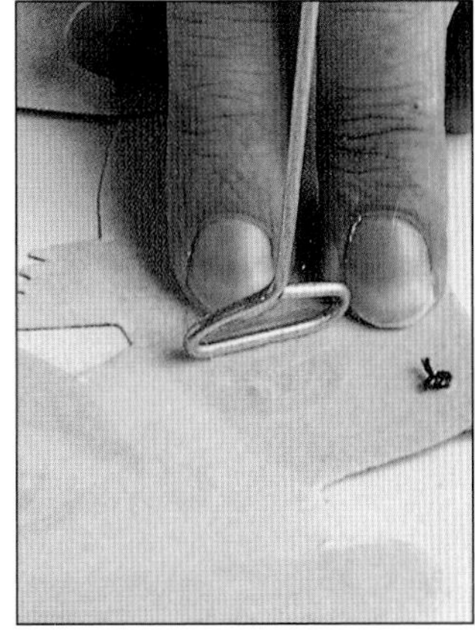

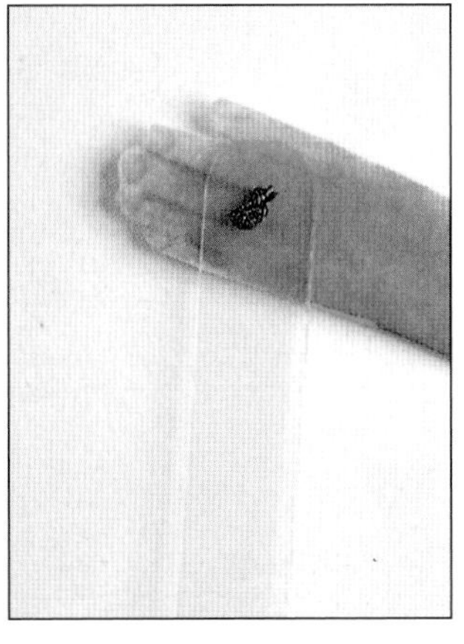

5 Cut out the puppet and join any moving parts. This is done now rather than earlier to avoid causing any damage while you are oiling the puppet.

6 Add the control rod and any additional controls if they are needed. It has to be accepted that normally the attachment of the controls will show – you can even build this into your design. If, however, you wish to make them less visible, you can attach a main control wire either with thread, or with a piece of clear acetate. Use clear contact glue; you may have to experiment to find a suitable glue as not all glues will adhere to the oiled surface.

7 A strip of clear acetate, attached by means of a knotted thread joint, may be used in place of additional control wires.

USING FELT PENS

Use either water- or spirit-based pens. Spirit-based colors tend to merge where the colors meet, giving at first a very subtle effect, though in time it is possible for the colors to *continue* merging and for the detail to be lost. Water-based colors, on the other hand, remain clear and crisp, but the price you pay is that the effect is more stark. Whichever type of pen you use, completely fill in blocks of color – light shading with separate lines of color is not effective.

USING RADIANT CONCENTRATED WATERCOLORS

Paint on the cardboard with radiant watercolours (or diluted, transparent dyes). Dr. Martin's Radiant Concentrated Water Colours or a comparable alternative are recommended. These colors do not mix to produce exactly the colors that are produced by mixing paints, and diluting them with water produces very different effects again.

MASKED BALL

★ ★

MATERIALS

Metallic foil cardboard 10 x 4 inches

Sequins

Crumpled tissue paper

Craft glue

Pencil

Craft knife and scissors

1 Draw around the template (page 222) onto the cardboard and cut out the mask. Cut out the eye holes. Put a thin layer of glue around one of the eye holes and cover with sequins.

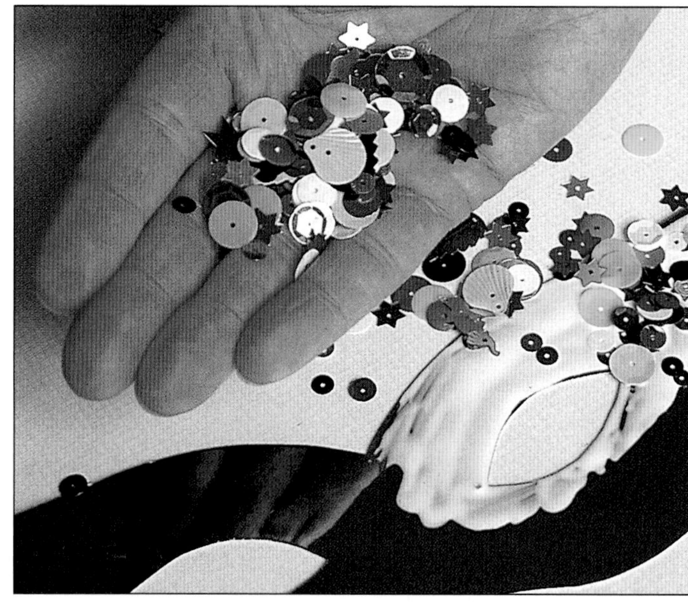

2 Put a little more glue on top of this and some more sequins. When all this is dry, put a thin layer of glue on any loose sequins. The glue is colorless when it dries.

3 Either repeat step 2 above on the other eye hole, or dip the bottom of crumpled pieces of tissue paper in glue and stick them around the eye hole.

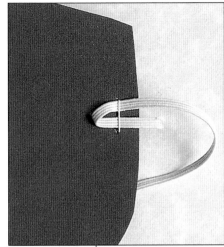

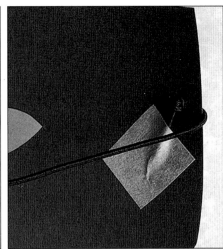

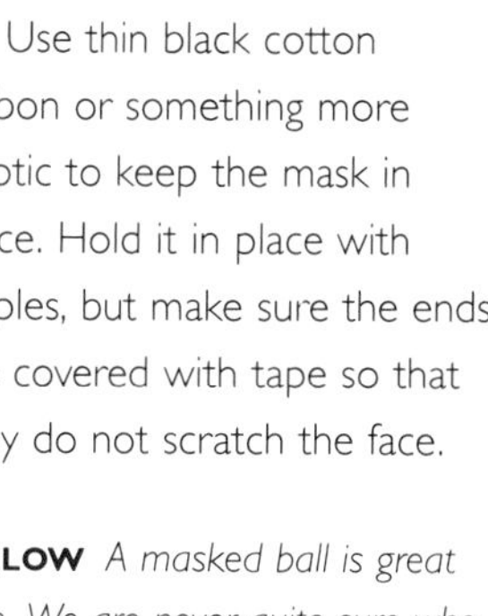

4 Use thin black cotton ribbon or something more exotic to keep the mask in place. Hold it in place with staples, but make sure the ends are covered with tape so that they do not scratch the face.

BELOW *A masked ball is great fun. We are never quite sure who is underneath the mask. You can cover this mask in sequins or crumpled paper, or a mixture of both decorations.*

TIP

There are many decorative variations of this mask; you could use small colored buttons or beads instead of sequins. Curl colored pipecleaners around a pencil and attach them to the top of the mask to make antennae.

Masked Ball

EYES AND EARS MASK

★★

MATERIALS

Pencil, scissors, and craft knife

Tracing paper

Light- to medium-weight cardboard in gray and black 11¾ x 8¼ inches

Scraps of pink, pale gray and green paper or cardboard

Glue

Elastic or ribbon

1 Trace the patterns from the single template on page 226. Draw the pattern onto the appropriate cardboard and cut out carefully, trying to make the curves as smooth as you possibly can.

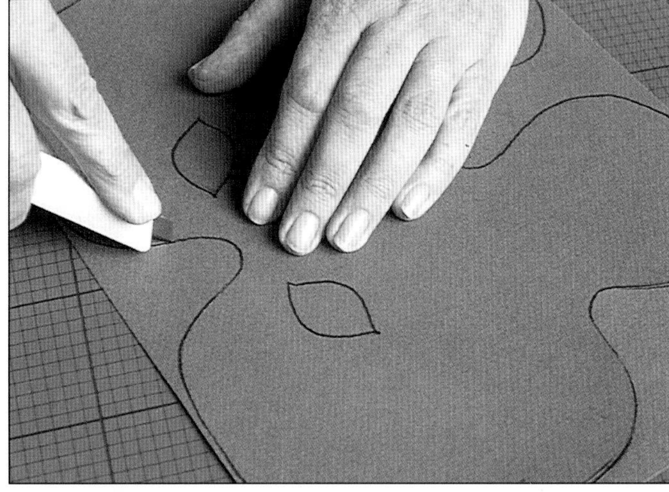

2 Cut out the ear linings from colored paper.

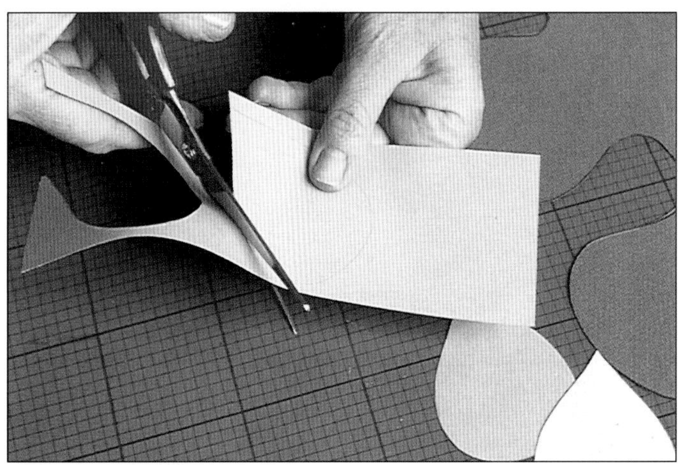

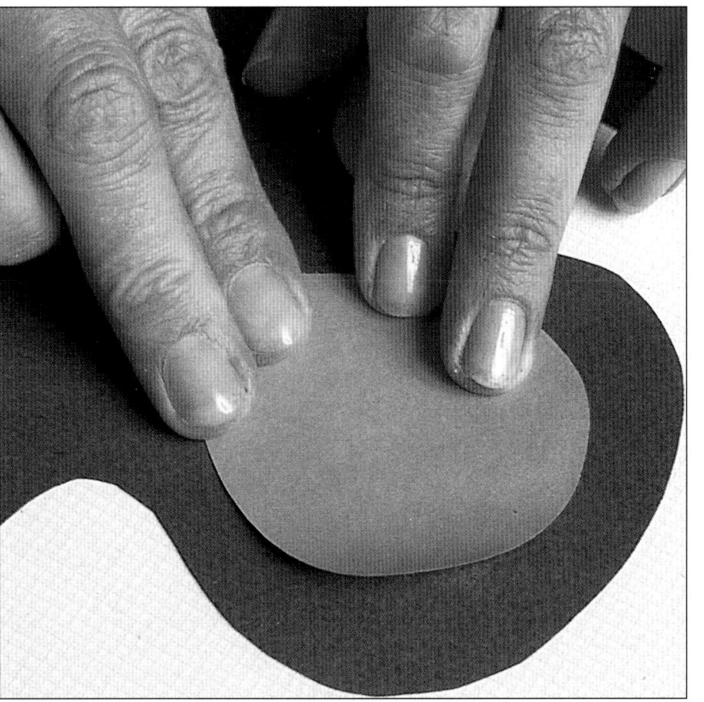

3 Glue the ear linings in place centrally on the ears.

4 Cut out the eye holes using the craft knife on a protected surface.

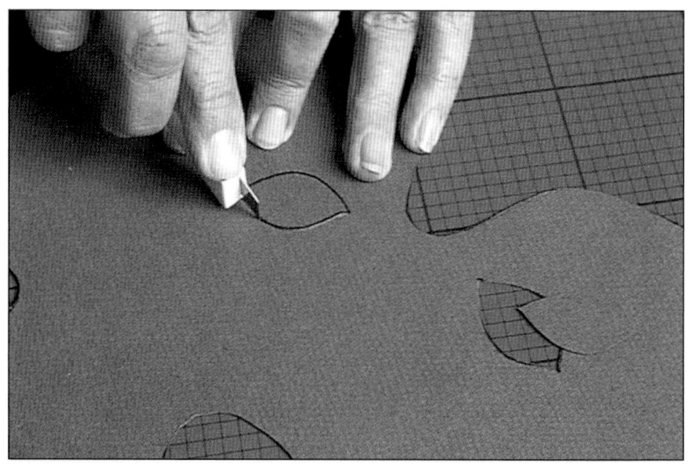

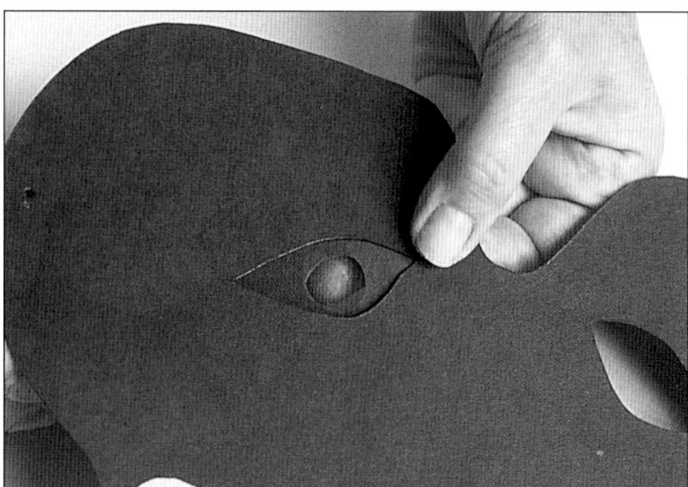

5 For the cat, cut scraps of green paper which will stick behind the eye hole and cut a much smaller hole in the center of each piece. Make holes on the sides of the mask for the elastic and tie to fit.

The masks shown here are both made from the same basic pattern, and you will probably think of other animals which can be created from the same template. Both cat and mouse can be made from a variety of colored boards, or the cardboard could be painted to create a tabby effect. The important thing to remember is that you are trying to represent the essentials of the animal – a mouse has large ears with pink insides; a black cat often has green eyes, and cats generally have pointed ears.

Eyes and Ears

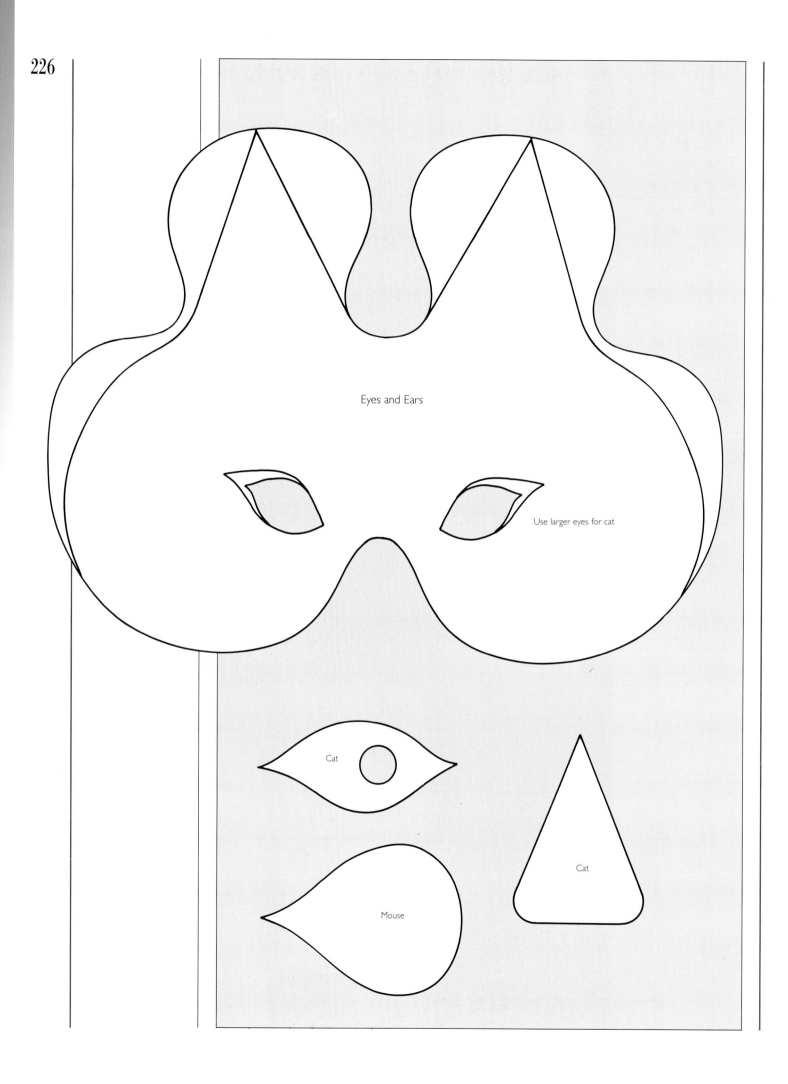

Use larger eyes for cat

Cat

Cat

Mouse

HARLEQUIN MASK

★★

MATERIALS

Pencil and ruler

Scissors and craft knife

Tracing paper

Cardboard for mask, about 20 x 20 inches

Clear glue and tape

Materials for decorating

Elastic for headband

1 Trace the pattern from the template on page 230 and enlarge it using a grid. Draw the pattern on the wrong side of the cardboard and cut out very carefully.
If you are using foil card for the basic shape, it will be necessary to cut the face area from some plain white cardboard first and then stick the foil in position on the main shape. The dotted lines on the template indicate this area. If you are using plain board, you only need to mark this area with a pencil.

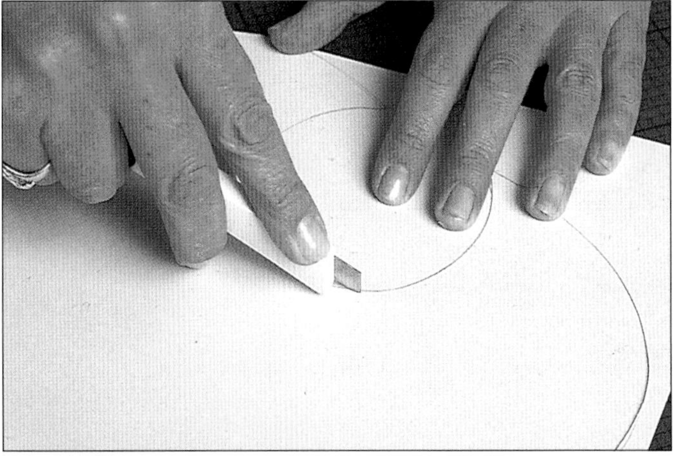

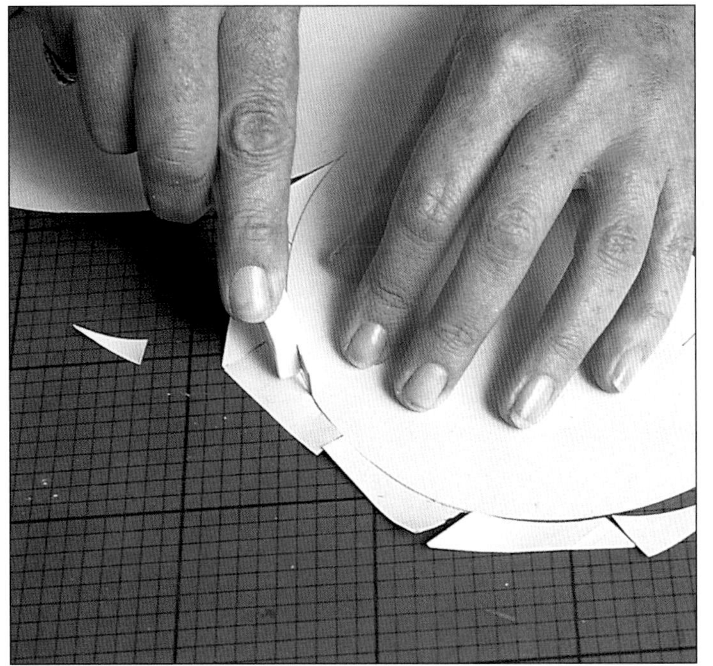

2 A diamond grid with the shapes 1½ inches apart has been used in this example, but this is quite arbitrary and other designs or measurements can be substituted. First mark your chosen design on the right side of the cardboard. Then cut up lots of pieces of decorative materials so that they will fit within the grid and arrange them.

3 When sticking the shapes in place, continue right to the edges. Cut away the excess areas from the wrong side when you have finished.

④ To give a neat appearance, braid or other materials may be stuck over the lines between the shapes.

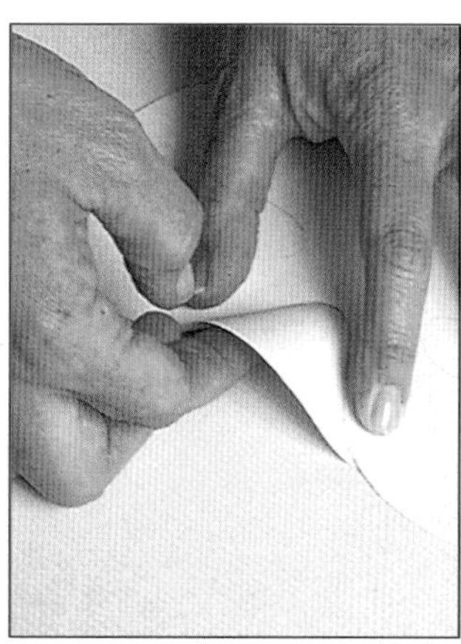

⑤ When the decoration is finished, the nose piece can be attached. First score along the line marked on the pattern and then curve the nose gently and anchor it in place on the rear side of the face piece.

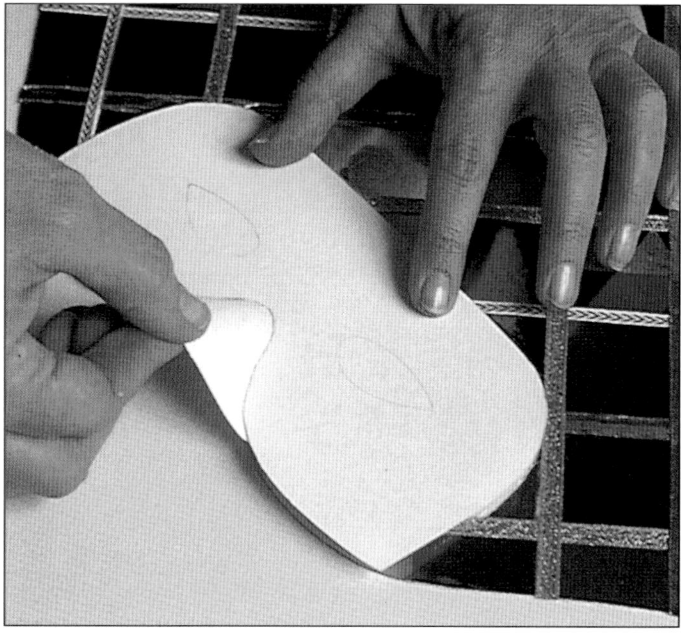

⑥ Glue the face piece in position on the mask.

⑦ Now cut out the eye holes. Finally make the headband by stapling elastic on each side. Cover the staples with layers of tape for the wearer's protection.

BELOW *This style of mask can be made to look very spectacular, offering ample opportunity for lavish use of decorative materials. In this example a variety of paper and cardboard has been used, including foil and fluorescent, patterned, and colored paper. In addition, pieces of leather and fabric have been introduced – a marvelous way of using scraps and leftovers from other projects. Traditionally, the Harlequin is dressed in patchwork, and this is why the costume is made up of different-colored squares.*

Harlequin

DRAGON MASK

★★

This dragon is a flat mask and is very simple to make. It can be as ornate and decorative as you want, depending on the materials you have available. The mask can be made to wear on the face or attached to a stick to wave in front of the face when appropriate.

MATERIALS

Medium-weight white cardboard 12 x 14 inches

Black or dark-colored paper 8 x 12 inches

Colored papers in 2 lengths of contrasting colors 2 x 12 inches

Gold or silver metallic marker

Paints and thin brush

Pulp shapes

Popsicle sticks

Colored translucent paper or tissue paper

Colored crinkle foil paper

Various metallic and colored candy cups

Craft glue

Pencil

Craft knife

Flat stick

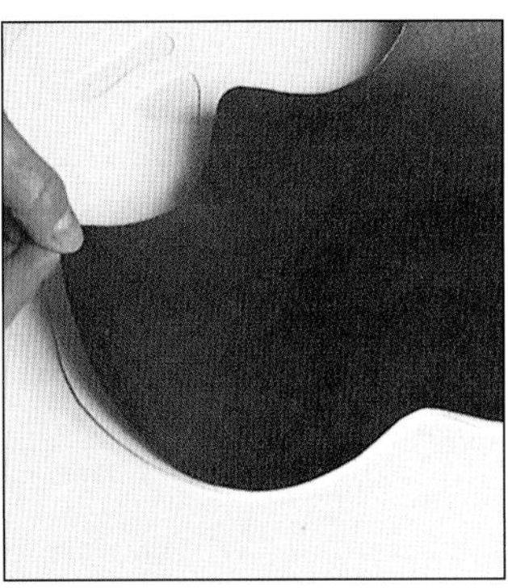

1 Draw around the template on page 234 onto the white cardboard and cut it out. Draw around the headdress onto the black or dark paper and cut it out. Glue this shape to the white cardboard.

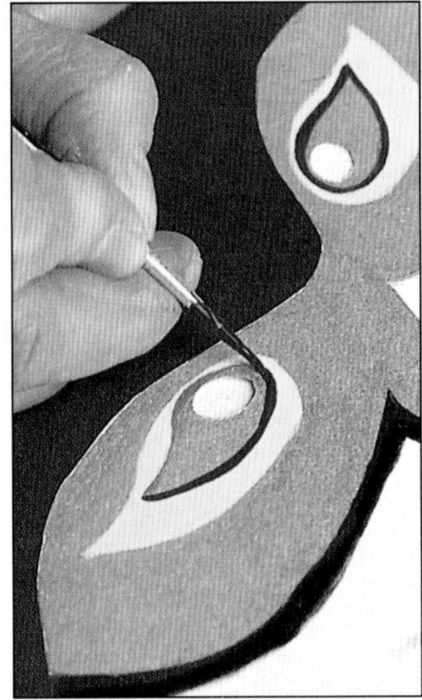

3 Add the final details of the face with red and black paint.

2 Draw the facial features with silver or gold metallic markers. Make the eyes and mouth big and bold.

4 When decorating the headdress, glue lots of brightly colored materials onto the black paper area. Do not be afraid of having lots of different colors and textures, but do aim for some symmetry to avoid ending up with a mess. Cut out three bright shapes from the crinkle foil and glue them onto the headdress.

5 Add painted or natural popsicle sticks, and glue painted pulp shapes, candy cups, or crumpled tissue paper onto them. Glue these to the top of the headdress. Roll up translucent paper or tissue paper and glue these rolls to the sides.

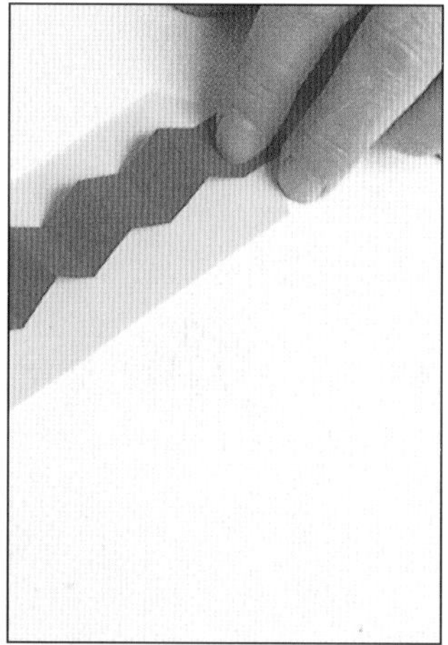

6 Make the tongue by taking a strip of colored paper 2 x 8 inches (or longer if you want). Fold over one end and make a point at the other. Take a piece of paper ¾ x 12 inches in a contrasting color and pleat it, making each pleat about ½ inch wide. Put a little glue on alternate accordion-pleated edges and glue it down the middle of the previous long strip of paper.

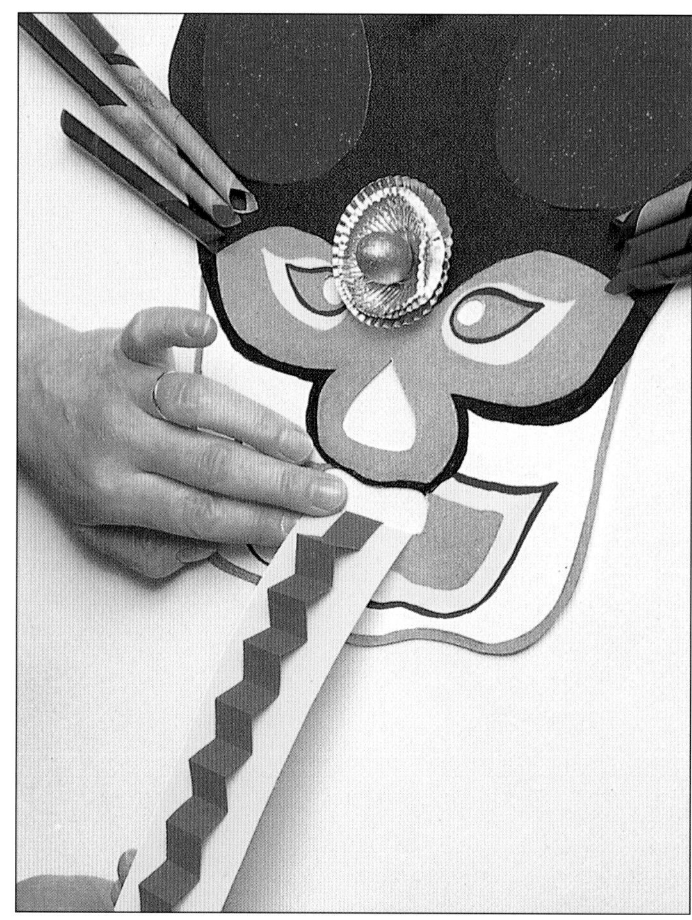

7 Hook the folded end of the tongue into the dragon's mouth and attach with tape, from behind. Glue a metallic candy cup or other decoration to the bottom of the tongue. This forms a basic tongue, but you could always add further decoration to it.

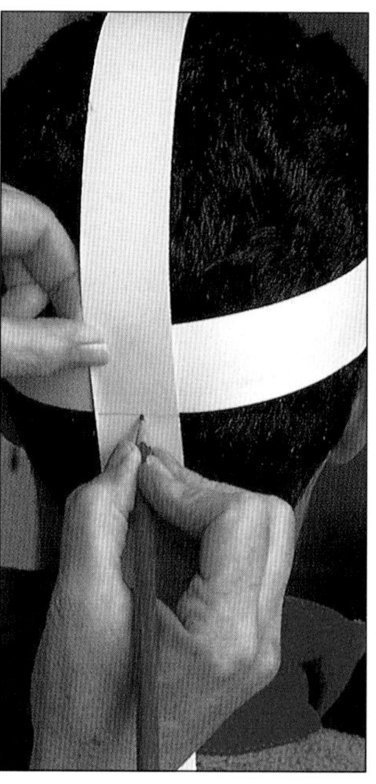

8 Attach the mask to a flat piece of wood positioned centrally on the chin area of the mask. Glue it in place and cover the glued end with clear tape.

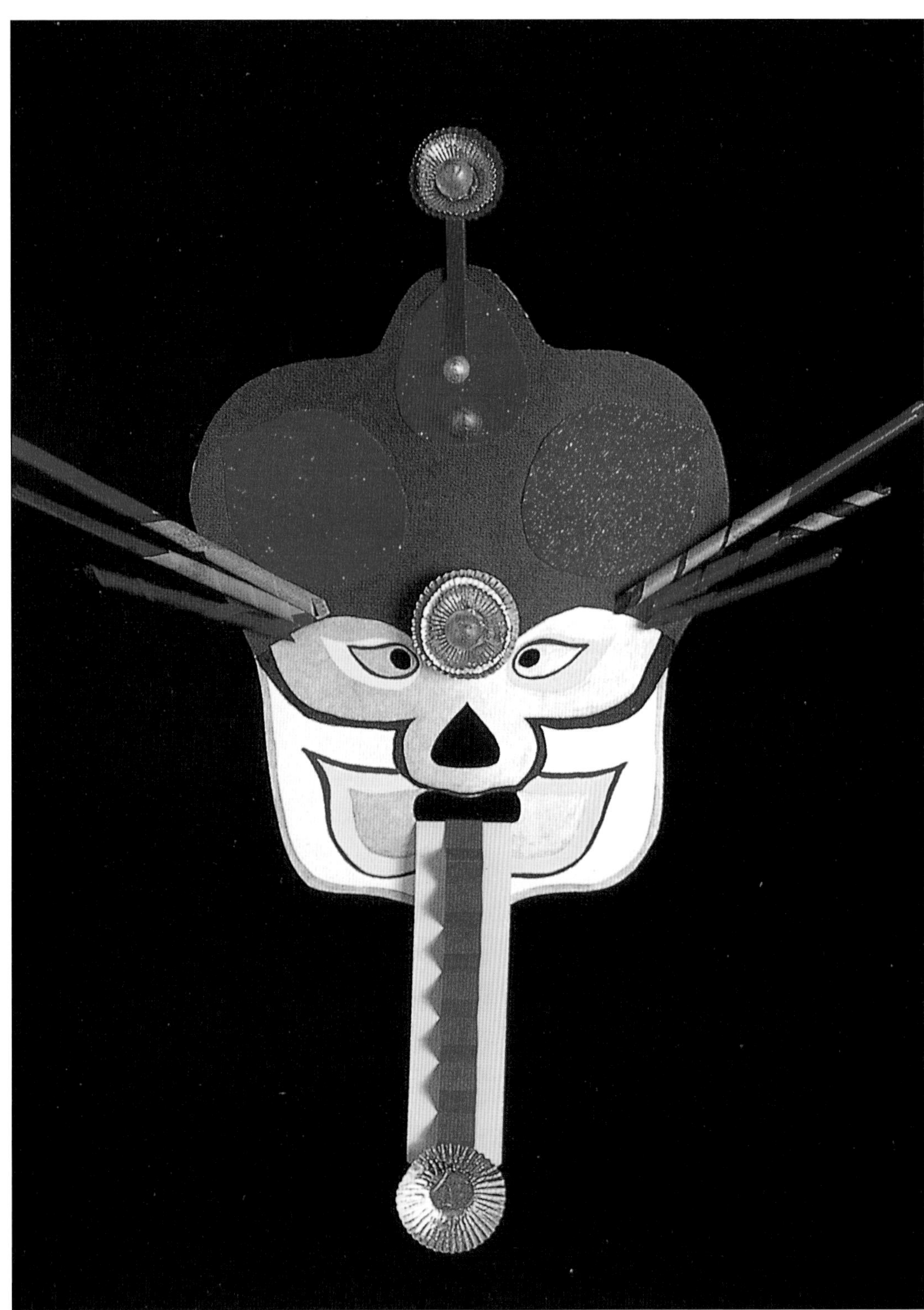

TIP

The wearer's nose could be painted a color – white or deep red – using face paints.

ABOVE *A very important symbol in all parts of Asia, especially China, Hong Kong, Tibet, Sri Lanka, and Indonesia, the dragon is a colorful and crucial element in many celebrations and festivals. Often the dragon is made into a large whole-head mask, sometimes with a large mouth, jointed jaws, huge bulbous eyes, and a large mane of colored hair.*

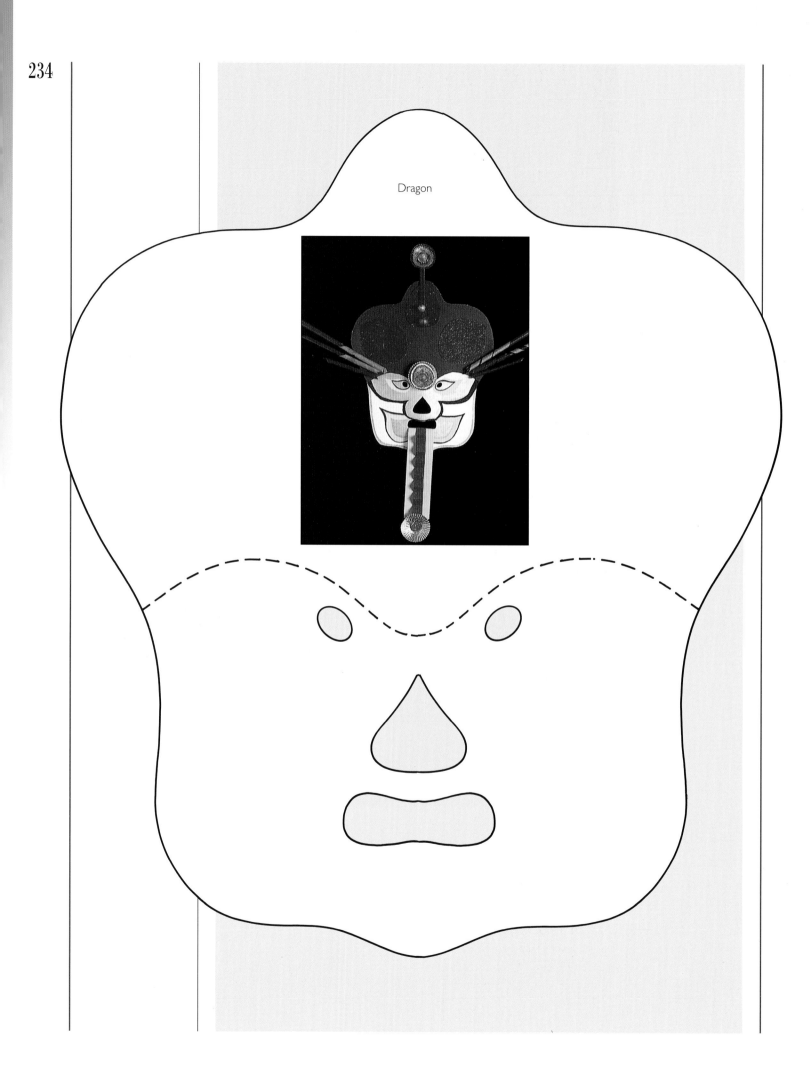

Dragon

LEO THE LION MASK

★★★

MATERIALS

Lightweight beige or light brown cardboard 11 x 28 inches (the grain running down the shorter side)

Another shade of brown cardboard 4 x 12 inches

Lightweight white cardboard 4 x 5 inches

Colored paper in black, beige, and white

Brown and pink paint and brushes

Cellophane tape

Glue

Paper clips

Craft knife and scissors

Pencil and ruler

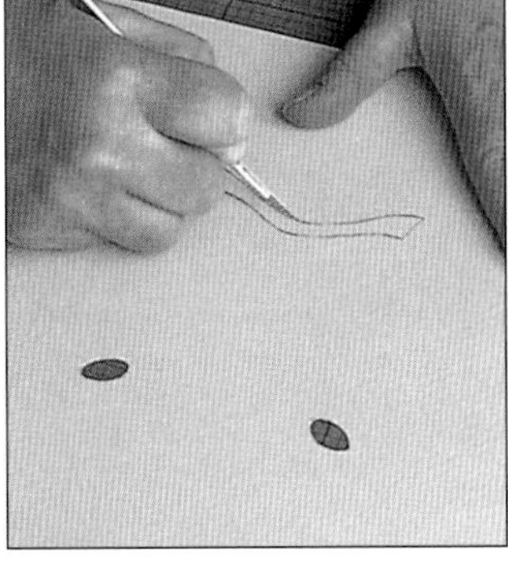

1 Lay out the large sheet of beige cardboard horizontally. Draw a light pencil line down the middle from top to bottom. Having enlarged the main part of the template (pages 238–239), lay it over the cardboard so that the pencil line is halfway between the eyes. Draw around the features. Cut out the eyes and mouth and make the ear slits.

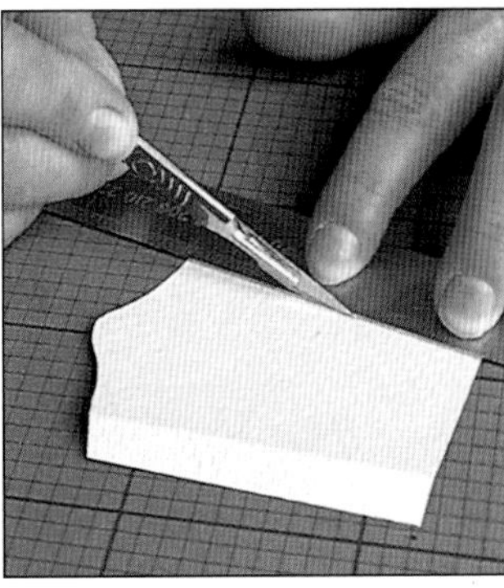

2 Place the chin template on the white cardboard and the ears and nose on the brown cardboard. Draw around them and cut them out. Score the sides of the nose along the line indicated on the template. Carefully bend them back to make flaps. Apply glue to the flaps and stick them in place.

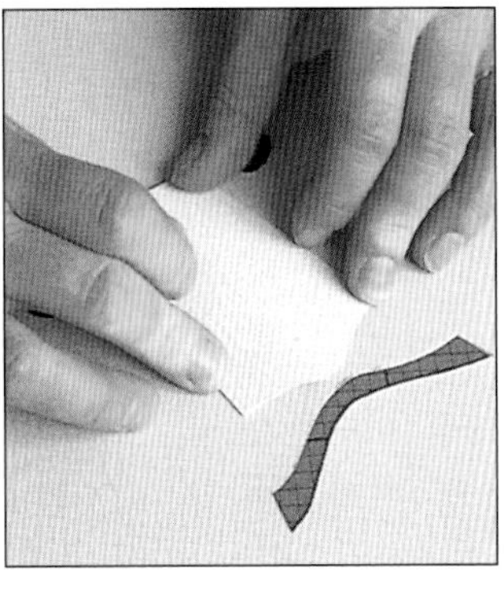

3 Gently push the sides toward each other so that the bridge of the nose is slightly raised.

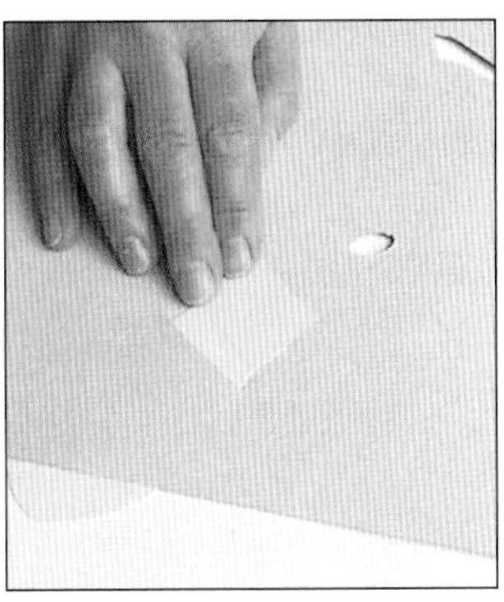

4 Slot the ears into the ear slots and hold them in place with tape on the back of the cardboard.

5 Make the hair with the three colored papers. You will need lots of hair in various lengths and thicknesses – a lion can be quite unkempt! Take a piece of paper, score and fold a line about ½ inch from the left edge to make the anchor strip. Cut strips between ⅛ and ¼ inch wide across the paper from the fold. Curl the thicker strips (see page 201).

6 Make short white straight hair and glue it to the chin. Fold back the anchor strip so that it is hidden beneath the hair. Apply glue to the side away from the hair. Glue the chin to the lion.

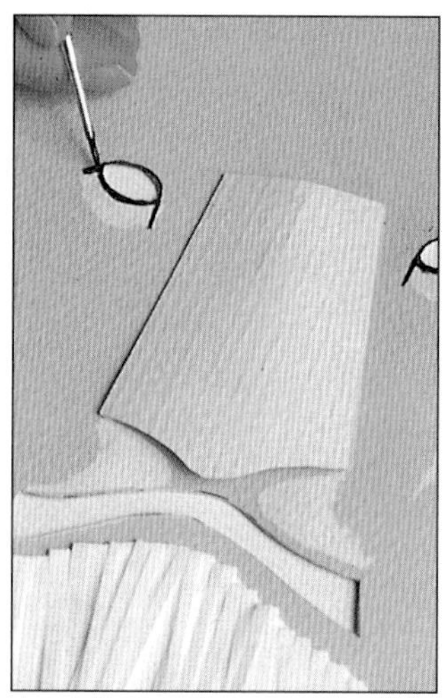

7 Accentuate the facial features with paint. He might need a pink nose and lines around the eyes.

8 Attach the rest of the hair to the lion. Put short pieces along the top of the head and longer pieces down the side of the face. Make the very long pieces go right over the top of the head and down the back. Add some shorter pieces to the back if required.

9 Bend the mask around the head of the wearer and fasten it into shape with paper clips at the top or bottom. Take it off and stand it on the table. You can staple the back of the head in place or, if the mask is to be used by different people, use the paper clips so that the fastening can vary according to the size of the head.

TIP

This method of mask-making can be used to make many other animals. To design your own mask, find a photograph of the animal you choose and make a large drawing of its most important features. Superimpose the tube shape onto this, then trace off the features, and you will have the basis of the new mask.

BELOW *Children love to roar behind this full-head lion mask. Easy to make from flat cardboard, the lion becomes three-dimensional at the very end. It can be adjusted to fit various head sizes.*

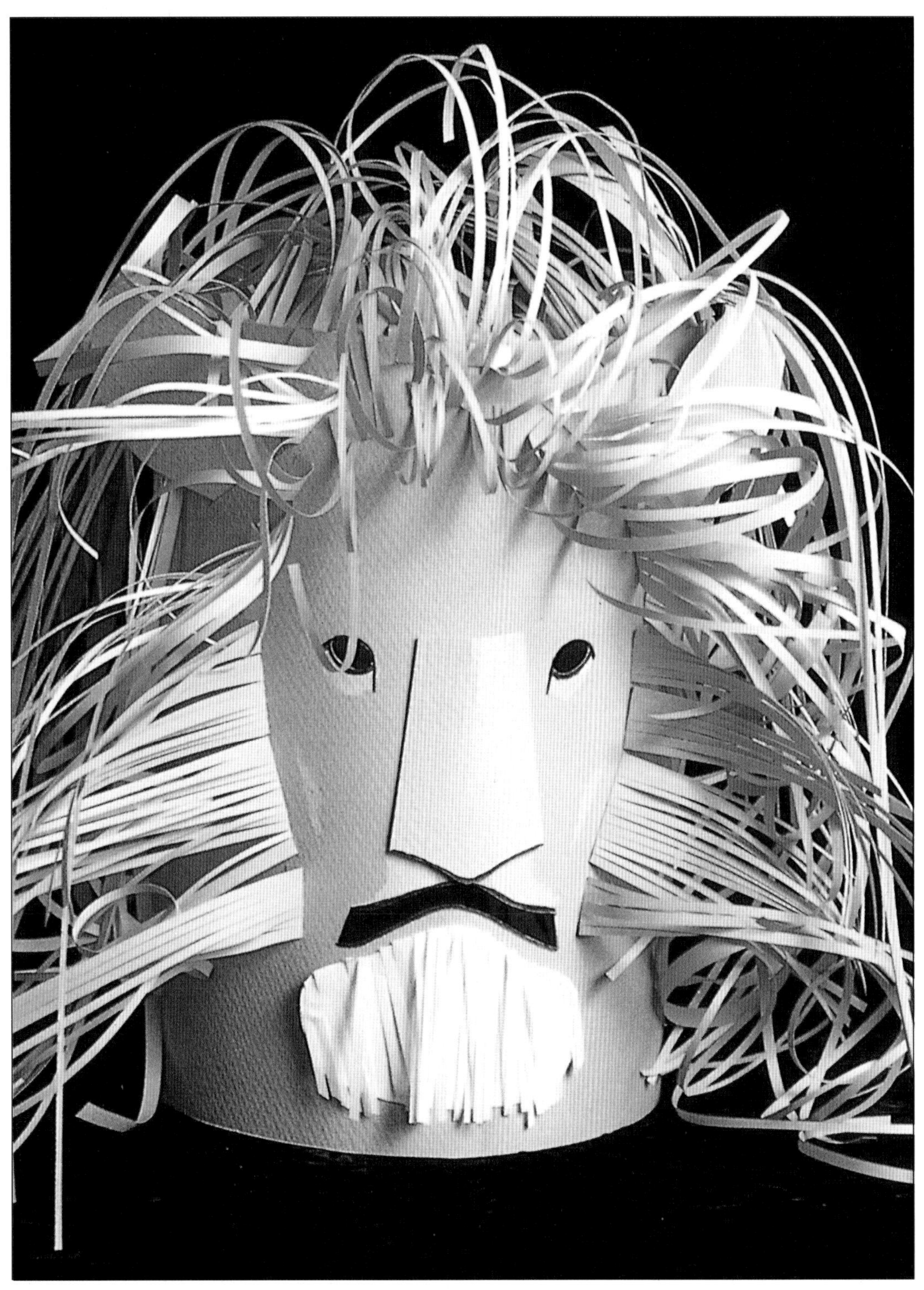

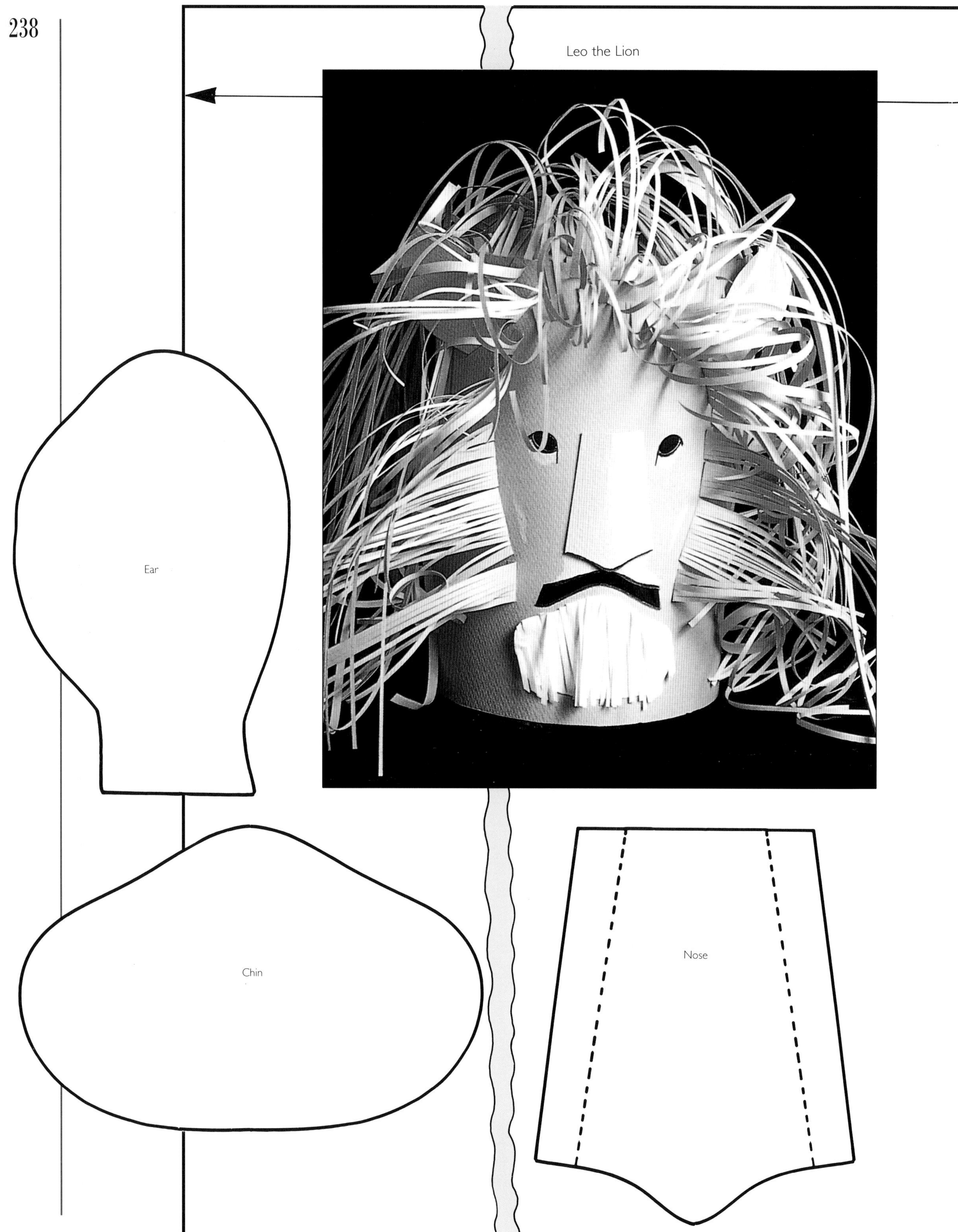
Leo the Lion
Ear
Chin
Nose

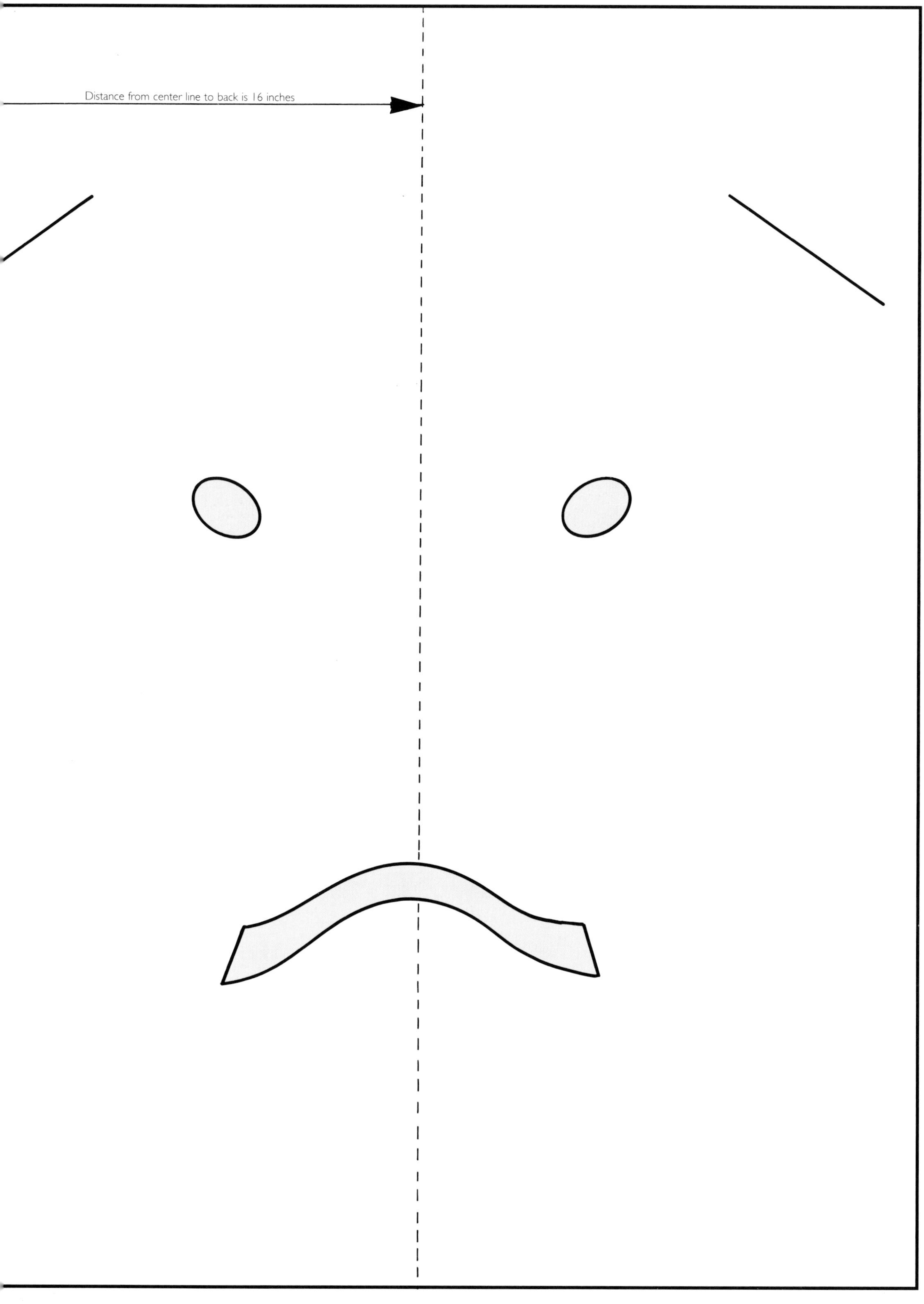

Distance from center line to back is 16 inches

HORSE HEAD MASK

★ ★ ★

MATERIALS

Two sheets brown cardboard, minimum size 16½ x 24 inches

Pencil and ruler

Craft knife and scissors

Cutting mat

Bone folder (if available)

Fur fabric of a suitable color or lightweight papers

Elastic

Cellophane tape

1 Trace the pattern from the template on pages 242–243 and enlarge. Draw the pattern on the wrong side of the brown cardboard and cut out; be very careful in cutting around ears and tabs.

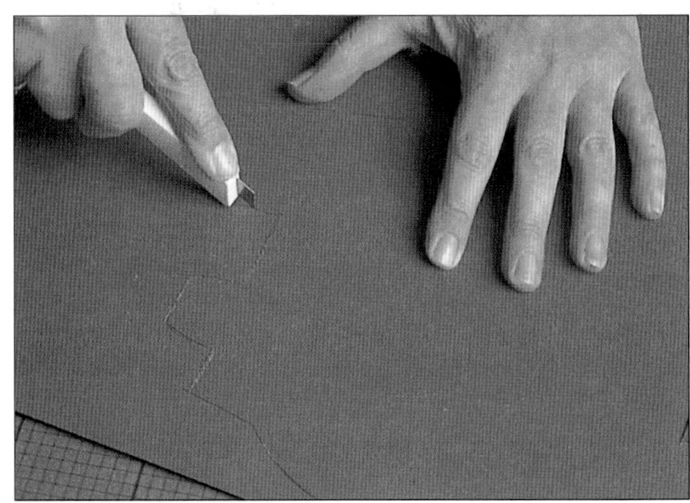

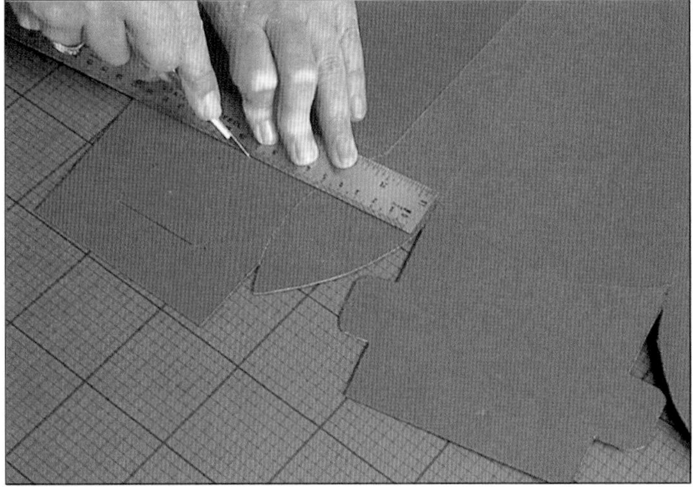

2 Now mark all the lines to be scored and the position of the slots for the tabs. This can be done at each end of the slot by piercing the cardboard with a pin. Score all the lines – if the cardboard is very thick, it will be necessary to cut partly through it. On the head part, gently bend the curve between the ears. Bend the side pieces from the outer edge of the ear to the nose and also the neck edge to the outer ear. The scored line from the inner edge of the ear to the nose should only be gently creased to give additional shaping to the mask. On the neck part of the mask, bend all the scored lines.

3 Check that the position of the slots is correct by aligning the mask parts. Then cut the slots. If the cardboard is thick, it will be necessary to cut out a thin sliver. It is better that the slot should be tight as it can always be enlarged. Now cut out the eyes as indicated on the template – note that a very small area has been cut away. Score the small curved lines and bend the two parts to the inside. Hold the two cut edges together with a piece of tape on the wrong side. Assemble the two parts – head and neck. Slot head sides together and then the head top. On the neck part, work from the top, being careful to align the lower tab before pushing the upper tab into position. Now join the two parts, making sure that the tabs slot in firmly.

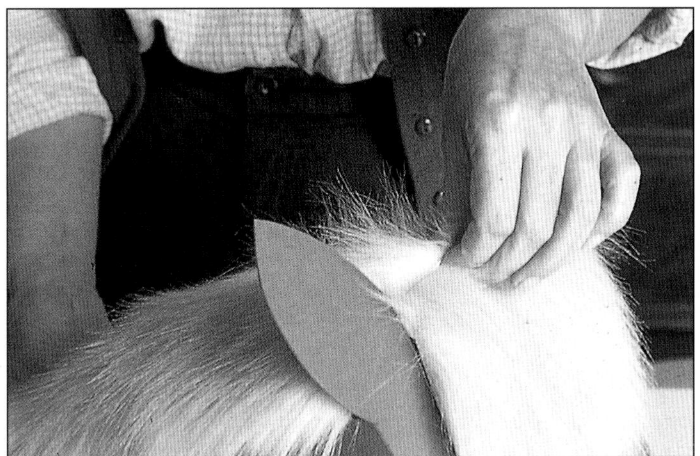

4 Cut a strip of fur fabric for the mane, which will fit from the top of the head to the bottom of the neck. Fold under a very narrow hem and glue it down – it will make the edge of the fur fabric stand up in a most realistic way. Apply glue down the center of the neck from the top of the head and glue on the mane. Hold in place until the glue dries.

Cut another piece of fur fabric to position between the ears and, using the same method, glue it in place. If fur fabric is not available, use various papers, such as colored tissue, crepe, and translucent papers, glued in layers and cut into narrow strips. This is the same method described in greater detail on page 235 for the Lion mask.

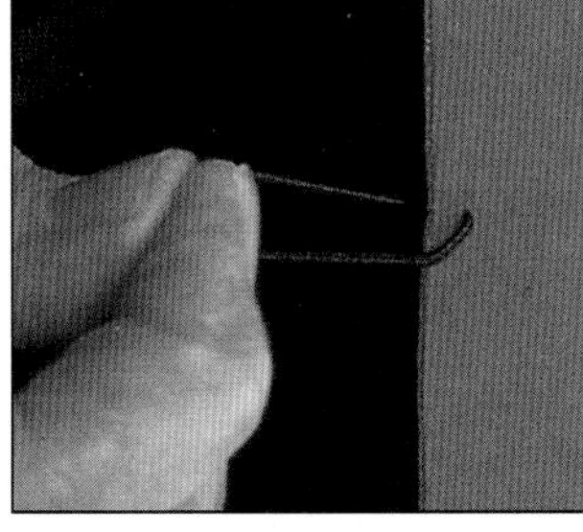

5 Finally, pierce the two holes marked on the lower jaw and thread the elastic through these holes. Tie so that the jaw is held in and looks horse-like rather than cow-like! If it is difficult to see through the horse's eyes, extra eye holes can be pierced.

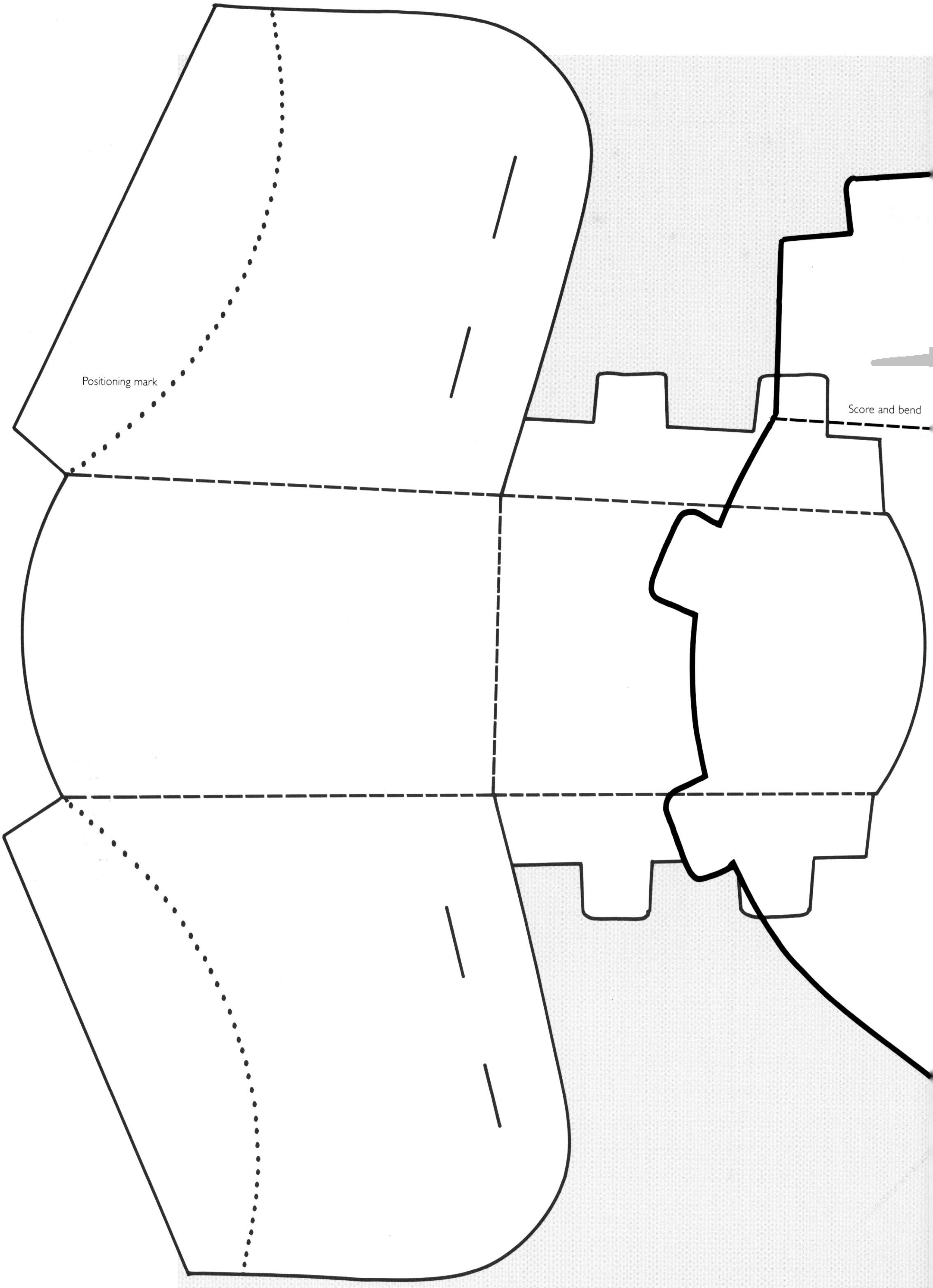

Positioning mark

Score and bend

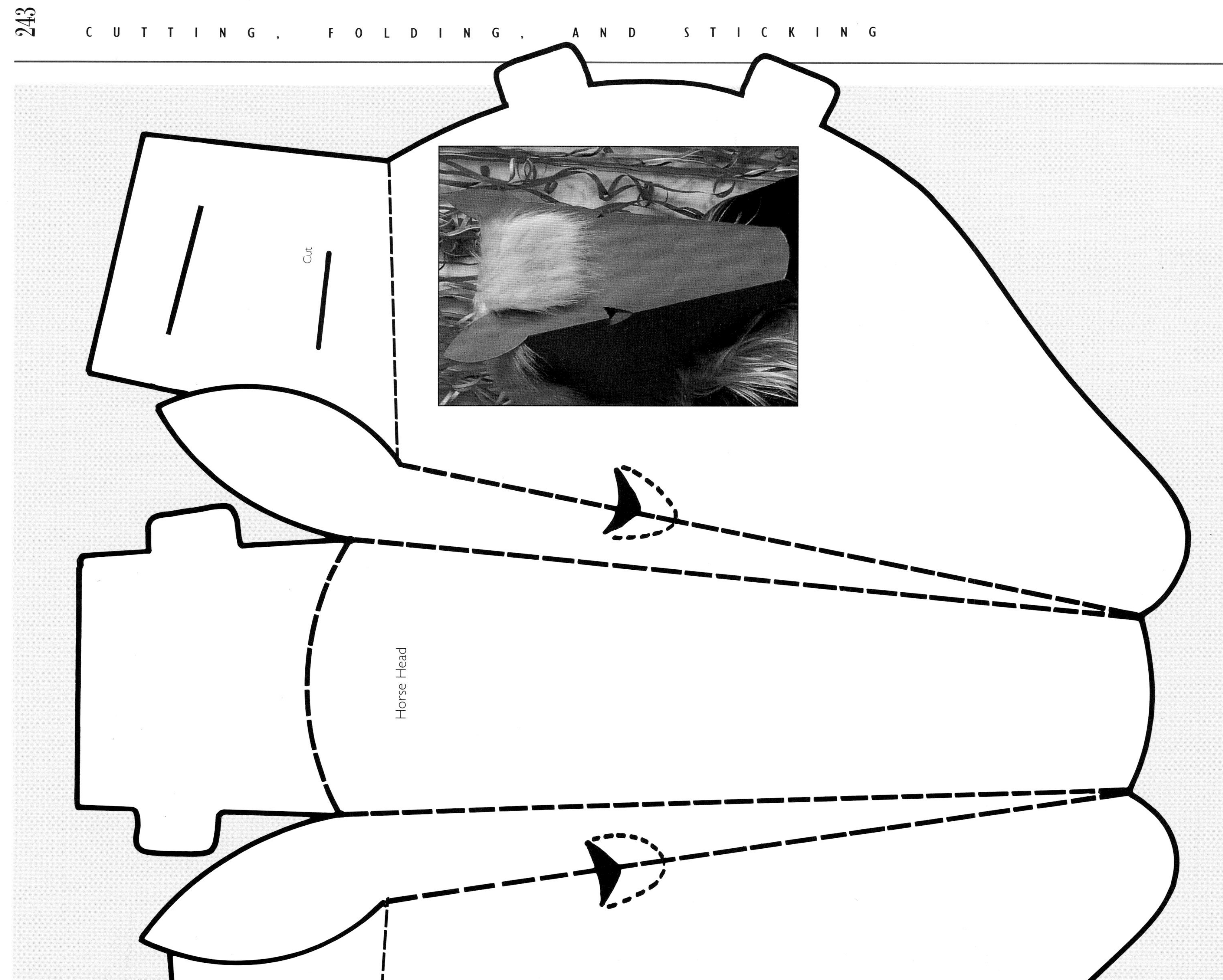
Cut
Horse Head

BELOW *The stylized horse head has been turned into a mask by using very simple paper engineering techniques. As with other designs in the book, when you create this design, the basic characteristics of the horse have been closely observed and incorporated into the pattern. All the lines have been simplified, and other animals can be created in this way – particular attention should be paid to ears, the width of the head, and the nose. The eyes will need great care – in this example, it has not been possible to cut the eye holes in the right place so small holes have been pierced to suit the wearer.*

CAROUSEL

★★

Recreate the cheerful atmosphere of the fairground by using brightly colored poster paints, sequins, beads, and glitter pens to decorate this carousel. The five prancing horses are suspended from a simple cardboard cone.

MATERIALS

- Drawing compass
- Pencil
- 11 x 16 sheet of white cardboard
- Scissors
- Craft glue
- Masking tape
- Poster paints
- Mixing palette
- Paint brushes in several sizes
- Glitter pens
- Sequins
- Tracing paper
- 11 x 16 sheet of white mat board
- Craft knife and cutting mat
- Long-nosed pliers
- 5 feet thin wire with a metallic finish in two or three different colors
- About 12 colored beads
- Needle

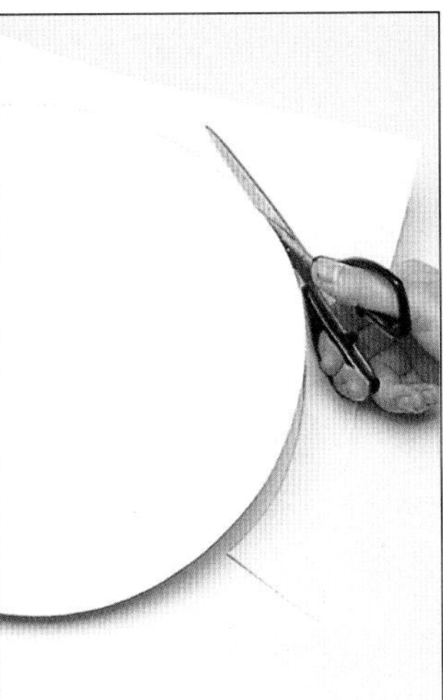

1 Using a drawing compass set at 6 inches, draw a circle with a diameter of 12 inches on the white cardboard. Now cut this out.

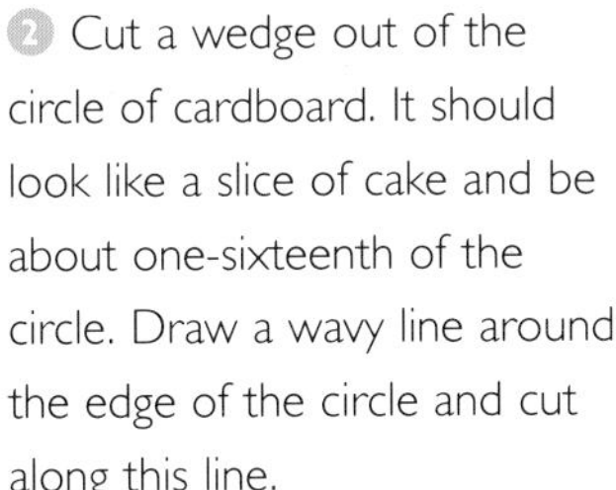

2 Cut a wedge out of the circle of cardboard. It should look like a slice of cake and be about one-sixteenth of the circle. Draw a wavy line around the edge of the circle and cut along this line.

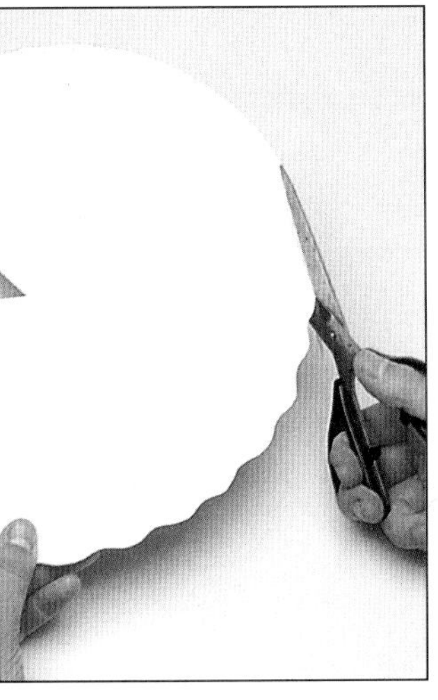

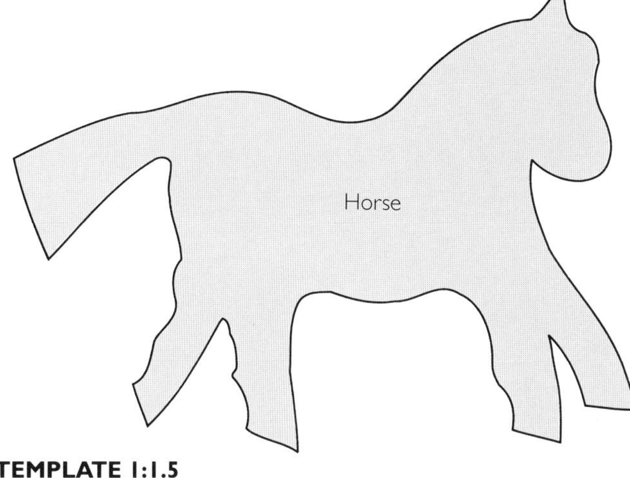

TEMPLATE 1:1.5

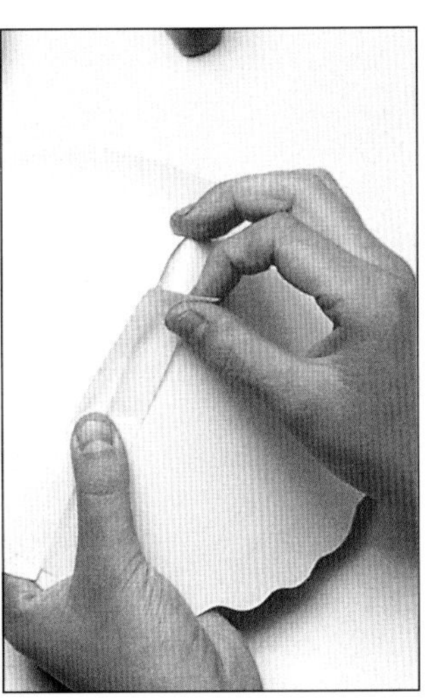

3 Bend the circle around to make a cone shape for the top of the carousel. Place a line of glue along the straight edge where you removed the wedge and lap the other straight edge over it. Press firmly and hold in place with a strip of masking tape until the glue dries. You will need to trim the wavy line where the cardboard edges have overlapped.

4 Use a pencil to mark lightly on the cone the guidelines of your chosen design. Paint in blocks or stripes of color.

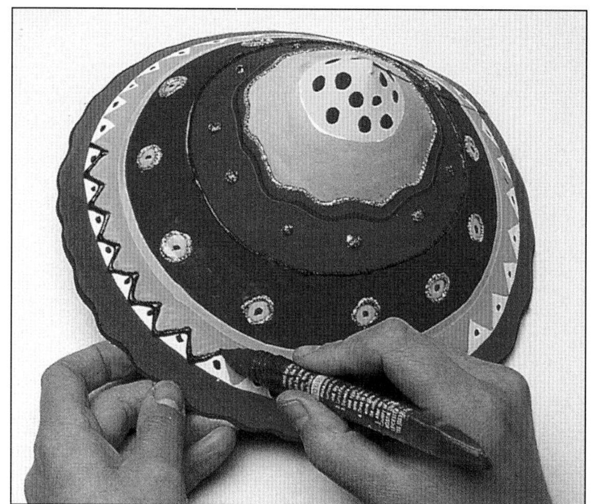

5 Use glitter pens to add more decoration and to emphasize the divisions between colors.

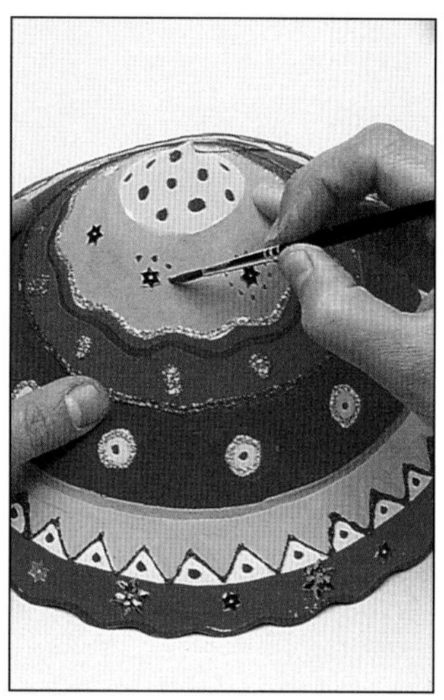

6 Once you have completed the cone, glue sequins around the edge. You may also like to add dots of paint to complete the effect. Paint the inside of the cone with a color that matches one used on the outside.

7 Trace the horse template from this book and cut it out. Use it as a guide to draw five horses on a sheet of white mat board. Cut these out using a craft knife and cutting mat.

8 On both sides of each horse, lightly draw in the hooves, mane, tail, and saddle. Now paint the main body of each horse in your chosen color.

9 Paint the mane, hooves, tail, and saddle, again on both sides. Paint more detail on the body and add the bridle. Use the glitter pens and sequins to add the finishing touches. Allow to dry.

10 To make each pole from which the horses hang, use pliers or scissors to cut two pieces of colored wire about 5 and 5½ inches long, one ½ inch longer than the other (this will be used to create a loop at the top). Twist the wires together, making a loop at the bottom. Thread a couple of beads on to the twisted wires for decoration. Repeat until you have six poles; one of these will be used to hang the carousel.

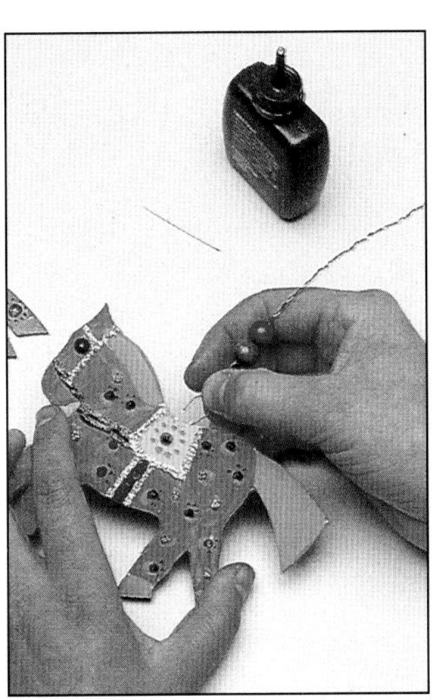

11 Make six little loops from colored wire, using pliers or scissors to cut it. Use a large needle to make two holes in the top edge of each horse's back. Take one of the wire loops you have just made and hook it over the looped end of one of the twisted wire poles. Add a drop of glue to each end of the wire loop and insert them into the two holes you have just made in the horse's back. Repeat this for every horse (the sixth loop is for hanging the carousel). Allow to dry.

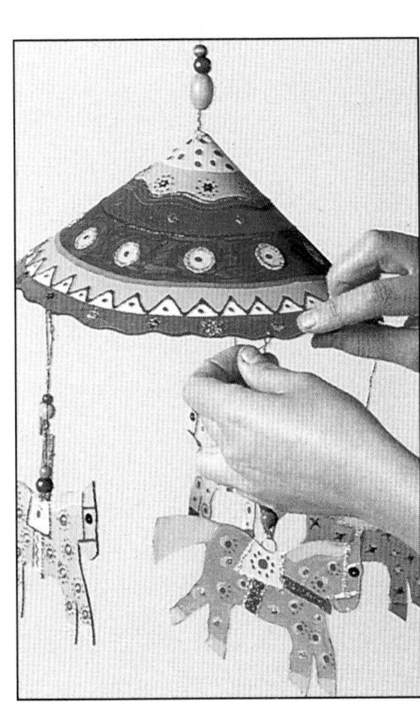

12 Use a needle to make five holes at regular intervals around the edge of the carousel. To attach the horses, simply push the ends of the twisted wire poles through the holes you have just made in the carousel and twist them around until they are secure. Place the last wire loop and twisted wire pole into the top of the carousel, using glue to secure the loop as in step 11. Allow to dry. Bend the top of the twisted wire pole around into a loop so that the carousel can be suspended.

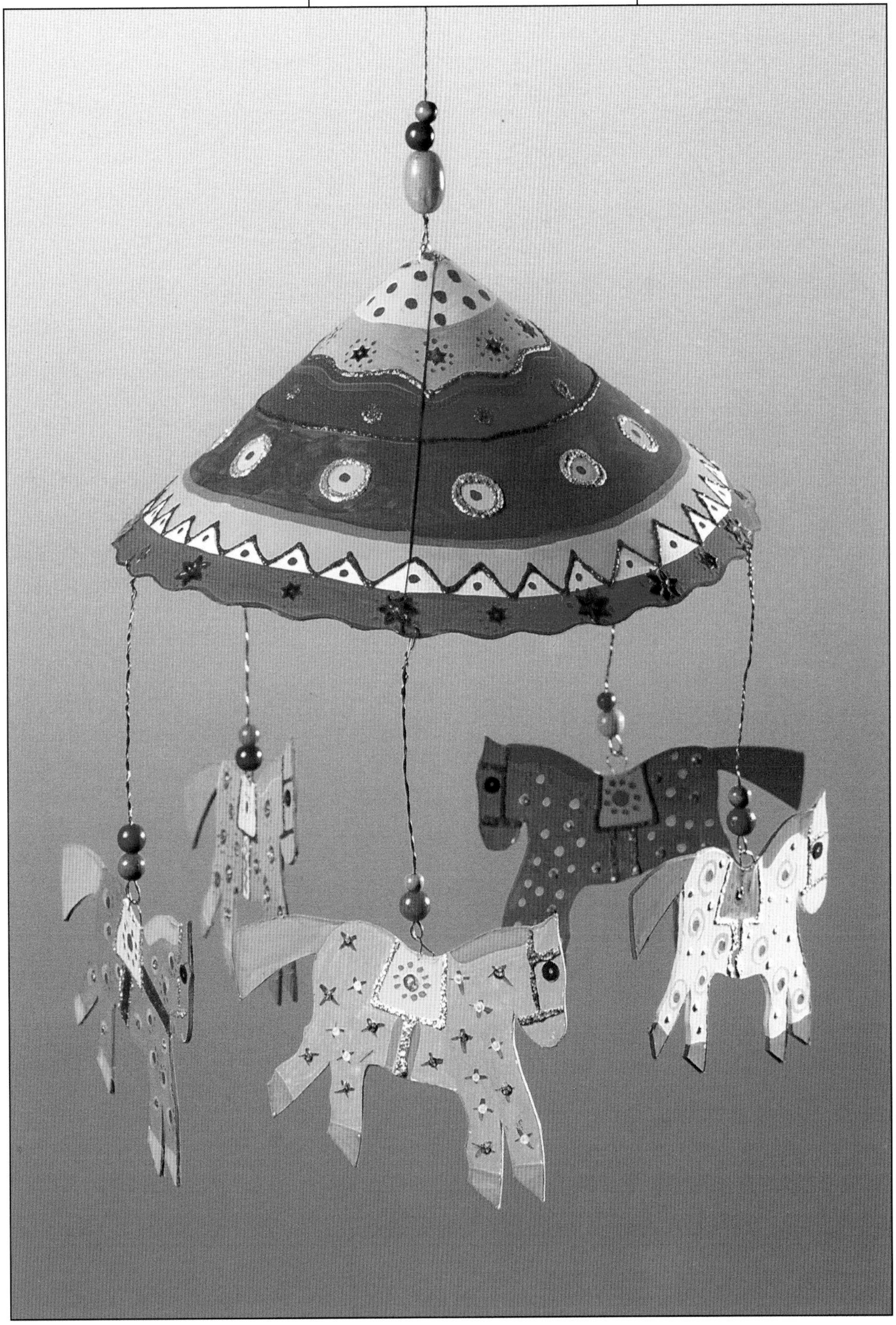

NOAH'S ARK

★★★★

"The animals went in two by two" is an endlessly popular theme. This Noah's Ark mobile is a project requiring some skill and is suitable for the more ambitious. A central three-dimensional ark is surrounded by pairs of animals made of colored cardboard with details added in poster paint.

MATERIALS

- Tracing paper
- Pencil
- 11 x 16 sheets of cardboard in each of the following colors: brown, white, yellow, pink, and gray
- Scissors
- Craft glue
- Masking tape
- Ruler
- Poster paints
- Mixing palette
- Paint brushes in several sizes
- 3 feet galvanized wire, 1/16 inch in diameter
- Silver spray paint
- 6 feet galvanized wire, 1/25 inch in diameter
- Long-nosed pliers
- Needle
- Cotton thread
- Paper clip

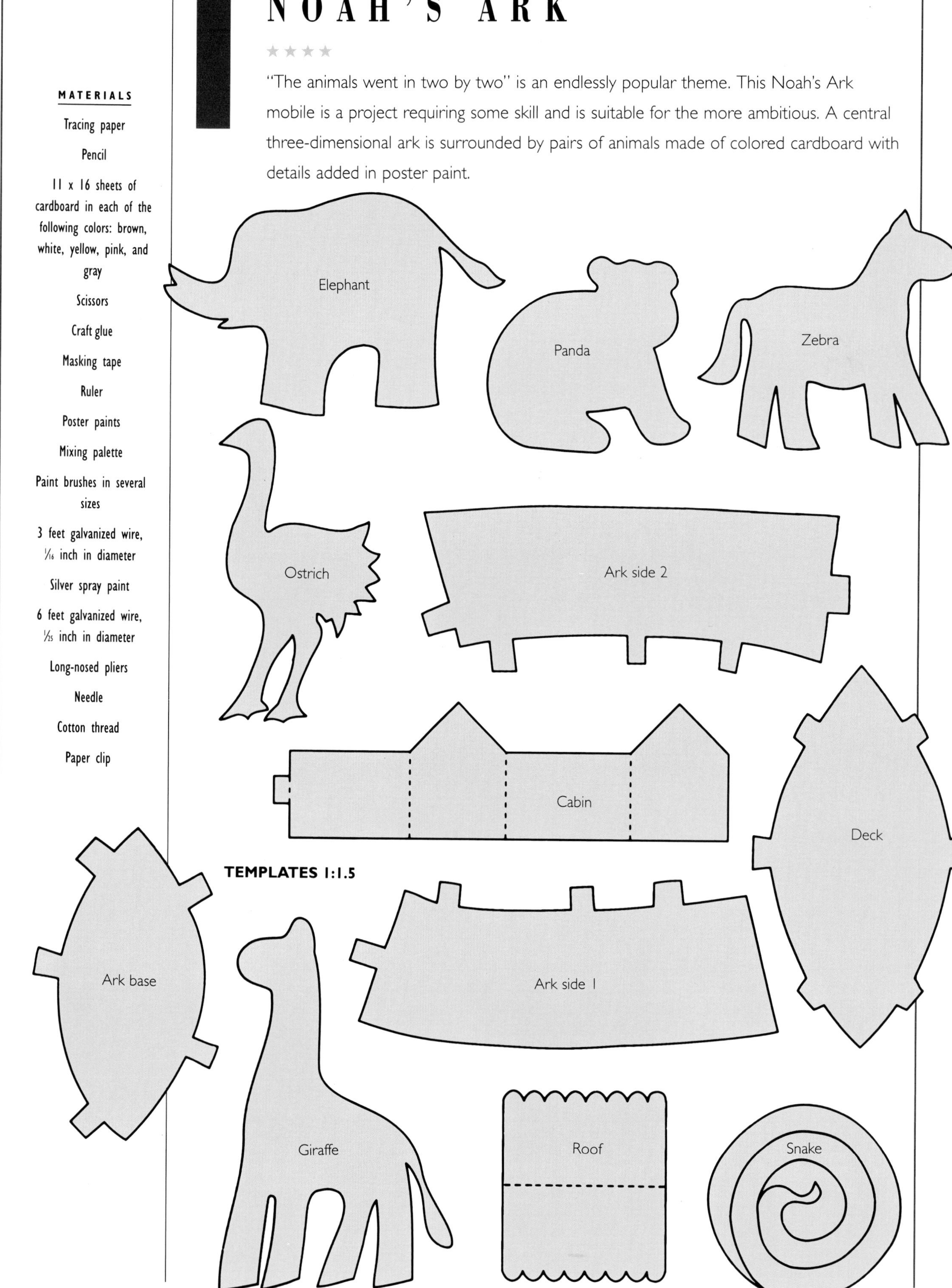

TEMPLATES 1:1.5

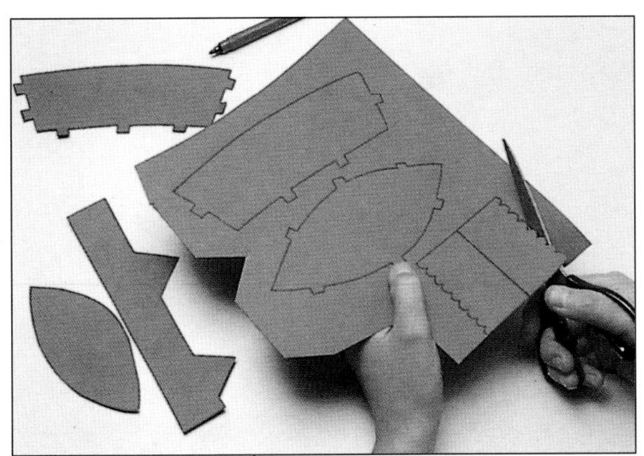

1 Trace the templates from this book for all the ark shapes, enlarge them to full size, transfer them to the brown cardboard, and cut them out.

2 Attach one side of the ark to the base by gluing the tabs and then securing them with masking tape. Do the same for the other side and then trim the base if you need to.

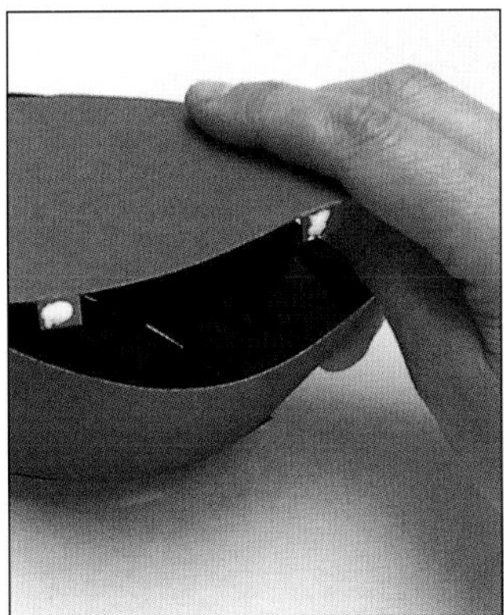

3 Once the sides are securely stuck, glue the tabs of the deck and insert it between the two sides of the ark.

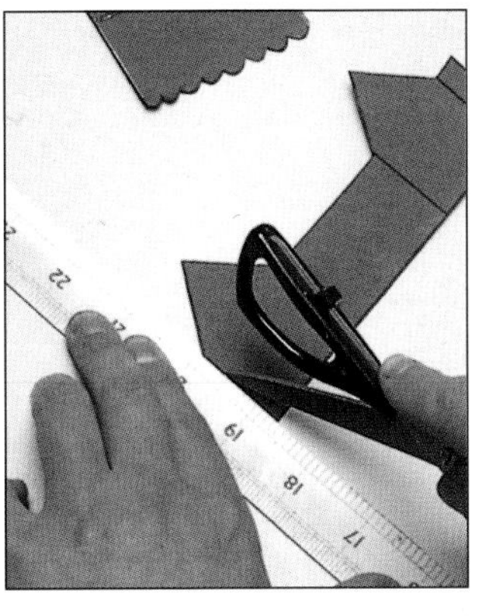

4 Using scissors and a ruler, score along the fold lines of the ark pieces – the fold lines are marked on the templates.

5 Fold the cabin and roof pieces along the scored lines. Fold the sides of the cabin around until they meet, then secure by gluing the tab. Now fold the roof along the middle and glue it to the cabin. Glue the cabin to the deck of the ark.

6 Using poster colors, paint details such as portholes, roof tiles, deck-boards, and so on on the ark.

7 Snip a paper clip in half, using the pliers, to create a hook. Use a needle to make two holes in the top of the ark ¼ inch apart. Put a drop of glue on each end of the hook and insert them into the holes in the top of the ark. Allow to dry.

8 The completed ark, with all its final details.

9 Trace the templates of the animals from this book, enlarge to full size, and transfer to cardboard. Cut out two of each shape, using yellow cardboard for the giraffes, gray for the elephants, black for the zebras, etc.

10 Paint both sides of the animals with the appropriate markings: give the zebras stripes, the giraffes patches, and so on.

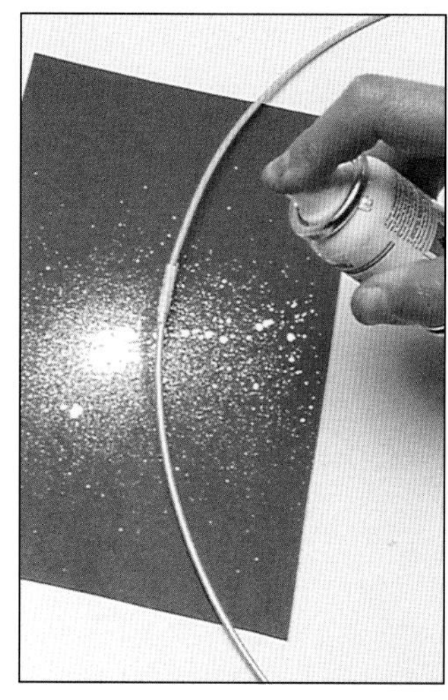

11 To make the frame, bend a piece of the thicker wire into a circle about 13 inches in diameter. Bind the joint with a piece of masking tape and spray the tape silver to match the wire.

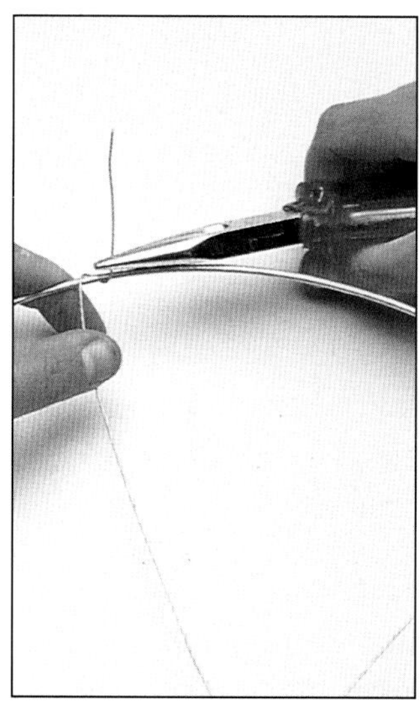

12 Cut three pieces of thinner wire 14½ inches long to reach across the diameter of the circle like spokes on a wheel. Use long-nosed pliers to twist them around the edge of the main wire circle.

13 Using a needle, attach a length of cotton thread to each animal at a point where it will balance when hung.

14 Use the pliers to cut six lengths of thinner wire about 4 inches long, and bend each end of each one into a hook. These will form the struts. Tie a pair of animals to each strut, one at each end.

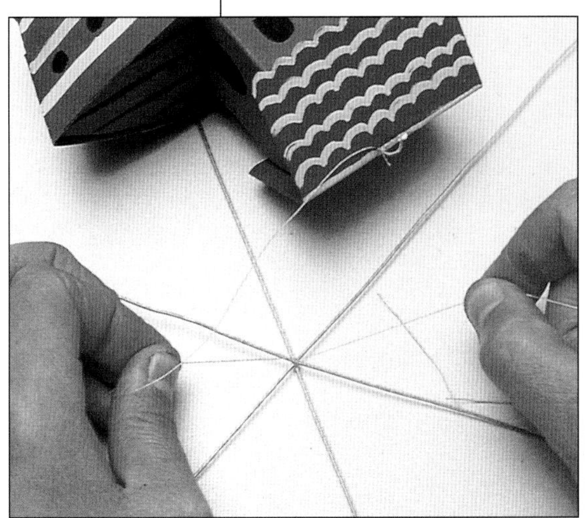

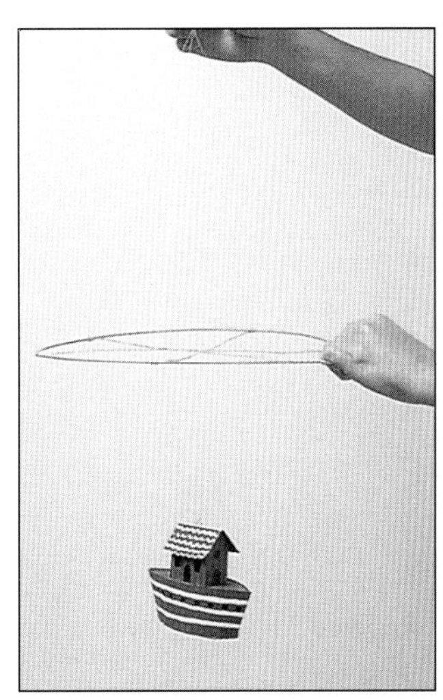

15 Tie a length of cotton thread to the hook in the top of the ark, then tie the other end firmly to the wires where they cross at the center of the circle. This holds the wires together as well as attaching the ark.

16 To hang up the wheel, cut six threads of equal length and tie them to the sides of the circle where the thinner cross-wires join it. Join all the untied ends of thread together and, once the circular frame is level, tie them in a knot. Create a loop to hang the mobile from.

17 Attach a length of thread to each strut from which the pairs of animals are hanging, and tie each strut to the circle where the cross-wires meet the edge of it.

SWIRLING SPIRALS

★ ★ ★

This project illustrates a great way of combining fluorescent cardboard of different colors with simple spinning spirals, resulting in a splendid psychodelic mobile.

MATERIALS

Scissors

4 or 5 16 x 24-inch sheets of fluorescent cardboard of different colors

Craft glue

Drawing compass

Pencil

11 x 16 sheet of mat board

Craft knife and cutting mat

Needle

Colored cotton thread

1 Using scissors, cut out six or seven pairs of squares from fluorescent cardboard in various colors, measuring anything between 4 inches square and 7 inches square. Glue the pairs of squares together, using different colors on each side. Make lots of different sized pairs of squares.

2 Using a drawing compass draw different-sized circles on the cardboard squares. Draw the circles freehand if you wish.

3 Cut out the circles and then cut into the circles to create spirals.

4 Cut up into a couple of the spirals to create double spirals.

5 Use a drawing compass to draw a hoop on mat board with an outer diameter of about 8 inches. The width of the hoop should be about 1 inch. Use a craft knife and cutting mat to cut out the hoop.

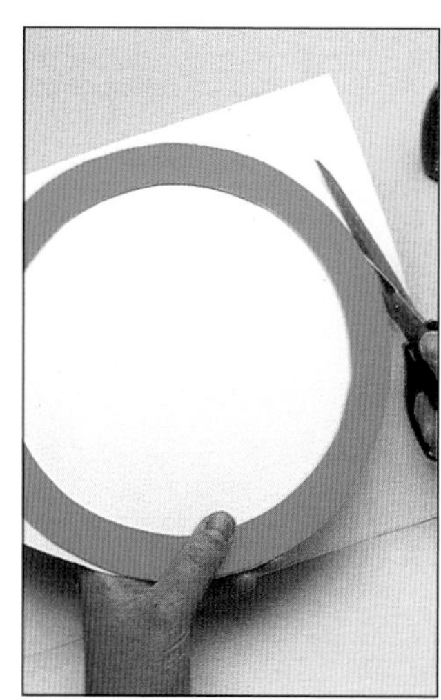

6 Glue one side of the hoop to the back of a piece of fluorescent cardboard and cut away the excess. Repeat with the other side of the hoop so that it is completely covered.

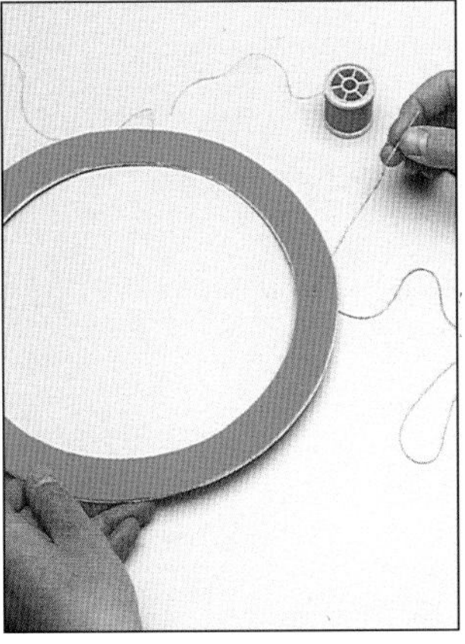

7 Thread a needle with brightly colored cotton thread and knot the end. By piercing the hoop with the needle, attach four separate lengths of thread to the hoop, knotting the end of each one and allowing equal distances between them. Pull the four lengths of thread together above the hoop and tie in a knot when the hoop hangs level.

8 Thread a needle with the same thread and knot the end. Thread this through the top of a spiral, then attach the spiral to the hoop by piercing the needle through the hoop and knotting it. Repeat for all of the spirals, spacing them evenly and so that they do not restrict each other's movement, and hanging them at different heights. Suspend the mobile and, if necessary, rearrange the spirals until you are happy with the effect.

PICTURE CREDITS

The publisher would like to thank the following artists and craftspeople whose work appears in this book: Mike Chase, David Currell, Judith Faerber, Gloria Farison, Vivien Frank, Paul Jackson, Deborah Jaffe, Robert J. Lang, Mike Palmer, Karen Reed, Nick Robinson, Yanina Temple, and Melanie Williams. For the handmade papers shown on pages 176–7, the publisher would like to thank Suzie Balazs and Gillian Johnson-Flint. Thanks also go to the artists who contributed their knowledge and expertise in the following areas: papermaking, Suzie Balazs; paper sculpture, Angela Freeborne; papier-mâché, Deborah Schneebeli-Morrell; and pulping, Madeleine Child.